BUSINESS POLICY

A MANAGEMENT AUDIT APPROACH

BUSINESS POLICY

A Management Audit Approach

BY

WILLIAM T. GREENWOOD

Professor of Management
Southern Illinois University

THE MACMILLAN COMPANY, NEW YORK
COLLIER-MACMILLAN LIMITED, LONDON

6 58
G 859 b

First Printing

Library of Congress catalog card number: 67–14417

THE MACMILLAN COMPANY, NEW YORK
COLLIER-MACMILLAN CANADA, LTD., TORONTO, ONTARIO

PRINTED IN THE UNITED STATES OF AMERICA

Dedicated to Roy C. Hall
My First Dean
College of Business Administration
University of San Francisco

PREFACE

This volume on Business Policy has been developed primarily to achieve the objectives of the course in a systematic versus an intuitive fashion. The Management Audit Approach has been developed over a period of twelve years of teaching the course at the graduate and undergraduate levels. Experiments conducted with senior undergraduate students revealed serious limitations in the latter's ability to apply analytically the theories, methods, and techniques learned in the business administration curriculum. This ability is of critical importance in the policy course, especially for the content of the core courses of management, economics, marketing, finance, accounting, production, and personnel. The variety of management, companywide, and departmental audits for the core-course fields presented in Part II has proven most effective in bridging the gap between theory and practice, and in developing problem-solving and decision-making skills in the course.

Because the policy issues in comprehensive business cases have been treated incidentally rather than systematically in most policy casebooks, an introduction to the nature and use of policy controls for strategic decisions is presented in Part III. The almost inseparable interrelationship of company strategies and policies is examined, and the types of policies for company and departmental activities are presented as necessary background material for the analysis of policy issues. Without this background, it is most unlikely that the undergraduate student, particularly, will be capable of distinguishing policy problems from goals, strategies, procedures, or rules problems. If this ability is not developed, the course title becomes, in fact, a misnomer.

The consideration of policy problems may be made from the perspective of the chief executive officer of the firm, that is, the policy formulator or administrator, or from the perspective of the many managers at all levels of the firm making decisions within policy control guidelines. In this book both perspectives will be considered inasmuch as most policy makers reach this position only after years of experience operating within policy controls. The multiplicity of policies in the firm, along with the conflicting goals often sought by varied policies, must be reconciled by management decisions, often at lower levels in the organization. The ability to recognize the variety of potential policy issues is therefore incumbent on middle management as well as on top management, and will be treated accordingly in the case problems in the book.

The multiple objectives of the policy course are delineated in Part I, and also evaluated in terms of their relative importance. The three major objectives of (1) discerning policy issues, (2) integration and application of core-curriculum course content, and (3) development of analytical, problem-solving, and decision-making skills are sought via the case method of instruction. To achieve these and the secondary, or by-product, objectives of the course, comprehensive, multi-functional, companywide case problems have been emphasized throughout the book.

The Business Policy cases in Part IV are presented in a cumulative sequence so that the skills of problem definition, management-audit application, policy analysis, financial analysis, and so on, can be systematically developed. The comprehensive Management Audit and strategy-policy cases are complemented by organizational environment, business growth stages, and audit appraisal and control cases. The growth stage group includes cases with problems of organizing a new business, undercapitalization, expansion limits, increasing competition, vertical integration, merger, changing industry conditions, and closedown or disposal of the firm. Internal environmental problems are treated with organization cases providing for analysis of the organizational structure and organizational behavior problems. External environmental problems of international expansion and social-political-ethical cases are also included. Final attention is given to the audit-appraisal-control functions of management, with analyses of budgetary, organizational, and companywide control problems.

The majority of the cases are concerned with a variety of manufacturing-company problems, but retail, wholesale, distributor, processor, and service-industry firms are also included. The emphasis throughout is on multi-function, companywide problems that emphasize problem detection and definition, as well as problem-solving skills. The systematic analysis of policy issues in these cases is facilitated by the interrelationship of the multi-problem cases.

The Business-Management Simulation Game in Part V adds the dynamic aspect of reality to business problem solving and decision making under competitive conditions. The game is particularly useful in testing the consistency of business strategies and policies over time—the capacity to resist the temptation to change strategies and policies at will in response to changes in competitive and environmental conditions.

ACKNOWLEDGMENTS

Individual case contributors to this book are identified in the Table of Contents, along with each case. Without these contributions, this Management Audit Approach to case analysis would not have been possible. Long-standing appreciation is expressed for the opportunity to teach the business policy course, starting in the early 1950's, provided by Dean Roy C. Hall, to whom this book is dedicated. Fremont Shull and Arthur Ely Prell of Southern Illinois University were most generous in teaching assignments and in arranging administrative support for the testing of innumerable cases before the final organization was achieved. Harvey Bishop and Edith Johnson of the Intercollegiate Case Clearinghouse at Harvard University provided permissions and case materials above and beyond the normal call of duty. Last, but not least, graduate students Kirby Madden and David Peach handled the endless details necessary to such an undertaking with meticulous care and perseverance.

W. T. G.

CONTENTS

PART I

THE BUSINESS POLICY COURSE: OBJECTIVES AND CONTENT

* *

INTRODUCTION

* *

Schools of business administration in the United States have experimented with various courses and methods to develop administrative skills for potential managers. The success of these experiments has been complicated by the difficulty of bridging the gap between descriptive theories and methods and their analytical application in business problem solving. One major vehicle used to overcome this obstacle has been the case method of instruction, and to this end its use in the business administration curriculum has increased significantly in recent years.

The Business Policy course in the undergraduate and graduate business curricula has been developed primarily as a case method course. It is designed in the undergraduate curriculum to integrate the knowledge and methods learned in prior business courses, and especially the courses in the core subjects: economics, accounting, management, marketing, statistics, production, and finance. The course is also used to develop analytical, problem-solving, and decision-making skills. Last, and hopefully not least, it emphasizes the analysis of "policy issues" in comprehensive, companywide business case-problems. The emphasis given these many objectives varies from school to school, and also in text materials used in the course.

DEFINED OBJECTIVES

The objectives of the business policy course were originally defined in a survey conducted for the American Association of Collegiate Schools of Business in the early 1950's. The findings of this survey indicated that "In those cases where such a course has been attempted, it is found under the heading of 'Business Management' or 'Business Policy'." Referred to in the survey as the "integrating course," it performs the function of a capstone for

3

all courses, theories, methods, skills, and techniques studied in the total business curriculum.[1]

More recently the objectives of the policy course have been defined in the Pierson and the Gordon and Howell studies of the business school curriculum. The Pierson study refers to the policy course in an integrative sense as follows: "It would mean an approach in the senior year to integration along business policy lines and avoidance of specialization in any one of the particular fields of business, beyond a very modest level."[2] The Gordon and Howell report provides a more complete statement of objectives. It recommends that "The capstone of the core curriculum should be a course in 'business policy' which will give students an opportunity to pull together what they have learned in separate business fields, and utilize this knowledge in the analysis of complex business problems. . . . [With] emphasis on the development of skill in identifying, analyzing, and solving problems in a situation which is as close as the classroom can ever be to the real business world, . . . the business policy course can concentrate on integrating what has already been acquired and on developing further the students' skill in using that knowledge."[3]

PRESENT USES OF THE COURSE

The present status of the business policy course has been presented in a recent survey of these courses in member schools of the American Association of Collegiate Schools of Business. This survey was conducted by Professor Charles Klasson of the University of Texas. Of 110 member schools, 46 responded to this survey. Of this number, 25, or 58 per cent, required the course as a final integrating, capstone course. One of the most significant findings of the study underscored the late development of this course, in spite of the recommendations of the association in the early 1950's. For example, only two schools required the course prior to 1950, five required it during the 1950's, and fifteen of the schools have made the course a core requirement since 1960.[4]

The two major uses of the course have been (a) for the integrative application of core course materials and (b) for the development of analytical and decision-making skills through the study of comprehensive cases which are multi-functional and multi-departmental in scope. With an almost exclusive use of case materials in the course until recent years, the overwhelming emphasis has been on these two objectives. Because of this, the student is

[1] "Professional Education for Business, Preliminary Report on Pilot Field Study, American Association of Collegiate Schools of Business," April, 1954, p. 73.

[2] Pierson, Frank C., and others, *The Education of Amercian Businessmen* New York; McGraw-Hill Book Company, Inc., (1959), p. 342.

[3] Gordon, R. A., and Howell, J. E., *Higher Education for Business* (New York: Columbia University Press, 1959), pp. 206–207.

[4] "Information About Undergraduate Business Policy Courses in American Schools— Survey Questionnaire Results." Klasson, Charles R., Department of Management, College of Business Administration, University of Texas, Austin, Texas, 1963.

advised to first consider the case method of instruction, and especially its purposes and methodologies.

THE CASE METHOD OF INSTRUCTION

The articles "Management and Training for Management" and "The Case Method of Instruction" by Pearson Hunt of the Harvard Graduate School of Business are presented in the latter part of this section. In the first article, Professor Hunt emphasizes the necessity of experience as opposed to theory training in the development of administrative skills. He therefore confirms the contention of the difficulty of bridging the gap between theory and practice in this process. In his second article, Professor Hunt describes in detail the case method of instruction. Emphasis is placed on the development of problem-solving skills for all levels of management practice. The discussion rather than the lecture method is proposed, for the purpose of developing effective communication skills and attitudes that will facilitate rather than deter group discussion in problem solving and decision making. The latter article was written by Professor Hunt a number of years ago, and some changes in his thinking will be found reflected in the first article.

While the case method of instruction has received widespread use in the business schools, it is not inconceivable that a student may arrive at the business policy course without prior case analysis experience. In the case method, emphasis is placed upon the development of analytical skills in problem solving and decision making; whereas the objectives of lecture and discussion methods in other courses emphasize the acquisition of knowledge. This difference in preparation may require adjustments for the policy course instructor, and a new role for the student. In this method the instructor has not traditionally provided the right answers, but rather has guided the student through a variety of problem-solving experiences so that he could develop and refine his own problem-solving, decision-making skills. Rather than learning principles of a subject, as in lecture courses, the student instead is developing "ways of thinking," and skills in problem solving and decision making.

In the policy course, the decision-oriented method of teaching is emphasized, and also the ability to reconcile different decisions of class members to yield widely accepted group solutions of the case problem. The responsibility for learning rests entirely upon the student. Under these circumstances, the development of student attitudes in the process of learning through the case method becomes an additional objective of the method. The necessity for open-mindedness, suspended judgment, the and exchange of ideas with fellow students under competitive conditions leads to refinements in individual decision-making skills. The ability to communicate is also improved as skills are acquired during group discussion and in making cooperative judgments.

The objective of developing efficient and effective decision-making skills serves as a criterion of success in the presentation of the course. This entails the new and unique roles and responsibilities assumed and developed by both the instructor and the student.

CASE METHOD LIMITATIONS

Unfortunately, too often the evaluation of comprehensive business cases leads only to open-ended discussion sessions instead of rigorous analyses. Rhetoric and strength of personalities have often prevailed over reasoned judgments. Lacking familiarity with and skill in the use of the tools of the logician, the students often spend their time ineffectually arguing their positions, hopefully to a " best analysis " of the case. Further limitations are found in the limited experience of students with actual business situations, and in their limited knowledge of basic business functions. Although the student should have completed courses in the basic functional fields consisting of theories, principles, and methods, an effective application of these theories and methods to case analyses is not readily achieved.

OBJECTIVES REDEFINED

The two major Business Policy course objectives identified in the American Association of Collegiate Schools of Business report are confirmed by the two business school studies: (a) the integrating-capstone function and (b) the development of decision-making skills. Unfortunately, other major objectives are often ignored, or only incidentally treated. To remedy these limitations, the course objectives may be delineated in the following order of importance.

1. *To discern policy issues, and to formulate and administer policies in the analysis of business problems*

The title of the course "Business Policy" has often become a misnomer because of the failure to adequately emphasize policy issues. The detection of policy issues as causes of problems, and the formulation and administration of policies are generic to the comprehensive nature of the business firm. This means that the student's experience in handling policy issues leads him to a consideration of their interdepartmental ramifications. In particular, policy issues are so pervasive in their effects throughout the organization that they inevitably become a decision of top management and companywide planning at the highest echelon of the firm. It is almost impossible to formulate an individual departmental policy without also projecting its interdepartmental ramification. As such, policy issues are the ideal type of problems for the students to evaluate in developing decision-making skills that affect the firm as a whole, as opposed to specialized functional or departmental problems. The role of policies in the course are treated in detail in Part III.

2. *To effectively integrate and apply the principles and methods acquired in the core curriculum*

Comprehensive cases include the full panorama of business functional problems. Questions of market forecasts, strategies, quotas, and product line policies are prevalent issues. Production capacity and utilization problems are perennial in manufacturing firms. Organization planning and staffing are necessary to all types and sizes of firms. Accounting control systems and financial analyses are keystones of any business analysis. Problems in management performance, development, and succession are among the most significant causes of failure for all businesses. Any attempt to analyze the company as a whole thereby entails not only the application of principles and methods from the basic business functions, represented by the core curriculum courses, but also their integrated application in the analysis of these cases.

3. *To develop analytical skills in over-all business problem solving and decision making*

While some individuals exhibit analytical skills and aptitudes early, for most, unfortunately, these skills must be painstakingly acquired. This acquisition is achieved best for the business student through repetitive analyses of comprehensive cases representing all sizes and types of business firms. Facility in discerning and defining basic problems, and their causes, is a major goal of this course. Refinements in the analyses of cases come both from depth and breadth case analysis experiences, and also through the development of an individual "administrative process."

BY-PRODUCTS OR SECONDARY OBJECTIVES

A number of by-product contributions of the case method in the Business Policy course are important enough to be considered as secondary objectives.

1. *To acquire vicarious business decision-making experience via the case simulations of actual business problems*

The development of self confidence is one of the major by-products of the case method of instruction. As the student analyzes business problems of different types of manufacturing, service, and trade organizations, his understanding of core course principles and methods take on new perspectives and meanings. As differing sizes and types of firms are presented, the student's confidence grows, in recognition of integrative relationships of the many business and management functions. As decisions are made from the perspective of the business consultant and chief executive of the firm, self confidence is an integral concomitant. The value of this self confidence cannot be underestimated, for its benefits are manifested in voluntary extensions of case analyses by the student, and in more intensive reviews of principles and methods contained in prior course work. When this self confidence is carried by the student to his first job following graduation, its value to the student and the company establishes the final touch of a "finished product" in professional business education.

2. *To develop communication skills*

Surveys of business firms perennially find "lack of communication skills" at the top of the list of the most significant limitations of business school graduates. The lack of writing skills is part of this deficiency, not only for the business school graduate but for practicing managers as well. The lifeblood of the business organization is the efficient and effective communication of operating information, orders, instructions, and reports through organization channels. The exercise of authority, and accountability for its use, require clarity, completeness, and conciseness in the communication of information. Students in the policy course develop writing skills in their reports on case analyses. These reports require not only clarity and conciseness, but also logical organization and tight, rigorous reasoning to substantiate particular positions and recommendations.

Oral communication skills are required and developed in class discussions and argumentations. Articulation skills not previously acquired by most students must be developed for logical and concise class presentations of case analyses and for successfully defending case analysis conclusions and recommendations against questioning by the instructor, and against argument and analysis by other students.

The value of both written and oral communication skills in future business positions is immeasurable. All future relationships with superiors and subordinates will provide critical tests on this score for assessing management and leadership potentials. Group discussions, conferences, and committees will separate the leaders from the non-leaders in terms of logical and persuasive communication of different positions and viewpoints. This particular "competitive" communication skill may be cited as an additional by-product of the case method as follows.

3. *To experience the defense of a position in a critical atmosphere*

The ability to defend one's reasoned position under competitive conditions provides the most realistic "simulation" of actual business decision making. This includes the opportunity to exchange, via the case discussion process, opposing ideas, analyses, and value judgments that are the hallmarks of decision making in a competitive economy and a viable business organization. The necessity of developing not only a sound case analysis but also the oral defense of this analysis against one's peers is vital to the development of attitudes and skills for an effective use of the administrative process. The maturation effects resulting from these experiences constitute significant by-products, or secondary objectives of the course. This dynamic aspect of the case method can be underemphasized, but we hope it will not be.

SUPPLEMENTAL COURSE CONTENT

While the exclusive use of case materials in the business policy course has historically prevailed, recent years have found many changes. The University of Texas' survey found that "all but six schools devote at least forty per cent of the total classroom time to case discussion." But there was also found an increasing use of lectures, with thirty-two schools (70 per cent) devoting up to 30 per cent of the classroom time to this function. Business gaming was the third most extensively used activity in the course besides cases. Eighteen (39 per cent) of the schools included business games, utilizing approximately 20 per cent of the course time. Other activities included the use of management audits, visiting lecturers, field trips, group presentations, buzz sessions, live case presentations, and plant visitations. In general these latter activities consumed less that 10 per cent of the total classroom time for each.[5]

The Texas report concluded with the statement "this suggests the need to supplement basic case materials with substantive textual materials of some type." To meet this need, supplemental course materials are presented in subsequent chapters of this book. A determination of these needs, and the trends in course materials to achieve them, are presented in the next chapter.

[5] *Ibid.*

1. MANAGEMENT AND TRAINING FOR MANAGEMENT*

—PEARSON HUNT

One often wonders how historians of the future will regard their own times when enough years have passed to make a judgement possible. It is my prediction that one of the things that will be found to characterize the second half of the 20th century is that it was the time when the masses of the people of the world realised that poverty could be conquered. That the governments of the world are responding to this realisation is evident everywhere.

Probably too many of those who desire to increase the world's wealth are of the opinion that all that is needed is the application of technology to natural resources, the building of roads, and so forth and so on. But those who have had experience with the management of economic affairs realise that people cannot make themselves rich merely by wishing to do so; they must accept the discipline and sacrifices which go with the advantages they desire to have, and, more important for my present theme, they must have among them persons with managerial ability to organise the people and the resources in efficient ways. The situation has been well summarised by a person from a country which has been making herculean efforts to improve itself (Chile), who said: " The problem does not lie in the setting of development goals or in attempting an artificial increase in productivity; the problem is to spread an adequate and effective economic formation. Our people must balance their desires and their capacities, and plans must be directed toward the creation of the aptitudes which are necessary if the people of the world are to have what they so strongly desire and what they can have if the resources are properly managed."[1]

If the resources are properly managed! We have had highly productive

* From *Scientific Business*, February, 1964. Reprinted by permission of Professor Pearson Hunt, Harvard University.
[1] Pedro Ibanez Ojeda, address to PACCIOS Meeting, Santiago de Chile, December, 1956.

techniques available to us for years but poor management has all too often caused economic loss where gain was expected. Perhaps it will be the contribution of this phase of history that the essential importance of management in any complex activity is recognised. At least it is my position, and the position of my Faculty, that management skills are fully as important as sources of energy for the operation of our society and for the reaching of the goals we seek. The growing number of Institutes of Administration throughout the world is evident that we are not alone in holding this opinion.

One most important point is often forgotten when one speaks of management. Too frequently we think of the manager only as the person with the final responsibility in a firm. In fact, persons who need the skills of managers are found at every level of a business, from the foreman who handles a small number of workers on to men at the so-called middle management level and up to the top management group. Management skills are called for at every level in a business, and that is why it is possible to operate a school for young men who wish to make management their professional field. We do not presume to have trained our graduates to undertake top management positions at once, but we do feel that they are prepared to take junior positions requiring management skills, and to make contributions to the over-all management activity within an organisation. Thus, when I speak of a manager, I refer to anyone at any level of authority whose work includes planning, control, and the co-ordination of the work of people.

I propose to divide this paper into two main questions. The first of these is whether management is a separate field of study, and especially whether such a subject should have the attention of a University Faculty. The second main question is this: if management is to be taught, how can it best be taught?

The answers which I am going to offer are matters of controversy. If space had permitted, I would have given a more balanced analysis of the advantages and disadvantages of the things which I am going to recommend, because they are topics which have interested me for some time, but, under the circumstances I shall become an advocate of the positions which my colleagues and I strongly support, because we are convinced that they represent the best solution to the problems raised.

Much of what I shall say will appear to be counter to the policies of older Faculties of British Universities. I value these University traditions myself. There are fields in which the traditional procedures are more desirable than those which I shall describe, but management education is not one of these fields. We are considering the training of the professional man who is to be active in the world of affairs. One who desires to be a teacher, or research worker, or theorist in the field of management needs to add further training in order that he may familiarise himself with all that has been done in this field, and develop his ability to think generally or in theoretical terms as well as in problem-solving conditions. This situation is not unusual, I believe, in the Professional Schools of a University.

After this introduction I now turn to the first of my questions. What is the subject matter of management education?

In trying to answer a question of this kind, I find that it is extremely important to look at the type of trained person whom we, as teachers, are trying to create. A programme in medicine for example, should not be designed without consideration of the knowledge and capacity which a medical doctor must have. If we can specify the capacities of a manager, we will have the best basis for the making of a curriculum for the training of managers.

Plentiful materials exists to describe the technical procedures that are available to managers—new ones seem to be elaborated every day. They are valuable, and we must teach them in our schools. But we shall not create young managers unless we realise that there is something much more basic that is needed. It is the type of mind, the attitude, or way of thinking, that characterises successful managers.

I believe that a manager can be described as a man who:

1. has a disciplined capacity of mind, leading to a capacity to think in explicit terms about the problems arising from the tasks which he must complete;

2. has a high ability to form organisations within which the work of others can be co-ordinated toward a commonly-shared end;

3. is prepared to carry the psychological burdens of taking decision despite the uncertainties of the future and of assessing the work of others;

4. has a strong sense of the social responsibility of those in management positions.

Turning to the first characteristic on the list, the way of thinking that characterises a successful administrator, I will suggest four sub-divisions to describe this capacity.

The first of these is the ability to analyse problems. Problems arising in the experience of an organisation come to the administrator confused with many facts of small importance and many side-issues, and the administrator must first make an analysis to see whether on one hand the question or problem has been properly stated, and whether on the other hand the facts offered to him are those which are pertinent to the situation. In this process he needs also to visualise what additional facts can be developed, given the time and the other limitations of the problem. The first criterion is in itself an ability requiring considerable skill and one that the student trained in theory finds it difficult to use, since he has been thinking about concepts as to which the irrelevant details have already been abstracted. In fact, I think that here we have one of the essential differences between theory and practice. The theorist is always working with the generalisation and going from point to point in his thinking without the necessity of constant clarification or definition due to frequent introduction of information that may or may not be pertinent.

Secondly, the administrator needs to know about the techniques of analysis that are available (they are rapidly increasing in number), so that he can select those which will give further information from the existing facts. Almost all administrators have been technicians in the course of the experience they have had leading to their present positions. They may have been accountants, lawyers, engineers, economists, and so on. The field of the experience is not important. From it they should be able to learn enough about the discipline of other fields to be able to make the selection which I have suggested.

Third is the capacity to think imaginatively. By this I mean that the administrator must take the problem which he has defined and analysed and turn it over, look at it from all points of view, manipulate it and see what will be the best solution under the circumstances—not simply the one dictated by tradition or the logic of some particular technique, but rather the solution which is the most successful under all the circumstances. Two types of thinking are required for this, operating in sequence. The first is the operation of the imagination to go as far as the mind's experience and its ability to transfer will let it go. The second is to bring the problem back to earth, by the observation of the factual situation, especially the existing limitations of the firm.

The fourth capacity has reference to all the preceding three; it is that the administrator must always think decisionally, for he is responsible for the making of a decision and many of his decisions will have to be the choice of one course of action out of a number of alternatives, none of which is attractive when compared to some ideal. There are a great many persons who have all the capacities of mind which are necessary for administrative work, except the willingness to accept the responsibility to make decisions and to stand behind them. It is one of the delights of the academic life, which I share, that one can stand away from a problem talking about its interesting aspects without ever having to make the tough decision at the end of the discussion. The administrator must be willing to do this and promptly and not shrink from the best available decision in the hope that delay may somehow change the situation or make a decision unnecessary.

I now turn to the second group of abilities related to the formation of organisations and work within them. The more important of the two characteristics which go with this condition is that the administrator must be willing to work with others. This means far more than that he is an acceptable member of a social group. A successful administrator is one who has learned that he, as well as others, benefits from frank discussion of problems and points of view. Teachers of administration often have to tell the students that they are not participating in group discussion simply to show how brilliant they are individually but rather to come with their best ideas, hear the ideas of others and leave with better ideas than any member of the group brought to the meeting. One who has experience with group work soon comes to anticipate such results and to be disappointed if they do not occur.

The second characteristic is the ability to organise the work of the group. This is a task requiring judgements about people, and their assignment to places in an organisation designed to perform the work of the firm in the most requisite manner. A recent book, "Exploration in Management"[1] (which I strongly recommend) makes clear the long-known but recently almost forgotten principle that the better type of organisation in the long run is that in which men know their jobs in terms of the work content of the role they occupy, the appropriate relationship of that role to other roles and the details of the policies which govern their companies for the purpose of co-ordinating their own work with the work of others. Now that we have been reminded of this matter, let us never forget it again.

One important part of the ability to organise the work of a group is to use delegation as the way in which members of the group will divide their work. Probably no subject of administration is more talked about than delegation. Most of us who have been considering the question could lecture for at least an hour on the subject without pause. Here I would merely like to point out one most frequently forgotten matter, which is that the man who delegates responsibility must, if the delegation is to be successful, accept the limitations which delegation involves. That is to say, the administrator who gives authority to someone to carry out part of the duties of the organisation, at the same time implicitly restricts himself from the many things which will serve to destroy the significance of delegation. He cannot, for example, delegate to someone, and then expect that person to do the task exactly as he would do it himself. One of the limitations of delegation is therefore the acceptance of the other man's way of solving problems. Furthermore, one cannot go over the head of the person to whom delegation has been made in case difficulties arise. There must always be a nice sense of the responsibilities of this sort of activity as well as the advantages.

The third group of characteristics of an administrator includes his willingness to look forward to the future and his acceptance of the risks that decisions under conditions of uncertainty always bring with them. It might be appropriate at this point to remark that a decision is the taking of a choice among a range of alternatives when there are no data which make clear which is the optimum choice. If the data did make it clear that one particular course is better than any other, then the administrator is not faced with the need to make a decision. The data have taken for him.

Altogether too many managers of various kinds of activities spend their time solving problems as they come to them. The problems that they have to solve seen to be those which happen to them from day to day. The real administrator is one who sees that these problems are solved, but looks ahead a week, a month, or even years, in order to define policies for today which will lead the organisation in the desired direction. In fact, it can be said that one of the major reasons why top management should not be concerned with daily details, important as they may be, is that the problems which require more imagination are even more important in the long run.

[1] Heinemann, London, 21s., by Wilfred Brown.

In saying that the manager must accept risks, I am saying that he must have a personality that does not insist on certain answers, for management is carried on in an uncertain world. At the same time, I must point out that a good manager does not accept risk thoughtlessly. One of the principles of management is always to have ready an alternative action, if it should turn out that one's estimates were inaccurate.

Every manager has to assess the performance of his subordinates. This work is still a matter of judgement, requiring the psychological stamina to take action that may seriously affect other people, despite the fact that an element of intuition is involved. The batteries of available tests do no more than reduce the area to which judgement is applied.

I have recently been very much attracted to studies which indicate that an important element in determining how far up the ladder of responsibility a man may go is found in his capacity to carry the anxieties resulting from making decisions which have a long time-span of uncertainty, and in assigning and judging subordinates in his organisation. At the moment we can hardly say that such a personality trait can be created in a school, but it can be recognised and encouraged.

And finally, and I am now speaking of conditions in the world at the present time and not as they were perhaps 50 years ago, the administrator must be a socially responsible man. In all countries people are becoming so conscious of the possibilities of social control, than an organisation cannot long succeed unless its management always considers how its purpose fits in with the basic policies of the society of which it is a part. In this connection, I am happy to say, more and more persons in positions of responsibility in private enterprise are able and willing to work out the appropriate relationship of the activities of their firm with the needs and desires of the society in which they operate.

I have not insisted that the administrator be a technician in any special one of the many fields which bear upon the management task. I have said that he doubtless is a technician in some field, and to me that is enough. Nor have I said anything which would indicate that the administrator would draw upon a single science for the knowledge and wisdom which he requires. Certainly economics will not be enough. It has been rightly said that "the economic man" is a creation of the intellect who would not be socially acceptable in any group of real persons with which he might associate. He is by definition gifted with only a selfish purpose in life, and he has far more accurate foresight of economic developments than anyone who has ever really lived. Nor can the administrator draw all he needs to know from psychology. "The psychological man" is by definition wholly preoccupied with the feelings and emotional reactions of persons with whom he may be in contact. While the administrator must know these feelings, he cannot devote himself exclusively to the way that people are going to feel about what he does, not insist that he will only do those actions which will be pleasing to all people at all times.

In other words, I am saying that the administrator cannot be trained by the study of courses which present a body of knowledge, such as economics, and then discuss its application to administrative problems. Rather the administrator needs to be trained by courses which pay attention to the problems of the administrator, and then look to economics and other fields, to see what parts of the structure of those fields will be useful to the administrator and the work he does. While this may seem to be only a reorganisation of words, in fact it is a very fundamental difference, which justifies the organisation of schools of management apart from schools of economics, engineering, and so on. In my mind's eye, I consider the field of administration as that area which lies between the subjects of which I have spoken, little explored, and probably containing theoretical considerations which are as yet not even imagined.

After these long introductory considerations I now state the proposition that management is itself a field of study apart from neighbouring fields of interest in the social sciences, where boundary lines are by no means rigid. And secondly, I would say that since this field is of such tremendous importance to society, and since as yet so little is known about the fundamentals of management, it is a field in which disinterested academic research is greatly called for. I would therefore argue that for two reasons the teaching of management is appropriate to a University. In the first place it is a professional field as worthy of attention as that of law, medicine, and so on. In the second place it is a field in which academic research will be richly rewarded because it is a field which has been so little explored as yet.

I now turn to the second major question to be covered in this paper, that is to say how to create in students the characteristics which I have been describing. My basic premise is that the definition of the nature of the product of our educational programme will in large part define the curriculum which should be offered to achieve that result. Therefore, the suggestions which I am about to offer are those which I believe will most surely develop the characteristics described above. I offer them in contrast to the traditional University education. Of course, the University's method have many values. For present purposes, however, I think that such things as reliance on lectures and the nature of the examinations usually given, tend to put too high an emphasis upon the individual brilliance of a man dealing with the abstractions and not enough emphasis on his abilities in handling detailed facts, dealing with people, and so forth.

In contrast, I shall argue that for the purposes indicated the teaching should be of the kind that is known in the United States as Student Centred. We are not alone concerned with pouring into the student's mind the accumulated knowledge in the subject of with concentrating attention purely on an abstract system of thinking. In fact we believe, as one of my colleagues some years ago expressed it that wisdom cannot be told. We have certain other ways of expressing this idea that may help to indicate my meaning. We say: the student learns by doing—and he learns what he does. For example, this paper may well be teaching something about management education to the reader, but he would learn more of the skills of the administrator from problems designed to make him do the kind of thinking which the administrator must do. There is a place for the presentation of principles in the form of a theory, but we believe that it comes later than the kind of training for a professional career with which we are now concerned. It has been our experience that most of the material of courses needs to be rearranged so that the subject is presented in an order that considers primarily the students general sophistication and his degree of knowledge of the subject.

Let me give an example from my own field of speciality, which is that of private finance. Shortly after the War, I collaborated with a Professor in Northwestern University, reconsidering the means of presentation of this field of study. We found that most professors were dealing with it in an entirely logical sequence, beginning first with the definition of the types of business organisation, such as corporations and partnerships, going back into history to show how these social organisations came into being, and then proceeding with a discussion of the way in which a new company is formed and financed. But all of us know that the problems of forming a company and financing it through its initial years are probably the most difficult of all the problems of finance, requiring the greatest sophistication and art in the whole activity of financial management. In other words, an outline which is perfectly logical, and doubtlessly very useful to a person who is already a trained theorist, presents the student with the hardest material first. We have changed this method of approach so that now we take the student into a going concern, a reasonably well financed, mature organisation. We begin there with day-to-day problems that face such a management and proceed outward to the more difficult problems of expansion, reorganisation and so forth. In fact, we end the course with the problems of promoting and financing a new enterprise, instead of beginning that way. We have been very pleased with the results.

The first of my propositions about the method of teaching, then, is that it must be student centred, and that this implies a considerably greater rearrangement of material than is commonly accepted.

We also insist upon discussion. In our curricula, time is allowed for students to meet together in groups after having studied the cases individually and before class. In some programmes, this is followed by the appointment of a reporter for each group who prepares to present the findings of the group to the entire student body in class. There follows an open discussion by the entire group under the leadership of the professor. In our own schools in the United States, where we have the students for a longer period of time, we usually make each student responsible for a defence of his position at any time.

At all events, the method of instruction which I am proposing requires time and opportunity for the students to meet together apart from the classroom.

This presents great difficulties in countries where students do not reside in the University, and where attendance has not been required. Nevertheless, I believe personally that this element is essential and that a way for its accomplishment must always be worked out.

Let me now describe briefly the method of instruction which has, in the field of Business Administration, come particularly to be associated with the Harvard School of Business—the case method. This method of instruction is not universally used in the United States or elsewhere, and I do not claim that it is essential that cases be used, but in the opinion of myself and my colleagues, the use of cases for instruction purposes has a particular virtue in throwing the problem to the student and in requiring him to acquire the habits of thought which are specified as those of the administrator.

I will try to explain this matter by analogy. History cannot be taught by the case method, but historians can. I shall define the teaching of history as the presentation of the whole panorama of the past arranged in such a way as to be understandable, and to lead us to some constructive thinking about what may happen in the future. The training of an historian, on the other hand, is the imparting of an ability to take tangled and incomplete evidence and to draw from it an accurate statement, which can then go down in the books as history. The contrast has sometimes been expressed as that between talking about and working with. It can also be described as an essential difference between theory and practice.

Every teacher makes his own choice of how to teach, and every method of teaching in the right hands achieves significant results. For teaching management, however, it is my conviction that the case method deserves more attention and use than any other.

So far, in talking about curriculum and method, I have tried to bring out three points, which are:

1. That the teaching must be student centred, not only in the classroom but in the order in which topics are presented;

2. that group work by students is essential;

3. that the students must work with concrete problems, not only with problems stated abstractly.

Before I conclude, I shall expand a little upon the last of these points. The type of instruction which I have been describing is often criticised by those who say that it transmits insufficient knowledge and information about the fields of study. In fact, the most common suggestion that I have received from professors is that our method would be improved if " a good theoretical background " were first laid out to the student by lecture. In my opinion, nothing could be farther from the truth, and I must reject this concept with all the force at my disposal. I do not reject the lecture process. I reject the concept that a theoretical structure should be built as a prerequisite to dealing with practical problems. The human mind is altogether too able to insulate parts of its knowledge from other parts. What we are trying to do is to assist the transfer of information within the mind from one problem to another by giving it to the students in situations where the need of information arises from a problem solving experience, and any theoretical structure is drawn upon with reference to an actual instance.

If one were to study thoroughly enough the curricula using the student centred method in most of the courses in business administration, he would find that a great deal of technical and functional material is imparted to the students; only not in the order in which the theorist would have presented it. It is, rather, presented in a way which leads to its being learned usefully— that is, in connection with conditions of problem solving. It is supplied in part by the case itself, in part in small statements or lectures by the teacher himself, and in part by reference work on the side of the student.

Another great misconception which seems to arise in the minds of many who are about to participate in courses of the kind I am describing is that we consider the teacher to be an unimportant factor, since the discussion is centred so entirely on the students. In fact, the phrase non-directive has come to be widely used in the United States. I cannot accept the idea that the teacher is simply a mirror or a rubber stamp for the activity of students. To me the conduct of the class by the discussion or the case method is one of the most challenging for a teacher. He has given the initiative to the student but he must constantly respond to the classroom in ways which will not force him to become didactic and yet will take the class in a direction which will be productive for the purposes of the course. It is a constant challenge and a very exciting one.

In conclusion, I would like to point out that I have been trying to define one area of education which I consider to be of sufficient intellectual and social importance to become a part of a programme of a separate faculty of a University. I have tried by defining the characteristics of the product to lead the way to my suggestions about the curriculum and the methods of teaching which are best suited to the goals to be desired. I have suggested certain points at which my ideas are so strongly in contrast with those of the traditional type of academic course that they should be emphasised. These are that the student should be taught by his own experience, guided of course by the professor, but not through the presentation of organised knowledge and theory as the professor knows it, that this usually requires a reorganisation of the curriculum of the course, and that all these things are greatly assisted by the use of case problems and group discussion.

As a final word, I should like to recall the statement of Holmes, who said a man's education really begins when what is called his education is over. We try to do in the University the things the University can do best, and especially to train the student in such a way that he may continue his development through his later experience. Ways of thinking are therefore far more important than memorised information.

2. THE CASE METHOD OF INSTRUCTION*

—PEARSON HUNT

I. THE CHARACTERISTICS AND GOALS OF THE METHOD

There are, of course, as many good ways of teaching as there are good teachers. A quotation from President Conant is appropriate: "What, after all, determines whether a given course is part of a liberal education or is merely prevocational training? Clearly, the outlook of the teacher." The case method, like any other method, can be used for narrowly professional courses or for courses in a program of general education. It is up to the teacher. In the author's opinion, however, too few teachers have considered the applicability of the case method to their subjects. This article is particularly addressed to these teachers, with the hope that they will give the method further thought.

The term "case method" has been applied to a number of ways of teaching, so the author wishes to define as specifically as possible the meaning of the term as it will be used here. The desired result of the case method is the ability to reason in dealing with problems in the area of the course. Appropriate use of theory, and the acquisition of factural material and procedural skills are also important goals, but the heart of the method is the use of problems to train the student to discover and then to fix in his mind *ways of thinking that are productive in the chosen field.*

A series of cases can be used to provide repeated and developing experience in the process of thinking, for the work on each case requires the kind of thinking which has been presented by John Dewey: the occurrence of a difficulty; the definition of the problem to be solved in working out the difficulty; the arrangement of facts and skills necessary for handling the difficulty; the

---

* From the *Harvard Educational Review*, Summer, 1951, pp. 3–19. Reprinted by permission of Professor Pearson Hunt and the *Harvard Educational Review*.

process of suggesting possible solutions, testing and elaborating the solutions that seem best; verification of the conclusions; and finally, an extension of the solution of the particular difficulty into a form of knowledge which will enable solution of other difficulties containing similar characteristics.

The word "decisional" has been used to contrast the case method with "expository" teaching. The case method is a type of the discussion method of teaching, in which students participate in group analysis of a problem, thus being trained to think by the interaction of individual attempts to reach a decision. Sometimes the problem is specifically stated in the text of the case, sometimes one of the objectives of the discussion is to determine what problems need to be solved. But it is essential that students attempt in their preparation and through discussion to solve the problem posed by the case. This must be a major part of any course using the case method as defined here. *Retained capacity to think* in the subject area is more likely to be created by group study of a range of possible solutions to cases than through the study of the explicitly stated generalizations of a subject area without the accompaniment of cases.

The case method can also be defined in terms of the materials made available to the student. There will be prepared "case problems" for discussion. The typical case will present the facts surrounding a problem. In general, the facts of the case need to be those which a person actually had at hand in connection with the problem. These facts may need to be supplemented by the student as part of his work. The bulk of the cases in a course should be so presented that the student can visualize the position of some person or group in the situation. His study then can include an attempt to make the decision from that point of view.

A group of cases making up a course will provide a series of experiences following a conceptual order chosen by the instructor, designed to provide the development of the desired power to think in the area covered by the course. Most of the cases in a collection must call for a choice to be made among reasonably possible alternatives. Such cases can be termed "issue cases." The reason for the insistence that a decision should be the goal of almost every discussion of a case is that the quality of mind termed "judgment" is not called for unless a decision must be reached. The discovery and naming of the considerations that must be weighed is only the prelude to the actual weighing process itself.

Most case collections contain a few cases where the issue is not of the type described. In such instances, care must be taken in the writing of the case and in its teaching to be sure that the student discussion will be directed toward reaching a decision. For example, a pair of cases might present differing behavior where at first glance there are similar circumstances. The question to be discussed from such material is "which of the slight differences in the facts can be considered the major explanations of the differing behavior?"

Another type of case will present a problem, but only part of the information necessary for its solution. In such a case, the problem is "what additional information is necessary, and how may it be obtained?" Such deviations from the issue case play very useful parts in an over-all plan, but they contribute to the case method only if nearly all of the cases are of the issue type described above.

In addition, it is altogether likely that the material for such a course will contain readings which are not cases, readings inserted at appropriate points to provide theoretical treatment, factual material, or procedural skills, which the current case material causes the student to desire. It is however, implicit in the case method that such background material would not be provided all at once as a separate section of a course. Such presentation has the disadvantage of insufficient motivation. More important, it presents the material apart from its use thus preventing the transfer process which is a vital part of problem solving.

The nature of "the case method" which the author has in mind can be clarified further by distinguishing two other types of educational material which are frequently referred to as "cases," but to which the author finds it desirable to give separate terms. An "instance" is a description of a problem whenever the description carries through to state what was done, and perhaps to analyze the results. An instance might be referred to as an exercise in the translation of complicated facts into the appropriate things to be considered, and then a demonstration of how this was done by someone else. Cases as often presented in social or medical study, and in the law school tradition, can usually be classed as "instances."

Another type of "case" is essentially an exercise in translating the problem's facts into such terms as can be substituted into some already known method, where the answer will follow from there on. Many (but not all) mathematical and engineering "cases" are classified by the author as "exercises" because there is no room for difference of opinion once the appropriate analysis of the facts has been made. The "excerise" is an experience in translation, rather than in judgment.

When confronted with the question of stating the goals of the case method, experienced teachers might state a maximum and minimum. The maximum goals are those which the teacher hopes to see his best students achieve, the minimum goals are those which will be reached by the students with the lowest passing grade.

The maximum goal of the case method is the development of a mind which has superior ability to transfer its powers from familiar types of problems to new ones. Persons with such minds also need the power to explain to others what is going on, that is, to verbalize their thinking. In contrast, as a minimum goal, most teachers of the case method would accept "direct learners," that is to say persons who can be observed to deal intelligently with the problems they face, although they are not able to explain the thinking process they have gone through. It is supposed that these students have an ability to generalize and transfer inarticulately without verbalization.[1]

On the other hand, failing grades would be awarded to some "lesson learners" who have the capacity to absorb facts and skills, but show no evidence of being able to think through new kinds of situations. It is clear that passing grades, sometimes of high rating, could be accorded to "lesson learners" under certain theories of education, while persons with high powers to deal with problems might be rated poorly because they lack certain substantive knowledge. Persons of the former sort, in courses taught by the case method, are usually found to spend a great deal of time organizing and reorganizing the facts in some manner, but never breaking over into a thinking process which produces a discovery leading to a solution.

The maximum and minimum goals which are implicit in the case methods can be restated more fully as follows. The minimum, itself a goal of considerable difficulty, is attitudes and habits of thought characterized by logical behavior in dealing with problems, such as:

(1) The power to analyze and to master a tangle of circumstances, by selecting the important factors from the whole set of facts, and by weighing their importance in context. In the eyes of an advocate of the case method this power of analysis is not to be interpreted as the power to derive and apply any "principles" in the sence that once the principles have been applied, the answer will come out mechanically.

(2) The ability to utilize ideas, to test them against the facts of the problem, to throw both ideas and facts into fresh combinations, thus discovering ways which make them appropriate for the solution of the problem at hand.

(3) The ability to recognize a need for new factual material or the need to apply technical skills to a problem, and the ability to assimilate such facts and skills as are needed for the solution of the problem at hand.

(4) The ability to use later experience as a test of the validity of the ideas already obtained, with flexibility to revise goals and procedures as experience is deepened. This is the key to continued learning after formal education ends.

Students who reach the maximum goal will, or course, have the minimum qualities just described. In addition they can be expected to have:

(5) The ability to communicate their thinking to others in a manner which induces thought.

(6) The ability to use ideas in theoretical form. That is to say, one should be able to create a coherent structure of generalized propositions from his problem-solving experiences. From this, one should be able to make inferences, both by adding the theoretical ideas of others as they are pertinent, and by one's own thinking on a high level of analysis.

---

[1] Actually, of course, if careful measurement were taken, the difference between the minimum and maximum student would probably be found to be one of degree rather than presence or absence of the qualities named.

(7) The ability to attain the goal simply, completely, and without any more waste than is necessary in any thinking about an unfamiliar problem. This has been referred to by Whitehead as the development of "style."

It is not a desired goal that a student should be able to think abstractly in the sense that he can make logical use of verbalization, follow logically from one general proposition to another, and so on, where the verbalizations are not meaningful in terms of the student's capacity to deal with problems as he faces them. Such power to deal unrealistically in symbols and abstractions is often impressive but constitutes in fact merely the appearance of learning. The real evidence of learning is the power to deal intelligently with problems at any level of generality. It is the author's own experience, and his observation with reference to others, that too much time spent acquiring the thought of others as stated in general terms may act as a bar to independent thinking.

II. EDUCATIONAL THEORY

The theory of education which can be deduced from observation of the case method can be stated as a series of propositions about the learning process. There is nothing novel in the statement below, yet its principles are often ignored in practice, so that it is desirable to state them explicitly as background for the rest of the discussion.

(1) *The material must be of interest to the student.* He must feel that it will contribute to his knowledge, if he contributes his application. Student interest can be obtained in many ways, of course. Cases, however, do have a quality which creates interest to an unusual degree.

(2) *Any successful learning process must require the student to think for himself, for learning is achieved by the interaction of ideas.*

Problem-solving, despite the seeming confusion of important and unimportant material, is a better basis for significant learning than the presentation of the elements of the subject in carefully compartmented, clearly worded statements. Although simplified and abstract statements are permissible and often desirable, they should be brought in where needed for solution of a problem, and they should not be used to develop a subject without frequent rechecking and new learning through a new problem-solving experience of appropriate difficulty.

In addition, the use of discussion in class demonstrates a third proposition.

(3) *Learning is affected by the whole environment of the learner.* Values are gained from group discussion, which are not gained from the work of a single person trying to handle an unfamiliar problem. In part this is a question of motivation, since no one likes to fall far behind the progress of his group. But more importantly, learning results from the encouragement gained from corroboration of one's own tentatively held ideas, and from the spirit of joint effort which comes from successful group work. Finally, and no less important,

group discussion trains the capacity to communicate to others the ideas that are running through one's own mind.

Outside the classroom, the use of cases has been found to stimulate group discussion as a part of preparation of assignments. This, in itself, is a considerable advantage over the more common ways of preparing an assignment.

Group discussion is also of help in dealing with an emotional problem in a way which advances maturity. A student comes to class with ideas and emotions which he needs to handle with reference to others. In a group discussion, the student can learn to change his views without thinking that he loses face, and to respect and use the ideas of others. He will be stimulated to this behavior by seeing his good ideas accepted and used by his colleagues.

The final proposition deserves separate statement, although it is included in the scope of the third:

(4) *Learning is affected not only by the nature of the material but also by the efforts of the teacher.* No matter how well the material has been designed and arranged, and how faithfully the student has worked, good teaching can magnify the results, and bad teaching can prevent most of them. For this reason, the question of teaching methods to be used in connection with cases is made a major section of this article and appears below.

III. WRITING CASES AND PLANNING A COURSE

As was said above, the case method presents material in a conceptual order chosen by the instructure to provide a series of experiences that are planned to develop judgment and the necessary skills and factual knowledge in the field covered by the course.

One of the important effects of preparing material for use with the case method is a change in the point of view of the case writer, if he has previously organized his course with a view to the orderly development of theory or the systematic presentation of facts.[2] The degree to which the use of the case method will change the order of topics and emphasis in a subject is underestimated by most of those who have not planned a case method syllabus. Most subjects have been developed over the years to present through text and lecture the problem areas seriatim, usually preceded by definitions, and perhaps

---

[2] For example, a course in history may be greatly changed if one pauses to ask why the student is being asked to study history. If the purpose is not to present a series of events that can be read as a sort of romance, but rather, say, to train one's ability to reach appropriate judgment about existing situations, a case might be set up on some current issue, where historical background will be most useful. A study of the current civil liberties controversy in the light of events in America during the threats of the Napoleonic Empire's expansion is an instance in point.

Or, if the student's attention is to be directed to the difficulty of properly recording "facts," he might be presented with some contradictory original evidence about an historical event and be asked to analyze it.

followed by problems where the partial analyses are used and integrated.[3]

Teachers are not the only ones affected by the substantially different pedagogic plan which the case method uses when contrasted with an ordered expository approach. Most students, on confronting the method for the first time, experience a sense of frustration that cannot be dispelled except by experience. Those who plan a course for students who are to have their first experience with the case method must be careful to introduce simple cases that will stimulate active discussion, to plan periods for summarization, or to use another device.

The syllabus which best fits the case method is one based on problems requiring analysis like that encountered by those actually dealing in the problems with which the course is concerned. Arrangement in suitable order for classroom use involves considerations of difficulty, of common methods of analysis, and matters of this kind. Briefly, problems should be selected which require the type of analysis that actually is necessary in practice in the field, yet so ordered that they present a continuity in the eyes of the student. Ordinarily the principal aspects of the subject should be covered more than once.

A procedure that has been found productive in developing a course to be taught by the case method may serve further to explain the ideas stated above. First, one should observe the existing background of the prospective students. This involves not only a survey of the content of courses already taken, but some attention to the manner in which the student has been trained to think. A similar analysis is desirable for the work which the students will be doing concurrently with the course being planned.

Second, a study of the traditional material usually used for the subject in question helps the teacher to find the types of problems which lie in the background of the training that is being given. Unfortunately, problems which lie in the background of the training that is being given. Unfortunately, problems suggested by a standard text, or simple illustrative examples, usually do not work at once into cases or ideas for cases because so often they have been simplified to fit some particular point in an orderly development of an expository type.

Conferences with persons who are using the kind of knowledge that the course is to convey are an essential part of the development of a course plan. These conferences should be devoted to the discovery of what kinds of knowledge, techniques, and judgment the person being interviewed is actually

---

[3] Even in such courses, teachers find cases useful. For instance, cases can be introduced to show the real situation from which an abstraction is drawn, or to provide a pool of facts from which students are trained to choose the facts pertinent to the abstraction that is being taught at the time, or to check a conclusion arrived at deductively. But all this is using cases in service to a method that is not the case method as the author has it in mind. Their use, however, may serve to prevent immunization against ideas that do not fit the accustomed structure of the subject.

using in dealing with problems.[4] When these are determined, cases can be sought which require the qualities of judgment that should be taught. It will be found that part of the information to be conveyed can be given in expository material, inserted at the proper time. Much factual matter, however, will occur in cases as necessary to the description of the problem at issue.

The reader who has been thinking of the traditional treatment of his subject while reading the above material will no doubt feel that a great deal more classroom time will be needed for a course taught by the case method. This is true, of course, if the same amount of material is to be taught. However, careful consideration will permit the omission of much material that traditionally is considered necessary. For instance, in the author's own field of corporation finance, the extensive detailed classification of the types of corporate instruments is omitted. Care is taken, however, to inform the students that they will eventually need to learn this classification, and materials for reference are made available.

The writing of cases is itself a process requiring great skill. The final text must be on a narrow dividing line. On the one hand, it must not state the "real facts," but rather the kind of evidence from which one would have to deduce the real facts in an actual situation. On the other hand, the case must be complete enough, and precise enough, to permit learners to think about the problem, and thus to learn to think. Wherever possible, each case should present an issue, and the student should identify himself with someone actually facing a problem. If this is impossible, care must be taken to provide some sort of choice to be made by the student, as for instance "what additional information is necessary before a decision can be made" or "what are the forces which cause this person to behave differently than in the case of so and so."

The problem to be solved may be stated explicitly in the first cases of a course, but it is well to write later cases so that one of the first things the student must do is to determine the problem which he is required to solve. Specific instructions outside of the case itself may be prepared to suit the particular condition of each student group at the time of the assignment.

The author feels very strongly that in every instance the problem presented must be one which is within the capacity of a student who is ready to use his brains. Difficulty is desirable, but bewilderment is to be avoided and blind trial and error is not to be encouraged. In fact, if a really intelligent student is confronted with a problem which he cannot solve with available case or reference materials, he demonstrates his intelligence by refusing to consider the problem. All this emphasizes the importance of presenting the basis for a reasoned choice in a case, or in actually available material. Material cannot be considered as available, even it if be physically on hand, unless time is

---

[4] An interviewer seldom finds a person who can state these matters directly. Usually several preliminary questions, such as "What facts did you have at hand?" are needed.

actually available for its use. If the material is inadequate, class discussion either goes in the direction of a " 'tis–'taint " argument or there is so much speculation that the discussion loses its semblance of reality. The need for appropriate basic material to keep the discussion from wandering off into unsupported hypotheses is the important need that people forget when they say that they can teach an entire subject from any one case.

It is also important that a good ratio of creative opportunity to gross work shall be maintained. Of course, a case which is split down so far as to present only the pertinent material loses much of its value. On the other hand, an enormous volume of irrelevant material usually has the effect of preventing the student from selecting the relevant facts in the time available to him. Cases for discussion in class need to be carefully edited with respect to length. Cases which are to be used for term reports or other longer assignments can contain more intricate problems and more irrelevant material.

IV. THE DISCUSSION METHOD OF TEACHING[5] AND THE PROBLEM OF EXAMINATION

Since the case method is a form of discussion teaching, the following paragraphs have been written about the discussion method, with emphasis on its use with cases. No one can be a good teacher who relies solely on a series of " do's " and " don'ts." Therefore it is unwise to give any listing of particular things to be done in all cases by all teachers.

First, it may be useful to review a few of the fundamentals for the success of teaching by discussion.

1. *There must be a basis,* (not only in the facts of the case problem, but also in the background of the knowledge and skills of the students) *for a reasoned difference of opinion to develop in the classroom.* Group discussion reaches minimum results if the teaching material (or the conduct of the class by the teacher) leads merely to a single line of analysis. A difference of opinion should develop, and the group should center on analyzing the reasons for the differing opinions so that each student may reach his own judgment. This is not to say that all case problems need to have indeterminate solutions, but only that there must be reasonable alternatives to examine and discuss. The decision-reaching process, not the decision, is the substance of the case method.

2. *There must be a leader to guide the discussion into productive channels.* Unless a group is exceptionally experienced in discussion, this leader will normally be the teacher. The functions of the teacher as a discussion leader are extremely complex, and will be discussed more fully below.

3. *There must be a " resource."* In other words, provision must be made for adding facts and skills to the discussion so that it does not proceed on the

---

[5] The author's organization of this section draws heavily on an unpublished manuscript by his colleague, Dr. K. R. Andrews.

basis of unverified assumption, and so that students can add to their knowledge of techniques as they deal with problems. The means of introducing this "resource" is one of the most difficult questions raised by the method, and more will be said of it below.

4. *There must be time to set aside for the relating of such generalizations as can be drawn from the discussion of a series of related problems to the "theory" of the subject area.* A thoroughly trained student should be able to read the literature of his subject, commonly expressed in abstract, sometimes in symbolic, terms, so that he can use the work of others to aid significantly in the solution of problems coming before him. He should also be able to think constructively about the generalized literature he has read, toward the goal of being able to write, himself, significant material at this level. This is a goal of the case method which is not always reached and sometimes not even recognized. But the power to deal with theory is certainly part of the necessary powers of a well-rounded mind.

In the classroom situation, the first thing to be noted is that at the first meeting of a class the teacher is the person on whom the students' interest enters. This centering of attention in the teacher remains in each class meeting throughout the course. No teacher can avoid being the key personality. The goal of group thinking with a minimum of participation on the teacher's part cannot be reached by any type of withdrawal on the part of the teacher. It will come from careful planning and leadership, sometimes of an extremely subtle kind.

Several writers have contrasted "directive" and "nondirective" leadership by teachers. One of the author's colleagues (Dr. C. I. Gragg) has coined the term "rapportive" to designate more accurately the desired relationship between teachers and students. Such a relationship may be established when the teacher's behavior tells the students that there is a genuine mutuality of interest present. Things are said and done in an attitude of equality of interest in the basic problems at hand—there is no evidence that the teacher feels himself a superior person, although he is recognized to be a person to be referred to as needed. Things are said and done in class in an attitude of suspended judgment toward the problem and toward the student. *All* the persons in the room are working on the basic problem, which is the way to learn as much as possible.

The desired learning results can be subdivided, conformably with the goals of education that were discussed above, into a series of processes. The teacher must use all his skill to lead the group to do well in any one of the things that it undertakes, and to select an order of processes that is likely to get the desired result efficiently. Those who are attempting the discussion method for the first time are usually impressed by the "inefficiency" of the use of class time. A certain amount of exploration down blind alleys is to be allowed, not prevented, for thinking through a new problem is always slow, and "scrapped ideas" are a normal part of the thinking process.

For this sort of group activity, class time is greatly needed. The usual college class period of 50 minutes is the very minimum that should be allotted for the discussion of a case. If scheduled class hours could be lengthened by 50%, the increased effectiveness of case method teaching would be far more than in proportion to the additional class time spent. Too short a class time, combined with a teacher's feeling of responsibility to "get across" certain materials during a term, often leads to too much direct lecturing on the part of the teacher.

In preparing for class, the teacher should remember certain principles that are basic to any teaching. (1) The teacher should always be conscious of what the class has already learned, not only in his own course, but in other courses. His expectations in this field should, of course, be realistic. Students have far less authoritative command over recently learned or once heard ideas than most teachers are prone to believe. (2) The teacher should visualize the students' preparation. He can learn from the way the assignment was given, and from the material in the case, the kind of work which most students will be likely to have done. To the maximum extent he should afford the students the courtesy of attempting to use the work that he believes they have done, instead of taking off on some tangent at the beginning of a class, for some alleged "surprise value." (3) While the teacher should be alert to prevent students from shifting responsibility to him, he should be ready at all times to add facts or to explain skills which are needed to continue a satisfactory discussion. The actual responsibility to learn should rest with the students because the student is the only person who can take this responsibility.

Any experienced teacher will recognize that all of these objectives are difficult to reach. Good teaching can never be perfect, it can merely try to be.

The characteristics of the process of reaching a good judgment, and certain questions that teachers may ask to stimulate this process in class, are: (1) One needs to maintain an attitude of suspended judgment until a problem has been thoroughly analyzed and the conclusions have been checked. Such questions as "Is it as easy as all that?" or "What weight did you give to the fact that——?" may be useful. (2) Any tangle of facts must be analyzed to define what the basic problem is and what the important facts are. Questions helping to keep on the track of such an analysis include "Can we solve that problem before we take up the question of—?" or "Suppose the facts you refer to were not the case—?" (3) The ability to transfer previously obtained ideas to the solution of a new problem is greatly aided by the stimulation of curiosity. "Is there any other way of looking at" or "Why do you suppose that this occurred—?" may be useful questions. (4) Another source of the transfer of ideas is the review of past experiences as they relate to a new problem. "Have we seen anything in past material that presents problems similar to this one?" or "Was there anything in your course in government that may help here?" will be useful. (5) Any group dealing with a problem is apt to deal with it superficially, if the analysis seems to be going along without friction. Poor teaching by the case method can encourage superficiality. The simple question, "Why?" to confront some student's assertion is perhaps as useful as any. "Can we be sure of that without further checking?" is another good question. (6) Habits of orderliness of analysis need to be stimulated. The virtues of a pause to review what has been done can be demonstrated by a brief summarization by the teacher himself, or some student (preferably previously warned) can be asked to summarize the discussion to date. Other ways of stimulating orderliness are the presentation of such questions as "How does your idea bear on the matter that has been discussed?" or even "Let's drop that now and take it up when it is more appropriate."

Of course the teacher's activity should not be confined to questions, and every sentence of a student should not be met by some questioning attitude on the part of the teacher. The questions need to be asked whenever in the teacher's judgment there is need to invite some progress in group thinking. So long as a class can proceed from volunteer to volunteer, with only a reasonable amount of scrapped thought, the teacher needs only to act as chairman. In this role, one of the most useful things that a teacher can do is to restate what a student has said in terms which are acceptable to this student, yet more precisely directed to the issue at hand.

What has been said in the previous paragraphs concerns the improvement of the student's ability to reason for himself. The teacher who handles a discussion group also has a duty to develop the student's ability to be an effective member of a group. (1) The ability to communicate ideas is the basic need for any group discussion. Asking a student to restate his own ideas when they are not well presented, or offering a restatement with a query as to its usefulness, or asking some student to say what he heard of the other man's remarks, (not in the decibel but in the intellectual realm) are all desirable processes. (2) Another needed attitude for full participation in group discussion is sensitivity to group feelings, including a willingness to share responsibility with others. (3) Still another capacity needed for group discussion is the understanding that a group is the understanding that a group member does not lose face when a tentative conclusion is shown to be wrong. In fact, one loses status with the group if he shows annoyance at such an occurrence, or in some other way shows that he is not willing to put his tentative ideas on the chopping block along with everyone else's. (4) Finally, a member of a group needs to develop a capacity to integrate what has been said during a discussion into something that represents progress in his own thinking, and that can be offered as a tentative statement of the group conclusions. It is sometimes useful to designate a student to have the function of summarizing the findings of the group during or immediately after a discussion. Assignment to go back over the discussions of several days and to attempt generalizations and summaries are also desirable at times. Such activities are referred to by some as "feed-back."

This list of the devices which the perfect teacher may use may appear frightening. They certainly disturb the author, for he is extremely conscious

of how often he has failed to meet one or another of the suggested requirements. It is in this respect that the "rapportive" attitude is a great help.
Students who are convinced that their teacher is trying just as hard as they
are will be more willing to be helpful, and will tend to fill in where the teacher
omits.

The teacher himself needs to generalize and summarize from his classroom
experience. Recently the author adopted the parctice of keeping a sort of
journal of the results he thinks were obtained from each class. Although the
comment on a day's teaching may amount to no more than a brief paragraph,
the author has found that this kind of thinking on paper has been very helpful
in planning for the progress of the course.

The problem of measuring the performance of students is not made easier
by the use of the case method. However, much that has been said with reference to examination procedure is as true of examining for case method
students as it is for others. Consequently, the following discussion can be
brief.

If class size permits, the teacher should have in mind pretty clearly before
the final examination what the capacities of his students are. This is especially
desirable for over-all matters such as "judgment" and "imagination." One
can never, of course, examine such abstractions directly. It is necessary to
translate the desired abstract qualities into observable behavior. A list of the
desired characteristics and the representative behavior can be drawn up for
any course. They will include the general goals which have been explained
above, and probably some specific things related to the subject material. If
such a statement be drawn up, the teacher can have it in mind, and the process
of evaluating students can become a continuous one, not just something to be
done at stated periods during a course.

While, in the author's opinion, the preservation of a proper student-teacher
relationship in the classroom prevents the regular grading of each recitation,
the teacher should be alert to note evidences of the desirable characteristics
that he is searching for, and to make a record of this observation with reference to the particular student. This can be done by a brief period of recollection after most classes. The author has developed, as most teachers have, a
system of shorthand notations which can be made during class with reference
to a student, so that his recollection is aided afterward.

Any major examination for a course taught by the case method will be in
part itself a case problem. The author is profoundly convinced that the integrative type of thinking which should be taught cannot be examined by any
series of short questions no matter how cunningly devised. Problem-solving
ability, then, will be tested by a problem.

It must be recognized, however, that a case used as an examination problem
is so used within rigid time limits. There are, therefore, three abilities taught
by the case method which cannot be tested in an examination. The first of
these is the ability to select from a complication of facts those which are

relevant and important to the issue at hand. The second is the ability to consider adequately many alternatives in analyzing a vague issue. A good examination does present facts that need to be winnowed out, and it does present alternatives, but the length of the examination period itself prevents the case from becoming very complicated in either respect. Finally, there is no opportunity to test one student's ability to use and build upon the ideas of others in a group.

An examination should also test the student's knowledge of the important factual material and skills that he should have acquired during the course. Further, it should test the student's ability to use wisely the writings of others on subjects related to the material of the course. The author suggests that the latter of these matters can be tested by giving appropriate quotations for critical analysis. Knowledge and skills, perhaps, can be tested by objective questions.

V. DIFFICULTIES CREATED BY THE METHOD

Any procedure that emphasizes certain goals inevitably under-emphasizes or distorts other desirable aims. Those who adopt the case method do so because they believe in the cardinal importance of training analytical power, as described above. They must be advised of the difficulties that the case method creates, not only to be able to warn students of them, but also to act against them. Many of the following difficulties can be overcome in large part by appropriate planning on the part of the teacher.

KNOWLEDGE AND SKILLS

Since the time for any course is limited, the time consumed by the case method in training reduces the available time for the teaching of facts and techniques. This difficulty exists despite the answers already given: that much of what is included in basic courses is not actually necessary, or that it can be provided to students by reference material. It must be overcome by the teacher, who will need to introduce factual information as it is pertinent to the case being discussed, or to the case that he is assigning. The teacher's responsibility to act as a " resource " is one that he must not forget. A variety of methods (lecture, text assignment, availability of reference material, specially written memoranda) can be used to satisfy this need.

Something of the same sort can be said with reference to technical skills, such as those of statistical procedure, which often cannot be dealt with directly without destroying the significance of the case discussion. Nevertheless, much can be done by way of review of a series of cases, where it can be pointed out that such and such a procedure would be a useful way of dealing with aspects of all the problems that have been covered, or by assigning technical reading and providing time for its development in class. Often, this can be done just before the cases in which the skills are useful. If done too far in advance, motivation is lost, and the time interval induces forgetting.

Despite all this possibility for guarding against the absence of factual information and technical competence, it must be conceded that a course taught by the case method cannot be expected to convey the same content as would be available in a course where facts and skills are the principal concern. Those who use the case method cannot at this point avoid their responsibility by saying that the thinking process is more important than factual knowledge, even though this is true. They do have the responsibility of showing the student that there is a body of factual knowledge and skills in the area. They should train the students to know when this kind of material needs to be used and where it can be obtained.

USE OF THEORY

A goal of the case method which was set forth above as one of those to be reached by the best students is the ability to generalize from the student's experiences, and then to use such abstractions deductively. An almost equally important goal is the capacity to read and use general treatments and theoretical presentations by others. Many teachers of the case method do not attempt to reach this goal, and in his classes the author is merely feeling his way toward it. It is undesirable, however, to leave the students as so many of them are left: with the ability to show that the generalizations of others do not fit particular experiences but without any feeling for the significance and usefulness of generalized and abstract thinking. While there are grave dangers in the use of deduction without constant reference to facts, one will always use some abstractions in his thinking about a problem. In fact, "transfer" is facilitated by attempts to generalize from particular experiences.

In dealing with this difficulty, the author has had some success with various devices: occasional assignments to review cases and to draw general statements from the problems studied with class discussion of the results; assignment of the writings of others on topics involved in recent cases, to see if the generalizations fit the problem studied; and constructive classroom discussions of the theoretical statements. Some critics of the case method say that students are thus made apt to fall into easy generalizations from too few instances. The author's experience indicates that this does not occur. Rather, students are inclined to be too ready to criticize generalizations because they do not suit the particulars of the cases they have seen.

VOLUME OF MATERIAL

It was stated above that cases need to be so edited that there is an adequate amount of significant material relative to the gross amount presented. Some critics have said that attention to this requirement prevents students with learning how to winnow out significant facts in difficult situations. Such a result would be undesirable. On the other hand, too much material relative to the student's available time usually leads to frustration, and not to progress. Good case writing can strike an appropriate balance. The critics should note, however, that even the more stripped-down cases give the student experience in seeing how facts can be stated and arranged in a useful manner. This in itself prepared him for the work of taking unedited material and selecting the significant portions.

BROAD SOCIAL PROBLEMS

It must be admitted that the "minimum" student in a case method course is apt to learn only the ability to administer the problems of individuals or single firms without any interest in ways and means of correcting the problems of society as a whole. On the other hand, persons poorly trained by more traditional methods often are able to deal glibly with the problems at the social level, without having any capacity to understand individual situations. Since we now live in a society where there is an increasing interrelationship between administrators at the "micro" level and administrators at the "macro" level, obtaining mutual understanding is a problem that deserves a great deal of further exploration.

In situations where the over-all social problem is recognized as not being the sum of the total problems of the individuals concerned—as in the area of juvenile delinquency—students who are asked to work only with problems of individuals may miss important over-all conditions. There is nothing about the case method which prevents the teacher in such circumstances from bringing out the differing nature of the total problem, either by a case at that level, or by readings, or by some other means. In fact, it is far better to approach the general problem after some experience with individual cases than more directly, since the background tends to prevent a superficial solution. An experience with several instances of delinquency, for instance, will deepen the understanding of the motives of an individual that lead to delinquency and to its cure, and will help in the choice of over-all methods to reduce the former motives and increase the latter.

Some critics of the case method argue that the use of actual problems tends to emphasize the status quo. That is to say, the environment is taken as the norm, and the cases are essentially problems in adjusting to this norm. There is no doubt that the case method prevents wholly abstract speculation on the social organization of a brave new world. But reformers trained by the case method are likely to see their ideas realized, for their proposals are likely to take into account of the individuals whose motivation is a pre-requisite to social change.

BIBLIOGRAPHY

In the general areas of the nature of the educated man, the theory of learning and the student-teacher relationship, the following references have been found most stimulating.

1. Whitehead, Alfred North. The Aims of Education. In *The Aims of*

Education and Other Essays. New York: Macmillan, 1929. Also in *Unseen Harvests.* (C. M. Fuess and E. S, Basford, ed.). New York: Macmillan, 1947.

2. Dewey, John. *How We Think.* Boston: D. C. Heath, 1910. Revised 1933.

3. Spring, Leverett W. Socratic Yankee: Mark Hopkins. In *Great Teachers.* (H. Peterson, ed.). New Brunswick: Rutgers University Press, 1946, Chap. 6.

4. Barzun, Jacques. *Teachers in America.* Boston: Little, Brown, 1945, Chap. 2: Pupils into Students; Chap. 3: Two Minds, One Thought.

Three readings are cited for their translation of the general goals of education into those suitable for specialized studies.

1. Fuller, Lon L. What the Law School Can Contribute to the Making of Lawyers. In *Education for Professional Responsibility.* Pittsburgh: Carnegie Press, 1948, 14-34.

2. Doherty, Robert E. *The Development of Professional Education.* Pittsburgh: Carnegie Press, 1950. Chap. IV: Education in Values; Chap. V: The Educational Task. Chap. IV also available as "Value Judgments in Professional Education," *Journal of Engineering Education,* November, 1949, *40,* 159-165 Chap. V also available as "An Undeveloped Phase of Engineering Education." *General Electric Review,* April, 1935, *38,* 164-168,

3. Donham, Wallace B. *Education for Responsible Living.* Cambridge: Harvard University Press, 1944. Chap. 18.

The first two of the following citations have to do with the general objectives of the case method, wherever used. The citations immediately following describe the use of the case method with different types of subject matter.

1. Culliton, James W. The Question That Has Not Been Asked Cannot Be Answered. In *Education for Professional Responsibility, op. cot.,* 85-92.

2. Cragg, Charles I. Because Wisdom Can't Be Told. *Harvard Alumni Bulletin,* October 19, 1940, *43,* 78-84.

3. Donham, Wallace B. The Case System in College Teaching of Social Science. In *Journal of General Education,* January, 1949, *3,* 145–156.

4. Teare, B. Richard, Jr. The Use of Problems and Instances to Make Education Professional. In *Education for Professional Responsibility,* op. cit., 135–150.

5. Means, James H. The Clinical Training of the Medical Student. In *Education for Professional Responsibility,* op. cit., 114–122.

6. Turner, Glen C. Teaching Business by the Case Method. *California Journal of Secondary Education,* October, 1938, *13,* 338–349.

7. Schell, E. H. The Case Method in Undergraduate Teaching. In *Journal of Engineering Education,* March, 1933, *23,* 539–542.

The first two of the following citations take up the effect of a case on students, and the teacher's problems under the case method. The next three items relate student and teacher experience under a discussion system. The final item is hard to classify, but it is most helpful in its suggestion of various ways of stimulating student thought.

1. Learned, Edmund P., Vandercook Chain Stores, Inc. *Harvard Business School Alumni Bulletin*, Autumn, 1949, *25*, 108–110, 133–136.
2. Glover, John Desmond and Hower, Ralph M. *Some Notes on the Use of "The Administrator."* Chicago: Irwin, 1950.
3. Cantor, Nathaniel. *The Dynamics of Learning.* University of Buffalo Press, 1946.
4. Kelley, Earl C. *Education for What is Real.* New York: Harper, 1947.
5. Polya, G. *How to Solve It.* Princeton University Press, 1948.

While the literature on the case method in the classroom is rather meager, there is a great deal on the discussion method. The first item cited is itself a bibliographical review. The next three citations are useful material of the manual type.

1. U.S. Department of Agriculture, Bureau of Agricultural Economics, *Group Discussion and Its Techniques.* Washington: Superintendent of Documents, 1942.
2. Sheffield, A. D. *Creative Discussion: Methods for Leaders and Members of Discussion Groups.* New York: Association Press, 1933.
3. National Industrial Conference Board, Studies in Personnel Policy. *Techniques of Conference Leadership.* New York, 1946.
4. Elliott, Harrison J. *The Process of Group Thinking.* New York: Association Press, 1928.

Recent intensive studies of the workings of groups trying to reach decisions have led to helpful ideas. The first of the following citations is a direct report by members of one such research group. The second is a popularization of their findings.

1. Bradford, L. P. and French, J. R. P. The Dynamics of the Discussion Group. In *Journal of Social Issues*, 1948, *4*, No. 2.
2. Strauss, Bert and Frances. *New Ways to Better Meetings.* Viking Press, 1951.

Finally, the author gratefully acknowledges the immense stimulation which he obtained from the writings of Professor Burton. Although these deal with education in a broader sense, they should certainly be a part of one's readings in studying the case method.

1. Burton, W. H. *The Guidance of Learning Activities.* New York: Appleton-Century Crofts, 1944.
2. Burton, W. H. *The Guidance of Major Specialized Learning Activities within the Total Learning Activity.* Cambridge, Massachusetts, privately printed, 1944.

PART II

CASE ANALYSIS TRENDS:
BUSINESS-MANAGEMENT AUDITS

* *

INTRODUCTION

* *

The case method of instruction, pioneered at Harvard University's Graduate School of Business, develops decision-making skills through the analysis of innumerable cases in a two-year program. Its essentially intuitive and pragmatic methodology is aimed at developing skills in decision-making and in the individual's administrative technique through the experience of evaluating many business case problems. While occasional recourse is made to specific fields of business knowledge, principles of management and principles of departmental or functional fields of business have not traditionally been emphasized. Because of this approach to the analysis of comprehensive business cases, the Harvard approach may be classified as an "unstructured" method of case analysis.

STRUCTURED METHODS OF CASE ANALYSIS

As stated in Part I, the business policy course provides for the integration of the core course fields of knowledge, principles, and methods, and their skilled application in the diagnosis and analysis of business problems and cases. The detection and resolution of policy issues in these cases is certainly an integral part of this analysis, or the course title is in fact a misnomer. Also inherent in this process is the necessity for the periodic appraisal of management, the over-all operation of the business, and departmental operations. Therefore, it appears that a refinement of analytic methodologies may be required for the achievement of *all* of the major objectives of the course.

A recent trend of note is the inclusion of materials in policy casebooks for more systematic approaches to the analysis of cases. While these approaches are contrary to the unstructured and intuitive approach of the original Harvard case method, they nevertheless provide refinements in and additions to traditional case analysis methods.

41

One of the earlier methods developed for the analysis of cases emphasized the evaluation of industry trends, and an appraisal of the competitive position of the company in its industry. This approach was then applied to a detailed breakdown of specific types of policy issues, structured in a cumulative order.[1] Another approach directed the student to the definition of the central problem, a determination and analysis of the significant aspects of the central issue, an investigation of alternative solutions, and thence to a conclusion resulting from the analysis. Intermediate steps included a pro-and-con factor analysis of all pertinent aspects of the case problem. This procedure was applied to cases organized by their increasing degrees of complexity. As a systematic approach, it can be viewed as a reinterpretation of the steps in the scientific method and their application to business case analyses.[2]

MANAGEMENT FUNCTION APPROACHES

A management function approach has been used by a number of writers through a classification of the problem issues in the following categories: (1) organizing functions, including delegation of authority, span of control, and the use of staff and service groups; (2) staffing functions, including recruitment, selection, training, evaluation, and retirement; (3) directing subordinates and evaluating the use of authority, communications, and motivation; (4) planning functions, including objectives, policies, procedures, and programs; (5) controlling functions of establishing standards of performance, evaluating performance, and taking action. In this approach, the basic and pervasive management functions and subfunctions are systematically treated, although not in the cyclical sequence often identified for the process. This method of case analysis appears to be the forerunner of the most recent trend. It has been promoted by partisans of the management process school who emphasize the use of management functions and their principles for the identification of underlying causes of business and departmental problems, since the latter are often more symptomatic than causal in nature.[3]

A refinement of the management function approach is found in the application of a cyclical sequence of the management process to business case problems. This approach provides cyclical sequential steps for analysis, including the following: (1) sizing up the problem by determining the critical factors; (2) defining organizational objectives; (3) formulating strategies; (4) controlling activities through effective communication; (5) application of leadership to the achievement of organizational goals; (6) analysis of industrial relations and interpersonal behavior problems; and (7) the final step,

---

[1] Newman, William H., and Logan, James P., *Business Policies and Central Management*, fifth edition (Cincinnati: South-Western Publishing Company, 1965).

[2] Raymond, Thomas C., *Problems in Business Administration*, second edition (New York: McGraw-Hill Book Company, 1964).

[3] O'Donnell, C., *Cases in General Management* (Homewood, Ill.: Richard D. Irwin, Inc., 1961).

decision making. All of these sequential steps in the management process are made within the framework of the social and economic setting, and emphasize the sequential or cyclical nature of the management function, decision-making process. In applying this process to the analysis of policy cases, a major objective is the development of systematic skills in the detection of business problems, their causal factors, and the making of decisions for the resolution of the problem.[4]

A cross classification analysis of business and management functions provides a matrix approach to the analysis of comprehensive cases. In this approach the business functions are cross classified with the management functions as follows: accounting, economics, finance, legal, management, marketing, and statistics are cross classified with planning, organizing-activating, controlling and evaluating. In addition to this matrix is another cross-classification matrix providing for analysis of behavioral problems in the firm. One axis of this matrix evaluates problems of man to himself, man to man, man to group, man to environment, and group to group. The matrix then cross classifies these problems with others of role, conflict-competition-cooperation, and adjustment to the economic, technological, and social conditions. While the schematic matrix approach is not applied in a detailed fashion, it does provide a unique overview of the interplay of a vast number of interrelated problems within the firm. Using the matrix structures as a guide, the student can evaluate business case problems in a logical-order sequence, with the development of the individual's administrative skills as a by-product.[5]

AUDIT CHECKLISTS

A more detailed systematic approach to case analyses has been developed in the form of organized checklists provided for both management and business functions. In one approach, these checklists provide an over-all analysis of the situation, including appraisals of the major internal and external factors, and of the skills and resources that determine company success. This is followed by a detailed checklist of management functions and subfunctions in the administrative process including basic objectives, corporate image, plans and strategies, and implementation of these through organization and control functions. This systematic approach is based on an innovative premise that failures in the performance of the management functions underlie the departmental and companywide problems. Thus business functional or departmental problems become more symptomatic than causal, since the performance of management functions in decisions affecting them often constitute underlying causal factors of success or failure within these functions and departments.[6]

[4] Johnson, Rossall J., *Executive Decisions* (Cincinnati: South-Western Publishing Company, 1963).

[5] Hargrove, Merwin M. *et al.*, *Business Policy Cases* (Homewood, Ill.: Richard D. Irwin, 1963).

[6] McNichols, Thomas J., *Policy Making and Executive Action*, second edition (New York: McGraw-Hill Book Company, 1963).

In another approach, a number of checklists are provided for administering the going concern as appendix materials for the systematic analysis of cases. These checklists apply to areas of general administration, boards of directors functions, and financial analysis. The first checklist provides for detailed function appraisals of corporate goals, policies, organization structure, staffing, management, decision making, leadership, and controls. The second evaluates the functions of boards of directors and their selection, organization, operational relationships, incentives, and special problems. The final checklist provides for a detailed financial analysis emphasizing balance sheet income statement, and combined statement analyses, with provision for the interpretation of these many statements. This compilation of company and management appraisal checklists is one of the most extensive found in business policy casebooks.[7]

EMERGING TRENDS: STRUCTURED CASE ANALYSIS METHODS

An emerging trend is quite clearly found toward more structured and systematic methodologies, and especially with the use of checklists for the analysis of comprehensive business policy cases. These checklists emphasize most the management functions and subfunctions, and also industry factors, board of directors' functions, financial analyses, and audit-appraisals of other business functions-departments. This trend correlates with the finding in Klasson's University of Texas report on " the need to supplement basic case materials with substantive textual materials of some type." Not only have checklists and methodological sequences been provided, but the variations of each have also increased.

The contributions of these structured approaches provide a number of cumulative improvements in case analysis methodologies. Systematic steps insure a more precise definition of the problem and preclude, in most instances, the inclination to treat symptoms as causes, especially for departmental function problems. Analysis of systematically delineated case factors and issues insures analysis in depth. The factor analysis approach dissects problems into their component parts and enables the student to analyze each detail at one point in time. Organization and structuring of analyses provides for a comprehensive overview of the many problems in a single case. This structure further enables the analyst to see more quickly relationships between various factors in the case.

Schematic grids provide an integration of problems to insure a comprehensive analysis rather than a tangental emphasis. The utilization of management-function checklists serves to sharpen detection of causal factors in the analyses. These checklists represent the most strategic decisions made by management in departmental and companywide operations, and are therefore highly

---

[7] Waters, L. L. *et al.*, *Administering the Going Concern* (Englewood Cliffs, N.J.: Prentice-Hall, Inc., 1962).

useful in detecting the major issues in a multi-problem, comprehensive business policy case. As structured approaches become more systematic, they also become more useful in providing analytical insights into the major underlying issues that might otherwise have gone unnoticed.

This review of structured and unstructured approaches to the organization and analysis of business cases appears necessary for one to recognize, if nothing else, recent significant refinements of teaching techniques for business case analyses. The unmistakable trend toward more systematic approaches in the use of checklists for analyses is found applied to industry, management, business, departmental, and environmental factors. These improved methods make it possible to develop more rapidly the student's skill in analyzing business policy cases. Learning through systematized experiences, the student progresses more quickly than he would through the trial-and-error or unstructured experience method. While the latter kind of learning may be the best kind, the time allocated for most business policy courses, particularly at the undergraduate level, is undoubtedly too brief for achieving the goals outlined for the course. Therefore, a number of detailed "checklist" or "audit" approaches are presented in this chapter in order to provide the most pertinent and applicable checklists available for business policy case analyses.

CASE ANALYSIS OUTLINE STEPS

If *all* of the objectives of the business policy course are to be realized, an organizational structure for the compilation, analysis, and presentation of case analyses should also be considered. Without this structure, integral parts of the case analysis may be ignored, and the multi-purpose nature of the course defeated. Such a structure would provide for the inclusion of the following:

1. *Statement of the major problem*—the essence of the case, the point beyond which one can no longer find a broader, more pervasive, or underlying issue.

2. *Outline of minor problems*—with facts and reasons. A hierarchical order of importance for the sequencing of these minor problems will be discussed following these steps.

3. *Existing major policy issues*—if any. This section will develop the ability to discriminate between goals, strategies, policies, programs, procedures, and rules by requiring a delineation of those policy issues which require formulation, administration, or revision.

4. *Major rejected alternative solutions*—with facts and reasons. This insures an adequate "search" for alternatives, as opposed to superficial analyses that lead to the application of the first alternative that may come to mind.

5. *Recommended solutions*—with reasons. These solutions should embrace and resolve all major and minor problems delineated in steps 1 and 2.

6. *Policy recommendations*. This step will require the completion of the goals cited in step number 3.

7. *Programmed implementation of recommendations and projected ramifications.* This step requires a time-sequence application of recommended programs and plans for achieving the recommended solution. It also requires a forecasting of ramifications, and the identification of negative effects of plans on interdepartmental problems.

MANAGEMENT AUDITS—A STRUCTURED APPROACH

A management audit is a systematic, checklist approach to the analysis of management functions and company operations and decisions. The checklist of questions is intended to present the most strategic decisions made by management in departmental and companywide operations. These audits vary considerably in scope, some covering the company as a whole, including all business and management functions, and many with specialized applications to departmental decisions or management functions.

The need for management audits as a comprehensive and systematic appraisal tool has been pronounced in the field of long-range financing. Both investment bankers and small business investment corporations face difficulty and costly processes of appraisals of industries and firms in meeting the tests of long-range success. Systematic approaches have been used historically, particularly by bankers and accountants, although the scope of their application has been limited.

The alternative to systematic approaches is basically an intuitive one, which relies on the breadth and depth of experience of the person making the appraisal. This approach probably finds its widest application among management consultants in this country. Also, intuitive appraisals are a highly significant part of the final decision in both short-range and long-range analyses of business firms. Exclusive reliance on the intuitive approach has been used more for appraising the management group and its functional performance than for general company operations and decisions.

A continuing need for management and business appraisals is occasioned by the annual planning decisions for business firms. When forecasts for the forthcoming year are made, an appraisal of the past year's operations should simultaneously be made. At this time, a particular need exists for more comprehensive and systematic approaches in order to achieve a higher degree of universality and validity in the appraisal of management and the operation of the firm.

MANAGEMENT AUDITS IN THE BUSINESS POLICY COURSE

The need for the management audit approach has also been found in the business school curriculum. This is particularly applicable to the integrative business policy course. This course not only requires a comprehensive review and integration of the knowledge learned in the functional fields of business before the final semester of the senior year, but also requires the development of analytical skills for the application of these principles and methods. In this course a significant transition must be made, a gap must be bridged, between the learning and understanding of basic subject principles and their analytical application in a comprehensive and systematic fashion. The limitations of the students in bridging this gap is often found in their lack of organized or systematic appraisal methods for case analyses in the business policy course. Their attempts to establish any hierarchical or sequential structure of core course principles and methods for analytical application to these cases invariably are found seriously wanting.

While the educational function of the student is well served by the provision of descriptive knowledge of theories, principles, and methods found in core course content, the corollary objective of skills development in the analytical application of this knowledge is not effectively met. To more effectively develop and refine these analytical skills, either basic core course content should be reorganized to better lend itself to analytical application in business problems and case analyses, or some other vehicle must be used to bridge this gap. Management audits appear to provide such a vehicle.

MANAGEMENT AUDIT TYPES

Unfortunately management audits are not a uniform appraisal instrument. In fact, the term is actually misleading because it is applied to systematic checklists for the analysis of management *decisions* in the over-all company and departmental decisions, rather than management functions alone. Most audit checklists found in the business periodical literature tend to be functional types, for specific departments, although a few comprehensive companywide audits are also found. Some audits apply only to operating management and its functions, and others apply to the board of directors.

The audit concept in traditional business operations is readily identified with external accounting audits performed by certified public accountants, or internal accounting audits performed by the company accountant or controller. In a broader sense, the concept is that one of the major responsibilities of the board of directors is to periodically audit the over-all activities of the company and, in particular, the performance of the management group. Essentially the audit of the over-all business might be defined as a measurement and evaluation of total organizational performance. Any measurement of the total enterprise must include a measurement of its functional or departmental units, as well as the individual and aggregate performance of its managers.

Management audits are defined by the Association of Consulting Management Engineers, Inc., in the Reading following this Introduction, as follows: "Just as a public accountant examines the books and records of a company and reports on its financial operations and conditions, management consultants study a business as a whole and in respect to all of its departments.

They consider its policies, organization, operating methods, financial procedures, personnel practices, and physical facilities and report on its over-all position. Whereas the accounting audit is concerned with the past transactions and present conditions, the management audit studies the present and looks to the future." It is particularly interesting to note that these over-all company measurements and evaluations are labeled "management audits."

This becomes more understandable when it is realized that because the over-all activities of the firm are primarily the responsibility of the top management group, the causal factors of success or failure will be traced ultimately to this group. On the other hand, this wide variety of activities, including departmental operations and activities external to the firm, does not find ready classification under the title "management audit." Nevertheless, the term has become generic. The title more properly could be a dual one; "management decision audit" for the decisions made in the many functions and departments within the business firm, and "management function audit" to include a detailed appraisal of the basic management functions and subfunctions. In fact, these two audits, embracing both management function and management decision checklists, constitute an evolving "management audit system." Hopefully, this systematic approach may eventually be the vehicle for the establishment of a "Certified Management Audit" for practitioners and theoreticians interested in raising their performance to the level of a profession. Since any comprehensive appraisal checklist must include the most important or "strategic" decisions made by management in *all* of its functions, internal and external to the firm, the evaluation of management decision making inherently includes every single area of activity within the business firm.

Management Function Audit. A comprehensive "management audit system" should be composed of two integral parts. The first part will apply a "direct" appraisal checklist to management functions, as outlined in Reading No. 2 by Lawrence Appley, President of the American Management Association. By evaluating management in terms of how well it performs its functions, a "direct" approach is taken, as opposed to an "indirect" approach that would evaluate management in terms of how well the business operates as a whole, and within specific departments. The latter approach would presumably evaluate how well management makes decisions for the company. When the board of directors is considered a part of management of the firm, its performance may also be audited with the criteria contained in Reading No. 3, "Appraising the Board of Directors."

Management Decision Audits. In the second part of the "management audit system," audit checklists are applied to decisions made for the company as a whole, and for each functional department. These decision checklists ideally should meet two criteria. First, they should include those decisions "most strategic" or most important to the success of the firm. Second, where possible these decisions should be structured in the checklist in a hierarchical and sequential order. This hierarchical sequence should first follow the order in which these decisions would be made in the annual planning-decision-making sequence. By following this order sequence, sub-optimization in decision making may be avoided. Also, implicit guides for decisions by subordinates in the organization will automatically flow from preceding decisions of broader scope and application to the firm.

ANNUAL PLANNING DECISION SEQUENCE

A survey of business and management audits in the business literature has produced the audits presented in the remaining portion of Part II. These audits have been developed by operating business managers, and the decisions included in these checklists are intended to represent the most strategic decisions affecting the particular functions or departments. The audits are grouped in the order of the annual planning decision sequence: management and boards of directors functions, long range and over-all company operations, marketing, production, personnel, finance, and accounting decisions. The logic of this sequence is as follows. The goals, strategies, and policies formulated by the Board of Directors and Executive Committees will determine over-all company decisions and plans constructed for both the long and short run. Audit systems for appraising the company as a whole are presented in Readings No. 4 and 5, utilizing the grandfather of management audits developed by Jackson Martindell, "The Management Audit." Martindell's over-all company appraisal provides for the analysis of the corporate structure, economic function, health of earnings, fairness to stockholders, research and development, directorate analysis, fiscal policies, production efficiency, sales vigor, and executive evaluation. This most comprehensive audit developed for the "scientific appraisal of management" also utilizes a point evaluation system for the relative importance of these functions to the company as a whole.

Marketing Audit. Once the company goals, strategies, and policies have been formulated, guidelines are available for making marketing forecasts, decisions, and plans. Appraisal of the marketing function and decisions are provided for in Reading No. 6, " Marketing Audit: New Management Tool," which audits marketing objectives, policies, organization, facilities, methods, procedures, and personnel. In addition to this audit, a more detailed analysis of marketing decisions is provided in Reading No. 7, "446 Checkpoints for Marketing Planning." These criteria are applied to the market, product, competition, market research, marketing plans, advertising, new products, economic policies, and the marketing department organization.

Production Audit. Production schedules and decisions should be derived from, and correlated with, marketing decisions and plans. In order to appraise the production function and decisions, an appraisal system is provided in Reading No. 8, " How to Appraise Mangement: Production Management."

Exhibit 1

	Profit Ratios	Asset Ratios	Debt Ratios	Sales Ratios
I. Profitability Measures	1 Net Profits Net Worth 2 Net Profits Net Sales 3 Net Profits Net Working Capital			
II. Liquidity Measures		4 Current Assets Current Debt 5 Fixed Assets Tangible Net Worth 6 Inventory Net Working Capital	7 Funded Debt Net Working Capital 8 Current Debt Inventory	
III. Leverage Measures			9 Total Debt Tangible Net Worth 10 Current Debt Tangible Net Worth	
IV. Turnover Measures				11 Net Sales Net Worth 12 Net Sales Net Working Capital 13 Net Sales Inventory 14 Collection Period

This audit provides for the analysis of production operations, facilities and equipment, purchasing and material control, and industrial relations.

Personnel Audit. Production, marketing, and over-all company decisions and plans are now translated into personnel needs for the company organization. The personnel functions and decisions are appraised in Reading No. 9, "The Personnel Audit: Gateway to The Future." Analysis is made of the administration of the personnel department, personnel planning, staffing, training, promotions and transfers, personnel rating, labor relations, employee services and benefits, health and safety, wage and salary administration, records and reports, departmental audit and review, personnel research, and miscellaneous items.

Financial-Accounting Audit. Over-all company, marketing, production, and personnel needs are finally translated into accounting and financial budgets and control systems. In Reading No. 10, "Comparing the Company with Its Industry by Ratios," an analysis of the financial health and financial decisions of the company is provided through the application of ratios to the company financial structure.

In the analysis of business policy cases, financial data is most often provided in the form of profit and loss, and balance sheet statements. In the analysis of balance sheet asset, liability, and ownership items, financial ratios have been applied, especially when industry ratios are available for comparison in the annual issues of *Duns Review and Modern Industry*. In applying these ratios, a systematic approach may be used by following the steps outlined in Exhibit I. The interpretation of these ratios, and their comparison with industry median ratios, are explained in detail in Reading No. 10.

In addition to the financial audit, the accounting control system may be audited as described in Reading No. 11, "Performance Standards For the Plant Accountant," wherein the accounting functions and decisions are evaluated in terms of the organization, administration, budgets and forecasts, management statements and reports, and cost control and profit plans.

Any appraisal of these functions and decisions for the company as a whole, and for specific departments, should ideally follow the sequence of the annual planning decision process. In this sequence the audit function provides not only an annual appraisal of managerial performance and managerial decision making within the business firm, but simultaneously provides the annual planning decisions and budgets for the year to come.

AUDIT FUNCTIONS IN THE BUSINESS POLICY COURSE

Business and management audits make a unique contribution in restructuring core course material in the business administration curriculum in the form of the most strategic operating decisions within business functional areas, sequenced in a hierarchical decision-making order. These audits will therefore serve two major functions in the policy course: (1) as a review tool for the student for the content of the core courses which he has studied in the business administration curriculum, and (2) as an organization of this material in a sequence that facilitates its analytical application to business policy course cases.

Since the final integrating business policy course emphasizes the integrated function of management decision making and problem solving, these individual departmental audits should not be considered as isolated applications. Their integration is accomplished by the sequential structuring of their application, and their interrelationships found in the companywide audit. This integration is furthet enhanced by the evaluation of policy issues, as discussed in detail in Reading No. 1, which follows.

MANAGEMENT AUDITS

* *

1. THE MANAGEMENT AUDIT*

—ASSOCIATION OF CONSULTING MANAGEMENT ENGINEERS

One of the services offered by many management consultants is the Management Audit. The demand for this kind of service has been increasing through the years. Some explanations of this type of service are offered here in answer to questions that have come to our members. What is a Management Audit? When is it called for? What are its potential values?

Just as a public accountant examines the books and records of a company and reports on its financial operations and condition, management consultants study a business as a whole and in respect to all of its departments. They consider its (1) policies, (2) organization, (3) operating methods, (4) financial procedures, (5) personnel practices, and (6) physical facilities, and report on its over-all position. Whereas the accounting audit is concerned with past transactions and present condition, the Management Audit studies the present and looks to the future.

Briefly, a Management Audit is an examination of conditions and a diagnosis of deficiencies, with recommendations for correcting them. It is basically constructive in its conception and objective in its approach. It has but one purpose—to help management better the position of the company.

The consultants who make such audits are men skilled in the techniques of analysis and research, seasoned by experience in similar situations, and trained to be always alert for one thing—a way to improve what they find. They analyze the policies under which the operation of the whole enterprise is conducted. They examine the organization structure and study each unit in detail, to gain a thorough understanding of its functions. They look into operating methods; each important step is studied in its relation to other steps and with the constant aim of improvement in mind. They give consideration to the company's human resources, always objectively and with respect to possible improvements in personnel practices. And of course the company's physical facilities come under the same close scrutiny.

* From the *ACME Reporter*, June, 1950, Vol. 1 No. 4. Reprinted by courtesy of the Association of Consulting Management Engineers, Inc.

The net result is a diagnosis of the present state of health of the business enterprise, with attention focused on what needs improvement and with clear-cut recommendations for effecting the improvements.

The company's management may request a Management Audit of all or a part of the business because of unsolved problems which are handicapping operations. Or an audit may be requested when an important change in top management is being made, when mergers are under consideration, or when the need for expansion or new financing is evident. Sometimes a company's management has audits made periodically, even when the business is progressing satisfactorily, as a check on its effectiveness and a means of self-improvement—much as a healthy man will ask his physician for a periodic check-up.

If the audit uncovers no major deficiencies or opportunities to increase effectiveness, the management can proceed on its course with confidence and assurance. If, as is usually the case, the audit does reveal possibilities for betterment, it is likely to pay substantial cash dividends.

The rate of change in business conditions is increasingly rapid, and each individual business must constantly adjust itself to this change by applying sound management principles to its operations under current conditions. The Management Audit is a useful, often an indispensable, tool of the management consultant in playing his part in this continuous and complicated process.

2. STANDARDS OF MANAGEMENT PERFORMANCE*

—LAWRENCE A. APPLEY

STANDARDS OF MANAGEMENT PERFORMANCE

(A standard of performance is a statement of conditions that exist when work is well done.)

A. PLANNING (PREPARATION FOR ACTION)

(Planning is setting objectives, forecasting future conditions, and determining the future course of action and policies required to attain objectives in light of forecasts.) Satisfactory performance in relation to planning has been attained when:

1. *There is adequate forecasting:* (Forecasting is the calculation of future events and conditions.)

Satisfactory attention has been given to forecasting when:

a. There are adequate records of comparison of past performance with forecast and of present performance with forecast on comparable terms and for extension of the same into the future.

b. Conditions bearing on achievement of objectives have been identified clearly—past and future.

c. Resources required (money, material, human, time) to meet the conditions (b) have been identified.

d. The events confirm the forecasts.

e. All necessary and no unnecessary information has been secured and used.

f. Arrangements have been made at minimum costs for special inquiry into significant facts not available elsewhere.

* From *Management at Mid-Century* (New York: American Management Association, 1954), pp. 17–20. Reprinted by permission of the American Management Association.

2. *Objectives are set:* Satisfactory attention has been given to setting objectives when:

a. There are definite, clear-cut, written and attainable

    (1) Long-range objectives.

    (2) Short-range objectives within the framework of the longer objectives.

b. The objectives cover all activities.

c. Objectives are carefully coordinated and balanced with each other and with those of the organization as a whole.

d. Objectives have been participated in and are understood and accepted by all those involved in their attainment to the degree of their responsibility.

e. Objectives are current and responsive to change.

f. Objectives are progressive and challenging.

3. *Courses of action have been formulated:* Courses of action have been formulated satisfactorily when:

a. There are written policies that set the boundaries of acceptable action.

b. Freedom of action is permitted within limits of established policy.

c. Policies have been expanded or revised to meet current problems and changing conditions.

d. Adequate research and analysis have been conducted to determine and evaluate alternate courses of action.

e. The requirements of the major responsibilities involved have been taken into account.

f. Procedures are specified where uniformity is required.

4. *Expected results have been specified, understood, and accepted:* This is satisfactory when:

a. Best possible and past performance have been considered.

b. Sustained performance at highest expected level is possible.

c. Provision is made for revising the level of expected results.

d. There is clarity of definition of results expected.

e. Results are measurable.

f. Common understanding and acceptance is reached between those who have to attain the expected results and those who require that they be attained.

B. ORGANIZING (A SECONDARY PLANNING ACTIVITY)

(Organizing is determining, assembling, and arranging the resources by function and in relation to the whole to meet the planned objectives.)

Satisfactory performance has been attained in relation to organizing when:

1. *There is a plan for arranging and relating resources:*

a. The plan assigns all functions, responsibility, authority, and accountability in proper relationships to attain the plan.

b. The plan provides proper allocation of resources according to quality, quantity, locations, etc.

2. *Resources have been determined:* Satisfactory attention has been given to determining resources when:

a. There is a definite estimate of resources required to activate plans.

b. There is an inventory of resources on hand.

c. Availability of additional resources or existence of surplus resources has been determined.

d. There is determination of how to balance resources required and those on hand.

3. *Provision has been made for assembling resources:* Satisfactory attention has been given to making provision for assembling the resources when:

a. Sources have been established.

b. Methods have been determined.

c. A time schedule has been established.

d. Assembly points have been identified.

4. *Factors to be appraised have been defined:* Such factors have been defined satisfactorily when:

a. They are in writing.

b. They are subject to measurement.

c. They affect the results.

d. They are sufficient to appraise the results.

5. *Means of measurement have been established:* Means of measurement have been satisfactorily established when:

a. A method of measurement has been set up for each factor.

b. The measurements are definite, concrete, practical, and appropriate to factor measured.

c. The measurements are consistent in application.

d. The measurements are based on identifiable facts.

C. EXECUTING

(Executing is carrying out the "plan" to obtain objectives.) Satisfactory attention has been given to executing when:

1. *Planned action has been authorized:* Satisfactory attention has been given to authorization when:

a. The decision to act and when to act has been made by appropriate authority.

b. The decision and the plan have been communicated to those responsible for executing; and is understood and accepted by them.

2. *The plan has been activated:* Satisfactory attention has been given to activating when:

a. Required resources have been properly assembled, arranged, and related at predetermined time and places.

b. Resources are prepared, tested, and ready to perform at the planned time and place.

c. Action begins on schedule.

3. *Actual results have been compared with expected performance:* Such comparison is satisfactory when:

a. Made soon enough to institute corrective action.

b. There is clear indication of variations from expected results.

c. Analysis has been made of reasons for variations.

d. Corrective action and opportunities for improvement have been determined.

4. *Action has been taken to maintain working relationships among resources in accordance with the plan and objective.*

3. APPRAISING THE BOARD OF DIRECTORS*

—WILBUR T. BLAIR

Everybody agrees that "management" is one of the major considerations in appraising potential company performance. Accordingly one would expect questions about the board of directors to be particularly important; the typical state statute, for instance, makes the director responsible for *managing* the business of the corporation, and the board is always shown at the top in organization charts.

Nevertheless, those interested in judging the probable success of corporations—security analysts, for instance—are likely to admit that they have devoted very little time to investigating the composition and performance of directorates. Nor does a scrutiny of the published material on directors reveal much about appraising the board in terms of the effect on the company's financial position.

What approach should be used? What factors should be considered? How is information obtained? The purpose of this article is to suggest answers to these unanswered questions. Although it is designed primarily as a contribution to the techniques of security analysis, the fact that its key is the "spotting" of strengths and weaknesses in boards of directors should make it a useful guide also for those directly concerned with improvement of company performance.

A summary study of the factors going into such an appraisal obviously cannot deal with all of approximately 447,000 United States corporations and over 2 billion shares listed on the New York Stock Exchange, and yet retain specificity of analysis and conclusion. Accordingly the present article deals only with the directorates of large industrial corporations, excluding public utilities, banks, insurance companies, and carriers. For convenience, the

* From the *Harvard Business Review*, January, 1950, pp. 101–113. Reprinted by permission of the *Harvard Business Review*.

appraisal factors will be considered under three headings: (1) composition of boards of directors, (2) performance of boards of directors, and (3) remuneration paid to directors. But first a few preliminary observations are called for about the role of directors and the way they are selected.

ROLE OF DIRECTORS

It might be emphasized, in beginning, that "management" is not the only consideration in a general appraisal and that the function of management is only in part the responsibility of the directorate. As a matter of fact, the division of responsibility between directors and executives varies widely with individual corporations. Perhaps a brief sketch of that relationship is appropriate here.

Important functions predominantly exercised by corporate boards are selecting the president, other top executives, and auditors; setting the salaries of the president and other officers; and appropriating sizable funds for new projects. Selecting depositaries for company funds and determining sources and amounts of working capital are functions of the board rather than of the executive management in over half of the larger corporations. As often as not, directors and executives share the responsibility for formulating and administering employee benefits and preparing stockholders reports. In a strong minority of corporations directors determine or approve company organization, financial relationships with subsidiaries, changes in product lines, and labor policy.

Selection of Directors. The mechanics of director selection are of secondary importance. What counts is the practice. Are the persons with the power of selection using their power to obtain the best available men on the board?

The duty of selecting directors is vested by law in the stockholders. The history of director selection, however, reveals that except in times of crisis the stockholders, although *electing* the directors, play a small part in actually *choosing* them. The use of proxies to elect the slate of directors nominated by the executives and incumbent directors results in stockholders' fulfilling a rather mechanical role in bringing about the election of persons chosen by either or both of these other groups. Most stockholders in large corporations recognize the futility of endeavoring to oppose the proxy machinery. (As the oft-quoted British statement maintains, it may be at least half true that it is often less difficult to upset a government than to turn out a board of directors.) In addition, the average stockholder is not interested in improving the quality of directors elected as long as the stock of the corporation is providing dividends and holding its own in the market.

There is no actual proof that greater stockholder participation at elections would improve the composition of directorates. Copeland and Towl point out that in closely held corporations where stockholders actively participate in selecting directors, an excellent board of directors is not always found.[1] It is their opinion, furthermore, that in corporations where there is a great diffusion of ownership and the directors are not actually selected by stockholders, the directors perform their functions more effectively than in closely held companies. It would seem that active stockholder participation in the selection of directors and the various mechanics designed to insure such participation are not in and of themselves sufficient to insure the election of a good board.

An executive will, in fact, when preparing a slate of director-candidates for submission to the board, endeavor in most cases to select persons who will meet with approval of the existing board, large stockholders, and other interested groups. He will, furthermore, probably take counsel with these groups in regard to qualifications and identity of persons to be nominated.

The listing in the proxy statement of candidates to be voted upon at the annual meeting of a corporation provides stockholders and others an opportunity to investigate the qualifications of such candidates. There is a growing school of thought, supported by the Securities and Exchange Commission among others, that greater detail with respect to qualification of directors should be set forth in the proxy statement. Such detail might include pertinent biographical material covering, at the least, principal occupation, other directorships held by the individual, and any dealings the candidate may have had with the company as a customer, supplier, attorney, or creditor. The SEC already requires the proxy notice to state the principal business of each director and his business with the company.

I submit that corporations for the most part have performed satisfactorily in the past in selecting members of their boards of directors, but that improvements may be effected in the future. Whether the directors are actually chosen by the executives, the incumbent directors, or the stockholders, is not important; what we are interested in is whether the group with the power of selection is keeping its standards for directors on a high plane.

The question of the means of evaluating that function leads directly to the first group of essential considerations, the composition of directorates.

COMPOSITION OF THE BOARD

A board's performance depends inevitably on the capabilities of its members. What the board actually does is, of course, the ultimate criterion in a management appraisal. Yet, I submit, no one can fully comprehend all aspects of directors' performance without first understanding the human relationships that motivated it. An appraisal of the composition provides us "leads" with which to approach the appraisal of performance. It makes possible the three-dimensional understanding of a board's acts and policies which, while not

[1] Melvin T. Copeland and Andrew R. Towl, *The Board of Directors and Business Management* (Boston: Division of Research, Harvard Business School, 1947), p. 178.

indispensable to us as passing observers, is nevertheless indispensable to us as analysts looking ahead.

Inside versus Outside Directors. One of the foremost issues at this point concerns the question of inside and outside directors—inside directors being active officers or employees of the company; outside directors being all others. Outside directors may be subdivided into (1) those who are substantial stockholders and (2) those who are not.

There is a wide variety of reasons why corporations elect outside directors. In a survey of nearly 3,000 outside directors made by the National Industrial Conference Board, however, the overwhelming majority were found to be elected either because they owned or represented large stockholdings or because they were prominent business executives, financial counsel, or lawyers.[2]

The real objective of a corporation in considering the proportion of inside and outside directors should be to secure *balance.* A well-balanced board will count toward a high rating for the management of a corporation. What is a balanced board? It is one which represents all the points of view needed by the particular corporation to promote sound management. These points of view may include manufacturing operations, sales, advertising, management techniques, economics, research, finance, law, and others, depending upon the company concerned.

In making management surveys of various corporations, an analyst will be confronted with boards of directors which are composed as follows: (1) all directors are full-time salaried officers; or (2) all directors are from outside the company except a few top executives; or (3) about half are full-time officers and the other half are from outside the company.

It is difficult to praise or condemn the composition of a board because of the single fact that it falls in any one of the above three classifications. The significant question is whether it fits the needs of the company concerned.

Such corporations as Standard Oil Company (New Jersey), Standard Oil Company (Ohio), Bethlehem Steel Corporation, and The American Tobacco Company, for instance, have no outside directors and yet have attained success in their highly competitive fields. In these companies, presumably, the particular advantages of inside directors outweigh the particular disadvantages. In general terms, the basic advantages and disadvantages to be weighed in considering a board composed largely of inside directors are as follows:

Advantages

1. Inside directors know the details of the business intimately.
2. The corporation is their primary interest.
3. They devote almost full time to the affairs of the company.
4. Firsthand participation by executives in policy making insures better executing of those policies.

---

[2] Paul W. Dickson, "Compensation and Duties of Corporate Directors," *Conference Board Reports,* Study No. 16 (New York: National Industrial Conference Board, 1946), p. 6.

5. A senior officer speaking as a director occupies a strengthened position.

6. Key executives can be attracted and held more easily.

7. With all key executives on the board, most important functions are represented when problems and policies concerning these functions are being considered.

8. Special or emergency board meetings can be held with greater facility.

9. The board may meet with greater frequency.

Disadvantages

1. Inside directors often lack the independence of outside directors because of a feeling of owing an allegiance to superior executives. A director should be in a position to deal on equal terms with the other directors and the executives of the company.

2. There is greater temptation for inbreeding and self-perpetuation.

3. There are no outside points of view on questions of finance, expansion, economics, and the like, with which executive management may be less familiar. The policies adopted by the board are not subject to review by disinterested persons scrutinizing the same from the standpoint of the stockholders as a whole or from the standpoint of public reactions and relations.

4. Unless officer-directors own a substantial portion of the company's stock, the stockholders are further removed from their representation than if the board were composed of outside directors.

5. The board of directors is almost a legal fiction because it does not exist as an independent supervisory body.

6. Because the board of directors is virtually eliminated, the officers incur a larger responsibility and, accordingly, are accountable for a higher degree of performance to stockholders and others.

7. The chief executive may head a virtual dictatorship, which may be beneficial at the moment but may cause great hardships to the company in the future if abused or when the chief executive is removed suddenly from office because of death or incapacity.

8. Difficulties are encountered in setting salaries and profit-sharing arrangements for director executives.

9. Members of an officer-board pass on their own fitness to be re-elected officers.

10. An adequate check on executives cannot be effected if executives and directors are the same persons.

11. Large shareholders who are not officers do not have a voice on the board.

12. The corporation already has the full-time services and abilities of the officers.

The second type of board, composed almost completely of outside directors, is the most recently developed of the three. It is found most frequently in public utilities, railroads, and financial institutions. One big manufacturing company which follows this theory of composition is the General Electric Company. For this type of board, obviously the advantages and disadvantages listed above are in effect reversed. Its advocates argue, in addition, that when a corporation becomes large and widely held, its more or less quasi-public character requires the trusteeship and fiduciary stewardship supplied by outside directors.

In dealing with this general question, one can find plenty of instances where the same type of board serves to the benefit of one corporation and to the detriment of another, because of special factors involved in the type of directors available, the location of the company, its product, its financial problems, and other items. But, in general, the appraiser should look with most favor on the board which is composed in almost equal proportions of inside and outside directors. Extremes in any direction are often dangerous, requiring special justification. The in-between form may have many of the advantages of both the other types without all the corresponding disadvantages. The presence of outside directors who are trustworthy and able, for example, does much to give stockholders and the public confidence in the enterprise; yet to secure the desired effect it is enough to have only a part of the board in that category.

The percentages of inside directors on the boards of 518 companies are set forth in Exhibit I. Note that the larger the company, the more likely it is to have outside directors.

Exhibit I
Composition of Corporate Boards

ASSET GROUP (IN THOUSANDS OF DOLLARS)	Board Includes Less than 50% Full-Time Paid Officers		Board Includes 50% or More Full-Time Paid Officers		TOTAL
	NUMBER	PERCENTAGE	NUMBER	PERCENTAGE	
Less than 1,000	26	39%	41	61%	67
1,000–9,999	95	46	110	54	205
10,000–49,999	87	61	56	39	143
50,000 and over	67	65	36	35	103
Total	275	53	243	47	518

SOURCE: Paul W. Dickson, *op. cit.*, p. 5.

Stockholder Directors. Most state corporation statutes do not require directors to own shares of stock in the company being served. As many observers have noted, large stockholdings by an individual do not assure that he will be a good director. Actually, though of course extent of stockholdings is no gauge of competency, the trouble may be that the typical large stockholder, rather than lacking the abilities of a director, simply does not have available the time to devote to the company. In such cases it is better for a competent and qualified agent to be appointed to represent the large stock-holdings. If he does have the time, however, the large stockholder may well be an able director.

Frequently, the interests of majority and minority stockholders are in conflict. This situation often arises in connection with the declaration of dividends. There have been many cases where large stockholder directors have insisted upon dividends being paid when, for the best interests of the corporation, the funds should have been retained in the treasury of the company. There have also been cases where large stockholder directors, because of personal income tax considerations, have opposed the payment of dividends which could have been declared without harm to the company and which the smaller stockholders would have liked to receive. The appraiser should be alert to such dividend policies.

Professional Directors. During recent years there has appeared in this country the so-called professional director. This type of director has long been common in England.

A professional director is an individual who devotes most of his time to his duties as a director of one company or a small number of companies. He possesses an adequate background of business experience. He is compensated for his services by payment of substantial remuneration which, in many cases, will be his only source of income.

In the NICB survey company executives were asked whether or not they favored well-paid directors who would serve on boards of several non-competing companies, hold no executive positions, and represent no particular groups. More than one half answered that they favored this type of direc-tor.[3] Most of the writers on this subject, however, oppose the service of pro-fessional directors.

As reasons for such opposition, these writers have given the increased possibility of friction with executives, on the one hand, and the desire for popularity with executives as a motive for failing to provide an independent check upon those executives, on the other hand. The alleged likelihood of perfunctory performance and of overconservative policies are further reasons.

It cannot be denied, however, that a professional director will probably be able to draw upon the many advantages afforded by time and diversified experience. It is also possible that he may be less susceptible to management collusion. In corporations where there is factional strife, the election of a professional director may be agreed upon by a group which otherwise would nominate one of its own less-capable candidates; he may likewise be accept-able to actively participating stockholder groups unable to agree on a common nominee from their own ranks.

---

[3] Paul W. Dickson, *op. cit.,* p. 18.

It is my judgment that the presence of professional directors on the board of a company should be looked upon with favor, unless, of course, it is found that there is friction between the professional directors and the executives. But the absence of professional directors on boards should not be regarded with disfavor if it appears that there is already "balance" on the board, performance of proper audit functions, and a competent group of executives.

"Big-Name"Directors. During the past 20 years considerable criticism has been leveled at certain corporations which have permitted "big-name" directors to serve on their boards without requiring them to perform full duties of directorship.

In discussing appraisal of boards of directors with representatives of some large institutional investors, I found that it is quite a common practice among analysts to appraise favorably a board merely because prominent names appear on the directorate list. It is obvious that this criterion does not provide any real information about the performance of the board in question. The board may meet most infrequently, and when it does convene, the session may be perfunctory. No knowledge is gained about attendance, research activities, asking of pertinent questions, and scope of matters considered by the board.

The practice of big-name directors serving in an inactive capacity on a board would seem to be as improper for the individuals in question as it is for the corporation. No person should permit his name to be used as a director of a company unless he actually has a share in directing the affairs of the enterprise. Court reports are abounding with cases of idle directors who became liable for mismanagement of corporations. The fact that they had merely loaned their names to the directorate was no defense.

Of course, the specific motives of the company in wanting to appoint such directors may be entirely honest, if mistaken in total import. The company benefits in public relations by having directors of national prominence. Also, these important big-name directors will often attract other competent persons to the directorship who, although not so prominent, have more time available to devote to the corporation.

Directors Representing the Public. During the past 15 years the theory has been advanced sporadically that directors representing the public (i.e., the goverrment) should serve on boards of directors. Most of the authorities who have made any detailed analysis of this proposition from a practical standpoint, however, have reached the conclusion that the principle is unworkable. Certainly the presence of such a director on a board would, in the rare event of its happening, be an unfavorable sign. The reasons for opposing this proposition are strong:

1. Political pressures would be exerted on the internal operations of the company.

2. The corporation would not benefit by securing special information from the government because the men selected would not ordinarily be close enough to those who develop and carry on government policies to be aware of any-

thing that was not open to all. If they were, they should not and would not reveal it.

3. The means that might thus be made available for securing special favors from the government would not be legitimate.

4. With a government director present, the other members of the board might not feel free to exercise independent judgment.

5. A government director would often be entangled in conflicts of interest.

Directors Representing Labor. There are a number of corporations which have elected to their boards directors representing employees. The main argument for this device is that it serves to keep labor informed about the problems of management and the expenses of operation and provides it a means of limited participation in policy making. The practice is, however, opposed by some labor leaders.[4]

One company on the West Coast has appointed a junior board of directors for each of its plants, composed of office, sales, and factory employees. Other companies have made similar moves. But the operations of such junior boards do not affect the activities of the senior board or regular industrial relations administration.

The writer regards boards having directors representing labor with some apprehension. A manufacturing enterprise must have labor, material, and capital to produce its products; nevertheless, it is not the function of labor to manage the affairs of the corporation. Nor are the standards of good management measured by a profit yardstick necessarily consistent with the standards of popular labor representation; the two are, in fact, often basically opposed.

The right to choose the management is vested in the owners—the stockholders, who in turn delegate to the directors the right to select the executives. It is quite foreseeable that friction, which would be detrimental to the company, and perhaps to labor as well, will arise in boards with labor representatives serving as directors.

Directors Representing Creditors. Investigation will sometimes reveal that certain directors represent company creditors. This situation usually indicates that the creditor occupies an influential position in connection with the management. Ordinarily, a corporation does not make available a seat on the board to creditors unless they are in a position to demand representation.

To be sure, the fact that creditors are represented on a board of directors of a company should not be construed, without closer examination, to mean that the management is necessarily ineffective and incompetent without such representation, or that the company's financial standing is shaky. Business history reveals that many financing institutions, in making large loans to a corporation, will insist upon representation on the board, not because the lender is of the opinion that the board is incompetent, but because the lender

[4] Loyall McLaren, *Annual Reports to Stockholders* (New York: The Ronald Press Company, 1947), p. 312.

will be in a better position to keep informed as to the use of its money and the debtor company's progress and operations. Even so, it is a fair inference that the company did not have the financial standing to resist the creditor's request.

Directors Representing Customers or Suppliers. Considerable question has arisen about the practice of electing directors who are executives of either customer or supplier companies. While it is possible to generalize concerning this subject and reach a conclusion that this type of director may not serve the best interests of the company, difficulty arises when an attempt is made to apply such a generalization to specific cases.

The most common objection to this type of director stems from the possibility of favoritism's being shown. It is the writer's opinion, however, that a complete investigation of business dealings between corporations and suppliers or customers who are represented on the board would reveal little favoritism which could be classified as contrary to company interests. Very few customer or supplier directors would venture to seek unusual favors which might be detrimental because of (1) the interests of fellow directors representing stockholders; and (2) the desire of officer directors to make a good earnings record for the company.

Moreover, customer or supplier directors are in a position to advance many suggestions for improving products or services and for lowering the material costs of items produced. During periods of economic recession, furthermore, it may be most helpful for corporations to have on their boards executives of prominent customers. The same argument may be advanced for having supplier directors during periods when materials are difficult to obtain.

Accordingly, it is submitted that the rating of a corporation's management should not be lowered because customers or suppliers are represented in the directorate, unless further investigation reveals evidence of favoritism. Interviews with corporate executives can be used to determine whether positive contributions are being made by such directors toward improving products or services and lowering material costs.

Expert Directors. During recent years there have been many discussions among businessmen concerning the use of so-called expert directors for the sake of specialized advice of one kind or another. Some of the smaller corporations utilize this device to obtain the services of an expert for the extremely low cost of a director fee.

Many executives of larger corporations believe that experts should be *hired* to consult with the board and officers of the company, thereby obviating the necessity of placing them on the board where they would be required to vote on many subjects other than their specialties. A board of directors composed largely of technical experts would not be a "balanced board" as heretofore described; and more general matters such as industrial relations, relations with the public, and board policies involving business judgment might not be given adequate consideration.

Among the individuals considered as experts are bankers, financiers, lawyers, accountants, advertising men, architects, real estate men, and engineers. Many of these might be tempted to accept directorships because of the hope of obtaining profitable connections with the corporation. This practice might narrow the freedom of choice and selection which is often desirable in connection with important business transactions.

In appraising a directorate consisting in part of experts, the important determination is whether the presence of this type of director causes any unbalance on the board. In addition, there is the question whether the corporation, by having an expert in a certain field on the board, is unduly limiting the expert talent which it might hire. If both the foregoing inquiries are answered in the negative, the rating of the management of the corporation in this respect should not be lowered; in particular cases where special problems of unusual magnitude face a company, the rating might well be raised.

Chairman of the Board. Of extreme importance is the ability of the chairman of the board of a company to guide the board's discussions. One of the most harmful situations which may render a board ineffective is the existence of cliques and dissensions among the members of the board. Frequently these dissensions arise during deliberations in connection with controversial issues. The chairman is usually in an excellent position to prevent personal hostilities from arising during the consideration of such issues. He must be impartial, honest, persuasive, and respected, and also must possess an abundance of leadership abilities.

The argument has been advanced that, because of his strategic position, the chairman of a publicly owned company should be chosen from outside the executive staff of the company to prevent the latter from dominating the board. This statement, like all generalizations, has its exceptions when applied to specific cases. Other things being equal, however, we should note with favor an outside director's holding the position of chairman in a large corporation whose stock is for the most part publicly held.

Age of Directors. Considerable information is available on the age of retirement for labor, white-collar workers, and executives, but relatively little has been published concerning the retirement of directors because of advanced age. While a number of companies prescribe retirement ages for employees, most make no requirement for directors. Standard Oil Company of New Jersey, an exception, retires directors at the age of 65.

A great deal is to be said in favor of directors not retiring as early as executives. Their duties may not be so arduous. In addition, for directors serving as counselors to the executives of a corporation, experience is a particularly valuable asset. Favorable judgment must be qualified, however, when the *average* age of the board is too high. I know, for instance, of two boards of seven men each where the average age is 72 and 73 years, respectively. A large percentage of vacancies, due to death or incapacity, would be most harmful to the welfare of both companies, yet they are running that risk more than seems necessary.

At the other extreme, of course, are boards consisting of too many young men to provide adequate experience. But we will not find this situation very often; immaturity of members is a rare complaint about boards of directors.

Tenure of Directors. It will be wise to examine the "turnover" history of the board being appraised. Rapid turnover usually indicates administrative incompetency, just as a lethargic rate of turnover during a long period is a sign that the board may be operating in a rut. Average turnover, according to tenure statistics, is about one directorship vacancy per year for most corporations. Modest increases in this rate, however, are not causes for alarm. A study of this subject by Copeland and Towl for the years 1925–1944 revealed that in every case substantial changes in the composition of the boards of 50 companies had taken place over the 20-year period.[5]

Refusal to be re-elected on the part of directors who have not served for as many years as might normally be expected may be an indication of dissensions within the board or between the board and the top executives. If examination should reveal that many able businessmen had served on the board and then *resigned*, there would be evidence of even greater internal dissatisfaction than if they had merely refused to be re-elected after serving to the end of their stated terms.

The practice of certain corporations of staggering directors' terms of office, instead of electing a full board each year, deserves attention. Although such companies are in the minority, the procedure has important advantages; and it is permitted, expressly or by implication, under the business corporation statutes of most states. The staggered terms are usually two or three years each. The advantages of such classification are as follows:

1. Directors are more likely to serve the company for a definite number of years than under the conventional year-to-year method of elections of all members.

2. There is less chance of sudden and complete changes being made in the personnel of the board.

3. Better continuity and stability of board policy are provided.

4. It is less confusing for stockholders to elect only a portion of the board. The fact that proxy statements and notices do not usually set forth names of the full board or of a slate of nominees for the full board makes it difficult for stockholders or appraisers to study the qualifications of all nominees and incumbent directors.

Size of the Boards. The recent figure of the National Industrial Conference Board indicate that for 535 nonfinancial corporations the number of directors per company ranges from 3 to 35. Few companies have more than 15

---

[5] Melvin T. Copeland and Andrew J. Towl, *op. cit.*, pp. 26–27.

directors, and the average is approximately 9. The average number of directors for companies with assets of $50 million or more is 12.[6]

Size is one of the appraisal factors. A board may be so large it is unwieldy and ineffective; or so small that, though effective as a working group, it does not ensure the diversity and background necessary for balance. While quality of composition is considerably more important, size may affect working ability so much that the potential of the board is seriously reduced.

Large unwieldy boards, furthermore, are a haven for inactive and, perhaps, "big-name" directors.

The size of the directorate has no necessary correlation with company size. National Dairy Products Corporation, with gross assets of $194 million, has 27 directors, while Gulf Oil Corporation, with assets of $523 million, has only 7 directors. Most authorities agree that a working board cannot exceed 10 or 15 members. Large boards, however, can avoid this difficulty by working through committees, as they frequently do. The real directors of companies with boards of over 15 members are often the members of the executive and financing committees.

The optimum size of a board depends, of course, upon many factors. Scope of corporate activities, complexity of operations, the number of stockholders and diversity of their stockholdings, and whether the business is local or national, are among the important ones.

Multiple Directorates. One of the most frequently heard criticisms has to do with multiple directorates. An individual with business of his own can hardly serve on the boards of a number of companies and have anything but a superficial knowledge of the complicated affairs of any one. There are men who are exceptions, but they are perforce rare; there are not enough of them to go around.

Directories of directors are available for determining the number of directorates upon which a member serves. If a director serves on more than five or six boards, his connections should be regarded prima facie as excessive. The fact that some of the companies are small is not an excuse; many small companies require as much time and ability as large corporations.

Conflicts of interest between companies not infrequently confront a multiple director. In any such dilemma of divided allegiance, he cannot be an asset to both companies—or, sometimes, to either one. Furthermore, he may subject himself and his corporations to liability for interlocking directorships.

Many of the arguments against multiple directorates are ignored by business men, because their experience has proved that there may be only a few persons available to a corporation who (1) are competent, (2) will undertake the responsibility, and (3) will perform in an outstanding manner. They base their reasoning on the premise "that it is much better to have a few hours

---

[6] Paul W. Dickson, *op. cit.*, p. 15.

from a very able man of quick perception and sound judgment than the full time of a less competent man." The presumption, however, is against such a possibility,

PERFORMANCE OF THE BOARD

The question of the quality of performance of a board of directors is a difficult one. The ultimate test, again, is what directors actually accomplish or fail to accomplish for their companies. But as a practical matter we cannot measure the particular contribution of the board to the success of the company or even evaluate directly the capabilities of individual directors. For our present purposes we must consider what seem to be evidences or signs of good performance or the opposite.

There is prevalent among many directors an opinion that their obligations commence when they enter the board room and cease when they leave it. In part, the opinion seems prompted by the fact that the only remuneration most of them receive is a fee for attending board meetings; also, most directors are preoccupied with their other business duties. In contrast, there stands the practice of those directors who communicate informally with the executives of the companies they serve at luncheons, by exchange of letters, committee meetings, telephone calls, or during visits to the company offices and plants.

The rating of corporate management should not go down when the powers of initiation of decisions have been vested in the executive group but, rather, when the directors have yielded also their powers of *supervision* of the executives or because they are not functioning effectively as *advisers* to the executives. Other "must" functions of the board are auditing the management periodically and making reports on company progress and quality of leadership.

A number of states have adopted statutes providing that, if a director is successful in defending any action against him arising out of alleged misfeasance of duty, he shall be entitled to indemnification by the corporation for his expense, including attorney fees in such amount as the court determines to be reasonable. The common law does not recognize such a right, but in states without such statutes corporate bylaws may provide for some sort of indemnification procedure. Since the rule puts a company in a better position to attract directors who are capable but who do not care to risk having to expend personal funds to defend themselves in court against groundless claims of stockholders, creditors, and others, the appraiser will want to check the state corporation statute and, if necessary, the corporate bylaws of the particular company.

Many boards of directors of large corporations, in serving as ratifying bodies for the decisions of executives, are interested merely in obtaining from the executives statistics concerning savings, increased profits, and lower operating expenses, without bothering to examine the means of accomplishing these results or the plans being considered for the future. These boards, and there are many, will receive low ratings when they are appraised.

Operating Boards. Just as detrimental to the progress of a corporation as "rubber-stamp" boards are the so-called "operating" boards. An operating board of directors is one that performs functions usually assigned to the company executives. Carrying out executive functions is not the correct role of a director. At law, directors have no power or authority except at properly convened board meetings.

The directorate should concentrate on its activities in policy making and policy revision. It must avoid crowding out the operating officials. If the board is dissatisfied with the way the executives are doing business, it should hire new ones, not take their places.

The disadvantages of operating boards should be so apparent from the foregoing discussion that giving them a low rating needs no further discussion.

Committees of Directors. One of the most effective means by which a board of directors may discharge its responsibilities, whether it consists of 7 members or 32, is through active committees. Standing committees may keep abreast of subjects concerning audits, finances, research, personnel, and public relations.

The membership of each of the committees may be small, thereby making it more workable. A committee can devote hours to a subject which the entire board, because of time limitations, must consider in a matter of minutes. Committee members, furthermore, have an excellent opportunity for asking management detailed and discerning questions.

The use of the executive committee for very many major decisions is an abuse of this device. Under the best procedure, major problems will be first considered by standing or special committees, then passed upon by the full board. The procedure of an executive committee's making recommendations to the full board permits the crowding of many important issues through that body, a result which is not so likely to happen when preliminary consideration is by standing or special committees.

Existence of Factions and Dissensions. Although it may be difficult to obtain information as to whether there are factions and dissensions on the board, trying to answer the question is indeed important enough to warrant considerable effort. Frequently, when such factions and dissensions exist on the board, the same conditions permeate down through the executive staff and the employees. Obviously, the chance of profitable operations suffers greatly from such conditions.

As has been stated earlier, it is the chairman of the board who carries the greatest responsibility for preventing factions and dissensions from developing within the directorate.

Research Activities, In virtually all industrial corporations there is a need for an active interest by the board in the subject of research. In the process of appraisal, we should develop a part-answer to the ever-present question whether an enterprise is abreast of the times in the fields of invention, management, operations, and sales.

It is not safe to conclude that the research activities of a company are sufficient simply because they consist of a research department and a vice president in charge of that function. Research results must be used; research activities must be integrated into other company operations. The board of directors, as much as any other group, must be constantly concerned with the over-all aspects of the research program if the company is to succeed in the manufacturing field.

Board Meetings. Reference has already been made to the principle that a board of directors can act only when convened in a properly called meeting. Although, as has been emphasized, the duties of directors do not begin when they enter the board room and end when they leave it, the board meeting is important because that is where the final deliberations and actions of the board take place. Therefore, the analyst will be especially interested in the frequency of board meetings, the attendance thereat, and the scope of the matters referred to the board.

Although the frequency of meetings is quite inconclusive evidence of a board's activities or ability, it does provide some indication of the time formally devoted by board members to company affairs. If boards of large industrial corporations meet less than quarterly each year, serious doubts should arise whether the board is sharing its responsibility in management.

From the NICB study of 535 companies in 1946, it appears that one out of every two companies meets monthly or more often. The tendency among smaller corporations is to meet quarterly; among companies with assets in excess of $50 million, directors meet once a month or oftener.[7]

Attendance is another important factor. Of the 3,905 directors covered by the NICB survey, almost 40% were present at every meeting held in 1945. At that time there were still wartime restrictions on travel. In excess of 65% of the 3,905 directors attended at least four out of five meetings that year. The qualifications of a director and his ability to ask discerning questions can contribute very little to the welfare of a corporation if he is frequently absent from meetings of the board of directors. Poor attendance suggests that board members may lack interest in the enterprise or that their abilities are not being utilized.

A corporation may gain many benefits if the items submitted to the directors are carefully chosen, so that prior consideration is given to the more important matters of policy and operations. According to the NICB figures, only about one out of four companies sends agenda to directors in advance of board meetings.[8] Yet sending out agenda and advance reports prior to board meetings is one of the best means of giving individual directors an opportunity

[7] Paul W. Dickson, *op. cit.*, p. 11.

[8] Francis Lusardi, "Keeping Corporate Directors Informed," *Conference Board Reports*, Studies in Business Policy, No. 24 (New York, NICB, 1947), p. 5.

to prepare themselves for the meetings. With advance notice, directors can and do find it profitable to discuss the problems to be considered with business associates who are not connected with the company, of course presenting the facts as a hypothetical problem if the situation is one of a competitive character or otherwise confidential. The opportunity for advance consideration is most valuable when coupled with informal discussions between the executives and the directors.

Reports to Members. Some companies follow the commendable practice of submitting reports to their directors during the interim between board meetings. Other companies submit reports only at board meetings. A number of them, it will be found, submit reports both between and at board meetings. A good appraisal will include a finding as to whether the company forwards reports to directors between board meetings and, if so, what subject matter is covered and in what form.

Many directors speak of their studying of company reports away from board meetings as " homework," indicating the use to which written reports are put. There are two reasons why this practice is an appraisal factor: (1) formal written reports can cover complexities which oral reports cannot; and (2) because of the usual short duration of board meetings there is not sufficient time to master the contents of a report made there.

Some 70% of the companies surveyed by the NICB had established the practice of sending interim reports to directors to acquaint them with operating and financial details.[9] In other words, there still are a substantial number whose failure to do so must weigh unfavorably in our appraisals.

REMUNERATION OF DIRECTORS

An important step to be taken to improve the boards of most large companies is to increase the remuneration of board members. This is probably the most underpaid group of individuals in the American business system today, in view of its responsibilities and at least potential services. The average outside director received approximately $850 during 1945, with other directors averaging $625.[10] By 1946, according to a study of 184 directors of large companies, about 3 out of 5 were receiving in the aggregate over $1,000 per year—an improvement, but still by no means sufficient.

The importance of director's functions, together with the desirability of providing incentives for the best men, makes the remuneration problem a vitally important one. From a strictly psychological point of view, the director who is receiving only a nominal fee for attending board meetings may unconsciously devote to the affairs of the company only as much effort and time as the fee seems to warrant. In the case of professional directors, for

---

[9] Paul W. Dickson, *op. cit.*, p. 10.
[10] *Ibid.*, p. 8.

whom salary is the prime incentive, the importance of compensation is obviously magnified.

A development of particular interest is the growing practice of paying salaries to directors. These, depending upon the size and earning capacity of the company, may range from $2,000 to $15,000 per annum. While a director who is compensated this way could not be expected to devote his full time to the company, neither would he, at the opposite extreme, limit his activities to the board room. He would be available for committee meetings, consultations with officers, plant visits, and reviews of reports. In addition, a substantial salary is an incentive for being constantly alert to ideas and plans which might improve company earnings and operations. This sounds, to be sure, like a rather intangible benefit, but it is by such constant awareness of the problems of the company and thinking about their solutions that directors, as well as executives, have brought into focus the ideas which have resulted in tremendous savings and earnings for many corporations.

We need not be concerned with the remuneration of inside directors if they are compensated adequately as officers of the company. In their executive capacity they are supposed to devote their full time to the corporation, although officers assuming a directorship of course undertake greater legal responsibility to stockholders and others.

Other reasons for deeming increased remunerations desirable include the fact that legal liability may jeopardize the director's personal fortunes. There have been many cases where, even after his death, his estate has been involved in litigation for years. Another reason is the fact that executives are likely to feel greater freedom in using the abilities of directors who receive reasonable compensation. In turn, most directors will not be willing to accept substantial compensation unless they are able to give to the corporation commensurate performance. Obviously, the company which recognizes the importance of all these factors should be rated up.

CONCLUSION

Perhaps it can serve as a conclusion to emphasize that in addition to all the specific factors set forth above there is the general criterion of what the stockholders think of the board of directors of their company. A low rating must go to the board which does not enjoy stockholder confidence, because without that confidence the success of the company may be placed in jeopardy.

The lack of confidence of stockholders may show itself at the annual meeting when it is apparent that stockholders are making many embarrassing questions concerning the performance of the board without receiving satisfactory answers.

The regulations of the SEC grant to stockholders the right to have proposals supported by a 100-word statement included in the proxy notice of the company. Such statements, where present, are specific evidence that certain stockholders lack confidence in the board and are of the opinion that it is not functioning properly.

The company which is endeavoring to gain the confidence of stockholders in its board of directors presumably deserves a high rating. One of the best ways of establishing this confidence is by making information concerning the board of directors available to the stockholders, both present and prospective. One excellent means of making such data available lies in the annual report.

Many companies do not publish the principal business affiliations of the outside directors. The mere fact that this information is listed in the proxy statement is not adequate; the proxy statement is frequently not preserved, and it is not distributed to prospective stockholders. Some companies, on the other hand, even publish photographs and brief biographies of all board members. As has been stated, there is a growing school of thought that the company's annual statement should set forth the qualifications of each director and the role he is expected to fill on the directorate.

Another phase of the stockholder relationship may be revealed in suits filed against directors by stockholders. Of course, there are many stockholder suits filed which are of questionable character and motive; but even these must be examined for their import. It has been developed that stockholders can exercise great control over a board of directors, and this control is quite likely to be manifested when the stockholders become dissatisfied. This dissatisfaction may result, for example, in the sale of the company's stocks in such volume as to create a bad market.

Securing the Necessary Information. During recent years, the practice has been prevalent among representatives of large institutional investors, corporate directors, and others, of visiting the head offices of large corporations. These visits have been for the purpose of obtaining detailed information regarding the operations of companies visited. Conferring with a number of these representatives leads me to believe that large corporations are usually most cooperative in making available information about their affairs.

It is often advisable to interview one or more of the outside directors to obtain facts concerning the directorates. If the analyst is alert, personable, intelligent, and clearly acting in good faith, he will discover from most directors interviewed considerable information concerning the performance of the boards on which they serve.

Of course this method of obtaining facts is not inexpensive, Many analysts cannot afford it. In addition, it is an investigation which will probably have to be repeated periodically, especially after major changes in the personnel of the board have been made or a new chief executive has been appointed. However, as I have suggested earlier, experience points very firmly to the conclusion that the analysis of corporate boards, while but one aspect of a general appraisal, is a fundamental part of an accurate over-all point of view, and as such it is usually worth the expense.

The following sources for information concerning boards of directors are available:

1. Annual statements
2. Registration statements filed with SEC
3. Listing statements—stock exchanges
4. Prospectuses
5. Interviews with the following:
   (1) Executives of the company
   (2) Directors of the company
   (3) Competitor companies
   (4) Labor unions
   (5) Trade associations
   (6) Other analysts
   (7) Government officials
   (8) Bankers
   (9) Stockholders and stockholder associations
6. Industry studies
7. Articles in newspapers and trade journals
8. Questions at stockholders' meetings

The foregoing list does not include minutes of board meetings because, in most companies, they provide an inadequate picture of board performance. It might also be repeated that evidence of stockholder dissatisfaction is often an important "lead" to internal trouble in the corporation. An unusual volume of stock selling, stockholder suits, proxy fights, and the active opposition of stockholder associations are all tentative indications that something may be wrong in management.

Of the eight methods outlined above, the two which in my own experience have proved most useful are (1) interviews and (2) asking questions at stock holders' meetings. It is usually possible, by exploiting these, to round out most of the factors that should enter into an appraisal of the corporation's board of directors.

4. HOW GOOD IS YOUR COMPANY? SCORE YOURSELF*

—BUSINESS WEEK

To rate your own management with this table, take the indicated number of points for each question if your answer is "yes." If it's "no"—or if you don't know the answer—the score is zero on each question. Add up the grand total. Then see (story below) how you rank with the "10 best managed companies." If your score is under 7,500, look for weak spots.

1. Corporate Structure (125 points for each "yes")
   a. Do you use product-division setups? _____
   b. Are you in best location? _____
   c. Do you know profit on each product? _____
   d. Are outside directors in majority on executive and finance committees? _____

   Total _____

2. Economic Function (100 points each)
   a. Do your main products help U.S. economic development? _____
   b. Is your share of total market growing? _____
   c. Do officers hold community posts? _____
   d. Are you in step with social changes? _____

   Total _____

3. Health of Earnings (150 points each)
   a. Do you fare well in business dips? _____
   b. Asset ratios stand up with competitors? _____
   c. Operating ratios, too? _____
   d. Have you escaped reorganization? _____

   Total _____

* Reprinted from the February 24, 1951 issue of *Business Week* by special permission. Copyrighted © 1951 by McGraw-Hill, Inc.

4. Fairness to Stockholders (175 points each)
   a. Do you pay 66⅔% of earnings in dividends (cash or stock)? _____
   b. Does dividend percentage match industry? _____
   c. Did you pay dividends (from earnings) through depression? _____
   d. Is half as much added to surplus consistently as is paid out in dividends? _____

   Total _____

5. Research and Development (175 points each)
   a. Do most research projects spring from that department? _____
   b. Does research have a budget? _____
   c. Have any processes been changed because of research? _____
   d. Any price reductions? _____

   Total _____

6. Directorate Analysis (225 points each)
   a. Was each director chosen for valid business reasons? _____
   b. Are you sure none of your directors represents politics, pressure, conflicting interests? _____
   c. Board independent of management? _____
   d. Is it an outside board? _____

   Total _____

7. Fiscal Policies (275 points each)
   a. Has inventory turnover increased? _____
   b. Do you co-ordinate manufacturing plans with estimated sales? _____
   c. Do you have long-time records handy on per cent of net income to net worth, net sales by products, labor and material costs, selling and administrative expenses? _____
   d. Does controller report to directors? _____

   Total _____

8. Production Efficiency (260 points each)
   a. Are costs in line with your industry? _____
   b. Do paper control systems save more than they cost? _____
   c. Are you certain there are no relatively unprofitable operations? _____
   d. Do top production men often operate on the floor? _____
   e. Is your labor dispute record good? _____

   Total _____

9. Sales Vigor (280 points each)
   a. Do you use a salesmanship school? _____
   b. Do your sales and technical staff know what the other is doing? _____
   c. Is turnover in dealers reasonable? _____

     d. Are you sure sales chief doesn't over-ride others in setting production schedules? _____

     e. Is there direct liaison between advertising, sales production? _____

                             Total _____

10. Executive Evaluation (600 points each)
     a. Is executive turnover moderate? _____
     b. Do you guard against nepotism? _____
     c. Do you have a system for selecting executives? _____
     d. Do salaries match your industry's? _____

                             Total _____
               GRAND TOTAL _____

Good management, like a good disposition, is something intangible. There is no way of measuring it objectively. But from time to time, somebody tries to work out a scale that will tell just how smart a company is.

Jackson Martindell, head man at the American Institute of Management, has developed the newest and most elaborate of these yardsticks (table, page 79). If you scored yourself 7,500 points or more as you ran down the questions, AIM figures you probably have a well managed company. If you topped 8,000, you're close to AT&T, General Foods, GM, du Pont, and six others of the top 10 companies in AIM's "scientific appraisal" (BW—Nov. 18'50, p. 98).

If your score is under 7,500, it's at least a hint that there are weak spots in your company.

Comparison. You can match your score against AIM's top 10. They are: AT&T—8,700; du Pont—9,300; General Foods—9,100; General Motors—9,000; Grand Union Co.—8,800; Merck & Co.—8,900; Pennsylvania Salt—8,500; Procter & Gamble Co.—9,200; Standard Oil (N.J.)—8,800; U.S. Plywood—8,400. Keep in mind that one of these companies scored zero for an entire category.

Basic Study. AIM's ratings are based on a broad-scale study of more than 2,000 companies. Of these, 243 met the standards for what Martindell figures is "excellent management."

Business Week's questionnaire is a streamlined version of AIM's. It condenses 300 questions into four or five key points in each of the 10 categories that Martindell and his staff use. It's a handy, though less scientific, way for top management to look in the mirror.

Factors Involved. AIM's ratings are based on Martindell's theories of good management, spelled out in a book, "Scientific Appraisal of Management," published by Harper Bros. last year.

Martindell gives a lot more weight to some of these categories than to others. For instance, he thinks that while a well-run research department is important, a company could still come out on top if its executives and top personnel programs rated high. You can see that by the fact that executives count, 2,400 points in the ratings, while research gets only 700.

Sales organization scores high, but Martindell stresses the fact that the sales department shouldn't dominate a company.

Also high on the list is the board of directors, in which, says Martindell, members other than company officers ought to have a strong voice.

Evaluation. In evaluating a company, AIM doesn't use all "yes and no" questions. It's able to weight each query, give partial credit where necessary. Sometimes answers come from published statistics or interviews with middle management on questions where top brass might give prejudiced opinions.

AIM believes that this is the best way to evaluate a company's management. Financial statements usually record the damage after it's been done.

5. THE MANAGEMENT AUDIT*

—JACKSON MARTINDELL

The Management Audit as developed by the American Institute of Management may be defined as a procedure for systematically examining, analyzing, and appraising a management's over-all performance. To determine this over-all performance, the Management Audit combines the evaluation of ten categories of appraisal, each a determination of the worth of the subject management in one category of the analysis, viewed historically, and in comparison with other organizations.

The Management Audit concepts were originally developed as a tool for investment appraisal. Within the past fifteen years, however, their use has been expanded to cover virtually all kinds and sizes of business organizations, as well as non-profit enterprises ranging from individual hospitals and colleges to the world-wide operations of the Roman Catholic Church.

As applied to a business organization, the Management Audit presents the qualities of the subject management relative to those of other managements in its particular industry, as well as in relation to the finest managements in other industries.

The ten categories of the Management Audit of business organizations are these:

Economic Function
Corporation Structure
Health of Earnings
Service to Stockholders
Research and Development
Directorate Analysis
Fiscal Policies

* From the *Proceedings of the Annual Meeting, Academy of Management*, 1962, pp. 164–171. Reprinted by permission of the Academy of Management and the author.

Production Efficiency
Sales Vigor
Executive Evaluation

These categories do not represent single functions of management, or pure variables.

In actual practice, preparation of a Management Audit of an organization consists of two distinct parts. The first is the compilation of data for analysis and evaluation. To insure completeness as well as comparability with data collected on other organizations, the American Institute of Management uses detailed prepared questionnaires covering management's performance in each appraisal category over a number of years. The information obtained through the Management Audit Questionnaire (questionnaires have been developed for a wide range of industries and types of business) is supplemented by interviews with members of management, directors, and a wide range of others associated with the company as employees, suppliers, competitors, customers, or investing owners. At the same time, material is assembled on the subject company's industry, to provide the comparative basis.

The second, actually significant portion of the Management Audit is the analysis of all information obtained. This result in the appraisal of individual categories and, from these, of the over-all performance of management appraisal, even with the systematic approach of the Management Audit, cannot be considered a science in the full sense of that word, since subjective judgment ultimately enters the appraisal. One of the values of the Management Audit, however, is the extent to which it permits judgment to rest on the widest possible base of substantive information, and on a uniform and general conceptual foundation. The most basic concept underlying the system is that management, wherever it is found, is *the art of purposeful action.*

ECONOMIC FUNCTION

The category Economic Function in the Management Audit is a unique contribution of the American Institute of Management, assigning to management the continuing responsibility for the company's importance to our economy. In effect, Economic Function, determines the *public value* of the company. This value is based on what the company has chosen to do— what products or services it produces—and how it does these things in the moral and ethical sense. It comprises such intangibles as the company's reputation and management's view and enlargement of the purpose of the enterprise. The *public* as referred to in Economic Function includes not merely the consumers of the company's products or its shareowners, but a number of distinct groups, all with varying interests, which the business organization must seek to satisfy (among them, its employees, suppliers, distributors, and the communities in which it operates).

The fulfillment of economic function is cumulative, in the sense that time alone can test a company's public value. A new corporation may quickly become an important element in our national life, but until it has endured trade cycles, met competition over the years, developed and replaced its management teams, and earned its reputation among its various publics, it cannot have achieved maximum Economic Function. It is by such outstanding companies as Procter & Gamble and Minnesota Mining and Manufacturing that the public value of new companies must be measured.

CORPORATE STRUCTURE

The category Corporate Structure in the Management Audit appraises the effectiveness of the structure through which management seeks to fulfill its aims. The organization structure of any company must expedite making and executing corporate decisions, must permit control of the enterprise, and must establish the areas of responsibility and authority of its executives. These are requirements that must be met regardless of the specific form of organization a company adopts; the American Institute of Management is not wedded to any particular organizational form in its appraisals.

In actual practice, the real form of organization of a company under study is seldom that of the nominal organization set out on the company's own organization charts. Published organization charts are, in fact, often so inaccurate in depicting the actual relationships and relative authorities within the company that they are of little use to the management analyst.

Companies that have developed product-division or other forms of decentralized organization have maximized the delegation of responsibility and authority, but they have not reduced the need for clear understanding of them throughout the organization. For the most part, corporations decentralize after the lines of authority have been well established; but at times, even large corporations have suffered as the result of a breakdown in the acceptance of exercise of authority. The classic example of this is still that General Motors Corporation in the early 1920's, when that company suffered an $85 million inventory loss because division executives failed to accept the authority of the principal executives.

HEALTH OF EARNINGS

The evaluation of earnings is concerned with the historical and comparative aspects of corporate income formation, not merely with the income itself. Health of Earnings must determine whether the profit potential of the corporations' assets has been realized in full. (By assets are meant not merely company-owned net equity but, in addition, the assets represented by whatever debt is included in capitalization—the net capital invested. These capital factors are represented in the production process by fixed assets in the form of land, plant, and equipment, or by more liquid assets including actual cash or, more remotely liquid, inventories. No matter what form they take, the paramount question is whether they have been employed at the optimum for the full realization of their potential.)

For both manufacturing and non-manufacturing companies the fruitfulness of capital can be determined by a study of the risk assumed in the employment of resources, in the profit returns upon their employment, and in the nature and distribution of the assets among various categories. Industrial enterprises are particularly suited to this analysis. Although the actual value of their assets (in particular, of their patents and processes) cannot always be determined exactly, one can at least trace the cost of their acquisition, the rates at which they have been depreciated, and the extent to which they have been employed profitably or unprofitably. While prepared information is seldom available for other categories of the Management Audit, the information required in Health of Earnings is usually on public record in a company's annual reports and in digests of its financial structure.

SERVICE TO STOCKHOLDERS

Appraisal of a company's service to stockowners rests chiefly on a three-part mandate that stockholders give the board of directors of corporations: first, that their principal not be dissipated or exposed to unnecessary risks; second, that the principal be enhanced as much as possible through the sound use of undistributed profits, and third, that they receive a reasonable return on the principal in the form of dividends, while their ownership interest is protected through preemptive rights. How well a company satisfies these three requirements determines its *fairness* to stockowners.

In addition, the appraisal covers the obligation that every company has today to provide *service* to its share-owners—primarily, to keep them well enough *informed* so that they can evaluate the progress of their investment in the company and participate in decisions that are likely to affect that investment. Even the financially inexperienced shareholder can review his own relationship with the company to determine whether or not the essentials of stockholder service are present. And while stockholder relations are less vital than sound dividend policies, they indicate a management conscious of its responsibilities—a fundamental of excellent management in any company.

For the specifics of analyzing fairness to stockowners, companies and industries differ too widely in what earnings they can pay out as dividends to set optimum ratios of dividends to net income or other absolutes. Rather, the ultimate return and capital appreciation are the important determinants of fairness to stockowners, not any particular or current percentage.

RESEARCH AND DEVELOPMENT

Because adequate research efforts over a period of years can assure company growth and improvement of its industry position, evaluation of company research policies is crucial to a Management Audit.

Our giant corporations, almost without exception, know the importance of research as a continuing activity, regardless of how well they pursue it. Too many smaller corporations, however, still look upon it with fear, and often do not undertake meaningful research at all. They could benefit immeasurably by greater boldness—if that boldness were based on a clear concept of what research is and can do and a realistic approach to budgeting and evaluating it.

Evaluating research results can show how well the research dollar has been employed, but it does not show whether or not management has realized the maximum from its research potential. For this reason, research must be examined comparatively and historically—in dollars expended, in the number of research workers employed, in the ratio of research costs and staff total expenses and personnel, in new ideas, information, and products turned out. These expenditures, examined with past research results, provide an estimate of management's willingness to employ research for *future* growth and health.

Some companies establish an arbitrary pay-out period to evaluate their own research results. This arbitrary system focuses attention on the need for research profitability, but it may actually discourage future research. The Institute's analysis of research success depends on no formula; it attempts, rather, to determine what part of the company's past progress can properly be credited to research and how well research policies are preparing the company for future progress.

DIRECTORATE ANALYSIS

The company directorate selects and guides operating management in the interest of the business owners and the public. In appraising its effectiveness, the American Institute of Management considers three principal elements:

1. The quality of each director and the contribution he makes to the board.
2. How well the directors work together as a team—whether they complement and stimulate each other. This, of course, is a principal test, since it is the board's actions as a group that affect the company.
3. Whether the directors act as trustees for the enterprise.

The trusteeship responsibility of the directorate can best be examined in those areas in which a partial conflict of interest exists between a company's executives and the business owners and public. One of the clearest of these is the area of executive incentives, and how well the directorate resolves compensation and other incentive problems provides an excellent key to its quality.

FISCAL POLICIES

While the fiscal history of a company—the result of all management actively expressed in measurable money terms—is appraised in the category

Health of Earnings, past and present financial policies are appraised directly in Fiscal Policies. This category includes three areas of study: the company's capital structure; its organizations for developing fiscal policies and controls; and the application of these policies and controls in different areas of corporate activity. The key problems are providing, controlling, and husbanding funds.

PRODUCTION EFFICIENCY

Evaluating production efficiency has obvious importance in appraising a manufacturing company. What is not so widely understood is that production efficiency or its equivalent, *operating* efficiency, is equally vital to non-manufacturing companies, whether they are in banking, insurance, transportation, communications, electric or other power, or any other field in which the end product is not a tangible good. Virtually all companies which are not merely agents for other companies must obtain and process some good or service before marketing it. This is the field of a company's over-all operation evaluated in the category Production Efficiency.

The analysis of present-day production management must be divided into two parts. The first of these may be termed the appraisal of "machinery and material management," since it evaluates the machanical production or processing of the company's products. This one part is often overemphasized, so that management's mastery of its machinery appears the major factor in production efficiency. However, a second aspect of production evaluation, that of "manpower management," is equally important. This facet of operations properly includes all personnel policies and practices for non-sales and non-executive employees developed by management. Only when both aspects are analyzed can over-all production in operating efficiency be appraised.

SALES VIGOR

Within single industries and even within single companies sales practices can vary broadly enough to represent different marketing principles. Between different industries the variations are often still greater. Yet the comparative appraisal of sales vigor must encompass all the forms that marketing can take —must, for example, enable the management analyst to compare the vigor of Procter & Gamble's consumer sales program, with its multimillion dollar advertising budget and scores of millions of customers, with the effectiveness of North American Aviation's sales essentially to one customer, the United States government.

Sales Vigor can, of course, be appraised despite these variations, but only after the marketing goals of each subject company have been determined and assessed. These goals, in turn, must be appraised in terms of the over-all goals of the entire organization. Then, as with other categories of the Management Audit, historical and comparative evaluation become possible, and how well past sales potential has been realized and how well present company sales policies prepare it to realize the future potential can be appraised. The treatment of sales personnel usually belongs in this category.

EXECUTIVE EVALUATION

Executive Evaluation is the most important single appraisal category of the ten that comprise the Management Audit. To a degree, of course, the other categories in this system of management appraisal also evaluate the organization's executives, since they appraise the results of executive thinking and action in each management function. But the quality of the executives themselves, their management philosophy, and the appropriateness of both to the purposes of the organization must still be appraised directly.

The American Institute of Management has found three personal qualities —ability, industry, and integrity—to be the essential elements for the business leader. These provide a framework for his evaluation in the Management Audit and should also be the criteria of the organization's leaders in selecting and advancing executives. Excellent management requires that executives work together in harmony, each with specific tasks contributing to the total effort, conscious that he is participating in this effort with men who command his respect. As a group the executives must regard the continuity of the corporation as an important goal, assuring it by sound policies of executive selection, development, advancement, and replacement. A key problem is to assure sound succession in depth.

UNIVERSALITY OF EVALUATION

The principles of the Management Audit remain valid regardless of the nature of the enterprise. All human activity is confronted with the same management problems. When two or more individuals get together in any common endeavor, wanting the best possible result, they must ask, "What shall we do, and how shall we do it?" In order to get good results, whether they are aware of it or not, they must follow fundamental tenets of management, which can be appraised.

SOCIAL FUNCTION

Whatever the undertaking, its impact upon the public welfare must be helpful rather than harmful. In the affairs of a church society, this value may be termed Social Function. In an educational institution, it is Academic Function. The principles of evaluation remain the same.

ORGANIZATION

The activities of two or more individuals—members of a management team once they unite in a common venture—create lines of authority and responsibility. They may be adjusted as the organization grows in size and consequence and progresses with its undertakings, but the extent to which authority and responsibility are made clear provides a basis for evaluation.

GROWTH

The enterprise must exhibit growth of facilities, whether these come from gifts or profits derived from merchandising goods or services. The health of that growth can be appraised.

MEMBERSHIP

Members, shareowners, or proprietors of an enterprise are encouraged to cooperate and contribute, whether through dividends or less material rewards. How this is done is a matter of techniques peculiar to the kind of enterprise and varying with circumstances and time. But that it shall be done activates fundamental management principles and permits evaluation of its effectiveness.

RESEARCH

Management of whatever kind seeks the most reliable, comprehensive, accurate, and up-to-date information available. Research and development includes study of any phase of group activity, with a view to betterment of either principles or techniques.

FISCAL POLICY

The financial and other resources of any group effort are the life blood of its activity. Where they are obtained—and obtained in proper quantity—the enterprise can continue to exist and grow. How well resources are found and used can be appraised. Fitting financial policies and practices to the immediate and long-term needs that experience indicates and then altering them as the result of study or alertness is a management principle closely related to survival.

TRUSTEESHIP

Whether called trustees, directors, or guardians, those overseeing an undertaking have the responsibility of determining its leadership. In this way they exercise the power of the organization. Appraisal can be made of how well they recognize that their authority needs the sanction of morality and creates obligations to assume responsibility for the welfare of the total enterprise, including the public and all individuals concerned.

OPERATIONS

The operations of an undertaking has a degree of effectiveness no matter what the product, service, or purpose. This is true even within the area of charitable, social, political, and spiritual endeavors. Every organization then, has production or operating problems, just as it has a research need; it must understand and solve these problems to be well managed.

SALES

Everyone is concerned with persuading others to accept him, his services his products, or his ideas, whether doctor, lawyer, merchant or priest. Every group activity must be sold or merchandized if the enterprise is to grow and prosper. The techniques to accomplish this vary with the enterprise, the occasion, and the purpose, but they can be assessed in terms of how well they persuade prospective purchasers, joiners, or whatever.

LEADERSHIP QUALITY

The quality of the leadership in any enterprise is the most important single aspect of the activity. The success of the executive group and the activity may depend on their integrity, ability, and industry, their devotion to the enterprise, their acceptance of responsibility, and their foresight in providing continued leadership after themselves. These qualities, all of which can be appraised, are not limited to the profit making corporation—they are fundamental wherever men join together for a common purpose, whatever the inspiration and the motive—commercial, divine or other.

In conclusion, administrative evaluation must recognize that for an organization to be well managed, it must have sound purposes and use good techniques. To be excellently managed, it must fit these techniques and practices within the framework of true administrative principles.

6. MARKETING AUDIT: NEW MANAGEMENT TOOL*

—PRINTERS' INK

Can you audit a marketing operation the way a company audits its finances? A handbook issued last week by the American Management Assn. wrestles with that question and comes up with an answer that seems to be yes and no. That is, yes, you can evaluate a total marketing operation. And, no, you can't do it with the same apparent mathematical precision of a financial audit.

Many companies are interested in the question and a few have tried to conduct marketing audits; that is, a thoroughgoing appraisal of their marketing operations on a regular, systematic basis. Others have discussed it. But the AMA handbook appears to be the first comprehensive study of what a marketing audit is, what it can accomplish and how it can be conducted.

Three statements—by Columbia University professor of marketing Alfred R. Oxenfeldt, assistant professor of marketing Abe Shuchman and Charles W. Smith, senior consultant of McKinsey & Co.—sum up the gist of the matter.

As the Messrs. Oxenfeldt, Shuchman and Smith see it, a planned analysis and appraisal of a company's marketing operations can produce real benefits It can also produce headaches, unless the audit is based on careful planning and organization, preceded by understanding.

Some marketing men who have conducted partial audits—share-of-market studies, sales analyses, distribution cost analyses, etc.—may think that the total marketing audit isn't new. In fact, the concept of an over-all, integrated and regular examination of the total marketing operation is quite new, and different. The piecemeal studies familiar to many marketing men are to a marketing audit what a recording of excerpts from My Fair Lady is to a front-row-center seat for the show. Or, as Shuchman puts it, "the sum of all the evaluations currently being made very rarely adds up to a marketing audit."

Just what is a marketing audit?

* From *Printers' Ink*, February 20, 1959, pp. 64–65. Reprinted by permission of the publisher.

Oxenfeldt says a marketing audit is "a systematic, critical and unbiased review and appraisal of the basic objectives and policies of the marketing

---

Seven elements in auditing marketing operations

1. • Objectives: Every marketing function should have a clearly stated objective.

2. • Policies: These should be studied together with the objectives because policies are the guides to achieving the goal represented by the objectives.

3. • Organization: Marketing appraisers should study whether the work load is equally distributed and if supervision of personnel is effective.

4. • Facilities: The physical structure of the marketing operation frequently is more susceptible to change than the operational elements. Therefore, it should be determined whether a company's facilities are the most efficient.

5. • Methods: These should be checked to determine if the methods used are the best for carrying out stated policies.

6. • Procedures: The difference between methods and procedures is one of degree. Methods are the means of carrying out policies to reach objectives while procedures are the specific steps —who does what and how.

7. • Personnel: Though the average company frequently evaluates personnel through periodic surveys, a marketing audit examination of employees should be conducted within the framework relating personnel to the stated objectives, policies and other elements of the operation.

---

function and of the organization, methods, procedures and peronnel employed to implement the policies and achieve the objectives."

Shuchman defines it as "a programed appraisal of *all* of the activities included within the marketing function." Many companies use even partial appraisals only when they get into trouble and need a way out. Shuchman emphasizes that the total marketing audit is "a prognastic as well as a diagnostic tool . . . a prescription for the sick firm, but it is also preventive medicine for the currently healthy and successful firm."

Smith emphasizes that the primary purpose of the audit is to disclose improvement opportunities. He also underscores perhaps the basic point: that the marketing audit is a management tool, and that its successful use depends to a great extent upon the chief executive officer.

In making an audit, the company will examine its market, its products and its marketing organization.

The market study will answer these questions:

- Who is buying what, and how?
- Who is selling what, and how?
- How is the competition doing?
- How are we doing?

In studying its product line, the company will want to know:

- Do we have too many products (or too few)?
- Does the line meet the demands of the market?

Obviously, an audit is a major undertaking. Its enthusiasts say the key words are "programed," "systematic" and "comprehensive." To those, some marketing men would add, "expensive," for it can cost a good deal, in time and money. There is another caution: unless an audit is properly organized and executed (under direction of top management) it can disrupt operations and affect morale adversely.

However, with the cautions observed, there seems little doubt that this kind of a how-are-we-doing examination can produce significant benefits, long-term and short-term.

Ideally, an audit would be conducted in two basic stages. The company could begin with an over-all, top-level study of the relationships among the various marketing functions. The objective here is to determine whether a proper balance of forces exists. The second phase would be an evaluation of each specific function, with each function sub-divided (for example, advertising would be studied from the point of view of company-agency relations, media selection, personnel development and compensation, etc).

In each phase, the experts agree, the auditors would want to base their appraisals on the seven elements outlined in the box on Page 93.

Of all the elements, objectives and policies are the key considerations. Objectives and policies, says Shuchman "are the base from which" the personnel, procedures and organization are derived. "In short," says Shuchman, the marketing audit is "primarily a re-examination and evaluation of objectives and policies."

Achieving this evaluation, of objectives, policies and other functional elements, requires answers to three basic questions: what kind of standards will be used, quantitative (and largely objective, employing statistics) or qualitative (and largely subjective, employing understanding and judgment); how will the evaluation program be scheduled, and who will conduct the audit.

Many companies prefer "outsiders"—management consultants—to conduct functional appraisals, on the grounds that this assures objectivity. On the other hand, the outsider cannot have the "feel" of the company that an experienced company executive would have. The choice is difficult. Oxenfeldt suggests an "outside-inside" task force to supervise the audit. The group would be made up of executives who are *not* involved in the function to be appraised but who know all the things an outsider might not have time to learn. Oxenfeldt suggests senior members of the marketing research department, the chief executive's personal staff members or members of the company's top management.

ALL A MATTER OF TIMING

On the matter of scheduling and timing, some rules of thumb are suggested:

• Audits should be made only as frequently as fundamental circumstances justify. For example, a share of market study every day would be ridiculous, but every year might be too infrequent; quarterly share of market analyses could be just right.

• Every aspect of the marketing operation should be evaluated at least every three years.

• No single part of a total marketing audit should be delayed too long after the other sections have been completed.

With proper timing and selection of auditors, the type of standards employed are crucial, Smith emphasizes.

Quantitative standards (numerical measurements such as share-of-market studies, warehouse tonnage and sales performance against quotas) are most frequently used. The quantitative appraisal can be made easily, frequently and by junior rather than senior executives. However, it has a basic disadvantage in that statistics are only a part of any story; they become meaningful only when refined through understanding and personal judgment.

Understanding and personal judgment are, of course, the essence of qualitative appraisals. However, making evaluations on the basis of personal judgments rather than measurable statistics is generally difficult to perform and such evaluations don't always win full confidence from all concerned. Still, the personal judgment factor is indispensable and a marketing audit made up only of numbers would be incomplete.

Since the point of an audit is to reveal the *potential* of the marketing operation, personal judgments on the basis of known statistics are essential.

There is no universal blueprint that every company could follow to conduct a marketing audit. However, these guide lines suggest a frame within which any company—employing imagination and initiative—can clearly determine how well it is doing. And, more importantly, how it could do better.

7. 446 CHECKPOINTS FOR MARKETING PLANNING*

—CRAIG S. RICE

Formal "marketing planning" is becoming an important activity in modern management. It is usually the function of responsible executives. It is generally based on a comprehensive collection of factual data, that is translated into specific plans.

A single omission of one vital factor can cause considerable executive embarrassment, costly delays and, worst of all, a disastrous market failure.

Our checklist was compiled to help avoid such an omission. It was prepared over a period of some years of marketing planning, budget planning, and product planning.

Not all points are necessary. The really capable marketing administrator can find the significant factors and ignore the unnecessary ones. He will separate the chaff from the grain. The checklist is designed to be sure no grain is overlooked.

This sort of list will provide you with a reminder of many things; angles, factors, and aspects that usually should be at least considered before a marketing plan is completed. You can read rapidly through it at almost any stage of the planning. At the beginning it will help you select and set up a list of factors that you want to cover in your planning. As you near the end of your planning, it will serve as a double-check to see that no important detail has been overlooked. It's all well and good to think big, but sometimes a little iron filing can jam-up big wheels.

Just a tool. The list will not do your thinking for you. It will not cover all aspects of every marketing plan on every marketing activity. While it is fairly comprehensive, it is only suggestive, not exhaustive. Further, no two people will necessarily classify all items under the same heading. Like all management

---

* From *Industrial Marketing*, October, 1957, pp. 188, 190–196. Reprinted by permission of the publisher.

tools, it should be used as a servant, not a master. The user should not attempt to cover every point, every time, but to use common sense and good judgment to pick and choose from the suggested list of about 100 points.

Here's how you might use this list. Let's say you have a marketing problem. It may be something big, like planning (or reviewing) the entire marketing of a product line. It may be that you only want to plan or review one aspect of marketing such as the market research, sales force activity, new product activity, etc. Read through this checklist under the appropriate headings. This will serve as a checklist of major factors that should be thoroughly handled, treated, and understood. In short, "checked off."

Some examples. Suppose you're planning or reviewing market research. This list will remind you to be sure to check seasonalities (they fluctuate widely on some products and not at all on others). It also will remind you that you might be wise to check your distributors' ideas and opinions. They frequently have suggestions that can be quite valuable, yet this is one of the many things even good marketing people forget to "check out."

Another example: If you're preparing a marketing plan, this list will remind you to set up a detailed time schedule, or check out your best distribution approach. Or, it will remind you to take a look at where you are, where you want to go, and how much it is likely to cost to get there. Unfortunately, these things are too frequently ignored in the normal enthusiasm of most marketing activities.

A marketing administrator who has at least a fairly thorough knowledge of each pertinent factor listed here, probably has an excellent foundation on which to institute sound scientific marketing.

MARKET FACTS
1. Market definition
2. The industry
Size
Trend
Product types
Cause of growth
Needs
Opportunities
3. Distribution
Company salesmen
Distributors
Manufacturers' representatives
Mill supply houses
Others
Numbers
Channel volume
Pricing
Policies
Advantages
Disadvantages
Peculiarities
4. Customers
Number
Major types
Location
Their sales volume
Their purchasing
Product types
Key purchaser
Quality standards
Ultimate user
Ultimate use
5. Major business split
Domestic
Export

Original equipment manufacturers
Processor
Other
  6. Market terminologies
  7. Market peculiarities

OUR PRODUCT

  1. Name
  2. Description
  3. Packaging and shipping
Specifications
Transportation
Responsibility
  4. Our market share:
By product
By period
By area
By dollars
By units
By per cent
  5. Advantages
Quality
Price
Promotion
Other
  6. Disadvantages
Quality
Price
Promotion
Other

COMPETITION

  1. Companies (general)
Number
Number each type
Number each size
Location
Characteristics
Policies
  2. Company income
Sales volume
Profits
Trends

  3. Company promotion
Salesmen budget
Advertising budget
Market Research budget
Other
  4. Salesmen
Selection
Training
Supervision
Salary
Quality
Performance
Morale
Reputation
Turnover
  5. Competitive product line
Kinds of products
Sales and share of market
Sales trends
Prices
Quality

MARKET RESEARCH

  1. General market facts
    (see above)
Research organization
Research function
Collection of facts
Analysis
Interpretation (significance)
Recommendation
Presentation to management
Influence on sales
Influence on profit
  2. Customers' opinions of:
Company
Products
People
Policies
Competition
  3. Distribution channel opinions
    of:
Company

Products
People
Policies
Competition
   4. Analysis of market trends
Total market
Successful products
Product quality differences
Product price differences
Other differences
Conclusions
   5. Published market data
Sources
Statistics
Significance
Trends
Conclusions
   6. Product suggestion sources
Research
Salesmen
Market research
Others
   7. New product's reasons for
      being
To fit market trends
To fill product line
To use production facilities
To increase profit
   8. New product screen
Relative quality
Relative promotion
Relative price
Market size
Market trends
Market opinions
Market loyalties
Market leader
Sales potential
   9. Seasonality of:
Total sales
Total production
Our product sales
Our production
   10. Market area potentials
Number of plants

Dollar volume
Kinds of industrial users
Trends
   11. Actual sales forecast by:
Product
Area
Month
   12. Purchaser potential by:
Industry type
Product type
Average volume
Modal volume
Median volume
Range of volume
   13. Market research services
Kinds
Costs
Value

MARKETING PLAN

   1. Industry facts
Volume
Trend
Products
Distribution
Promotion
Customer types
Purchaser attitudes
Prices
Costs
Profit
Cause of growth
Opportunities
   2. Our product
Name
Description
Quality
Sales
Distribution
Promotion
Distribution channel attitudes
Purchaser attitudes
Price
Cost

Profit
Advantages
Disadvantages
  3. Competition
Name
Description
Quality
Sales
Distribution
Promotion
Purchaser attitudes
Price
Cost
Profit
Advantages
Disadvantages
  4. Problems
Market
Industry
Distribution
Customers
Competition
Product quality
Cost
Price
Profit
Promotion
  5. Opportunities
Market
Distribution
Purchaser attitudes
Product quality
Product price
Promotion
  6. Objectives
Product sales
Product market share
Product trend
Distribution quotas
New customers
  7. Recommendations
Distribution
Product quality
Product price

Product promotion
Regional quotas
Monthly quotas
Product quotas
Promotion budget
Promotion strategy
Product strategy
Cost vs. sales
Time schedule
  8. Future plans
Product type
Cost reduction
Product improvement
Promotion improvement
Price improvement
Short term plans
Long term plans

SALES FORCE
ADMINISTRATION

  1. Number
  2. Location
  3. Job specifications
  4. Salary incentives and bonuses
  5. Sources of salesmen
Listing
Analysis
Evaluation
  6. Selection of salesmen
Requirements
Application
Testing
Interviewing
Evaluation
Selection
Orientation
  7. Training and instruction
Individual
Group
Rating
Demonstration
Practical Work
Testing
Recording

8. Sales quotas:
By product
By month
By territory
9. Work plans
By product
By month
Territory
Customer selection
10. Expenses
Automobile
Other allowances
11. Published instructions
Selling tips
Product technology
12. Selling aids
Samples
Manuals
Display material
13. Sales meetings
Purpose
Program
Evaluation
14. Conventions
Customer
Trade
15. Contests
Type
Purpose
Evaluation
Policy
16. Daily reports
Purpose
Kind
Use
Value
Review
Analysis
17. Salesman evaluation
Method
Timing
Correction
18. Turnover
Rate

Reasons
Corrections
19. Morale evaluation
Method
Timing
Correction
20. Termination
Interviews
Checklists
Notations
Finances
Reasons
Evaluation
Recommendations
Reports
Records
Action taken

ADVERTISING

1. Budget by:
Product
Period
Media
2. Research
Market data
Product sales
Purchaser opinion data
Copy suggestions
Art suggestions
Media suggestions
3. Media alternatives
Trade shows
Business papers
Catalogs
Direct mail
General business magazines
Publicity
Movies
Point-of-purchase displays
Product tags
Other
4. Media criteria
Budget

Frequency
Reach
Timing
Audience
Copy strategy
   5. Copy
Market facts
Basic strategy
Product seasonality
By season
By media
   6. Art strategy
   7. Agency
Size and trend
Clients
Personnel
Reputation
Attitude
Basic policies
Services
Functions
Limitations
Location
Advantages
Disadvantages
Contact
   8. Advertising testing
Area selection
Media
Ad design
Timing
Goal
Budget
Research
Results
Evaluation
Validity
   9. Advertising coordination with:
Market research
Product research
Production
Sales force
Top management

NEW PRODUCTS

   1. New product committee
Purpose
Policy
Basic philosophy
Personnel
Roles
Rules of action
Organization chart
Position in chart
Mechanical procedures
Reports
Minutes
   2. New product suggestions
      program
Sources
Mechanics
Disposition
   3. New product selection
Criteria
Screening
Disposition
   4. New product timing
By date
By product
By sales estimates
   5. New product recommenda-
      tion
Product description
Use
Sales
Costs
Price
Profit
Promotion
Production schedule
Marketing schedule
General strategy
Selling points
Advantages
Disadvantages
Conclusions

ECONOMIC POLICIES

1. Costs
Of goods
Advertising
Selling expenses
Administration
Market research
Product research
Overhead
Costs in dollars
Costs in per cent of sales
2. Quantity discounts
3. Price policies
4. Return goods policies
5. Sales analysis
Purpose
Contents
Use
Originator
Receiver
6. Sales analysis
By product
This period
Last period
Dollars
Units
Per cent change
Internal reasons
Market reasons

MARKETING DEPARTMENT

1. Organization
Job titles
Job specifications
2. Personnel qualifications
Training
Experience
Ability
3. Basic policies
Objectives
Role
Philosophy

4. Marketing plan
Originating team
Team action
Evaluation
Correction
5. Sections
Order department
Advertising
Salesmen
Market research
Product research
Sales records
6. Market testing
Originator
Methods
Evaluation
Action
7. Liaison with:
Top management
Product research
Production
Accounting
Purchasing
Legal
Personnel
Public
Trade
Other

SUMMARY OF MARKETING

1. Gathering facts (Where are we?)
Industry
Competition
Product
Promotion
Cost
Strong points
Weak points
2. Setting the goal (Where are we going?)
In industry
By product

By customer
By channel
By promotion
   3. Planning the route (How are we going to get there?)
Product strategy

Promotion strategy
Price strategy
Time schedule
Short range
Long range

8. HOW TO APPRAISE MANAGEMENT: PRODUCTION MANAGEMENT*

—OLIVER J. GREENWAY

My objective is to try to give you some suggestions in the area of manufacturing and its related functions, and in Industrial Relations which you may find worthy of consideration.

FOUR VITAL AREAS

Gentlemen, I cannot over-emphasize the importance of these areas of an industrial organization. Of course the areas already discussed by Bill Wiley and those to be presented by Ray Rich are important. They are vital. But can you afford to neglect an evaluation of that part of the company on which probably three-fourths of its income is spent each year? Can you omit from your studies the area which makes the product on which a company's income depends? . . . the area that controls, and thereby primarily determines, its costs? . . . which buys, maintains, and replaces the equipment in which a very substantial portion of a company's dollar investment is placed? Can you neglect the area that is responsible for buying the materials used by a company? . . . which selects, trains, and pays its people? . . . which builds its reputation for service, quality and performance?

Let me ask you this question: would you think as much of a Works Manager who effected a clear savings of $2,000 a week (through methods changes or astute purchasing, for example), as you would of a Sales Manager who increased annual sales by $1,000,000? In my company, it is exactly the same thing. One hundred thousand dollars a year saved is equal to one million dollars in sales.

Now, I am talking specifically about four general areas in an industrial organization:

* From the *Bulletin of the Robert Morris Associates* Supplement, November, 1953. Reprinted by permission of the publisher.

1. Production Operations;
2. Facilities and Equipment;
3. Purchasing and Material Control; and
4. Industrial Relations.

I believe it is important that you make at least some evaluation of these vital areas of a company, if you are really going to know whether that company is a sound risk.

"YOU DON'T HAVE TO BE A SPECIALIST"

Obviously since most of you, at least, are not industrial plant specialists, you cannot be expected to appraise the technical aspects of these operations. However, you don't have to be a specialist. By alert observation and the kind of answers you get from appropriate questions, you should be able to determine how capably the operations are being performed. I should like to urge you, at least, to take three steps in this direction:

1. Meet the guy who is responsible. Have at least one thorough personal talk with him.

2. Walk through the production area of the plant—and get an impression of the atmosphere.

3. Find out what management's attitudes, practices, and goals are in these areas.

You don't have to be a specialist to decide whether the man (or men) responsible for these parts of a company's operations are alert, dynamic, aggressive, hard-hitting. You don't have to be a specialist to discover whether the atmosphere is crisp, efficient, orderly, friendly. You don't have to be a specialist to determine how far-sighted a company is or is trying to be, or how progressive it is. At the very least, by taking a look for yourself, you will be able to determine whether you need a specialist's assistance and opinion.

TAKE A LOOK FOR YOURSELF[1]

If you are persuaded to take a look for yourself, and I hope that you are, what are the things to look for? I should like to highlight a few points in each of these areas as being of major significance.

First, let's look at Production Operations and some general aspects of it. In no area is thoughtful, far-sighted and well-implemented planning more important. Are there long-range and clear-cut objectives? Are they known and understood? Are they in harmony with other divisions of the Company? How are they being implemented? What is the record of achievement? Is there a realistic time table? The answers you get to these questions alone (and the evidence produced to substantiate the answers) should give you an excel-

---

[1] EDITORS NOTE: For a more detailed appraisal, check list referred to at end of this reading.

lent picture of the calibre of the men who are responsible for these functions.

More specifically in the general area of operations, what is the comparison between the plant's production capacity and its real output over a significant period of time? If the plant is operating well below capacity, unit costs will leap because of overtime, overloaded equipment, and so forth. Is production relatively level throughout the year, or are there seasonal or occasional swings resulting in layoffs, idle equipment, poor morale? And more important in terms of evaluating the company's future, how realistically has it grappled with problems of this kind, what has it done and what does it plan to do about them?

And still under the general heading of production operations, let me suggest that you look at the three areas of cost, quality and customer service. Proper management attitudes backed up by effective programs would be of major significance to the soundness of any company. Proper management attitudes in these three areas have always been of basic importance. And, based on the economic predictions we have available, they will be increasingly important during the next few years.

LET US LOOK AT THE COST PROBLEM FIRST

Management should be continually aware of costs . . . they should know what they are and they should be doing something about them. There should be a conscious and continual reduction program. There should be a vigorous long-range program aimed at methods improvement. I suggest that you try to get some information on the productivity trends for both direct and indirect labor. You undoubtedly agree that this trend must be steadily upward if the business is to continue successfully. And this upward trend, in most cases, can be realized only through methods improvements; it can never be achieved for any substantial period of time by a squeeze on labor. Attempting to achieve it by squeezing the work force is the Communist way and I am delighted to see that it is backfiring already in outbursts by the working people, such as we recently saw in East Germany. No, productivity can only really be increased through methods improvements and this will happen only when there is thoughtful and deliberate and long-range effort in this direction. Remember, when I save my company one hundred thousand dollars a year, I am doing the same thing for the company that our Sales Manager is doing when he goes out and sells a million dollars of product.

THE SECOND MAJOR AREA IS QUALITY

I would want to be assured that the management is quality minded. Is there a continual emphasis on quality on the part of those who are making the product, as there undoubtedly is on the part of those who are selling the product? The product must satisfy market requirements and be at least equal to good competition. Good vendor relations must be maintained to assure a steady flow of good materials. There must be a minimum of customer returns of defective material. High customer returns because of defective materials can quickly, almost overnight, destroy customer confidence in a product. The percentage of customer returns must be judiciously examined. The manufacturing processes should be controlled to assure the desired final quality for the optimum in lowest possible production cost, fewest rejects and repairs with the least possible inspection.

THE THIRD MAJOR AREA IS CUSTOMER SERVICE

By customer service I mean making good delivery promises and making good on the promises. Where a product has to be manufactured to order, the order, production, shipping, and delivery cycle must be quick, crisp and efficient. Where products are shipped from stock, all efforts should be made to see that stocks are well balanced and that deliveries can be made quickly.

Yes, the attitudes towards cost, quality and customer service are an excellent key to the health of a business; so look for the existence of programs in these three areas.

THE THREE M's

Now, if I may, I should like to leave the area of Production Operations and turn to the three remaining areas:
1. Facilities and Equipment;
2. Purchasing and Material Control; and
3. Industrial Relations.

The three M's—Machines, Material and Manpower. Most of the Company's money is spent in these areas.

I should like to suggest that you first ascertain the relative financial significance of these areas to the particular company with which you are concerned. It will vary. In my own company, approximately half of our costs are in human energy, and a fourth in raw materials. Obviously, therefore, we are even more concerned about a wage increase than we are about a price increase in our raw materials. In another company, the opposite might well be true. Yes, a basic economic factor in you evaluation of any company is the relative financial significance of each of these three areas. Let's look more closely at them.

FACILITIES AND EQUIPMENT

Undoubtedly you will find that most companies you investigate will have the major portion of their financial investment tied up in the plant itself and in equipment. In terms of the building facilities themselves, management awareness of geographical factors are important. Is the plant located in the best place when you consider the company's sources of materials? . . . its sources of manpower? . . . its marketing problems?

Answers to these questions may seem obvious to you, particularly if the company is located in a community with which you are already familiar and if you already know something about the nature of its operation. But you can find out a lot about the calibre of the Plant Manager by seeing how much he has thought about these problems and what he has effectively done and is planning to do in the future.

Take a look at the building itself. Is there room for expansion? If not, can additional space be acquired economically and quickly when it may be needed and in a desirable location? Only a few days ago I learned of a company in New York which obtained space for additional facilities after considerable searching, at an awkward location and at excessive expense, only to find later that they could have done much better right around the corner. Talk about acres of diamonds . . . a little foresight and planning could have saved them substantial sums of money.

Another key to the calibre of a company which you can use in the area of physical facilities is the amount of thinking that has been done regarding decentralization versus centralization. If the company's operations are confined to one location, what is the risk of interrupted production which might be caused by fire, explosion, or just strike? The recent fire at General Motors is an alarming example of what can happen in this situation; a small organization can be ruined.

You may remember that one of the three things I urged you to do in taking a look for yourself was to walk through the production areas of the plant. It often is surprising how much you can find out in a quick tour of this kind. For example, what is the plant's general appearance? How is the light? . . . ventilation? . . . washroom facilities? . . . safety? . . . And above all, is it neat, clean and orderly? Have you ever seen any business produce efficiently and serve quality products from a disorderly house, whether it be a bank, a store, a restaurant or a factory? A cardinal principle for any industrial organization is that "Good workmanship, high production, sound personnel relations and final quality of product are definitely dependent on Order, Neatness and Cleanliness of Plant." You don't have to be a specialist, and it doesn't take much time to get a good picture in this area.

I know there is no need for me to tell you how important equipment is to any company. It usually represents a high portion of the company's assets. It is the key to higher production as well as steady production. In this highly competitive and technological era in which we live, improvements are constantly being made in equipment which have a way of obsoleting older equipment, sometimes overnight. I think it is important for you to ascertain whether this company's equipment is modern and up-to-date. And what the plant management is doing to keep it so with equipment research, development and improvement programs.

I think you will also agree that plant equipment should be maintained in good condition. All good companies realize its importance and operate a preventive maintenance program to insure uninterrupted production, low cost and high quality. However, I think you would be surprised to know how many companies do a relatively inadequate job in preventive maintenance. It's an easy area to neglect, until the day when your neglect catches up with you. In order to use money for other purposes, some companies have been known to cripple along with obsolete and poorly conditioned equipment only to wake up one day to the surprising knowledge that they can't produce efficiently and are consequently faced with new equipment and rehabilitation expense beyond what they are able to cope with at that time. How well you know that one man can ruin his automobile in 20,000 miles while another can get good operation for 100,000 miles. Far-sighted planning for equipment replacement and an active preventive maintenance program are both indications of a sound company with a future, and the absence of these would indicate a fly-by-night to me. It's one more way of telling the Men from the Boys.

Another illuminating question you may want to ask, after you've seen the plant's equipment yourself, is how much money the company spends for maintenance and repairs. This is often a clue to the age and condition of the equipment.

PURCHASING AND MATERIAL CONTROL

Now, let us consider the crucial areas of Purchasing and Material Control. Of course your first problem is to discover how important the purchasing function is in the particular company you are studying. Other important considerations in assessing the importance of this function are whether the materials used are technically complex and what percentage of the unit product cost is determined by the cost of materials. Furthermore, are any important items subject to abnormal economic conditions such as Government controls, patents, rareness, monopoly, geographic or political problems?

Assuming that the purchasing of materials is an important consideration (and it usually is), what should you find out about it? I should like to suggest two major areas for your investigation.

First, investigate the controls that are exercised over purchases. Is authority centrally placed, and tightly held? And is there thorough and regular clearance with all appropriate departments of the company before major purchases are made? I know of one company in which it was decided to place an order for four times the normal turnover requirement in an item in order to obtain a real price advantage. Ordinarily, this would have been highly commendable. However, this was not discussed with the Engineering Division, which shortly afterwards issued a change which completely obsoleted the material. It had to be scrapped. What looked like a wise move that would make a profit turned out to be a substantial loss because of inadequate controls and clearance procedures.

Second, investigate the attitudes and procedures used to keep abreast of technological developments in the field, to constantly discover and use new sources of supply, new and better materials at lower prices. Is the attitude one of aggressive and progressive thought and investigation? What is the achievement record, and what are the future plans?

The illustration which I just mentioned regarding inadequate controls and clearance involves, of course, the related function of in-plant material control. Gentlemen, I believe it would be hard for me to exaggerate the importance of this one function to the financial success or failure of any organization.

Think, for a moment, of what can happen if Material Control is inadequate. If there is a larger inventory than is needed, capital which should be used for other constructive purposes is frozen, and hazards of obsolescence are greatly increased. Furthermore, excessive storage costs would normally be involved. If, on the other hand, a company's inventory is insufficient, the result all too often is work stoppages, production and factory losses, poor morale in the work force and customer dissatisfaction because of delays. A company cannot survive very many experiences of this nature, particularly now and in the years ahead of us.

Or think for a moment of the effects of such obvious things as poor records, poor storeroom control of receipts and issues, theft, inaccurate inventory statements and therefore misleading financial reports. Let me give you a tragic example from my own knowledge. A company, whose name I won't mention (but let me assure you it is not mine) coasted through the year with monthly statement which definitely indicated a good year was shaping up. But at the end of the year, after the annual inventory was taken, approximately FIVE HUNDRED THOUSAND DOLLARS of physical inventory could not be accounted for. It was simply errors in records. So, what looked all along like a good profit year, suddenly proved to be a loss year for that company. Both the Works Manager and the Plant Production Manager were fired. But the horse, gentlemen, had already been stolen. That was a personal tragedy for several individuals and it seriously damaged the company itself.

There have been several dramatic cases, recently publicized, of large thefts of valuable materials which went along undiscovered for surprisingly long periods of time. You know of some of these cases. Possibly it even happens in banks. Good material control . . . what can be more important? I urge you to check the methods used for this purpose by the company you are investigating. Are they modern? . . . efficient? . . . adequate? Are inventories maintained at the optimum level? Is the material turnover rate high enough? Are records and storage facilities adequate to prevent obsolescence, deterioration and pilferage? Are inventories taken frequently and accurately to prevent startling annual surprises? I do not see how you can afford to overlook at least raising questions like these with the man responsible for this area of the company's operations. And, if you have time, request proof.

INDUSTRIAL RELATIONS

Finally, folks, I would like to turn to the area of Industrial Relations. There is no better key to the calibre of leadership which a company has than its

Industrial Relations' attitudes and policies. No company can be any better than the people it employs. And, in most companies, a major portion of costs is involved in this area of "human energy." There are the usual general questions you need to have answered, similar to those already raised regarding Facilities and Equipment, Purchasing and Material Control. How important are the people? How much money is involved? What percentage of the product cost is represented by wages and salaries, and how does this compare with other companies in similar fields? What is the source of supply? Is the company dependent on relatively skilled personnel, or on unskilled people, and are they available?

I should think that a quick survey of a company's labor relations would constitute an essential inquiry for you. Is the labor force organized, and if so, what are the Unions involved? What is the history of its labor relations in terms of strikes, stoppages, arbitration cases and grievances? And of particular importance—if the company is not organized, is it likely that it soon will become organized, by what Union, and what would the results be if that happened?

The alertness of the management can be measured in large part by the company's employment practices and results, its wage and salary administration programs, its health, welfare and fringe benefits, and its emphasis on training and development.

There are, in addition, several quick clues to the morale of the work force which might be helpful. Strikes or work stoppages of course (though the presence of these does not always indicate poor management by any means). But in addition, ask for a comparison of this company's absence and lateness record with companies in similar industries. Or get a comparison of its labor turnover rate in the industry involved. Or its unemployment compensation costs.

I know that I need not remind you that almost every company you will investigate is a competitive institution. It is, therefore, wise to compare it with its competitors, including the field of Industrial Relations. And remember, when you compete for people, you compete in a geographical area as well as in a skilled group or in an industry. If the company lags behind the others in the area in wages, in fringe benefits, in both financial and non-financial incentives, the chances are most likely that it will have to come in line at some point if it stays in business. And you can look for increased costs in this area if that is the case.

Just two other points in the field of Industrial Relations: First, I suggest that you glance at the level of management compensation. Is it enough? Is there a financial incentive program for management in terms of bonus or profit sharing? This is most important. And second, is the company aware of and does it generously fulfill its community and social obligations? Does it encourage active participation in community organizations? Does it participate as a company? Here again is an illuminating clue to the calibre of its management.

Let me tell you a story which I think you will find interesting and perhaps helpful. When I was searching for a location for one of our plants, I found it beneficial to visit several of the plants in the areas that interested me. I recall visiting one plant which very greatly impressed me in every respect except one. The Manager himself guided me through his beautifully equipped and orderly plant and he proudly explained the equipment and processes of the operation and the accomplishments which had been made and what he was planning for the future. Yes, I was very much impressed. Here was a fellow who was really on the ball in all but one thing—Human Relations. Do you know this guy didn't speak to one person on that entire tour. It was just as if the plant were empty. Shortly after that I visited another plant of about the same size and here I was impressed with an absolute contrast. The Manager of this plant, in my opinion, was a real leader. His plant was not only in fine condition and producing efficiently but, what was so important, he had the human touch. It was here that I could quickly sense that harmony, willing cooperation and high productivity prevailed. The man seemed to know every workman in the plant and he exchanged smiles and greetings with all of them.

He too had some special pieces of equipment of which he was proud, but his technique of explaining it to me was quite different. He would take me over to the operation, introduce me to the operator, and then ask the operator to describe the operation to me. With amazing pride these operators would give me the whole pitch even to the cost of the machine, its productivity and how much better it was than the old one it had replaced. Need I elaborate any further or even suggest which plant was the better operated?

Well—there you have it. I believe these areas are vitally important in any company: Production Operations . . . Facilities and Equipment . . . Purchasing and Material Control . . . Industrial Relations. Just take a look at them for yourself. Meet the man responsible. Walk through the production areas. Find out what management's attitudes, practices and goals are. I believe it will pay you real dividends.

I. MANUFACTURING

A. PLANT

1. In what type of facility does the Company perform its operation?
   a. Where located?
   b. Owned or leased?
   c. Size of areas?
   d. Is any of space unused at present?
   e. Where would any expansion take place?
   f. Cost of space?
   g. In what condition is the facility?
2. Has any consideration been given to decentralization?
3. What degree of security is there against strike, sabotage, etc.?
4. Is the plant safe from fire, explosion, etc.?

5. Is location good for raw materials, market and source of labor?

6. Is plant well lighted and ventilated?

7. Is good housekeeping maintained?

B. EQUIPMENT AND FACILITIES

1. Are they modern and up-to-date?

2. What portion is general purpose equipment?

3. What portion is special purpose equipment (i.e., peculiar only to this Company's process)?

4. Is it in satisfactory condition?

5. Is a preventive maintenance program used?

6. Is an equipment replacement program in effect?

7. Is all equipment being used?

8. Is there any equipment on the books at value not being used which is obsolete or worn out?

9. What is the ratio of maintenance expense to direct labor? Is this too high? If so, why?

10. Are good safety practices employed for personnel protection?

C. PLANT OPERATIONS

1. Is the plant well laid out to provide efficient and orderly process of production, material handling, stores and associated functions?

2. At what level of capacity does the plant generally operate?

3. If sales fluctuate, what is done to minimize effect on plant operations?

4. Is the capacity greater than needed or insufficient?

5. Is there a definite program established to obtain improvement, simplification and economies in equipment, methods, processes, materials, labor and overhead?

6. What is the worker productivity both direct and indirect? What is the trend?

7. Does the Company use an incentive system? What type? To what extent is it employed? What is its effectiveness?

8. What effort has been made to obtain level production?

D. PRODUCTION PLANNING AND CONTROL

1. Is a sound and efficient program for production planning, scheduling and control in effect?

2. Are production schedules made as far in advance as possible to insure availability of materials, level manufacturing loading and minimum turnover and movement of workers?

3. What is the record on meeting customer delivery promises?

4. Is there good control over movement of work-in-process materials and is this inventory kept at a minimum consistent with an efficient manufacturing cycle?

E. QUALITY

1. Is top management quality minded?
2. Does the Company use modern quality control techniques?
3. How does this Company's product compare with competitors?
4. Are there markets of any significance which this Company cannot serve because quality does not meet the requirements?
5. What is the in-plant performance on rejects and repairs? Is it excessive?
6. Is the product uniform?
7. Does the Company have a materials conservation and salvage program which provides the best method of utilization and disposition?
8. Are customer returns of defective material excessive?
9. Does top management include a review of product quality reports?
10. Is the quality function used for:
    a. Better vendor and customer relations?
    b. Reducing manufacturing costs?
    c. Product improvements?
    or limited to inspection activity only?

F. COST CONTROL

1. Are costs known and is effort made with any success to control them?
2. What products are unprofitable and are steps being taken to make them profitable? Is intelligent use made of the cost data in setting sales prices, valuing inventories, etc.?
3. Have standard operating ratios been established and do they make intelligent use of them?
4. Are budgets used effectively?
5. What is the break even point? If it is high, what steps are being taken to reduce it?
6. How would the Company fare in any recession in business? Is there a planned program of what would be done if there is a down turn in business of 10%—20% etc.? Can economies be effected immediately?
7. Are costs increasing or decreasing, and why?
8. Are the cost methods adequate? Are they calculated for the purpose of providing an historical record or are they used to control operations?
9. Are sufficient reserves maintained for equipment and materials inventories?
10. Are non-recurring expenses identified and separated from regular operating expenses?
11. Is vigorous control exercised over indirect expense?

G. RESEARCH AND ENGINEERING

1. What importance does the Company place on research for the (a) improvement of its existing products, manufacturing equipment and processes,

and (b) development of new products, manufacturing equipment and processes?

2. Are the research activity objectives in harmony with the overall Company objectives, and is its active program well directed to accomplish effective results?

3. In the development of new products, manufacturing equipment and processes, has proper consideration been given to:

    a. Future market volume and profit potential?

    b. Product quality?

    c. Review of manufacturing considerations?

    d. Sufficient trial runs on a pilot basis to avoid " bugs " when in factory production?

    e. Standardization of equipment and materials?

    f. Economy in manufacturing?

    g. Simplification of processes?

    h. Minimum labor content?

    i. Minimum of maintenance?

    j. Caution against over-engineering?

    k. Use of existing inventories of materials?

Is all of this done before project authorization is given? What has been the Company's experience?

H. PURCHASING

1. How important is the purchasing function to the operations? Are purchasing specialists used?

2. Do purchased materials represent a large percentage of the product cost?

3. Do items purchased have technical complexity?

4. What is the annual value of purchases?

5. Are adequate controls exercised on commitments by members of management such as the financial officer, works management, engineering, sales, purchasing agent?

6. In what manner are the controls maintained?

7. Do you consider the purchasing function a profit making operation or is it used only as a facilitating service?

8. Are any of the important purchased items subject to abnormal economic conditions such as governmental control, patents, rareness or monopoly?

9. Is reciprocity practiced and, if so, to what extent?

10. How is purchasing performance measured?

11. If the Company has multiple plant operations, is the purchasing centralized or decentralized and what benefits accrue from method used?

12. Are relations with vendors good? How is this determined?

13. How are vendors selected?

14. Are there automatic checks and balances for:

    a. Control of requisitioning authority?

  b. Distribution of paperwork to all persons who should have information?
  c. Matching or orders, invoices and actual receivals?
  d. Inspection of receivals?

15. Does the procurement group keep abreast of technological developments and are they constantly searching for new sources of supply, new and better materials and methods, and lower prices for the operations?

I. MATERIAL CONTROL

  1. Are modern and efficient methods employed to control inventories?
  2. Are inventories maintained at the optimum level?
  3. Is turnover rate high enough?
  4. If inventory size and balance get out of line, is explanation requested of steps being taken to revert to a normal position?
  5. Are materials properly and efficiently recorded and stored to provide minimum of obsolescence, deterioration and pilferage?
  6. Are modern materials handling methods used for transportation and storage?
  7. Is a good system for physical inventory of materials in effect to obviate any surprises in loss or value?

II. INDUSTRIAL RELATIONS

  A. What is the management's attitude on industrial relations as a whole and how well is it set up to handle this important function?
  1. What is the title of the person in charge of Industrial Relations? (Place on organization chart will indicate to a great degree the attitude of management.)
  B. Does the Company employ good programs for:

  1. Employment?
  2. Wage and Salary Administration?
  3. Medical Care?
  4. Employee Welfare?
  5. Employee Services?
  6. Training?
  C. Is the Company unionized? If so, how long has it been unionized? What is the Union? Suggest a review of the contract for any peculiar conditions. What is the Company-Union relationship?
  D. What is the morale of the employees and their attitude toward the Company?
  E. What is the rate of employee turnover as related to (a) the area in which the Company is located, and (b) its competitors'?
  1. What is the unemployment insurance experience?

F. What is the record on absenteeism and lateness as related to (a) the area in which the Company is located, and (b) its competitors'?

G. Does labor make unreasonable demands resulting in restriction of output, featherbedding, inflexibility, etc.?

H. On employee wage rates and fringe benefits, how does the Company compare (a) with the area in which it is located, and (b) with its competitors'?

I. If the Company is out of line on employee wage rates and fringe benefits, is it not probable that it will ultimately be obliged to get in line with the area and its competitors?

1. What are the potential long term costs of the fringe benefits?
   a. Insurance
   b. Pensions, etc.
     Are they actuarially sound? Funded or non-funded?

J. What effect would such a cost increase have on its operations?

K. Is there an effective training program for all key personnel?

L. Are all key positions protected with trained replacements?

M. Is the Company training personnel for the expansion of its operations?

N. Is there harmony and cooperation existing among key employees and between departments and divisions?

O. Does the Company have good two-way communications throughout the organization?

P. Does the Company have an effective program to enlighten employees on the true economic "facts of life"?

Q. Is front line supervision functioning effectively and are they paid properly?

9. THE PERSONNEL AUDIT: GATEWAY TO THE FUTURE*

—ERNEST O. MILLER

A small company, with its plant in a rural community some miles from the city in which the executive office was located, decided to improve its management of the personnel function. While a clerk had handled the personnel detail in the past, a personnel adviser was hired to advance the function more competently. To assist him in planning and launching his program, a personnel audit was decided on. Since the company was not staffed to undertake such an audit, a consulting organization was retained to work with the personnel adviser and the management in conducting the audit.

An audit is a flexible tool the full value of which can only be gained by designing it to cope with the problems of a particular situation. A personnel audit can include, if available, an appraisal of the number and type of grievances and the number which reach arbitration, an analysis of arbitration decisions, turnover ratios for various classes of personnel, recruiting and employment costs, staffing ratios as related to total employment and sales, supervisory ratios, accident frequency and severity measures, workingmen's compensation costs, unemployment compensation costs, area wage and salary surveys, analysis of wage and salary practices and merit review programs, benefit plan participation ratios, etc. These techniques permit us to quantify the audit and give us a basis for comparison when future audits are undertaken. Unfortunately such measures are rarely found in the situation where the need for an audit is most pronounced. This was the case in the situation being considered; so the procedures of the audit had to present "the art of the possible."

* From the *Personnel Journal*, September, 1961, pp. 1–8. Reprinted by permission of the publisher.

THE APPROACH

In view of the lack of quantitative data available for use in the audit and since the function being audited was in fact just being launched, an approach appropriate to the needs and limits of the problem was developed. This approach was described in the introduction to the audit as follows: "This audit is designed to better prepare the company to plan realistically the direction and amount of effort that will be expended to move ahead successfully (in this functional area). The audit . . . has three phases:

" a. An analysis of the current activities of the personnel department;
" b. A survey of the thoughts and opinions of management on the personnel function and its activities; and
" c. A survey of the attitudes of the employee group toward those aspects of management and the services provided that relate to their well-being as individuals and their satisfaction with the organization."

On the completion of phases (a) and (b) of the audit, since many important problems were uncovered, problems needing immediate action, the decision was made by management not to proceed at that time with the third phase of the audit. (This was an unfortunate decision since it overlooked the fact that the basic measure of the success of a personnel program is in its impact on the attitudes and motivation of employees. It also deprived the company of a reliable bench mark against which it could later evaluate the success of its efforts to improve its programs and measure the return it was receiving on the increased investment it was making.) The first two phases of the audit will be discussed in detail below.

PERSONNEL DEPARTMENT ACTIVITY ANALYSIS

While a general statement of the responsibilities of the personnel department and the personnel adviser was available there was marked disagreement among members of the management group as to what the department was doing, how it was spending its time and money and why it was spending it in these ways. To obtain a factual answer to this question the personnel adviser kept a daily record of his activity, tabulated in half-hour units, for a three and a half month period. Management agreed that this was a fairly typical three and a half months and accepted it as representative of how the personnel adviser spent his time.

The activity data collected in this way was tabulated by function, by judged level of professional competence required to assure satisfactory performance and by the operations involved. The functional areas used for the tabulation were:

1. *Department Administration:* administrative direction and review of the whole employment relations program.

2. *Planning:*
   a. Policy Formulation—recommending new or changed policies and practices.
   b. Programming—planning and developing programs designed to carry out accepted policies.
   c. Organization—recommending revisions or extensions in overall organization and inter-unit relationships.

3. *Staffing:*
   a. Job Analysis—identifying and describing jobs.
   b. Recruiting—discovering and securing manpower.
   c. Selection and Placement—screening applicants through testing and interviewing; making initial adjustments for new employees.

4. *Training:* all types from job to executive.

5. *Promotion and Transfer:* includes terminations, severance pay and exit interviews.

6. *Personnel Rating:* periodic evaluation of employee performance and potential.

7. *Labor Relations:* collective bargaining, negotiations, contract administration and grievance handling.

8. *Employee Services and Benefits:*
   a. Communications—in-plant communications including publications, handbook, suggestion system, bulletin boards, etc.
   b. Counseling—aid and advice to individual employees.
   c. Other Services—financial aids, recreation, administering pensions, insurance, unemployment compensation, etc.

9. *Health and Safety:* sick leave, hospitalization, medical benefits, safety programs, etc.

10. *Wage and Salary Administration:* wage surveys, payroll management etc.

11. *Records and Reports:* records of all industrial relations functions, preparation of reports on work of the division.

12. *Audit and Review:* checking programs against policies, evaluation of current policies, program and practices.

13. *Research:* conducting studies of current policy and practice, analysis of records.

14. *Overhead and Miscellaneous.*

These functional areas were the same as those used by Yoder,[1] in order that Yoder's survey data on personnel ratios and costs could be used to compare with our data.

The basis for the tabulation for judged level of professional competence required was:

[1] Yoder, D. and Wilson, L. P., "How Much Do Personnel Activities Cost?", Pers. Vol. 30, #2, Sept. 1953.

Level 1: Activities at this level, because of the technical aspects or contacts involved, must be handled by the personnel adviser.

Level 2: Activities at this level may be handled by either the personnel adviser or an assistant.

Level 3: Activities at this level can be adequately handled by a secretary or clerk. Examples: filing, completing routine reports, posting notices, etc.

The operational categories used for classifying the data were:

Investigating: Reviewing files, records or literature and interviewing people for background material and facts related to a problem Ex.: discussion with a supervisor of an accident, review of files on 25 year dinner, etc.

Planning: Time spent in evaluating facts as they relate to what will be done in the future.

Executing: Carrying out the activity.

Recording: Reducing to writing relatively routine kinds of information where operations are essentially those of listing and entering.

Evaluating: Reviewing critically the results of actions taken.

Reporting: Communicating to others or for the files the results of investigations, activities and evaluations.

The results are presented in Tables 1–5.

Table 1

Personnel Adviser Activity by Functions
(9/20/54 – 1/4/55)

Function	No. Half Hour Units	Company Percent	Percent Industry Budget[1]
1 & 2: Administering, Planning Policy and Organizing	57	4.3	11.9
3. Staffing	44	3.3	18.6
4. Training	35	2.6	9.8
5. Promotion and Transfer	41	3.1	2.2
6. Personnel Rating	0	0.0	2.1
7. Labor Relations	191	14.3	7.5
8. Employee Services	398	29.7	15.3
9. Medical, Health and Safety	290	21.7	16.2
10. Wage and Salary	51	3.8	4.1
11. Records and Reports	76	5.7	5.3
12. Audit and Review	56	4.3	1.3
13. Research	14	1.0	1.7
14. Overhead and Miscellaneous	86	6.4	4.0
Total	1339	100.0	100.0

[1] YODER, D. and Wilson, L. P., "How Much Do Personnel Activities Cost?"; Pers. Vol. 30, #2, Sept. 1953.

Table 1 indicates how the personnel adviser spent his time by functional area. Labor relations, employee services and medical, health and safety programs took up 65.7% of his time. In contrast with this, the average practice in industry at the time of the audit (1955) was to spend approximately 39.0% of the personnel budget in these areas. At this company the low areas in terms of time spent were administration, planning, policy, organization, staffing and training. While staffing requirements were a function of turnover and expansion, and so the need in this company was less since there was little turnover and with increased automation, a reduction in the work force, the other areas were probably not receiving the attention they deserved.

Table 2
Personnel Advisor Activity by Level
(9/20/54 – 1/4/55)

Level	No. Half Hour Units	Percent
Level 1	493	36.8
Level 2	514	39.4
Level 3	332	24.8
Total	1339	100.0

Table 3
Personnel Advisor Activity by Operation
(9/20/54 – 1/4/55)

Operation	No. Half Hour Units	Percent
Investigating	267	19.9
Planning	210	16.4
Executing	387	28.9
Recording	112	8.3
Evaluating	70	5.2
Reporting	293	21.8
Total	1339	100.0

Table 2 shows the level of activity in which the personnel adviser was engaged. Only 36.8% of his time was spent in activities the difficulty of which required a person of his training and ability; 63.2% of his activity could have been successfully handled by an assistant or clerk. Even assuming half of the activity in Level 2 should be assigned to Level 1, only 56.0% of the time spent would have been at the appropriate level of difficulty. This fact when added to the evidence of serious understaffing suggested that a personnel assistant should have been added to the personnel department.

Table 3 is self-explanatory. It indicated too little time was being spent in Planning and Evaluating.

Table 4 shows where the personnel adviser needed help the most. The data suggested that the personnel assistant could make an immediate contribution by assuming responsibility for the details involved in employee services, medical, health and safety, records and reports and miscellaneous.

Table 4

Personnel Adviser Activity by Function and Level
(9/20/54 – 1/4/55)

Function	1	%	2	%	3	%	TOTAL	%	Time in Function %
1 & 2: Administering, Planning, Policy and Organizing	41	71.9	9	15.7	7	12.2	57	100	4.3
3. Staffing	12	27.2	27	61.3	5	11.3	44	100	3.3
4. Training	18	51.4	15	42.8	2	6.8	35	100	2.6
5. Promotion and Transfer	9	21.2	24	58.5	8	20.3	41	100	3.1
6. Personnel Rating	0	0	0	0	0	0	0	0	0
7. Labor Relations	138	72.2	38	21.0	15	7.8	191	100	14.3
8. Employee Services	94	22.9	182	44.3	134	32.8	410	100	29.7
9. Medical, Health and Safety	72	24.8	166	57.3	52	17.9	290	100	21.7
10. Wage and Salary	13	25.4	28	55.0	10	19.6	51	100	3.8
11. Records and Reports	10	13.1	11	14.4	55	72.5	76	100	5.7
12. Audit and Review	50	89.4	0	0	6	10.6	56	100	4.3
13. Research	10	71.4	2	14.3	2	14.3	14	100	1.0
14. Overhead and Miscellaneous	28	32.5	12	13.9	46	53.6	86	100	6.4
Total	493	36.8	514	39.4	332	24.8	1339	100	100.0

Note: The data in the table is reported in half-hour units.

Table 5 lists the percent of companies who had reported activity in each of the 14 functional areas. This indicates the extent to which functions performed by the personnel department are generally accepted. Also reported in the table are the personnel ratios by functional area from a 1954 survey of industry practice and for the company. (A personnel ratio is commonly computed as the number of employees in the personnel department for each 100 employees in the company.) An inspection of Table 5 indicates the company was badly understaffed by industry standards. Only in the labor relations and employee services areas did the time spent by the company match general industrial practices.

The company had one employee in the personnel department for 300 employees. This was a personnel ratio of approximately 0.33. For companies of the same size the median personnel ratio from a survey of industrial companies was 0.86 in 1954, 1.00 in 1953. The ratio in 1954 varied from below 0.64 to above 1.27. For manufacturing companies in 1954 the median ratio reported was 0.70 while it was 1.00 for the construction industry. Regardless

Table 5

Personnel Activities and Ratios: Industry vs. Company Practice*

Function	Firms Reporting %	Personnel Ratios— All Industry—'54	Personnel Ratio— Com- pany—'54
1 & 2: Administering, Planning,	98	.04	.014
Policy and Organizing	86	.03	
3. Staffing	94	.10	.011
4. Training	78	.07	.009
5. Promotion and Transfer	83	.04	.010
6. Personnel Rating	64	.02	.000
7. Labor Relations	83	.05	.048
8. Employee Services	97	.10	.099
9. Medical, Health and Safety	97	.21	.072
10. Wage and Salary	85	.05	.013
11. Records and Reports	94	.09	.019
12. Audit and Review	63	.02	.014
13. Research	73	.02	.003
14. Overhead and Miscellaneous	58	.07	.021

* Toder, D., "How Much Do Personnel activities Cost?", Pers., Vol. 31, #s, November, 1954; Yoder, D. and Wilson, L. P. "Salaries and Ratios in Industrial Relations: 1954," Pers., Vol. 31, #1, July 1954.

of the comparison made, the personnel function in the company, by general industrial standards, was understaffed. At least one full-time employee preferably at the personnel assistant level, should be added to the department. This would raise the ratio to 0.67 and would have been in line with general practice.

With this addition to staff the areas not receiving sufficient attention could be more adequately covered. The personnel assistant could assume responsibility for all of the Level 3 activity and most of the Level 2 activity as reported. The personnel assistant would spend most of his time on employee services, medical, health, safety, records and reports and miscellaneous filing and office routines. The personnel adviser would spend more time on planning, policies organization and training.

The analysis as reported here led to these recommendations:

a. A personnel assistant should be added to the personnel department.

b. A systematic time-activity record system should be installed in the personnel department for budget development and management control purposes.

c. The personnel department should develop a functional budget based on the 14 functional areas used in this report.

d. Another activity audit should be conducted in about a year to determine the direction and extent of change in the department's activities. This can then be related to the objectives as set by management based on the data here reported.

SURVEY OF MANAGEMENT OPINION

The analysis of how time and money was being spent by the personnel adviser was not sufficient for a review of the impact of the function as then managed or as a basis for planning the future development of the function. Since the personnel function is an essential line function it is the line organization which had to set the pattern. As a device for systematically getting line management opinion a questionnaire was developed which a number of managers were asked to complete.

The questionnaire was completed by the president, plant manager, plant superintendent, assistant to the president, a few of the supervisory group and the personnel adviser. This group was the authority structure for the plant. By having each level of management represented it was possible to assess how successfully the president and plant manager made their philosophies and policies known and understood by lower organizational levels and how well they understood, in turn, the thinking and problems of these levels. The personnel adviser gave the staff view on how well words represented practice and how effectively philosophy was translated into deeds.

When the questionnaire was given to these members of management the consultant on the assignment discussed with each man what was being done and why. The written introduction to the audit questionnaire said:

Everything that is done in a business is accomplished through and by people, with the aid of the tools provided by the stockholders and the planning, guidance and controls provided by top management. The personnel function represents a recognition of the fundamental importance of people.

The effectiveness of a personnel program is measured by its contribution to the overall objectives of the business, both economic and social.

For the company, a sound, well-rounded personnel program should result in greater cooperation, higher productivity, lower unit labor costs and more efficient use of capital.

For the employees, a good personnel program should result in greater job satisfactions, higher living standards and greater security.

To periodically assess the extent to which objectives are being achieved is good management. To provide a basis for assessment and a point of departure for future planning an accurate record of current personnel policies and practices, both formal and informal, is essential. This questionnaire is designed to guide a systematic recording of current practice. An evaluation of practices against the criteria of latest personnel thinking constitutes a Personnel Audit.

A Personnel Audit is concerned with the more formal aspects of the personnel function. To determine the degree of success of personnel activities in building a loyal, satisfied work group, the findings of the Audit should be supplemented by a survey of the attitudes of the employee group.

The facts obtained from the Audit and the Survey of Attitudes will guide us in our efforts to build a stronger organization. Measuring the effectiveness and efficiency of a personnel program requires a detailed analysis of what is being done, by whom, when and how.

This questionnaire has been developed for the purpose of recording the existing personnel organization, policies and practices.

Most of the questions are phrased so as to ask "What are we doing?" The answer to this question should be followed by an explanation as to "how" it is being done.

The steps in making the Personnel Audit are—

1. Obtain information on existing conditions. What are we doing?
2. Evaluate existing policies or practices. Are they effective? Are they worthwhile (paying off)? Are we doing too much or too little or is the program out of balance?
3. Identify and consider what we are not doing. Ask why not. Should we?
4. Formulate recommendations for improvement. Set up a time table for changes.
5. Follow-up and evaluate the results of the changes.

The questionnaire raised questions about personnel policies, the personnel department's organization and functions, employee recruitment, selection and placement, induction and follow-up of new employees, training and personnel development, transfer, promotions and separations, compensation, employee security and benefits, employee services, activities and facilities, personnel records and forms, labor relations, plant rules and regulations, communications, community relations and other miscellaneous activities.

Some sample questions are as follows:
- Who recommends establishment of or changes in policy?
- What controls are exercised to assure compliance with established policy?
- What are the personnel responsibilities of line management? Are they defined and understood?
- What records are kept of applicants interviewed, hired, rejected, held in reserve, source and method of recruitment?
- Are applicants measured against job specifications?
- What is the existing program for supervisory and management development?
- How are employee records and performance review results used in connection with selection for transfer and promotion?
- Is there a job evaluation program?
- How do the company's pay rates and other compensation practices (including fringe benefits) compare with other plants in the immediate geographical area and with other companies in the same industry?
- What personnel records are maintained, what analyses are made and to whom are they reported?
- What important practices and understandings have developed that are not spelled out in the labor contract?
- What methods are used to communicate to (1) supervisors and (2) employees information on matters of interest or importance to the company and/or its employees?
- Do company management members participate and cooperate in community programs and activities?

When the completed questionnaires were returned the responses of each management member were listed in the order of his organization level for each question. In this way the consistency of report and opinion by level and, in this case, by location at the executive office or plant could be assessed. For each question a brief summary statement of the current situation, the evaluation of the current situation and the recommendations flowing from this review and evaluation was made. For example, for a question on training for hourly workers, the audit report showed:

CURRENT SITUATION

The primary emphasis in training employees is on-the-job-instruction by supervisory personnel. There is a modified apprenticeship program which is not working too well because of difficulties with the union. Employees can take courses either at an educational institution or by mail and be reimbursed by the company if they have obtained prior approval and successfully complete the course.

EVALUATION

In terms of the amount of employment activity the current training pattern for hourly employees is the only realistic one that could be established. Its success obviously depends on how skilled the supervisors are in instructing and training. It is probable that all supervisory personnel could profit from training in training. For upgrading purposes a man must wait until he is on the job before having an opportunity to learn the job. Many aspects of plant operation could be taught by company personnel in "off-hour" courses. This would tend to provide better trained personnel for higher level jobs when openings do occur. There is a need for general training of personnel in the economics of the industry, the use to which the product is put and the part each man plays in the manufacture of a quality product.

RECOMMENDATION

To achieve maximum results from an employee training program where supervisory personnel conduct the training requires that the supervisory personnel know how to train. The supervisory group should be trained in job instruction. Consideration should be given to the development of training programs to cover the operating and maintenance responsibilities of higher jobs to be given to hourly personnel by company personnel. More general courses in the economics of the industry and developments in the uses of the product might also be considered.

Hourly people should be encouraged to take courses at local universities or by correspondence that will increase their level of technical knowledge used in the operation of the plant.

When each specific question had been analyzed in this way the recommendations were consolidated into a summary. This summary listing was reviewed with management to develop an order of priority in which the problem areas should be approached. It, of course, also gave management a framework within which to appraise progress against goals periodically.

RESULTS

Action was taken on the basis of the evidence developed by the audit. The personnel department was enlarged. A program plan was developed. A procedure for periodic review and reconsideration of the function was installed. The personnel function was revitalized and began to make its full contribution to the successful management of the company.

Future audits that might be undertaken by this company would be very different from the first audit. Better records and quantification of significant aspects of the program will permit a more sophisticated review and comparison of performance in the areas where records and quantification are possible. In the other areas the concern will be on the rate of progress from the base line recorded in this first audit.

AND SO...

The audit function is an indispensable supplement to routine reporting activity, a supplement that uses existing records and reports but also concentrates on the nuances of performance, the currently non-quantifiable aspects of getting the job done. All organizations require an audit function but it can be located either within or outside the organization. If within the organization it will frequently need the stimulation of contact with an external audit group.

Personnel involved in auditing activity must be of high integrity and ability. The knowledge and experience input for an audit group will vary depending on the nature of the assignments received and the training and development mission of the group.

There is no set audit procedure. Audits are oriented toward facts and, in opinion rather than factual areas, toward multiple opinions from a sample of respondents from the groups interested in and concerned about the activity. Audits should be designed to help line management to do a better job, not as punitive instruments of exposure. A manager on whom a highly critical audit report is prepared should be given the opportunity to correct the conditions subject to criticism before any general distribution of the audit report is made.

Audits have become common practice in financial activities. They can also be used effectively with the management group, employee groups, general organization structure, policies and procedures, marketing, manufacturing, personnel, public relations and research and development. Auditing is a control concept as general in its possible application as there are activities to control.

10. COMPARING THE COMPANY WITH ITS INDUSTRY BY RATIOS*

—WILLIAM E. WESTERDAHL

One area often overlooked by accountants in providing management with information to guide its decisions toward the desired goals of perpetuating the business and making a profit is the financial structure of the business. Much has been written about reducing costs, accounting practices and procedures, break-even points, reporting to management, organization, etc., but comparatively little appears regarding the basic financial structure of a business. However, if managers were asked to state their foremost problem, financing the business—or lack of financing for it—would be close to the top among the answers, especially in the smaller companies. Often it is only an apparent lack that simply means unwise use of available funds. On the other hand, management often is not aware that financial structure is a problem. Managing a company involves directing and coordinating the research, production, distribution, and financial functions into a smooth working combination. Much effort is directed toward selling, producing and developing new products, but perhaps too little time is taken with the fourth function—financial planning and control.

Every year studies are made of the causes of business failures. These studies are based on the opinions of creditors and information on credit reports. The conclusion usually is that about 90 percent of the failures are management failures—inexperience or incompetence. This would indicate that management often needs guidance in making decisions. In the March 1960 issue of *Dun's Review and Modern Industry*, it was reported that of 2,612 manufacturing firms that failed, inadequate sales and competitive weaknesses were indicated as principal symptoms. In these areas accountants' reports and opinions probably could not have helped much. However, 11.8 percent had receivable

* From the National Association of Accountants *N.A.A. Bulletin*, November, 1961. Reprinted by permission of the publisher.

difficulties, 10.9 percent had excessive fixed assets and 4.8 percent had inventory trouble. Only 7.8 percent were reported as failing because of heavy operating expenses.

In other words, business failures attributable to poor financial structure were about five times greater than those due to excessive expenses. If these were the predominant reasons for the business failures, perhaps the accountants should have spent more time on determining financial structure weaknesses and emphasizing to management that it is important to build a sound structure. And, if this is the condition among the companies that have failed, we can assume that many firms, while still solvent, are struggling with the same problems and could be in serious trouble if their sales volume were to drop appreciably.

RATIOS AS OBJECTIVE GUIDES

Executives with accounting or financial background generally are aware of the financial weaknesses in a company but often it is difficult to communicate these ideas to other members of management. When the accountant expresses his opinions, such as "there isn't enough working capital" or "inventory is too high" or "we have too much invested in fixed assets," etc., the executive may feel that it is the accountant's opinion against his own. He may discount the importance of the accountant's findings, ignoring the probability of their factual basis, and thus the situation remains uncorrected. Unless these ideas or situations are communicated to top management in such a way that it can readily understand the situation and see that improvement is necessary, the company will continue to operate under handicaps.

A very effective way to emphasize to management that certain parts of the financial structure are out of balance is to compare the company's figures with those of other similar companies. For example, suppose that the inventory in a particular company is high. The accountant may go to the general manager, production and sales managers, and point this out to them. They, on the other hand, may be perfectly satisfied that the inventory is "all right"; they are always able to deliver to the customers, never have any short-run production headaches, and perhaps have recently built an addition to warehouse the inventory, so there is no space problem. It is the accountant's opinion against that of the other executives, and the accountant may be outvoted.

On the other hand, suppose the accountant were to bring out the fact that the company, in comparison with an average of, say, fifty other companies in the industry, had twice the inventory that the others did, the matter is no longer only the opinion of the accountant. The fact cited becomes an indicator that perhaps the company is carrying too much inventory.

Or it may be fixed assets. Often management is proud of having a large plant with an abundance of equipment so it can "make anything," and its buildings may be a monument to the president. The financial executive can rather quickly become unpopular with the plant superintendent and general manager if he shows any resistance to expansion of plant and equipment. However, if he is able to show management that, in comparison with some 30 or 40 other firms in the same line of business, the average investment ratio of fixed assets to net worth is, say, only 40 percent and that in the company 90 percent of the net worth is tied up in fixed assets, perhaps management will take a more objective look at the problem, rather than just feeling that the accountant is "too conservative."

Comparisons are not easy. One of the difficulties in comparing one company to another is the fact of dissimilarity in size. If we were to compare the dollar figures of two or more companies, this would not be very meaningful. However, effective comparisons can be made through the use of ratios. Even here, there are pitfalls but there are sufficient reliable advantages to render the endeavor fruitful. The main hazard is comparison of average against individual conditions. A ratio is a computation expressing the relationship of two sets of figures. It may be expressed as either a percentage, such as the profit divided by sales to yield profit as a percent of sales, or as a multiple, such as current assets divided by current liabilities to give the common current ratio.

Ratios may be classified as static ratios, referring to balance sheet items; operating ratios, showing the relationship of expenses to sales; and velocity ratios relating income and expense items to certain balance sheet items.

SOURCES OF COMPARATIVE RATIOS

The question arises as to what ratios are significant. Every year Dun & Bradstreet publishes "Fourteen Important Ratios" for a number of different lines of business These are:

1. Current assets to current debt.
2. Net profits on net sales.
3. Net profits on tangible net worth.
4. Net profits on working capital.
5. Net sales to tangible net worth.
6. Net sales to working capital.
7. Collection period.
8. Net sales to inventory.
9. Fixed assets to tangible net worth.
10. Current debt to tangible net worth
11. Total debt to tangible net worth.
12. Inventory to working capital.
13. Current debt to inventory.
14. Funded debt to working capital.

These ratios are published for 12 retail lines, 24 wholesale lines and 36 manufacturing lines. Figures for each of the ratios are provided for upper, median and lower quartiles of responding companies. This information is usually published during the last quarter of the year, covering the previous calendar year.

Robert Morris Associates, a national association of bank loan officers and credit men, also publishes information on a number of different lines of business. This includes composite balance sheets the items of which are expressed as a percent of total assets, as well as composite condensed income statements, with costs expressed as a percent of sales. There is a supplementary study which expands the income statement classifications to:

Net sales	Other general administrative expense
Cost of sales	All other expenses net
Gross profit	Profits before taxes
Selling and delivery expense	Income taxes
Officers salaries	Net profit or loss

These are likewise reported as a percent of sales. In addition to the composite balance sheets and income statements, Robert Morris Associates also publishes the following ratios for the lines of business treated:

Current ratio	Sales/Inventory
Net worth/Fixed assets	Sales/Fixed assets
Net worth/Debt	Sales/Net worth
Sales/Receivables	% profits/Net worth
Cost of sales/Inventory	Sales/Total assets
Day's sales in inventory	% profits/Total assets

Other ratios may be calculated from balance sheet figures. The Robert Morris Associates' figures are not by quartiles. However, the information is broken down by total asset size: firms under $250,000, $250,000 to $1 million, $1 million to $10 million and, in a few cases $10 million to $25 million, enabling companies to make comparisons with firms in their own industries and corresponding asset-size groups.

The Robert Morris Associate's figures include about 90 lines of manufacturing, 44 lines of wholesalers, 36 lines of retailers, plus laundries and dry cleaners, bottlers (soft drinks), and seed companies. The information generally becomes available by late summer for the previous calendar year and may be obtained from the member banks or from the home office of Robert Morris Associates.

Another source of financial statement ratios is found in trade associations which collect these data and make them available to their members.

RATIO ANALYSIS IN CORRECTING UNSOUND CONDITIONS

It is apparent that many different ratios are available for use. There may be some question as to which are of particular significance. Let us examine some which can be used to ferret out conditions which should be corrected. It may be well to break them into categories that may be considered serviceable to disclose what part of the business is out of line. These categories might be:

Inventory	Fixed assets	Profit
Accounts receivable	Financing	Sales activity

Inventory Ratios. Perhaps one of the prime causes of business failures and voluntary liquidations has been either excessive or unbalanced inventory. Except for speculation, management seldom plans to build an excessive inventory. Ratios will not reveal unbalanced inventory but they can be used as a guide to determine if the inventory totals are in line with those of other firms in the industry, or with goals set by management in forecasting financing requirements. These ratios include the following:

1. Inventory to working capital. This shows how the least liquid portion of current assets stands to the total.
2. Sales to inventory. This could indicate too much or too little inventory for the sales volume.
3. Cost of sales to inventory. This shows the inventory turnover.
4. Day's sales in inventory. This also indicates inventory turnover but may be more impressive when presented to management.

There are several dangers from excessive inventory. As discussed later, it uses too much of the working capital so that the company is no longer in a position to meet its current obligations with cash and accounts receivable. Another danger is obsolescence. When inventory fails to turn within a reasonable length of time, there is chance of deterioration or of some new product superseding the product being manufactured. Another danger is that the price of the raw materials may fall. Then the inventory would have to be written down, involving larger losses than if the inventory were at a nominal level.

There is still a fourth problem. It has been estimated that the cost of carrying excess inventory, including interest on investment, runs between 15 and 22 percent per year. This includes storage costs, insurance, taxes, etc. When the inventory is excessive conditions may necessitate plant expansion to house the inventory, with an accompanying increase in fixed costs. Thus, costs increase without adding value to the product.

There are, of course, dangers from having inadequate inventories. These include the incurring of excessive out-of-stock conditions, placing many small orders which add to paper work and receiving costs, and which increase production costs because of additional setups, short runs, etc.

An Accounts Receivable Ratio. Funds tied up in accounts receivable are not available for other purposes. Average collection period is a good guide to compare the company's collections with the industry for evaluating the effectiveness of the credit and collection functions.

Fixed Asset Ratios. Only a certain amount of net worth should be tied up in fixed assets. Ratio guides to point out the degree of soundness of a company's financial structure in this respect are:

1. Fixed assets to net worth.
2. Sales to fixed assets. This ratio may disclose that a business has too large or too small a plant for the sales volume. In making comparison of sales to

fixed assets, another problem confronts us. Fixed assets are normally carried at the original value less depreciation. If the assets were purchased in years when the value of the dollar was higher than now, and they have been heavily depreciated, this would result in a very high ratio. On the other hand, a low ratio could reflect an excessive valuation of fixed assets. Thus, if the company's ratios are out of line with the industry ratios, much judgment must be used before drawing specific conclusions in this area.

Financial Ratios. Financing the business can be divided into two major categories: (1) procurement of funds from the owners, long-term financing, and short-term sources ("sourcing" of funds) and (2) proper balance and allocation of available funds among cash, accounts receivable, inventory, and fixed assets (rationing of funds). Allocations relate to such ratios as have already been discussed. Ratios which might be useful in evaluating balance in the source of funds would include:

1. Current assets to current liabilities.

2. Current debt to net worth. This could indicate that suppliers may be furnishing too much capital.

3. Total debt to net worth. This supplements the current debt to net worth ratio and should disclose undercapitalization.

4. Funded debt to working capital. This is a test to see if a business could liquidate long-term debts from working capital. If this ratio is over 100 percent

Exhibit 1

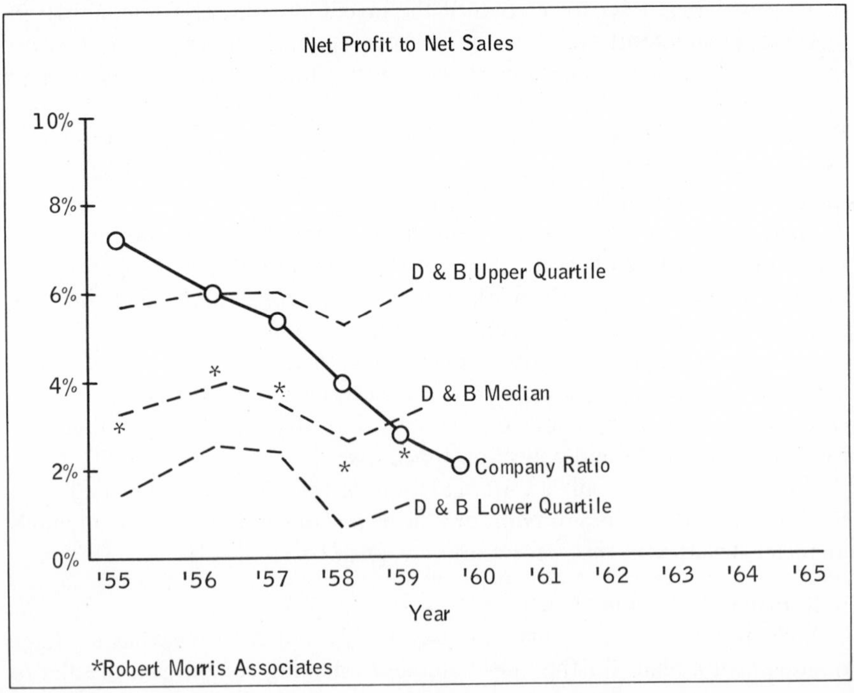

*Robert Morris Associates

it could indicate that too great a portion of the company's funds is invested in fixed assets.

Profit. Ratios to test profit showings are probably used by most companies today. Management generally watches the profits-to-sales ratio very closely, sometimes overlooking other ratios which are more significant in controlling business operations. Ratios useful for comparing the profitability of a company with others in the industry are:

1. Profit to sales (Exhibit 1). This is a check to determine if margins are in line with those of other companies. Where information is available, it should be supplemented by a comparison of gross profit to sales.

Exhibit 2

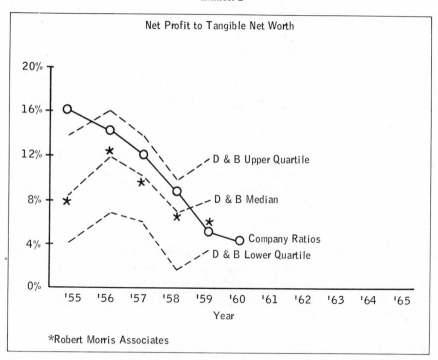

2. Profit to net worth (Exhibit 2). This is a test of the ability of management to earn a return on the owner's investment. It is recommended that the going interest rate on so-called "safe" investments, such as government bonds or bank savings, be considered as the "break-even" point. Profit above this figure is necessary to attract capital where there is more of an element of risk than on "safe" investments.

3. Profit to total assets. This is a test of the ability of management to earn a return on all assets used in the business.

In using profit ratios in comparative analyses, it is essential to know whether the profit figures are before or after income taxes. A further problem in comparability of profit ratios may arise in a closely held corporation, with the question of owner-managers' salaries. Owners may be drawing more (or less) than the going salaries for managers. For making a comparison of the company profit with that of the other businesses, it is suggested that the owner determine what he would pay a professional manager to perform his job. This figure would be substituted for the actual owner's salary, and the pre-tax and after-tax profit figure used for making comparisons. But it must be remembered that deduction of a true salary figure assumes that this is also done in the data with which comparison is made.

Sales Activity. Ratios can be used to determine whether or not a company is "over-trading" or "under-trading." These ratios would include:

1. Sales to working capital.
2. Sales to net worth. This is a check to see if the owners have invested too little (or too much) for the sales volume, and if the capital is being used efficiently.
3. Sales to total assets. This supplements the sales-to-net-worth ratio and may show that a business is using too much capital belonging to creditors.

THREE KEYS TO SOLVENCY

Three ratios among all those available can be considered as "keys to solvency." They test the ability of a company to weather a storm in case of a recession or other form of setback. These ratios—fixed assets to net worth, working capital to sales and inventories to working capital—are probably the most important ones management should watch in guiding a company through periods of stress.

The Relationship of Fixed Assets to Net Worth (*Exhibit 3*). Fixed assets are described as the land, buildings, equipment and furniture at book value, less accumulated depreciation. Net worth is described as the owners' capital invested in the business after deducting all intangibles such as goodwill, patents, trademarks and the like. A company's investment in fixed assets should be in proper relationship to its tangible net worth. There is no one answer as to what this relationship should be; it depends upon the line of business. A point to consider is that the more the fixed assets are built up, the higher are the accompanying fixed costs such as depreciation, insurance, taxes, maintenance, heat, light and power. This in turn raises the break-even point and the company may have trouble in making a profit if sales drop off.

"Plant-minded" management often feels that it is successful if it has an attractive building and the very latest equipment. If there is an increasing demand for its product, it may feel that it must expand in order to capitalize on this increasing demand and presumably make more profit. It may overlook the fact that, when more and more of its net worth is invested in plant

Exhibit 3

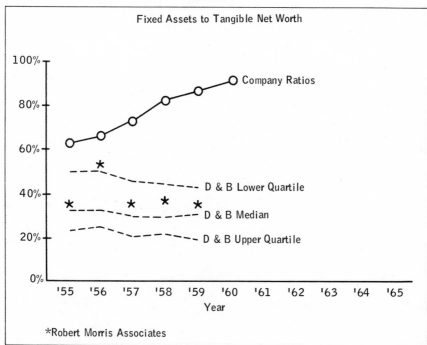

Fixed Assets to Tangible Net Worth

*Robert Morris Associates

and equipment, there are less funds available for working capital needs such as accounts receivable, inventory, cash, etc. Thus, it may be in a position that, while it has the capacity to meet the greater product demand, it does not have the working capital available to support this increased volume. This is the unhappy situation in which a higher break-even point results, and yet the company must of necessity curtail its sales volume because of the lack of funds for carrying inventory and accounts receivable.

The Relationship of Working Capital to Sales (Exhibit 4). Another fundamental is that the working capital of an enterprise should be in proper proportion to its sales. The working capital is described as the difference between the sum of the current assets and the sum of the current liabilities. A small retail store operating on a cash basis and with a good inventory turnover may be able to get along quite comfortably on $5,000 of working capital. However, if the owner were suddenly to expand it to a large department store, where he had to carry accounts receivable and a much larger, and probably slower turning, inventory, obviously the $5,000 of working capital would be grossly inadequate and he would be in serious trouble.

There is no universal answer as to what the working-capital-to-sales relationship should be. A comparison should be made with the industry ratios to guard against "over-trading," previously mentioned. Businessmen feel that the more they sell, the more profit they make. This can be true;

Exhibit 4

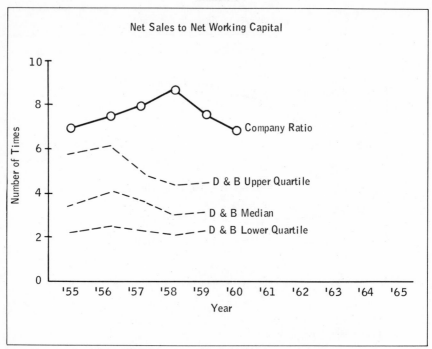

however, additional sales volume usually means more capital is tied up in accounts receivable and in inventory. If the additional capital is not provided for by the company, it must borrow, generally by obtaining short-term loans or by delaying payments to creditors. In this situation the company could be in serious trouble if sales volume were to drop and it could not meet its current obligations. As one banker put it, "You can go broke just as quickly by selling too much as by selling too little."

The Relationship of Inventories to Working Capital (*Exhibit 5*). The third key to solvency is the relationship of inventories to working capital. Here again, we have different relationships in different industries but, in general, a company's investment in inventories should be kept within the amount of its net working capital. When inventories exceed net working capital, the current liabilities (debts that must be paid within one year) exceed the cash, marketable securities and accounts receivable which represent claims on funds due within one year. Thus, the company would be forced to liquidate some of its inventory in order to meet its current obligations should it run into a period of stress. This could occur just when customers were slowing down on their buying and it might mean selling the inventory at a considerable discount.

TRENDS ARE IMPORTANT

Very often a single comparison of a company ratio against published information may not bring a significant trend to light. Also, because it takes con-

Exhibit 5

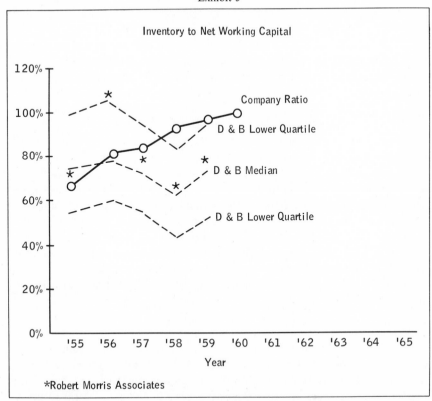

Inventory to Net Working Capital

*Robert Morris Associates

siderable time to prepare, compile and publish statements, industry figures are not available for quite a few months. For these reasons, ratios for a number of years plotted on graph paper, one sheet for each ratio, are highly practical. Generally, the industry ratios will not vary too much from year to year unless the general economic conditions change considerably. Thus, when the company statement is prepared and the ratios are calculated and put on the graph paper, a good comparison can be made immediately with other companies in the industry, on a basis which relies on the picture of a series of years.

One big advantage in plotting these ratios is that it makes it possible to point out to management the direction of the trend. A comparison of company ratios versus industry ratios in a given year might indicate a healthy situation—yet the trend may be in the wrong direction. That is why the exhibits which have been given for particular ratios cover a number of years and illustrate how trends may be followed. In all of them it has been found useful to plot the Dun & Bradstreet figures for the upper, median and lower quartiles. Available Robert Morris Associate's ratios are indicated on the graphs with an asterisk. Superimposed on this is a heavy line which indicates the company's ratio. Thus, at a glance, management not only can compare its ratios with the published ones but also can see significant trends.

The question always arises: when is a ratio out of line? It is suggested that a particular ratio be analyzed closely to determine reasons for variance whenever it is outside the upper quartile or lower quartile range. Company ratios are in line with the "middle half" of the companies included in the sample when they are between the upper and lower quartiles. In other words, one-fourth of the firms are "better" than the upper quartile and one-fourth of the firms are "worse" than the lower quartile of the middle two.

COMPARISONS WITH OWN INDUSTRY MOST SIGNIFICANT

It has been assumed throughout the discussion that a portion of the hazards of ratio comparisons would be overcome by making company comparison with other firms in the same industry. While some of the ratio figures may be approximately the same in many manufacturing lines, the industry character-istics might make a comparison with a composite of all industry quite invalid. For example, for the five-year period ending in 1958, the median of the fixed assets to tangible net worth among the shirt manufacturers was about 7 percent, while the median among the petroleum manufacturers was about 87 percent. Some of the ratios do have wide varance based on the nature of the industry, so it is well to compare with the industry rather than with any composite average.

ONE TYPE OF HELP

A well balanced financial structure is important to the well-being of a com-pany. Management seldom has unlimited capital; it is desirable to extract the most value from available funds. Whenever too much is invested in one segment of a business, another segment generally suffers. Too much invest-ment in a business as a whole indicates an inefficient use of capital.

There are few formulas that show what the optimum use of capital should be. However, much valuable guidance may be obtained by comparing com-pany ratios with industry ratios and by determining the reasons for unusual variances. An excellent selling tool for accountants to use in pointing out the unusual to management is a graph of company and industry ratios empha-sizing trends as well as variances.

The caution sounded throughout this article should be re-emphasized now. Ratios are guides only. There may be perfectly good reasons why the company's ratios vary significantly from the published information. The important thing in the use of ratios is to be aware of the fact, when the com-pany's figures are significantly different from the industry, and to determine the reasons for variance. Also, ratios are not to be used as a strait jacket. For example, it may be wise to build inventory if a material is threatened or, in the expansion of a plant, it may be wise to build for the anticipated volume five years from now, even though, for the next few years, the fixed-assets-to-net-worth ratio may be out of line. However, the use of ratios does have its place and is an excellent guide for management's decisions.

11. PERFORMANCE STANDARDS FOR THE PLANT ACCOUNTANT*

—CURTIS W. SYMONDS

It is surprising that the valuable operating tool of performance standards has so long been confined to the factory level. The opportunity to extend this type of measurement to the realm of supervisory, administrative, and executive positions represents a challenge which, until quite recently, has gone completely unanswered. However, two major factors have been largely responsible for a small beginning which has now been made and which is rapidly becoming a growing trend towards the development and use of performance standards for members of the top and middle management groups.

The first has been a gradual awareness of the fact that standards for the hourly worker have done more than merely establish a useful base for budgets and cost control. It has also opened up a two-way street of communication between the employee and his immediate supervisor which gives each a common understanding of what is expected and just what constitutes satisfactory performance on the job. The somewhat belated discovery has now been made that managers, engineers, and cost accountants will respond in much the same way and that the introduction of written performance standards for their jobs provides exactly the same type of personal incentive and creates desire to equal or better the established level of performance.

The second consideration, and the one which has probably done the most to accelerate the use of performance standards, has been the rapid post-war expansion and growth which has taken place throughout industry. The unprecedented demand for trained men to be moved up quickly into positions of greater responsibility has placed on management the burden of finding a better means of evaluation and appraisal of the individual. The idea of written performance standards has been borrowed from the factory to form the missing link betweeen the job description and the performance review.

* From the *N.A.C.A. Bulletin*, June, 1957, pp. 1299–1303. Reprinted by permission of the publisher.

The task of preparing suitable performance standards is not a simple one and, understandably, becomes more difficult for each successive level of responsibility within the organization. It is obviously easier to agree on adequate standards for the employee whose output can be measured in so many units per hour than it is to describe a satisfactory level of performance for the vice president of the company, whose efforts cover a wide field of endeavor and take the form of judgments and directives. There are, however, certain very basic principles to be followed which make it possible to analyze and define the performance desired for any function at any level of responsibility. In approaching the subject of performance standards for the first time, the case history of their development and use for the job of plant accountant at Sylvania Electric Products Inc., provides an example of the techniques employed in a field in which the company's rapid growth had focused attention on the need for qualified personnel.

SELF-DESCRIPTION; RECOGNITION OF FIVE JOB AREAS

The decision was made at the outset to have the standards prepared by the plant accountants themselves. It was felt that group participation in establishing the performance standards would make them much more readily acceptable than if they were drawn up by higher authority and simply handed down for use. This not only proved to be true but it was later found that, in settling their own standards, the accountants voluntarily proposed a much higher level of performance for themselves than an outside committee would have suggested.

The job description, itself, provided the starting point as a means of defining the areas of responsibility and the description of specific duties to be performed. This soon proved to be entirely too brief and too general in nature, and was expanded into a lengthy list covering every conceivable function performed on a daily, weekly, monthly, or annual basis. After considerable discussion and review, the preliminary listing was next condensed to a summary of the major important functions and responsibilities common to all plant locations and grouped under the following general headings:

1. Organization.
2. Administration.
3. Budgeting and forecasting.
4. Management statements and reports.
5. Cost control and profit planning.

The stage had now been set to consider the development of individual performance standards which would provide an explicit and measurable yardstick for each facet of these broad areas of job responsibility.

THE STATEMENT EVENTUATES

To accomplish the objective, a working definition of a satisfactory standard was agreed upon as "a statement of conditions existing when a good job results," and a decision was reached to avoid generalities which would not lend themselves to measurement. With these goals in mind, standards covering organizational responsibilities were established. They prescribe that as to organization aspects of the plant accountant's work, performance is up to standard when:

1. The plant accounting department is properly organized and adequately staffed to carry out its functions in an efficient and economical manner.

2. Personnel are properly selected and trained to handle their specific duties and the workload is effectively delegated.

3. Job descriptions and performance standards are established and maintained for each member of the department.

4. A performance review and post-appraisal interview is conducted with each employee at least once a year.

5. An active training program is maintained for the development of subordinates.

6. Departmental salaries are reviewed on a scheduled basis and appropriate action taken.

It is interesting to note here that these six standards which the group set covered duties and responsibilities which were not even mentioned in the company's written job description for the plant accountant. In preparing these particular standards, the accountants had voluntarily assigned to themselves certain definite functions for which they recognized responsibility and, in so doing had established, a high level for satisfactory performance. The same philosophy went into the consideration of their various administrative duties which proved to be the most numerous of the several groups. It was specified that administration of the plant accountant's job is up to standard when:

1. All standard practices and established accounting policies of the company are properly followed.

2. Procedures are established for the adequate protection of petty cash funds, inventories, equipment, and other assets under plant control.

3. Payroll calculations are prepared accurately on a weekly schedule and suitable safeguards are provided for the disbursement of wages to employees.

4. All purchase commitments are made in written form on approved purchase requisitions, in line with established budgets.

5. Vendors' invoices are matched with supporting documents for approval and payment by the due date and all cash discounts are taken.

6. Miscellaneous sales of materials, supplies, and services are supported by shipping papers and invoiced on a current basis.

7. Employee expense accounts conform to established company policies and are submitted for reimbursement within the current month.

8. An approved procedure is followed for the monthly valuation of raw and in-process inventories.

9. An accurate and systematic method is employed for the recording of the production of finished goods by code number.

10. Inventories of raw and in-process materials are reviewed for obsolescence at least twice a year.

11. An approved program is followed for the retention and destruction of records.

12. Completed staff work is performed for the plant manager in connection with routine and administrative functions.

This section of the performance standards also went well beyond the rather brief outline to be found in the job description claimed and broad areas of administrative control which more clearly defined the scope of the plant accountant's participation as a member of the management team. At the same time, standards of how these duties should be performed were described in precise and measurable terms. Following on to standards for budgeting and forecasting, it was found that these were somewhat easier to express, since they contained elements of mathematical accuracy, could be related to established time schedules and dealt, in general, with the more readily recognized working tools of factory cost accounting. It was offered that budgeting and forecasting performance is up to standard when:

1. Annual manufacturing budgets and fixed and variable budgets are prepared on a uniform and consistent basis and are issued on schedule.

2. Standard costs reflect the predicted manufacturing costs at predetermined volume levels within an accuracy of at least 5%.

3. Standard allowances for materials, labor, and overhead provide for effective comparison to actual performance at various production levels within the limits of the budget.

4. Manufacturing budgets reflect the gradual attainment of average standard costs and measure the effect of volume variance for each calendar month.

5. Annual permanent property budgets are prepared and issued on schedule together with supporting detail where necessary.

6. Three-month manufacturing forecasts are prepared monthly which correctly interpret current operating conditions and accurately predict significant variances from standard cost.

7. Standard-type costs are prepared on the basis of engineered labor standards, analysis of specific operating efficiencies, and allocation of overhead expenses by cost center.

8. Cost estimates on new types and new projects are submitted as required, which fairly present the expected cost and operating efficiency.

9. All operating budgets present realistic and attainable objectives based on analysis of past performance and scheduled improvements.

These statements constituted a forthright expression of exactly what the plant accountants felt was expected of them and at what level of performance they should be measured. Going on to the area of management statements and reports, the group placed particular emphasis on the reporting function of the plant accountant, recognizing the value and importance of prompt and effective communication in this critical area of their job responsibility. It was represented that, for management statements and reports, performance is up to standard when:

1. Manufacturing cost reports are prepared for each product or operating location and are issued by the 8th working day of the following month.

2. Cost comments are prepared for management which present a brief and informative analysis of significant trends and current variances from standard.

3. Prompt and effective corrective action is initiated or recommended on costs areas which are off standard.

4. Special reports are instituted as required by operating conditions.

5. Monthly turnover reports are prepared and issued for all raw material inventories.

6. All reports are subject to continuing review to simplify preparation and improve the timeliness and utility of the information.

7. Obsolete reports are discontinued.

Again, the comprehensiveness of the standards may be noted. The group went on to the last section of the performance standards, dealing with cost control and profit planning. This side of the work proved to be the most difficult to define in terms of measurable performance, since it dealt with areas of creativity and job enlargement. The group insisted, however, that the areas of cost control and profit planning be strongly emphasized even though certain generalities were found necessary. The resulting statement was that cost control and profit planning performance is up to standard when:

1. A system of budgetary control of manufacturing expenses is established and followed.

2. Special expense requests are initiated as required and an adequate follow-up is maintained.

3. Active participation is taken in the profit improvement program.

4. Inventories of raw materials and supplies are kept within established "bogies" for turnover.

5. Accounting routines are performed in a manner which will lead to a gradual reduction of auditing costs.

6. Reserve balances are properly established and controlled.

7. Cost consciousness is developed in all departments of the plant through effective cost reporting.

8. Cost reductions are planned which will maximize profits rather than minimize overheads.

TWO FAVORABLE RESULTS

Although these performance standards have been drawn up to meet the needs of one particular company, the functions described and the level of performance indicated will be found readily adaptable to the needs of the industrial cost accountant in almost any line of business. The results of this work have been twofold. The preparation and issuance of formal written performance standards has given management a uniform and consistent means of evaluation and appraisal against stated objectives which provides a sound basis for counseling and for promotion. The greatest benefit, however, has probably accrued to the plant accountant, himself, whose efforts in creating acceptable standards of performnace have opened up new horizons for him in the field of professional management. In short, the very act of thinking in terms of specific objectives and how to meet them has inevitably led to improvement in work performance.

BUSINESS-MANAGEMENT AUDIT CASES

* *

1. KARGL INSTRUMENTS, INC.*

—C. R. KLASSON

and

K. W. OLM

On July 15, 1963, Mr. D. W. Hubbard, vice-president and general manager of Kargl Instruments, Incorporated made the following comments regarding the main problems that had confronted him since assuming his present position with the company in October, 1961.

Up until today, I believe that getting our sales effort organized was my main problem. It certainly absorbed most of my time. Now that we have developed a good sales organization, our main problem has shifted to the production area. To support an increased level of sales activity, we need to make some personnel changes in the shop; we need to organize a production control section; and we need to double shop capacity. Since we diversified our product line our sales prospects have increased to the point where we may have some difficulty producing what has been sold. We are under pressure to finance an expanded level of production and at the same time have increased product development expenditures. Undoubtedly, the most important project during the next few months will be to establish plans to increase our capitalization to support planned growth which we are certain will come.

COMPANY HISTORY

Kargl Company of San Antonio, Texas, the predecessor of Kargl Instruments, Incorporated, was founded by Mr. Gilard Kargl in the early 1940's to perform aerial surveys and to design and fabricate needed equipment for photogrammetry. Mr. Kargl, a civil engineer by training, became one of the pioneers in the photogrammetry field when he began mapping with the use of

* Reprinted by permission of The Board of Regents, The University of Texas and Professors C. R. Klasson and K. W. Olm, University of Texas.

aerial photographs in the middle 1920's. He became interested in determining the best route for a proposed railroad in the hill country west of central Texas. The railroad was never constructed, but his interest in improving aerial surveys resulted in a life-long association in the new industry.

Prior to establishing his own firm, Mr. Kargl had been active in organizing many of the aerial photographic firms in Texas, including Edgar Tobin Aerial Surveys, Jack Ammann Photogrammetric Engineers, and Muldrow Aerial Surveys, to mention a few. For each of these firms Mr. Kargl designed and built a wide variety of photographic and photogrammetric equipment including in 1929 the first autofocusing rectifier ever built in the United States.

Kargl Company was organized in 1949 as a corporation for the purpose of designing and manufacturing precision photo-optical instrumentation. The majority of business done from 1949 to 1959 was prototype design and fabrication of aerial cameras, viewers, projectors, rectifiers and other aerial film handling equipment. The firm sold its services and products to various agencies of the federal and state governments, major oil companies and other private industrial firms, and to foreign companies and government agencies in Mexico and various Central American countries.

COMPANY OPERATIONS THROUGH 1961

Over the years, Kargl Company had come to enjoy an excellent reputation for making high quality precision photogrammetric instruments. This success reflected the untiring and creative efforts of Gilard Kargl, whose primary interest focused upon designing new equipment which could solve new and challenging problems in the photogrammetric field. Being a designer and engineer, Mr. Kargl had little interest in the administrative aspects of his company from the start. No administrative staff was maintained other than a secretary and one clerk. The accounting and financial records were maintained by a part-time bookkeeper at his personal residence. In 1955, Mr. Ray Kelsey, a graduate engineer trained in the photo-optics field, joined the organization and for five years assisted Mr. Kargl in evaluating new designs, supervising the manufacture of all equipment, and assisting in the general management of the company.

During the initial years of operation the company had never employed over twenty employees and had operated on a very informal basis. Manufacturing and office operations were conducted in a building which was located on a five acre tract of land owned by Mr. Kargl. With primary emphasis on the design and fabrication of precision instruments, a minimum of attention was devoted to sales efforts since no sales organization of any kind had been established nor were any full-time salesmen employed prior to 1961. Sales were largely the result of personal contacts of Mr. Kargl and his small technical staff and by the fine reputation of Kargl in the photo-instruments field.

Sales volume and profitability of the company varied considerably from year to year. Gross sales reached a peak of approximately $200,000 in 1956, and a low of approximately \$100,000 in 1960. Net profits on sales were considered to be good in the years 1956–58. Sales volume during the 1949–1960 period did not increase significantly because Kargl Company had concentrated primarily upon research and development activities while minimizing production activities. During this period the company primarily fabricated prototype instruments for their customers. Also, inasmuch as Mr. Kargl had assumed the major responsibility for design and engineering work, the amount of inhouse contracts was necessarily limited by the small technical staff.

Recognizing the growth potential for Kargl Products and his lack of interest in the managerial aspects of the business, Mr. Kargl from time to time attempted to interest qualified persons to buy into the company. Early in 1961 he succeeded in finding an investor who was willing to take over the management of his company. In May, 1961, Mr. Kargl sold eighty per cent of the outstanding stock of Kargl Company to a small group of investors headed by Mr. Harry Evons. Mr. Evons held substantial interests in several local enterprises and had been actively engaged in business for approximately twenty years. The sale was consummated with the understanding that the three new stockholders would assume major responsibilities for the management of the company, allowing Mr. Kargl to devote his full attention and efforts to designing new photogrammetric equipment.

REORGANIZATION OF THE COMPANY, 1961

Mr. Harry Evons, as the major stockholder, immediately began a reorganization of the company. He was installed as chairman of the Board of Directors and President, and he began looking for a qualified general manager to handle the day-by-day operations of the company. Of the other two major stockholders, one was elected corporation secretary and the other was elected corporate treasurer. Mr. Gilard Kargl retained twenty per cent of the stock and membership on the Board. He assumed the position of executive vice-president, with complete freedom to devote his time and talent to improve the design of existing photogrammetric products and to design new products for the company.

Mr. D. W. Hubbard, with an extensive background in military and civilian aviation and aircraft sales administration, joined the company in October, 1961, as vice-president and general manager. Mr. Ray Kelsey who had left the company in 1960, rejoined the company in July, 1962, as chief engineer and director of research and development. Kelsey's initial responsibilities also included manufacturing, purchasing, and production control activities.

During the first several months after reorganization, the Board of Directors served as a management committee meeting every week for purposes of making operating decisions and hiring additional personnel as required. Only a few changes were made while the new management group gradually formulated its products and market strategy and established appropriate operational procedures and policies to guide overall company operations. After

Mr. Hubbard was hired in October, 1961, the Board began to meet only once a month, and members anticipated meeting only on an annual basis beginning in 1964. Harry Evons, the president, moved his personal office to the company on March 1, 1963, and began to take an active part in the Company. At that time the name was changed from Kargl Company to Kargl Instruments, Inc. in order to provide the public with a more correct description of the major interests of the company. The other stockholders anticipated taking no active part in company operations other than making major policy decisions from time to time.

The general manager and the chief engineer were usually invited to meet with the Board, and a representative of the Company's auditing firm also attended meetings occasionally.

OPERATING PHILOSOPHY OF NEW MANAGEMENT

The new Board of Directors adopted an operating philosophy designed to promote growth as rapidly as possible with the available technical, manufacturing, and financial resources of the company. Long-term gains in the form of capital appreciation of their investment was desired in place of immediate payment of earnings in the form of dividends.

Growth was to be accomplished primarily by a process of (1) product diversification, (2) concentration of research talent on projects and products which promised significant returns, and (3) solicitation of ideas and products from outsiders in need of technical assistance in design, development and fabrication of prototype products.

No specific guidelines were established for the proposed product diversification program. The new owners were determined to add more products to the present line of photogrammetric equipment which was considered to be very limited. They also wished to add other non-related product lines to level out seasonal and cyclical variations in sales commonly experienced when selling large budget items primarily to the federal and state governments and a few major industrial firms. Since the salaried engineering staff had talents largely restricted to the photogrammetric industry, internal expansion was restricted to those fields until additional engineering talent could be acquired.

Widespread product diversification was encouraged by soliciting from any interested party new and unique designs and ideas needing further research and development provided that the idea promised some reasonably long-term profitable relationship. Exhibit 1 illustrates the policy established to handle new product ideas submitted by persons outside the company.

While the company was determined to emphasize its research and development orientation, it was also determined to develop its manufacturing capability. New product ideas which were likely to develop ultimately into products manufactured by Kargl were favored over ideas where no manufacturing business was likely to develop. Management recognized that many

Exhibit 1

Kargl Instruments, Inc.
8123 Broadway
San Antonio 9, Texas

Kargl Instruments, Inc. is happy to consider ideas submitted by people outside of our company, but it has become necessary to establish a policy to mutually protect both the company and persons who submit ideas for our consideration.

We cannot receive or evaluate any disclosures from persons outside the company except on the understanding that our evaluation of disclosure entails no obligation on our part. It must be expressly understood that no confidential relationship is to exist concerning any information or material submitted to us. The submitter's rights are to be defined solely by patent protection he has or hereafter may acquire. Large numbers of disclosures are sent to us for our consideration. So many are submitted, in fact, that we cannot undertake to return all material; therefore, you are advised to retain a duplicate of all documents and material in your disclosure. In the event we decide that we have no interest in your disclosure, no reasons for our decisions will be given because to do so may require the release of information we do not wish known outside of our company.

If you wish to make a disclosure in accordance with the above conditions, please sign and date one copy of this agreement and return it to us with suitable material describing or illustrating your idea, and retain the other copy for your files.

> Very truly yours,
> D. Wm. Hubbard
> Vice Pres.-Gen. Mgr.

I have read and understand the terms outlined above and agree to the conditions set forth.

Subject: _____

Date:_____ Submitter:_____

ideas might not get beyond the prototype stage, but all proposals not specifying at least the fabrication of one prototype were rejected. Usually, the company sought to obtain a research and development contract that included provisions for the fabrication of up to 100 units of the item. They did not refuse to consider contracts calling only for a single prototype where it was felt there was a good possibility of additional orders as well as commercial marketing potential.

OPERATIONAL ACTIVITIES AS OF 1961

At the time of the reorganization, Kargl Instruments was firmly entrenched in the photo-optical instrumentation field with a limited line of well established commercial products along with a highly qualified, if small, research and development staff available for consultation on special problems in the photo-optical field. The research and development capabilities of the company were gradually expanding under the leadership of Mr. Kargl and Mr. Kelsey until they utilized a staff of fifteen persons in the Engineering Department by October 1963.

The 1961 line of photographic products included three models of aerial cameras with prices ranging up to $3,500 (the 1963 line of aerial cameras ranged up to $10,000 in price); a line of camera mounts; a patented tilt recording aerial camera; an autofocusing rectifier designed to remove range displacement present in aerial negatives; several models of copy cameras ranging from a small vertical model priced at $8,500 to a large horizontal model priced at $25,000; and a reflecting projector. Because of the high value and custom nature of each of these items, they were usually manufactured only to customer order. On rare occasions, items were manufactured for inventory when sales prospects appeared promising and if costs of producing an additional unit were very favorable. Through the years the company had maintained a camera and instruments repair service until this activity was discontinued in early 1963 because they were interested in directing activities to more productive areas in line with new policies. A local camera repair service was available for use by customers.

Technical proposals (bids) were submitted to various U.S. government and military agencies to obtain research and development contracts. Of some thirty proposals submitted during a two-year period, two contracts were awarded to Kargl Instruments. Industry average for contract awards was reported to be approximately one out of 20 submissions. One contract awarded by the United States Air Force Aeronautical Chart and Information Center called for the design of a special combination camera and projector while the other contract awarded by the United States Geodesy Intelligence Mapping Research and Development Agency (GIMRADA) contracted for a micromap camera to produce seventy milemeter photographs of military maps.

NEW PRODUCT DEVELOPMENT PROGRAM

New product development was the joint responsibility of Messrs. Hubbard, Kelsey, and Dick Evons. This group met periodically to evaluate new product ideas. On occasion Mr. Kargl was informally consulted. After preliminary screening, potentially new product ideas were presented to the President and to the Board of Directors for further consideration and action. Mr. Hubbard, the general manager, stated, " We are interested in almost any product which requires design, development, and fabrication work to produce, even though we are primarily in the photogrammetric equipment business." Mr. Kelsey, the chief engineer and head of research and development, felt that the company's current line of photogrammetric equipment was very small and therefore tended to place the company in a position where they were adversely affected by cyclical fluctuations in the market demand for these products. He was concerned with broadening the product line to reach a diversified market that could help to minimize sudden drops in demand for the company's products. Mr. Dick Evons was very interested in developing non-related products which would not be tied in any way to the photo-optical instrument business.

NEW PRECISION INSTRUMENTS

During the eighteen-month period after the reorganization of the company, a number of new photo-optical instruments were added to the company line including an aerial film viewer; a roll film dispenser; and an image motion compensation camera mount attachment. Along with these new products, the company had received a number of contracts for design improvement and manufacture of a number of photographic instruments. Micro-Film Systems Incorporated contracted with Kargl to redesign and manufacture 100 units of a card-roll-card microfilm duplicator (desk type). These units had an approximate retail price of $1,200. Many microfilm products were still in the idea stage, and the company felt that this would be a worthwhile field to exploit. Special research attention was being devoted to a small company information retrieval system and a microprinted-circuit camera designed to reduce electronic circuit drawings and subsequently micro print functioning circuits directly on a glass plate. The product development committee felt that successful solution of technical problems encountered in these two projects would likely open up a dynamic and profitable market for the company.

NEW NON-OPTICAL PRODUCTS

An unusual product area which the company entered came about when an inventor of a complex mechanical nutcracker brought his product to the company and requested them to manufacture and market it for him on a royalty payment basis. This product had been manufactured and sold with moderate success almost five years previously. After being examined in detail by the product planning group, they decided the product had definite possibilities as a profitable sideline item, provided that the design could be improved by using some of the existing design talent available within the firm. After several months of consideration, the decision was made by the Board of Directors to proceed with the development and marketing of the product. The decision was made by the Board of Directors to proceed with the development and marketing of the product. The decision was felt to be in keeping with the broad company policy that proposals will be accepted if they provide for a continuing arrangement whereby the company can design, develop the prototype, arrange for production, and market the product at a profit.

Since the nutcracker was not related to the company line, and Mr. Kargl was mildly apprehensive about his long-established reputation for quality scientific equipment, a decision was made to organize a new products division to be called Krak-All Products, to serve as a coordinating and marketing unit for household and related institutional products. With the exception of overhead allocations, a separate set of accounts was to be established and maintained for the Krak-All Products Division.

The Krak-All line was expanded quickly by the addition of an ice cube cracker, which was identical to the nutcracker except for different cracking surfaces, and by the addition of a portable folding steel outdoor cooking grill.

Other products in the houseware and miscellaneous line under consideration and invarious stages of development by October 1, 1963 were a powered can opener, a portable insecticide spray gun, and a small tank gauging mechanism. The development of the spray gun had been completed but the device was not in production. The tank gauge had been patented by the inventors, but production was delayed until a market potential could be established.

Following an informal market survey, an industrial products design consultant was retained to improve the appearance of the nutcracker while company engineers improved the mechanical features of the product and constructed a prototype model suitable for high-speed diecasting operations. Pre-production models were market tested with results judged very favorably by management. Kargl Instruments, Inc. arranged for a booth to introduce the product to a group of manufacturers' representatives attending the semi-annual National Housewares Show at the McCormick Place in Chicago in July, 1963. Based upon the advice of several merchandising experts at the show, the proposed retail price of $5.95 was raised to $7.95 in order to provide a better product image and to cover more intensive advertising and promotion expense. Initially the company had not intended to give advertising allowances, but this was changed to provide for a 25 per cent allowance. Based upon the favorable market reaction, a decision was made to distribute Krak-All products on a national basis. The uniqueness of the product resulted in the company being given editorial recognition and publicity in such magazines as *Family Circle*, *Modern Metals* (September, 1963), and on the nationally televised program "The Price is Right."

The original display box was designed by an industrial designer. Soon thereafter it was redesigned to provide a more suitable visual display for the nutcracker and ice cracker. The new box featured a transparent insert through which the device could be viewed. A contract was entered into with a firm that had suitable diecasting capacity to manufacture the product, and the capability to package, inventory and ship to customer accounts according to orders received from the Krak-All Division. An initial order of 5,000 units was placed with the sub-contractor. The contract provided for a schedule of price concessions on orders ranging from 5,000 to 100,000. By October, 1963 an additional order for 25,000 was placed, and by that date the products were being marketed through nearly one hundred speciality stores, gift shops, and major chains. The company had established a channel of distribution through a group of 20 manufacturer's representatives. Krak-All retained the rights to sell certain key accounts in major cities around the country on a direct basis.

The promising developments in the Krak-All line resulted in the hiring of an experienced distribution executive to assume control of the Krak-All division. Mr. Jules Sterling was appointed vice-president of Krak-All Products in September, 1963.

SALES

Kargl Company had no sales organization of any kind and no full-time salesmen until October, 1961, when Mr. Hubbard was hired as executive vice-present and general manager. Sales prior to this time were by word of mouth, limited efforts of the technical people, mainly Mr. Kargl, and as a result of selective direct mailings. Mr. D. W. Hubbard sold copy cameras to the oil industry on a part-time basis for Kargl while he was associated with a large local aerial mapping firm in 1958 and 1959. During his initial months in his new capacity with Kargl Company, Mr. Hubbard spent a considerable amount of his time developing new house accounts and soliciting business from existing customers, several of whom were known to him from previous contacts.

In September, 1962, Mr. Hubbard prepared a sales projection for all photo-grammetric products based upon their past performances, known prospects, and future potential. State highway departments that were currently installing their own departments or divisions for photogrammetry included fifty pros-pects with a potential sales ranging from $500,000 to $2,000,000 over a period of several years. Large consulting engineering firms currently organizing internal photogrammetric departments in attempts to avoid subcontracting represented a maximum of 1,000 potential customers with sales ranging from $250,000 to $1,500,000 over a period of several years. Aerial surveying and mapping firms that bid on government contracts or performed work for selected clients represented an additional 200 firms with a potential sales volume ranging from $400,000 to over $1,000,000 over a several-year period. Government agencies having internal photogrammetric divisions and depart-ments represented an almost unlimited potential for Kargl Instruments sales. Foreign government agencies currently forming or expanding internal depart-ments also represented a great potential, especially in Central and South America where photogrammetry was beginning a rapid growth period. One of the largest and as yet untapped sources of sales was industrial firms which were adding photogrammetric capabilities to solve internal research problems. Typical prospects for this group included the American Can Company, Goodyear Tire and Rubber Company, Aeroflex Corporation, and Northern Pacific Railroad. Because of the potential sales to new customers and because the company was faced with only a few major competitors, Mr. Hubbard projected a significant increase in the photogrammetric end of the business for the next three to five years.

Early in 1963 Keuffel and Esser's new Photogrammetric Systems Division had contacted Kargl Instruments, Inc. requesting them to consider an agreement whereby they would market Kargl's products on a world-wide basis with specific orders being placed by K. & E. f.o.b. San Antonio, Texas. In March, 1963, a decision was made by the Board of Directors of Kargl Instruments to accept the marketing arrangement extended by Keuffel and Esser. The marketing agreement called for the distribution of major Kargl photogrammetric products under the K. & E. label throughout the world. Kargl Instruments, however, retained exclusive selling rights in the three state area of Texas, Oklahoma, and Louisiana because they did not want to lose their long-established key accounts in the oil industry, several of whom were on the verge of placing orders for equipment. The K. and E. association provided Kargl with a world-wide marketing organization for its photogrammetric equipment. Mr. Hubbard and the Board of Directors considered the arrangement very desirable since they realized the benefits to be derived from the world-wide marketing efforts of a company with K. and E.'s excellent reputation and still continue to establish major sales policies. Along with the sales contract, several products sold by K. & E. were offered to Kargl Instruments for design improvement and manufacture if they were interested and capable of improving them. One of the most promising of these products was a 35 mm microfilm camera, with an approximate retail price of $6,500. Kargl received an initial order for twenty-five redesigned units, with more orders to follow if the product sold well. In commenting about the overall sales potential of the business, Mr. Hubbard stated that the company was definitely attempting to develop a balance between the various types of products produced. Mr. Hubbard felt that graphic arts products represented a very large product potential in that all major oil companies and industrial firms with large drafting rooms and internal photo service departments were potential customers. In the area of research and development he also felt that the potential with government agencies was unlimited since the company had recently obtained a security clearance. For the non-photogrammetric products, it was projected that the company could sell between 50,000 and 100,000 Krak-All products priced at $7.95 during the first season (1963–64). They also estimated that a maximum of 1,000 scale engraving machines could be used in precision machine shops, and these would sell for approximately $850. No estimate of actual sales of these machines for the current year was made, however. Aerial camera sales of sixty units were made between 1949 and 1955. Camera sales in subsequent years fell to a minimum of six in 1961. A substantial recovery of aerial camera sales was noticed in 1962 when fifteen were sold, and higher dollar volume sales were predicted for 1963 and subsequent years.

See Exhibit 3 for projected, received, and delivered sales for Kargl Instruments for fiscal years 1962, 1963, and 1964.

Exhibit 3

Sales Projected, Received and Delivered

Fiscal years 1962, 1963, and 1964

Fiscal years	Sales Orders		
(April 1–March 31)	PROJECTED	RECEIVED	DELIVERED
1962	$140,000	$170,000	$150,000
1963	435,000	290,000	235,000
1964	844,000	470,000*	175,000*

* For first five months of fiscal year only.

Source: Interview with company management.

FACILITIES

Kargl Instruments, Inc. housed all of its operations in a modern, air-conditioned masonry building which included over 13,000 square feet of floor space. Floor space was allocated on the following basis:

	Square Feet
Engineering	3,505
Production	5,436
Light assembly	495
Administration	1,524
Warehouse	2,654
Total	13,614

Along with all engineering design and drafting work which was conducted on the second floor, photographic and optical laboratory facilities were also maintained. The photographic lab was capable of processing aerial roll film, performing contact and projection printing and maintaining an inplant photographic facility. While the company did not manufacture lenses, they did maintain optical facilities for testing lenses.

The well equipped production facilities enabled the company to build prototype models of most products they designed or contemplated manufacturing. Identical facilities were used for model building and basic production operations. Production facilities included a sheet metal fabrication shop, an electric and acetylene welding shop, a wood shop, a wiring shop, a painting shop including bake ovens, and associated machining equipment such as lathes, drill presses, milling machines, presses and grinders.

These facilities were designed and layed out for intermittent production, and were considered unsuitable for other than very small scale production.

PRODUCTION OPERATIONS

Prior to July, 1963, Kargl Instruments actively contracted for research work where the company would design a product for a client on a fixed fee basis. Normally such contracts called for the delivery of product specifications and a prototype model. Because of the desire of company management to expand their manufacturing operations concurrently with contract design work, a policy was established whereby the company was no longer interested in simply procuring design work. After July, 1963, the company restricted contract design work in that they required minimum production runs of designed products. Because of the unique nature of photogrammetric equipment, such orders were normally limited to between five to twenty-five units of a given item. The highly specialized nature of the product and the generally limited market tended to restrict order quantities. Consequently, Kargl Instruments' manufacturing operations were best described as "job shop" operation. Because of the nature of Kargl's market for most of their products, production facilities were essentially a model shop designed to develop prototypes rather than to produce in any quantity. Once a product was released by the engineering department, three successive models were developed. First, a developmental model, which was used to prove the design concept, was made. Second, a prototype model was made to prove the actual design of the product. And finally a pre-production model was made to check the production tooling. See Exhibit 4 for a schematic model of the product development sequence at Kargl Instruments.

The engineering and manufacturing departments worked together very closely and in harmony. Upon receipt of a new contract a project number was assigned, a budget was established, and an engineer was assigned to supervise the project. The design engineer worked very closely with the production shop when fabricating the developmental, prototype, and preproduction models. Because of the smallness and informality, the engineer, especially if it was Mr. Kargl, often performed some of the machining operations of the first model.

As a direct result of the new management's attempt to increase the sales volume and profitability of the company, the production requirements had continued to increase noticeably since the beginning of 1962. As of August, 1963, the company had a number of orders in house which called for the manufacture of production models. Production jobs in process included a card-roll-card microfilm duplicator of which 100 units were required; the fabrication of twenty-five microfilm cameras; a forthcoming order for twenty 105 mm microfilm cameras; and a possible order for five other products for 100 units each. Mr. Ray Kelsey, the chief engineer, who also supervised the production operations indicated that he expected the current shop force of fifteen people to more than double at the end of 1963. He also estimated that $40,000 worth of new production equipment would be required to handle the

Exhibit 4

Product Development Sequence

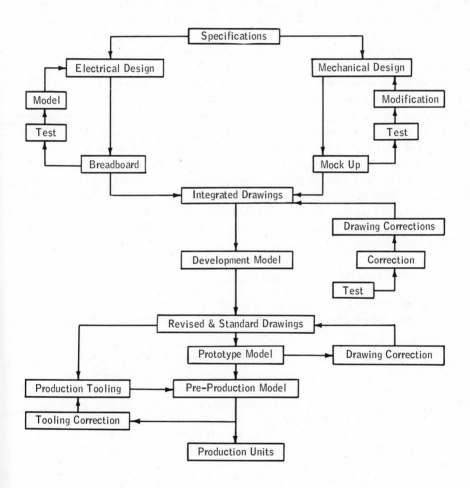

Source: Company officials

increased manufacturing activities. One shortcoming was the lack of space for line assembly operations. However, plans were in process to provide space for assembly in the proposed expansion of the physical facilities scheduled for late 1963. An additional 9,000 square feet of floor space was planned to house expanded production operations which would include additional machining capacity and line assembly operations. The additional building at the rear of the present building was estimated to cost approximately $65,000. Erection started in October, 1963, and was scheduled to be completed by December 1, 1963.

Prior to the expansion of the production facilities of Kargl Instruments, the company had maintained informal control over production. With more manufacturing orders coming into the house, increased scheduling problems began to develop. Conflicting demands for available equipment and manpower, and problems of coordinating current projects began to emerge by mid-1963. Recognizing the need to formalize production control, a department was established. A shop superintendent who had formerly been with Kargl and who recently was shop supervisor at a local air base was employed to relieve Mr. Ray Kelsey of that responsibility.

As of 1963, the engineering department had a backlog of orders in house which would keep the department busy until the end of 1963. Mr. Kelsey directed twelve people in the engineering department, three of whom were engineers and the remaining nine were draftsmen and designers. Lead time for new products through the engineering department ranged anywhere from a minimum of three months to a maximum of six months depending upon the complexity of the product involved. More basic research was assumed by Mr. Kargl, with the total development time of some projects requiring as much as a year or more.

ORGANIZATION AND PERSONNEL

Mr. Hubbard, general manager of Kargl Instruments, made the following comments about organizational and personnel changes since he had been with the company:

During the past several months we have been making a number of key organizational changes that we felt were necessary to facilitate the planned growth of the company. Since I came with the company in October of 1961, we have added the following positions to the organization—director of sales, chief of engineering, office manager, and purchasing agent. These were all considered to be necessary functions and positions which had to be established in order to carry out the increased volume of business acquired. The people who assumed these positions, however, each performed a variety of functions above and beyond those designated by their official titles. You can understand that in any small organization this is a typical situation especially when you cannot afford to hire help for all the work that needs to be done.

At the present time we are employing forty-five people. Of this number seven are classified as administrative personnel, thirteen as engineering personnel, and the remaining twenty-five as production personnel. At our present rate of planned growth, we anticipate doubling our engineering and production personnel by the end of 1963. Just recently, a man was hired to fill our last key slot in the production

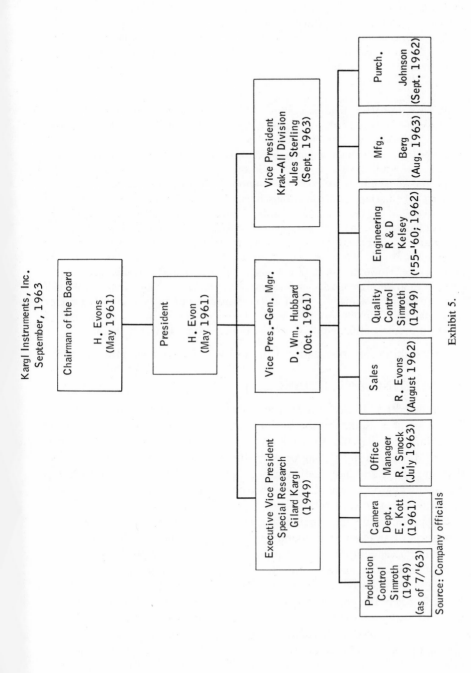

Kargl Instruments, Inc.
September, 1963

Chairman of the Board
H. Evons
(May 1961)

President
H. Evon
(May 1961)

Executive Vice President
Special Research
Gilard Kargl
(1949)

Vice Pres.–Gen. Mgr.
D. Wm. Hubbard
(Oct. 1961)

Vice President
Krak–All Division
Jules Sterling
(Sept. 1963)

Production Control
Simroth
(1949)
(as of 7/'63)

Camera Dept.
E. Kott
(1961)

Office Manager
R. Smock
(July 1963)

Sales
R. Evons
(August 1962)

Quality Control
Simroth
(1949)

Engineering R & D
Kelsey
('55–'60; 1962)

Mfg.
Berg
(Aug. 1963)

Purch.
Johnson
(Sept. 1962)

Source: Company officials

Exhibit 5.

163

organization. The new shop superintendent will start to work within the next month. With this addition we feel that we have all the key positions well manned with qualified personnel, all of whom take a personal interest in the product and its performance characteristics. We are well aware of the fact that we have a very high overhead payroll cost at present, but we felt it was necessary to hire key department heads in order to facilitate the planned increase not only in engineering but as well in production operations. Our overhead per hour will decrease as production increases.

We have a very unique organization of people here at Kargl Instruments. First, you have probably noticed that we have a relatively young organization of highly qualified personnel each in their own fields and with extensive experience in all phases of the photo optical industry. Second, there is not a man in this organization who has not worked with someone else in the organization in the same field somewhere and sometime in the past. It is impossible to assess the value of such past working relationships and friendships of the people in this shop. Third, I feel we have one of the best balanced boards of directors I have ever seen. Each board member has a unique background, extensive business experience in his own specialty, and readily avails himself to the operating management of this company.

Administratively, we have not attempted to formalize all operations to any great degree. However, we have gradually begun to establish standard operating procedures in the area of sales, engineering, accounting and manufacturing. We still feel that we are essentially a small and informal operation even though some of these changes gradually have been made. This is one of the definite advantages of the small business firm, and we hope we can keep it that way as we grow.

See Exhibit 5 for organizational chart of Kargl Intruments, Inc.

ACCOUNTING AND FINANCE

Detailed sales forecasts for each product line were not made more than one year in advance. Some members of management believed that things changed so rapidly that they did not have time to do required planning in any great detail. Mr. Evons did not agree with this viewpoint. He felt quite strongly that long range and intermediate range planning had to be done by the top management group, even at the sacrifice of certain other activities. He insisted that planning was too vital to postpone because of daily detail work.

The president decided that better planning could be obtained with the formation of an executive committee. Effective October 17, 1963, the executive committee, composed of the president, the three vice presidents, and the head of engineering and sales were to meet weekly for the purpose of developing operating plans on a short-term, intermediate-term and a long-term basis. In the words of the president, once the plans were formulated, they were then going to evaluate how they were doing in relation to those plans and forecasts. By this process they would be able to decide where they were and where they were going, and thereby overcome the tendency to get fuzzy about their objectives. He intended, he stated, to keep those areas vital to success sharply in focus.

While he anticipated a detailed plan for the ensuing year, he recognized that they did not have the staff to develop anything but a general plan for a five-year period.

During the summer months, for example, operating management spent approximately ninety-five per cent of their time on problems which were projected six months in advance and only about five per cent of their time on problems which extended beyond a year in advance. These ideas were to change with the active participation of Mr. Evons and the imposition of his policies.

Each department head submitted a budget for the following fiscal year based on sales projection provided by the director of sales. Personnel, material, administration, and shop overhead budgets were used to prepare a cost of sales budget. Capital expenditures were also included in departmental budgets. Departmental budgets were consolidated into an overall company budget which became the basis for next year's operations. However, Mr. Hubbard indicated that these budgets were merely guidelines for each department head and were not formally approved by the Board of Directors. From time to time changes were required in original estimates because of variations in product orders. Each month the company accountant prepared for Mr. Hubbard a report in which the month's activities were summarized financially and accumulated on a monthly basis. The report included selling price, total sales revenue, cost of sales, and gross profit for each product sold by the company. The report also included a breakdown of administrative overhead, net profit before taxes on total sales, increase or decrease of sales to date over last fiscal year, a cash flow statement, a cash position statement, and end of month bank balance.

The company was in the process of developing a cost accounting system for their inhouse research and development work as well as the production work. Cost standards on completed production were available for reference. The company recognized the value of keeping cost accounting records and they were determined to have as simple a system as was possible to generate needed records.

Kargl Instruments, Inc. was a private corporation, and as of September 1963, had not made a public offering of stock and had not anticipated making such an offer in the near future. While it was a closed corporation, management offered stock to all company employees on a special purchase plan The key officials were granted a stock option plan as a special incentive.

With the expanding level of sales, the initial capitalization of the business had proved inadequate to finance overall company operations. Working cspital was tight since the company sought to finance current operations primarily by short-term bank loans. It was indicated that once a sales contract was received from a reliable purchaser, it was relatively easy to obtain funds from a local bank to finance the project. The company had established excellent working relationships with a large local bank in San Antonio. With careful cash planning, they had developed an excellent credit rating. In view of the planned expansion of the business the company had established a policy whereby no cash dividends would be paid out of earnings until the desired expansion had been realized. The Board of Directors assumed primary responsibility for financing the expanded operations of the company. When the rapid growth made substantial additional funds necessary late in 1962, the Board of Directors sought to obtain long-term capital for the business without resorting to a stock sale. The best available source appeared to be through a Small Business Department Corporation, but after checking into the possibilities of this particular source, it was decided that it would be unadvisable to pursue this avenue. The Board of Directors next considered a public sale of stock, but after further examination felt that it was not practical to attempt to place a public stock issue then since the company had not had sufficient time to establish a good earnings record and an issue at that time would adversely affect the market price of the stock. Consequently, serious consideration was given to accepting offers from several local investors who had expressed an interest in investing in Kargl Instruments, Inc. Kargl had already gained a national reputation for the high quality instruments they produced and was also beginning to establish a regional reputation as a growing company with good prospects for capital appreciation. Because of the apparent growth potential of the company and possibilities for appreciation of its stock, several local investors had expressed interest in getting in on the " ground floor."

As of November, 1963, $60,000 of additional stock had been sold. The Board of Directors plan to make available a limited amount of additional stock to interested local investors and then arrange for long-term financing to further the continuing need for expansion indicated by the increased demand for products from " Kargl's " customers.

2. ACME BRASS MANUFACTURING COMPANY*

—GRANT C. MOON

and

CHARLES H. SPENCER

The fiscal year ended June 30, 1949, had been very disappointing to the stockholders of Acme Brass Manufacturing Company of Detroit, Michigan.

This family-controlled firm was incorporated in 1906 for the manufacture of brass castings, valves, and cocks as original equipment for makers of gas ranges, driers, and heating appliances. The company was successful for several years but met sharp reverses during the 1930's, and was on the verge of bankruptcy in 1938 when Mr. Robert T. Herbert, son of the founder, bought out his two brothers and reorganized the company.

Heavy indebtedness made it impossible immediately to replace inefficient, outmoded equipment with modern machinery. Very little progress had been made on this problem prior to World War II and the very low earnings that had been made during the base period, 1936 to 1939, subjected the firm to heavy excess profits taxes. Again, because of this and other wartime factors, the company was prevented from modernizing its facilities as rapidly as needed to keep abreast of competition.

From 1938 on the management had been practically a one man operation, but in September 1947 Herbert told his son-in-law, Grant C. Willman, then production manager, that he intended to have Willman become familiar with the commercial and financial phases of the business. Before these intentions could be carried out Mr. Herbert died suddenly in November 1947 and Willman was made president and treasurer.

Before joining Acme Brass in 1939 Willman had been employed in the Chevrolet Division of General Motors, where he had received training in warehouse management, supplemented by training in sales and in analysis of dealer costs and earnings. This experience had convinced him of the importance of close control of costs and also of the advantages of efficient

* Reprinted by permission of Mr. Grant C. Moon, Small Business Administration, Washington 25, D.C., and Charles H. Spencer.

organization with clearly defined chain of command and areas of responsibility and authority.

Fortunately a new cost system had been put into operation in October 1947 and was functioning well when Mr. Willman assumed his new responsibilities. This system provided him with a daily analysis of labor variance from standard in each department and enabled him to keep a close control on manufacturing costs.

Early in 1948 Willman requested the company's auditors to survey the entire organization and submit their recommendations. The auditors compiled and submitted a complete report including organization charts job descriptions, and recommendations for implementing their proposals. Just at the point where Willman undertook to act on the auditors' proposed reorganization, sales began declining.

According to Mr. Willman, Acme Brass did not enjoy any important advantage over its competitors during the late 1940's. Prices on about 85 percent of the company's lines were approximately the same as quoted by the firm's major competition. Acme's prices on air cocks and water gauges, which comprised most of the remaining 15 percent, were about 2 to 5 percent higher than the general industry level. The quality of the Acme Brass product in 1948 was said to have been on a par with competition, but possessed of no particular superiority.

Exhibit 1

Acme Brass Manufacturing Company
Comparative Condensed Operating Statements

	June 30, 1946	June 30, 1947	June 30, 1948	June 30, 1949
Net Sales	$904,899	$1,486,514	$1,237,265	$920,651
Cost of Sales	786,043	1,302,687	1,039,316	824,227
Gross Profit	118,856	183,827	197,949	96,424
Expense or Loss	71,001	114,054	121,540	123,379
Net Operating Profit (Loss)	47,855	69,773	76,409	(26,955)
Other Income	6,616	9,108	9,195	14,162
Other Deductions	3,324	8,266	4,010	504
Net Profit (Loss) before Federal Income Tax	51,147	70,615	81,594	(13,297)
Provision for Federal Income Tax	24,000	26,255	31,500	(4,900)*
Net Income After Taxes	$ 27,147	$ 44,360	$ 50,094	$ (8,397)
Net Worth	$207,901	$ 252,261	$ 297,355	$306,718**

* Tax Loss Carryback.

** Company realized $17,760 from sale of 296 shares of capital stock @ $60.00 per share.

The shortages created by World War II made a ready market for almost all types of manufactured goods and, in its fiscal year 1946–1947 Acme Brass had been able to operate at full capacity and sell its output at prices which permitted the realization of a satisfactory profit. However, as the supply pipelines began to be filled, demand slackened and buyers took a closer look at prices and values.

In fiscal 1947–1948 Acme Brass experienced a decline in sales of $249,249 from the previous year. However, even though selling and administrative expenses increased by $12,700,[1] Acme was able to reduce manufacturing costs by $263,371 with the result that, after other charges, net profit before Federal income taxes increased by $10,979. During the following year the company sustained a further decline in sales of $316,614—from $1,237,265 to $920,651. The cost of sales fell by only $215,089, however, and advertising expense increased by almost $4,700,[1] more than offsetting a decrease of $2,800[1] in administrative and general expense. The net reduction of $94,891 in earnings before income taxes resulted in a net loss of $13,297 before a tax loss carryback. See Exhibit 1 for condensed operating statements and Exhibit 2 for comparative balance sheets.

A study of the profit and loss statements for the fiscal years ended June 30, 1947 and 1949 reveals the following:

Net sales	$565,860 decrease
Cost of sales	478,460 decrease
Gross profit	87,403 decrease
Selling and advertising	9,325 increase
Administrative and general[2]	5,807 increase
Other income	5,054 increase
Other deductions	7,762 decrease
Net profit before Federal income taxes	83,912 decrease

Acme Brass was unionized and wage scales were negotiated with U. A. W. representatives. The union scale for the plant was somewhat lower than that paid by the automobile manufacturers but, whenever a higher scale was agreed to by the auto companies, Acme Brass was under pressure to raise its own wage level. For several years following World War II higher wage scales were negotiated every year; otherwise the company would have lost its skilled workers to firms paying the prevailing wage scale. These increases prevented the reduction of manufacturing costs in direct proportion to declining sales.

The higher selling expense reflected the greater effort put forth to maintain the company's position in the face of keen competition. The increased amount

---

[1] Case writer's note: The "selling and administrative" figures were supplied by the case firm from actual records and given as approximations.

[2] Figures supplied by the case firm and given as approximations.

Exhibit 2

Acme Brass Manufacturing Company

Comparative Balance Sheets at June 30, 1949 and June 30, 1948

ASSETS	June 30, 1949	June 30, 1948	Increase Decrease*
Currents assets:*			
Cash	$33,642.78	$26,850.49	$6,792.29
Trade notes and accounts receivable	44,629.46	90,379.02	45,749.56*
Claim for refund of federal taxes on income	4,900.00	0	4,900.00
Inventories	138,704.49	180,649.91	41,945.42*
Prepaid taxes, insurance, and miscellaneous accounts	25,096.19	**	25,096.19
Total Current Assets	$246,972.92	$297,879.42	$50,906.50*
Other assets	**	1,512.91	1,512.91*
Property, plant, and equipment	148,457.31	144,104.38	4,352.93
Deferred charges.	**	25,262.85	25,262.85*
	$395,430.23	$468,759.56	$73,329.33*
LIABILITIES			
Current liabilities:			
Notes payable to bank	$4,315.33	$19,441.27	$15,125.94*
Accounts payable and accrued expenses	67,190.64	119,170.27	51,979.63*
Federal taxes on income	1,407.57	32,792.85	31,385.28*
Current maturities on long-term indebtedness	3,300.00	0	3,300.00
Total Current Liabilities	$76,213.54	$171,404.39	$95,190.85*
Long-term indebtedness	12,498.10	0	12,498.10
Capital stock and surplus:			
Common stock	139,800.00	125,000.00	14,800.00
Capital surplus	26,425.41	23,465.41	2,960.00
Earned surplus	140,493.18	148,889.76	8,396.58*
Total Capital Stock and Surplus	$306,718.59	$297,355.17	$9,363.42
	$395,430.23	$468,759.56	$73,329.33*
Ratio of current assets to current liabilities	3.24 to 1	1.74 to 1	

* Miscellaneous accounts and deposits which were classified as " Other assets " at June 30, 1948, and prepair taxes, insurance, and other expenses which were classified as " Deferred charges " at June 30, 1948, have been classified as " Current assets " at June 30, 1949.

of administrative and general expense resulted partly from Willman's attempt to implement the recommendations of the company's auditors with respect to the organization, and partly because of increased legal and other expenses incurred upon the death of Mr. Herbert. Willman began a retrenchment program soon after the downward trend in sales became evident. The reorganization program was largely abandoned. Clerical work was simplified and wherever possible supervisory jobs were consolidated. Mr. Willman directed that all purchase orders must be referred to him for advance approval.

Exhibit 3.

Building Plan, Acme Brass Manufacturing Company

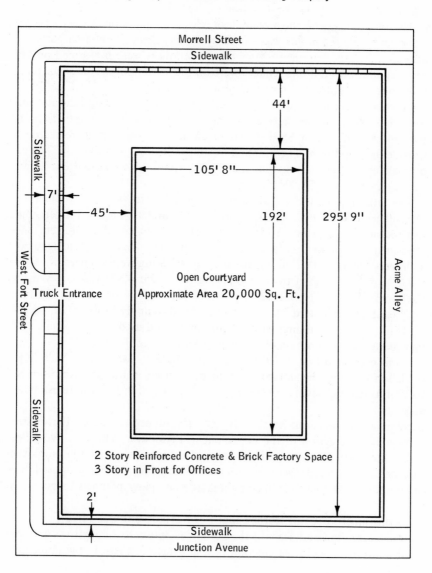

All of these steps proved insufficient to arrest the unsatisfactory trend of earnings.

The high wage rates prevailing in the Detroit area were only partially responsible for Acme's excessive manufacturing costs. The company occupied 96,000 square feet in a three-story building at the corner of West Fort Street and Junction Avenue. The dimensions of the building were approximately 300 feet by 200 feet; a central open courtyard, 106 feet by 192 feet, took out an area of approximately 20,000 square feet in the center of the building. See Exhibit 3. Trucks entered and left the court through an arched driveway in the center of the front section of the building.

The foundry was on the second floor, cleaning operations were on the first floor, and sand for molds was stored in the basement. Purchased parts were also stored in the basement. Machining operations were performed on both the first and second floors. Offices were on the third floor. Some space on the first floor was rented to an outside firm.

Elevators were inadequate for the company's operations and did not meet the requirements of the Detroit building code. A reliable contractor estimated that an expenditure of $50,000 would be necessary to put the elevators in satisfactory condition. The building repair bill in 1947 was $17,160. The cost of coal for heating was as much as $7,302 annually, while real estate taxes were approximately $7,800 a year.

The situation had been discussed at length with the stockholders. In December, 1948, a decision was reached to purchase vacant property in a Detroit suburb on which a modern one story plant could be erected. Soon afterward an option was taken on some land in Plymouth, Michigan, and architects' plans and elevations for the new building were prepared.

The estimated cost of the new building was $195,500. It was believed that the company could realize $237,500 net from the sale or trade of the plant on West Fort Street and Mr. Willman planned to apply $150,000 of the proceeds on the new building, with a bank loan being used for the balance. No immediate major purchase of new equipment was contemplated.

It was estimated that monthly savings of $4,952 in wages plus $436 in the reduction of fringe benefit costs could be realized in the new location. See Exhibit 4. Annual savings in the cost of heating and in taxes were estimated at $8,067.

Negotiations were undertaken for the simultaneous sale of the existing plant and the erection of the new plant in Plymouth. When the West Fort Street factory was advertised for sale, Mr. Willman called the employees together and showed them the architects' drawing of the proposed new building, so that they would not think the company planned to go out of business.

At this juncture it was learned that Ford Motor Company had purchased a large tract of land adjacent to the site under option to Acme Brass and that Ford planned to begin the erection of a new factory there in the immediate future. Mr. Willman and the other stockholders realized that if they went ahead with their plans they would be forced to match Ford wage scales or lose their skilled workers to better paying jobs at the Ford Plant.

Exhibit 4

Acme Brass Manufacturing Company
Schedule of Possible Monthly Savings

To be effected by the trading of present plant for one better suited to the company's production requirements.

1. Supervision	Tool engineer to take over tool room supervision in addition to his present duties.	$395.00 (sal)
2. Supervision	Eliminate one supervisor in the foundry by consolidating cleaning, molding, and melting operations.	370.00 (sal)
3. Supervision	By relocating the buffing department, the foreman in Department 18 can supervise the workers in the latter department.	312.00 (hrly)
4. Timekeeper	Eliminate one in Department 15, since timekeeper in charge of Departments 16 and 21 can also handle Department 15. Timekeeper in Department 18 can take care of work for Department 19.	211.00 (hrly)
5. Cost	By moving the standards office adjacent to the cost office C. Bowman will be able to assist both E. Muer and C. Overton, thereby eliminating M. Cullen.	245.00 (hrly)
6. Trucker	By changing from coke to oil or gas fired furnaces we will save the hauling of the coke as well as approximately 4 hours labor each day cleaning out the coke pit.	310.00 (hrly)
7. Furnace Helper	By making change mentioned in No. 6 we are anticipating a saving in furnace helpers since there will be no charging of coke (direct labor).	250.00 (hrly)
8. Set-up Man	By consolidating Department 15 with Departments 16 and 21 we can eliminate at least one set-up man and possibly a second one— one man only.	272.00 (hrly)
9. Watchmen and Firemen	By installing automatic gas or oil fired boilers we can eliminate 3 men.	1100.00 (hrly)
10. Gate Guard	Eliminate one	240.00 (hrly)
11. Janitor	Eliminate one.	205.00 (hrly)
12. Maintenance	Eliminate three men.	842.00 (hrly)
13. Office	Eliminate at least one girl	200.00 (sal)
	Total Monthly Savings	$4952.00

The above amounts are based on a comparison of $100,000 per month business in the present building as against $100,000 per month in a new building.

In addition to the savings computed above, we should save in fringe benefits, based on the above amount, the following:

> 2.5% for Vacations
> 1% for Old Age Benefits
> 1.3% for Unemployment Compensation
> 3% for Bonus
> 1% for Compensation
> ─────
> 8.8%

8.8% times $4,952 = $435.78 monthly savings on fringe benefits.

The cost of coal for heating for the fiscal year ended 6/30/48 was (represented by 678 tons @ $10.77 per ton) $7,302.06

Exclusive of the basement, we are now heating 73,000 square feet. The approximate size of the new building would be 45,000 square feet, reducing the size by about 42 per cent and also reducing the fuel cost by that amount. Therefore the minimum saving would be $3,066.87

Franchise taxes, real and personal property taxes for the year ended 6/30/48 were $19,176.88

It is hoped that we will be able to locate in an area nearby which will enable us to retain the same working force and still take advantage of lower taxes. A conservative estimate of tax savings $5,000.00

$250,000.00	Possible sale proceeds on old building
12,500.00	Commission
$237,500.00	Net realized from the sale or trade
150,000.00	To apply on new building
$87,500.00	Cash for operating expenses
30,000.00	Moving expenses (including purchase of minor pieces of new equipment)
$57,500.00	Increase in working capital

3. KENTUCKY FOOD STORES, INC.*

—JOSEPH L. MASSIE

During the first two weeks of April, 1962, Mr. W. L. Murray, General Manager of the Kentucky Food Stores, was preparing plans for the next year to be presented to the annual meeting of the members. Mr. Murray had been the chief salaried manager of the cooperative, retail-owned warehousing and buying organization for fourteen years and therefore was intimately familiar with its policies and problems. He felt that the organization had been successful in meeting its original objectives but he was aware of additional opportunities open to the group. In addition, several important problems had developed in the preceding year which needed management's attention. He felt that it was his job to make specific recommendations to the 84 members who were to meet on the fourth Tuesday of April. He was preparing these recommendations.

HISTORY OF KENTUCKY FOOD STORES

The Kentucky Food Stores had been organized in Lexington, Kentucky, a town of 75,000 population, in May 1944 by 32 independent grocers to buy and warehouse products for its members at low cost. This group of grocers had become acquainted through the activities of the Lexington Grocers Association formed in 1938. The original association had been organized for the purpose of encouraging individual retail operators to become better acquainted and to exchange ideas concerning mutual problems. Prior to its formation several independent grocers located within a mile of one another had not even met. Previously, the feeling had been that if one independent operator visited another, the purpose was to gain competitive advantage by comparing prices and discovering new practices. After its formation, the

* Reprinted by permission of the Southern Case Writers Association and Professor Joseph L. Massie.

association changed this feeling into a friendly and trusting relationship and served as a means of educating the independent grocer in better methods of operating his business.

During the early part of World War II the independent grocers had been able to operate profitably. Wartime rationing regulations enabled them to obtain their share of scarce merchandise and allowed them to maintain their competitive position with the chains since all stores sold under the same price ceilings. By 1944 it appeared that the war would end in victory; the grocers began to wonder what was going to happen to them when peace came. The incorporation of the Kentucky Food Stores was part of their answer. Each member paid for a membership in the Kentucky Food Stores which rented a warehouse and began to purchase from national distributors in large lots.

In 1948 the organization completed a new warehouse which served approximately 60 members each of whom had invested $1,500 in the cooperative. Mr. Murray at this time accepted the position of General Manager of the Kentucky Food Stores and ceased to operate his own independent grocery. Soon after, with the purchase of appropriate refrigeration equipment, the services of the organization were expanded to supply produce and vegetables.

Exhibit I
Growth of Kentucky Food Stores

Year	Number of Members	Total Sales
1945	32	N.A.
1948	60	$1,496,059
1949	N.A.	1,865 709
1950	N.A.	4,084,741
1953	105	4,811,192
1954	N.A.	5,264,859
1955	N.A.	5,394,878
1956	N.A.	5,347,481
1957	N.A.	5,451,280
1958	N.A.	5,847,115
1959	80	5,141,139
1960	88	6,190,740
1961	84	5,808,632

During the decade of the 1950's the cooperative warehousing operation expanded gradually in terms of member firms and gross sales volume as outlined in Exhibit I. By 1962 84 members provided a volume of $6,000,000 annually. The statements shown in Exhibits II and III indicate the financial picture at the time Mr. Murray was preparing his recommendations.

Exhibit II
Balance Sheets for 1960 and 1961 for Kentucky Food Stores

Assets

	1960		1961	
Current				
Cash	$100,147.74		$60,283.91	
Accounts Receivable	41,372.17		8,674.62	
Notes Receivable	13,700.00		39,900.00	
Merchandise Inventory	382,954.62		399,262.76	
TOTAL CURRENT ASSETS		$538,174.53		$508,121.29
Fixed				
Real Estate	$29,664.49		$29,664.49	
Building	149,391.22		152,376.84	
Refrigeration Equipment	7,663.38		7,663.38	
Trucks	21,446.41		21,446.41	
Warehouse Equipment	12,169.44		19,605.22	
Furniture and Fixtures	8,171.51		8,449.31	
GROSS FIXED		$228,506.45		$239,205.65
TOTAL ASSETS		$766,680.98		$747,326.94

Liabilities

	1960		1961	
Accounts Payable	$114,175.83		$89,799.87	
Notes Payable	176,000.00		145,400.00	
Accrued Payroll Taxes	2,250.61		2,378.15	
Accrued Income Taxes	2,050.93		5,864.35	
Accrued Expenses	9,830.83		13,810.45	
Members Refunds and Rebates	3,163.01		2,383.18	
Reserve for Depreciation	55,322.76		66,143.26	
Capital Stock	267,100.00		253, 200.00	
Surplus-Paid-In	66,400.00		87,800.00	
Surplus-Earned	70,387.01		80,547.68	
TOTAL LIABILITIES & CAPITAL		$766,680.98		$747,326.94

DESCRIPTION OF OPERATIONS AND POLICIES IN 1962

The objective of the Kentucky Food Stores was to buy and warehouse products in large volume and to pass the resulting savings to its members. Its policies were formed to provide a financially sound operation which would minimize operating costs but which would yield little or no profit. It was felt that the profit should be made by the independent grocer helped by the service from the cooperative.

The chief achievement of the cooperative can be expressed in terms of its ratio of operating expense to sales. This ratio ranged from 3.25 percent to

Exhibit III

Income Statements for 1960 and 1961 for Kentucky Food Stores

	1960		1961	
Gross Income				
Gross Sales		$5,774,971.02		$5,995,202.70
Less—Cost of Sales:				
Beginning Inventory	$377,536.11		$382,954.62	
Purchases	5,650,144.39		5,865,044.62	
	$6,027,680.50		$6,247,999.24	
Ending Inventory	382,954.62	$5,644,725.88	399,262.76	$5,848,736.48
Gross Profit		$130,245.14		$146,466.22
Discounts Earned	$73,184.67		80,871.94	
Advertising Revenue	2,977.00		3,040.00	
Interest Received	265.00		760.39	
Hauling and Drayage	17,576.77	94,003.44	19,720.00	104,392.33
TOTAL INCOME		$224,248.58		$250,858.55
Deductions				
Salaries and Wages	$129,750.48		$144,764.75	
Rent	5,121.50		5,551.04	
Interest	10,095.66		9,263.46	
Taxes	12,976.25		14,327.67	
Depreciation	12,708.76		10,820.50	
Other Deductions	42,181.62		48,028.50	
Contributions	318.78		256.22	
Accrued Income Tax	233.87		729.18	
TOTAL DEDUCTIONS		213,386.92		233,741.32
Net Taxable Income		$10,861.66		$17,117.23

4 percent. It was felt that this percentage was 2–2½ percent better than the operating percentage for other firms with similar activities. This differential enabled the member to gain a competitive advantage on the cost of goods delivered to his retail outlet.

Pricing policies of the cooperative were quite simple. Twice a month a Stock Bulletin was issued to members which listed all of the items available through the warehouse. This bulletin informed members of the price per carton, f.o.b. the warehouse dock, and suggested a retail price per unit which could be used by each member as a guide to his own retail pricing. It also gave prices by its competition on key items. Supplements to this bimonthly bulletin were issued when changes of prices were necessary and new items were introduced. Prices were computed by using a percentage markup which remained stable: 2 percent markup plus the 2 percent cash discount received by the cooperative from the distributors on general groceries and produce;

2 percent (the amount of the cash discount) on canned milk, coffee, sugar, tobacco and cigarettes; 1 percent on drop shipments (items delivered directly to retail store by distributor); $1\frac{1}{4}$ percent on poultry and fish; zero mark upon soaps and shortening. Other services provided by the cooperative were optional and were charged for only if used by the individual member.

Each member secured from the cooperative most of his requirements for the 6,000 items of merchandise handled by the Kentucky Food Stores. However, because the cooperative did not handle frozen foods, bottled drinks, milk, bread, and other commodities sold by the retailer, the cooperative supplied only about 33 percent of the gross sales of the typical member. That is, if Blankenship grocery purchased $200,000 worth of merchandise from Kentucky Food Stores, it probably grossed $600,000 in sales per year.

For the first 10 years of operations, Kentucky Food Stores allowed members to buy on credit up to 75 percent of its membership fee with payment due in three days. Need for additional working capital to handle a larger inventory ultimately demanded either an increase in the membership fee or payment on a cash and carry basis. The members then voted to change its terms to strictly cash on delivery, a step which freed $70,000 in funds for handling increased inventory.

Even after an addition to the warehouse increased its space to 42,000 sq. ft., Mr. Murray believed that the available space could not service any significant increase in volume of sales. Merchandise was received by rail and trailer trucks and moved by fork lift truck to the proper location in the warehouse. All items were given a code number which determined their location on the floor. These same codes were used by the bookkeepers in recording transactions and by the order selectors in the filling of individual orders. In this manner the selector did not backtrack since he merely proceeded from the smallest code number to the largest in the same order in which the items were stacked in the warehouse.

Warehousing had recently developed several problems as a result of the geographical location of members and the variations in the scale of operations among members. Exhibit IV presents an analysis of sales by size of purchases and geographical location. The problems of handling merchandise for those members in Lexington differed from the problems of handling merchandise for outlaying members.

Stores buying $50,000 worth of merchandise did not require the variety of merchandise that stores buying over $100,000 required. The greater variety of merchandise handled by larger stores increased the difficulty of storing items properly in the limited space of the warehouse. Therefore the larger volume members were required to contribute additional funds to the cooperative to help finance the increased inventory.

Inventory control was handled by use of IBM cards. A separate card represented a case of merchandise. All cards were kept in a tub file and were checked weekly by the buyer. Out-of-stock items were listed daily and ordered immediately. The time required from making an order to receipt of the goods varied; in most cases it was approximately one week. As member stores became larger and carried a greater variety of items, the pressure on space in the warehouse increased. Turnover of inventory therefore became a problem which Mr. Murray had to watch carefully.

Exhibit IV
Sales Analysis of Kentucky Food Stores for 1961

22 members purchases $100,000.00 and up

8 members in Lexington	$1,374,499.75	23.75%
14 members out of Lexington	1,977,893.57	34.00%
22 total members	$3,352,393.32	57.75%

21 members purchases $50,000.00 to $100,000.00

6 members in Lexington	$440,927.65	7.75%
15 members out of Lexington	914,079.22	15.75%
21 total members	$1,355,006.87	23.50%

41 members purchases up to $50,000.00

10 members in Lexington	$264,158.21	4.50%
31 members out of Lexington	837,074.12	14.25%
41 total members	$1,101,232.33	18.75%

Summary

14 members in Lexington	$2,079,585.61	35.8%
60 members out of Lexington	3,729,046.91	64.2%
	$5,808,632.52	100.00%

22 members (each purchases $100,000 or more)	$3,352,393.32	57.75%
21 members (purchases of $50,000 to $100,000)	1,355,006.87	23.50%
41 members (purchases up to $50,000.00)	1,101,232.33	18.75%
	$5,808,632.52	100.00%

The question of adequate financing continually had been watched closely by the Board of Directors and the General Manager. Immediately after its formation, the cooperative quickly achieved a high credit rating with national distributors. Membership fees were increased when the need for additional funds was evident. Over the years a small surplus had been created by operating at a small profit upon which taxes were paid. Bank borrowing was used to provide funds for carrying some of the inventory. Since the terms of purchases for many items included a 2 percent discount for cash payment in ten days, the cooperative concentrated on maintaining sufficient funds to take all cash discounts.

A basic policy of Kentucky Food Stores from its inception was to provide each member with similar services regardless of size or location. For example, the price of merchandise was uniform to all members regardless of the number of units purchased. The management of the cooperative always considered this policy first when making any changes in services performed by the cooperative. The variety of characteristics of the 84 member groceries in-increased the difficulty of holding to this policy.

ORGANIZATION

The organization of the buying and warehousing corporation was purposely kept simple. Mr. Murray felt that the primary reason that his operating expenses were low was due to the absence of a number of highly paid executives. Exhibit V illustrates the positions in the organization including all personnel. All of the officers of the corporation were owners of independent groceries; members of the Board had no operating duties and received no salaries. The general manager served as chief executive officer and handled all marketing, storekeeping, and transportation functions. The officers and a finance committee handled all financial matters. The assistant general manager served as warehouse superintendent and handled routine personnel matters. The advertising manager operated independently of the warehouse operation; his chief duty was to help the independent grocery owners in the preparation of cooperative advertising. The buyer was occupied in handling orders for merchandise and controlling inventory.

PERSONAL PROFILE OF MR. MURRAY, GENERAL MANAGER

Mr. Murray, as President of the original Retail Grocers Association and one of the independent grocers who recognized the need in 1944 for a buying cooperative, felt that the small independent grocer could exist only if some means of increasing efficiency could be found. Although he had been happy and successful in the operation of several small groceries, he accepted the position of General Manager in 1947 when it became apparent that the first general manager of Kentucky Food Stores lacked the necessary knowledge and experience. He left his own retail groceries netting $12,000 to accept the position of General Manager which at that time paid only $5,000.

The management philosophy of Mr. Murray had evolved from his early experiences as an owner of retail groceries and as an employee in a wholesale grocery company. In 1962 at an age of 62 he identified himself with a movement to strengthen the position of the small independent grocer through helping him meet the strong competition from large organizations with their chains of supermarkets and their aggressive merchandising techniques. He felt that these large organizations had few advantages which could not be neutralized by aggressive actions of independent owners. He observed: "We do not hope to buy a case of canned goods cheaper than others can buy it

Organization of Kentucky Food Stores

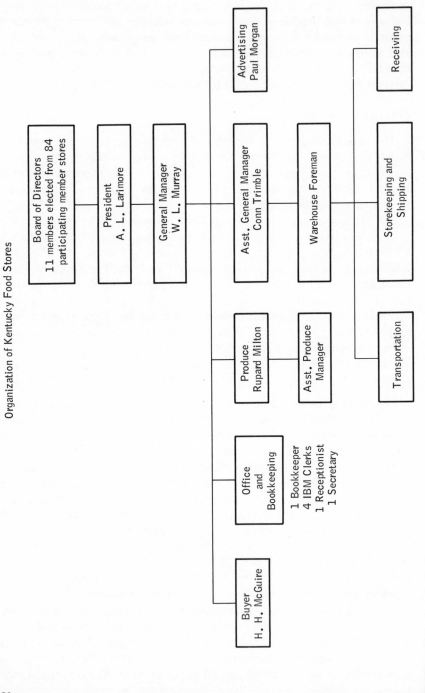

Exhibit V

but we do expect to be able to buy it for $1.00 if others can buy it for $1.00." At times, especially in the early days of the cooperative, he recalled that it had only been necessary to remind a distributor of the laws against price discrimination in order to obtain the desired supplies of merchandise at the price charged to competitors.

Mr. Murray felt that the chief problem facing the independent grocery owner was to improve the merchandising of his products. Some owners, he believed, became content with their current revenue from their business and failed to see promising opportunities. Some owners did not have the time to give attention to the many special phases of their business, such as the meat department, advertising, and store arrangement. However some owners were young and aggressive but needed assistance in meeting their problems.

Mr. Murray stressed the importance of finding new merchandising techniques which appealed to the customer. He felt that some competitors had been successful in using trading stamps. Some members of the cooperative had been successful in using contests; others had provided special attractions such as a train for children while their mothers were shopping. Mr. Murray believed that the number of devices was limitless and that it didn't make much difference which ones you used as long as you found those that appealed to your particular customers.

TRANSPORTATION AND ADVERTISING

Kentucky Food Stores offered extra services to its members on an optional basis. Two of the most important were delivery of goods from the warehouse to the member stores and joint advertising. Each of these services were offered at a charge which was considered only sufficient to cover the extra costs. A charge of $1-1\frac{1}{2}$ percent of gross purchases of each participating member was made for delivery of the goods to the door of the member grocery. A charge of 1 percent of gross purchases was made to cover joint advertisements in Lexington newspapers. Costs of these services were segregated and matched against the revenue received from the charges.

Four tractor-trailer trucks were used to make deliveries to member stores once a week along a sheduled route. Those members who preferred to pick up their orders at the warehouse were allowed to do so and were not charged for delivery. Exhibit VI is a map of the territory in which members were located showing those members on a scheduled delivery route and those members who provided their own delivery. This map also gives the population of each county in the territory. Members who picked up their own orders were allowed to obtain their orders as frequently as they wished. There was no schedule of hours for these pickups; consequently, at times the loading dock at the warehouse was crowded.

Each of the four trucks used for making deliveries to member stores was able to carry purchases valued from $5,000 to $8,000. It was estimated that

Exhibit VI

Location of Member Groceries of Kentucky Food Stores

Legend

● Delivered by trucks of Kentucky Food Stores

○ Picked up at warehouses by member grocers

‖ Delivery routes of Kentucky Food Store trucks

Numerals show population of counties in
thousands

25¢ per mile covered the cost of trucks. Deliveries to the north of Lexington
were made on Tuesdays; to the south on Wednesdays; to the south and southwest on Thursdays. One route to the south was traveled on alternate Mondays.
Usually two or three trucks were required on each of these runs.

Joint advertising was added as a service in 1950. An advertising committee
was formed which met weekly to determine those items to be featured in a

given week. The promotion was planned and carried out by Mr. Morgan, the advertising manager. Although all members were required to contribute 1 percent of their gross purchases to advertising, those members who felt that they could be served better by advertising in their own local newspapers (most of which were weekly) were able to obtain credit from the cooperative by presenting evidence that they had placed their advertising directly. However, since the Lexington newspapers had a wide circulation in the territory, all members in Lexington and a number of members in other counties participated in the joint advertising.

COMPETITION AND SALES POTENTIAL IN KENTUCKY FOOD STORES' TERRITORY

The population of Fayette County in which Lexington was located increased by 31 percent between 1950 and 1960 with an even greater increase in per capita income. Similar rates of increase were experienced by those counties contiguous with Fayette; however, other counties in the territory had had little increase in the decade and in many cases the population had actually declined. The cash income of the outlying mountain counties was extremely low. Many of these counties were declared in a distressed area by the federal government in 1961.

Chain stores had moved aggressively into Lexington during the decade of the 1950's. In 1962 sixteen large chain supermarkets operated by four national companies were in Fayette County. Three of these companies offered trading stamps with the customers' purchases. These companies, however, had opened few stores in other counties in the territory and in several cases had closed the stores that they had had. Mr. Murray understood that one of these chains had a policy to operate only those stores that could gross $1,000,000 in sales annually. He felt that if this were true, the opportunity for independent members was great since a sales of $500,000 annually was considered a nice size store in his organization. He considered the opportunity in those counties with no chain outlet as being especially good. However, if a member store became especially successful and large, there was always the risk that it would seel out to a large chain. Two member stores in Lexington had already sold to different chain firms.

The management of Kentucky Food Stores did not make formal market surveys and did not use the statistics relating to market potentials other than the actual population figures. Until 1962 the cooperative group did not have a formal plan for expansion into those areas which appeared promising. Historically, new members had been obtained on the initiative of the independent grocery stores already in existence. Mr. Murray pointed out that a quick look at the map (Exhibit VI) would indicate that there were gaps in the territory. A number of independent groceries in the territory could be serviced efficiently if the cooperative decided to promote further expansion.

LABOR RELATIONS

Until 1961 Kentucky Food Stores had operated without a union. On August 1, 1961, the Brotherhood of Teamsters initiated an organizing campaign among the employees of the cooperative. In an election on September 1, the workers voted to accept the union as their bargaining agent by a count of 13–7. During October and November 1961, the union met with the management in an attempt to agree on a union contract. All issues were discussed and agreement reached on such matters as wages, hours, and benefits. The only troublesome issue involved the recognition by management of a union shop. At this point the management made it clear that it was quite willing to negotiate with the union on all other matters but that it did not believe that it should force all employees to join a union. On December 15, 1961, the union called a strike and stationed pickets outside the warehouse. Immediately the management requested the member groceries to cooperate with Kentucky Food Stores by providing their own transportation for their purchases. The office personnel, managers, and seven workers who did not strike continued filling orders in the warehouse. Immediately the management began to hire new personnel as permanent employees to help maintain operations. In less than a week a new labor force had been recruited; moreover extra workers were hired because of the relative inexperience of the new people. At the time Mr. Murray was preparing his recommendations, the union was continuing to picket the warehouse, but the basic operations of the firm continued. The management felt that it would be difficult to make any great changes in operations if the labor picture remained insecure. However, gradually it began to appear that operations could continue in spite of the union actions.

PLANS FOR THE FUTURE

The management of Kentucky Food Stores had for several years considered various possibilities for expanding its services to members. In 1961 it had expanded its lines of merchandise with the addition of the classification known as Health and Beauty Aids. The success of this addition was not certain by April 1962 although there were indications that it could be very successful. The reasons that the line had been added were: (1) the individual items were not large and therefore warehousing space could be made available in the existing location without significant overcrowding; (2) the customary markups of the items in the classification were large enough to provide promising opportunities for both the cooperative and the individual members; many members already were carrying these items in their groceries but were obtaining them from other sources.

The question of whether to add frozen foods to the line had been considered for several years. In fact, the addition to the warehouse had provided for the future purchase of frozen food equipment at a cost of $200,000. Mr.

Murray commented: "We will have to go into frozen foods some time but the question is—when?" Although the markup in handling frozen foods was favorable, several factors had prevented the management from actually taking the step. The chief uncertainty involved the efficiency with which the cooperative could deliver the items to its members. One cause of this uncertainty was the action by health authorities which threatened to require a refrigerated truck which would keep all deliveries at zero degree temperature. Some competitors who currently handled frozen foods were using insulated bags for delivery. If these bags were acceptable to the health authorities in the future, the management of Kentucky Food Stores felt that it could enter the frozen food business without further delay. The chief drawback of the use of a refrigerated truck was the inefficiency involved in delivering frozen foods to all outlying members. In areas around Lexington, there was no problem in operating refrigerated trucks as efficiently as competitors could. Yet according to the management's policy, if the service was to be offered to some members, the same service must be available to all members.

For several years the management had been seeking a satisfactory location in which to build an entirely new warehouse and to sell the present warehouse. This location could be outside the city as long as rail and highway facilities were adequate. The existing warehouse, $112' \times 380\frac{1}{2}'$, completely covered the present lot and thus could not be expanded further. It was well located so that a sale would not be difficult. The debt on the existing building had been reduced and thus financing would not be a serious problem. The decision to move, however, was interrelated with other plans for expansion and, therefore, depended on other actions by the members.

PLAN FOR SELECTED STANDARDIZED SUPERMARKETS

Mr. Murray had felt that the operations of the Kentucky Food Stores had made it possible for the independent grocery to remain in competition with the larger marketers by minimizing the costs of buying and warehousing. Although Kentucky Food Stores had previously concentrated on buying and warehousing, it appeared that in the future it might be advisable to develop a plan which would expand its activities into merchandising.

The plan would be to obtain an identifying name which would be used only by a carefully selected number of supermarkets placed in choice locations. New stores would be organized by Kentucky Food Stores and leased to independent owners. The location of the store, the layout of merchandise, the scale of operations, and other characteristics of the retail operation would be controlled by Kentucky Food Stores. The plan would necessitate the hiring of several specialists for meat operations, planning layout, etc. Kentucky Food Stores would thus provide technical advice to the independent owners. This extra service would be financed by payment of 1 percent of the retail sales of each store in the plan. The owners would be required to follow the general recommendations of the specialists hired by the cooperative and the super-markets would have standardized characteristics. One possible version of the plan might require that accounting records be kept in the main office of Kentucky Food Stores.

Under this plan the retail outlet would be owned and operated by an independent grocer who would receive merchandising help from Kentucky Food Stores. The main financial requirement of the member grocer would be sufficient capital to handle his inventory. The building would be built to specifications set by the cooperative. It would be owned by a third party and leased to Kentucky Food Stores. In this way the cooperative would be able to increase its sales without the necessity of owning additional real estate; yet it could control the use of the favorable locations and any goodwill which might be created.

New problems would develop as the result of placing this plan into effect. First, the expense of maintaining the merchandising specialists would necessarily be shouldered by the owners of the supermarkets operating under the plan. Second, the extra volume which would be generated by the plan would require the construction of a new warehouse. Third, the present members would not want to help create new retail competition which would adversely affect their existing groceries. Fourth, experiences with similar plans indicate that the relations between the independent owner and the specialists could be strained by the number of controls placed on the independent owner. In similar plans it has been found that the owners felt their independence was curtailed causing them to prefer to operate less efficiently but with more freedom.

OPINIONS OF INDIVIDUAL MEMBERS ABOUT THE FUTURE OF THE COOPERATIVE

In the cooperative association, the attitudes and opinions of individual members were considered to be very important. In fact, many of the members of Kentucky Food Stores felt that the degree of success of the organization depended directly upon the close relationships among its members.

In order to keep touch with members' opinions, the cooperative made considerable use of committees. Important committees included the Executive Committee, the Promotional Board, and Advertising Committee, and a Meat Committee. Each of these committees met weekly and maintained close contact with current operations.

The Board of Directors also met weekly. Although some members of the board lived at some distance from Lexington, attendance at the meetings was good. Topics for discussion ranged from basic policies of the cooperative to detailed questions about the immediate future.

The feeling among the members concerning the reasons for the continued life of Kentucky Food Stores centered around the buying power of the organization. One of the members summed up this advantage: "Before my affiliation with Kentucky Food Stores, I was employed by one of the large chain stores for several years. This work led me to realize that success in this field was almost entirely dependent upon the existence of a large buying organization. Kentucky Food Stores has provided the small independent with such an organization."

The members were conscious of problems facing the organization. One member, who had been affiliated with the cooperative from its inception, expressed the opinion that if the organization had begun merchandising had begun merchandising activities ten years sooner, the large chain organizations might have been discouraged from expanding in the area.

One member pointed out another problem: "Being a retailers' cooperative we place considerable emphasis upon the individual member's independence. I believe that another problem is that we are too independent." He explained that although Kentucky Food Stores was a cooperative organization, contact among members was too brief. Many of the member firms were located at considerable distance from other members with the result, he believed, that a continuous flow of communication among members was not maintained. This "excessive independence" was especially unfavorable to an effective merchandising program.

With respect to the new plan for standardized supermarkets, the attitudes of members appeared to be highly favorable. However, an interesting human factor appeared. A majority of existing members were confident of the possibilities of the new program for *other* members. Only a few felt that they might want to operate under the plan themselves. Different reasons were given for this paradox. One member stated that if he were younger, he would be interested. Another felt that some of the technical parts of the plans were not to his liking. Although no member mentioned the point explicitly, it appeared that the members were quite aware of the effect of the new plan on their independence in operating a store. The value placed on this independence appeared to be very high. The fact that any new system might improve operations did not mean that they would be willing to give up some of their independence in order to operate more efficienctly. They were quite sure, however, that others should be interested.

One member who planned to operate under the new plan, if adopted, expressed a high degree of optimism that he would be able to capture a substantial share of the market which was presently held by several chain stores. In supporting this view he pointed out: "Not only will we be able to compete with the chains on the basis of price, but we will also have a large advantage which the chains do not possess—the personal touch." He explained that large chains had long suffered from the disadvantage that they were "foreign" investments which did little to benefit the community. "Their disadvantage" he said, "will be our advantage."

4. E. W. WALTON COMPANY*

—SAMUEL A. POND

In November 1959 Mr. Robert E. Lowery was elected President of the E. W. Walton Company. Prior to his election he had been treasurer of the company for seven years, and prior to that assistant to the president for two years. He succeeded Mr. J. C. Hodges who had been president since 1916, and who died at the age of 73 in September 1959.

In June 1962 the board of directors of the company was agreed that the company should expand its operations. Consideration was being given to retaining a consulting firm, to conduct a study of the company's manufacturing facilities.

HISTORY OF THE COMPANY

The E. W. Walton Company was in the business of manufacturing, selling, installing, maintaining and repairing elevator systems. The headquarters and manufacturing facilities of the company were in St. Paul, Minnesota. Service centers were maintained in Milwaukee, Duluth, Rochester, and Minneapolis.

The company had been incorporated in 1906 by Mr. E. W. Walton and Mr. J. C. Hodges as two of the three incorporating stockholders. Financial difficulties resulted in a reorganization of the company in 1916 at which time Mr. Walton left the company and Mr. Hodges took over the management. During the years of Mr. Hodges' stewardship the company grew in size to a sales volume of almost $4 million in 1959 and made money in every year except three of the depression years in the 1930's. A nine-year financial summary is attached as Exhibit 1.

* Reprinted by permission of Professor Samuel A. Pond, Stanford University.

Exhibit 1

E. W. Walton Company

Nine-Year Financial Summary
Consolidated Statements

	1953	1954	1955	1956	1957	1958	1959	1960	1961
Balance Sheet									
Current assets	$1,039,308	$ 933,417	$ 958,750	$1,083,219	1,153,240	$1,240,209	$1,306,119	$1,195,822	$1,242,650
Current liabilities	355,290	254,093	251,608	332,222	356,977	350,279	351,070	269,761	320,525
Net working capital	$ 684,018	$ 679,324	$ 707,142	$ 750,997	$ 762,263	$ 889,930	$ 955,049	$ 926,061	$ 922,125
Prepaid and deferred items	47,343	63,344	69,383	86,197	72,457	85,239	67,694	69,587	89,483
Property (net)	273,684	280,813	286,347	285,168	305,598	284,556	284,132	241,863	236,224
Total stockholders equity	$,1005,045	$1,023,481	$1,062,872	$1,122,362	$1,174,318	$1,259,725	$1,306,275	$1,237,511	$1,247,832
Common stock equity per share	$ 358	$ 364	$ 378	$ 400	$ 418	$ 448	$ 465	$ 449	$ 455
Operating									
Net sales	$3,213,597	$2,849,590	$2,972,482	$3,265,535	$3,620,352	$3,728,283	$3,982,223	$4,005,878	$4,148,507
Cost of manufacturing	$2,183,175	$1,917,056	$2,031,333	$2,187,629	$2,458,578	$2,524,024	$2,707,377	$2,839,533	$2,840,378
Manufacturing expenses	351,909	349,982	362,612	398,404	436,667	421,736	487,745	544,246	459,486
Selling and administrative expenses	457,632	467,938	461,737	506,298	559,432	602,345	655,454	668,507	758,314
Provision for federal taxes	128,410	58,578	58,808	85,678	85,618	89,788	63,893	(22,213)	46,000
Total costs and expenses	$3,121,126	$2,793,554	$2,914,490	$3,178,009	$3,540,295	$3,637,893	$3,914,469	$4,030,073	$4,104,178
Net income	$ 92,471	$ 56,036	$ 57,992	$ 87,526	$ 80,057	$ 90,390	$ 67,754	$ (24,195)	$ 44,329
Cash dividends	28,100	28,100	28,100	28,038	28,100	28,100	28,100	27,870	27,325
Increase in earnings retained	$ 64,371	$ 27,936	$ 29,892	$ 59,488	$ 51,947	$ 62,290	$ 39,654	$ (52,065)	$ 17,004
Per share of common stock									
Net income	$ 32.80	$ 20.00	$ 20.20	$ 31.20	$ 28.50	$ 32.00	$ 24.00	$ (8.78)	$ 16.18
Dividends	$ 10.00	$ 10.00	$ 10.00	$ 10.00	$ 10.00	$ 10.00	$ 10.10	$ 10.10	$ 10.00

THE ELEVATOR INDUSTRY

Companies in the elevator industry usually manufactured components required for an elevator, installed elevators including the planning and engineering, and/or maintained and serviced elevators after their installation. Both hydraulic and electric power were used in the industry, the former for low rise (usually freight) elevators, and the latter for high rise[1] elevators.

Each elevator installation was a distinct and unique engineering problem. Since World War II intricate electronic control systems had been developed so that, as an example, elevators automatically responded to a preponderance of calls in a given direction. These control systems were in their most advanced state in the fast, well-coordinated banks of elevators in high rise hotels and office buildings.

There were many hundreds of companies in the industry throughout the United States. These ranged from small enterprises engaged in minor maintenance and servicing work to the fully integrated giants of the industry. Two companies fell in this latter category. They were the Otis Elevator Company and the Westinghouse Electric Corporation. Together these two companies accounted for over one-half of industry sales and most of the technological improvements.

Industry growth closely followed new construction. There were serious slumps during the two world wars and during the depression in the 1930's. Since 1945 the industry responded (1) to the unprecedented increase in building construction throughout the country, and (2) to expiration in 1945 of the Otis patents on control systems, which brought many new and smaller companies into the business.

The primary role of the E. W. Walton Company in the industry was that of a fully integrated *regional* manufacturer. A study made by the company in January 1961, indicated that in the year 1960 the company had 27.78% of the North Central market for electric elevators, 16.5% of the dumb-waiter market, and 3.24% of the hydraulic elevator market.

MANAGEMENT AND ORGANIZATION

On July 15, 1962, the officers and directors of the company were the following:

Name	Position	Age	Date of Employment	Date of Election as Officer Board Member
R. E. Lowery	President and Director	54	1950	1959 as President
W. J. Taylor	Vice President Engineering and Director	60	1921	1952 as Director
H. Jensen	Vice President Contract Sales and Director	57	1930	1953 as Director

[1] In the St. Paul area a high-rise elevator was usually defined as one serving a building 10 or more stories in height.

Name	Position	Age	Date of Employment	Date of Election as Officer Board Member
L. P. Herron	Vice President Resale and Director	65	1919	1955 as Director
T. N. Jones	Director (Co. attorney)	70	(not an employee)	1955 as Director
L. A. Ford	Treasurer	46	1960	1961 as Treasurer

An organization chart of management relationships within the company is attached as Exhibit 2.

Members of the board of directors held 46% of the outstanding common stock in approximately equal portions except Mr. Jones, who owned only one share so that he could be eligible for board membership. Two trusts, established under the wills of two early stockholders, held 31% of the common stock. The balance, or 23%, was held by 20 key employees. The company had an option to purchase the common stock from a terminating employee (or stock that was held by the estate of a deceased employee), at 56% of the book value. Such shares were then resold to deserving employees.

The common stock held by the two trusts was not voted in recent years. Since 1916 the management of the company had not been challenged by stockholder action.

OPERATIONS OF THE COMPANY

The manufacturing facilities of the company were concentrated in three buildings in St. Paul, Minnesota. The main plant was built in 1911. Adjacent to the factory was the office building that was built in 1929. The factory had a Mechanical Department which made elevator cars, machines, rails, governors and brakes. The Electrical Department made controllers, switches, floor selectors and accessories.

In July 1962 the plant had been working a 56-hour week for over two years. The cost of premium pay was averaging $30,000 to $40,000 a year.

The products manufactured were sold in three different ways:

1. By the Contract Sales Division whose function was to obtain contracts for the installation of elevators in new buildings.[2] This business was limited to the North-Central area. Sales were made by competitive bidding on jobs as they came to market. Contacts with architects were particularly important, as the architect frequently specified which elevator companies were to be permitted to bid. In the 17 months ending May 31, 1962, contract sales were $2,139,000, producing a net operating loss of $105,000.

2. By the Resale Division which sold elevator equipment f.o.b. St. Paul to

[2] Generally speaking the company confined its installation and modernization installations to low rise elevators, and did not attempt to compete with Otis and Westinghouse for the high rise business.

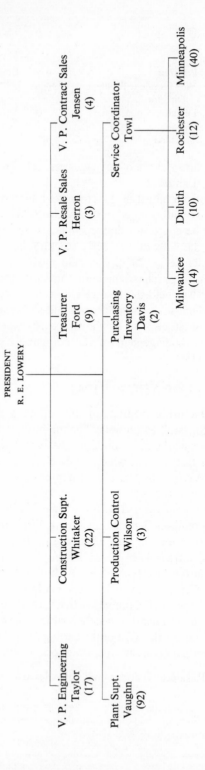

Exhibit 2

E. W. Walton Company

Management Organization Chart

PRESIDENT
R. E. LOWERY

V. P. Engineering
Taylor
(17)

Construction Supt.
Whitaker
(22)

Treasurer
Ford
(9)

V. P. Resale Sales
Herron
(3)

V. P. Contract Sales
Jensen
(4)

Plant Supt.
Vaughn
(92)

Production Control
Wilson
(3)

Purchasing
Inventory
Davis
(2)

Service Coordinator
Towl

Milwaukee
(14)

Duluth
(10)

Rochester
(12)

Minneapolis
(40)

194

independent elevator companies throughout the United States and Canada. The major part of this market was in the Middle West. Ninety per cent of the business came from less than 30 accounts out of a maximum of 250 to 300 customers on the books. Sales volume in the 17 months ending May 31, 1962, was $1,477,000, producing an operating profit of $34,000.

3. By the Service Division which modernized, repaired, and maintained elevator equipment through offices in Milwaukee, Duluth, Rochester and Minneapolis. Contracts ranged from full maintenance contracts (under which the company practiced preventive maintenance by early replacement of wearing parts as well as necessary repairs and service) to partial maintenance contracts, to inspection contracts only. Modernization of obsolete elevator equipment was a significant portion of this division's business. Sales volume totaled $2,274,000 in the 17 months ending May 31, 1962, producing an operating profit of $327,000. See Exhibit 3 for a somewhat different breakdown of income attributable to these service centers.

Exhibit 3
E. W. Walton Company

Income Summary

(IN THOUSANDS)

	1957	1958	1959	1960	1961
St. Paul*	(1)	36	(17)	(108)	(56)
Foundry**	—	(23)	(5)	(77)	—
Service	280	279	279	229	250
Operating profit	279	286	257	44	194
Employee bonus	99	100	121	74	95
Income tax	103	108	79	(22)	46
	202	208	200	(8)	53
Other income (expense)	3	12	11	(16)	(9)
Net profit	80	90	68	(24)	44

* "St. Paul" denotes company's total manufacturing operations in the St. Paul plant with appropriate assignment of corporate overhead.

** Foundry operations were discontinued in November 1960.

FINANCIAL SUMMARY

The company had been profitable in each of the past nine years except 1960. Earnings on stockholder equity, however, had decreased in this period from over 9% to 3.5% in 1961.

The working capital position in these years included cash running 15% to 20% of current assets, and a current ratio averaging in excess of 3:1. This liquidity had been the product of a modest dividend policy and a relatively constant property account. There had been no fixed indebtedness and bank borrowings were occasional and seasonal, not exceeding $200,000 in any one year.

COMMENTS OF MR. R. E. LOWERY, PRESIDENT

Mr. R. E. Lowery, President of the company, was a Northwestern graduate. Prior to joining the company in 1950 he had been associated with another company in auditing work. His views on his company and its problems were as follows:

You know, J. C. Hodges was quite a fellow. He ran this business—make no mistake about it. You couldn't argue with him. You couldn't even make a suggestion. The Board of Directors was just a rubber stamp for whatever he wanted to do.

He was a nut about details and figures—read every piece of mail that came in the office. I'll never forget how he took inventory when I first joined the company. He had the whole office force down here on Christmas Day pricing inventory by hand. He didn't trust calculators. He had the answer for all kinds of problems buried in old files in his desk. "Don't tell me how to run this business. I had the answer to this one 20 years ago."

He had a knack of picking good men and then keeping them with him. These are the same men that are with me now. We're lucky to have them. They're very able and competent and they keep the business going. But it was a shock to all of us when Mr. Hodges died. He was 73 and he hadn't been too well or active in the last few years but even so we did not expect it.

About six weeks after his death in 1959 the board elected me President. There was one other person here in the company who wanted the job. Mr. Hodges did not believe any of us could take over. That's why he kept on working.

It's been important since then to come to some reasonable re-evaluation of people's worth. We've made changes in personnel such as consolidating our Service Centers under Mr. Towl and bringing in a new plant superintendent. We've raised salaries a good deal. We still need to fix responsibility better and to get some decisions made *away* from this office. Things are different now. I'm not the whole answer to everything, but it's hard to change from a one-man shop.

Business is booming and has been for several years, but our net has been decreasing. Mr. Hodges was dead set against expansion especially in the years just before his death. He was afraid of another downturn like in the thirties. We could increase our business a good deal right now if we had the manufacturing facilities. As it is we're scheduling heavy overtime. It's pretty expensive.

Of course lack of space is just part of it. We could always lease 25,000 square feet of space close by. The question is what would we do with it. Our board couldn't agree on this. That's why we are considering using a consultant. They'll take a look at our manufacturing facilities including inventory handling and other matters in this area. We expect them to be a big help.

Our biggest decision was in 1960 when we closed down the foundry in Mankato. The equipment and buildings were old and labor costs were twice what they should have been. A new superintendent we brought in did not work out. We ran in the red over $50,000 in 1960 alone. The only question was whether we could buy the kind of castings we needed here in our St. Paul plant. As soon as we found this out we decided we belonged in the elevator, not the foundry, business.

When I first became President I felt I was a referee. Now it's different. Now I spend my time looking for ideas, trying to evaluate and act upon the good ones. Morale and enthusiasm are important. An insurance company has been trying to sell me an annuity program which would be cheaper if long years of past service were not counted. That's insane. The old timers are responsible for this company. The leading architects and contractors in this area know all our people and have faith in them. That's why we're successful.

COMMENTS OF MR. H. JENSEN, VICE-PRESIDENT, CONTRACT SALES DIVISION

Mr. H. Jensen, Vice-President Contract Sales, was a Minnesota graduate who had joined the company in 1930. He had been in charge of contract sales since 1952, and a director since 1953.

I don't know why it was but J. C. Hodges never paid much attention to contract sales. He left me alone which was a good thing because you couldn't suggest anything to him. Well, you might suggest something once but never twice. Hodges was a master psychologist. He handled each of us differently. Just when you'd get thoroughly disgusted and ready to quit he'd say or do some little thing that set you up.

Hodges, of course, picked Lowery to be President long before his death. Now the board operates just the way it did before he died. That's one of our big troubles. In my opinion the board doesn't live up to its responsibilities as a Board of Directors. What's worse, they're not sure what these responsibilities are.

Right now we're hemmed in by our limited production facilities. Any increment is an overtime increment. I keep saying we should go to a second shift but no one wants to act on this. I can only assume there are good reasons for not doing so.

I realize our contract sales business is losing money. That's always been the case. On the other hand you can't operate a repair and service business unless you manufacture as well. Ninety per cent of our service contracts came to us because we made the original installation, and then the customer contracted with us for service in the future.

The way for this company to expand is by increasing our resale business. We could do this overnight just by sending out a flyer. We're in the middle of the biggest building boom the country has ever known, and we're not taking advantage of it.

I suggested to Mr. Lowery he ought to hire a consultant. I don't know exactly what they ought to do but I know what we need around here. That's a few facts on which to make a decision.

COMMENTS OF MR. L. P. HERRON, VICE-PRESIDENT, RESALE DIVISION

Mr. L. P. Herron, Vice-President, Resale Division, joined the company as a stenographer in 1919, and has been a vice-president for the past eight years.

The best way to expand our business is to expand the number of our Service Centers. This is hard to do because it's awfully tough to support a salesman who is trying to drum up service business in a new area. What we should do is buy out existing businesses and build on this as a base.

The Resale business could be expanded easily. Right now we just take business as it comes our way. Our salesmen go out on the road only when there's a call for them. The contract business gets the call on our manufacturing capacity so we can't push too hard.

One of our difficulties in the past has been the lack of a design engineering group. For instance some years ago we redesigned our signals and operating fixtures and these subsequently became our biggest quantity item. Somehow or other our design engineers always get swallowed up in production engineering so that we don't have the product development we should have.

Of course our real bottleneck is the availability of space. We'd be a long way ahead with more room.

COMMENTS OF MR. W. J. TAYLOR, VICE-PRESIDENT AND CHIEF ENGINEER

Mr. W. J. Taylor, Vice-President and Chief Engineer, had a night school engineering degree and joined the company in 1921.

The big change in this business is that our product is getting more complicated. This is particularly true in electronic controls where we've done most of our design work. Controls and relays that go with them seem to be getting smaller all the time.

We're getting into other areas as well. We've just designed new pumping units for a small hydraulic elevator. Last year we installed our first gearless elevator at Minnesota. This last was a big project for us and technically difficult. J. C. Hodges would have no part of a gearless machine but we think it means new business that we're now technically ready to handle.

COMMENTS OF MR. L. A. FORD, TREASURER

Mr. L. A. Ford joined the company in 1960 as Controller. He graduated from the University of Chicago Graduate Business School in 1939.

My view is that Mr. Lowery's big job is to draw people out so that they will accept responsibility. I never knew Mr. Hodges but it's my understanding that everybody was used to getting answers from him. Mr. Lowery does not have the same detailed intimate knowledge of the business so he depends much more on all of us.

It's very difficult to bring about change in an employee-owned company. As an example we would like our Purchasing Agent, Mr. Jim Davis, to analyze make-or-buy situations more systematically. Mr. Davis looks upon his job primarily as one involving purchasing and inventory control. He has been on the job since 1935, before that was a caddy for Mr. Hodges and is now one of the major stockholders in the company.

We don't know our costs at all accurately. Everybody is figuring like mad but the information that we have is inadequate for control purposes. We are just now starting to revise our procedures to collect information around profit centers.

COMMENTS OF MR. S. C. REAGEN,
MANAGER (MINNEAPOLIS) SERVICE CENTER

Mr. S. C. Reagen was manager of the Minneapolis Service Center, having been transferred from the Rochester Service Center two years ago.

Our volume here in Minneapolis is in excess of $1 million a year. Our backlog right now is $320,000 compared to $80,000 in January 1962.

I have made some changes since I took over here in Minneapolis. I believe we've got to be competitive in bidding on modernizing jobs even though we have to trim our margins. Modernizing an old elevator system can be a big expensive proposition involving our most modern controls. When the job is over, and we have a satisfied customer, we can sign him up for a service contract and make our money later.

Just think of the buildings just in Minneapolis that will have to modernize their elevators if they want to compete with new buildings in renting space. This is where our market potential lies, and we're not, at this point, doing any more than taking the business that comes in the door.

Mr. Hodges had no direct experience (or even interest) in the Service Business. Since Mr. Lowery brought me here to Minneapolis, I've had more latitude in getting and pricing jobs than in my 20 previous years with the company. My problem is getting delivery date committments from the St. Paul factory. Our production facilities are so tied up that I have to be very careful only to bid on a job where I have a reasonable chance of delivery.

COMMENTS OF MR. DONALD TUCKER,
MANAGEMENT CONSULTANT

We are very pleased at the prospect of working with the E. W. Walton Company, and believe we can be of some help to them.

Their product is well thought of in the Middle West. The elevators here in our own building were installed by Walton.

When Mr. Lowery first talked to us it was in terms of an inventory control and schedule job. This concept has been broadened so that we would now like to study facility planning in all of its phases.

My preliminary opinion is that Walton is fabricating a good many items which they would be better off to buy. Production scheduling needs to be improved as well so that their delivery schedules can be met more promptly. Inventory and manufacturing cost controls should provide more refined cost allocations. In other words, there are a number of things that need study if we are to make recommendations for an expansion in production.

$$*\qquad*\qquad*$$

On June 29, 1962, the management consultant made a formal proposal to Mr. R. E. Lowery, "To meet the goal of a facility with greater production capacity." A copy of this proposal is attached as Exhibit 4.

Exhibit 4

E. W. Walton Company

June 29, 1962

Mr. R. E. Lowery, President
E. W. Walton Company
220 Swarthmore Avenue
St. Paul, Minnesota

1–3111

Dear Mr. Lowery:

We are pleased to submit this proposal for providing assistance in your facilities planning, as discussed in the meeting with you and Messrs. Donald Tucker and John L. Trillich of our firm, on June 21, 1962. As a result of this meeting, as well as previous contacts with you and your associates, we feel confident that we have a clear understanding of your problems and can provide the assistance you desire.

As we understand the situation, you feel that one of the major obstacles to increasing production capacity to meet current and anticipated demand is the lack of sufficient manufacturing space. At present, you are considering the possibility of moving out of the present Swarthmore Avenue plant and relocating to a better facility. There are, of course, many inter-related factors affecting a decision of this magnitude, such as the possibility of major renovation to the present plant, consolidating manufacturing and service operations, site location, methods of financing, building and departmental layout, and many other aspects. Never having faced this situation before, you feel that it would be advantageous to seek outside assistance and guidance in the over-all program and in evaluating the various alternative means to meet the goal of a facility with greater production capacity.

Our firm has on its staff a number of specialists who have conducted studies which were closely related to the problems you now face. Our projects in this area have ranged from general assistance to a client involved in expansion problems, such as yours, to a single specific detailed aspect such as the site selection or the financial planning.

Proposed Approach We propose to approach the problem of facilities planning for E. W. Walton Company through a series of inter-related steps, as follows:

1. Determine, through observations and discussions with key management personnel, present operating methods and procedures, particularly as they relate to space and facilities. Where applicable, we will make recommendations for changes. Specific areas for study will include:

a. Material and product flow
b. Scheduling and inventory control
c. Purchasing and make-or-buy
d. Fabrication and assembly

2. Establish the criteria for an improved manufacturing facility. These criteria would involve consideration of

a. Operations to be performed, both immediately and in the future.

b. Capacity requirements, in terms of quantity, size of units, methods of operation, and possible new products.

c. Site location in terms of accessibility by employees, need for proximity to suppliers and/or customers, and other considerations.

d. Special features (e.g. high-bay, crane-ways).

3. Having established and mutually agreed upon the criteria for a new facility, evaluate various alternatives. In addition to a careful evaluation of your present facility in terms of its potential to meet the criteria we will consider the economic feasibility of leasing an existing facility, purchasing an existing plant, and building a new plant.

4. Advise on the financial and cost aspects of a possible relocation including such factors as:

a. Economic justification for moving production operations.

b. Possible consolidations with service and other company activities.

c. Available financing alternatives including lease-back, use of Minnesota Development Corporation, and the more usual methods of bank financing.

5. Assist in selecting industrial realtors and work with realtors in determining areas for potential location, establishing criteria for building evaluation, evaluating specific facilities in terms of E. W. Walton's requirements, and generally assisting in the selection of a new facility. If you so desire, we can conduct a search for and evaluation of facilities without disclosing your company name.

6. Assist in laying out production and other facilities, recommend modifications to the selected facility, and advise on the many aspects on the implementation of a move.

As we have indicated above, we will be working closely with you and your associates throughout the course of this project. We will give you periodic informal reports at appropriate times and, as they are developed, we will submit to you various diagrams, sketches, and layout drawings. At the conclusion of our work we will submit an informal written report summarizing our findings, conclusions, and recommendations.

Very truly yours,
Authorized Contracting Officer

PART III

BUSINESS POLICIES:
CONTROLS FOR STRATEGIC DECISIONS

* *

INTRODUCTION

* *

"Business Policy" is the most widely used title for the final integrative, capstone case analysis course in the business core curriculum. Its objectives have been extensively treated in prior chapters. While many analytical methodologies, both structured and unstructured, have been used to achieve some of the course objectives, in only one instance has the policy objective been systematically approached.[1] Since the course has been assigned the explicit title of Business Policy, it would appear consistent that development of the ability to discern policy issues, and to formulate and administer policies in the analysis of business problems, should, by definition, be its primary objective. Unfortunately, this objective has neither been explicitly sought in most existing approaches nor developed in any organized or systematic fashion. It is the intent of this chapter to define the framework of policy issues in comprehensive business case problems, to provide reference materials for the strategic decision-policy areas of business operation, and to examine a systematic approach to their analysis.

Business policies provide control guides for decision making. They insure a minimum level of consistency and uniformity in making decisions affecting basic or strategic company practices. They are specifically applied to business problems that recur frequently, and under similar but not identical circumstances. Policies also provide control limits or guides which minimize the risks of delegated decisions. As such, they facilitate the delegation of decision making to the lowest possible level in the organization, where time requirements force decision making at the point of action.

Without policy controls and guides, lower level management decisions are subject to the risks of inadequate experience, skills, and knowledge, and decision making inconsistent and incompatible with basic company practices.

[1] Newman, William H., and Logan, James P., *Business Policies and Central Management*, fifth edition (Cincinnati: South-Western Publishing Company, 1965).

These practices relate particularly to those activities of the company that constitute its major comparative-competitive advantages. The mix of advantages or utilities that cause market segments to purchase from particular companies must meet minimum levels of consistency and uniformity. If the product line, price, quality, service, etc., fluctuate in their level of performance, market segment customers will seek other firms where their preferred mix of utilities can be depended upon. As the British say, "it is their custom" to patronize particular firms, as long as consistency and dependability are provided in basic strategic company practices. In short, they insure the competitive success and therefore survival of the company.

Policies provide control limits and guides that insure the optimum achievement of the range and hierarchy of company objectives. They provide for the implementation and preservation of long range strategies of the company. They are primarily a planning tool of management in resolving problems that recur under similar conditions. This similarity requires that these decisions approach a "standard practice" of the firm, and yet provide flexibility for decision making under changing circumstances, while optimizing decisions by maintaining minimum levels of consistency.

POLICIES AND STRATEGIES

Policy control guides are particularly applied to the strategic decisions of the firm, those that constitute the array of comparative-competitive advantages which thereby become the "basic practices" of the company. Competitive survival, success, and growth require a number of strategically successful practices, for the long and short run, which are pervasive to all company and department functions. These practices, to be continuously successful, must meet minimum levels of consistency and uniformity, and policy control guides are provided to insure that delegated decisions contribute to continued competitive success. Therefore an array of strategies become more readily identified in the array of business and departmental policies used for the control of these delegated "strategic decisions."

The nature of company strategies is discussed in Reading No. 1 in this part, "How to Evaluate Corporate Strategy." The evaluation criteria include, first, the test of internal consistency, and, second, consistency with the external environment in which the firm operates and competes with other firms. Other criteria of acceptable risk, timing, and workability provide pragmatic tests for evaluating the potential success of strategy decisions.

The interrelationship of goals, strategies, and policies further indicate the interdepartmental nature of policies. The best view of company goals and strategies is found in a study of its policies. Policies portray the relative importance of the goals-mix of an organization, and provide for optimizing them through consistent and compatible controls over strategic decisions.

Just as policies are a subfunction of company goals and strategies, they are also guides for the use of other types of plans, such as procedures and rules.

When problems recur under identical circumstances in a highly repetitious manner, standard operating procedures are developed to provide a "one best way" for their resolution. These procedures in turn serve to achieve policy, strategy, and organization goals. Therefore a comprehensive set of business policies facilitates the development of standard operating procedures, and also internal checks and balances against obsolete, overlapping, and superfluous procedures.

POLICY CONTROLS FOR DELEGATED DECISIONS

Policies facilitate the formulation of a management-organization policy of "delegation." Without policy controls, extensive delegation of decision-making authority would be impossible because of the risks of inconsistant decisions, especially those with legal ramifications. Before the price fixing scandal in the heavy electrical equipment industry recently, corporate policies controlling prices existed in only a small fraction of the firms in the industry. After the court sentences and fines were meted out, the overwhelming majority of firms had established and written policies recommended by their legal counsels.

The importance of policies is sometimes overlooked when we realize that the majority of small and medium size firms have developed only incomplete, if any, policy statements, expecially in written form. This apparent contradiction of actuality and theory is purely illusory. A variety of "standard practices" is found in all of these firms. They are by necessity meeting minimum levels of consistency and uniformity in their basic company practices, and if they were to change their location, product line, price, quality, etc., their customers would most probably discontinue their "custom" of patronizing them. In every purchase made, basic buying motives and utilities are satisfied. If these utilities start to fluctuate and change, it is not likely that customers will continue to buy from the same firms.

An understanding of business policies is important to all managerial jobs at all levels in the organization. While the formulation and administration of policies is a function of higher level management, their application and ramifications are found especially at lower levels. The Business Policy student benefits by learning how to use policy guides in his future employment, and from studying policy ramifications and problems as they apply throughout the firm. In subsequent policy cases attention will be given to both the policy administrator, and the values and problems of utilizing the policy control guides by all operating managers.

MANAGEMENT DECISION VERSUS OPERATING POLICIES

The descriptions of business policies to this point have emphasized their nature as control guides over delegated decisions. In their application to repetitious problems under similar conditions, they provide the flexibility required for true managerial discretion in making decisions versus application of particular procedures or rules. Since this delegation of decision-making discretion and authority is an imperative for all growing business organizations, when the discretion is taken away via the use of procedures and rules for decision making, business *management* policies no longer exist.

In spite of the requirements of management decision policies, we find innumerable so-called business policies providing controls over basic company practices. Unfortunately, many of these basic company practices require precise controls of "standard operating procedures" and rules. As major strategic decision areas, they become identified as basic business policies in the lexicon of the businessman. But the final test of business policy controls, as distinguished from other types of management planning and decision guides and controls, is the maintenance of an area of discretion within which the individual manager exercises his decision-making authority.

This semantic problem of management versus operating policies becomes more than an academic one if the full benefits of policy control guides for delegated decisions is to be achieved. But in the analysis of business policy cases, the dual classification of policies must be applied in order to avoid the stalemate of this semantical trap.

POLICIES AND THE TOTAL IMAGE

An overview of policy benefits is provided in Reading No. 2, "Written Policies Help 9 Ways." Consistency and continuity, delegation and coordinated teamwork, training and good human relations are primary among these benefits. While some arguments are presented against putting policies in writing, the benefits of clear cut, consistently applied policy controls more than offset the minor problems arising from their implementation in written form.

The accumulated value of company policies is seen in the personality, character, and philosophy—or image—of the organization. For the most part, these important "images" of the company are the result of the composite of all company policies, the basic standard practices by which the company is known as a whole. Here we see that the whole is greater than the sum of its parts. While particular functional and management-organization policies may well constitute the major comparative-competitive advantages or strategic decisions for the company, the totality of all policies provides a "company image" with an impact that most often supersedes particular company practices. For this reason the public relations function in the organization has assumed increasing importance in recent years. This function integrates and synthesizes all corporate policies and practices into a complementary whole. More and more purchases and decisions affecting the selection of firms by buyers are made because of the impact of the "total image" of that firm. And again, this "total image" is for the most part the personality and character of the firm, as manifested in its basic company practices, ideally spelled out in written policy form.

HIERARCHICAL SEQUENCE OF POLICIES

Just as the annual planning decision sequence determines an ideal system for auditing management decisions, policies should also be hierarchically structured. Following such a structure provides additional benefits for policy formulation and review. As a result, policies have priorities assigned in the decision sequence, and thereby prevent sub-optimization of policies formulated at lower hierarchial levels.

The hierarchy of policies starts with their formulation by the board of directors. The functions and duties of the board emphasize long range and over-all objectives, and their relative priority to the firm. Long range strategies are then formulated to match the skills and resources of the firm with particular market segments, and optimized against strategies of other firms in the industry. Policy formulation is next, and actually one of the most pervasive functions of the board. Long range, companywide, and strategic operating policies fall within the responsibility of the board. These policies are sometimes reserved for executive or policy committees that in most instances include members of the boards among their membership.

Externally imposed policies receive high priorities to avoid the formulation of contrary or contradictory policies. Federal, state, and local legislation and regulations provide constraints on internal policies. The external environment is composed of an ever-increasing number of interest and pressure groups whose influence on internal business operations and policies requires policy adaptation, if not outright formulation. Labor unions, for example, make and break company policies in the collective bargaining process. Increasing needs and demands from the community influence the formulation and change of business policies affecting business financial contributions, participation in civic affairs, political activities, industrial development programs, etc. Last, but not least, the customer is the prime external environmental influence on the structure and composite of company policies. Public relations policies, therefore, are formulated or approved by the board, particularly insofar as they represent the companywide image, or composite of strategic company decisions and policies.

MARKETING POLICIES

With the customer as the prime " public," the second step in policy formulation is the marketing function. In this function or department of the company is found the second largest number of policy statements. Customer market segments are identified and protected with policy controls, insuring that the variety of marketing activities optimize the achievement of marketing goals, without serious inconsistencies in decision making at the lower organizational levels.The panorama of marketing policies is examined in Reading No. 3, " The Concept of the Marketing Mix." The elements of the marketing mix start with the product line policy, followed by policy decisions that parallel the basic marketing functions. The market forces bearing on the marketing mix are identified as customer buying behavior, trade or middlemen behavior, competitor or industry position, and governmental controls. Basic marketing strategy and policy decisions are then reconciled or optimized both within the firm and the department, and with the important environmental influences and constraints. The element of strategy becomes increasingly important because of the varieties of individual and group behavior involved, and the dynamic element of change.

The hierarchical sequence of policy making applies to departmental policies as well as to the company as a whole. Market segment potentials are usually forecast, and then matched with product lines and product mixes. The matching process applies particularly to quality, price, service, advertising, and sales promotion policies. Consistency, not only within but also between policies, is a function of the process. Quality and price policies must be compatible and, in fact, particular departmental policies become integral and complementary parts of overall departmental policies. The extensive variety and interrelationships of these marketing policies and their dynamic environmental behavior are also treated in detail in Reading No. 3.

PRODUCTION POLICIES

Following the formulation of marketing policies, consideration for achieving the customer and marketing goals must be translated into production or operations goals and policies. Repetitive questions of make or buy, facilities and equipment growth rates, capacity utilization and economic lot quantity production runs, inventory levels, purchasing and subcontracting trends, and range or diversification or productive capacity are only a few of the decisions guided and controlled by production policies. In Reading No. 4, "Production Policy," a variety of production management and operating policy issues are discussed. It should be noted that in this function-department a greater number of operating policy decisions are found than for the managerial types with subsequent discretion for decision making. Systems, standard operating procedures, and rules provide the majority of decision controls here. But coordination must be achieved with policies of other departments, and for the company as a whole.

PERSONNEL POLICIES

The largest number of policy statements in most organizations apply to the personnel function. This is occasioned by the emphasis on consistency and uniformity in the formulation and administration of policies affecting employee relations. This is a simple but explosive question of fairness and equity in resolving those recurring personnel problems under similar, but rarely identical circumstances. Company policies can and will change, but most often they maintain a high level of consistency. Recruitment policies for some companies emphasize the hiring of relatives and friends. Contrarily, more firms follow the policy of *not* hiring relatives to avoid internal cliques and nepotism problems. Questions concerning the use of tests, interviews, training, appraisal, wages, and salaries require uniform answers and practices. The range of employee benefits and services is a function of company personnel policy, or should be, at least. Labor-management relationships in the collective bargaining process reflect the company philosophy, attitude, and policies governing these relationships. A detailed picture of the extensive number of personnel policies is provided in Reading No. 5, "Personnel Practices in Factory and Office: Manufacturing." The 174 personnel problem topics affecting factory and office workers require personnel policy formulation to avoid perennial grievances resulting from apparent, if not real, inconsistencies in the resolution of these recurring problems. A detailed view of the differing policies applied to these 174 decision areas is provided in the 1964 National Industrial Conference Board Studies in Personnel Policy, No. 194, from which these 174 topics have been abstracted.

The personnel policy formulation process also has a hierarchical and sequential order. Personnel manning tables provide for the calculation of personnel needs by types and numbers in order to meet production schedules, marketing programs, and service or facilitating departments in the organization. These numbers and types in turn influence recruitment, selection, orientation, induction, training, wage and salary and other policies. The "other" policies, in this instance, could include the full range of 174 policy practices outlined in Reading No. 5.

Personnel policies both affect and are affected by other company and management policies. Leadership philosophies, communication and motivation practices, and the whole tone of management direction functions reflect the composite of personnel policies in the firm. To the extent they do not reflect them, the grievance machinery is sure to receive overtime use.

FINANCE-ACCOUNTING POLICIES

Once the management planning and policy making functions have been applied to the marketing, production, and organizational-personnel problems, their implementation and control still require activation by financial resources and policies, and also by accounting systems, policies, and procedures controls. Recurring decisions must be controlled for questions of long term sources of funds, financing growth from profits, dividend amounts and stability, owning versus leasing facilities and equipment, credit extension, etc. An analysis of these policies is presented in Reading No. 6, "Financial Policies." Policy decision criteria for types of funds required, for differing sources and institutions from which they may be acquired, criteria used by the sources in approving requests for funds, and the general application of solvency criteria to the different types of capital required and used by the firm are examined. The policy criteria treated in this article are extremely important in case analyses for eliminating naïve recommendations for the indiscriminate request of funds from inappropriate sources, or by firms without the requirements of these sources of capital.

Once financial goals and strategies are controlled with a network of policies, the question of standardizing financial practices in detail is provided for by accounting systems, procedures, and a set of policy standards that apply to the performance of this function. In Article No. 7, "Riding Herd on Accounting Standards," the problem of uniformity in the compilation of financial data by "issuing" organizations and the "users" of this data for control decisions is examined. Problems of standardized measurements are involved in meeting the needs of many groups such as the owners, creditors, labor unions, department managers, and the many levels and branches of government. Therefore rather precise minimum levels of consistency and standardization are required for these decisions.

While it is true that production and accounting functions lend themselves to the most extensive use of systems and procedures for the "one best way" resolution of their recurring problems, policy questions are also found. The standardization sought and achieved must also remain flexible and adaptable to change. The impact of change, coming from both external and internal dynamics, affects accounting policy questions, and changes in policies in other functional activities in the company also affect them.

POLICY INTERDEPENDENCY

One of the most distinguishing characteristics of policy control guides is their interdependency. Marketing product line, quality, price, promotion, and distribution policies must not only be compatible with, but also affect and help determine one another. If a particular product line and mix is predetermined and correlated with a matching market segment potential, concomitantly the quality, price, etc., must "fit" these predetermined policy goals. Also, if any one of these policies is changed significantly, the other policy goals must also be changed accordingly, or be defeated in their achievement. This interdependency applies also between functional policies. Accounting control policies must serve the prior needs of finance, personnel, production, and marketing policies and goals. The accounting data must meet consistency standards that enable the achievement of product pricing, especially insofar as production and personnel "stabilization policies" seek sustained employment levels and economic-lot-size production runs. Financial policies affecting dividends and re-investment for financing growth will limit or enhance organizational planning policies providing for management development and succession.

The interdependency of company policies requires that this function be performed at the highest level in the organization in order that interdepartmental ramifications can be projected for new policy formulation, and for policy changes within each department. This also requires that all policy guides be integrated into a composite that optimizes the policy function for the organization as a whole. This integrative function is therefore the essential characteristic that makes the study of "business policy" problems ideal for the final integrative capstone course in the business school curriculum.

POLICY UTILIZATION

Once again the twofold aspect of the policy administrator and the affected decision makers are emphasized. Every manager tends to find many of his departmental decisions have ramifications outside his department. Delegated decisions must first be made within the limits of policy controls, especially for those strategic decisions basic to company success. Secondly, these decisions must be consistent and compatible with strategic-policy decisions of other departments. Inconsistency in decision making in either case may seriously affect company success, and in the process set precedents for future decisions that cannot be tolerated. It is often said that there is no such thing as a decision that is an exception to a policy control guide, that in fact the exception constitutes a precedent that becomes a modification or change of the policy. This is particularly true for decisions in handling personnel relations problems, and also for marketing policy decisions where the possibility exists that the "exception" may become known and requested by other customers. Therefore policy issues are at least of equal importance to the individual managerial decision maker at all levels in the organization as to the policy formulator and administrator at the top.

Because of the inherent interdepartmental and integrative nature of business policies, emphasis on the discernment and analysis of policy issues as the major objective of the course is readily understood. Since this objective is only incidentally considered in the structuring of materials and methods in all but one business policy approach to date, the following readings on policy issues are provided to fill this void. Study of the many policy issues should therefore provide for the achievement of the following objectives:

1. the ability to distinguish policy issues from goals, strategies, and procedures problems.

2. a comprehensive review of policy issues for all functional activities in the company.

3. a study of policies in the hierarchical sequence in which they should be considered in their formulation and change.

4. the development of an appreciation for the interdepartmental and integrative nature of policy decisions—the function of this integrative nature preventing indiscriminate changes in departmental policies contrary to the minimum levels of uniformity and consistency required in basic company practices.

STRATEGY-POLICY TYPES

* *

HOW TO EVALUATE CORPORATE STRATEGY*

—SEYMOUR TILLES

No good military officer would undertake even a small-scale attack on a limited objective without a clear concept of his strategy. No seasoned politician would undertake a campaign for a major office without an equally clear concept of his strategy. In the field of business management, however, we frequently find men deploying resources on a large scale without any clear notion of what their strategy is. And yet a company's strategy is a vital ingredient in determining its future. A valid strategy will yield growth, profit, or whatever other objectives the managers have established. An inappropriate strategy not only will fail to yield benefits, but also may result in disaster.

In this article I will try to demonstrate the truth of these contentions by examining the experiences of a number of companies. I shall discuss what strategy is, how it can be evaluated, and how, by evaluating its strategy, a management can do much to assure the future of the enterprise.

DECISIVE IMPACT

The influence of strategy can be seen in every age and in every area of industry. Here are some examples:

• From the time it was started in 1911 as the Computing-Tabulating-Recording Co., International Business Machines Corporation has demonstrated the significance of a soundly conceived strategy. Seeing itself in the data-system business at a time when most manufacturers were still preoccupied with individual pieces of equipment, IBM developed a set of policies which resulted in its dominating the office equipment industry.

• By contrast, Packard in the 1930's was to the automobile industry everything that IBM is today to the office machine industry. In 1937, it sold over 109,000 cars,

* From the *Harvard Business Review*, July–August, 1963, pp. 111–121. Reprinted by permission of the publisher.

compared with about 11,000 for Cadillac. By 1954 it had disappeared as an independent producer.

Strategy is, of course, not the only factor determining a company's success or failure. The competence of its managerial leadership is significant as well. Luck can be a factor, too (although often what people call good luck is really the product of good strategy). But a valid strategy can gain extraordinary results for the company whose general level of competence is only average. And, conversely, the most inspiring leaders who are locked into an inappropriate strategy will have to exert their full competence and energy merely in order to keep from losing ground.

When Hannibal inflicted the humiliating defeat on the Roman army at Cannac in 216 B.C., he led a ragged band against soldiers who were in possession of superior arms, better training, and competent " noncoms." His strategy, however, was so superior that all of those advantages proved to be relatively insignificant. Similarly, when Jacob Borowsky made Lestoil the hottest-selling detergent in New England some years ago, he was performing a similar feat—relying on strategy to battle competition with superior resources.

Strategy is important not only for aspiring Davids who need an offensive device to combat corporate Goliaths. It is significant also for the large organization faced with a wide range of choice in domestic and international operations. For instance, the following corporations are all in the midst of strategic changes, the implications of which are worldwide in scope:

• Massey-Ferguson, Ltd., with 26 factories located around the world, and vying for leadership in the farm-equipment industry.

• General Electric Company and Westinghouse Electric Corporation, the giant producers of electrical equipment who are recasting their competitive policies.

• Singer Sewing Machine Company, trying to make its vast assets yield a greater return.

DYNAMIC CONCEPT

A strategy is a set of goals and major policies. The definition is as simple as that. But while the notion of a strategy is extremely easy to grasp, working out an agreed-upon statement for a given company can be a fundamental contribution to the organization's future success.

In order to develop such a statement, managers must be able to identify precisely what is meant by a goal and what is meant by a major policy. Otherwise, the process of strategy determination may degenerate into what it so often becomes—the solemn recording of platitudes, useless for either the clarification of direction or the achievement of consensus.

IDENTIFYING GOALS

Corporate goals are an indication of what the company as a whole is trying to *achieve* and to *become*. Both parts—the achieving and the becoming—are important for a full understanding of what a company hopes to attain. For example:

• Under the leadership of Alfred Sloan, General Motors achieved a considerable degree of external success; this was accomplished because Sloan worked out a pattern for the kind of company he wanted it to be internally.

• Similarly, the remarkable record of Du Pont in the twentieth century and the growth of Sears, Roebuck under Julius Rosenwald were as much a tribute to their modified structure as to their external strategy.[1]

Achieving. In order to state what a company expects to achieve, it is improtant to state what it hopes to do with respect to its environment. For instance:

Ernest Breech, chairman of the borad of the Ford Motor Company, said that the strategy formulated by his company in 1946 was based on a desire to "hold our own in what we foresaw would be a rich but hotly competitive market."[2] The view of the environment implicit in this statement is unmistakable: an expanding over-all demand, increasing competition, and emphasis on market share as a measure of performance against competitors.

Clearly, a statement of what a company hopes to achieve may be much more varied and complex than can be contained in a single sentence. This will be especially true for those managers who are sophisticated enough to perceive that a company operates in more external "systems" than the market. The firm is part not only of a market but also of an industry, the community, the economy, and other systems. In each case there are unique relationships to observe (e.g., with competitors, municipal leaders, Congress, and so on). A more complete discussion of this point is contained in a previous HBR article.[3]

Becoming. If you ask young men what they want to accomplish by the time they are 40, the answers you get fall into two distinct categories. There are those—the great majority—who will respond in terms of what they want to *have*. This is especially true of graduate students of business administration. There are some men, however, who will answer in terms of the kind of men they hope to *be*. These are the only ones who have a clear idea of where they are going.

The same is true of companies. For far too many companies, what little thinking goes on about the future is done primarily in money terms. There is nothing wrong with financial planning. Most companies should do more of it. But there is a basic fallacy in confusing a financial plan with thinking about the kind of company you want yours to become. It is like saying, "When

---

[1] For an interesting discussion of this relationship, see A. D. Chandler, Jr., *Strategy and Structure* (Cambridge, Massachusetts Institute of Technology Press, 1962), pp. 1–17.

[2] See Edward C. Bursk and Dan H. Fenn, Jr., *Planning the Future Strategy of Your Business* (New York: McGraw-Hill Book Company, Inc., 1956), p. 8.

[3] Seymour Tilles, "The Manager's Job—A System Approach," HBR January–February 1963, p. 73.

I'm 40, I'm going to be *rich*." It leaves too many basic questions unanswered. Rich in what way? Rich doing what?

The other major fallacy in stating what you want to become is to say it only in terms of a product. The number of companies who have got themselves into trouble by falling in love with a particular product is distressingly great.[4] Perhaps the saddest examples are those giants of American industry who defined their future in terms of continuing to be the major suppliers of steam locomotives to the nation's railroads. In fact, these companies were so wedded to this concept of their future that they formed a cartel in order to keep General Motors out of the steam locomotive business. When the diesel locomotive proved its superiority to steam, these companies all but disappeared.

The lesson of these experiences is that a key element of setting goals is the ability to see them in terms of more than a single dimension. Both money and product policy are part of a statement of objectives; but it is essential that these be viewed as the concrete expressions of a more abstract set of goals—the satisfaction of the needs of significant groups which cooperate to ensure the company's continued existence.

Who are these groups? There are many customers, managers, employees, stockholders, to mention just the major ones. The key to corporate success is the company's ability to identify the important needs of each of these groups, to establish some balance among them, and to work out a set of operating policies which permits their satisfaction. This set of policies, as a pattern, identifies what the company is trying to be.

THE GROWTH FAD

Many managers have a view of their company's future which is strikingly analogous to the child's view of himself. When asked what they want their companies to become over the next few years, they reply, "bigger."

There are a great many rationalizations for this preoccupation with growth. Probably the one most frequently voiced is that which says, "You have to grow or die." What must be appreciated, however, is that "bigger" for a company has enormous implications for management. It involves a different way of life, and one which many managers may not be suited for—either in terms of temperament or skills.

Moreover, whether for a large company or a small one, "bigger," by itself, may not make economic sense. Companies which are highly profitable at their present size may grow into bankruptcy very easily; witness the case of Grayson-Robinson Stores, Inc., a chain of retail stores. Starting out as a small but profitable chain, it grew rapidly into receivership. Conversely, a company which is not now profitable may more successfully seek its survival in cost reduction than in sales growth. Chrysler is a striking example of this approach.

[4] See Theodore Levitt, "Marketing Myopia," HBR July–August 1960, p. 45.

There is, in the United States, a business philosophy which reflects the frontier heritage of the country. It is one which plays a high value on growth, in physical terms. The manager whose corporate sales are not increasing, the number of whose subordinates is not growing, whose plants are not expanding, feels that he is not successful. But there is a dangerous trap in this kind of thinking. More of the same is not necessarily progress. In addition, few managers are capable of running units several times larger than the ones they now head. The great danger of wholehearted consumer acceptance or an astute program of corporate acquisition is that it frequently propels managers into situations that are beyond their present competence. Such cases—and they are legion—emphasize that in stating corporate objectives, bigger is not always better. A dramatic example is that of the Ampex Corporation:

From 1950 to 1960, Ampex's annual sales went from less than $1,000,000 to more than $73,000,000. Its earnings went from $115,000 to nearly $4,000,000. The following year, the company reported a decline in sales to $70,000,000, and a net loss of $3,900,000. The *Wall Street Journal* reported: "As one source close to the company put it, Ampex's former management 'was intelligent and well-educated, but simply lacked the experience necessary to control' the company's rapid development."[5]

ROLE OF POLICY

A policy says something about *how* goals will be attained. It is what statisticians would call a "decision rule," and what systems engineers would call a "standing plan." It tells people what they should and should not do in order to contribute to achievement of corporate goals.

A policy should be more than just a platitude. It should be a helpful guide to making strategy explicit, and providing direction to subordinates. Consequently, the more definite it is, the more helpful it can be. "We will provide out stockholders with a fair return," is a policy no one could possibly disagree with—or be helped by. What *is* a fair return? This is the type of question that must be answered before the company's intentions become clear.

The job of management is not merely the preparation of valid policies for a standard set of activities; it is the much more challenging one of first deciding what activities are so strategically significant that explicit decision-rules in that area are mandatory. No standard set of policies can be considered major for all companies. Each company is a unique situation. It must decide for itself which aspects of corporate life are most relevant to its own aspirations and work out policy statements for them. For example, advertising may be insignificant to a company which provides research services to the Defense Department, but critical to a firm trying to mass-merchandise luxury goods.

It is difficult to generalize about which policies are major, even within a particular industry, because a number of extraordinary successfull companies appear to violate all the rules. To illustrate:

[5] "R for Ampex: Drastic Changes Help Solve Big Headache of Fast Corporate Growth," *Wall Street Journal*, September 17, 1962, p. 1.

● In the candy industry it would seem safe to generalize that advertising should be a major policy area. However, the Hershey Company, which is so successful that its name is practically the generic term for the product, has persistently followed a policy of no advertising.

● Similarly, in the field of high-fidelity components, one would expect that dealer relations would be a critical policy area. But Acoustics Research, Inc., has built an enviable record of sales growth and of profitability by relying entirely on consumer pull.

NEED TO BE EXPLICIT

The first thing to be said about corporate strategy is that having one is a step forward. Any strategy, once made explicit, can quickly be evaluated and improved. But if no attempt is ever made to commit it to paper, there is always the danger that the strategy is either incomplete or misunderstood.

Many successful companies are not aware of the strategy that underlies their success. It is quite possible for a company to achieve initial success without real awareness of its causes. However, it is much more difficult to successfully *branch out into new ventures* without a precise appreciation of their strategic significance. This is why many established companies fail miserably when they attempt a program of corporate acquisition, product diversification, or market expansion. One illustration of this is cited by Myles L. Mace and George G. Montgomery in their recent study of corporate acquisitions:

"A basic resin company . . . bought a plastic boat manufacturer because this seemed to present a controlled market for a portion of the resin it produced. It soon found that the boat business was considerably different from the manufacture and sale of basic chemicals. After a short but unpleasant experience in manufacturing and trying to market what was essentially a consumer's item, the management concluded that its experience and abilities lay essentially in industrial rather than consumer-type products."[6]

Another reason for making strategy explicit is the assistance it provides for delegation and for coordination. To an ever-increasing extent, management is a team activity, whereby groups of executives contribute to corporate success. Making strategy explicit makes if far easier for each executive to appreciate what the over-all goals are, and what his own contribution to them must be.

MAKING AN EVALUATION

Is your strategy right for you? There are six criteria on which to base an answer. These are:

1. Internal consistency.
2. Consistency with the environment.
3. Appropriateness in the light of available resources.

[6] *Management Problems of Corporate Acquisitions* (Boston: Division of Research, Harvard Business School, 1962), p. 60.

4. Satisfactory degree of risk.
5. Appropriate time horizon.
6. Workability.

If all of these criteria are met, you have a strategy that is right for you. This is as much as can be asked. There is no such thing as a good strategy in any absolute, objective sense. In the remainder of this article I shall discuss the criteria in some detail.

1. IS THE STRATEGY INTERNALLY CONSISTENT?

Internal consistenty refers to the cumulative impact of individual policies on corporate goals. In a well-worked-out strategy, each policy fits into an integrated pattern. It should be judged not only in terms of itself, but also in terms of how it relates to other policies which the company has established and to the goals it is pursuing.

In a dynamic company consistency can never be taken for granted. For example:

Many family-owned organizations pursue a pair of policies which soon become inconsistent: rapid expansion and retention of exclusive family control of the firm. If they are successful in expanding, the need for additional financing soon raises major problems concerning the extent to which exclusive family control can be maintained.

While this pair of policies is especially prevalent among smaller firms, it is by no mean limited to them. The Ford Motor Company after World War II and the New York Times today are examples of quite large, family-controlled organizations that have had to reconcile the two conflicting aims.

The criterion of internal consistency is an especially important one for evaluating strategies because it identifies those areas where strategic choices will eventually have to be made. An inconsistent stretegy does *not* necessarily mean that the company is currently in difficulty. But it does mean that unless management keeps its eye on a particular area of operation, it may well find itself forced to make a choice without enough time either to search for or to prepare attractive alternatives.

2. IS THE STRATEGY CONSISTENT WITH THE ENVIRONMENT?

A firm which has a certain product policy, price policy, or advertising policy is saying that it has chosen to relate itself to its customers—actual and potential—in a certain way. Similarly, its policies with respect to government contracts, collective bargaining, foreign investment, and so forth are expressions of relationship with other groups and forces. Hence an important test of strategy is whether the chosen policies are consistent with the environment—whether they really make sense with respect to what is going on outside.

Consistency with the environment has both a static and a dynamic aspect. In a static sense, it implies judging the efficacy of policies with respect to the environment as it exists *now*. In a dynamic sense, it means judging the efficacy of policies with respect to the environment *as it appears to be changing*. One purpose of a viable strategy is to ensure the long-run success of an organization. Since the environment of a company is constantly changing, ensuring success over the long run means that management must constantly be assessing the degree to which policies previously established are consistent with the environment as it exists now; and whether current policies take into account the environment as it will be in the future. In one sense, therefore, establishing a strategy is like aiming at a moving target: you have to be concerned not only with present position but also with the speed and direction of movement.

Failure to have a strategy consistent with the environment can be costly to the organization. Ford's sad experience with the Edsel is by now a textbook example of such failure. Certainly, had Ford pushed the Falcon at the time when it was pushing the Edsel, and with the same resources, it would have a far stronger position in the world automobile market today.

Illustrations of strategies that have not been consistent with the environment are easy to find by using hindsight. *But the reason that such examples are plentiful is not that foresight is difficult to apply.* It is because even today few companies are seriously engaged in analyzing environmental trends and using this intelligence as a basis for managing their own futures.

3. IS THE STRATEGY APPROPRIATE IN VIEW OF THE AVAILABLE RESOURCES?

Resources are those things that a company *is* or *has* and that help it to achieve its corporate objectives. Included are money, competence, and facilities; but these by no means complete the list. In companies selling consumer goods, for example, the major resource may be the name of the product. In any case, there are two basic issues which management must decide in relating strategy and resources. These are.

- What are our critical resources?
- Is the proposed strategy appropriate for available resources?

Let us look now at what is meant by a " critical resource " and at how the criterion of resource utilization can be used as a basis for evaluating strategy.

Critical Resources. The essential strategic attribute of resources is that they represent action potential. Taken together, a company's resources represent its capacity to respond to threats and opportunities that may be perceived in the environment. In other words, resources are the bundle of chips that the company has to play with in the serious game of business.

From an action-potential point of view, a resource may be critical in two senses: (1) as the factor limiting the achievement of corporate goals; and (2) as that which the company will exploit as the basis for its strategy. Thus, critical resources are both what the company has most of and what it has least of.

The three resources most frequently identified as critical are money, competence, and physical facilities. Let us look at the strategic significance of each.

Money. Money is a particularly valuable resource because it provides the greatest flexibility of response to events as they arise. It may be considered the "safest" resource, in that safety may be equated with the freedom to choose from among the widest variety of future alternatives. Companies that wish to reduce their short-run risk will therefore attempt to accumulate the greatest reservoir of funds they can.

However, it is important to remember that while the accumulation of funds may offer shortrun security, it may place the company at a serious competitive disadvantage with respect to other companies which are following a higher-risk course.

The classical illustration of this kind of outcome is the strategy pursued by Montgomery Ward under the late Sewell Avery. As reported in *Fortune:*

" While Sears confidently bet on a new and expanding America, Avery developed an *idée fixe* that postwar inflation would end in a crash no less serious than that of 1929. Following this idea, he opened no new stores but rather piled up cash to the ceiling in preparation for an economic debacle that never came. In these years, Ward's balance sheet gave a somewhat misleading picture of its prospects. Net earnings remains respectably high, and were generally higher than those of Sears as a percentage of sales. In 1946, earnings after taxes were $52 million. They rose to $74 million in 1950, and then declined to $35 million in 1954. Meanwhile, however, sales remained static, and in Avery's administration profits and liquidity were maintained at the expense of growth. In 1954, Ward had $327 million in cash and securities, $147 million in receivables, and $216 million in inventory, giving it a total current-asset position of $690 million and net worth of $639 million. It was liquid, all right, but it was also the shell of a once great company."[7]

Competence. Organizations survive because they are good at doing those things which are necessary to keep them alive. However, the degree of competence of a given organization is by no means uniform across the broad range of skills necessary to stay in business. Some companies are particularly good at marketing, others especially good at engineering, still others depend primarily on their financial sophistication. Philip Selznick refers to that which a company is particularly good at as its " distinctive competence."[8]

In determining a strategy, management must carefully appraise its own skill profile in order to determine where its strengths and weaknesses lie. It must then adopt a strategy which makes the greatest use of its strengths. To illustrate:

[7] "Montgomery Ward: Prosperity Is Still Around the Corner," *Fortune*, November 1960, p. 140.

[8] *Leadership in Administration* (Evanston, Illinois, Row, Peterson & Company, 1957), p. 42.

• The competence of *The New York Times* lies primarily in giving extensive and insightful coverage of events—the ability to report "all the news that's fit to print." It is neither highly profitable (earning only 1.5% of revenues in 1960—far less than, say, the *Wall Street Journal*), nor aggressively sold. Its decision to publish a West Coast and an international edition is a gamble that the strength of its "distinctive competence" will make it accepted even outside of New York.

• Because of a declining demand for soft coal, many producers of soft coal are diversifying into other fields. All of them, however, are remaining true to some central skill that they have developed over the years. For instance:

—Consolidation Coal is moving from simply the mining of soft coal to the mining *and transportation* of soft coal. It is planning with Texas Eastern Transmission Corporation to build a $100-million pipeline that would carry a mixture of powdered coal and water from West Virginia to the East Coast.

—North American Coal Company, on the other hand, is moving toward becoming a chemical company. It recently joined with Strategic Materials Corporation to perfect a process for extracting aluminum sulfate from the mine shale that North American produces in its coal-running operations.

James L. Hamilton, president of the Island Creek Coal Co., has summed up the concept of distinctive competence in a colorful way:

"We are a career company dedicated to coal, and we have some very definite ideas about growth and expansion within the industry. We're not thinking of buying a cotton mill and starting to make shirts."[9]

Physical Facilities. Physical facilities are the resource whose strategic influence is perhaps most frequently misunderstood. Managers seem to be divided among those, usually technical men, who are enamored of physical facilities as the tangible symbol of the corporate entity; and those, usually financial men, who view physical facilities as an undesirable but necessary freezing of part of the company's funds. The latter group is dominant. In many companies, return on investment has emerged as virtually the sole criterion for deciding whether or not a particular facility should be acquired.

Actually, this is putting the cart before the horse. Physical facilities have significance primarily in relationship to over-all corporate strategy. It is, therefore, only in relationship to *other* aspects of corporate strategy that the acquisition or disposition of physical facilities can be determined. The total investment required and the projected return on it have a place in this determination—but only as an indication of the financial implications of a particular strategic decision and not as an exclusive criterion for its own sake.

Any appraisal of a company's physical facilities as a strategic resource must consider the relationship of the company to its environment. Facilities have no intrinsic value for their own sake. Their value to the company is either in their location relative to markets, to sources of labor, or to materials; or in their efficiency relative to existing or impending competitive installations.

[9] *Wall Street Journal*, September 11, 1962, p. 30.

Thus, the essential considerations in any decision regarding physical facilities are a projection of changes likely to occur in the environment and a prediction about what the company's responses to these are likely to be.

Here are two examples of the necessity for relating an evaluation of facilities to environmental changes:

• Following the end of World War II, all domestic producers of typewriters in the United States invested heavily in plant facilities in this country. They hypothesized a rapid increase of sales throughout the world. This indeed took place, but it was short-lived. The rise of vigorous overseas competitors, especially Olivetti and Olympia, went hand in hand with a booming overseas market. At home, IBM's electric typewriter took more and more of the domestic market. Squeezed between these two pressures, the rest of the U.S. typewriter industry found itself with a great deal of excess capacity following the Korean conflict. Excess capacity is today still a major problem in this field.

• The steady decline in the number of farms in the United States and the emergence of vigorous overseas competition have forced most domestic full-line manufacturers of farm equipment to sharply curtail total plant area. For example, in less than four years, International Harvester eliminated more than a third of its capacity (as measured in square feet of plant space) for the production of farm machinery.

The close relationship between physical facilities and environmental trends emphasizes one of the most significant attributes of fixed assets—their temporal utility. Accounting practice recognizes this in its treatment of depreciation allowances. But even when the tax laws permit generous write-offs, they should not be used as the sole basis for setting the time period over which the investment must be justified. Environmental considerations may reveal that a different time horizon is more relevant for strategy determination. To illustrate again:

As Armstrong Cork Company moved away from natural cork to synthetic materials during the early 1950's, management considered buying facilities for the production of its raw materials—particularly polyvinyl chloride. However, before doing so, it surveyed the chemical industry and concluded that producers were overbuilding. It therefore decided not to invest in facilities for the manufacture of this material. The projections were valid; since 1956 polyvinyl chloride has dropped 50% in price.

A strategic approach to facilities may not only change the time horizon; it may also change the whole basis of asset valuation:

Recently a substantial portion of Loew's theaters was acquired by the Tisch brothers, owners and operators of a number of successful hotels, including the Americana in Florida.[10] As long as the assets of Loew's theaters were viewed only as places for the projection of films, its theaters, however conservatively valued, seemed to be not much of a bargain. But to a keen appraiser of hotel properties the

[10] See "The Tisches Eye Their Next $65 Million," *Fortune*, January 1960, p. 140.

theater sites, on rather expensive real estate in downtown city areas, had considerable appeal. Whether this appraisal will be borne out is as yet unknown. At any rate, the stock, which was originally purchased at $14 (with a book value of $22), was selling at $23 in October 1962.

Achieving the Right Balance. One of the most difficult issues in strategy determination is that of achieving a balance between strategic goals and available resources. This requires a set of necessarily empirical, but critical, estimates of the total resources required to achieve particular objectives, the rate at which they will have to be committed, and the likelihood that they will be available. The most common errors are either to fail to make these estimates at all or to be excessively optimistic about them.

One example of the unfortunate results of being wrong on these estimates is the case of Royal McBee and the computer market:

In January 1956 Royal McBee and the General Precision Equipment Corporation formed a jointly owned company—the Royal Precision Corporation—to enter the market for electronic data-processing equipment. This joint operation was a logical pooling of complementary talents. General Precision had a great deal of experience in developing and producing computers. Its Librascope Division had been selling them to the government for years. However, it lacked a commercial distribution system. Royal McBee, on the other hand, had a great deal of experience in marketing data-processing equipment, but lacked the technical competence to develop and produce a computer.

The joint venture was eminently successful, and within a short time the Royal Precision LPG-30 was the leader in the small-compuer field. However, the very success of the computer venture caused Royal McBee some serious problems. The success of the Royal Precision subsidiary demanded that the partners put more and more money into it. This was no problem for General Precision, but it became an ever more serious problem for Royal McBee, which found itself in an increasingly critical cash bind. In March 1962 it sold its interest in Royal Precision to General Precision for $5 million—a price which represented a reported $6.9 million loss on the investment. Concluding that it simply did not have sufficient resources to stay with the new venture, it decided to return to its traditional strengths: typewriters and simple data-processing systems.

Another place where optimistic estimates of resources frequently cause problems is in small businesses. Surveys of the causes of small-business failure reveal that a most frequent cause of bankruptcy is inadequate resources to weather either the early period of establishment or unforeseen downturns in business conditions.

It is apparent from the preceding discussion that a critical strategic decision involves deciding: (1) how much of the company's resources to commit to opportunities currently perceived, and (2) how much to keep uncommitted as a reserve against the appearance of unanticipated demands. This decision is closely related to two other criteria for the evaluation of strategy: risk and timing. I shall now descuss these.

4. DOES THE STRATEGY INVOLVE AN ACCEPTABLE DEGREE OF RISK?

Strategy and resources, taken together, determine the degree of risk which the company is undertaking. This is a critical managerial choice. For example, when the old Underwood Corporation decided to enter the computer field, it was making what might have been an extremely astute strategic choice. However, the fact that it ran out of money before it could accomplish anything in that field turned its pursuit of opportunity into the prelude to disaster. This is not to say that the strategy was " bad." However, the course of action pursued *was* a high-risk strategy. Had it been successful, the pay-off would have been lush. The fact that it was a stupendous failure instead does not mean that it was senseless to take the gamble.

Each company must decide for itself how much risk it wants to live with. In attempting to assess the degree of risk associated with a particular strategy, management may use a variety of techniques. For example, mathematicians have developed an elegant set of techniques for choosing among a variety of strategies where you are willing to estimate the payoffs and the probabilities associated with them. However, our concern here is not with these quantitative aspects but with the identification of some qualitative factors which may serve as a rough basis for evaluating the degree of risk inherent in a strategy. These factors are:

1. The amount of resources (on which the strategy is based) whose continued existence or value is not assured.
2. The length of the time periods to which resources are committed.
3. The proportion of resources committed to a single venture.

The greater these quantities, the greater the degree of risk that is involved.

Uncertain Terms of Existence. Since a strategy is based on resources, any resource which may disappear before the payoff has been obtained may constitute a danger to the organization. Resources may disappear for various reasons. For example, they may lose their value. This frequently happens to such resources as physical facilities and product features. Again, they may be accidentally detroyed. The most vulnerable resource here is competence. The possible crash of the company plane or the blip on the president's electrocardiogram are what make many organizations essentially speculative ventures. In fact, one of the critical attributes of highly centralized organizations is that the more centralized they are, the more speculative they are. The disappearance of the top executive or the disruption of communication with him, may wreak havoc at subordinate levels.

However, for many companies, the possibility that critical resources may lose their value stems not so much from internal developments as from shifts in the environment. Take specialized production know-how, for example. It has value only because of demand for the product by customers—and customers may change their minds. This is cause for acute concern among the increasing number of companies whose futures depend so heavily on their ability to participate in defense contracts. A familiar case is the plight of the airframe industry following World War II. Some of the companies succeeded in making the shift from aircraft to missiles, but this has only resulted in their being faced with the same problem on a larger scale.

Duration of Commitment. Financial analysts often look at the ratio of fixed assets to current assets in order to assess the extent to which resources are committed to long-term programs. This may or may not give a satisfactory answer. How important are the assets? When will they be paid for?

The reasons for the risk increasing as the time for payoff increases is, of course, the inherent uncertainty in any venture. Resources committed over long time spans make the company vulnerable to changes in the environment. Since the difficulty of predicting such changes increases as the time span increases, long-term projects are basically more risky than are short ones. This is especially true of companies whose environments are unstable. And today, either because of technological, political, or economic shifts, most companies are decidedly in the category of those that face major upheaval in their corporate environments. The company building its future around technological equipment, the company selling primarily to the government, the company investing in underdeveloped nations, the company selling to the Common Market, the company with a plant in the South—all these have this prospect in common.

The harsh dilemma of modern management is that the time span of decision is increasing at the same time as the corporate environment is becoming increasingly unstable. It is this dilemma which places such a premium on the manager's sensitivity to external trends today. Much has been written about his role as a commander and administrator. But it is no less important that he be a *strategist*.

Size of the Stakes. The more of its resources a company commits to a particular strategy, the more pronounced the consequences. If the strategy is successful, the payoff will be great—both to managers and investors. If the strategy fails, the consequences will be dire—both to managers and investors. Thus, a critical decision for the executive group is: What proportion of available resources should be committed to a particular course of action?

This decision may be handled in a variety of ways. For example, faced with a project that requires more of its resources than it is willing to commit, a company either may choose to refrain from undertaking the project or, alternatively, may seek to reduce the total resources required by undertaking a joint venture or by going the route of merger or acquisition in order to broaden the resource base.

The amount of resources management stands ready to commit is of particular significance where there is some likelihood that larger competitors, having greater resources, may choose to enter the company's field. Thus, those companies which entered the small-computer field in the past few years are now faced with the penetration into this area of the data-processing giants. (Both IBM and Remington Rand have recently introduced new small computers.)

I do not mean to imply that the " best " strategy is the one with the least risk. High payoffs are frequently associated with the high-risk strategies. Moreover, it is' a frequent but dangerous assumption to think that inaction, or lack of change, is a low-risk strategy. Failure to exploit its resources to the fullest may well be the riskiest strategy of all that an organization may pursue, as Montgomery Ward and other companies have amply demonstrated.

5. DOES THE STRATEGY HAVE AN APPROPRIATE TIME HORIZON?

A significant part of every strategy is the time horizon on which it is based. A viable strategy not only reveals what goals are to be accomplished; it says something about *when* the aims are to be achieved.

Goals, like resources, have time-based utility. A new product developed, a plant put on stream, a degree of market penetration, become significant strategic objectives only if accomplished by a certain time. Delay may deprive them of all strategic significance. A perfect example of this in the military sphere is the Sinai campaign of 1956. The strategic objective of the Israelis was not only to conquer the entire Sinai peninsula; it also was to do it in seven days. By contrast, the lethargic movement of the British troops made the operation a futile one for both England and France.

In choosing an appropriate time horizon, we must pay careful attention to the goals being pursued, and to the particular organization involved. Goals must be established far enough in advance to allow the organization to adjust to them. Organizations, like ships, cannot be " spun on a dime." Consequently, the larger the organization, the further its strategic time horizon must extend, since its adjustment time is longer. It is no mere managerial whim that the major contributions to long-range planning have emerged from the larger organizations—especially those large organizations such as Lockheed, North American Aviation, and RCA that traditionally have had to deal with highly unstable environments.

The observation that large corporations plan far ahead while small ones can get away without doing so has frequently been made. However, the significance of planning for the small but growing company has frequently been overlooked. As a company gets bigger, it must not only change the way it operates; it must also steadily push ahead its time horizon—and this is a difficult thing to do. The manager who has built a successful enterprise by his skill at " putting out fires " or the wheeler-dealer whose firm has grown by a quick succession of financial coups is seldom able to make the transition to the long look ahead.

In many cases, even if the executive were inclined to take a longer range view of events, the formal reward system seriously militates against doing so. In most companies the system of management rewards is closely related to currently reported profits. Where this is the case, executives may understandably be so preoccupied with reporting a profit year by year that they fail to spend as much time as they should in managing the company's long-term future. But if we seriously accept the thesis that the essence of managerial responsibility is the extended time lapse between decision and result, currently reported profits are hardly a reasonable basis on which to compensate top executives. Such a basis simply serves to shorten the time horizon with which the executive is concerned.

The importance of an extended time horizon derives not only from the fact that an organization changes slowly and needs time to work through basic modifications in its strategy; it derives also from the fact that there is a considerable advantage in a certain consistency of strategy maintained over long periods of time. The great danger to companies which do not carefully formulate strategies well in advance is that they are prone to fling themselves toward chaos by drastic changes in policy—and in personnel—at frequent intervals. A parade of presidents is a clear indication of a board that has not really decided what its strategy should be. It is a common harbinger of serious corporate difficulty as well.

The time horizon is also important because of its impact on the selection of policies. The greater the time horizon, the greater the range in choice of tactics. If, for instance, the goals desired must be achieved in a relatively short time, steps like acquisition and merger may become virtually mandatory. An interesting illustration is the decision of National Cash Register to enter the market for electronic data-processing equipment. As reported in *Forbes*:

"Once committed to EDP, NCR wasted no time. To buy talent and experience in 1953 it acquired Computer Research Corp. of Hawthorne, California. . . . For speed's sake, the manufacture of the 304's central units was turned over to GE. . . . NCR's research and development outlays also began curving steeply upwards."[11]

6. IS THE STRATEGY WORKABLE?

At first glance, it would seem that the simplest way to evaluate a corporate strategy is the completely pragmatic one of asking: Does it work? However, further reflection should reveal that if we try to answer that question, we are immediately faced with a quest for criteria. What is the evidence of a strategy "working"?

Quantitative indices of performance are a good start, but they really measure the influence of two critical factors combined: the strategy selected and the skill with which it is being executed. Faced with the failure to achieve anticipated results, both of these influences must be critically examined. One interesting illustration of this is a recent survey of the Chrysler Corporation after it suffered a period of serious loss:

"In 1959, during one of the frequent reorganizations at Chrysler Corp., aimed at

[11] "NCR and the Computer Sweepstakes," *Forbes*, October 15, 1962, p. 21.

halting the company's slide, a management consultant concluded: 'The only thing wrong with Chrysler is people. The corporation needs some good top executives.'"[12]

By contrast, when Olivetti acquired the Underwood Corporation, it was able to reduce the cost of producing typewriters by one-third. And it did it without changing any of the top people in the production group. However, it did introduce a drastically revised set of policies.

If a strategy cannot be evaluated by results alone, there are some other indications that may be used to asses its contribution to corporate progress:

• The degree of consensus which exists among executives concerning corporate goals and policies.

• The extent to which major areas of managerial choice are identified in advance, while there is still time to explore a variety of alternatives.

• The extent to which resource requirements are discovered well before the last minute, necessitating neither crash programs of cost reduction nor the elimination of planned programs. The widespread popularity of the meat-axe approach to cost reduction is a clear indication of the frequent failure of corporate strategic planning.

CONCLUSION

The modern organization must deploy espensive and complex resources in the pursuit of transitory opportunities. The time required to develop resources is so extended, and the time-scale of opportunities is so brief and fleeting, that a company which has not carefully delineated and appraised its strategy is adrift in white water.

In short, while a set of goals and major policies that meets the criteria listed above does not guarantee success, it can be of considerable value in giving management both the time and the room to maneuver.

[12] "How Chrysler Hopes to Rebound," *Business Week*, October 6, 1962, p. 45.

2. WRITTEN POLICIES HELP 9 WAYS*

—LOUIS CASSELS

and

RAYMOND L. RANDALL

You can improve management efficiency by putting your company's policies on paper.

That's the testimony of scores of firms, ranging from giants such as Sears, Roebuck & Co. to up-and-coming smaller organizations like the Milton Roy Company of Philadelphia, makers of controlled volume pumps. Both companies cited have achieved excellent results with carefully written policy and procedure manuals.

There was a time, in the recent past, when many forward-looking managers feared that written policies would lead to rigidity in adminstration, curb creative thinking, and interfere with executive development by preventing experimentation at lower echelons.

Now the trend in well managed firms is unmistakably toward more specific and authoritative policy guidance from the top.

Management consultants Booz, Allen & Hamilton recently polled 337 firms to determine their current attitude on policy. They found that "the majority . . . have stated policies in all major functional fields, and find them extremely valuable in the conduct of their business."

Although many companies still do not commit all their policies to writing, the survey showed, "the tendency to do so is increasing." The largest organizations have written policies governing about half of their operations. The extent of policy coverage tends to decline with company size, but even among smaller companies Booz, Allen & Hamilton noted "an active effort to develop more formal policy patterns."

The experience of companies large and small points up nine good reasons for spelling out policy in authoritative, written form. The reasons are:

1. WRITTEN POLICIES PROMOTE DEEP DELEGATION OF AUTHORITY

This fact, to which many companies bear witness, directly contradicts the notion that a rule book will paralyze initiative in lower echelons. The truth is that real delegation is more likely when an executive is reasonably assured that his subordinates will act in a given situation as he would act himself. Clearly defined and well communicated policies help to give him this assurance.

Subordinates are more willing to take responsibility for operating decisions when they know they can cite an accepted company policy as justification for their action.

2. WRITTEN POLICIES PROMOTE MANAGEMENT BY EXCEPTION

This is listed by H. J. Phillips, Jr., vice president for administration planning of U.S. Steel Corp., as one of the principal advantages of a policy manual. Specifying in advance how frequently recurring problems are to be handled frees the overworked senior executives from many repetitive, time-consuming decisions.

A corollary benefit, noted by C. E. Ware, Jr., supervisor of organization planning of Allegheny Ludlum Corp., is that internal communication channels are cleared of a vast amount of inquiry-and-response correspondence relating to routine decisions.

This means that, when an exceptional problem does arise—the kind that really warrants a fresh management decision—the organization is geared to transmit it speedily to the top and back. Upper-echelon executives have time to give it the thoughtful consideration it deserves.

3. WRITTEN POLICIES PROMOTE CONSISTENCY

This consideration looms large with big outfits such as Standard Oil of California, which place high value on policy manuals. But it is pertinent to smaller organizations, too. The modern corporation is a person not only in the eyes of the law, but in certain respects also in the eyes of its employes, customers and suppliers. That is to say, people expect a company's left hand to know what its right is doing. Personnel policies that vary widely from one unit to another are extremely damaging to employee relations.

Inconsistency in the treatment of customers and suppliers, either between one branch of the company and another, or from one time to another, can be bad for business. The uniformity of administration which flows from formal, company-wide policies is the best insurance against these dangers.

4. WRITTEN POLICIES PROMOTE CONTINUITY

As one management researcher put it, written policies are a "means of transmitting the company's heritage" from one generation of executives to another. The accumulated wisdom that a senior executive carries in his head is lost when he leaves the company. But if past experience and judgement are distilled into policy, and captured on paper, successors can avoid some of the pitfalls and blind alleys which have already been adequately explored.

5. WRITTEN POLICIES PROMOTE PLANNING

"One of the major benefits we have found through the publication of our policy and procedure manuals," says Robert T. Sheen, president of the Milton Roy Company, "is the fact that the actual process of writing down policies helps to clarify management thinking." The top executives responsible for drafting a policy manual are made aware of gaps, contradictions and fuzziness in existing policies which may have seemed quite adequate so long as no one had to explain them in writing.

Since the value of a policy manual depends on the extent to which it anticipates problems, the managers who compose it must think ahead. Thus, policy formulation becomes a stimulus to long-range planning.

6. WRITTEN POLICIES PROMOTE TEAMWORK

There is no better vehicle for creating and maintaining an institutional viewpoint at all levels of an organization. A well prepared policy manual enables lower-echelon managers and specialists to see the over-all picture as the chief executive sees it—the company's goals, the basic principles that underlie its specific policies. They can see how their particular responsibilities dovetail into a bigger plan.

7. WRITTEN POLICIES PROMOTE UNDERSTANDING

As Charles E. Redfield points out in his classic text on "Communication in Management": "The written word is not distortion-proof, but it suffers less from distortion than does its oral counterpart." Any executive who has witnessed the remarkable transformation that a simple fact can undergo in passing along the company grapevine must shudder at the thought of what happens to a carefully calculated policy by the time it has been handed down through several echelons by word-of-mouth.

8. WRITTEN POLICIES PROMOTE TRAINING

There has been a growing realization in the past few years that generalized training in management skills, while essential, is by no means the end-all and be-all of executive development programs. In a practical business context, you need to develop managers who know how your company does things. A policy manual can be an invaluable aid to the orientation of young or newly hired managers. If conscientiously studied, it can be as effective as months or years of coaching in preparing a man to function smoothly as a member of a closely meshed organization.

9. WRITTEN POLICIES PROMOTE GOOD HUMAN RELATIONS

Attitude surveys show that people work better when they know what is expected of them. They feel more secure because the ground rules are right there in black and white. Buck-passing in both directions is minimized, because neither superior nor subordinate can claim—as both often do when a verbal instruction boomerangs—that management wishes were misunderstood.

A policy manual gives a superior a ready-made answer to the alibi "I didn't know." It gives a subordinate protection against a capricious boss who may be inclined to attribute his own unreasonable whims to company policy.

So much for the dividends. What are the arguments against putting your company's policies in writing? Four principal objections are raised. None of them, however, is insurmountable.

The first is that certain policies are best kept confidential. If announced to the world in an official company manual, they could cause trouble with organized labor, competitors or the government. No realistic executive would deny the force of this argument. But it need not be controlling. Confidential policies comprise a relatively small proportion of the the total policy picture. They can be omitted from the regular manual and promulgated either verbally or in a written supplement of carefully restricted circulation.

There is one important warning: Never include in your official manual any statement of policy which is essentially contradicted by an actual policy that is kept in confidence. Ignore the whole subject in the manual if you feel you must, but do not say one thing publicly when you privately mean another.

This kind of duplicity is invariably detected sooner or later by subordinates, who thereupon begin to regard the entire policy manual as undependable eyewash. A policy manual can be silent even on an important subject without destroying confidence in its over-all authority. It cannot be hypocritical.

A second objection, often raised by smaller organizations, is that policy manuals cost too much to produce. "We can't afford to get out of those fancy books," argued the president of one small but growing company. "It's easier and cheaper for us to lay down our policies in letters and memoranda."

It's easier, all right—but is it really cheaper? Careful cost-accounting studies show that it costs the average organization at least $1 to produce a letter or memorandum. Multiply that unit cost by the vast number of individual questions and answers that must flow through the correspondence system when there are no clear-cut policies for handling routine problems, and you quickly exceed the cost of a simple manual.

A good policy manual doesn't need to be fancy. The most efficient type is an inexpensive loose-leaf notebook. Policy statements, classified and indexed by subject, can be printed or mimeographed (depending on the number of copies required) on separate pages so that revisions can be made easily by substituting an entire page or section.

What about the executive time that goes into writing out the policy statements? There is no denying that it involves a lot of work—work that must be done at the highest management level and carefully reviewed by the chief executive himself. But this expenditure of time is justifiable on two grounds: The first is that top management has no function more clearly its own, nor more urgent, than policy formulation. The second is that the time spent in preparing a clear policy pronouncement will be made up many times over by the executive man-hours saved in eliminating repetitive routine decisions.

A third objection is that written policies tend to remain on the books long after they are obsolete. This is a real pitfall. Unless you are willing to take the trouble to avoid it, you'd better not undertake to publish a policy manual. Even the wisest policies can become outdated quickly in today's business world. If your manual is going to be an effective management tool, and if it is to have the unquestioning respect that is essential to its role, it must be frequently reviewed and revised.

Although each senior manager should be held responsible for keeping an eye on the general state of policy in his particular area, it is usually advisable to have one person or department assigned to the task of keeping the manual itself up to date.

Every time a letter or telegram goes out that has the effect of changing policy, a formal revision of the manual should quickly follow. Otherwise, lower echelons will fall into the bad habit of relying on informal sources—including word-of-mouth—to justify departures from the policies spelled out in the manual.

The fourth argument is that written policies may reduce management flexibility and become a strait jacket for the organization.

This criticism can validly be directed only at poorly conceived manuals that attempt to spell out all of the rules in great detail. A good manual, as such companies as Sears and International Harvester have demonstrated, can actually encourage flexibility by carefully delineating the areas where the company's mind is made up, and those in which it welcomes the exercise of managerial discretion.

It is quite easy to make clear in the wording whether a given set of instructions is mandatory or just advisory. When you say that something " shall," " will " or " must " be done under certain circumstances, you are laying down the law and are entitled to demand strict compliance. But you can use other words to convey the idea that here is an area where subordinates are free to use their own judgment if circumstances seem to make company policy inappropriate.

Such words and phrases as "may," "generally recommended," "in most cases" and so on have a clearly permissive flavor.

Although policies and procedures are often included in the same manual, it is a good idea to distinguish between them in the format. Mixing them up may give a false impression of rigidity, since many companies are far more dogmatic about procedures (i.e., the form to be used, the office to be notified, etc.) than about substantive policies.

State your policies in broad, clear language, explaining the rationale behind them and marking off the boundaries within which individual discretion may be exercised. Then, on a separate page, you can go into the details of procedures. This will help to keep subordinate managers from feeling hemmed in by enormously detailed instructions that have more to do with paper work than policy. It will avoid the impression that "the company has changed its policy" when it has really only changed the number or mailing date of a clerical form.

When all of the pros and cons are weighed, it is easy to see why more and more companies are getting their policies on paper. The Booz, Allen & Hamilton survey, summing up the views of scores of executives who have tried it, puts the case for written policy in these words:

"It builds on proved decisions of the past, conserving executive energy for new decisions; it creates an atmosphere in which individual actions may be taken with confidence; it speeds administration by reducing repetition to routine; it supports consistency of endeavor across a large group through the years. It stabilizes the enterprise. It frees top management so that more creative consideration can be given to the problems of today and the new programs for tomorrow."

3. THE CONCEPT OF THE MARKETING MIX*

—NEIL H. BORDEN

I have always found it interesting to observe how an apt or colorful term may catch on, gain wide usage, and help to further understanding of a concept that has already been expressed in less appealing and communicative terms. Such has been true of the phrase " marketing mix," which I began to use in my teaching and writing some 15 years ago. In a relatively short time it has come to have wide usage. This note tells of the evolution of the marketing mix concept.

The phrase was suggested to me by a paragraph in a research bulletin on the management of marketing costs, written by my associate, Professor James Culliton (1948). In this study of manufacturers' marketing costs he described the business executive as a

" decider," an " artist "—a " mixer of ingredients," who sometimes follows a recipe prepared by others, sometimes prepares his own recipe as he goes along, sometimes adapts a recipe to the ingredients immediately available, and sometimes experiments with or invents ingredients no one else has tried.

I liked his idea of calling a marketing executive a " mixer of ingredients," one who is constantly engaged in fashioning creatively a mix of marketing procedures and policies in his efforts to produce a profitable enterprise.

For many years previous to Culliton's cost study the wide variations in the procedures and policies employed by managements of manufacturing firms in their marketing programs and the correspondingly wide variation in the costs of these marketing functions, which Culliton aptly ascribed to the varied " mixing of ingredients," had become increasingly evident as we had gathered marketing cases at the Harvard Business School. The marked differences in the patterns or formulae of the marketing programs not only were evident through facts disclosed in case histories, but also were reflected clearly in the figures of a cost study of food manufacturers made by the Harvard Bureau of Business Research in 1929. The primary objective of this study was to determine common figures of expenses for various marketing functions among food manufacturing companies, similar to the common cost figures which had been determined in previous years for various kinds of retail and wholesale businesses. In this manufacturer's study we were unable, however, with the data gathered to determine common expense figures that had much significance as standards by which to guide management, such as had been possible in the studies of retail and wholesale trades, where the methods of operation tended toward uniformity. Instead, among food manufacturers the ratios of sales devoted to the various functions of marketing such as advertising, personal selling, packaging, and so on, were found to be widely divergent, no matter how we grouped our respondents. Each respondent gave data that tended to uniqueness.

Culliton's study of marketing costs in 1947–48 was a second effort to find out, among other objectives, whether a bigger sample and a more careful classification of companies would produce evidence of operating uniformities that would give helpful common expense figures. But the result was the same as in our early study: there was wide diversity in cost ratios among any classifications of firms which were set up, and no common figures were found that had much value. This was true whether companies were grouped according to similarity in product lines, amount of sales, territorial extent of operations, or other bases of classification.

Relatively early in my study of advertising, it had become evident that understanding of advertising usage by manufacturers in any case had to come from an analysis of advertising's place as one element in the total marketing program of the firm. I came to realize that it is essential always to ask: what overall marketing strategy has been or might be employed to bring about a profitable operation in light of the circumstances faced by the management? What combination of marketing procedures and policies has been or might be adopted to bring about desired behavior of trade and consumers at costs that will permit a profit? Specifically, how can advertising, personal selling, pricing, packaging, channels, warehousing, and the other elements of a marketing program be manipulated and fitted together in a way that will give a profitable operation? In short, I saw that every advertising management case called for a consideration of the strategy to be adopted for the total marketing program, with advertising recognized as only one element whose form and extent depended on its careful adjustment to the other parts of the program.

The soundness of this viewpoint was supported by case histories throughout my volume, *The Economic Effects of Advertising* (Borden, 1942). In the chapters devoted to the utilization of advertising by business, I had pointed out the innumerable combinations of marketing methods and policies that might be adopted by a manager in arriving at a marketing plan. For instance, in the area of branding, he might elect to adopt an individualized brand or a family brand. Or he might decide to sell his product unbranded or under private label. Any decision in the area of brand policy in turn has immediate implications that bear on his selection of channels of distribution, sales force methods, packaging, promotional procedure, and advertising. Throughout the volume the case materials cited show that the way in which any marketing function is designed and the burden placed upon the function are determined largely by the overall marketing strategy adopted by managements to meet the market conditions under which they operate. The forces met by different firms vary widely. Accordingly, the programs fashioned differ widely.

Regarding advertising, which was the function under focus in the economic effects volume, I said at one point:

> In all the above illustrative situations it should be recognized that advertising is not an operating method to be considered as something apart, as something whose profit value is to be judged alone. An able management does not ask, "Shall we use or not use advertising," without consideration of the product and of other management procedures to be employed. Rather the question is always one of finding a management formula giving advertising its due place in the combination of manufacturing methods, product form, pricing, promotion and selling methods, and distribution methods. As previously pointed out, different formulae, i.e., different combinations of methods, may be profitably employed by competing manufacturers.

From the above it can be seen why Culliton's description of a marketing manager as a "mixer of ingredients" immediately appealed to me as an apt and easily understandable phrase, far better than my previous references to the marketing man as an empiricist seeking in any situation to devise a profitable "pattern" or "formula" of marketing operations from among the many procedures and policies that were open to him. If he was a "mixer of ingredients," what he designed was a "marketing mix."

It was logical to proceed from a realization of the existence of a variety of "marketing mixes" to the development of a concept that would comprehend not only this variety, but also the market forces that cause managements to produce a variety of mixes. It is the problems raised by these forces that lead marketing managers to exercise their wits in devising mixes or programs which they hope will give a profitable business operation.

To portray this broadened concept in a visual presentation requires merely:

1. a list of the important elements or ingredients that make up marketing programs:
2. a list of the forces that bear on the marketing operation of a firm and to which the marketing manager must adjust in his search for a mix or program that can be successful.

The list of elements of the marketing mix in such a visual presentation can be long or short, depending on how far one wishes to go in his classification and subclassification of the marketing procedures and policies with which marketing managements deal when devising marketing programs. The list of elements which I have employed in my teaching and consulting work covers the principal areas of marketing activities which call for management decisions as revealed by case histories. I realize others might build a different list. Mine is as follows:

Elements of the Marketing Mix of Manufacturers
1. *Product Planning*—policies and procedures relating to:
   a. Product lines to be offered—qualities, design, etc.
   b. Markets to sell: whom, where, when, and in what quantity.
   c. New product policy—research and development program.
2. *Pricing*—policies and procedures relating to:
   a. Price level to adopt.
   b. Specific prices to adopt (odd-even, etc.).
   c. Price policy, e.g., one-price or varying price, price maintenance, use of list prices, etc.
   d. Margins to adopt—for company; for the trade.
3. *Branding*—policies and procedures relating to:
   a. Selection of trade marks.
   b. Brand policy—individualized or family brand.
   c. Sale under private label or unbranded.
4. *Channels of Distribution*—policies and procedures relating to:
   a. Channels to use between plant and consumer.
   b. Degree of selectivity among wholesalers and retailers.
   c. Efforts to gain cooperation of the trade.
5. *Personal Selling*—policies and procedures relating to:
   a. Burden to be placed on personal selling and the methods to be employed in:
      1. Manufacturer's organization.
      2. Wholesale segment of the trade.
      3. Retail segment of the trade.
6. *Advertising*—policies and procedures relating to:
   a. Amount to spend—i.e., the burden to be placed on advertising.
   b. Copy platform to adopt:
      1. Product image desired.
      2. Corporate image desired.
   c. Mix of advertising: to the trade; through the trade; to consumers.
7. *Promotions*—policies and procedures relating to:
   a. Burden to place on special selling plans or devices directed at or through the trade.
   b. Form of these devices for consumer promotions, for trade promotions.

8. *Packaging*—policies and procedures relating to:
   a. Formulation of package and label.
9. *Display*—policies and procedures relating to:
   a. Burden to be put on display to help effect sale.
   b. Methods to adopt to secure display.
10. *Servicing*—policies and procedures relating to:
    a. Providing service needed.
11. *Physical Handling*—policies and procedures relating to:
    a. Warehousing.
    b. Transportation.
    c. Inventories.
12. *Fact Finding and Analysis*—policies and procedures relating to:
    a. Securing, analysis, and use of facts in marketing operations.

Also if one were to make a list of all the forces which managements weigh at one time or another when formulating their marketing mixes, it would be very long indeed, for the behavior of individuals and groups in all spheres of life have a bearing, first, on what goods and services are produced and consumed, and, second, on the procedures that may be employed in bringing about exchange of these goods and services. However, the important forces which bear on marketers, all arising from the behavior of individuals or groups, may readily be listed under four heads, namely the behavior of consumers, the trade, competitors, and government.

The outline below contains these four behavioral forces with notations of some of the important behavioral determinants within each force. These must be studied and understood by the marketer, if his marketing mix is to be successful. The great quest of marketing management is to understand the behavior of humans in response to the stimuli to which they are subjected. The skillful marketer is one who is a perceptive and practical psychologist and sociologist, who has keen insight into individual and group behavior, who can foresee changes in behavior that develop in a dynamic world, who has creative ability for building well-knit programs because he has the capacity to visualize the probable response of consumers, trade, and competitors to his moves. His skill in forecasting response to his marketing moves should well be supplemented by a further skill in devising and using tests and measurements to check consumer or trade response to his program or parts thereof, for no marketer has so much prescience that he can proceed without empirical check.

Below, then, is the suggested outline of forces which govern the mixing of marketing elements. This list and that of the elements taken together provide a visual presentation of the concept of the marketing mix.

Market Forces Bearing on the Marketing Mix
1. *Consumers' Buying Behavior*, as determined by their:
   a. Motivation in purchasing.

    b. Buying habits.

    c. Living habits.

    d. Environment (present and future, as revealed by trends, for environment influences consumers' attitudes toward products and their use of them).

    e. Buying power.

    f. Number (i.e., how many).

2. *The Trade's Behavior*—wholesalers' and retailers' behavior, as influenced by:

    a. Their motivations.

    b. Their structure, practices, and attitudes.

    c. Trends in structure and procedures that portend change.

3. *Competitors' Position and Behavior*, as influenced by:

    a. Industry structure and the firm's relation thereto.

        1. Size and strength of competitors.

        2. Number of competitors and degree of industry concentration.

        3. Indirect competition—i.e., from other products.

    b. Relation of supply to demand—oversupply or undersupply.

    c. Product choices offered consumers by the industry—i.e., quality, price, service.

    d. Degree to which competitors compete on price vs. nonprice bases.

    e. Competitors' motivations and attitudes—their likely response to the actions of other firms.

    f. Trends technological and social, portending change in supply and demand.

4. *Governmental Behavior—Controls over Marketing:*

    a. Regulations over products.

    b. Regulations over pricing.

    c. Regulations over competitive practices.

    d. Regulations over advertising and promotion.

When building a marketing program to fit the needs of his firm, the marketing manager has to weigh the behavioral forces and then juggle marketing elements in his mix with a keen eye on the resources with which he has to work. His firm is but one small organism in a large universe of complex forces. His firm is only a part of an industry that is competing with many other industries. What does the firm have in terms of money, product line, organization, and reputation with which to work? The manager must devise a mix of procedures that fit these resources. If his firm is small, he must judge the response of consumers, trade, and competition in light of his position and resources and the influence that he can exert in the market. He must look for special opportunities in product or method of operation. The small firm cannot employ the procedures of the big firm. Though he may sell the same kind of product as the big firm, his marketing strategy is likely to be widely different in many respects. Innumerable instances of this fact might be cited.

For example, in the industrial goods field, small firms often seek to build sales on a limited and highly specialized line, whereas industry leaders seek patronage for full lines. Small firms often elect to go in for regional sales rather than attempt the national distribution practiced by larger companies. Again, the company of limited resources often elects to limit its production and sales to products whose potential is too small to attract the big fellows. Still again, companies with small resources in the cosmetic field not infrequently have set up introductory marketing programs employing aggressive personal selling and a " push " strategy with distribution limited to leading department stores. Their initially small advertising funds have been directed through these selected retail outlets, with the offering of the products and their story told over the signatures of the stores. The strategy has been to borrow kudos for their products from the leading stores' reputations and to gain a gradual radiation of distribution to smaller stores in all types of channels, such as often comes from the trade's follow-the-leader behavior. Only after resources have grown from mounting sales has a dense retail distribution been aggressively sought and a shift made to place the selling burden more and more on company-signed advertising.

The above strategy was employed for Toni products and Stoppette deodorant in their early marketing stages when the resources of their producers were limited (cf. case of Jules Montenier, Inc. in Borden and Marshall, 1959, pp. 498–518). In contrast, cosmetic manufacturers with large resources have generally followed a " pull " strategy for the introduction of new products, relying on heavy campaigns of advertising in a rapid succession of area introductions to induce a hoped-for, complete retail coverage from the start (cf. case of Bristol-Myers Company in Borden and Marshall, 1959, pp. 519–533). These introductory campaigns have been undertaken only after careful programs of product development and test marketing have given assurance that product and selling plans had high promise of success.

Many additional instances of the varying strategy employed by small versus large enterprises might be cited. But those given serve to illustrate the point that managements must fashion their mixes to fit their resources. Their objectives must be realistic.

LONG VS. SHORT TERM ASPECTS OF MARKETING MIX

The marketing mix of a firm in large part is the product of the evolution that comes from day-to-day marketing. At any time the mix represents the program that a management has evolved to meet the problems with which it is constantly faced in an ever changing, ever challenging market. There are continuous tactical maneuvers: a new product, aggressive promotion, or price change initiated by a competitor must be considered and met; the failure of the trade to provide adequate market coverage or display must be remedied; a faltering sales force must be reorganized and stimulated; a decline in sales share must be diagnosed and remedied; an advertising approach that has lost effectiveness must be replaced; a general business decline must be countered. All such problems call for a management's maintaining effective channels of information relative to its own operations and to the day-to-day behavior of consumers, competitors, and the trade. Thus, we may observe that short range forces play a large part in the fashioning of the mix to be used at any time and in determining the allocation of expenditures among the various functional accounts of the operating statement.

But the overall strategy employed in a marketing mix is the product of longer range plans and procedures dictated in part by past empiricism and in part, if the management is a good one, by management foresight as to what needs to be done to keep the firm successful in a changing world. As the world has become more and more dynamic, blessed is that corporation which has managers who have foresight, who can study trends of all kinds—natural, economic, social, and technological—and guided by these, devise long-range plans that give promise of keeping their corporations afloat and successful in the turbulent sea of market change. Accordingly, when we think of the marketing mix, we need to give particular heed today to devising a mix based on long-range planning that promises to fit the world of five or ten or more years hence. Provision for effective long-range planning in corporate organization and procedure has become more and more recognized as the earmark of good management in a world that has become increasingly subject to rapid change.

To cite an instance among American marketing organizations which has shown foresight in adjusting the marketing mix to meet social and economic change, I look upon Sears Roebuck and Company as an outstanding example. After building an unusually successful mail order business to meet the needs of a rural America, Sears management foresaw the need to depart from its marketing pattern as a mail order company catering primarily to farmers. The trend from a rural to an urban United States was going on apace. The automobile and good roads promised to make town and city stores increasingly available to those who continued to be farmers. Relatively early, Sears launched a chain of stores across the land, each easily accessible by highway to both farmer and city resident, and with adequate parking space for customers. In time there followed the remarkable telephone and mail order plan directed at urban residents to make buying easy for Americans when congested city streets and highways made shopping increasingly distasteful. Similarly, in the areas of planning products which would meet the desires of consumers in a fast changing world, of shaping its servicing to meet the needs of a wide variety of mechanical products, of pricing procedures to meet the challenging competition that came with the advent of discount retailers, the Sears organization has shown a foresight, adaptibility, and creative ability worthy of emulation. The amazing growth and profitability of the company attests to the foresight and skill of its management. Its history shows the wisdom of careful attention to market forces and their impending change in devising marketing mixes that may assure growth.

USE OF THE MARKETING MIX CONCEPT

Like many concepts, the marketing mix concept seems relatively simple, once it has been expressed. I know that before they were ever tagged with the nomenclature of "concept," the ideas involved were widely understood among marketers as a result of the growing knowledge about marketing and marketing procedures that came during the preceding half century. But I have found for myself that once the ideas were reduced to a formal statement with an accompanying visual presentation, the concept of the mix has proved a helpful device in teaching, in business problem solving, and, generally, as an aid to thinking about marketing. First of all, it is helpful in giving an answer to the question often raised as to "what is marketing?" A chart which shows the elements of the mix and the forces that bear on the mix helps to bring understanding of what marketing is. It helps to explain why in our dynamic world the thinking of management in all its functional areas must be oriented to the market.

In recent years I have kept an abbreviated chart showing the elements and the forces of the marketing mix in front of my classes at all times. In case discussion it has proved a handy device by which to raise queries as to whether the student has recognized the implications of any recommendation he might have made in the areas of the several elements of the mix. Or, referring to the forces, we can question whether all the pertinent market forces have been given due consideration. Continual reference to the mix chart leads me to feel that the students' understanding of "what marketing is" is strengthened. The constant presence and use of the chart leaves a deeper understanding that marketing is the devision of programs that successfully meet the forces of the market.

In problem solving the marketing mix chart is a constant reminder of:

1. The fact that a problem seemingly lying in one segment of the mix must be deliberated with constant thought regarding the effect of any change in that sector on the other areas of marketing operations. The necessity of integration in marketing thinking is ever present.

2. The need of careful study of the market forces as they might bear on problems in hand.

In short, the mix chart provides an ever ready checklist as to areas into which to guide thinking when considering marketing questions or dealing with marketing problems.

MARKETING: SCIENCE OR ART?

The quest for a "science of marketing" is hard upon us. If science is in part a systematic formulation and arrangement of facts in a way to help understanding, then the concept of the marketing mix may possibly be considered a small contribution in the search for a science of marketing. If we think of a marketing science as involving the observation and classification of facts and the establishment of verifiable laws that can be used by the marketer as a guide to action with assurance that predicted results will ensue, then we cannot be said to have gotten far toward establishing a science. The concept of the mix lays out the areas in which facts should be assembled, these to serve as a guide to management judgment in building marketing mixes. In the last few decades American marketers have made substantial progress in adopting the scientific method in assembling facts. They have sharpened the tools of fact finding— both those arising within the business and those external to it. Aided by these facts and by the skills developed through careful observation and experience, marketers are better fitted to practice the art of designing marketing mixes than would be the case had not the techniques of gathering facts been advanced as they have been in recent decades. Moreover, marketers have made progress in the use of scientific method in designing tests whereby the results from mixes or parts of mixes can be measured. Thereby marketers have been learning how to subject the hypotheses of their mix artists to empirical check.

With the continued improvement in the search for and the recording of facts pertinent to marketing, with further application of the controlled experiment, and with an extension and careful recording of case histories, we may hope for a gradual formulation of clearly defined and helpful marketing laws. Until then, and even then, marketing and the building of marketing mixes will largely lie in the realm of art.

REFERENCES

Borden, Neil H., *The Economic Effects of Advertising*. Homewood, Ill.: Richard D. Irwin, 1942.

Borden, Neil H., and M. V. Marshall, *Advertising Management: Text and Cases*. Homewood, Ill.: Richard D. Irwin, 1959.

Culliton, James W. *The Management of Marketing Costs*. Boston: Division of Research, Graduate School of Business Administration, Harvard University, 1948.

4. PRODUCTION POLICY*

—CHARLES L. JAMISON

CHANGE OF MATERIALS BY MANUFACTURER

Only a small percentage of the products of nature are consumed without some kind of processing; by far the bulk of raw materials must be processed. The change in form ranges from simple to very complex transformation. In American industry, the dollar value added by manufacturing is more than three times the dollar value of the products of extractive industries—agriculture, forestry, fisheries, and mining. Manufacturing is financially the most important segment of American business.

Decisions made by manufacturers in regard to production techniques are vital to the success of every processing company. Topping all decisions are those pertaining to the changes in raw materials that are possible to make them most useful to consumers. Fibers are spun and woven into textiles. Metals are refined and fashioned into articles that can be used by other producers or by consumers. Clay products are processed and molded into building materials. Forest products are made into boards and plywood, which in turn are made into furniture and other useful things. Food products from the farm are processed to preserve them or to make them more palatable for human consumption. Chemicals are refined, mixed, blended, and passed through intricate processes to create products such as our ancestors never dreamed of.

Decision as to which materials will be worked with is closely related to the type of business selected as a major undertaking. In some cases what to make is decided first, and the proper material then is selected. In other cases it may be decided to work with one material rather than another, the type of product becoming a secondary decision. For example, a manufacturer of women's

* Charles L. Jamison, *Business Policy*, Chapter 26, (C) 1953. Reprinted by permission of Prentice-Hall, Inc., Englewood Cliffs, N.J.

dresses is more interested in the style of the product than in the material. He may use cotton, wool, silk, or some synthetic fabric. In contrast, a chemical manufacturer owning a rich deposit of chemical salts may search for ideas that will best utilize and make his chemicals salable.

Assembled articles such as machines and appliances, motor vehicles, furniture, and a multitude of other things, require careful attention to design. The first step in manufacturing plans is to decide on design. The salability of the product is of utmost importance; therefore, its utility, appearance, and durability influence its design. Then consideration is given to cost of manufacture. The design may have merit as to customer appeal, but cannot be made economically. Again more efficient processes than those originally specified by the design engineer may be substituted without changing the over-all design. Although decisions of this sort may be classified as minor decisions, they still constitute a part of manufacturing policy.

MATERIALS

The objective of a manufacturing company is to produce articles intended for a specific purpose. Some articles can be made from any one of a variety of materials. The decision as to what materials best suit the purpose revolves around a number of considerations such as availability, cost, durability, and ease of processing. New discoveries in chemistry and metallurgy are making available alternative materials for almost every purpose. Some substances have qualities superior to others. Aluminum is substituted for steel because it weighs less and does not corrode. Plastics are unbreakable and undentable, but are too costly for articles requiring large quantities of material, such as automobile bodies and fenders. Magnesium is lighter than aluminum but requires care and skill in handling. These are a few examples of the relative properties of materials.

Managers of manufacturing face a perpetual challenge to keep abreast of scientific development. Not only that, but changing transportation costs, the exhaustion of supplies in one locality, government demands for armament, and rapidly rising prices limit or cut off the source of supply of materials formerly depended upon. A switch to some other source or some substitute material then becomes imperative. Substitution of a new material for one old and tried is hazardous. The new material may not give the service that the old one gave. It may prove harder to process and for that reason may run up manufacturing costs. Customer acceptance of a product somewhat depends upon customer acceptance of the material from which it is made. That is why research into materials and adoption of the most suitable ones is a decision of major importance.

DIVERSIFICATION

A basic policy that affects manufacturing operations is whether to simplify or diversify the line of products. This is primarily a marketing decision, but it still is a problem of manufacturing. Efficiency in producing is increased with repetition. In general, factory managers oppose diversification. Established routines become matters of habit. Mental processes and manual movements follow the same groove. There is no delay for thinking things through, no experimenting with methods, no doubt as to results. Here again we deal with men, machines, and materials. Repetition reduces costs of labor, machine setup, and utilization of materials.

The first time a worker performs an unfamiliar operation he is slow and awkward. With each repetition of the operation his skill increases. Not only can he work faster, but the quality of his work improves. Manual dexterity can be attained only after long, patient practicing. That is true of typists, musicians, golf players—any activity that requires mental and muscular coordination. The most skilled workers are those who have performed the same operations again and again for months and years. To change a worker's task means the slowing down of his movements, hence, less productivity per hour. Experiments have been conducted with shifting workers at intervals from one task to another to introduce variety into their work. The results have been greater contentment and an over-all increase in efficiency. Diversification of products may introduce diversification of tasks. So long as the skills attained in one task can be carried over into another, no great loss of effort may result.

When skill is transferred from worker to machine, the setup of the machine takes time and requires an investment in fixtures and tools. Each change in setup adds to cost of operations. If the operator of the machine makes the change, the time he spends is unproductive. If a millwright sets up the machine, his time must be paid for, and in the meantime both the worker and the machine are idle. In case diversified products require the introduction of new and different machines, there is the further cost of the new equipment with the accompanying idleness of the discarded machine. The more completely mechanized the factory the greater the urgency for long runs of the same product.

As to the effect of diversification on the utilization of materials, a change of materials may necessitate a change of workers' habits, and may call for machine adjustments. Factory supervisors and workers who have become accustomed to handling one kind of material are frustrated when they have to work with materials that require different handling.

MANUFACTURING PROCESSES

Where there is a variety of choices, decision must be made as to the best process to use. As a rule, there is one best process for achieving a desired result. Management must find that process and plan operations accordingly. Research is constantly discovering new and better ways to do things. Each company that conducts research is on the alert to pioneer in such discoveries. But no research department has a monopoly on brains. What one company discovers may benefit another. As stated in Chapter 20, new ideas can be patented, but the rights to use patents are interchanged by cross-licensing arrangements. It is good business for any company to adopt the best process whether that company originates the process or not.

In some lines of manufacture, particularly continuous flow industries like oil refining, new processes must be adopted when competitors adopt them. Otherwise, operating costs may become too high by comparison for the backward company to continue in business. Or the quality of product may be inferior to that of competitors. The change in process may be so radical that a complete change in manufacturing facilities will become necessary. This calls for top management decision. Examples would be the tanning of leather, the curing of meats, the refining of metals, where chemical and electrolytic processes replace more time-consuming and costly methods theretofore regarded as the best way.

Of relatively minor importance are decisions between alternative processes in metal working industries. A metal part may be formed into the proper shape by any one of several methods. For instance, a piece of metal may be cut to a specified shape on a lathe or some other suitable cutting tool. Its shape may be formed by casting into a mold. It may be forged into the desired shape; or it may be extruded through dies that will give it the shape desired. Processes for joining two pieces of metal together vary. They may be bolted, riveted, welded, or forced together under pressure. Design engineers may decide that one process rather than another will give the most satisfactory joint for the particular product and may write the specifications accordingly. Under some circumstances the process by which parts are fashioned makes no difference in design. For example, consider a transfer machine that will move a casting for an automobile cylinder block automatically through 42 machines which cut and drill 530 operations on the piece of metal, completing it ready for assembly. The finished work meets the most exacting specifications and is in every respect as satisfactory as it would have been if 42 or more different workmen had placed the piece in each of 42 different machines, one after the other.

Decision as to what process to use then rests on the production control department. . . . Suggestions as to the most suitable process from a manufacturing point of view may flow up to production control from factory supervisors. Where a well-integrated system of production control has been installed, each process used must have the final sanction of the production control department, but design engineers and all others concerned with the product generally are consulted and their assent obtained.

PLANT LOCATION

A top management decision of outstanding importance is the selection of a suitable location for a manufacturing plant. In making this decision, materials, men, and markets are the primary considerations. If the needed materials can be found in almost any locality, as clay for making bricks, then closeness to a profitable market is the determining factor. If materials are not near the consumers' market, the deciding factor is the relative cost of transporting materials to a factory located near the market, or transporting the finished product from factory to market. Bulky materials that are largely wasted in processing, as ores bearing a small percentage of metal, are worked where they lie. A few pounds of metal are cheaper to transport than a ton of ore. Where bulk is not lost in processing, one ton of raw material equaling one ton of finished goods, other factors are considered beside proximity to materials. One of these factors may be the availability of labor.

In weighing the labor factor, thought must be given to the number of workers available at a given location, their skill for the tasks required of them, wage rates in that particular market, and the willingness of workers to conform to the industrial pattern—that is, whether they would have enough appreciation of the opportunity to be employed in the kind of jobs offered to be willing to work diligently and to observe the rules of the game.

As to consumers' markets, goods eventually must get to market. The question is, how long will it take and how much will it cost to get them there? The closer the factory is to the market, the more favorable will be the answer to the foregoing question. When the market is nation-wide, some goods must be transported long distances no matter where the factory is located. Thickly populated areas undoubtedly will consume more goods than sparsely populated areas, and a location near the largest markets would minimize transportation of finished goods. However much one may theorize about the choice of location in relation to consumers' market, the fact is that manufacturers with thoroughly analytical staff advice seem to give little consideration to that factor. For example, an electrical manufacturer with plants on the East Coast makes electric irons for the entire country at a plant located in California.

Other factors affecting plant location for peculiar types of industries are power and climate. Industries requiring quantities of electrical power cluster around sources of cheap power. Aluminum and many chemical industries are in this class. The glass industry has located near sources of natural gas. The steel industry at one time found proximity to coking coal to be a major factor. As to climate, the textile industry formerly sought humid climates where the breaking of thread due to its becoming dry and brittle was reduced to a minimum. Now mills can be humidified and located anywhere, if other conditions are favorable.

The foregoing discussion pertains to selection to geographical location. Having decided on that, the selection of a site next must be considered. In making this decision such factors are considered as cost of land, room for expansion, local taxation, accessibility to workers' housing, and probably local legal restrictions. Another important factor is transportation facilities. Industries that have bulky freight in and out usually seek a location along a railroad line, although transportation by truck gives that factor less importance than it once had. A few industries find location adjacent to navigable waterways an important consideration because of cheap water transportation.

FACTORY DESIGN

Efficient factory operation cannot be reached with poor plant design and layout. Each type of product calls for a different kind of factory. Some light manufacturing industries can be operated in any quarters that have four walls and a roof. In large cities loft buildings provide suitable quarters for such industries. Space can be rented, with power, light, and heat furnished. Garment enterprises, job printing businesses, and a variety of specialty work shops solve their problem of location by renting the amount of space needed. But most manufacturing companies find it expedient to have factories designed for their particular needs.

Ideally, an efficient layout is planned first and a building designed to surround it. First, the processes must be listed in sequence to insure a smooth flow of work from materials to finished product; movement from one operation to the next should cover as little distance as possible. Then the amount of space needed for each process is computed. All of these figures added together give the total floor space needed. Whether the factory should be single or multistory depends upon the cost of land and the area available. Construction costs of a multistory building usually are higher per cubic foot than a single story building. Nevertheless, a more compact unit can be obtained by going into the air. Multistory factory buildings still are being built, but a greater number, built on relatively low cost land, are confined to one story.

Laying out the machinery in a factory is a scientific operation. Layout engineers plan on paper where machines and equipment should be placed, but they know that their theoretical layout may not be practical. A factory laid out according to the plan probably would have to be changed when put into actual operation. To move heavy machines once they have been bolted to their foundations is expensive. A compromise, therefore, is struck. In a three dimensional model of the factory, built to a scale probably one-thirtieth the size of the actual factory, the layout engineers place miniature models of every machine to be used. These models can be purchased from the companies that specialize in making them. Miniature conveyors and miniature models of operators are also placed in position. The layout is studied and criticized by practical operating men. The miniature equipment is shifted around until everyone is satisfied that a real factory so laid out can be operated efficiently. Then a layout is drawn on paper following the adopted plan. So seriously do layout engineers take this playhouse procedure that one company spent $17,000 for models with which to lay out a single factory. The subsequent expense of mistakes in the final factory layout would greatly exceed the cost of this preliminary planning.

QUALITY CONTROL

Standards of quality commensurate with the intended utility of the product and the price at which it is offered require top management decision. Decisions so made must be followed by systematic controls to insure quality standards. In considering quality, consumers' goods may be regarded as falling into three general classes—durable goods, semidurable goods, and consumption goods. Durable goods are furniture, household appliances, automobiles, and similar products that have a life expectancy of many years. Semi-durable goods are those that wear out quickly when used, as shoes and clothing. Consumption goods are those destroyed in giving personal satisfaction—food, fuel, and cosmetics. Durable goods can be made to last a hundred years or more. Some furniture still in use is even older than that. It is the policy of manufacturers to give to purchasers of goods the quality that will measure up to their expectations—the more quality put into goods the higher their cost and the higher the selling price. Consumers generally do not want to possess things for too long a time. Where a style factor is involved, people will discard things that are out of style even though they still have utility.

Research into consumer expectations enables manufacturers to judge how much durability to put into articles in the "durable" classification. Less durability generally means lower manufacturing cost and consequently lower selling price. It is essential that price be within the means of the income class whose patronage is sought. What has been said of durable goods applies also to semidurable goods. As to consumption goods, the Pure Food and Drug Administration of the Federal government sets standards of purity which must be observed by all producers. Conscientious producers would not knowingly offer goods for sale that would be harmful to consumers. They set their own standards of purity and see to it that their products are thoroughly inspected to assure that quality.

Quality of producers' goods, like that of consumers' goods, must meet the expectations of purchasers. Power plants, railway equipment, machinery, and things of that sort must not fail when put into use. All of them require periodic maintenance, of course, after they have been installed, for they are put to hard usage no matter how well they are made. Nevertheless, a recognized standard of quality is observed if a manufacturer of producers' equipment expects to stay in business with repeat orders. Because the protection of quality is so essential to all manufacturers, control over quality is a responsibility delegated to the inspection department. . . .

PLANNING FOR PRODUCTION

Although planning for production is far down the scale from top management planning, it nevertheless is of vital importance to the success of a business and generally requires top management approval. Production planning is an application of the principle of separating planning from doing. Some manufacturers produce for stock; others produce to customer's order. The former group manufacture standard goods that are placed in stock and supplied to customers when demanded. The latter group do not produce until they have a customer's order. Usually, the order specifies some feature that differentiates the product from all others of its kind. Such enterprises are sometimes known as job order shops. The bulk of manufactured goods in the United States is made for stock. A list of those products would include many thousands of items. Manufacturers producing to customers' order generally are the heavy industries making special machinery, railway equipment, and some construction materials. A few things for personal use are made to order, too, but this branch of industry is relatively small.

The objective of control in a factory producing for stock is to insure a steady flow of work. Each department, each machine, each worker must be assigned enough work to be kept busy. Idle machines, idle men, and idle materials absorb expense and produce nothing. Planning production so that no one will have assignments beyond his capacity while others have too little to do is handled by a group of planners known as the production control department. . . .

The production control department releases authority to produce, whether production is for stock or to fill customers' orders for non-standard products. But production control must be informed that production is desired. Information regarding stock comes from inventory records of finished goods on hand, supplemented with information regarding market demand. When inventory records show that stock is accumulating, it indicates that sales are not keeping up with production. It is a warning to investigate market conditions. Market analysis is made by the market research staff. It is apparent that close coordination must exist between the sales department and production control. In the final analysis it is the sales department that decides what is to be produced, how much, and when.

Order control originates with a customer's order. The order, or a copy of it, comes to production control. There it is analyzed and all necessary papers are prepared to authorize production. In a job order shop it is just as important that men and machines be kept busy as in a flow control shop. One way to insure an even distribution of work is to group orders for similar products and then to schedule production somewhat as it is done in flow control. When working from a backlog of unfilled orders, production control can plan for efficient production more effectively than is possible if each order is put into production as soon as it is received.

TECHNIQUE OF PRODUCTION CONTROL

Planning production involves a system of records and reports, an explanation of which is an aid to understanding the complexities of manufacturing management. As has been stated, production control authority originates in the sales department and is relayed to the production control department. The tlater is a staff department without line authority over the men in the factory. When it is said that authority to produce is released by production control we mean that plans to produce are prepared in that department, and, in theory, transmitted to the factory manager for execution. He may follow the plans or he may disregard them. If he chooses to disregard the plans, he will be held accountable to top management. It is presumed that a system of production planning has been introduced with the sanction of top management. It is further presumed that the factory manager has accepted the idea and will do all in his power to make it work.

The records that are prepared for articles to be assembled from an assortment of parts are as follows:

1. A master bill of materials, which is a list of all materials that go into the product, the quantity of each, and where it is to be obtained—that is, purchased, taken from stock, or manufactured.

2. A master route sheet, which is a list of the sequence of operations, the machines to be used, the special tools and fixtures required, and the identifying numbers of any engineering drawings.

3. Engineering drawings for the article.

4. Processing instructions to supplement the abbreviated statement of processes shown on the route sheet.

The foregoing records become a part of a permanent file. When repeat orders are received at a future date the file can be consulted, and a repetition of the planning is unnecessary. When it is decided to set production in motion, a series of office forms are filled in from data contained in the permanent file. The following is a list of papers made up by clerks in the production planning office:

1. An order bill of material, which is headed by the name of the article to be manufactured, its identification number, and the number of units to be made. A list of the number of pieces of each part is written after the name and identification number of the part. Where materials and parts are to be obtained is indicated by "S" for stores, "P" for purchase, or "M" to manufacture.

2. An operations sheet, showing the sequence of operations. On this sheet the necessary tools, jigs, and fixtures are shown. At the head of the sheet is shown the date work is to start and the date it is to be completed. The time schedule for each operation is indicated after a description of the operation.

3. Requisitions authorizing the withdrawal of materials, parts, tools, measuring gauges, and other appliances the worker may need.

4. In some cases processing instructions for use of the foreman or individual workers, with sections of drawings when needed to supplement written instructions.

5. Identification tags to follow the work through the shop, and move tickets to instruct move men where to move the work from operation to operation.

This is a bare skeleton of the paper work needed to transmit authority to the work floor. The idea is that foremen and workers should be given written rather than oral instructions covering every detail of their duties. Instructions that go out are not the end of production control. Reports must come back to inform the production control department when the various operations have been completed. The control department with the aid of a device known as a control board can watch the progress of a production order, and can observe when schedules are not being followed.

METHODS ANALYSIS

The objective of methods analysis is to find the one best way to do things. It may involve such revolutionary changes in equipment and processes as to demand approval at higher levels of management. Methods engineers are specialists who constantly study operations in order to save time and effort and to improve workmanship. Improvements of the most elementary sort are in simplification of manual movements—the arrangement of materials, tools, and machines to minimize the motions a worker must make with his hands, feet, or body. This probably will call for a rearrangement of the work place. From this type of simplification, methods improvement can extend to re-modeling an entire factory. Special purpose machines, modern material handling equipment, improved lighting, ventilation, and noise reduction all fall within methods improvement.

When large capital outlays are involved, methods improvement recommendations should go to top management for approval. For simpler improvements, the authority of the foreman may suffice. Not all suggestions for methods improvement originate with methods engineers. Workers themselves observe shortcuts and are encouraged to make suggestions. Foremen, too, are a fertile source of ideas. Indeed, the acceptance of changes at the operating level is essential to success in making improvements produce the desired results. Workers are likely to resist change unless they have participated in developing the idea.

ACCOUNTING CONTROL

Facts widely used by management for gauging the effectiveness of policy execution at the manufacturing level are derived from accounting reports. Their design originates in the systems section of the accounting department, but requires acceptance by the manufacturing management. Operating men are not skilled in clerical work; they do not do well in keeping records and do not want to be bothered with them. Nevertheless, control over manufacturing calls for continuing reports of what is being done.

Mention has been made of the paper work involved in controlling production. Accounting control embodies figures that go into the statement of earnings and the balance sheet, and is a thing apart from production control. Assets and expenses affect accounting. Fixed assets in the factory include machinery and equipment of all sorts. Every item of equipment must be accounted for. Every item is identified by name and preferably a serial number. If it is scrapped the accounting department must be notified. If it is moved from one department to another, accounting records should be changed. All maintenance and repairs should be recorded and systematically reported. All inventories of raw materials, work in process, and finished stock, as well as factory supplies, are current assets and must be accounted for. Where they go and how much goes to this or that must be reported if accurate accounting records are to be kept. As long as inventories are on hand they are assets which appear on the balance sheet.

Consider, for example, the importance of a physical count of inventories. The time was when a factory would be shut down while all persons able to count tallied everything lying around that had value. Modern accounting keeps a running record of receipts and issues of materials and supplies. Control is effected by requiring that nothing be issued without a requisition. The requisitions are prepared in advance by the production control department. The stores ledger is kept by a materials control section, which in many companies is part of the accounting department. Little or no clerical work is required of operating personnel. All that is required of them is co-operation. Even the most carefully kept perpeutal inventory records of balances on hand must be verified from time to time by an actual physical count. In this work production control is expected to co-operate.

COST CONTROL

Comparison of actual costs with standard costs summarizes the efficiency of manufacturing activities. Manufacturing management must be satisfied that the controls are reasonable. The use of cost figures as a measure of efficiency creates occasional controversy. Operating personnel have two reasons for being suspicious of costs. First, when the efficiency of foremen is rated by their ability to keep costs at a minimum, foremen are prone to question the accuracy of the figures. Second, when bonuses are paid to manufacturing executives as a percentage of cost savings of their departments, they are skeptical of the yardstick with which actual costs are compared, and they also question the way actual costs are computed.

There can be little disagreement as to prime costs—labor and materials. A given number of hours of labor multiplied by the wage rate gives correct labor cost. A given number of units of material times a price per unit is correct material cost. However, in connection with the latter cost figure, some misunderstanding may arise when a change is made from first-in-first-out method of pricing to last-in-first-out. This probably can be explained to the executive's satisfaction, but the allocation of overhead expense is somewhat arbitrary. To avoid misunderstandings about cost accounting, many companies offer to executives courses of instruction in the application of cost accounting. Even then there may be disagreement. Accountants themselves are not in agreement as to procedures. That being true, it is too much to expect non-accountants to accept accounting figures on faith, especially when the figures affect their incomes, or promotions, or even the retention of their jobs.

CO-ORDINATION

Manufacturing activities must be co-ordinated with sales; purchasing must be co-ordinated with manufacturing. A complete system of production control generally keeps production in line with sales. As soon as sales fall off, production orders are cut back. When sales increase production is increased. This can be accomplished in one or a combination of four ways. (1) Add more employees and speed up production. (2) Run an extra shift. (3) Expand production facilities by adding more equipment. (4) Contract work to outside producers. Management may object to all these measures. There is an optimum number of workers who can work together efficiently in a given amount of space. Workers on night shift generally are less efficient; moreover, a premium wage rate sometimes must be paid for night work. Expansion of plant capacity requires capital which may lie idle if the spurt in business should prove to be temporary. Farming out of orders to other producers overcomes the three preceding objections, but control of quality is not assured, and the profit on the extra business must be paid to the subcontractor.

Purchasing is a preliminary step to manufacturing. Excessive purchases mean accumulation of inventories with the danger of attendant losses. An aim of production control is to keep purchases co-ordinated with production activity. If the control works smoothly no exessive purchases will be made. But more disturbing is a shortage of materials because of the inefficiency in the purchasing department. This situation can be corrected only by a co-ordinating executive at the top, probably a vice-president or even the president. Of course, in times of material shortages no effort of a purchasing department can procure what is not procurable. This is particularly true under a plan of government allotment of materials during rearmament activities.

IMPACT OF LABOR POLICIES

Interruption of production due to labor disputes brings the labor relations department into direct conflict with the manufacturing department. Three kinds of strikes may interrupt production. (1) Authorized strikes, which usually occur as a result of disputes over labor contracts. When a contract is being negotiated union leaders may call a strike as a show of strength to enforce their demands. (2) "Wildcat" strikes, which are not called by top-labor leaders but are a local expression of dissatisfaction, usually over interpretation of contract provisions. In each of the foregoing situations the labor relations department is more or less involved. (3) Slow-down strikes, in which

workers do not leave the job but willfully retard production. Such distur-
bances may result from dissatisfaction with the foreman's enforcement of
discipline. The industrial relations department cannot be held responsible for
that.

Since the objective of the production department is to keep production
moving at an even rate, touchy situations with employees should be avoided,
if at all possible. Close co-operation between manufacturing and labor relations is imperative. A contented, interested, well disciplined work force is the
ultimate aim of both departments.

THE MANUFACTURING BUDGET

General policy on manufacturing is translated into a plan of action in the
form of a manufacturing budget. A budget in its simplest form is a statement
of proposed activities or expenditures. A master budget for the company as a
whole is a matching of expenditures against income. Income is the outside
limit of what can be spent. Plans to spend must be trimmed to fit income. All
the money that is spent producing goods must be recovered from income
obtained from sales. The manufacturing budget is an advance plan for producing what the sales department estimates can be sold. The plan usually is
projected for a year and is revised from month to month as business conditions change. At some point dollar estimates must be translated into units of
finished product. That translation is made when the manufacturing budget is
prepared.

The manufacturing budget is a statement of the number of units to be produced in a year. The total is broken down into a schedule of production. The
quantity to be produced each day, each week, and each month is set opposite
the proper division of a time schedule. The capacity of the plant, or a division
of the plant, limits the schedule for a single day. Some point within that limit
is an attainable goal. In some situations a schedule of 80 per cent of capacity
will allow a cushion for unforeseen delays. If apparent orders should be far
below capacity, the principle of economic operations applies. It is uneconomic
to run through small driblets. It may be better to run through more in one
month than can be sold and not to produce any the next month.

With these considerations in mind, a schedule is made, usually on a month
to month basis. A production schedule is illustrated in Figure No. 1. Note
that the same amount is not scheduled for each month; the quantity varies
to accommodate other demands on the machines. The cumulative total, however, comes out at the end of the year as equal to estimated annual sales.
Notwithstanding the care exercised in making plans, actual achievement
rarely squares with the plans. In order to compare progress with the plan, a
monthly report of actual production is made. Over and under production can
be seen by comparing actual with planned production. Production schedules
are revised accordingly.

| ITEM | January | | | | | |
| | SALES | | PRODUCTION | | CUMULATIVE ESTIMATES | |
	Expect	Actual	Quota	Actual	Sales	Prod.
A	100		160		100	160
B	200		170		200	170
C	40		50		40	50
D	600		500		600	500

| ITEM | February | | | | | |
| | SALES | | PRODUCTION | | CUMULATIVE ESTIMATES | |
	Expect	Actual	Quota	Acutal	Sales	Prod.
A	200		150		300	310
B	180		140		380	310
C	60		70		100	120
D	480		500		1080	1000

| ITEM | December | | | | | |
| | SALES | | PRODUCTION | | CUMULATIVE ESTIMATES | |
	Expect	Actual	Quota	Actual	Sales	Prod.
A	140		160		1920	1920
B	100		170		1800	1800
C	30		20		480	480
D	700		800		7200	7200

Actual to be filled in at end of month.
Excessive discrepancies require revision of budget.

Fig. 1. Manufacturing budget.

SUMMARY

Only a small percentage of the products of nature are consumed without some form of processing. Change in form ranges from simple to very complex operations constituting the greatest segment of business activity. The objective of manufacturing is to produce articles designed for a specific purpose. The most suitable materials must be used, which calls for policy decisions as to their durability, ease of processing, availability, and cost. Manufacturing costs are lowest when confined to one product and one process, but the demands of the market call for diversification. However, manufacturing management usually has a choice between several processes. Plant location and plant design effect manufacturing economies. Standards of quality commensurate with the intended utility of a product and the price at which it is to be offered require managerial decisions as to quality standards. Although the details of planning for production are worked out far down the scale from top management, it is nevertheless a matter of vital importance to the success of a business that the planning be well done. The technique of production control must be understood by top management. Methods analysis is essential to efficient operation and cannot be left to chance. Accounting figures are necessary for proper control, especially cost figures. All manufacturing operations must be co-ordinated with sales efforts. Labor policies have an impact on manufacturing practices, and vice versa. The manufacturing budget is a part of the over-all budgetary control.

5. PERSONNEL PRACTICES IN FACTORY AND OFFICE: MANUFACTURING*

I. Employment Procedures
    1. Sources Used in Recruiting
    2. Use of Private Employment Agencies
    3. Travelling Expenses for Pre-employment Interview
    4. Types of Employment Interviews
    5. Centralized Employment Screening
    6. Work References
    7. School References
    8. Personal References
    9. Use of Credit Reports
    10. Testing Programs
    11. Minimum Hiring Age
    12. Probation Period
    13. Merit Rating Programs
    14. Providing Work References
    15. Hiring Relatives of Employees
    16. Exit Interviews
    17. Outside Employment (Moonlighting)
II. Hours of Work and Pay Practices
    18. Normal Work Day
    19. Pay for Overtime (Over 8 Hours)
    20. Normal Work Week: Hours
    21. Normal Work Week: Days
    22. Pay for Work on Sixth Day
    23. Pay for Work on Seventh Day
    24. Pay for Work on Sunday

* From NICB *Studies in Personnel Policy* No. 145, 1964, pp. ii–vii. Reprinted by permission of The National Industrial Conference Board.

67. Athletic or Recreation Field
68. Recreation Clubhouse
69. Recreation Room
70. Employee Library
71. Retired Employees' Clubs
72. Christmas Parties
73. Company Picnics
74. Open House Programs
75. Company Religious Activities
76. Service Awards Program
77. Long-Service Clubs
78. Company Parking
79. Daily Transit Assistance
80. Housing Assistance
81. Blood Banks
82. Company Gifts to Employees
83. Work Uniforms
84. Paying for Soiled Clothes
85. Company Cafeteria
86. Mobile Lunch Facilities
87. Vending Machines
88. Credit Unions
89. Loans to Employees
90. Temporary Living Expenses (New Employees)
91. Moving Expenses (New Employees)
92. Sale of Company Products to Employees
93. Company Stores
94. Retail Discounts to Employees
95. Sale of Non-Company Products to Employees
96. Special Services for Employees

V. Time off With Pay
97. Paid Time Off: Death in Family
98. Paid Time Off: Illness in Family
99. Paid Time Off: Trial Witness
100. Holiday Pay
101. Paid Time Off: Voting
102. Time Off for Christmas Shopping
103. Salary Continuance: Summer Military Encampment
104. Paid Time Off: Jury Duty
105. Paid Time Off: Medical Appointments
106. Paid Time Off: Marriage
107. Maximum Vacation Allowance
108. Service Required for Vacation Allowances

6. FINANCIAL POLICIES*

CHARLES L. JAMISON

FINANCIAL DECISIONS

Managing business finance involves decisions as to volume of capital required, the sources of capital, and its allocation to fixed assets. Figure 1 shows capital

Business arch

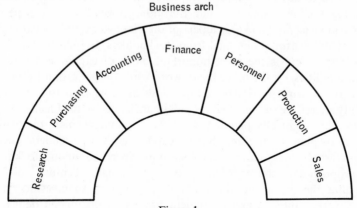

Figure 1.

as the keystone supporting the business arch. It is in some respects the most important segment of the business structure. Within itself it has structural characteristics which may be termed capital structure. This, like any physical structure, should be the product of planning and forethought.

A corporation's capital structure appears on the credit side of a balance sheet, as illustrated in Table 1. The main classification of items embraces

* Charles L. Jamison, *Business Policy*, Chapter 24, (C) 1953. Reprinted by permission of Prentice-Hall, Inc., Englewood Cliffs, N.J.

Table 1

Credit Side of a Corporation Balance Sheet

Liabilities and Present Worth

CURRENT LIABILITIES

Accounts payable		$204,350
Notes payable		100,000
Accrued taxes		1,500
Total current liabilities		$305,850

FUNDED DEBT

First mortgage bonds		250,000
Total liabilities		$555,850

STOCKHOLDERS' EQUITY

Capital stock	750,000	
Surplus	264,250	
Total proprietary interest		$1,014,250
Total liabilities and present worth		$1,570,000

current liabilities, funded debt, and stockholders' equity. *Current liabilities* generally are defined as debts that must be paid within a year. Although money owed to anyone is capital employed in a business, current liabilities are not regarded as planned capital. But money owed for a longer period in what is known as *funded debt* is a part of the planned capital structure. More important still is capital obtained from stockholders. In industrial companies *stockholders' equity* is the most important block of capital structure. Railroads and utilities, on the other hand, work with a larger proportion of long-term borrowed capital. Managerial decisions as to whether to borrow or to sell equity shares are the most vital of all financial decisions. Ideally, financial structure is thoughtfully planned. For example, management might decide as part of its plan to raise one-third of capital funds from lenders, one-third from preferred stockholders, and one-third from common stockholders. These proportions were regarded as conservative half a century ago for the reason that the degree of obligation to pay money to investors in each category varies. Interest and retirement provisions on funded debt are inescapable liabilities. The obligation to pay dividends on preferred stock is not so pressing. On common stock there is no legal obligation whatever except in case of liquidation. A businessman would be foolhardy if he assumed a liability to pay a fixed sum each year for the use of every dollar of his capital. The risk would be cut by two-thirds if he pledged the income from only one-third of the capital. If income in any one year does not measure up to expectation, the common stockholders can go without dividends, and the preferred stockholders can be asked to defer their dividends until earnings are better.

The primary consideration in deciding upon the proper capital structure is ability to assume the risk of contracts with investors. A secondary consideration is the prevailing state of the securities markets. In an orderly securities market three types of investors are found: (1) those seeking investments that insure security of principal and regularity of income; (2) those who are less concerned with recovering their principal than with assurance of regular income; (3) those who are willing to assume risk to capital and income in the hope that the value of the investment may increase and that the income will increase proportionately. Bonds satisfy investors in the first group; preferred stock those in the second group; common stock those in the third group. An even balance between the three types of investors rarely is found in practice. When business is booming and speculative fever runs high, common stocks are in greatest demand. When business faces an uncertain future, when stock prices are low and investors are disinclined to speculate, bonds are in greater demand. Between the two extremes there is a varying interest in preferred stocks. Corporations requiring new capital usually follow the most expedient course at the time they need funds. If common stocks can be readily sold at high prices, financing may be in common stocks. If relatively better prices can be obtained for preferred stock, then that form of security may be offered to the public. If bond interest rates are low or investors are in a conservative frame of mind, bonds may be the best available source of capital. In simple language these are the factors that in the end determine capital structure, regardless of any preplanning that may have been done.

VOLUME OF CAPITAL REQUIRED

The size of the business largely determines the amount of capital required, although decisions concerning expansion are closely related to capital decision. Capital is invested in two types of assets, fixed assets and current assets. The fixed capital of a manufacturing company is its land, buildings, machinery, and equipment. The fixed capital of a store is land, building, and store fixtures. The fixed capital of an electric power company is its generating plants, power lines, transformer stations, and offices. Each type of business also must provide for an adequate fund of working capital that is invested in current assets. For a manufacturing company the proportions may be two-thirds fixed and one-third working capital. For a store the proportions may be one-third fixed and two-thirds working capital. For an electric power company the proportions may be seven-eighths fixed and one-eighth working capital.

A capital fund must be provided sufficient to pay for all the fixed assets. Some of this money may be borrowed, or all of it may be obtained from stockholders. The investment may be reduced if buildings are rented, as is likely in the case of a store. Many small manufacturing companies also rent space in which to operate. Working capital is composed of cash, stocks of materials and salable goods, and money owed by customers. The proportions may be 20 per cent cash, 40 per cent inventories, and 40 per cent accounts receivable. The proportions vary according to each company's policies and the nature of its business. The important thing to determine is what the policies are to be and to provide enough capital to execute the policies properly.

As a rule, capital is not provided for expansion until expansion plans are completed. Before work is begun, however, the capital should be in hand, If the necessary founds cannot be obtained, the plans should be abandoned. Companies which violate this rule must finance expansion from working capital. This practice depletes working capital and may lead to trouble. A company in that predicament is said to have overexpanded. In a desperate attempt to extricate itself, management may be obliged to obtain capital on ruinous terms. It is apparent that a policy of expansion must be tempered by the availability of the requisite capital.

SOURCES OF CAPITAL

The largest reservoirs of capital seeking investment are to be found in institutions that control pools of individual savings, such as life insurance companies and saving banks. Total savings in normal years equal as much as seven or eight billion dollars. In the year 1944, savings amounted to 22 billions. In 1932, individuals spent more than one billion dollars of previous savings. Much of the large amount was, and still is, paid into insurance companies or deposited in savings banks. Insurance companies have reserves of more than 50 billions which must be invested in income-producing securities. Bonds of public bodies (Federal, state, and municipal) are the safest investments for insurance companies. A good share of insurance company investment is in mortgages, but a considerable sum is placed in corporate bonds and a few choice stocks.

It is estimated that seven million individuals own corporate stocks. Shares are acquired by purchase on stock exchanges or are bought from investment banking houses. Stocks bought on stock exchanges put no new capital into the investment stream—they just transfer ownership from one investor to another. The funds acquired by the seller, however, may find their way, directly or indirectly, into new securities. Shares bought from investment banking houses do inject new capital. Investment bankers are professional marketers of new securities, some of which are bought by individual savers and some by institutions that in turn are depositors of savings of individuals. By one means or another, savings find their way into the coffers of governmental bodies or into business. State and municipal governments build capital assets in the form of highways, bridges, and public structures with the proceeds of bond sales. Some of these assets produce revenue and some do not. Interest and retirement of principal are paid from revenue, if there is any, or from taxation. Some of the savings exchanged for Federal government bonds also are invested in capital assets.

Savings that have found their way into industrial securities generally earn income for the investors. Such income flows to investors in the form of dividends or interest, and some of it may repay the principal. Not all of this money is spent by security holders. Much of it is added to their savings and seeks reinvestment.

THE BEST RESERVOIR TO TAP

Decision as to which reservoir to tap is influenced by the ease with which investors may be persuaded to risk their savings, and the cost of the capital—underwriting expense and interest. Assume for a moment that, if a business corporation had free choice in selecting a source of capital funds, the choice would be individual investors in common stocks. But conditions are better at one time than at another for the sale of this type of stock. Lack of interest on the part of investors in an investment that does not guarantee a fixed return and never will repay the principal would be an unfavorable condition. The only way an investor in common stock can recover principal is to sell to someone else. If investors in general have lost interest in common stocks it would be hard to find a market, except at a very low price. That would not be a good time to offer new common shares to the public. While some buyers might be found if the price were low enough, an unreasonably large number of shares would have to be sold to bring in the desired amount of capital.

A few investors who might not buy common shares would be interested in preferred stock. When market prices for common are low, they probably would also be low for preferred. Nevertheless, a better price per share could be had for preferred than for common, and a given amount of new capital could be raised with fewer shares of the former than of the latter. The issuing company, however, would assume an obligation to pay a regular dividend on the preferred. At least no dividends could be paid on previously issued common until preferred dividends had been paid.

At times when interest rates are low because a mass of funds is seeking investment, the sale of bonds may be the cheapest source of capital. Purchasers of bonds may be reached through investment banking houses acting as middlemen. Investment bankers take a profit that may range from $1 to $5 on each hundred. The amount of cash realized from that sort of transaction shrinks by the amount of the bankers' profit. More cash under certain circumstances can be realized by the sale of large blocks of bonds directly to insurance companies. There is no middleman's profit in such transactions. There are other advantages in selling to insurance companies, to be discussed in a later section.

INSTITUTIONS WHICH DEAL IN SECURITIES

Rounding up the savings of individuals is a professional undertaking which has become the business of investment bankers. As a rule a corporation wishing to sell new securities does not have the requisite knowledge or the organization to sell the securities directly to the public. Therefore, it sells an entire issue to an investment house, which in turn sells the securities where- ever a market can be found. Persons who have money to invest are accustomed to going to investment bankers for advice and the ultimate purchase of suit- able stocks or bonds. As a merchant in securities the banker has a clientele of investors large and small whose requirements are varied. Like any mer- chant he carries a full line, consisting of bonds, preferred stocks, and common stocks of assorted varieties issued by different types of companies. Before he can sell he has to buy. Before he buys, he investigates. With expert knowledge of securities and the investment needs of his customers, he is in position to render valuable advisory services.

When a company approaches an investment banker for funds for long term financing, the company states its requirements. The banking house desires assurance that the security will provide a sound investment for its clients. Therefore, before a purchase is made, the banker conducts an ex- haustive analysis of the company. A preliminary investigation is limited to the financial history of the company, its apparent stability, and probable future prospects. If the proposition appears to have merit, a more exhaustive in- vestigation is made of physical assets and managerial policies. Financial records are checked by auditors; physical plant is checked by engineers; the company's legal entanglements are checked by lawyers. If the banker still is satisfied that the risk is reasonable, negotiations are entered into regarding protective provisions of the contract with prospective investors, interest rates on bonds, dividend rates on preferred stock and the price the investment house is willing to pay. This price usually is one, two, three, or more points below the price at which the security may be sold to the public. The in- vestigation is so expensive that only large issues of several hundred thousand dollars yield enough profit to pay this expense and leave any margin for the service of the banker and the risk he runs.

Securities offered to the public, if transactions cover state lines, must be registered with the Securities and Exchange Commission. The registration certificate, filed in triplicate, is available to the public. It must contain a full and complete disclosure of the financial affairs of the company and its obligations to investors. Severe penalties are imposed on officers and directors if any false statements are found in the document. The great detail required and the complete accuracy of facts presented necessitates extensive audits and legal opinions which cost the procurer of new capital many thousand dollars. These expenses and the fees of underwriters have the effect of reducing the amount of capital available for use in the business, and are an argument for avoiding public offering of securities if funds can be raised by any other means.

INVESTMENT TRUSTS

An increasing number of individual savers lack confidence in their own judgment to manage the investing of their accumulated funds, and therefore entrust their money in investment companies, which in a roundabout way supply capital to business. The assets of American investment companies are somewhere between three and four billion dollars. This capital has been contributed by individual savers. The practice of investment companies generally is to make purchases of stocks and bonds in the investment markets. They do not underwrite new issues of securities as do investment banking houses. Nevertheless, when they buy securities from other investors, funds flow into the hands of the seller, who seeks replacements. By some roundabout process the millions of investment funds that find their way each year into investment trusts supply capital to industry.

A few management companies supply capital directly to industry. They get the money by selling their own stocks or debentures to the public. Investors in the securities of such companies have the benefit of diversified investments, relying on the judgment of the executives of the management companies for the safety of their capital. Investment companies of any type make exhaustive investigations of the companies in which they own securities, which is a safeguard to the amateur investor.

BANKS OF DEPOSIT

Deposits are made by the public in two types of banks—commercial and savings. The business of commercial banks is to receive and protect demand deposits. They must be prepared to return deposits whenever depositors call for their money. Commercial banks, therefore, may invest depositors' money chiefly in short-term loans or readily marketable government bonds. Although they may invest in mortgages within limits, commercial banks are not a ready source of permanent capital. But they do supply funds to business for working capital needs.

Savings deposits are left with banks for safety. They cannot be withdrawn on demand and can be invested in long-term securities provided maturities are properly rotated. Since savings banks pay interest on deposits, it is necessary that income be earned on their investments. However, the banks are strictly regulated by law. Only high grade securities are eligible because safety of principal is an important factor. Therefore, banks depend on seasoned securities, those that have an established market and are issued by companies that have a long record for conservative management. Corporations rarely get new capital directly from savings banks, but many billions of dollars of savings deposits help to finance business in a roundabout way.

INSURANCE COMPANIES

Insurance companies, instead of looking to the securities markets for sound industrial investments for their reserves, find it advantageous to deal directly with corporations seeking new capital. Direct dealing in this manner eliminates the middle-men whose services otherwise would be used. Direct placement of securities is less expensive, less time-consuming, and less complicated. Registration with the Securities and Exchange Commission is not required.

This saves time and considerable expense. Terms of the debt arrangement can be made to fit the needs of both borrower and lender. This simplifies the process. When securities are offered to the public they must fulfill the requirements of only one investor. Although return to the insurance company may be a little higher, it is not more costly to the borrower because of the saving in fees and expenses. A close relationship exists between borrower and lender throughout the life of the loan. On occasions, when interest rates have been falling, insurance companies have consented to replacing existing loans before maturity with new loans at a lower interest rate.

Objection to direct placing of loans is raised by investment banking houses. It channels the choicest securities to institutional investors and leaves less attractive ones for investment banking firms to handle. In some years more bonds have been placed directly than through security markets. This weakens their position as service adjuncts to business. It further is contended that insurance companies are not as thoroughly experienced as securities underwriters and sometimes have used poor judgment in granting loans. Borrowers, it is said, sometimes overextend themselves because of the ease of getting funds from insurance companies.

STATE OF THE SECURITIES MARKET

As stated earlier in this chapter, capital structure in some cases is preplanned, but generally it is shaped by expediency. Although financial planners may have decided upon a desirable proportion of bonds, preferred stock, and common stock before they approach the investment market, the plan more often than not must be modified. The prevailing investment fad or the relative cost of floating securities is the determinant of whether bonds or stock are to be issued, and what kind. Except for companies whose policy is to "trade on the equity" most corporations prefer to raise capital from the sale of common stock. If the market at the time is not favorable for the sale of common stock, it may be expedient to offer preferred stock convertible into common at a price that approximates what would have been considered satisfactory had it been possible to sell common stock at the time of the initial offering.

Factors that affect the market for common stock are:

1. *Current Position of the Business Cycle.* When the cyclical trend is upward investors are optimistic; when it is downward they are cautious about risking their funds in what are regarded as speculative investments.

2. *Fear of Inflation.* Capital flees from fixed principal investments to inflation hedges. Owners of equity shares have an interest in corporate property after all debts have been paid. The value of land, buildings, machinery, and inventories rises as the value of the dollar declines. The sales value of products goes up and the profit margin in terms of dollars also rises. Theoretically dividends also increase, but they usually lag behind the devaluation of the dollar.

3. *The Ebb and Flow of the Fad for Speculation.* Speculators buy shares in the hope of making a quick profit. They bid up the price of stocks and create active markets in which new issues can be disposed of to the public at favorable prices.

The convertible feature of preferred stocks can be explained by the following example: Consider a securities market in which the price of common shares is relatively low. Investors are uncertain as to the future prospect for continuing dividends on common stock. They know, however, that a sound company will pay the contract rate on preferred shares even though common dividends are lowered or altogether discontinued. Some time in the future common dividends may exceed thòse on preferred, and the market price may rise proportionately. Under such circumstances a certain class of investors will pay proportionately more for preferred shares than for common. Say, they would be willing to pay $100 a share for a 5 per cent preferred stock. The price of the common at that time may be $35. Under the contract printed on the preferred stock certificate each share may be converted into two shares of common at any time within five years. Should the price of common go above 50 during that interval, it would be profitable for the holders of the preferred to convert. In effect the issuing company would have sold common shares at $50 at a time when the market was only $35.

If the state of the market should be such that preferred shares could not be sold readily, it might be possible to sell debenture bonds containing a similar conversion provision. At some time in the future the bonds might be converted into common shares when the market price made such conversion profitable. In that event the issuing company would be just as well off as though it had sold common originally at the conversion price.

TRADING ON THE EQUITY

Regardless of financial expediency a studied policy of "trading on the equity" substantially increases earnings on equity capital when interest rates are low and profit margins are high. The advantage of such a policy can be illustrated by a company able to earn 10 per cent on the capital invested in its business. Suppose its credit was good enough to enable it to borrow money at 4 per cent. With a capital structure made up of $250,000 of bonds and $750,000 of stock, or a total of $1,000,000, a profit of 10 per cent would amount to $100,000. The interest on the bonds would be $10,000. The remaining profit of $90,000 would be available for dividends on common stock. The rate of earning on the common stock would be 12 per cent. This is 2 per cent more than could be earned on the common if all the capital had been raised from that type of security. Suppose the proportions had been reversed, and that bonds had been 75 per cent and stock 25 per cent of the capital. Interest on $750,000 of bonds would be $30,000, which would leave $70,000 for the common stock, or 28 per cent. The greater the amount of borrowed funds in proportion to equity capital the greater the rate earned on equity capital.

Two conflicting objectives may influence the making of financial policy. One objective is to protect the company against the liability that a fixed debt imposes; the other is to maximize earnings on common stock. If managers are large owners of common stock they may have a selfish interest in increasing their income by following the latter course. In view of the relatively small stock ownership of most managers, such an objective does not prevail. This may partly explain why so many companies retire debt as quickly as possible when circumstances have made it necessary to borrow.

OWNING VERSUS LEASING

Capital tied up in fixed assets may produce less profit than the same amount of capital used as a working fund. Institutional investors who would not care to take the risk of investment in equities will buy fixed assets from a corporation and lease them back for a long term. Some universities have invested endowment funds in land and buildings purchased from large stores and factories. Life insurance companies have made similar investments. The advantages to investors are:

1. Return on capital is higher than it would be on sound bonds.

2. Income is assured if the tenant is a well established, efficiently managed business.

3. Principal is secure because the property has a value that probably will not depreciate below the amount invested. Indeed, it probably will increase in value, because the tenant in most cases is required to keep the property in repair and probably will improve it in order to increase its efficiency.

The advantages to borrowers are:

1. Capital formerly invested in fixed assets is made liquid and can be used to finance inventories, to carry accounts receivable, and to provide other needed working capital.

2. The amount of capital raised on the property greatly exceeds what could be raised if the property had been mortgaged and mortgage bonds sold. Usually not more than 60 per cent of the value of property can be borrowed on a mortgage, whereas, when property is sold outright, 100 per cent of its value can be raised. The tenant's use of the property is in no way changed when he becomes a tenant.

3. The property of educational institutions is tax free. Until tax authorities began to question the propriety of the practice, funds invested in income producing properties in some jurisdictions were not taxed. Doubts have been raised as to whether business corporations are not transferring property to tax exempt institutions for the purpose of avoiding taxes. Any subterfuge to avoid taxes is frowned upon.

Some chain store companies induce private investors to build the type of store they want, and then rent the property on a long-term lease. Manufacturing companies rent space in loft buildings and manufacturing centers, thereby conserving their capital for more active employment in the business. Like trading on the equity this is one way to get the maximum return on business capital.

REINVESTMENT OF EARNINGS

Much business expansion is financed with funds created by the business, either from retained earnings or from funds accumulated in depreciation reserves. After all fixed charges are paid, including interest on bonds and dividends on preferred stock, the earnings that remain are available for dividends on common shares. A distribution of 70 per cent of the residual amount is regarded generally as conservative. Few companies year in and year out follow a practice of paying exactly 70 per cent of earnings in dividends. In some years they distribute more; in some years less.

Many large manufacturing companies have financed expansion almost entirely from reinvested earnings. It is the simplest and least expensive way to get new capital. Accordingly, when an expansion program is being carried out, there is a tendency for companies to reinvest stockholders' money rather than to give it to them in the form of dividends. It is not unusual for a company to distribute as little as 30 per cent of earnings. Stockholders may complain that they and not the directors should be allowed to judge whether or not they want to increase their equity in a company. Why don't the directors distribute all the earnings and then invite stockholders to buy additional shares with their dividends? If they want to keep their money in business, it is argued, they will buy more stock. If they do not wish to do so, they are free to do as they please with their share of earnings.

A practice followed by some rapidly expanding companies has been to pay reasonably generous dividends and then to offer *privileged subscriptions* to stockholders whenever new capital is needed. The privilege consists in offering an opportunity to buy shares at a price somewhat below the prevailing market price. That is to say, a stock selling at 50 may be offered to stockholders at $45. If they wish to subscribe they can save $5.00 on each share; if they do not they can sell their *rights*. Suppose a company is offering each stockholder the privilege of subscribing for one new share for every five old shares. The holder of 100 shares has the privilege of subscribing for 20 new shares, which he can buy for $100 less than the prevailing market price. Since he holds 100 shares, each right is worth $1.00. Each stockholder receives a warrant which certifies that the holder is entitled to subscribe for a stated number of new shares at $45 per share. A warrant is somewhat like a stock certificate, and can be assigned and sold in the market. The purchaser then acquires the privilege to subscribe. He already has paid for the warrant and, although he pays only $45 a share for the stock, he is only a little better off than he would have been had he bought stock in the market.

DIVIDEND POLICY

Instead of maintaining dividends at a uniform rate year after year, a policy of paying whatever rate seems prudent may be adopted. There is an increasing tendency for companies not to try to maintain a uniform rate on common stock. Earnings fluctuate widely. If a company with fluctuating earnings should pay the same rate each year the percentage of profits distributed would vary from year to year as earnings are up or down. It has been observed that companies do not always pay out a fixed proportion of earnings. The distribution may be as little as 30 per cent, or it may be more than 100 per cent when past earnings are dipped into. Even without a uniform dividend rate, yearly variation in dividends is not as great as yearly variation in earnings. When earnings are low the dividend rate may be reduced, but not in the same proportion as the drop in earnings. When earnings are high the dividend rate may be increased, but not in the same proportion as the increase in earnings.

The strongest argument against attempting to maintain a regular rate is that the risks of business must be passed on to someone. Every participant in business enterprise cannot be guaranteed a fixed income, since sales and profits are not guaranteed. The common stock holder is the residuary claimant and, therefore, must be content with what is left after all other claimants have received their shares. It is considered an unwise policy to put management in the position of having to squeeze a fixed amount out of business in order to maintain the dividend at a regular rate. Management's responsibility is to direct the business as efficiently as possible, not to cut corners, nor to neglect maintenance, nor to turn a quick dollar at the expense of future customer and public relations.

On the other side of the argument, it is contended that individual investors whose investment in business has been solicited have a right to demand a regular income. Uncertainty as to yearly dividends drives them away from common stocks. This objection is met partly by some companies. A regular dividend at a rate that is reasonably sure to be earned is paid year after year. Extra dividends are paid when earnings warrant. The rate may vary from time to time, or the extra may not be paid at all in years of low earnings. When stockholders get an extra dividend they have reason to be pleased, but they should not depend upon it.

Another argument for regularity in dividend rate is the stabilization of price in the stock market. When new capital is needed from the sale of additional stock, a segment of the investing public, disinclined to speculate, is attracted to stock with a record of stable dividends and relatively stable market price.

STOCK DIVIDENDS AND STOCK SPLITS

Allied to dividend policy is a policy of increasing the number of shares in the hands of existing stockholders by splitting the shares or by issuing stock dividends. Either of these devices increases the number of shares without requiring additional investment. A stock split means that one share of new stock is given for one of old; or it may be two for one, or three for one, or four for one. There is no limit to the ratio, but generally it is in multiples of whole shares. A $100 par share may be split into two $50 shares, or four $25 shares. Surplus account is not altered. All that is done is to change the number of shares in the capital stock account and the value of each share.

Stock dividends, on the contrary, require a bookkeeping entry transferring an amount from surplus account to capital stock account. A portion of surplus so transferred to capital necessitates the issue of enough new shares to stockholders at the prevailing declared value of each share to equal the fund taken from surplus. Stock dividends usually are less than 100 per cent although there is no reason why they should not be more.

The primary argument for splitting stock is to reduce the price in the market. It is believed that investors are more inclined to buy low priced than high priced shares. Although $100 shares give a holder just as much equity in a company as four times as many $25 shares, the average investor seems to like to own a large number of shares. Because of this preference, market prices of low priced shares are somewhat higher relatively than high priced shares. That is to say after a stock split four shares may command a price of $27.50 per share, whereas one share before the split may have been selling at $100.

The secondary argument for splitting stock is that the dividend per share on a greater number of shares will be smaller although the aggregate distribution of profit will be the same. Nevertheless, persons disposed to criticize corporations for the profits they distribute are much less critical if the distribution is $2.00 a share than they would be if it were $8.00 a share. The same arguments apply to diluting the number of shares by stock dividends.

MANAGEMENT OF WORKING CAPITAL

Insolvency can be avoided by wise management of working capital, an objective that is attained by established policies of financial management. Insolvency results when a businessman incurs debts that he is unable to pay when the obligations fall due. Creditors require payment in cash. Therefore, good financial management anticipates all claims by seeing that ample cash is on hand. Provision of an adequate cash balance is a primary duty of the finance department. But capital must be kept at work. Cash lying idly in the bank is not working. To keep it working, capital must be circulated. In a manufacturing business it first goes into materials; to this is added labor cost. The product of that process is salable goods. The goods must be sold as quickly as possible, usually on credit. The amounts owed by customers become accounts receivable, which must be collected when they are due. Cash once more comes into the business ready for another turn around the circuit. With each turnover a profit is made that increases the fund of cash. Figure 2 illustrates the circulation of working capital.

The components of working capital are cash, accounts receivable, and inventories, in the order of their liquidity. Cash is entirely liquid. Investments in government bonds also are regarded as liquid because they can be quickly converted into cash. Temporary investment in such securities earns a small income. When accumulating cash to meet some impending large outlay it is

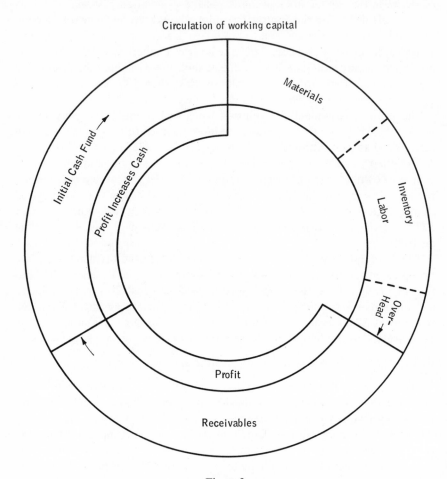

Figure 2.

the practice of companies to buy that type of temporary investment security. Accounts receivable generally can be depended upon to produce cash in due time if the credit of customers is sound. But accounts can only be collected in accordance with credit terms. Credit policy determines credit terms and is the joint responsibility of sales and finance. The shorter the credit terms the more quickly the money can be collected. Turnover is accelerated by shortened credit terms, a factor that can be controlled. But to bring the money in when it is due requires collection pressure. This is the responsibility of the credit manager who reports to the treasurer in many companies.

Slow turnover of inventory can retard efficient use of working capital even more than slow turnover of accounts receivable. This is something beyond the control of the finance department. However, they can exert influence over the production department and recommend procedures that will stimulate inventory turnover. This is another example of the need for co-ordination between finance and other departments.

SUMMARY

Managing business finance involves decisions as to the volume of capital required, the sources of capital, and its allocation to fixed assets and current assets. The size of a business determines the amount of capital required, although expansion policy may be limited by the amount of available capital. The largest reservoirs of capital seeking investment are to be found in institutions which control pools of individual savings. Some individuals invest directly, but their savings go largely into industry through insurance companies and savings banks. Rounding up the savings of thrifty people is a professional undertaking that has become the business of investment houses. Investment trusts place a large volume of capital in industry. Short-term financing can be obtained from banks of deposit. In recent years insurance companies have become extensive investors in the securities and assets of industrial companies. Capital structure follows prescribed principles. Some types of business are justified in going into debt. Some adhere strictly to equity financing. One way to stretch capital is to allow a fiduciary institution to own fixed assets and to lease them on long-term contracts.

Companies with wide profit margins can expand with reinvested earnings. Dividend policy varies in different companies. Stockholders to some extent prefer to have their equity built up by reinvested earnings rather than to take all the profit in dividends. When that policy is followed the holdings of stockholders are increased through stock dividends and stock splits. The management of working capital is one of the most important duties of financial management.

7. RIDING HERD ON ACCOUNTING STANDARDS*

—HERMAN W. BEVIS

The general topic for this session, "The Future of Accounting," is so broad that time permits discussion of only some one aspect of the subject. A good place to start is with the unsolved problems of the present. Certainly one of these is a proper perspective with regard to the determinations of, and compliance with, appropriate accounting standards.

Some public comments appear to come quite close to advocacy that uniform accounting standards in some degree of detail be imposed on all businesses. Important advantages, it has been claimed, would result. If the proposition were as easy as it sounds, and were free from serious disadvantages, one could properly question why it had not been achieved long ago.

The course toward uniformity is, however, neither simple nor obvious. Quite aside from the enormous practical problems of definition, we must consider whether uniformity would help or hinder adjustments to new conditions. We are living in times of rapid change. Scientific developments are influencing the economy at an ever faster rate, and the future threatens to arrive before we are ready for the present. The accounting profession must improve its ability to adjust to the needs of the times.

It is also pertinent to examine whether the super-regulation implied by any extensive degree of imposed uniformity is compatible with the very foundations of our free enterprise system.

* From *The Accounting Review*, January, 1961, pp. 9–16. Reprinted by permission of the American Accounting Association.

I have deliberately chosen this word "standard" to avoid having to choose among several which are more commonly used, such as, "principle," "procedure," "practice," "policy," "method," etc. Understandings as to the meaning of these latter seem to vary widely in practice.

This paper was presented at the annual meeting of the Association at The Ohio State University on August 31, 1960.

THE FRAMEWORK

In examining the question of accounting standards, uniform or otherwise, it is necessary to consider the fundamental nature and purpose of accounting. I start with the broad definition of accounting as the measurement and communication of financial and other economic data. Its end product is information. The end purpose of this information is to assist someone in formulating judgments and making decisions. Thus, it is important always to bear in mind that *usefulness* is inherent in the full discharge of the accounting function. Accounting is not an art that is practiced for its own sake.

Communications of economic data generated in any one organization may be for internal, or for external, purposes. This discussion deals only with financial reporting to external persons, and of all the organizations which do this—government, institutions, associations, businesses—is further limited to those which are profit seeking.

Since we are not dealing in a realm of natural, universal "truths," data must always be measured and communicated in accordance with a set of man-made standards. Frequently there is more than one logical way of treating any given data, depending upon whose logic is employed. Of course, custom or other forms of consensus may favor one over others in some situations. Be that as it may, whenever the particular standards used by the issuer have a significant effect, it is important that they be understood by the user. In other words, information about standards used is an important part of the communication process.

Standards used in the measurement and communication of data must be practicable for the issuer and useful to the user. They must be practicable in that, providing always that the accountability requirements of stewardship are met, they must be capable of being applied without undue effort and delay by the issuer in originating the data. In other words, the benefits of the information must be at least as great as the cost—it being clear that benefits are often proportional to timeliness. As to usefulness, the standards must result in communication of data addressed to the users' informational needs and capable of being comprehended by the knowledgeable among them.

In tracing the role of standards for the measurement and communication of economic data, we have confined the parties at interest to two: the issuer, and the user. Note that the accountant does not appear as a principal at all. It may be well, then, to devote some attention to the nature of these issuers and users.

TYPES OF ISSUERS OF ECONOMIC DATA

At a superficial glance, it might appear that uniform standards for financial and other economic data might be developed for all issuers as one body. Unfortunately for this line of thinking, there are important differences among businesses which can have pronounced effects upon the accounting standards which may be appropriate for them. These differences (other than the obvious ones turning upon the natures of operations) could probably be set forth in various ways. Here are two important ways of distinguishing their characteristics:

First, one might classify issuers *according to freedom to establish selling prices, or to recover from revenues all types of costs and expenses incurred.* Categories of companies which would be affected differently by these factors would include:

Regulated utilities.

Companies supervised to a certain extent, such as banks and insurance companies.

Suppliers to the government where allowable contract costs are a factor in determining selling prices.

"Captive" suppliers to companies substantially larger than themselves which also sell on something approaching a cost-plus basis.

Other companies, shaded according to their relative competitive positions in their markets.

The extent of freedom in the described areas can have an important bearing not only on the income statement, but also on the bases for stating and classifying assets and liabilities (or even including them at all) in the balance sheet. For example, standards for balance sheet treatment of certain costs in property or inventory accounts, or credit amounts, as fairly carried to the income accounts of future periods, may properly be different among the several types of businesses enumerated. The problem is further complicated by the fact that many complex companies have portions of their business falling in two or more of the categories enumerated, which suggests that different standards may be appropriate for the same item in the same company.

Secondly, many accounting standards rest heavily upon an *assumption of permanence* of the organization issuing accounting data. In actual practice, the probable validity of this assumption ranges from less to more in the following categories of users:

Small businesses, particularly those under-capitalized or otherwise not well established.

Any company, large or small, with a record of losses and with unsure prospects, particularly those with an appreciable amount of debt. (Mention of debt introduces another variation—the fact that an assumption of permanence of *relationship* may differ as to equity and creditor interests while, at the same time, the "going concern" assumption for the enterprise as a whole is reasonable.)

Companies with a well-established competitive position, and an effective research program to help maintain that position.

Companies the continuance of which involves a high degree of public interest, such as utilities, a major supplier of a product or service essential to the government, or an economic institution the demise of which would be an unsettling factor in the economy of an area, region or even the entire country.

Some accounting standards might preferably differ, for example, between the electric utility serving a huge metropolitan area, and the new electronic company whose whole future depends on its research. Within the same company, do not—and should not—accounting standards *for the same type of transaction* differ, say, between the operation in the United States and that in any foreign country where there is a high degree of economic and political uncertainty?

Looking at issuers alone, then, one encounters diversity bearing upon appropriateness of accounting standards. Let us now examine the users of economic data.

TYPES OF USERS OF ECONOMIC DATA

Financial reporting must take cognizance of the needs of the recipients, or it has not fulfilled the full measure of its usefulness. These needs vary widely: the interest of the banker in the "pounce" value of assets is substantially different from those of the regulatory body or taxing authority; and these, in turn, still differ from that of the investor in equity securities. One might classify external users of economic data into a number of groups, including the following:

Owners and prospective owners of equity constitute a broad group of users of financial and other economic data issued by profit-seeking businesses. This group, perhaps, is the one most frequently though of in connection with financial reporting, but even it is anything but homogeneous. One way of subdividing the group would be according to closeness of identification with the enterprise, such as:

Owner-managers.
Corporate owners of a substantial percentage of equity interest.
Other managing and nonmanaging holders of substantial nonliquid interests.
Stockholders of listed and registered companies whose shares are readily marketable.

Another grouping might be according to present intention as to the duration of the investment, such as:

Speculators.
Long-term investors.
Owners intending to sell whole companies.
Prospective buyers of whole companies.

A third possible means of subdividing the owners of equity might be according to the nature of the investor, such as:

Individuals.
Mutual funds.
Institutional investors.
Pension and welfare funds.
Other corporations.

While many of these groups of equity owners have needs for information and preferences as to accounting standards in common, there are sufficient differences to warn against complacent assumptions of homogeneity.

Creditors, another group of users of financial and other economic data, range from short-term to long-term and their interests might vary accordingly.

Labor might be considered still another group among users of financial data which could well be interested both in the type of data supplied and in the standards by which it is compiled. Labor's interest in these respects might also differ, however, according to whether it is opportunistic, or a " partner " interested in perpetuating an enterprise on a sound basis which is fair to it.

A fourth group among users of economic data would be *government*. In subdividing this broad field, one might list categories of recipients of financial reports with widely different interests, such as:

Taxing authorities.
Regulatory authorities, such as for public utilities, railroads, airlines, etc.
Supervisors of depositaries, such as for banks, insurance companies and savings and loan associations (sometimes government has the added function of guarantor).
Customers, as in military procurement.
Those governmental functions attempting to act as economic stabilizers or stimulants under adopted national policies.

Some users have established standards for measuring and reporting some portion, or all, of the data which they need as, for example: taxing, regulatory and supervisory authorities; the military services; trustees of bondholders, through indentures; buyers and sellers of businesses; and parties to construction contracts. In some cases, the custom-devised standards tend to be comprehensive. In others, they modify only in specified respects the issuer's own standards. Some users are powerful enough in relation to issuers, and consider the matter of sufficient importance, that they have actually required the issuer to depart from standards which he otherwise would have chosen for measuring and communicating data—not only to themselves but to other parties as well.

Now, it is probably fair to say that each issuer of data has its own personality, as does also each user. This might suggest that each issuer agree with each separate user of its data on the standards for measurement and communication. However, this is manifestly impracticable and the foregoing enumeration of some of the differences among issuers and users was not made for the purpose of advancing such a solution. What the analysis *does* suggest are these two points: that penetrating research is required to support accounting standards advanced for any degree of widespread use; and, second, that any standards which are so proposed should always be accompanied by a definition of the groups for which they are intended. This has not always been made clear, for instance, in bulletins issued by the AICPA Committee on Accounting Procedure.

Thus, part of the problem is: which standards, for which issuers, for which users?

PROBLEMS OF IMPOSING UNIFORM STANDARDS

Assuming that certain standards have emerged as appropriate for widespread use, a second part of the problem emerges, namely, shall they be forced upon the issuers, and, if so, how? Profit-seeking organizations are units of a free enterprise system, only a few groups within which have any portion of their accounting controlled by external legal forces through regulation or other supervision. Even the federal income taxation law, to which all the businesses under discussion are subject, provides that taxable income shall be computed by methods of the taxpayer's choosing (with imposition of the Commissioner's method under certain circumstances *as the exception*). And the SEC, which has jurisdiction over certain of the reports of a group of companies relatively small in number but great in importance, has wisely confined its requirements to full and fair disclosure with only a minimum of prescription of accounting standards to be uniform for all.

Statutory and administrative law give force to such standards as have been imposed by agencies regulating utilities, the supervisory agencies, the Renegotiation Board, the taxing authorities and similar governmental units. A few standards—not many—derive from other laws.

Of course, the future could see standards imposed upon all issuers through additional laws regulating all of industry along the lines of a socialized nation. Whether or not the individual accountant might consider this preferable to the existing free enterprise system of this country (which I, for one, do not), in considering legally imposed accounting standards of the future it seems best not to assume that extensive uniformity will be mandated by regulatory law.

Incidentally, where any of the standards deriving from government sources have been sweeping, even for issuers presumably rather homogeneous, three lessons have been learned: first, the standards always fail to provide comparability in many important details; second, the more extensive and detailed the prescribed standards, the more exceptions and loopholes and the more difficult the enforcement; and third, inflexible standards which are continued after change in the conditions for which they were once suitable can commence to hide a state of affairs rather than fairly reflect it.

On the last point: a shift in emphasis from the balance sheet to the income statement occurred for most financial reports decades ago, but is considerably short of accomplishment in industries discharging depositary functions. Much of the lag can be attributed to the influence of the governmental supervisors, whose principal objectives are to safeguard the interest of the depositors. This concentrates attention on asset valuation, reserves, liquidity, margin of safety, and other aspects of the balance sheet, rather than the reporting of income to the investor.

The other external force (beside the authority of the law) which can cause an issuer to change or adopt a standard is custom. The appeal of conventionality, of conformity, seems to be growing, particularly among managements of public corporations. In this area professional accountants may be helpful in reporting custom or consensus along with an analysis of the basic underlying forces. But it must be remembered that such a role is advisory, not regulatory.

Incidentally, it is appropriate to take note here of the ideas that the resources of the American Institute of CPAs should be utilized to determine what are acceptable accounting standards and that the weight of its authority should be invoked in enforcing them. There is, of course, every reason why members of the Institute and of the American Accounting Association should assist in articulating standards in general use, in formulating tentative standards for new situations, and even become driving forces towards these ends. However, any illusions as to the extent of authority of the Institute to impose them upon issuers should be quickly dispelled. The Institute's direct authority runs only to those CPAs who voluntarily choose to take membership in it, and this does not even include all CPAs. It has no authority which runs directly to the issuers of accounting data, although its influence is increased to the extent of reliance placed by the SEC on Institute bulletins.

Another unifying influence in some industries has been the trade association. The members of an industry through their trade association have recommended in some instances certain standards as appropriate for financial and statistical data of the industry. Such voluntary steps toward greater uniformity should be encouraged and assisted by professional accountants, particularly for problem areas peculiar to an industry.

To summarize this point, some accounting standards have been introduced under authority of law and some by agreement or custom. However, procedural standards *in any detail*—certainly for data to nongovernmental users —remain largely determined by individual issuers within allowable tolerances which can, for some areas, be rather wide.

Before leaving the subject of externally imposed standards, brief reference must be made to one phase which deserves a whole treatise by itself—the practical problem of definition. Great obstacles exist here. Consider for a moment, for example, the relatively simple matter of fixed assets. In a uniform system would one catalog of property units be applicable to all businesses in the United States? If not, how many would be needed for different industries and different sizes of companies? What detailed rules for capitalization of overhead expenses and for depreciation would be needed? How can this be done across the board? And if it were done, would the uniform reporting, suggesting as it would a uniformity in underlying conditions be *better* reporting? George O. May likes to illustrate the point by the example of a freight car, which, having been wrecked and rebuilt, bears either its old number or a new one, with the accounting varying greatly according to the choice made.

ACCEPTING REALITY AND DEALING WITH IT

While accountants should make their contribution toward standards acceptable in similar situations for homogeneous groups (and this could be all that those who call for greater uniformity are suggesting), it should be obvious that diversity will continue to be more characteristic than uniformity in any beyond the broadest areas while our free enterprise system continues. Accountants, therefore, would be misguided if they did not continue to devote attention to useful financial reporting where accounting standards are diverse. The fact of the matter is that present-day financial reporting *is* useful and that this is not happenstance. Those who dwell upon illustrations of inconsistency between companies and reason from these that present-day financial reporting ranges from the useless to the misleading exhibit something considerably less than the balanced judgment of a professional man.

In connection with maintaining a practical, professional attitude toward accounting standards of the future there are these seven points which, it seems to me, accountants should bear in mind.

First, standards which an issuer devises within acceptable limits as appropriate in its situation are not necessarily self-serving, and injurious to outside interests. In fact, the issuer has an *obligation* to exercise judgment here as a part of its stewardship. It seems the fashion these days to brand with suspicion, as adverse to the public interest, internal decisions and policies of "business" while at the same time warmly endorsing our system of free enterprise. Some businesses and businessmen are the extremists which will be found in any group, but they can and should be dealt with in the individual case rather than by blanket indictments directed at all business. Certainly, accountants (trained, as they are, in objective determinations) should not fall into loose thinking in this regard. Standards are not necessarily bad because they are issuer-created.

Second, continual emphasis should be given to the vital principle of full and fair disclosure. This is not new, but seems occasionally to drop from sight. This was recommended by the Institute to the New York Stock Exchange, and to the SEC, in the early 1930s. It has never been fully developed.

There is room for a great deal of improvement in the degree to which issuers describe to users of data those standards used which have an important effect on the data communicated. Without engaging in distinctions between principles, policies and practices, *any* of these which affect the data to an important degree and which might be different among issuers might well be disclosed.

Third, there should also be continual emphasis on the strong safeguard to meaningfulness of data deriving from consistency in the application from one period to another of standards chosen by an issuer. The principle became vital with the shift of emphasis from the balance sheet to the income statement and, at the present time, results in far greater comparability of income among companies than some would have the public believe. This can and should be demonstrated in actual cases by accountants as reassurance to users of data.

Fourth, the Institute should clear up what appears to be some current confusion about the meaning of the phrase "generally accepted accounting principles" as used in the short-form opinion. Are the "principles" referred to few and broad, or many and detailed? Do the words "generally accepted" refer to the one—the only—way, or to a foundation in theory and in use of a standard chosen, perhaps, from among many? I suspect that the original meaning of the phrase has been twisted by time, and believe that the new Accounting Principles Board should straighten it out quickly. Furthermore, to the extent that future bulletins and other pronouncements are intended to enumerate "principles," they should always be accompanied by identification of the classes of issuers and users to which they do not, or do, apply.

Fifth, professional accountants should devote more attention than at present to accounting standards imposed upon issuers by taxing, regulatory, and other governmental users of data. Some of these standards are being imposed on the grounds that they are sounder than those of the issuer where, in reality, they are designed solely to further the objectives of the governmental unit.

No one would deny the government the right to have data—say, net income—measured and communicated to it in such manner as best to effectuate approved public policy. But professional accountants should be alert to distinguish for all concerned between standards designed to this end and those appropriate for other users of the same issuer's data. Above all, if the governmental agency is under illusions as to the appropriateness of its standards for other purposes, when this is not the case, accountants have an obligation to assist in the required clarification.

Sixth, accounting research and thought should be concentrated on fundamental and widely pervading factors which have a bearing on standards appropriate for many issuers and many users. There will probably not be many of these, but such as there are will be of far greater importance than the details with which accountants sometimes are prone to concern themselves.

For example, is there, or is there not, general agreement among the various elements of our economy that financial reports should show the extent to which the economic capital of the issuer has or has not been preserved? If the answer to this were clear, many of the standards for accounting during a changing price level would be easier to establish.

Take another example: it is national policy to minimize fluctuations in the economy. Do widely used accounting standards conform with this policy? Straight-line amortization of any asset against income tends to accentuate fluctuations in an issuer's net income. On the other hand, amortization by units of production or other bases which vary with the volume of operations tends to minimize them. Is rethinking required here?

Selection of subjects of sufficient depth and breadth to be appropriate for research and pronouncement will, I believe, be one of the most difficult problems of the new Accounting Principles Board.

Finally, a realistic solution to reasonable demands for more comparability of data should be developed. The first step here is to distinguish which pressures are susceptible to practical solution. Then, where reasonable common standards can be developed, or where they already exist but an issuer desires to break new ground, it may be preferable to press for *additional disclosures* by an issuer to show the effect on data of applying common standards—a "norm"—as compared with its own.

The logic of this approach, as contrasted with attempting to require the issuer to *adopt* the common standard (which, as has been discussed, may be largely impracticable anyway), is that the issuer is left with freedom for innovation while at the same time the request for comparability is met. Freedom for innovation, inviting continued progress in accounting, provides a far sounder base from which to launch into a future almost certain to be characterized by rapid change. It is much better than uniformity imposed by external authority with its accompanying tendency toward regimented stagnation.

In closing, the strongest plea of all that I could make with regard to future determinations of accounting standards is that professional accountants not consider this their exclusive jurisdiction. The accounting profession will have reached its full maturity when it has the humility to recognize that the formulation of standards for the measurement and communication of financial and other economic data requires the effort of a team, of which it is only one of the members. At that point, its stature will never have been higher. The composition of the initial task forces of the Accounting Principles Board is indeed an encouraging start in the right direction.

POLICY—STRATEGY CASES

* *

1. THE ARLA CHEMICALS COMPANY*

—EDMUND P. LEARNED

and

FRANCIS J. AGUILAR

"If you want to know what our major problems are in 1962, I would say that they all involve some aspect of product planning," commented Mr. Schetty, Commercial Director of The Arla Chemicals Company. "Our business is being squeezed on three sides. For one thing, we are in danger of losing our primary raw material, baurite. Secondly, the market conditions for our most important by-products, the acid group have been changing, but we are severely hindered by external forces from adapting to this change. Finally, with respect to our other important by-product, ferannal, our customers for this material have been introducing a new process in which no ferannal is required."

Mr. Rybert, President of Arla, commented, "These problems with our suppliers and markets have to be solved. The quickening pace of Europe's economic integration makes the situation more urgent because we expect our competition to increase considerably. I might add that the Company must also consider the possibility of diversifying into new fields of the chemical business."

THE COMPANY

The Arla Chemicals Company was a middle-sized chemical firm producing a number of basic inorganic chemicals,[1] all of which were long-established

---

* Copyright 1962, by l'Institut pour l'Etude des Méthodes de Direction de l'Entreprise (IMEDE), Lausanne, Switzerland. Reprinted by permission. The names of the company, its executives, its raw materials, and some of its products have been disguised.

[1] Chemical products are often subdivided into two broad categories, organic and inorganic. The inclusion of some hydrocarbon in the molecular structure of a chemical product qualifies it as organic. Most of the organic chemicals are derived from petroleum, coal, or natural gas sources. The better-known basic industrial chemicals, such as soda ash, calcium carbide, ammonia, caustic soda, hydrochloric acid, and sulphuric acid, are inorganic chemicals.

items in industry. The firm had grown with the industry and enjoyed the reputation of being a reliable producer of quality chemicals. Arla was located in one of the European Common Market (ECM) countries and was near the borders of two other ECM nations.

Established shortly after the turn of the century, the Company had sales of 76 million Swiss francs in 1960, employed almost 1,300 persons, and had no significant financial obligations outstanding. Exhibits 1 and 2 show financial data for selected years.

Arla's management had traditionally been proud of the firm's technical competence, and they considered their technical staff to be among the foremost in their sector of the chemical industry. The firm's strength was largely due to low-cost and efficient production processes, which allowed it to sell high-quality chemicals at competitive prices.

Arla also sold their patented processes and equipment through a wholly owned subsidiary. This small engineering company often designed complete plants based on Arla operations. Where it did so, this subsidiary would normally assign its own engineers to supervise the construction of the plant, to start the system in operation, to train the customer's personnel, and to assure successful operation of the plant. By 1962, plants and equipment had been sold in most parts of the world.

ARLA'S PRODUCTS AND MARKETS

Arla's principal product was feran. The Company used the most common process of making feran, in which two valuable by-products, a sulphurous material and ferannal, were also produced. These by-products had to be profitably sold for the successful operation of the overall business.

Originally, Arla simply made sulphuric acid from the sulphurous material and sold it and all of the unprocessed ferannal to industrial customers. Over the years, however, as the production of feran increased, the Company began to introduce new derivative products in order to market the consequently increasing volume of by-products.

All of the Company's major products were grouped into three categories: feran; the acid group, which was originally developed to dispose of the sulphurous content of the baurite; and the ferannal group. Of total 1960 sales, feran accounted for abour 66 per cent, the acid group of products for about 24 per cent, and the ferannal group of products for about 10 per cent Exhibit 3 shows the product and product group sales for 1960 and also shows the product sales volumes for selected years. Exhibit 4 displays the product and process relationships in 1962.

FERAN

Company operations centered about the production of feran. (The process is shown by a double line in Exhibit 4.) All of Arla's other products were

Exhibit 1

The Arla Chemicals Company

Balance Sheet Before Distribution of Profits, 1958-1960
(In Thousands of Swiss Francs)

		1958		1959		1960
Current Assets						
Cash		3,032		4,158		3,317
Notes Receivable		1,593		1,933		2,063
Accounts Receivable		3,441		7,852		8,313
Govt. Securities		4,220		615		2,521
Investments		7,176		7,117		7,037
Inventory		12,037		10,809		11,626
Total		31,499		32,484		34,877
Fixed Assets						
Equipment and Buildings	44,646		46,107		51,992	
Reserve for Depreciation	36,325		39,206		41,652	
Net Equipment and Buildings		8,321		6,901		10,340
Land		260		235		235
Patents and Good Will		—		—		—
Total		3,581		7,136		10,575
TOTAL DEBITS		40,080		39,620		45,452
Current Liabilities						
Accounts Payable		7,824		7,543		9,008
Provision for Taxes		2,363		1,976		2,766
Matured Coupons		57		63		42
Total		10,244		9,587		11,816
Fixed Liabilities						
Debenture		164		82		—
Total		164		82		—
Capital Reserves and Profits for Distribution						
Common Stock		17,000		17,000		17,000
Legal Reserve		1,700		1,700		1,700
Capital Surplus		300		300		300
Equipment Replacement Reserve		4,100		4,100		6,200
Reserve for Inventory Valuation		1,000		1,000		1,000
Employee Welfare Reserve		3,150		3,430		4,560
Profits for Distribution		2,422		2,421		2,876
Total		29,672		29,951		33,636
TOTAL CREDITS		40,080		39,620		45,452

Source: Company records.

Exhibit 2

The Arla Chemicals Company

Profit and Loss Statement and Distribution of Profits Statement, 1953–1960
(In Thousands of Swiss Francs)

	1958	1959	1960
PROFIT AND LOSS STATEMENT			
CREDIT			
Operating Income less Operating Expenses	2,594	2,434	4,342
Financial Revenues from Investments and Accounts Receivable*	827	1,020	1,133
Carryover from Preceding Year	1	2	1
Total	3,422	3,456	5,476
DEBIT			
Provision for Corporate Taxes	750	750	1,600
Charitable Funds and Grants	250	285	1,000
Profits for Current Distribution	2,422	2,421	2,876
Total	3,422	3,456	5,476
DISTRIBUTION OF PROFITS STATEMENT			
Taxes Withheld on Dividends	750	750	900
Statutory Share (Directors' Compensation)	170	170	200
Cash Dividends Paid to Stockholders	1,500	1,500	1,750
Carried Over to Following Year	2	1	26
Total	2,422	2,421	2,876

* Arla carried accounts receivable for their customers at the bank rates of interest for comparable loans.
Source: Company records.

originally manufactured in order to sell profitably the by-products, which were produced in a fixed relationship to the production of feran.

Feran was a basic inorganic chemical, about half of which was used by the paint industry and the rest by a wide range of other industries. Most of Arla's feran sales were made within the ECM. Because of the industrial applications for this product, the market for feran was strongly affected by the swings of industrial activity, particularly by those of the paint industry.

Certain of Arla's executives expressed the opinion that the feran industry had not been aggressive enough over the years and had consequently lost ground to other products. They felt that more industry research should have

Production and Sales, Selected Years, 1926–1960

Products	Production (Tons)								Sales in 1960	
	1926	1927	1938	1939	1949	1950	1959	1960	Thousands of Sw. Frs.	% of Total Sales
Main Product										65.8
Feran	21,593	24,397	43,179	40,501	33,408	35,006	44,498	45,722	50,008	65.8
Acid Group										24.5
Sulphuric Acid	17,702	17,575	58,007	55,076	57,030	51,489	126,213	159,712	9,691	12.7
Phosphoric Acid	—	—	45	56	191	175	724	299	21	—
Simple Superphosphate	—	—	—	13,701	76,279	32,326	26,198	20,284	1,380	1.8
Triple Superphosphate	—	—	6,384	3,699	3,307	2,822	15,310	26,098	5,224	6.9
Complex Fertilizer	—	—	—	—	—	—	2,083	1,922	769	1.0
Other Products (e.g., detergents)	—	—	—	—	—	—	2,526	2,263	1,611	2.1
Ferannal Group										9.7
Ferannal	672	700	5,142	4,891	4,001	3,460	5,158	6,025	2,002	2.6
Food Additive	—	—	—	—	19	339	2,774	3,953	5,367	7.1
									76,073	100.0
Total Sales (Millions of Swiss Francs)	21.8	24.5	50.7	48.8	46.2	44.2	69.6	76.1		

Note: 1. For convenience, local currency has been coverted into Swiss francs.
2. All franc values have been adjusted to a 1960 base.
Source: Company records.

Exhibit 4.

The Arla Chemicals Company

Product and Process Relationships

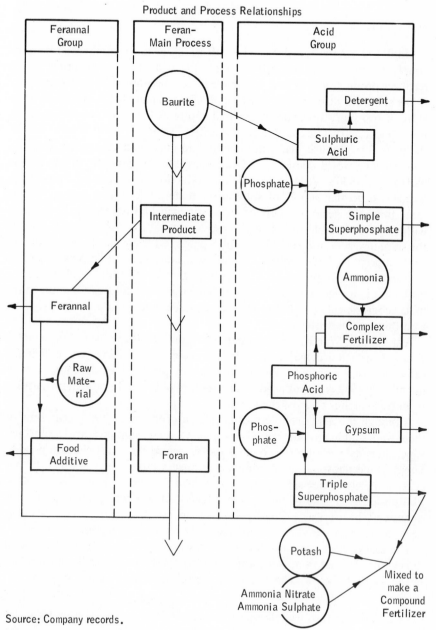

Source: Company records.

been carried out to improve the product, so that it could be better used in current applications and also introduced for new applications. They stated that, while world sales of feran had increased slightly in absolute terms, feran's share of the total market in which it competed was actually decreasing.

THE ACID GROUP

Until 1937, Arla had disposed of all its by-product sulphurous material simply by producing and selling sulphuric acid. The introduction of the fertilizer products at this time was made largely because of adverse conditions in the sulphuric acid market. Since sulphuric acid had always been difficult to store or transport, other producers had had repeatedly to dump their output in the local market[2] as supply temporarily exceeded demand. Consequently, the price for sulphuric acid traditionally had fluctuated very much. Furthermore, as the world demand for feran increased substantially in the second half of the 1930's, Arla increased its production of feran and found itself faced with greater supply of sulphurous material than ever before. At the same time, the general supply of sulphuric acid had outgrown the demand within the marketable area. Under these circumstances, Arla began to process the sulphuric acid into simple superphosphate fertilizer, phosphoric acid, and triple-superphosphate fertilizer. These new products permitted Arla profitably to dispose of its sulphuric acid excess in new markets and also alleviated the problem of storage. Up to 1962, Arla had been the only feran manufacturer in its geographical area that processed sulphuric acid into derivative products —in this case, fertilizers.

After World War II, the local pattern of industrial chemical requirements changed, and the demand for sulphuric acid greatly increased until it far exceeded the supply available from feran by-products in the area. Consequently, by 1962 Arla was producing one-third of its sulphuric acid production from free sulphur to meet these needs.

Although the acid group consisted of ten products by 1960, only four of these were sold in any substantial amounts. Of these, sulphuric acid and triple-superphosphate fertilizer accounted for 80 per cent of the acid group sales. Simple superphosphate and complex fertilizers represented another 12 per cent, while the other six products accounted for the remaining 8 per cent. Phosphoric acid, one of these six products, actually was produced in great quantities, but it was primarily used as an internal intermediate product, because no significant demand existed for it outside the Company.

The markets for these products were diverse. The sulphuric acid was sold direct to industrial users within the 100- to 150-kilometer radius mentioned in the footnote below. The fertilizers were sold to farm supply distributors.

---

[2] Transportation costs limit the sulphuric acid market to a radius of about 100 to 150 kilometers from the producer.

Transportation costs limited this market to a radius of 150 kilometers.[3] The other products were normally sold through agents in Europe.

THE FERANNAL GROUP

The one constantly strong market for ferannal was the food processing industry, where it was used in the production of a certain expensive food additive. Arla had been selling its ferannal to a number of intermediate product manufacturers who produced additives for the food processing industry. No one customer purchased more than 20 per cent of Arla's normal ferannal production.

Starting in 1949, Arla began producing the additive itself and selling it through distributors to food processors. By 1962, the value of the additive sales was about 2.5 times that of ferannal sales.

THE PROBLEMS OF BAURITE SUPPLY

Since 1955, Arla had encountered growing difficulty in obtaining its requirements of baurite at what Company executives considered a reasonable price. As a result, Arla had suffered a baurite cost disadvantage vis-à-vis their competitors, while the baurite market had remained a seller's market. An even more serious problem was that world political moves were threatening further to reduce the free supply of baurite. Arla's management was seriously worried about the long-range possibility that free supplies would become permanently reduced, especially since Arla was the only feran manufacturer in their local area wholly dependent on this supply.

Arla's founders located the firm so as to take advantage of nearby baurite deposits. These sources became uneconomical to work shortly before the First World War, and subsequently, the Company had to import all of its baurite from outside sources at the world commodity price. Arla typically purchased baurite from a number of suppliers in normal shipment amounts. The price for baurite was determined on the commodity exchange market in Paris.

Two unusual conditions caused the baurite world commodity market to be very volatile. First, the United States' tariffs effectively segregated this large supply and demand sector from the world market. Second, many of the large baurite users outside the United States owned or controlled their own sources; these users came in and out of the baurite market only to meet fluctuations in their requirements. By purchasing baurite when the demand for feran was high[4] and dumping baurite when the overall demand for feran was low,

[3] The 150 kilometers refers to overland transportation. In Arla's case, a seaport lay within this distance, which permitted bulk distribution of fertilizer overseas. Sulphuric acid, on the other hand, was not commonly transported overseas because of the difficulty and expense of handling and storing this chemical on board ocean vessels.

[4] The only major use for baurite was for the production of feran.

these firms applied an adverse pressure to the baurite market, which caused wide fluctuations in the price.

Arla was subject to the full swing of these prices for their complete supply of baurite. On the other hand, its large competitors, who met most of their requirements from their own sources, were subject to these swings only for their marginal needs. Up to 1962, Arla had been able to offset its baurite cost disadvantage by means of production savings and the profitable sale of its feran by-products.

Arla's management was worried, however, that the recent advantageous position of the baurite sellers in the free market was becoming a permanent condition. If this were so, Arla would find itself at an even greater disadvantage than in the past, since there would no longer be those periods of excess baurite supplies during which Arla could favorably negotiate purchase agreements. A factor which contributed to this pessimism was that a large percentage of the better baurite sources[5] were located in the under-developed and politically unstable areas of the world. There was pressure within most of these countries to appropriate the mining operations and to nationalize them. As Mr. Schetty explained: " If they (the inhabitants of these countries) ever seize the source facilities, they will not stop there. Then they will want to produce the chemicals themselves rather than sell the baurite on the world market, more as a matter of prestige than of good economics. What is even more worrisome is that they will damage or destroy the baurite facilities in their ignorance of these facilities' economic value to their nations. In either event, there will be less baurite in the free market."

Arla's top management had not yet attempted to study the economics of this problem. As one member said: " We have a number of major choices. We can continue our present method of purchasing baurite and take our chances. There will always be some baurite available at a price. Or we can invest in baurite facilities, either on our own or with others. However, this is a new business to us, and the source facilities can involve enormous investments. Then there is always the possibility of arranging long-term supply contracts, but it is going to be expensive to interest the suppliers at this time because of the present seller's market. And, of course, with the political situation as it is, we are not certain that we can rely on the performance of such a contract in the future. First, we shall have to select a course of action. Then, if we select any joint ventures, we must also decide what kind of partner we want."

THE PROBLEMS OF THE ACID GROUP

Changing requirements in the fertilizer market had confronted Arla with two major problems. First, there was a technical problem in that the Company's fertilizers no longer met the new specifications. Then, there was the

[5] Deposits of baurite exist in most parts of the world.

business problem of obtaining suppliers for any new raw materials which would be needed. The success or failure with which these problems were met would clearly affect the whole product balance within this group.

Traditionally, farm supply distributors had purchased the necessary ingredients for compound fertilizers and mechanically mixed these for the farmer according to his required proportions. One of the most common inorganic compound fertilizers contained potash, superphosphate, ammonia sulphate, and ammonia nitrate. This mixture was referred to as a "three-element" fertilizer, since the latter two chemicals served to provide nitrogen in the two different forms required by plants. In the late 1950's, farmers began increasingly to favor a chemically integrated single-pellet fertilizer because of its technical advantage over the former multi-pellet mixture.

To meet this new demand pattern, Arla had devised a chemical process to combine phosphoric acid, ammonia nitrate, and ammonia sulphate into a complex fertilizer with two of the major components. The potash would then be mechanically mixed in and the final combination formed into individual pellets. The new complex fertilizer was expected fully to meet the new requirements of the market.

Having solved the technological problem of producing a competitive complex fertilizer, Arla then encountered the problem of obtaining the required ammonia nitrate supply. Both the phosphate- and the nitrogen-product manufacturers were competing for the new complex fertilizer market. The nitrate manufacturers, on the one hand, could either purchase or manufacture the needed phosphates without any trouble. On the other hand, Arla had encountered serious resistance in obtaining the necessary nitrates for a sufficient production of complex fertilizer, and it was unable by itself to manufacture the nitrates economically.

Mr. Schetty summarized the nitrate-purchase problem in these words: "We simply cannot buy the needed ammonia nitrate under reasonable conditions. The only price that they (the nitrogen-product manufacturers) will quote is designed to discourage us from competing with them in the complex fertilizer market. Their terms of sale, which positively exclude us from a large portion of our natural market, pose an even more serious problem. The nitrogen suppliers allege that agreements among the nitrogen-product manufacturers discourage the sale of nitrates to a customer if the resulting end products are to be exported to another West-European country. This means that if we want to produce a complex fertilizer containing their ammonia nitrate, we cannot market this fertilizer in our neighboring countries. These countries now purchase over 35 per cent of our fertilizer production and could represent a much higher share in the future. If we should lose our overseas markets as a result of the establishment of fertilizer-producing feran plants in the under-developed countries, we would have to turn to our ECM market in order to offset these sales losses, since the home market within our distribution range is nearly saturated. Under the most severe export losses, we would have to expand our sales in neighboring countries by close to 50 per cent of their current level in order to maintain overall sales."

In discussing the nitrate-manufacture problem, Mr. Schetty said: "Engineering studies have shown that the smallest economical plant would provide substantially more ammonia nitrate than we could use. And, of course, there is no market in which to sell the excess, since the nitrogen-product manufacturers fully control the nitrate market. Besides, the production of the nitrate is technically difficult, and we are not anxious to contend with these problems."

It appeared to the researcher that two reasons dominated the arguments in favor of actively pursuing the fertilizer market. First, the line of products had been profitable and promised to remain so. Second, Arla's executives were concerned about an expected deterioration of the general sulphuric acid market over the next ten years[6] and were anxious to maintain a marketing outlet which could absorb the firm's future excess sulphuric acid supply.

Concerning the course of action to be followed, Mr. Schetty stated: "We studied the possibility of fighting the unfair restriction imposed on us by the nitrogen-product manufacturers by requesting relief from our government or from the ECM authorities. Another possible solution would be to try to form a joint operation to manufacture the complex fertilizer with one of the small nitrogen-product manufacturers in this area who is not prepared to enter the complex fertilizer market by himself. Although this type of firm might be a party to any existing agreements, we do have one point of bargaining leverage; namely, that the ECM authorities will probably disallow such agreements on the grounds that they violate the covenants of the Treaty of Rome. The small nitrogen-product firm knows that the eventual breakdown of the industrial agreements will leave him much less protected than ever before, and we are offering him a long-term relation in a profitable business."

THE PROBLEMS OF THE FERANNAL GROUP

The well established food additive market for ferannal became unsettled in the late 1950's when a new process was discovered which permitted the production of the same additive more cheaply without the use of ferannal. Two factors worked against Arla's defensive move of increasing its own production of the food additive: a raw material problem and a market saturation problem.

While Arla could recycle ferannal in its main process so as to obtain feran, a much greater marginal profit could be realized by using the ferannal itself to produce the food additive. As for the firm's competitive position, management determined that Arla could produce the additive at the same cost or

---

[6] In the past, the manufacture of ammonia sulphate required a large quantity of sulphuric acid. Mr. Schetty estimated that the need would lessen because of technological developments.

even at a slightly lower total cost than the manufacturers using the new process. This was possible because Arla would not have to pay for the costly transportation of ferannal.

In order to produce the food additive, Arla required another raw chemical, with the trade name Huzon, which was available from only one manufacturer. Despite a concerted effort to arrange for the favorable supply of Huzon on a long-term basis, the supplier continued to demand a price which Arla executives considered about 30 per cent too high.

In the face of this unacceptable situation, Arla's management investigated the possibility of producing its own Huzon. It was determined that the smallest economic plant would produce about twice the Huzon needed to process the ferannal resulting from Arla's feran production. In the process of making Huzon, a by-product chemical was also produced. According to Mr. Schetty, no market existed for either Huzon or its by-product in the local region because of the tight control held by the aforementioned manufacturer. There was a possibility of selling these chemicals to distant manufacturers, but even there the competition would be very severe. Mr. Schetty finally commented: "If we could find one or two customers who would purchase 80 per cent of our Huzon by-product on a long-range basis, we would go ahead with the plant."

Should Arla solve the Huzon supply problem, a number of officers pointed out, there still remained the problem that the additive market was already tight. In view of the substantial additional facilities Arla would introduce, the industry's production capacity for food additive would far exceed the normal demand.

THE PROBLEMS OF DIVERSIFICATION

A number of the less senior members of top management felt strongly that Arla had to consider diversifying into new areas of the chemical industry in face of the long-term trends. During the course of the field study, however, the researcher noted in this group traces of an opinion that the top executives would be very reluctant to allow Arla to enter fields with which they were not technically acquainted.

Many arguments were advanced in favor of diversification. Diversification was said to be indispensable in order to:

1. Reduce the dangers of an increasing difficulty in obtaining baurite.
2. Compensate for the cyclical behavior of the feran market.
3. Anticipate the long-term threat of a vanishing market for feran, especially in light of the possible entry of new manufacturers at the sources.
4. Move into areas with greater growth prospects than the inorganic chemicals area in which Arla had been active.

Organic chemical products, especially the more elaborate organic fertilizers, were of most interest to the Arla management. It was recognized, however, that the Company's executives did not have the breadth of technical and business knowledge to ensure, by themselves, the success of diversification into this area. Consideration was, therefore, given to the relative advantages of (1) hiring qualified people to start new operations, (2) setting up a joint operation with a company in the organic chemical field, or (3) merging with such a company.

Discussing the steps taken to diversify, a plant manager remarked that inquiries about opportunities were being made by the Company's officers through their personal and professional acquaintances, and that the Company was doing some new product research. Mr. Parmi, who was in charge of research, mentioned: "New product research is largely confined to areas related to our present products. Neither I nor my staff are properly qualified to investigate fully the possibilities in organic chemicals." Another executive added that some general exploration into possible joint ventures was being done also by the engineering subsidiary.

If Arla should decide to diversify by means of partnership or merger, it could offer a prospective participant a large plot of excellently located property on which the new operations could be constructed. It could also offer any potential non-European partner its general know-how of operating in Europe. It could not, however, offer a ready marketing organization for the new products. First, because Arla's marketing experience was restricted to a narrow line of inorganic chemicals. Second, because management recognized that it had, to some extent, neglected marketing over the years, and that this area would require further development before it could be considered an asset in negotiation.

In recognition of the difficult marketing problems that diversification would entail, one executive remarked: "We must be prepared to merge with or, preferably, to absorb another company which will provide us with an entrée into new fields. Our engineering company has gained us world-wide renown in our industry. We should capitalize on that renown. Any possible merger must take into account the possible extension of our commercial organization in such a way as to replace our now dominant technical orientation with a marketing outlook."

Mr. Klare, Executive Vice President, summed up his thoughts on the subject with this comment: "Any expansion should be based on our technical strengths, which center about certain inorganic chemical processes. The organic chemical industry, about which we know relatively little, technically or otherwise, is rapidly growing, and changes take place quickly. This means that you have to be very careful in selecting an area to enter, because by the time you build the plant and start producing, the technologies involved can change so that you no longer have a market."

J. W. STERN & SON, INC.*

—ANCEL G. TAFLINGER

As of May 1956, Mr. Gilbert Stern, President and General Manager of J. W. Stern & Son, Inc., *plumbing contractors*, was convinced that the firm was losing money on volume currently running at a rate of $125,000 per year. He believed that the expected loss was largely a function of the firm's objectives and method of operation.

J. W. Stern & Son, located in a large mid-western city, was a family-owned corporation controlled by the elder Mr. Stern, who had begun to taper off his part in actual operations. The general management function was devolving on his son, Gilbert, a man in his late thirties. A younger son, Morris, was reaching a level of experience which would enable him to take over field supervision of the ten plumbers employed by the firm. Both sons were licensed journeyman plumbers but an attack of poliomyelitis had forced Gilbert to give up working in the field.

The elder Mr. Stern had emigrated from Russia at the age of 16, settling in the city in 1901. Seeking a trade, he had become an apprentice plumber and secured his journeyman license in 1908. Two years later, he accepted an offer from his employer to become a partner by contributing $250 in cash, equal to the value of the firm's assets at that time.

The partners developed a reputation for high-quality work and were able to draw living expenses and still divide substantial profits every year. During the early part of World War I, however, they agreed to dissolve the partnership. Mr. Stern, taking one-half of the cash, tools, materials and other assets,

* All names have been disguised. This case was prepared by Prof. Ancel G. Taflinger, State College of Washington, as a basis for class discussion. It does not purport to demonstrate or illustrate either correct or incorrect methods of dealing with problems of a business firm. Copyright 1957, by Ancel G. Taflinger.

set up his own business as a licensed master plumber, engaged principally in "jobbing"[1] work.

By 1928, Mr. Stern had built up a volume of more than $100,000 per year, employing 25 plumbers, and had moved out of the field of jobbing into contracting on new installations. During this period he did all of his own office work, acted as his own field superintendent, did some of the actual work as a Master Plumber, and set up his own layouts and specifications as needed.

The depression years and the decrease in new building hit the business hard, with an estimated loss of over $100,000 in the period from 1929 through 1931. He attempted to carry out all his contracts in full even though chances were poor that the client would be able to make full payment. Some completed work was never paid for. In spite of his losses, however, Mr. Stern refused to take refuge in bankruptcy and, over the next few years, succeeded in paying off all debts in full. Throughout his career, he has never been refused any desired amount of credit by any of his suppliers.

Losses and lack of capital resulting from the depression made it difficult to rebuild the firm. However, by cutting costs to the limit, working very long hours, and doing only the highest-quality work, Mr. Stern was able to recover to a considerable extent. By the beginning of World War II, he had developed a volume which returned a comfortable income.

The years following World War II saw a basic change in plumbing contracting. Whereas Mr. Stern had been able to estimate jobs with great rapidity due to their similarity, it was now necessary to work largely from architect's drawings and engineering specifications. This required analysis of plans to determine the number and size required of each piece of piping, each fitting, and each fixture to complete the job, and determination of the contractor's cost for this material. It was then necessary to estimate the amount and cost of labour required to install all of the materials plus the cost of testing to be sure specifications were met. (See Exhibit 3 for a partial estimation sheet.)

When his illness forced Gilbert out of field work, he took over the duties of estimator. As more complex jobs came up, it might require three days to a week of paper work to estimate a $25,000 job in order to bid on it. Although Mr. Stern realized the necessity of this, he still tended to resent the idea of what seemed to him to be a "non-productive" work. He also felt that such office fixtures as filing cabinets were unnecessary. He consented to the purchase of an adding machine only after a fatigue-induced error of $1,000 was discovered in an estimate.

In addition, the late 1940's and early 1950's saw what amounted to a proliferation of small plumbing firms consisting of non-union partnerships who took over many of the smaller jobs at greatly reduced prices. Development of mass building operations by general contractors sharpened competi-

---

[1] Jobbing—a trade term referring to repair or maintenance work on old plumbing, as against installation of new equipment.

tion among the larger plumbing firms. The net result was a decline in gross margins for all small and medium-size firms.

"This puts us in a real bind," Gilbert Stern pointed out. "You'd think these guys would have more sense than to cut their own throats. I suppose some of them don't know their real costs well enough for accurate estimating. Then, too, some of them are real 'dogs' who bid on first-class work and expect to do the poorest job they can get away with. But the ethical firms still have to meet those bids if they want the jobs."

According to Gilbert, plumbing firms fall into five general classifications. Starting with the largest, he described these categories as follows:

1. The very large contractor, often owned or directed by expert managers who know nothing of plumbing work. They have staffs of engineers and operate in the areas of consulting, engineering and contracting on a national or international scale. Experimental and cost-plus jobs are common. Few of these firms do less than a million dollars a year with some running into tens of millions.

2. Highly selective companies doing a volume of around one million dollars yearly on a bid basis. Usually well-managed and with plenty of capital, they seek contracts for hospitals, laboratories, skyscrapers, large industrial plants and the like. Many of them engage in high-grade jobbing or maintenance work on a contract basis. Commonly, they have staff engineers for their own work.

3. A group of firms in the range of $250,000–$500,000 per year, with one or two well above that figure. These companies do not offer engineering service and work from plans or specifications. Contracts in the $25,000–$50,000 range are the standard for these firms and very keen competition exists for the plumbing in single stores, small plants, government installations, blocks of residential housing, and similar projects. Practically all the volume of such firms is done within a single metropolitan area.

4. A group classified by Gilbert as "robber" or "dog" firms using legal but unethical methods. Usually small in size, they bid on any kind of piping or sheet-metal work, including heating, plumbing, sewers and other relatively small jobs. Using non-union workers, they operate in "hit-and-run" fashion, trying only to be sure that the work will hold for the standard one-year guarantee period. It is this group which does most damage to reputable firms by low bids which leave practically no margin on first-class work.

5. The local or neighborhood plumber, usually skilled in heating, plumbing and air conditioning, who rarely works on a contract basis for other than service contracts. About the only member of the plumbing fraternity who has contact with the ultimate user, he depends heavily on fast-service jobbing, with occasional new construction in dwellings or small buildings. Commonly, he operates from a retail store carrying fixtures and appliances. His location is of great importance and is usually in a shopping center in metropolitan areas.

"All of these groups differ widely in personality of the ownership or management people, the tools and equipment they use, their operating methods, and the type of work they look for," said Gilbert Stern. "We don't feel that the first and fifth of these categories offer us any competition. We're not interested in the little guy's jobs, and we couldn't possibly swing the kind of contract the big firms handle. We'd like to move into the second group but we don't have the capital for their jobs that really pay off."

Exhibit 1

Adjusted Balance Sheet

J. W. Stern and Son, Inc.
Comparative Balance Sheets for Fiscal Years
Ending June 30, 1953–1955

ASSETS	1953	1954	1955
Current Assets:			
Cash in Bank	$5,235.63	$10,416.52	$5,761.04
Accounts Receivable	7,420.24	4,203.46	10,961.76
Inventories	1,717.59	1,689.55	2,293.39
Bond Deposits		201.00	
Total Current Assets	$14,373.46	$16,510.53	$19,016.19
Fixed Assets:			
Land	$1,000.00	$1,000.00	$1,000.00
Building	5,000.00	5,000.00	5,000.00
Trucks and Equipment	4,427.55	4,761.86	4,761.86
Furniture and Fixtures	330.00	330.00	330.00
Less: Accumulated Depreciation	2,395.86	3,564.36	4,799.72
Total Fixed Assets	$8,361.69	$7,527.50	$6,292.14
TOTAL ASSETS	$22,735.15	$24,038.03	$25,308.33
LIABILITIES AND NET WORTH			
Current Liabilities:			
Accounts Payable	$1,685.56	$1,825.93	$5,885.28
Accrued Payroll Taxes	254.38	266.68	331.78
Accrued Taxes (Other)	157.83		
Total Current Liabilities	$2,097.77	$2,092.61	$6,217.06
Long Term Debt:	$14,844.44	$16,704.34	$15,128.64
Total Debt	$16,942.21	$18,796.95	$21,345.70
Capital and Net Worth:			
Capital Stock (Common)	$5,000.00	$5,000.00	$5,000.00
Earned Surplus	792.94	241.08	1,037.37(d)
Total Capital and Net Worth	$5,792.94	$5,241.08	$3,962.37
TOTAL LIABILITIES AND NET WORTH	$22,735.15	$24,038.03	$25,308.33

* Unpaid Salaries and Loans.
(Inaccurate information and poor accounting procedures might account for lack of balance.)

"At the moment, we're trying to straddle the third group, although it offers the keenest competition. One of our problems in moving into it is capital. (See Exhibits 1 and 2.) We try to operate on an average gross margin of around ten per cent, but we run into the 'fifteen per cent rule'. In this business, fifteen per cent of a contract price is withheld for 45 to 90 days after the job is completed to see whether the work is satisfactory. With high volume, that wouldn't be so bad because we'd have a string of withheld payments coming in all the time. At our volume, it's a real headache."

"Sometimes, too, we get a call from a general contractor who finds a low bidder was a 'dog' that he doesn't want on his job," Gilbert added. "He offers us the job because of our reputation, but only if we meet the other

Exhibit 2

J. W. Stern and Son, Inc.
Comparative Profit and Loss Statements for Fiscal Years
Ending June 30, 1953–1955

Total Sales Billed	$70,062.68	$52,676.10	$52,367.15
Cost of Sales Billed	30,663.90	20,246.49	20,949.32
Gross Profit on Operations	39,398.78	32,429.61	31,417.83
OPERATING EXPENSES			
Salaries and Wages	31,106.02	25,046.78	21,641.78
Truck Expense	1,759.75	1,554.99	1,070.74
Permits	187.39	65.45	129.92
Rentals	223.17	99.00	132.00
Advertising		22.00	55.00
Insurance	1,162.31	1,107.05	1,044.78
Telephone and Telegraph	601.37	783.62	850.08
Union Dues & Health Fund	900.20	902.23	1,515.60
Sub-Contract Payments	172.08		2,521.20
Payroll Taxes	474.33	410.26	599.43
Other Taxes	389.70	382.88	339.71
Legal and Audit Expense	330.00	181.50	247.50
Office Expense (General)	132.88	266.42	365.24
Heat and Light	370.93	294.50	400.44
Depreciation Expense			
Trucks and Tools (5 yr.)	885.50	885.50	952.36
Building (20 yr.)	250.00	250.00	250.00
Furniture & Fixtures (10 yr.)	33.00	33.00	33.00
Total Operating Expenses	38,978.63	32,285.18	32,148.78
Net Profit on Operations	420.15	144.43	730.95(d)
Interest Expense	150.00	128.15	544.50
NET PROFIT FOR PERIOD	$270.15	16.28	1,275.45(d)

(d) Deficit

Note: All figures contained in this statement have been altered by introduction of a common factor.

Exhibit 3
J. W. Stern and Son, Inc.
**Job Estimate—Master Sheet*

NO.	ITEM	PAGE REF.	OUR COST
1.	Fixtures	2	4,224.00
2.	Soil Pipe (Rainwater—1205; Sanitary—2110	4	3,315.00
3.	Water Pipe	6	2,000.00
4.	Hangers, sleeves	Est.	275.00
5.	Insulation (Bid by Wilmuth Bros.)	—	1,530.00
6.	Staging—None needed	Est.	—
7.	Permit	2	83.00
8.	Hot Water Tank, delivered w/saddles (205 gal.)	Bid	1,128.00
9.	Hot Water Tank trim	Est.	35.00
10.	Street Water Conn.—to prop. line only	8	750.00
11.	Extend Wat. Serv. to Bldg. w/hydrant	8	1,895.00
12.	Street Gas Conn. & ext. into bldg.	8	150.00
13.	Extend Gas Serv. to Bldg. (included Item 12)	—	—
14.	Interior Gas Piping	Est.	50.00
15.	Floor Drains (11 @ $38.00) (including labor)	7	418.00
16.	8″ vent flashings (13 @ $4.00)	Est.	52.00
17.	Paint unfin. surf. of enam. fixt. (incl. in labor)	—	—
18.	Valve tags and frames	Est.	10.00
19.	Gas Hot Water Heater, delivered	Bid	633.00
20.	Flue piping for heater	Est.	15.00
21.	Hot Water Circl. Pump & acquastat	Est.	75.00
22.	Sump pump	Bid	190.00
23.	Thermostatic Mixing Valve	Bid	231.00
24.	Wall Hydrants (4 @ $18.25)	Est.	73.00
25.	Pressure reduction valve	3	95.00
26.	Hot Water Tank Stand	Est.	30.00
27.	Access Panels (for conductors) (9 @ $5.00)	Est.	45.00
28.	Excavation for water line	Bid	550.00

Materials and sub-contract work	$17,852.00
Labor to install and test	7,750.00
Travel	500.00
Payroll Tax	450.00
Total cost	$26,552.00
Plus 10% overhead charge	2,655.00
Total Estimate	$29,207.00
Actual Figure Quoted on Bid	$28,900.00

* This exhibit shows the master sheet and one sub-sheet of an 8-page estimate.

Note: "Bid" in the column headed "Page Ref." indicates a bid by a supplier to furnish the item at the price noted.

price. We call it shopping. It's all very nice that people have so much confidence in us, but it sure doesn't do much for our profit ratio."

"We've got a mighty good reputation in the city and the surrounding area," said the elder Mr. Stern, "principally because I've always insisted that we must do a first-class job regardless of the price. The trouble is that nowadays most people don't know a good job of plumbing when they see it, and a lot of those who do know just don't care. Still, there are some general contractors who want a good job. We often get calls asking us to bid on a particular job that we'd like to do, and we have to refuse it because Gilbert

J. W. Stern & Son, Inc.

Sub-sheet # 2 Project _____

ESTIMATE FOR   Fixtures (Dalton-Ingersoll)

Item	No. Req.	Cost Each	Total Cost
Floor Toilet	2	$46.50	$93.00
Floor Toilet (w/9500 seat)	4	48.00	192.00
Lavatories	7	39.60	277.20
Lavatory w/wrist fitting	1	52.65	52.65
Bradley Fountain (washing)	4	89.25	357.00
Urinal	8	64.00	512.00
Slop Sink—enameled	4	76.00	304.00
Drinking Fountain	1	63.00	63.00
Classroom sink	14	54.25	759.50
Slop Sink—v.c.	1	91.00	91.00
Wall Toilet (blow-out)	7	97.00	679.00
Wall Toilet (siphon)	5	103.00	515.00
Stainless Sink	1	55.00	55.00
Electric Cooler	1	273.75	273.75

Total Fixture Cost $4,224.10

ESTIMATE FOR   Permit

60 fixtures @ $1.00	$60.00
11 Floor Drains @ $1.00	11.00
10 Roof Drains @ $1.00	10.00
H.W. Tank & Htr.	2.00
Total Permit Cost	$83.00

doesn't have the time to estimate it. As he gets more experience, I'm hoping to see him fast enough to estimate a job in half the time he needs now. That way, we can bid on twice as many jobs and get our volume up to carry this overhead."

"As far as I can see right now, we're on the ragged edge," Gilbert summarized. "We've got to establish ourselves firmly in that third category I mentioned, or we're going to wind up in the 'dog' class. To move up, we've got to increase our overhead so we can do our estimating faster, bid on more jobs, and give better and faster service. We've got to have more capital to carry the overhead and, on a ten per cent gross, that doesn't grow on trees.

As it stands now, we're losing money every month. We're too big to compete with the little outfits and too little to compete with the big ones. I'm beginning to wonder, seriously, if our only solution isn't to drop into the 'dog' class deliberately and start cutting every corner we can. With the pride we've always had in our work and our reputation, I'm not sure we'll be able to live with ourselves but, in a cutthroat business like this, what the hell can you do?"

DETROIT FORGE AND GEAR COMPANY*

—THOMAS J. McNICHOLS

Providing executives for ten or twenty years in the future was the most pressing problem confronting the top management at Detroit Forge, according to James F. Jensen, vice-president of research and development.

When George R. Anderson, the former vice-president of production, became president of the company in 1950, he formed an administrative committee from his headquarter's organization. (See Exhibit 1.)

In 1951 Mr. Anderson found that he was facing an increasing load of policy decisions on matters which required opinions and advice of representatives or heads of several departments. He therefore established on an experimental basis four committees on *sales, engineering,* and *production* policies, one for each plant. Membership on each committee was drawn from the principal department heads and their immediate assistants. The plant manager and plant accountant served in each case, and the committees were to include individuals directly concerned in the particular plant's sales, production, and engineering problems as well as some general representatives. It was intended that the chairmanship would rotate periodically. Although some executives served on the policy committees of more than one plant and a few were on all four, no executive was chairman of more than one. To begin the experiment, Mr. Anderson appointed three vice-presidents as chairmen as follows: Mr. Nathan to head the Toledo committee; Mr. MacDonald the Gary committee; Mr. Jensen the Pontiac committee; while Henry Degen, plant manager, was appointed initial chairman of the Detroit committee. His recognized managerial ability and the unique problems of his plant, which employed 1,100 of the company's 3,600 employees, made him a logical choice for the position.

* From McNichols, Thomas J., *Policy Making and Executive Action* (New York: McGraw-Hill Book Company, 1959), pp. 514–531. Reprinted by permission of the McGraw-Hill Book Company and Dr. Thomas J. McNichols.

Manufacturing a wide variety of parts, chiefly for the automotive industry, the Detroit Forge and Gear Company operated plants in Detroit, Michigan; Toledo, Ohio; and Gary, Indiana. Originally opening in 1912 as a heavy-

Exhibit 1

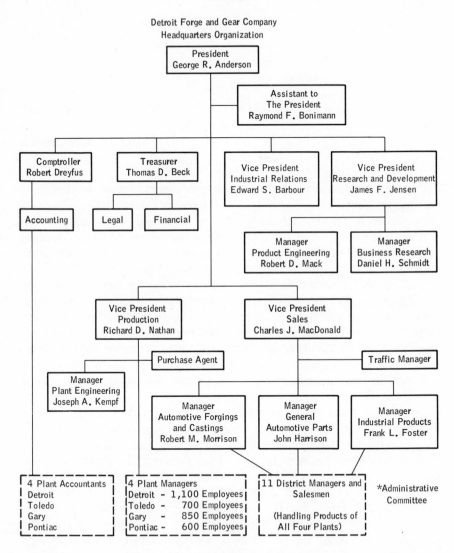

Detroit Forge and Gear Company
Headquarters Organization

President
George R. Anderson

Assistant to
The President
Raymond F. Bonimann

Comptroller
Robert Dreyfus

Treasurer
Thomas D. Beck

Vice President
Industrial Relations
Edward S. Barbour

Vice President
Research and Development
James F. Jensen

Accounting

Legal

Financial

Manager
Product Engineering
Robert D. Mack

Manager
Business Research
Daniel H. Schmidt

Vice President
Production
Richard D. Nathan

Vice President
Sales
Charles J. MacDonald

Purchase Agent

Traffic Manager

Manager
Plant Engineering
Joseph A. Kempf

Manager
Automotive Forgings
and Castings
Robert M. Morrison

Manager
General
Automotive Parts
John Harrison

Manager
Industrial Products
Frank L. Foster

4 Plant Accountants
Detroit
Toledo
Gary
Pontiac

4 Plant Managers
Detroit - 1,100 Employees
Toledo -   700 Employees
Gary   -   850 Employees
Pontiac - 600 Employees

11 District Managers and
Salesmen

(Handling Products of
All Four Plants)

*Administrative
Committee

forging shop, the Detroit plant supplied manufacturers of conveyors, general machinery, and production-type machine tools. Production of parts for trucks was begun during World War I and over-all capacity was further expanded during the 1920's. By the purchase of two small companies in 1926, volume production of automobile parts was begun. One of the purchased plants was at Gary, Indiana, and included light and heavy stamping and electroplating facilities; while the other plant was a foundry in Toledo, Ohio. In 1946 the company purchased a government-built plant it operated during the war in Pontiac and used its well-equipped metal-cutting machine shop for the production of automotive parts.

The company had always been operated with relatively little decentralization of responsibility except in the production department. As the Gary, Toledo, and Pontiac plants had been acquired, their sales had been handled by the established sales organization from the company's downtown Detroit headquarters, and most accounting, engineering, and industrial relations functions were handled in the same manner.

One of the purposes of the committees was to develop the operating and second-level managers by giving them a chance to sit in on committees with vice-presidents where they would have opportunity to have their opinions heard on matters of policy. A centralized business organization tended to develop good specialists. As a result, Mr. Jensen believed men proficient in their own chosen profession or department often failed to have full appreciation for and understanding of other viewpoints and the problems and contributions of other departments. The president, by requiring committee work of this nature—forcing men with different backgrounds and personalities to come together, to interchange views on the current problems—forced the men in the second and third levels of management to educate each other: accounting people in sales and labor relations, manufacturing people in credit and purchasing, and others similarly. Through this committee work, in addition to getting certain tasks accomplished more effectively, it was hoped to develop better understanding of other departments and common company objectives—factors that were considered important in executive development.

The membership of the policy committee on sales, engineering, and production for the Detroit plant,[1] as an example, was composed as follows:

Sales
    Mr. MacDonald, vice-president, sales department
    Mr. Morrison, manager, automotive forgings and castings, sales department
    Mr. Foster, manager, industrial products, sales department
Engineering
    Mr. Jensen, vice-president, research and development
    Mr. Mack, manager, product engineering
Production
    Mr. Nathan, vice-president, production
    Mr. Degen, plant manager, Detroit plant (chairman of the committee)
    Mr. Kempf, manager, plant engineering

[1] The story of the Detroit plant policy committee is presented in some detail as representative of the activities of all four committees.

General
  Mr. Dreyfus, comptroller
  Mr. Schmidt, manager, business research
  William A. Paddock, plant accountant, Detroit plant

The letter which the president wrote to the men he appointed to membership on the new committees was supplemented by a memorandum prepared by the assistant to the president which specified procedure and functions as follows:

OUTLINE OF PROCEDURE FOR POLICY COMMITTEES ON SALES, ENGINEERING, AND PRODUCTION

Object. To aid the President in establishing new or revised business policies, he will appoint standing Policy Committees whose duties shall be (1) the orderly consideration of matters jointly affecting sales, engineering, production, and other departments, and (2) the submission of proposals to the President for executive approval and issuance, based on decisions reached through such consideration.

Committee Conduct. Each chairman shall be responsible for the conduct and the activity of his committee. Full meetings will be held at his call, which should be at intervals not greater than six months. The place of such meetings should be at an office of the plant represented.

Each chairman shall prepare an agenda for each meeting called and shall submit it to all members of his committee sufficiently in advance to permit any necessary preparation and to assure full and complete discussion.

For consideration of matters which do not justify a full meeting but which should not be delayed unduly, the chairman may present it to his committee by letter.

Minutes. Skeleton notes of discussions and of the opinions of members of each committee shall be taken and copies of such memorandum minutes shall be signed by the chairman and copies submitted to the President and to each member of the committee. If there is no written correction within a reasonable time, it shall be assumed that the members approve of the minutes as submitted.

Jurisdiction. The members of committees will serve in a staff capacity in all committee activity and no change is made or intended in regular line authority or responsibility through creation of the committees.

Committee consideration should be directed toward the review of existing policies that could be contributing adversely to the results of an operation and to the formulation of recommended changes to old policies and to new policies that will benefit the company.

Any approved policy recommended through a committee will be administered through the regular line organization.

Attendance and Voting. Various department representatives may be members of a committee to develop full discussion and reveal all available essential information, but action on any resolution for submission for formal approval of the Presiednt shall be by votes of each senior department representative member of the committee.

Resolutions. The chairman shall initiate, or on request prepare, resolutions to be acted upon by the committee.

Unanimous action on resolutions is not essential, but dissenting members may and generally should submit their views at the time of submission of the resolution to the President.

Upon majority adoption of resolutions, they shall be typed on a special form, bear an identifying Policy Committee number (a separate series for each committee) and shall be signed by the committee chairman and the voting senior department representatives.

After approval by the President, the Policy Committee resolution will become an executive order to all concerned and will remain in force until amended or cancelled by later resolution or by order of the President.

The Detroit plant manager noted that although he was designated chairman of the Detroit committee at the start, the chairmanship would be rotated from time to time. With three vice-presidents, including his own immediate superior on his committee, he felt that the meetings should be kept very informal and planned to hold them in his own office at a T-shaped table arrangement. Since many of the problems the committee would consider were unique to his plant, he considered it fortunate in some ways that he would be the first chairman. He anticipated little difficulty serving in this capacity since he would be most intimately acquainted with the plant and its product problems and would be secure in speaking up boldly on the facts as he saw them. Indeed, he felt he would be doing less than his duty to the company if he hesitated to do so.

Shortly after the formation of the committee, the works manager wrote as chairman to each of the other members asking for suggestions for the agenda for the first meeting. Excerpts from the replies follow in the sequence received:

REPLY FROM MR. SCHMIDT, MANAGER, BUSINESS RESEARCH

Generalizing, I feel that your agenda for this meeting should include as much of the following as time will permit:

a. Product

Design, materials, production specifications

b. Marketing

Volumes by classes, pricing policy and price control effects, field service

c. Manufacturing

Facilities, optional methods, standards, supplies—to order or for stock, quality control, production controls, cost controls, research, material procurement and labor sources

As and if time permits and importance of the subject demands, the agenda may include the subjects of cost analysis: financial and statistical reports; personnel, public and customer relationships in all their phases; purchasing and storekeeping practices including expediting; inventory control; government relations (local); membership, activities and contributions to civil, municipal and industrial organizations; taxes; legal problems; credit; plant expansions; new-product acquisitions; standardizations; integrations; coordinations; organization structure and planning; plant engineering projects; patents, copyrights and trade marks; competition, etc.

REPLY FROM MR. KEMPF, MANAGER, PLANT ENGINEERING

I suggest that you may wish to consider for inclusion on the agenda of the first meeting:

Consideration regarding the proposed requirement of a high-speed forging press and accompanying reduceroll for the intended purpose of improving the plant's position in the competitive forging market.

I might mention the following projects also: Purchase and installation of a new steam boiler and construction of new Forge Shop Material Storage Warehouse without necessarily recommending that you include them on the agenda, as studies for both are progressing.

REPLY FROM MR. DREYFUS, COMPTROLLER

The overhead rates for Detroit plant must be revised to reflect increases in labor rates, higher prices for materials, supplies and services, substantial change in Detroit's product mix.

I suggest that our committee obtain a forecast of Detroit sales volume to serve as a basis for the overhead study. The overhead rates are intended to reflect average conditions—therefore, the forecast should be projected as far into the future as possible. Past forecasts for our purpose have been for only a year, but forecasts for longer periods will provide more valuable cost information.

The previous forecast, made in November of 1948, is shown with the actual shipments in tons for the 1949 and 1950 fiscal years.

	Forecast for Fiscal 1949 (Tons)	Shipments, Fiscal 1949 (Tons)	Shipments, Fiscal 1950 (Tons)
GROUP 1			
Machine-part forgings	1,600	1,614	1,747
Gear and sprocket forgings	300	600	955
Other industrial forgings	700	707	636
GROUP 2			
Brake-drum forgings	5,000	6,310	5,814
Axle and crankshaft forgings	3,150	2,820	2,594
Tandem axle parts	*	*	758
Other automotive forgings	700	823	278
GROUP 3			
Leaf springs	2,400	1,310	855
Coil springs	3,500	4,132	3,257
Automobile bumpers	1,425	1,237	789

* Included with "Other automotive forgings" in 1949.

The subjects that the committee will consider will require considerable study of cost information. The basis for the cost reports should be established carefully in order to provide information that will serve the committee's purpose.

For the purpose of judging the profit results of specific products, we use costs that reflect manufacturing burden and S.E.A. & G.[2] expenses that have been allocated at average or normal rates to provide a measuring device that does not fluctuate with temporary fluctuations in volume. If we allocated actual burden to specific products, the cost results would reflect so many divergent influences that they would be extremely difficult to judge. The use of average or normal rates, however, requires a reasonably accurate forecast of future volume.

REPLY FROM MR. PADDOCK, DETROIT PLANT ACCOUNTANT

I suggest the following subjects to be included on our agenda:

1. Type of costs required which will be most effective for cost controls and establishing sales policy.

2. Method of presentation of pricing information to the Sales Department.

3. The preparation of specific cost information on specific designs and products for general information

After the above have been determined, it will be necessary for us to review our cost procedures to determine if they are adequate to furnish the information desired. It may be found that it is desirable to make changes in our departmental cost presentation, possibly the establishment of new department budgets, and a re-allocation of overhead.

REPLY FROM MR. MACK, MANAGER, PRODUCT ENGINEERING

I would like to suggest that the matter of developing a fabricated, stationary type, No. 12 balancing beam be placed on the agenda for our first meeting. This subject was an active item on the agenda of the now-dissolved Product Development Committee.

REPLY FROM MR. NATHAN, VICE-PRESIDENT, PRODUCTION DEPARTMENT

I would suggest that your agenda include an item relating to a critical analysis of the following three product classes: machine-part forgings, gear and sprocket forgings, and leaf springs.

REPLY FROM MR. JENSEN, VICE-PRESIDENT, RESEARCH AND DEVELOPMENT

I am listing below several items which I believe might very well be given consideration by the Policy Committee although it is obvious that not all of them should be introduced for the first meeting. However, I believe that Item No. 1 is the most important one and probably will be present on the agenda of several meetings:

1. General review of Detroit plant profit performance

2. Consideration of effects of elimination of low-profit product lines

3. Consideration of effect of change from production of our present trailer draft gear type if current service tests on new development prove satisfactory[3]

4. Consideration of desirability of extending participation in defense material products

---

[2] Sales, engineering, administrative, and general.

[3] In 1951, "fifth wheels" were produced at the Toledo foundry. Other parts were fabricated at Detroit.

5. Consideration of long-range position of Detroit plant, assuming gradually increasing competition and possible decline in automotive demand

REPLY FROM MR. FOSTER, MANAGER, INDUSTRIAL PRODUCTS, SALES DEPARTMENT

I recommend that consideration be given to evaluation of purpose, function, availability, and timing of cost data for pricing purposes, required by sales for the diversified markets now served by Detroit plant industrial products.

REPLY FROM MR. MORRISON, MANAGER, AUTOMOBILE FORGINGS AND CASTINGS, SALES DEPARTMENT

The burden placed on Detroit plant by charges for S.E.A. & G. are assuming unreasonable proportions for the type of highly repetitive business in which most of the plant is now engaged. The limiting effect on high volume and repetitive sales of a generally fixed charge (per unit produced) for S.E.A. & G. should be recognized and the advisability of replacement by a sliding scale based on gross business by product or plant as a whole be considered as an advisable replacement.

REPLY FROM MR. MACDONALD, VICE-PRESIDENT, SALES DEPARTMENT

I recommend that you consider a study of the earning potential of the plant on both a long-range and short-term basis, by products, with particular consideration given to effects occasioned by broad variations in volume.

AGENDA PREPARED BY MR. DEGEN, CONSOLIDATING ALL SUGGESTIONS

June 11, 1951

Committee Members:

Regarding my letter of May 28, wish to thank you for your suggested subjects to be considered at our first meeting to be held June 20. Listed below are subjects for discussion:

1. Profit performance of
   a. Detroit plant
   b. Specific products
2. Volume effects on
   a. Manufacturing overhead
   b. S.E.A. & G. expense
3. Selection of product for marketing
   a. Automotive
   b. Industrial
   c. Defense
4. Costing information for
   a. Purpose of sales
   b. Purpose of plant cost control

After complete discussion of the subjects, committee should define our objectives and make definite proposals for proper procedure of action.

The policy committee on sales, engineering, and production for Detroit

Exhibit 2

Detroit Forge and Gear Company

Selected Sales Statistics, 1946–1950, Detroit Plant (Dollar Figures in Thousands)

	Group 1. Industrial Forgings						Group 2. Automatic Forgings								Group 3. Spring Shop					
	MACHINE PARTS		GEAR AND SPROCKET		OTHER		BRAKE DRUMS		AXLE AND CRANKSHAFT		TANDEM AXLE		OTHER		LEAF SPRINGS		COIL SPRINGS		BUMPERS	
	SALES	PROFIT	SALES	PROFIT	SALES	PROFIT	SALES	PROFIT	SALES	PROFIT	SALES	PROFIT	SALES	PROFIT	SALES	PROFIT	SALES	PROFIT	SALES	PROFIT
1946	783	41	521	(146)	514	48	1,090	139	862	96	*		723	122	742	57	2,133	191	302	(10)
1947	1,139	83	655	48	835	88	1,220	172	1,091	159	*		879	153	1,037	96	2,511	228	538	64
1948	1,116	123	637	44	921	95	2,080	130	1,394	119	*		1,005	175	877	37	3,045	270	601	65
1949	837	64	556	36	829	82	2,501	290	1,459	147	*		1,136	197	791	28	2,728	243	651	68
1950	983	84	653	40	791	106	2,050	245	1,212	133	852	187	698	107	463	(36)	2,164	194	476	53

( ) Indicate loss.

* Included with "Other Automotive Forgings."

321

plant convened at 10:00 A.M. on Wednesday, June 20, 1951, with all members in attendance. Excerpts from the minutes of the meeting follow:

The first item of discussion on the agenda was a review of the profit performance of Detroit Plant. The chairman presented a statement which showed the total yearly profit performance of the Plant for the past three decades. The statement indicated profits as a percentage of total net sales, before taxes and after annual adjustments. Sales statistics for major classes of product, covering the years 1951 to the present, were also submitted to the group. (See Exhibit 2.) It was pointed out that the decades of the 1920's and 1930's represented a complete major business cycle. The average yearly profits for the Detroit Plant during this cycle were 10.2 per cent of net sales.

The chairman questioned what a desirable profit objective for the Detroit Plant should be. One of the committee members suggested that the monthly profit objective of the Detroit Plant should be expressed in terms of total dollars rather than as a percentage of net sales because of the major variations of profit margins which exist for the various products, and the various markets in which the Detroit Plant sells its products. Several other members stated, however, that such a procedure would not give adequate consideration to monthly fluctuations in sales volume and product mix. After considerable discussion, it was generally agreed that profit objectives would have to be considered and analyzed for each individual class of product. As an over-all broad objective, it was agreed that plant performance should be measured on the basis of a profitable return on investment.

At the present time, the company has approximately $8,000,000 invested in the Detroit Plant, including fixed assets, plus working capital. During periods of high-volume production, this investment should bring a return of 10% after taxes. Considering the present tax rates, this would require a 20% return on investment before taxes. It was stated that the Plant has a yearly sales potential of 16 to 17 million dollars on the basis of our present dollar value. Profits on this amount of net sales would depend upon product mix, break-even point for a specific product, volume of business above this break-even point, pricing policies, and other factors. At maximum production, however, the profit goal should be a 20% return on investment before taxes. A minority believed that this goal was a little too high considering the Detroit Plant's class of products and the highly competitive markets for which it is producing.

It was emphasized that efforts must be directed toward obtaining the type of business and volume necessary to achieve a 20% return on investment. The Plant has several marginal and also loss items at present which must be carefully analyzed in order to determine what future course of action must be recommended.

Brief Review of Several of Detroit Plant's Products. After considerable discussion, the comptroller suggested that the committee devote its immediate attention and efforts to manufacturing, pricing, and sales of leaf springs and gear and sprocket forgings. These are some of the more important trouble spots which require further attention and analysis, representing the areas where the potential for improvement is the greatest.

Costing Information. Regarding the last item on the agenda, Mr. Foster, the manager of industrial product sales, requested that the Sales Department be given more adequate cost information to assist in the making of decisions regarding products to be manufactured and establishing sales prices for these products. Cost estimates on individual piece parts and products would materially assist the Sales Department in their pricing function.

Organization and procedures must be developed to prepare this information quickly and accurately for the Sales Department. He furthermore requested that the Sales Department be furnished with actual costs, whenever requested, in order to determine whether the Company made or lost money on specific products and orders, and also to assist in the pricing of subsequent orders.

The Committee agreed that proper steps must be taken to give the Sales Department the information they require. The chairman will appoint a subcommittee comprising representatives of the Sales and Accounting Departments in order to study this problem further and outline procedures to be used.

Suggested Topic for Next Meeting. It was suggested that the principal item on the agenda for the next Detroit Policy Committee meeting should be the subject of leaf springs. The Committee should determine whether this should be maintained as a class of product. If so, then the unprofitable items in this class should be segregated from the profitable ones, and the Committee should determine if anything can be done with these items. Mr. Paddock, the plant accountant, will prepare the necessary analyses and statistics for the various products in this class for the Committee's review at the next meeting.

Meeting adjourned at 5:00 P.M.

Note to Committee Members. The chairman has appointed the following subcommittee to analyze the problem of supplying the Sales Department with adequate cost information: Mr. Foster, Mr. Degen, and Mr. Paddock.

The work of the sub-committee on cost information for pricing was carried out in a highly informal manner and was completed before a second full meeting of the policy committee. The plant manager met with his assistant and the plant accountant on several occasions to discuss the matter. Although not present at the time of the meetings because his own office was located at the company headquarters, Mr. Foster's views were well known and taken into consideration because he was in daily contact with the plant by telephone and generally visited in person about once a week. The initial problem was to price the miscellaneous, low-volume, and special-order industrial springs and forgings orders which frequently required special design and tool set-up. While the plant manager and plant accountant thought there should be a follow-up to determine adequacy of price in relation to cost but ruled out actual costing of every order as unnecessarily expensive, it was soon apparent that consideration should be given to pricing procedure on all products. The problem of coordinating customer delivery requests and plant production schedules became involved, and the plant members of the committee at first favored authorization for direct contact with the salesmen on prices and deliveries. However, an agreement was reached with the Sales Department that plant and sales should each designate a man or men to handle the details of pricing and scheduling, and that direct communication between them should be authorized.

The plant accountant asked the comptroller to express his point of view on the latitude to be allowed the plant in developing figures to pass directly to the Sales Department. He replied as follows:

October 3, 1951

Herewith is a clarification of the position of the general office accounting department concerning the degree to which we wish to participate in obtaining pricing information from Detroit plant for the sales department.

Our reason for wishing to participate in initiating requests for, and submitting reports of cost information, is that there are so many meanings to the term "cost." There are actual costs, normal costs, standard costs, conversion costs, marginal value costs, and imputed costs, in addition to such formula costs as are now required by OPS regulations. By participating in the request for, and the reporting of, cost information, we hope to assure that the right type of cost is requested, and that the recipient of the information understands the type of information he has received.

Whenever prior agreement has been reached by the sales department and the plant about the type of information they request for pricing purposes, we do not wish to participate. We do, however, ask that this type of information be clearly designated as "pricing information."

For your use in developing plans for expediting the submission of pricing information, you may follow these general rules:

1. Provided a clear understanding is reached as to the type of information required, requests for pricing information which originate at general office may go direct from the sales department to the individual designated by you and the plant manager to receive such requests. The information may be transmitted direct from the individual to the sales department.

2. We have no primary interest in request for pricing information which originate at the plant for use by plant personnel, and leave the handling of that problem to your discretion.

3. Any request for cost information which originates in the general office should clear through the general office accounting department. Any report of cost information from the works for the use of any general office department should clear through the general office accounting department.

4. We have no primary interest in requests for cost information that originate at the plant for use by plant personnel, and leave the handling of that problem to your discretion.

If the above does not clarify the position of the general accounting department as it concerns requests for, and reports of, pricing information and cost information, we shall be pleased to receive your further questions.

In preparation for the next meeting of the Detroit plant policy committee, the plant accountant and the assistant plant manager prepared a report on leaf springs. After it was ready the plant manager, plant accountant, assistant plant manager, and plant product engineer met to consider it and drew up the summary, conclusions, and recommendations. The group agreed that for purposes of presentation to the policy committee, the plant manager should sign the recommendations and the plant accountant should sign the body of the report. The plant manager's summary and conclusions are quoted below:

LEAF SPRINGS[4]
ANALYSIS OF PROFIT RESULTS BY DESIGN

This report presents a digest of the facts that were developed from an examination of all phases of the manufacturing methods, the manufacturing costs, and the results that were obtained after the application of the selling prices by the sales department.

In order to save the time of the committee members, we are setting forth below the conclusions that were drawn from the data that was assembled for analysis:

1. Cost variations are related to product design.

2. The preponderance of orders received is for small quantities, primarily heavy types for large trucks and mobile industrial equipment.

3. The price schedule—being based on weight—does not sufficiently recognize cost variations which are due to design and to small quantities. Even the extras that are listed in the price schedule are applied on the basis of weight.

4. Too many designs are sold for the volume of business received.

5. It is important that the sales department be given promptly the necessary pricing information reflecting the above.

The costs that were used in the calculations that resulted in the final results of the report are predicated on the best possible production efficiencies that are attainable with our present manufacturing methods. This is not necessarily the production efficiency that we are experiencing at this time:

As a result of the conclusions set forth above, we submit the following recommendations:

1. The current price schedule should be withdrawn from use.

2. The price quoted to customers should have relation to design and quantity on order—Detroit Plant to furnish pricing information accordingly.

3. If the action recommended above conflicts with government pricing regulations, immediate steps should be taken to obtain whatever relief is possible under the regulations.

4. If no relief is possible, orders should not be accepted from marginal customers for small quantities.

The second meeting of the policy committee on sales, engineering, and production for Detroit plant convened at 9:50 A.M. on Wednesday, November 28, 1951:

The meeting opened with a general discussion of the report, on the analysis of profit results for leaf spring product class. The following points were considered:

1. Would Detroit be better off without this product class?

2. Should we be more selective of the orders which are accepted from customers?

[4] The company formerly manufactured leaf springs for two independent automobile manufacturers. This volume was lost when one redesigned its car with a new type suspension in 1947 and the other in 1949.

3. Would the amount of absorption of fixed expense, which was obtained by the retention of this product class, warrant its continuation?[5]

Recommendations made by Detroit plant in the report were reviewed. It was pointed out that, because of Government regulations, it will be necessary to continue to price these products in accordance with the current price schedule and, therefore, it cannot be withdrawn from use.

It was agreed, however, that, if we continue in the production of Recommendation No. 2, namely, "The price quoted to consumers should have relation to design and quantity on order," should be accepted but modified as follows:

"Sales department to change existing schedules and procedure for quoting on new designs as soon as Detroit plant can furnish the necessary information, and as soon as regulations will permit. (Information to be prepared by the plant on the basis of the figure that will permit the plant to better its overall performance if the job is taken at that price.)"

Mr. Foster stated, in connection with Recommendation No. 4 ("If no relief is possible, orders should not be accepted from marginal customers for small quantities"), that he is not accepting short orders, except from regular customers who have relied upon us in the past for these parts.

It was suggested that, if leaf springs continue to be loss items after a reasonable time but not less than one year has elapsed after we begin "free pricing," then the product class should definitely be discontinued. ("Free pricing" contemplates pricing procedure after the expiration of Government regulations controlling prices.) It was agreed that, at such time, the prices quoted to customers should have reasonable relationship to design and quantity on order as recommended in the plant's report.

It was pointed out that competition, in the main, sets the price for these products. It was also pointed out that the use of these parts is on the decline.

The meeting adjourned at 12:30 for lunch and reconvened at 2:00 P.M.

The subject of pricing information was discussed in the afternoon. A general discussion followed covering the aims and objectives. The plant manager went into considerable detail in order that the committee might be informed of the planning that was being done on this item. It was agreed that the centralization of responsibility and a definite assignment of individuals to the details would eliminate the major portion of the problems now experienced. An organization chart (see Exhibit 3) was presented to the committee, which indicated the delegation of responsibility and the general lines of communication. A suggestion was made and agreed to by the Chairman that a flow chart be prepared for the Committee. (See Exhibits 4, 5, and 6.)

[5] The comptroller stated that for the purpose of looking at adequacy or inadequacy of prices it was a company policy to consider depreciation of replacement cost. With a product as important as the leaf spring class, requiring much factory space and management time and attention, it was appropriate that the figures used for study should include burden charges representing the appropriate share of management costs and overhead. Implied in a decision to discontinue the product was an assumption that the facilities would be used for other more profitable purposes. Space was one of the pressing problems at the Detroit plant, and there would be no problem utilizing the space if the product class was discontinued. Machinery and equipment was largely special purpose and would not be used.

The Chairman then asked for items to be considered at the next meeting of the Policy Committee. It was agreed that the following would be discussed:

1. A Policy for Detroit plant overtime operations—whether or not the plant should be scheduled for five- or six-day operations.

Exhibit 3

Detroit Forge and Gear Company
Proposed Organization for Pricing Information at Detroit Plant

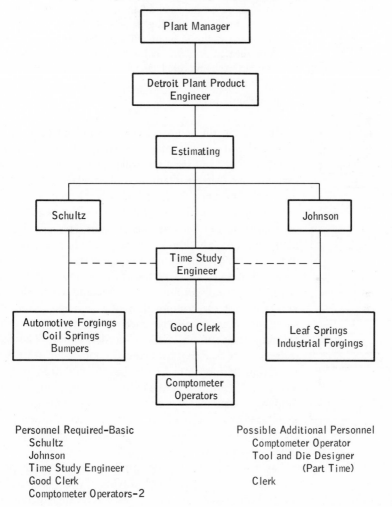

Personnel Required–Basic	Possible Additional Personnel
Schultz	Comptometer Operator
Johnson	Tool and Die Designer
Time Study Engineer	(Part Time)
Good Clerk	Clerk
Comptometer Operators–2	

2. Sales forecast for a five-year period beginning 1952. This is essential for the re-allocation of overhead, the development of standard costs and variable budgets,

and from the standpoint of planning material inventories and determination of labor requirements.

It was suggested that the Chairman appoint a committee to study the causes for the excessive overtime operations of Detroit plant during the years 1950 and 1951.

There was a tentative understanding that Mr. Morrison and Mr. Foster would immediately begin work on a sales forecast for a five-year period beginning 1952. It was suggested that Detroit plant project production volume and cost of manufacture on the basis of the products already booked and which make up backlog of approximately 15,000 tons. It is expected that the plant will be able to forecast shipments predicated on this backlog, and give a reasonably close estimate of the expected manufacturing costs and profit results.

The meeting adjourned at 5:00 P.M.

Mr. Jensen, the senior vice-president and head of the research and development department, served as a member of each of the four policy committees including that for the Detroit plant described above. He stated that as of January, 1952, no positive recommendations or resolutions had been submitted to the president to be approved and become executive orders. The Detroit plant committee had never actually voted on any proposition. Generally, the committees had resulted in clearer understanding of what the specific problems at each plant were, just where profits came from and more detailed knowledge of the composition of costs and profits. In some instances, committee meetings had resulted in the clearing away of obstacles to needed action. The committees were serving to bring second- and third-level management men into the policy formulation process. The senior members of the committees contributed their guidance, particularly in policy thinking, while the junior members brought detailed and intimate knowledge of specific problems, whether representing local or general office viewpoints.

The committees did serve to state clearly the ramifications of major problems, usually the first and major step toward solving them. Nevertheless, Mr. Jensen stated that the committees were still considered experimental and might be discontinued if they did not soon prove an effective and efficient management process. The committees had not been operating long enough to appraise what they had or could accomplish in a positive way. The top management of the company was not wholeheartedly in favor of "committee

Exhibit 4

Detroit Forge
and Gear
Company

Flow Chart for
Pricing Infor-
mation Prior to
December, 1951

Customer

Sales Department
Request for
Pricing Information

Comptroller

Detroit Plant
Accounting

Operating
(Plant Manager)

Estimate of Time
and Material,
Detroit Plant
Product Engineer

Detroit Plant
Accounting

Plant Manager

Comptroller

Sales Department

Customer

management." Committee discussion was fine; however, it was Mr. Jensen's experience that a committee functioned only as effectively as the chairman operated. Committees could not actually be responsible for decisions or relieve line managers from responsibility.

Exhibit 5

Detroit Forge and Gear Company

New Flow Chart for Pricing Information, December 17, 1951

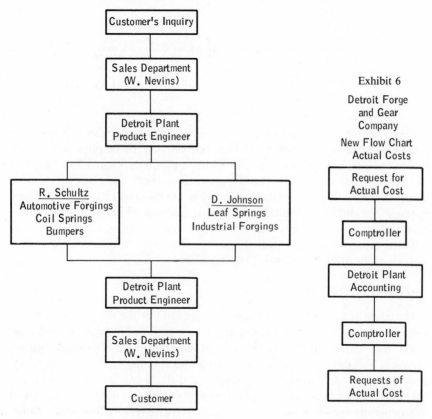

Exhibit 6

Detroit Forge and Gear Company

New Flow Chart Actual Costs

The decision on leaf springs at Detroit resolved the kind of problem that could be handled most effectively in committee. This was a product the company had made for many years. Profit performance of the product, since discontinuance of high-volume production for automobiles, had not been bad enough to receive sharp attention from either sales or production managers who would build a strong argument for abandoning the entire line. However, a committee, representing the views of the several divisions concerned, permitted a positive decision to be made.

4. THE AMERICAN PACKING COMPANY*

—RANDOLPH G. KINABREW

The American Packing Company is engaged in the slaughtering and processing of cattle and hogs into a full line of fresh beef, cured pork, and bacon. It also operates a modern cannery in which it produces Vienna Sausage, beef stew, potted meats, corned beef hash, gravy, sliced beef, and chili. In addition, its product line includes weiners, smoked sausages, and lunch meats. These products are distributed through wholesale markets which operate in thirty-six states and two foreign countries.

The company was incorporated under the laws of a Southern state in 1946 with an authorized capital stock of $1,100,000.

OPERATING FACILITIES

The plant is located on a 70-acre tract of land at the edge of a Southern town of about 15,000 population. Operating facilities include slaughtering, rendering, and cold storage areas and equipment; mechanized cutting, grinding, and mixing equipment; cooking and canning equipment; mechanized conveyor lines for packaging weiners and sliced bacon; scales, and internal floor transporting and handling equipment. This equipment is housed in a two-story masonry building with 85,000 square feet of floor space. Other facilities in this building include lockers for the 540 employees, first aid rooms, offices for Federal meat inspectors, and storage rooms.

Other buildings owned by the company at this site include a modern metal building with concrete floor for storing canned meats, a frame building used as a warehouse, an office building and cafeteria of brick construction, and two large cattle barns of frame construction with concrete floors and metal roofs.

---

* Written for the Southern Case Writers' Association. Reprinted by permission of the Association and Professor Randolph G. Kinabrew.

Rolling stock consists of 31 passenger automobiles, 19 refrigerated delivery trucks, and 10 tractors with trailers for over-the-highway delivery.

Total assets of the company were valued at $4,315,946 by the end of 1960.

EARLY HISTORY

The company has grown from a small livestock business and retail meat market operated by the father of the present owners into a fully developed regional meat packing enterprise with annual gross sales of about $25,000,000 within a relatively short period. The founder of the business, Mr. J. C. Young, Sr., operated a meat market in the downtown area during his lifetime and bought and sold livestock. The business became the property of four sons of the founder, including the present owners, upon the death of their father in 1930. One brother sold his interest and left the business in 1932; a second owner withdrew in 1936, leaving the remaining two brothers, Mr. B. L. Young and Mr. J. L. Young, as joint owners.

One member of the family who withdrew from this business entered the automobile business in which he has had a very successful experience. The other member who withdrew entered business on his own initially and became a cattle buyer for this company at a later date. He is employed by the company in this capacity at the present time.

The remaining two brothers added hard work to the training which their father gave them and built a remarkable business through a series of expansions in capacity and additions to and improvements in products. Company growth has taken place within the framework of policies established and followed by the founder. Operations and expansions have been financed entirely from earnings. The company has never made use of outside capital. The owners have never taken money out of the business except for their salaries.

COMPANY DEVELOPMENT

The first experience with company growth occurred during the period of transition in ownership after the death of the founder. A horse-drawn wagon was used to sell and deliver fresh meat to residential customers, in addition to operating the retail meat markets. The use of the mobile sale and delivery unit enabled the company to serve a new group of customers. It proved to be profitable and was continued and emphasized thereafter in the operation. Expansion of the market by the use of the wagon increased the demand for a greater output volume. Management became interested in obtaining additional equipment for slaughtering meat animals and processing and storing fresh meat. The need for capital was discussed with a banker in the community. The banker was unwilling to extend credit at this time because of the risk involved. He advised management to purchase the equipment which was desired from the manufacturer on the installment plan.

Management declined this advice and undertook to develop its own financial resources by making the very best use of assets which it possessed. The immediate objective at this time was to acquire 500 head of cattle and $10,000 as beginning resources for the first venture into expanding capacity.

By 1936, the company had acquired the cattle and capital which was considered by management as the minimum necessary to justify constructing permanent installations and expanding production capacity. It had also acquired other assets in building, land, and some miscellaneous holdings. All of these assets were purchased or developed by using the earnings of the company. In that year, the owners constructed a small masonry building on the present plant site. This building contained a kill-floor, processing room, and cold storage room. It represented an investment of $3,000.

The fundamental nature of the company did not change for the next several years. It was able to sell all the fresh beef and cured pork it could produce and followed the pattern of deepening production facilities and increasing capacity to produce these products as capital was accumulated through its own earnings. As physical facilities were expanded, new and more efficient processing equipment was added and greater quantities of fresh and processed products were marketed under the company brand name. A fleet of modern refrigerated delivery trucks was obtained to serve merchants in the principal marketing areas. A sales force was organized to call on retail outlets at least twice a week. During this period the company maintained a consistent advertising campaign which included newspapers, movie theaters, radio spot announcements, point-of-sale display materials, and retail demonstrations. By 1950, annual sales receipts had risen to $4,000,000, even though sales were restricted to the state in which the company was located. The company had not become engaged in interstate commerce.

A major change in the nature of the company was made in 1950 when it began producing sausages and bologna. This development came about in an informal manner through the interest of an employee of the company. This employee was a butcher whose employment was somewhat irregular. On one occasion, he left the company and attempted to go into the meat market business in a nearby town. After failing in this venture, he returned to the American Packing Company and maintained his interest in developing processes for making sausages and bologna. He was provided with some facilities and encouraged by the management to continue experimenting with these processes. Eventually, he produced a type of bologna which was gray in color. It was sent for examination to a firm in Chicago from which the company purchased spices. Through the assistance of the spice company, the processes were improved and a satisfactory product was made.

The spice company assisted in developing processes for manufacturing other processed meat products. A sausage kitchen and canning operation were installed. Thereafter, the American Packing Company was regularly engaged in the production of a wide variety of sausages and canned meats.

A modern two-story canning plant addition was constructed in 1953 which doubled sausage and canning capacity. Products from this operation contribute a substantial amount to total sales. It is estimated that canned meats are the most important product today from the point of view of sales volume.

Still another significant change occurred in the company in 1952 when federal meat inspection was instituted. This development, of course, established quality standards for all food products and allowed for the shipment of these goods in interstate commerce. This was very important for the marketing of all products, but it provided a very special advantage in the marketing of surplus fresh meat which could not be withheld from the market very satisfactorily and for the marketing of canned meats which could be shipped long distances without refrigeration. The present sales area for fresh meat includes Alabama, Arkansas, Florida, Georgia, Louisiana, Mississippi, New York, Pennsylvania, South Carolina, and West Tennessee. Canned meat is sold in 36 states, England, and Puerto Rico. The company has a sales force of 26 employees, in addition to jobbers and brokers who handle company products. Annual sales reached $26,000,000 by 1960.

COMPANY POLICY

The framework of major long-range policy of this statement is well established from evidence obtained from informal statements of officers and three published statements along this line. The first recorded statement of company policy is found in a reprint from *Meat Magazine* for November, 1950. A quotation from that article states:

The elder Mr. Young, who died in 1930, was a sound, conservative businessman who believed in operating strictly within the limitations of his own capital. The present operators attribute to their father a great share of the credit for their amazing success. They still operate under the same policies he established and expand their business only when they can do so on their own capital.

The second statement on this subject is contained in an article published in a local newspaper in January, 1953, as follows:

Working closely together, the brothers make a perfect team . . . , the president handles livestock purchases and farm operations; . . . the vice president directs plant operations, where an efficient staff has been assembled.

The third statement is in the analysis section of a private report dated April, 1961, as follows:

This company, long prominent in the area it serves, has, for the past few years, sold about as much as its plant facilities are capable of producing. Thus, its volume has been relatively steady. Earnings have been good, and are retained, at least in part, to expand both tangible net worth and net working capital.

GROWING WITH OWN CAPITAL

The above statements point out in a forceful way the influence of the attitude of the founder upon the manner in which company growth has been financed Consistent adherence to the policy of financing growth from company. earnings has provided management with a high degree of independence from external pressures. Internal financing and independence in decision-making are regarded as objectives of the company as much as growth itself. Consequently, decisions are made in an atmosphere of informality and deliberate action. Policy decisions are developed by the management team in line with the long-run objectives of the company. Operating decision-making is very decentralized. These decisions are made within the framework of company policy and the knowledge and experience of supervisory personnel. There is a minimum of decision-making at any level through the exercise of internal authority or under circumstances of emergency or necessity.

Internal financing is more than a company policy which has been adhered to because of difficulty in using alternative means of obtaining capital. It has become an effective way of expressing a philosophy of management. The company seeks to do business on a continuing basis. One slogan associated with selling company products is, " Can I sell him again ? " This is a convenient expression of a desire not only to gain but also to hold customers for repeat sales. Management recognizes the effect of the company on the local agricultural economy by providing a ready market for livestock from local farms. Likewise, it provides employment and income for nonagricultural workers. At the same time, management seeks to continue providing these eternal economies to the community without exposing itself to the necessity of yielding to undesirable pressures through temporary unfavorable conditions in the market.

As an illustration of how this philosophy of management may be implemented in routine transaction, it was pointed out in conversation with officers that the company has been able to avoid the impact of unfavorable market conditions in procurement. As a result of its independent financial position, it has been free to withdraw from the supply market in temporary periods of high prices for meat animals. It is common practice to compete with large and small buyers on an orderly basis and simply maintain its relative position in the supply market when prices are unfavorable. No evidence was found to indicate that the company is in a competitive race to increase short-run volume or long-run capacity. It tends to increase volume when direct cost conditions are quite stable.

The greatest cost of growing within the limitations of its own capital probably is in the area of overhead cost. For several years prior to 1959, additional production capacity was added by constructing more building space and installing new equipment on the basis of immediate needs of various operations. Eventually, the capacities of major line operations became uneven, and operating the plant at its most efficient level did not necessarily allow each function in the over-all operation to perform at its most efficient level. Under these circumstances, those operations which had been over-expanded in terms of capital investment were being operated at less than the most efficient level; while functions which were under-expanded were being over-utilized. Of course, some of the operations may be utilized at the most efficient level at any rate of utilizing the capacity of the plant. Nevertheless, the capacities of the operations are not co-ordinated and high overhead costs cannot be avoided under the circumstances unless more uniform capacities are created in the seqeunce of production operations.

This problem may be illustrated by the relationship of the hog-killing floor to the pork-processing operations. Normally, this unit operates only two days per week and handles from 550 to 660 hogs per day. The other pork-processing units operate five days per week and handle a maximum of 1,200 hogs per week, or an average of about 250 per day. The killing floor is equipped with modern machinery and is quite efficient when operated at capacity, but it is a high-cost operation as it is used in this situation because the machinery is idle about one-half the time other units are operating.

In 1959, management realized the effects of this situation and decided to plan subsequent expansions of plant capacity in order to bring about more uniformity of production operations. One officer stated that "we caught up with ourselves." An outside consultant was brought in to develop a master plan by which the company would continue to grow by phases. The phases are arranged in an order of priority and scheduled so that one phase would be completed each year until completion of the master plan. A resident industrial engineer is employed to assist the company in attaining the objectives of the master plan.

THE MANAGEMENT TEAM

The American Packing Company is owned and managed by two individuals, the president and the vice president. Each of these two persons owns one-half of the outstanding stock. Likewise, there is some division of management responsibility. The president is responsible for the purchasing of cattle, calves, and hogs; while the vice president is responsible for plant operations, including the development of new products. Both the president and the vice president have a son active in the management of these respective areas. Also, each owns and manages other private business interests. The president has extensive holdings in farm operations, livestock growing, and feeder lots; while the vice president owns a local residential construction firm. Both of these men are widely recognized as successful businessmen working together in the packing business and as individuals in their personal enterprises.

Within the packing company, there is strong evidence of an informal approach to decision-making. The informality of management was discussed without hesitation by all persons interviewed. The president emphasized the lack of formality in the making of decisions. " We know what we are supposed to do," he explained, "and we simply do it." Knowledge of the business was pointed out by him as the factor which he regarded as most responsible for success. On the other hand, there was no indication of a disposition to vary from the fundamental policy of operating and expanding within the limitations of the company's capital. Decisions are made within the scope of this policy and through an informal process of free, thorough, and extensive discussion by all company personnel concerned with issues involved in those decisions. It is more of a process of developing decisions rather than making decisions.

In addition to the informal character of decision-making, there is a prevailing attitude within management of eagerness to import scientific and technical knowledge from organized and well-established groups outside the business. There is a strong desire to do business with other companies on a continuing basis and to cultivate the residual effects of exchanging information which is mutually beneficial. New ideas are applied to constructing new plant facilities, selecting and operating improved equipment, and developing new

TABLE 1

South's Share of Animals Marketed, Meat Produced, and Meat Purchased, 1955

Type of Product	Per Cent of United States Total
Meat Animal Marketings	22
Meat Production	17
Meat Purchased	25
Hog Marketings	12
Pork Production	16
Pork Purchased	32˙
Cattle and Calf Marketings	28
Beef and Veal Production	19
Beef and Veal Purchased	20

Source: *Meat Consumption Trends and Patterns*, U.S. Department of Agriculture, Agricultural Marketing Service, Agricultural Handbook Number 187, Washington, D.C., page 25.

processes and products. Because of this " open-door" policy toward new ideas, practices and techniques tend to change quite frequently; but the fundamental policies of co-operative teamwork and independent financing tend to endure.

THE POLICY OF LONG-RUN GROWTH

The American Packing Company has been in a position to sell about all it could produce and expand its capacity through the years because of the extent of the market through which it obtains its supply of beef cattle and the market in which it sells beef and pork. Table 1 indicates that the Southern area is an exporter of meat animals and an importer of meat. A breakdown of the quantities in Tables 2 and 3 shows that the area markets more beef cattle than it slaughters, and consumes far more than it markets or slaughters. By 1959 all of the individual states in the area show a surplus of marketings of cattle over slaughterings. They are presumed to be exporters of feeder cattle to the Corn Belt. Negligible quantities of cattle are shipped into the states in the area as finished slaughter cattle. Instead, beef is shipped in as dressed weight. Packers in the area have had a surplus supply of cattle of all grades in relation to slaughter capacity. Of course, the major supply problem has been and continues to be that of obtaining quality grades of finished cattle from feeder lots. Buyers must exercise extreme selectivity in this regard. The growth in the supply of cattle in the South has paralleled the diversification of agriculture in the area.

The South does not slaughter enough cattle to supply its consumer market. A breakdown in the estimate of quantities consumed by states for selected years (Table 3) shows that the majority of the states have been and continue to be deficient in quantities of beef domestically available in relation to quantities domestically consumed. Beef consumption is regarded as a function of per capita personal income and population. The states in the area vary in respect to changes in both of these variables; however, the over-all, long-run change in both variables has been upward during the period of long-run growth of the company.

The situation in respect to pork differs from that of beef. The Southern area is deficient in the marketing and slaughtering of hogs; yet, it is a heavy consuming area for pork. Only 12% of United States hog-marketings are in the South and 16% of pork production, while the people in the South purchase 32% of the total pork purchased in the United States. Area packers import about 1/3 of the hogs processed and sellers import 1/2 of the pork sold. Because the South is a relatively low income area and per capita consumption of pork is a declining function of per capita personal income, the area ranks very high in per capita consumption of pork. The past structure of personal income distribution has tended to broaden the market for pork. The high cost of importing an adequate supply of hogs, together with what appears to be an elastic demand for pork, requires a very efficient and large-scale processing operation in order to realize a profit in this phase of the meat packing business. The American Packing Company is moving in this direction by increasing the pork processing capacity of its operation. The ratio of production to consumption in the market area indicates that there is considerable room for expanding before the market is saturated.

TABLE 2

Commercial Marketings and Slaughter of Cattle by Selected States and for Selected Years

Years	Commerical Marketings (1,000 Head)	Commerical Slaughter (1,000 Head)	States
	77	86	South Carolina
	227	420	Georgia
	207	246	Florida
	635	205	Kentucky
1947	403	299	Tennessee
	345	230	Alabama
	352	124	Mississippi
	366	140	Arkansas
	409	216	Louisiana
	56	69	South Carolina
	208	290	Georgia
	202	186	Florida
	493	193	Kentucky
1950	306	279	Tennessee
	220	164	Alabama
	280	69	Mississippi
	244	49	Arkansas
	172	148	Louisiana
	143	121	South Carolina
	384	537	Georgia
	304	401	Florida
	467	227	Kentucky
1955	409	531	Tennessee
	436	236	Alabama
	387	185	Mississippi
	258	111	Arkansas
	302	228	Louisiana
	108	93	South Carolina
	277	262	Georgia
	326	287	Florida
	481	189	Kentucky
1959	352	348	Tennessee
	359	177	Alabama
	401	229	Mississippi
	318	112	Arkansas
	263	180	Louisiana

Source: *Commercial Livestock Slaughter*, U.S. Department of Agriculture Marketing Service, Statistical Bulletin No. 231, July, 1958, and *Agricultural Statistics*.

The economic situation in respect to canned meat, sausages, and lunch meat is intermediate between that of beef and pork. These products are made

TABLE 3

Estimate of Total Beef Consumption by Selected States for Selected Years

State	Head of Cattle			
	1945	1950	1955	1960
S. Carolina	227,800	246,800	296,200	279,700
Georgia	371,400	455,300	487,300	530,800
Florida	300,600	344,000	514,700	628,900
Kentucky	247,400	279,500	307,800	345,300
Tennessee	301,000	345,500	398,000	450,200
Alabama	318,200	351,300	293,300	371,300
Mississippi	236,300	245,000	234,500	255,100
Arkansas	205,100	225,700	233,400	213,200
Louisiana	232,700	349,600	380,100	429,600

Source: Compiled from United States Departments of Agriculture and Commerce Statistics.

from low-grade meat animals and sold in an elastic market. Both of these factors are favorable for a meat cannery in the Southern area. Again, The American Packing Company has not only expanded capacity, but also has tailored its operations in the right directions.

SUMMARY OF COMPANY POLICY

Operational decisions are made by the management of The American Packing Company within the framework of very definite company policy. Knowledge of experienced personnel is the guiding force at this level. The common bond of skill and knowledge of the meat packing business invites teamwork and co-operative effort.

Decisions in respect to changes in procedures and products are made through the assistance of outside technical personnel and through consideration by management as a group. This is evidenced by the presence of a resident industrial engineer and by the eager acknowledgment of valuable assistance obtained from suppliers.

The long-run company policy of growth was formulated and is maintained within the environment of the economic conditions in which the company exists. It may be that the company could not have survived and maintained its position in the supply and consumer markets without expanding operations.

TABLE 4

Commercial Marketings and Slaughter of Hogs by Selective States for Selective Years

Years	Commerical Marketings (1,000 Head)	Commerical Slaughter (1,000 Head)	States
	335	407	South Carolina
	760	1,284	Georgia
	427	667	Florida
	812	541	Kentucky
1945	895	743	Tennessee
	591	514	Alabama
	310	214	Mississippi
	663	277	Arkansas
	568	444	Louisiana
	1,966	399	South Carolina
	3,178	1,460	Georgia
	1,446	453	Florida
	1,417	845	Kentucky
1950	1,178	1,411	Tennessee
	947	539	Alabama
	399	146	Mississippi
	784	213	Arkansas
	633	193	Louisiana
	429	390	South Carolina
	1,340	1,599	Georgia
	405	525	Florida
	1,142	1,033	Kentucky
1955	996	1,528	Tennessee
	1,064	671	Alabama
	371	247	Mississippi
	318	245	Arkansas
	290	184	Louisiana
	591	857*	South Carolina
	2,028	2,596*	Georgia
	494	543*	Florida
	1,593	1,949*	Kentucky
1959	1,450	2,078*	Tennessee
	1,215	1,616*	Alabama
	630	928*	Mississippi
	378	599*	Arkanasas
	244	410*	Louisiana

* Average Estimate

Source: *Commercial Livestock Slaughter by States*, 1944–57, Statistical Bulletin No. 231, U.S. Department of Agriculture, Agriculture Marketing Service, Washington, D.C., July, 1958. *Agricultural Statistics.*

TABLE 5

Estimated Total Pork Consumption by Selected States for Selected Years

State	Head of Hogs			
	1945	1950	1955	1960
South Carolina	1,197,140	1,311,660	1,570,840	1,646,340
Georgia	1,930,660	2,388,090	2,555,560	2,499,860
Florida	1,123,000	1,752,000	2,080,000	2,803,000
Kentucky	1,436,000	1,634,000	1,801,000	1,720,000
Tennessee	1,605,000	1,842,000	2,155,000	2,037,000
Alabama	1,540,000	1,804,000	2,038,000	2,153,000
Mississippi	1,135,000	1,169,000	1,128,000	1,366,000
Arkansas	1,010,000	1,092,000	1,140,000	1,144,000
Louisiana	1,503,550	1,869,090	2,032,000	2,064,940

Source: Compiled from *Commercial Livestock Slaughter by States*, 1944–57, Statistical Bulletin No. 231, U.S. Department of Agriculture, Agriculture Marketing Service, Washington, D.C.

Meat Consumption Trends and Patterns, U.S. Department of Agriculture, Marketing Service, Agriculture Handbook No. 187, Washington, D.C.

Agricultural Statistics, U. S. Department of Agriculture, Washington, D.C.

The policy of internal financing was formulated through the experience of the founders of the business.

THE FUTURE OF THE COMPANY

The son of the vice president is very interested in the future of the company and is concerned about long-run prospects, as well as alternative directions in which the business may develop in the future. He is a young man, active in the management of the company. After graduating with a bachelor's

TABLE 6

Gross Sales of The American Packing Company, Selected Years

Years	Sales
1950	$4,000,000
1952	12,000,000
1958	24,300,000
1959	24,700,000
1960	24,800,000

Source: Obtained from the Company.

TABLE 7

Comparative Condensed Operating Statements of The American Packing Company for Selected Periods

	Year Ending		
	Dec. 31, 1958	Jan. 30, 1960	Dec. 31, 1960
Sales and Misc. Revenues	$24,268,207	$24,701,240	$24,822,923
Operating Costs and Expenses	23,840,896	23,825,594	24,255,182
Operating Profit	427,310	875,646	567,740
Income Taxes	224,922	472,981	302,146
Net Profit after Taxes	202,388	402,665	265,592

Source: Private report.

TABLE 8

Comparative Balance Sheets of The American Packing Company for Selected Dates

	Dates		
Items	Dec. 31, 1958	Jan. 30, 1960	Dec. 31, 1960
Cash	$383,490	$621,033	$247,381
Marketable Securities	198,336	488,622	296,184
Notes Receivable	3,345	2,630	1,174
Accounts Receivable	740,054	745,065	1,091,796
Inventory	708,681	714,628	894,622
Fixed Assets	1,433,505	1,587,169	1,784,789
Total Assets	$3,467,511	$4,159,147	$4,315,946
Due Banks			
Notes Payable			
Accounts Payable	258,070	310,379	431,015
Accruals			
Taxes (Except Fed. Inc.)			
Federal Income Taxes	174,922	420,481	202,146
Long-Term Liabilities (Current)			
Fixed Aassets	1,433,505	1.587,169	1,784,789
Total Current Liabilities	$459,993	$730,860	$633,161
Long-Term Liabilities			
Reserves			
Preferred Stock			
Common Stock			
Capital Surplus			
Earned Surplus	3,007,518	3,428,287	3,682,784
Net Worth (Prop or Part)			
Total Liabilities	$3,467,511	$4,159,147	$4,315,945

degree from a university in the state in which the business is located, he enrolled in a graduate school of business administration, where he made an enviable record and earned the master of business administration degree. He maintains that there is little justification for enlarging the scale of the present operation just for the sake of expanding; but if the company should encounter rising costs and external dis-economies, it may be necessary to make further fundamental changes in the nature of the business. Such a change may be brought about by any one or more of the following alternatives:

1. Establish a new plant similar to the present one and in the same general market area. This is a horizontal expansion which would convert the company into a multi-plant organization.

2. Add a new product to the present product line, possible dog food, which would be sold under either the brand name of the present line or a new brand name for this single product.

3. Develop a new product line in the chemical field to utilize by-products of the present business. Opportunities of this type may be discovered in the manufacture of plastics and cosmetics.

4. Stabilize volume of present operation and expand the business through industrial acquisitions in the field of canned meat containers, sausage casings, and other packing house supplies.

5. Stabilize present operation and make acquisitions in areas unrelated to the meat packing business.

Undertaking any of these alternatives will impose upon management new responsibilities which will require the establishment of new company goals and policies which will have major effect upon the nature of the company. The extent of change in company goals and policies will vary with the particular alternative course of action chosen for future company development. The future character of the business depends upon the range of choice of alternatives available to management today, the actual choice made by management, and the policy framework in which the decisions are to be implemented.

SHORT-RUN PROBLEM (Assimilated in reference to this company)

In the pork processing division of the company, the layout is arranged so that the product flows through the following sequence of operations: hog-kill floor, rendering room, chill room, cutting room; one-half of dressed weight flows into canning department and one-half into pork curing room, and into shipping room.

All operations are at full capacity except the hog-kill floor. Assume the equipment in the hog-kill floor as being utilized at one-half capacity. Also, assume the live weight of hogs to yield 56% in dressed pork, excluding lard. It is estimated that one-third of the work force of the company is employed in the pork processing division and divided equally among the six operations in that division.

An estimated one-third of fixed assets is in the pork division. All operations in that division have an equal amount of fixed assets, except the hog-kill floor where equipment value is double that of other operations.

An estimated one-third of accounts receivable and inventory is directly related to the pork division.

PART **IV**

BUSINESS POLICY CASES

* *

INTERNAL ORGANIZATIONAL ENVIRONMENT: ORGANIZATIONAL STRUCTURE AND BEHAVIOR

* *

1. NEW ENGLAND DEACONESS HOSPITAL*

—JAMES C. HODGETTS

For several years Mr. Robert D. Lowry, Executive Director, had been considering the use of the Unit Manager System[1] at Deaconess Hospital. He thought that this system might help solve the problem created by the present shortage of persons with nursing skills. On March 28, 1962, Mr. Lowry and selected members of his organization heard Mr. Duane T. Houtz discuss the Unit Manager Pattern.[2]

During the next several months, the Unit Manager System and its possible use at Deaconess was discussed widely by many persons at all levels of the Deaconess organization. On June 19, 1962 Mr. Lowry decided to discuss the Unit Management System with key management personnel who might be affected by it if it were installed at Deaconess. During the discussion he recorded comments made at the interviews. These comments were as follows:

RESULTS OF INTERVIEW WITH MISS HOWLAND, DIRECTOR OF NURSING, JUNE 20, 1962:

Miss Howland offered the following suggestions and comments:

"A unit should not be over 34 beds."

"The unit should be the same size as now controlled by one head nurse."

"The system would result in better patient care because the nurse would have more time with the patient."

"The morale of the nurses would be better because nurses want to take care of patients."

"Better housekeeping and maintenance would result because the head nurse is patient-care oriented and the unit manager would be administratively oriented."

"Certain problems would result:

---

* Reprinted by permission of Professor Hodgetts.
[1] See Appendix I.
[2] See Appendix II.

a. Anything new or different is a problem in itself.

b. The head nurse may resent or be jealous because of the loss of responsibility. She will lose status.

c. The Doctors will not like it. They want just one head. They are accustomed to this being the head nurse. He may have to see two people instead of one. This takes time."

" The head nurse should not be under the unit manager."

" The unit manager would report to administration."

" The head nurse and the unit manager would have to have a high degree of cooperation."

" The status of the unit manager would be the same as that of a head nurse."

" It should be started on an experimental basis in an area where the head nurse wants it."

RESULTS OF INTERVIEW WITH MISS WINGER, CHIEF DIETITIAN, JUNE 20, 1962:

Miss Winger offered the following suggestions and comments:

" The unit could be any size, a floor, a building, a section, or any unit."

" It would improve patient care."

" Certain disadvantages would result:

a. Unit manager might antagonize my [dietary] employees. The unit manager will not understand the employees and their jobs.

b. There will be a conflict of authority between the unit manager and staff dietitians [assistant dietitians]."

" The food handlers should be responsible to the staff dietitian, not the unit manager. They cannot report to two people."

" The relationship of the staff dietitian and the unit manager would have to be one of cooperation."

" The unit manager should have training in personnel and business administration. She should have hospital experience with at least a college education."

" The position would be on the same level as, or higher than, that of a staff dietitian."

" The system should start in one unit with an agreeable head nurse who is interested in the program."

" The unit manager could take over much of the paper work of the staff dietitian, giving her more time to supervise and discuss diets with patients."

" The duties of the unit manager must be clearly defined or it would not work."

RESULTS OF INTERVIEW WITH MISS MUNN, HEAD NURSE, JUNE 21, 1962:

Miss Munn offered the following suggestions and comments:

" If the unit manager system is installed, the head nurse should not report to the manager unless she is a nurse."

"The manager would take dietary, housekeeping, clerical, and maybe some nursing responsibilities away from the head nurse."

"Nursing should be left to nurses."

"A lot of adjustments would have to be made in order to get cooperation between the head nurse and the unit manager."

"If the unit manager were a nurse, she would have the same status as a supervisor [nursing]. If not, she would be on the same level as a secretary which is below that of a head nurse."

"This system would give the head nurse more time for nursing matters because there would be less interference from non-nursing matters."

"The doctors would not be satisfied. They want to go to one person rather than two."

"If the head nurse did not take care of doctor's orders, she would not know what was going on in the unit."

"If the patients went to someone else, the head nurse would not know their problems."

"The unit manager would have to have experience in administration, nursing, and housekeeping. She would need training in Business Administration and Medical Secretarial Practice. She should be a registered nurse if she is to be in charge of nursing service."

"The unit manager should be in a unit of about 50 beds, 24 hours a day. This would be very difficult."

"A nurse assumes a lot of responsibilities. This person would have to be well qualified to do this."

RESULTS OF INTERVIEW WITH MISS PRESTON, ASSOCIATE DIRECTOR OF NURSING, JUNE 21, 1962:

Miss Preston offered the following suggestions and comments:

"The unit manager would take over the administrative duties of the head nurse. This would permit the head nurse to do more nursing."

"It should result in more efficiencies in non-nursing activities. The unit manager would not have to go through as many levels as the head nurse."

"The unit manager should be able to develop better systems in the unit."

"The head nurse would not like the system because she is used to being the key figure in the unit."

"The unit manager would be at the same salary as the head nurse but would work a straight eight-to-five shift with weekends off. The head nurse would not like this."

"Maybe the unit manager should be under nursing rather than under administration. Other hospitals have changed to this idea."

"If the unit manager is aggressive, she would get into nursing problems."

"The physical layout of this hospital is not good for this system."

"If the system is started it should be started in one unit at a time."

"It would create dual authority with the head nurse."

"The unit manager should be a Junior College major in business. She should be about the same age as the head nurse. Hospital experience would not be necessary."

"The unit manager would be at the same level as the head nurse, but this would be a problem."

RESULTS OF INTERVIEW WITH MISS HOWELL, HEAD NURSE, JUNE 25, 1962:

Miss Howell offered the following suggestions or comments:

"The unit manager would take over the various routine functions now done by nursing. This would take care of non-nursing jobs on the floor for which the Head Nurse is not trained."

"I have volunteered my section as an experimental unit."

"The head nurse and the unit manager would have to have a high degree of cooperation. Neither should report to the other. The head nurse would report to the supervisor [nursing] and the unit manager would report to Administration."

"The unit manager would have about the same status as the Head Nurse."

"The system would help the head nurse with non-nursing duties so that she could supervise better, train better, and be closer to the patient."

"The only trouble, I see, is the possibility that the unit manager might limit supplies and equipment to nursing. They would not be nurses and would not understand the profession."

"The unit manager should be a college graduate or a medical secretary. She should be trained in administration."

"This person [unit manager] is going to need a lot of help from the head nurse."

"It may have a hard time getting started because:

a. Many nurses will not want to change.

b. Many nurses will not want to give up authority.

c. There is a lot of opposition to it from head nurses."

"It will aid the team system. The assistant head nurses will become team leaders. A team is assigned to specific patients rather than one nurse giving T.P.R.'s, another medications, etc."

RESULTS OF INTERVIEW WITH MRS. PEACOCK, EXECUTIVE HOUSE-KEEPER, JUNE 26, 1962:[3]

Mrs. Peacock offered the following suggestions or comments:

"We have two kinds of maids, discharge maids and room maids. The discharge maids would have to work under too many unit managers. They should continue to report to housekeeping supervisors."

"The unit manager should be able to understand people and should have considerable intelligence but no formal training would be needed."

"The unit manager would be on the same organizational level as a supervisor in housekeeping."

"The maids would resent taking orders from the unit manager unless she was extremely skilled in handling maids."

"The system could create problems because the unit manager might want things done too rapidly."

APPENDIX 1

Most hospitals are organized in some manner similar to the following partial Organization chart:

[3] Mrs Peacock had not heard of the Unit Manager System prior to this meeting.

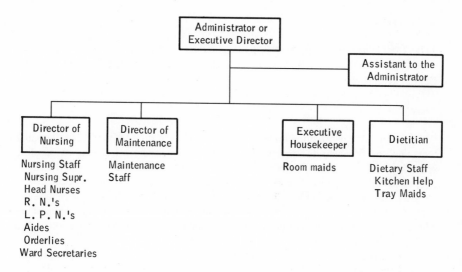

Under the Unit Manager System the chart could appear as follows:[4]

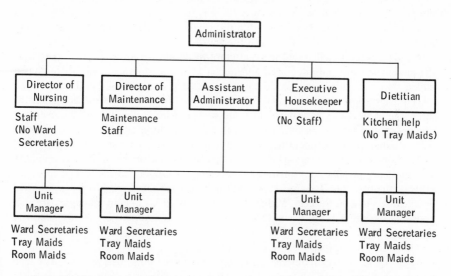

Each Unit Manager would be over a patient care unit.[5] The unit would also have one or more head nurses who would report to the Director of Nursing Services or to a supervisor. The head nurse would be in charge of Registered Nurses, Licensed Practical Nurses, Aides, Students, and Orderlies. The Unit Manager would be in charge of all non-nursing personnel in the unit.

[4] This type of structure would not necessarily be used at Deaconess
[5] A unit could be any number of rooms or wards in which patients are attended

APPENDIX II

THE UNIT MANAGER PATTERN
by Duane T. Houtz, Assistant Director of University Hospital—S. Hillis Health Center, Gainseville, Fla.

Presented before the New England Hospital Assembly, Boston, Massachusetts, March 28, 1962

The demands for qualified nurses throughout the country are not presently being met, and the forecasts for the future are cause for concern. Looking at possible solutions to this problem, management is designing the hospital around the nurse to save time and steps, studying work simplification techniques to utilize more effectively the nursing hours available, instituting automation to eliminate or reduce the time necessary for specific nursing procedures, and providing ancillary personnel who are continually supplying more of the functions originally the responsibility of the Registered Nurse.

Early in the 1900's, industry adopted the basic management techniques of first defining the position and then selecting the best qualified person, but hospitals have been slow to adopt some of the proven methods developed in related fields. In defining the job of the head nurse and nursing supervisor, it appeared that many of the duties assigned to them by hospital administration could be performed by nonprofessional personnel. Similarly to the way that the ward secretary has accepted many of the clerical duties of the staff nurse on the unit, a floor manager can supply many of the administrative details to the ward.

A nurse, recently frustrated in an attempt to obtain certain food, remarked that the patient is "not only doctored and nursed, but also administered." It might be added that the patient is also doctor-administrated and nurse-administrated. The mechanics of operating a hospital, including all of the activities from admission to discharge of a patient, have developed into such a melee of detail that the nurses and doctors can become absorbed in administrative procedures and forms so as to interfere with their primary functions—hence, the need for a new concept in management.

The floor manager program being developed at the University of Florida Teaching Hospital consists of six unit managers, each supervising one of the 64-bed specialty units of the hospital. This includes a unit manager for Ob-Gyn, Medicine, Surgical Specialties, General Surgery, Pediatrics, and Psychiatry. Lay unit managers are also coordinating areas such as the Operating Rooms, Rehabilitation, X-ray, and the Clinics, but my main topic of concern is the unit manager as she operates on the patient floor, supplementing the Registered Nurse.

The original written requirements for the position of unit manager were a college degree plus one year of supervisory experience; however, our experience has indicated that neither the college training nor the supervisory experience is nearly as important as some familiarity with a hospital's functions and organizational structure. Experience in a hospital department such as Admitting, the Business Office, or Personnel is a great advantage, especially in the initial phases of training for a unit manager.

The job summary for the position of unit manager is almost as broad as that for an administrator, assistant administrator, or nursing supervisor. The description includes the following:

1. Assists in the administration and coordination of all services within the hospital, as they affect each patient on the unit.

2. Assists in preparation of budgets and allocation of funds.

3. Directs procurement and maintenance of supplies and equipment.

4. Directs and supervises ward clerks and couriers.

5. Cooperates with Nursing Service, the medical staff, and administration in formulating policies that pertain to the unit.

6. Represents administration within the unit, and acts as liaison between administration, the patient, and each of the services.

7. Maintains contact with patients, relating administrative detail.

At the present stage in the development of this position, the most time-consuming functions might be labeled (1) interservice communication, (2) supply and maintenance, and (3) supervision of clerical and auxiliary services.

1. *Interservice communications and relationships.* Initially, the unit manager must understand and be able to interpret her own role and objectives. In addition, in order to work effectively with each of the servicing departments within the hospital, she must assess its concept of the unit manager system, its goals, functions, and any difficulties which might affect their relationship. She must be able to evaluate procedures, analyze problems, communicate these to the proper individuals, and conceive and promply implement improved methods in a joint effort with the nursing and medical staffs. She must earn their respect by maintaining the highest standards of service, first to the patient and then to each of them. In effect, the unit manager has the opportunity—by her standards, performance, ability to communicate—and the responsibility to weld all of the contributing services into a cooperative and effective team.

In the development of this program, various groups within the hospital have envisioned the role of the unit manager somewhat differently. This in the past has created frustrations for the unit manager, for anyone's happiness in his position depends upon how closely four pictures of his job correspond: what one thinks he should be doing, what he wants to be doing, what he is doing, and what others think he should be doing. Recent progress by administration in more clearly defining the position and in providing more adequate orientation for unit managers promises to reduce this problem.

A frequent criticism of the system has been, "I wish we had just one person to go to who could speak for the entire floor and take action," or "To whom do we go for this problem—the unit manager or the supervising nurse?" These criticisms indicate that the division of responsibility on the patient floor is not always clearly delineated. It is debated as to whether a unit can operate as efficiently with divided authority and responsibility under a unit manager and a nurse, or whether one person should be in charge as in the traditional head nurse pattern.

There has been divided sentiment expressed over the pattern presently employed at the University of Florida Hospital; some persons feel that the system would eventually evolve into having one person responsible, while others feel that this sort of division has been in effect for years in comparable situations such as with the dean of a medical school and the hospital director, so why can't it work in this situation?

In fact, this organizational structure should eliminate a conflict of authority, in that it delegates the responsibility for the administration of the nursing care program to the supervising nurse and the responsibility for the operation of the ward to the unit manager, in both cases on a 24-hour-a-day, 7-day-a-week basis. Whenever the unit manager cannot be reached, administrative decisions are referred to the senior person in the Admitting Office, who in turn handles the problem or refers it to the Assistant Director on call.

2. *Supply and Maintenance.* The unit manager is responsible at all times for the stocking and maintenance of all supplies—medical, surgical, sterile, pharmaceutical, dietary, clerical, etc. She is also held responsible for instruments, major equipment, furnishings, and care of the physical plant itself.

After determining, in conjunction with the medical and nursing staffs, the essential levels of floor stock and equipment to be maintained, the unit manager orders the various items in accordance with departmental procedure and then checks to ensure delivery and adequate quantity. Whenever an item cannot be provided, the unit manager is the one who (like the head nurse) borrows or improvises to meet any emergency.

The unit manager is responsible for all items which must be charged to the patient's account, and she and her staff ensure that all accounts are properly recorded.

Experience has indicated that the supply and maintenance function of the unit managers is one of the most time-consuming of their responsibilities. Far more time is being spent and has been spent in this area to date than was anticipated by administration. As the hospital becomes more established, this function should take substantially less time.

3. *Supervision of clerical and ancillary services.* The unit manager is responsible for hiring, training, and supervising all clerical personnel on the floor. She is also responsible for the transportation of patients and supplies from her floor to all other areas of the hospital. To this end she is accountable for the most productive implementation of each employee's time and capabilities, and for the control of the group's standards, performance, cooperation, morale, development, and discipline. She must be thoroughly familiar with the duties and responsibilities of the ward clerk, and often in case of a clerk's absence she must fill the position herself. She supplements the clerical functions on the floor, personally handling such things as personnel schedules, payroll reports, sick leave and vacation records, and salary recommendations.

With the clerical staff on the floor the unit manager provides these services to the unit: transcribing of physician's orders, handling of medical records, admissions, discharges, transfers, assignment of beds (in coordination with admitting office), handling of all traffic on the floor, all telephone calls, the floor paging system, and greeting and answering questions for anyone who may come to the nursing unit.

The unit manager's task of training and supervising the floor clerks has been a considerable one because of the high turnover among the clerks. The University of Florida Hospital is located in a university community which provides well-qualified persons to fill these positions but has the disadvantage of excessive turnover. The student wives are often employed as clerks have to this date spent considerably less than one year in this position, on an over-all average. This turnover rate has greatly increased the amount of time necessary for the unit manager to spend with the clerks. It should be pointed out, however, that if the nursing supervisor had the responsibility of training all of the ward clerks, this would be an almost insurmountable task. As our hospital develops a corps of career people, it should become less of a problem for the unit manager to train and supervise the clerical personnel.

TRAINING FOR THE UNIT MANAGER POSITION

In the three-and-a-half years that our unit manager system has been in operation, there have been seventeen persons filling the six unit manager positions on the patient floors. The turnover in this positions has, of course, slowed down the overall progress for this pattern of organization; however, it has greatly helped in formalizing the qualifications needed by a person filling the job and in clarifying the training program necessary to give a new unit manager the required background. A key attribute for an applicant is that she be a career person, similar to the nursing supervisor who has accepted her position as a life-long career.

At the present time our training program for a new unit manager consists of the following:

1. A period of clerkship during which she can become completely familiar with the duties and responsibilities of the floor clerks, and at the same time she can gain an over-all impression of the organization and operation of each hospital department as it relates to the patient floor.

2. An extensive interview schedule with each hospital department head. These interviews enable the department head to educate the unit manager as to the role of his individual department and of its relationship to the patient and the floor; the unit manager, meanwhile, meets a great number of the people in the hospital with whom she will have day-to-day contact.

3. An apprenticeship in which she works with the other unit managers on their floors, learning the procedures for purchasing, personnel, requisitioning supplies, etc.

The time necessary for training the unit manager has varied depending upon her background, but it takes a minimum of a month before she can begin to feel really at ease in her position. At the end of three to six months she should be capable of handling almost any problem and of carrying out the responsibilities associated with any supervisory position.

COST OF OPERATION

Detailed cost figures are not now available to outline exactly how much this pattern of supervision runs in comparison to the typical head nurse pattern. Neither have we had adequate time to determine the number of minutes the nurse spends at the patient's bedside. The nurse is freed from many of the functions that she has historically been performing, but the statistical data are not yet available to substantiate our impressions that the patient is seeing more of the nurse. Cost and nursing-time studies are under way at the present time. However, it is felt that the system does not cost any more than a system in which nursing personnel are performing the tasks presently being done by our unit managers. The unit managers and the supervising nurses feel that it would take a nurse to replace each unit manager if we were to abandon the system at this time.

In a published report from (Mt.) Sinai Hospital of Baltimore concerning a floor manager pattern, it was mentioned that one of the most serious risks with this sort of program is the loss of key personnel within or directly responsible for the program. The lack of an administrator during the first year of operation of our hospital, the turnover among the unit managers, and the normal growing pains experienced by a newly-opened medical center have definitely slowed down the progress of the development of this pattern of organization. However, it does appear that the basic philosophy of this sort of organizational structure is sound enough to have carried it through some tough spots and laid the groundwork for a pattern of administration that can more effectively utilize the nursing hours available.

Recently a visiting hospital director made this observation of our unit manager system: " It seems to work here. I suspect that, like the Western Electric experiment, it appears to be productive simply because the people concerned *want* it to work."

2. CONVAIR–FORT WORTH*

—HALL H. LOGAN

Convair–Fort Worth, a Division of the General Dynamics Corporation, was in 1956 one of the largest aircraft manufacturing facilities in the country engaged primarily in making products for the U.S. Air Force.

There were 4,367,000 square feet of factory space in the Fort Worth Division with extensive surrounding area. The facility adjoined Carswell Air Force Base on the west. The Carswell landing strip lay between the two facilities and was used by both.

CAFB was one of the Strategic Air Command Bases at which bombers of the USAF were stationed. In almost every period of CAFB history, some of the aircraft stationed there were manufactured by Convair–Fort Worth.

COMPANY HISTORY

The name " Convair " was chosen in lieu of the longer title of Consolidated Vultee Corporation. The latter was adopted upon the merger of two major companies. The oldest company in the Vultee group dated back to 1925 when Eddie Stinson, a pioneer in aviation, and several Detroit businessmen formed what later became the Stinson Aircraft Company. Several corporate changes, mergers, and acquisitions occurred prior to the merger of Vultee and Consolidated Aircraft Corporation. The latter had its beginning in 1923.

During World War II Convair operations expanded to 13 divisions throughout the nation, with peak employment exceeding 101,000. There were eight manufacturing plants, three modification plants, a research division, and a transpacific air line known as Consairway. The Fort Worth facility was completed by the government in 1942 and had been operated as a government-owned facility by Convair continuously since that date.

* Produced from activities of the Southern Case Writers' Association. Reprinted by permission of Professor Logan and the Association

Between 7 December 1941 and 15 August 1945, Convair delivered more than 350,000,000 pounds of airframes, or nearly 13 per cent of the total output of the nation's industry. This poundage comprised more than 28,000 completed aircraft and approximately 5,000 equivalent planes delivered as spares (replacement parts).

Convair was merged into the General Dynamics Corporation on 29 April 1954 and comprised about 75 per cent of General Dynamics' operations. Convair operated three plants in California until 1958 when Convair–Astronautics, a new $40 million facility, was added. The Fort Worth plant and the Navy Bureau of Ordnance Aerophysics Laboratory for Research and Development at Daingerfield comprised the Texas operations.

CHARACTERISTICS OF THE AIRCRAFT INDUSTRY

The industry as a whole was subject to large volume fluctuations, and individual manufacturers experienced even greater ups and downs. The nature of much of the product and processes of manufacture could be best described in the industry's own terminology as "exotic" and new designs as "out on cloud nine."

Time was of great strategic importance. Once a new design concept was "bought" and given the go-ahead by the Military, the pressure was on. The Material and Tooling people put pressure on the Design Engineers for advance information in order that planning could be started on down the line, long lead-time materials ordered, and sub-system vendors selected. This same process was repeated at the major subsystem vendor's plants. There were radically new and complex problems of design, materials, and processes to be resolved. Seldom did time permit the development of perfection at any step before proceeding to the next. So, of necessity, problems were worked in parallel rather than in series, calling for continual coordination.

Change was a fundamental characteristic of the industry. Original designs were subsequently improved; better processes developed; quantities were changed by the customer; and new objectives and capabilities were suggested by Convair or requested by the customer. Conditions were very fluid through the delivery of the first production article.

Changes continued but at a decreasing rate. Most early articles differed considerably in configuration.[1] Somewhere down the line changes slackened to the point where they would be accumulated or held up for incorporation in successive blocks or lots of aircraft. Design changes continued throughout the entire production contract and even beyond as aircraft were modified in retrofit programs at Air Force bases. More extensive modifications were performed at the manufacturers' plants or special modification centers.

---

[1] "Configuration" had a much broader meaning than outward appearance. It was more often used to describe internal construction and the part numbers comprising assemblies or the total product.

RECENT ORGANIZATION PROBLEMS

Convair–FW was typical in most respects of large companies in the aircraft industry. Reorganizations were commonplace because of the continual recurrence of the causes for change in organizational structure.

EMPLOYMENT

Employment at Convair–FW rose rapidly when the plant opened in February 1942 to a peak of 30,000 by the close of 1943; declined by 7,000 in five months; then drifted on down to about 21,700 at the close of 1944; increased 1,000 in the first three months of 1945; and dropped sharply at the close of the war to 6,100 in early 1946. Then, in one year, employment doubled to 12,000 and maintained this until mid-1948 when it rose to 19,000 by mid-1950 and accelerated to 31,000 by October 1951; declined at a constant rate to 17,000 at the beginning of 1954; bottomed out at 16,000 in the spring of 1955; rose to 27,500 in the spring of 1957; and then dropped sharply to 21,000 by the close of the year.

Convair–FW had partially alleviated the gap in production and tooling work between the B-36 and B58 prime contracts with rather large subcontracts for major components of the B-52, F-102, and F-106. The last B-36 had been delivered in 1953. The first B-58 was flown on schedule in November 1956.

THE EFFECT OF PRODUCT

The B-58 was a revolutionary new weapon system.[2] Its reported speed of mach 2 was more than double that of other bombers[3]; It was the country's first supersonic bomber. Only currently developed fighter aircraft could match its speed. The 2 to 1 ratio of speed did not, however, reflect the increased capabilities of the new weapon system. The B-58 was highly automated; much of the automation and radically new performance represented new breakthroughs in the state of the art. (Sub-system costs were roughly 50 per cent of total cost.) Such progress was not attained without problems of considerable complexity. Weight and space were very critical design limitations. More parts required machining to closer tolerances which previously were made by metal forming. Greater heat problems required sandwich type construction with honeycomb cells between, bonded by new adhesive processes that were developed with the early models. Problems in the electronic and associated fields were beyond most people's understanding.

---

[2] An oversimplified definition of "weapon system" in the aircraft industry is the complete airplane, any weapon or missile if specially designed for the airplane, and all associated. support equipment for operational requirements.

[3] Mach 1 is the speed of sound. At sea level it is about 670 miles per hour. Mach 2 would be 1340 miles per hour.

CONTRACT INNOVATION

It had been the custom for the Air Force to make a prime contract with an aircraft company to manufacture the airframe and to assemble and deliver a completed aircraft. However, sub-systems, engines, and occasionally other major components were purchased under separate contracts from specialists in each product and supplied by the Air Force to the prime contractor for assembly in the delivered article. One agency of the Air Force would procure engines, and one or more would procure sub-systems. So more than one agency of the Air Force was involved in approval of changes; others in funding; others in schedules; etc. In light of the continual change and development inherent in the industry, it was obvious that there was need for much coordination. Both the government and the contractors were concerned. Critical time was being lost. It was alleged that Russia could better our time from conception of a design to operational status.

With the advent of supersonic aircraft and with its increased complexity in design and tolerance, simplification in program administration became almost mandatory. Coming at this time, the B-58 prime contract was awarded to Convair–FW on a basis almost as new as the aircraft itself. "Weapon-System Management" was the terminology used to describe Convair–FW's full authority and responsibility to design, procure, tool, manufacture, flight test, and support a total weapon system. This responsibility included management, design, and manufacture of the basic aircraft, sub-systems, ground support and test equipment, and several types of missles or "pods." The latter were carried below the fuselage of the aircraft. The only significant exclusion from the Convair–FW contract was the four jet engines, which were purchased by the Air Force from the General Electric Company.

The Weapon-System Concept created many new situations in Convair–FW organization structure and procedures. Particularly was this so in the procurement area, where procurement and contractual relations with some twenty sub-system vendors were handled.

ORGANIZATION PHILOSOPHY

Over the years, Convair–FW favored a functional type of organization insofar as it was practical. In general, product specialization had been the basis for separate organization units only when the volume of work warranted. Consequently, the organization units devoted to one product were at the lower levels of the Division structure and at department level only in major assembly areas where large fixed base tooling set the organization pattern.

Figure 1 is the Division Organization Chart showing the emphasis on horizontal structure at the top level. The Program Director B-58 illustrates a rather recent novelty in organization theory. This top executive was a high-level "project coordinater." His responsibilities were to see that all phases of the B-58 Program progressed according to plan, to resolve differences, and

Division Organization: Convair - Fort Worth
A Division of General Dynamics Corp.

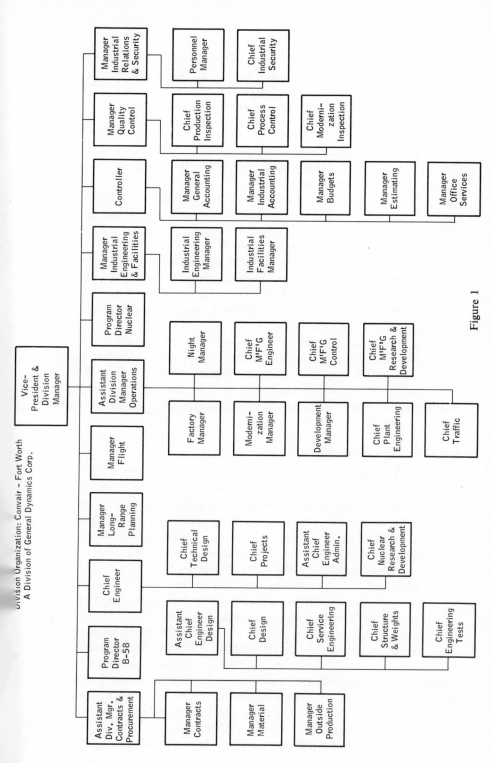

Figure 1

361

to keep the Division Manager informed of significant problems and progress on the B-58 Program. Other contracts were at this time occupying large portions of the manufacturing capacity.

CUSTOMER SUPPORT

In March 1957, the Vice-President and Division Manager, Mr. Harrington, felt that it was time to plan for the support of the B-58 Weapon System after delivery to the Air Force. There was need for an early look at support because Convair responsibilities were greater under the Weapon-System Management Concept and the customer's expectations had also undergone changes in the past few years.

The first B-58 had been flown on schedule in November 1956. Though delivery of production models was at least a year away, considerable organization rebuilding might be necessary. Spares support for the B-36 was at a very low volume. The need for assistance to the customer at Air Force bases had dwindled until the Aircraft Service Group in the Engineering Department had been reduced to a dozen people.

As the Industrial Engineering Department was responsible for systems, procedures, and organization studies, the Department Manager assigned Mr. Alden to the B-58 customer service problem. No instructions or ground rules were given Mr. Alden. He began his study by sizing up the support task and by locating those functions most closely associated with the support program.

THE MEANING OF CUSTOMER SUPPORT

Customer Support was one of several terms used to describe the contractor's services and assistance to the customer following delivery of a new weapon system or any major product. Contractors were very interested in assuring that the customer received the maximum in per cent of operational readiness and effectiveness from their products. Such service was common for military articles. The principle was similar to the machinery manufacturer's service of installation and initial operation of a major machine in a customer's plant. Military articles required more post-delivery assistance, and for a longer period. This was the result of the high degree of complexity of the products. Furthermore, each military product usually represented a radical new development for which time was not allowed to extensively prove the article before delivery. Though the many new developments were laboratory tested extensively in the best simulated conditions of later operational environments, it was not always possible to predict the combinations of actual environmental conditions, i.e., the elements of nature, operation of the article under tactical conditions, and physical handling and maintenance by G. I.s who were often subject to high turnover.

A Customer Support organization could have over-all responsibility for logistic support and offer a single point of contact for the customer regarding any aspects of support. These general responsibilities involved some or all of the following: a close liaison with the customer to promote good relations with those customer's agencies providing logistic support; the analysis of customer's needs to develop adequate programs and assist in negotiating these with the customer; the administration of all off-site activities in support of products; the production of handbooks as required by contract; the determination of training requirements and the conduct and evaluation of training programs; performance of maintenance analyses; recommendations for provisioning, ordering, and direction of the delivery of spare parts; and the obtaining of data and statistics that would help to better serve the customer and improve the product.

FORECASTING THE GENERAL TASK

The number of aircraft and pods that the company hoped to make would be a major factor in determining the total support program. This could be anywhere from $100 million to a possible $500 million.

Forecasting in defense industries was very difficult and hazardous. The time span from inception of a major aircraft design to the end of a production contract could be from two to ten years. Some products never reached the production stage. The threat of obsolescence was a deterrent to long-range contractual commitments by the Department of Defense. Successive carry-on contracts were the custom. The principle of carry-on contracting was more logical under annual Congressional appropriations.

At the time, Convair–FW was delivering on the first contract for 13 aircraft and an undisclosed number of pods. These were developmental models and destined for early flight tests. Detail parts manufacture was beginning on the second contract, for ships 14 through 30. These were to be flight test models. Negotiations were under way by the Contracts Department for the first production models, ships 31 through about 75. Convair expected that the contracts would eventually be extended to 350 or 400 aircraft, plus proportional orders for pods and ground support equipment.

The B-58 Program did not provide for a prototype article *per se*. The first thirty ships were destined for various phases of an extensive test program by Convair. Provisions were made for later conversion of a majority of these ships to tactical configuration and for the removal of excess instrumentation. A Customer Service function would have no major responsibility for assistance or support of flight test ships—only to be aware of future problems.

LOCATION OF ORGANIZATION ELEMENTS

Mr. Alden's analysis of pertinent organization elements revealed the following:

The Aircraft Service Group was presently, as it had been during the B-36 Program, at the fourth level below the Division Manager in the organization structure. This

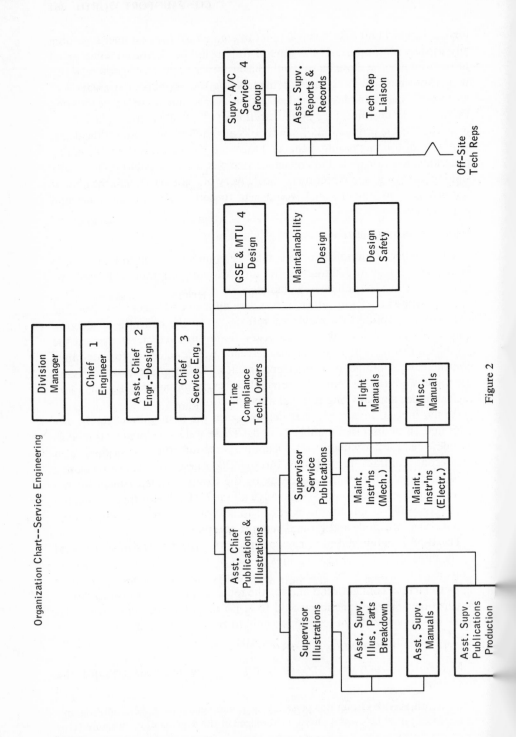

Organization Chart--Service Engineering

Division Manager

Chief Engineer 1

Asst. Chief Engr.-Design 2

Chief Service Eng. 3

Time Compliance Tech. Orders

Asst. Chief Publications & Illustrations

Supervisor Service Publications

Supervisor Illustrations

Flight Manuals

Misc. Manuals

Maint. Instr'ns (Mech.)

Maint. Instr'ns (Electr.)

Asst. Supv. Illus. Parts Breakdown

Asst. Supv. Manuals

Asst. Supv. Publications Production

GSE & MTU 4 Design

Maintainability Design

Design Safety

Supv. A/C Service Group 4

Asst. Supv. Reports & Records

Tech Rep Liaison

Off-Site Tech Reps

Figure 2

364

was the first level devoting full attention to customer service. The Chief of Service Engineering, at the third level, had some interests which were closely related to other Design Groups, Refer to Figure 2 and Appendix A.

The Government Furnished Property (GFP) Section of the Material Department, at the fourth level below the Division Manager, was the first organization unit devoting full attention to spares. Refer to Figure 3 and Appendix B.

The Spares Section of the Contracts Department, at the fourth level down, was the first organization unit devoting full attention to spares. Refer to Figure 3 and Appendix C.

The Manufacturing Control Accumulation Area, at the fifth level down, was concerned principally with the physical handling of spares. Refer to Figure 4 and Appendix E.

Mr. Alden also reviewed available information on other companies' organizations for customer support. Refer to Figures 5 through 7.

SOME EXECUTIVE VIEWPOINTS

Mr. Alden had a number of conversations with department and area managers and with persons at lower levels to determine the realistic working relations that currently existed.

Mr. Garland, Chief of Service Engineering, was a man in his early forties who had been with Convair for over fifteen years. He had been closely associated with the post-delivery phase of the B-36 Program. His experience and capability had earned him the high respect of many Air Force officers. Mr. Garland was not considered an aggressive person. He was more inclined to take a considerate approach than to move headlong into a controversial matter. This trait had its advantages insofar as dealing with the customer was concerned.

Mr. Garland believed that the stature of Service Engineering, or those functions that would be directly related to Customer Support, should be elevated in the organization structure. Design of Ground Support Equipment (GSE) and Mobile Training Units (MTU) was, however, an engineering function more closely related to design than to service, although these products were used almost exclusively in the post-delivery phase of a program. Those engineers designing GSE and MTU required close liaison with Design Engineers on the aircraft. It was felt that better coordination between these design groups could be maintained if both were in the Engineering Department. It was necessary for those designing support equipment to figuratively "look over the shoulder " of the engineer who designed the aircraft. There was some concern that the GSE Designers might have to wait until the aircraft design was complete and then work from official completed drawings, if they were in any department other than Engineering. On the other hand, the Tech Reps[4] who used the support equipment were able to offer many suggestions

[4] Technical Representative—a term used for company representatives working at off-site assignments The majority of the men were engineering graduates—or the equivalent.

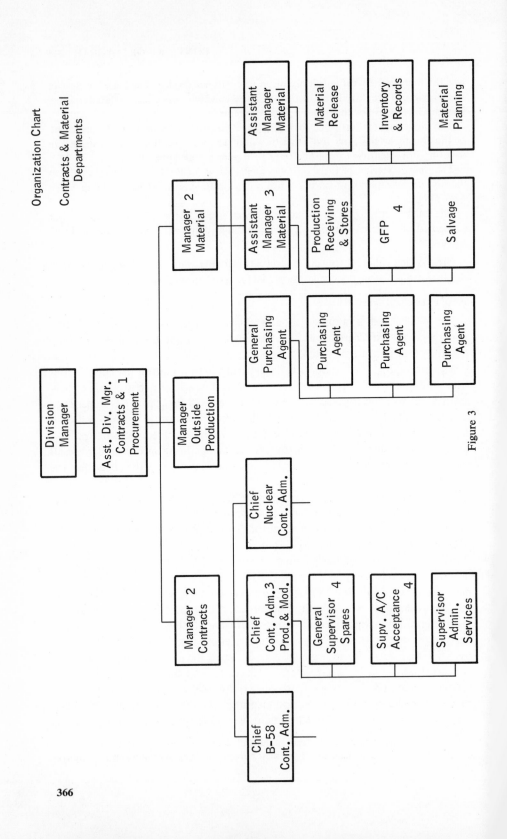

Organization Chart

Contracts & Material Departments

Figure 3

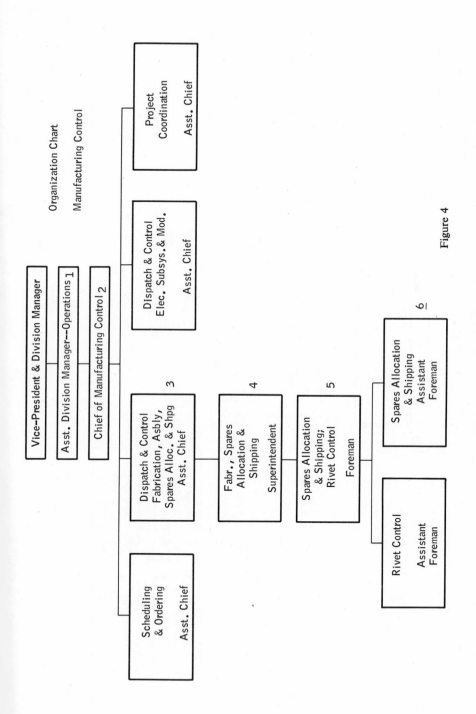

Organization Chart

Manufacturing Control

Vice-President & Division Manager

Asst. Division Manager—Operations 1

Chief of Manufacturing Control 2

Scheduling & Ordering
Asst. Chief

Dispatch & Control
Fabrication, Asbly.,
Spares Alloc. & Shpg 3
Asst. Chief

Dispatch & Control
Elec. Subsys. & Mod.
Asst. Chief

Project Coordination
Asst. Chief

Fabr., Spares
Allocation &
Shipping 4
Superintendent

Spares Allocation
& Shipping;
Rivet Control 5
Foreman

Spares Allocation
& Shipping
Assistant Foreman 6

Rivet Control
Assistant Foreman

Figure 4

367

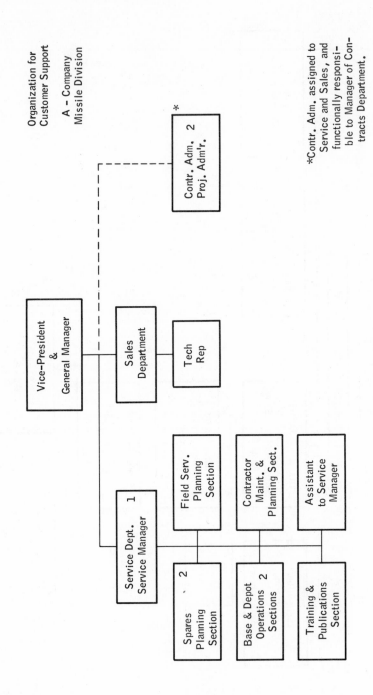

Organization for
Customer Support

A – Company
Missile Division

Vice–President
&
General Manager

Sales
Department

Tech
Rep

Contr. Adm.   2
Proj. Adm'r.   *

Service Dept.   1
Service Manager

Field Serv.
Planning
Section

Contractor
Maint. &
Planning Sect.

Assistant
to Service
Manager

Spares   2
Planning
Section

Base & Depot
Operations   2
Sections

Training &
Publications
Section

*Contr. Adm. assigned to
Service and Sales, and
functionally responsi-
ble to Manager of Con-
tracts Department.

Figure 5

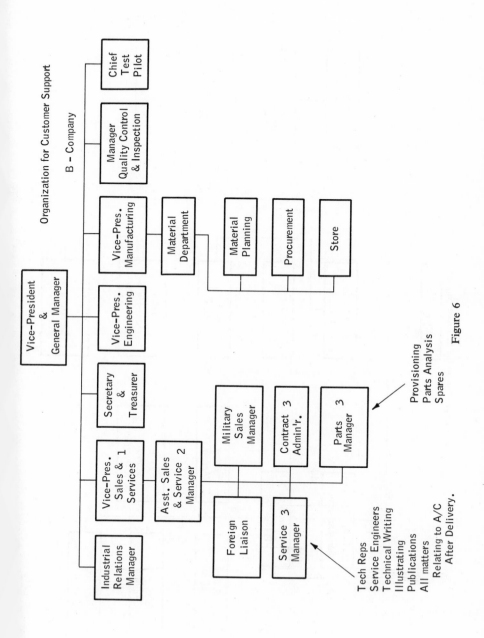

Organization for Customer Support

B – Company

Figure 6

Organization for Customer Support--C- Company

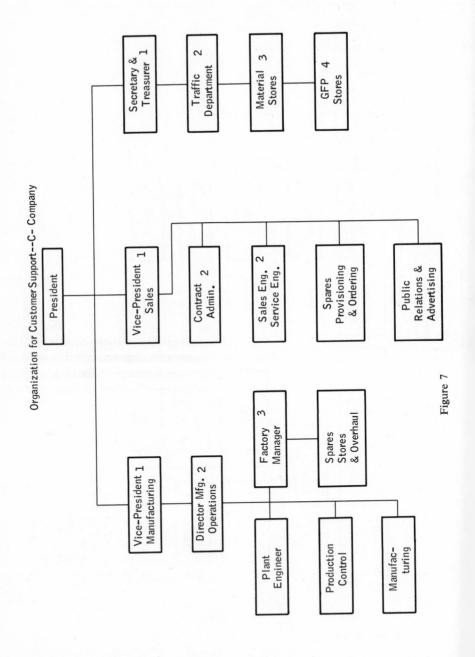

Figure 7

as to the manner of use, protection in field handling, etc., for the design of support equipment.

There would also be a problem of manning the Customer Service Department with capable Tech Reps who were skilled engineers; and it was quite evident that, because of the complexity of the B-58, a number of different skills would be required. It had never been easy to interest Design Engineers in taking a job as a Tech Rep. Some engineers objected to any job classification that did not include the title " Engineer."

The principal reason for elevating the organization level of Customer Support would be to effect a more comparable position with Engineering and other major functions of the Division. Post-delivery support of the B-58 was going to be a greater problem than on the B-36 because of the highly complex character of the total weapon system. This being so, there was some feeling that Customer Support Management should be on an organization level where it could exert influence in proportion to its responsibility.

It was a general belief that post-delivery problems were minimized by those departments involved with future models and other tasks, e.g., it was alleged that production departments gave preference to production parts over spare parts and that Design Engineers were so deeply involved in new designs that they were reluctant or slow to respond to requests to review what they, or some other engineer, designed many months before.

Mr. Williams, Manager of Contracts, seriously objected to the removal of the Contract Spares Section from his responsibility. He felt that all Division functions should remain in their present location and that a high level Director of Customer Service should be appointed who would report directly to the Division Manager and keep him informed of Customer Service problems and progress. The Director of Customer Service would also make contacts with the top echelons of the Air Force agencies and base commands. To prevent duplication of regular functional department responsibilities, the Director would be limited to a very small staff, possibly a secretary and three strictly staff personnel, to gather data and run down inquiries.

Mr. Williams was sympathetic to the combination of the GFP Section of the Material Department with the Contract Spares Section. However, in all sincerity he said he was not asking for the responsibility of the Spares GFP organization of several hundred people but, if Industrial Engineering recommended it and Management approved, he would do what was considered best for the Division. He believed that the technical problems of spares provisioning were greater than the more mechanical reordering, storing, and issuing activities in the Material Department. Furthermore, it was not logical to separate the contract administration function by placing the spares administration in another department and to leave the administration of production and other phases in the Contracts Department. (Most spares contracts were addendums to the production contracts.) Mr. Williams believed that the philosophy of functional organization should be maintained and extended to the Customer Support Program.

Mr. Baker, Industrial Engineering Manager, believed that eventually all functions relating to customer support should be centralized under one Manager of Customer Service. The content of such a department he proposed as follows:

Function	Presently in
Spares Receiving, Stores, and Issue	Material Dept.—GFP Section
Spares Requisitioning	Material Dept.—GFP Section
Provisioning of Spares	Contracts Dept.—Spares Section
Reports and Records	Eng. Dept.—A/C Service Group
Administration of Off-Site Activities	Eng. Dept.—A/C Service Group
General Management of Customer Service Activities	(No one department)
Program Planning for Customer Service	(No one department)

Mr. Baker further explained that a Director of Customer Support, as advanced by Mr. Williams, would be weak and ineffective in getting immediate cooperation and results from in-plant managers. He understood that the San Diego Division had moved in the direction of putting more functions under one head after an earlier experience, with less centralized authority, in support of the F-102.

Mr. Dunlap, a man in his late thirties, had served as Supervisor of Off-Site Activities in charge of Tech Reps at several Convair operations, particularly on the B-36 Program. He was one of the "older" Tech Reps. He had a high regard for Mr. Garland and generally confirmed most of the latter's comments.

He related firsthand some of the feelings that Engineers had for the Tech Rep assignment. Some felt that a person lost out on promotions and opportunities when away from the main plant. There was the problem of moving one's family and school problems for those with older children. Often the living facilities were high for value received, although the Tech Rep usually received some compensation for living expenses.

Mr. Dunlap believed most Design Engineers would benefit by a year in the field. The B-58 was going to require some highly skilled specialists for field assignments. It might be more logical to man the Customer Service Department with a basic core of Tech Reps and, as special problems developed, to send the desired Design Engineer as a specialist to the field for one day or two months until the problem was solved.

Mr. Dunlap further stated that it seemed reasonably certain that Convair's task would include maintenance of aircraft at CAFB and the training of ground crews. One plan calls for training AF crews at CAFB on a sixteen-week rotating basis. Each sixteen weeks the crews for one squadron (fifteen ships) would be trained and then would move out with their ships to their permanent base. There would be an overlap in the schedule in that a new crew would come in every eight weeks.

Tech Rep and Spares Rep services would be required at the several permanent bases, probably about 50 per cent of the task at CAFB for six months, then declining to two Tech Reps for two years. Approximately 45 to 50 ships would be stationed at each permanent base.

This program indicated that the Convair Manager of Operations at CAFB would be on a hot spot to give service. The program would be under pressure to maintain schedules. Although not officially so, the Manager would in essence be working for the U.S. Air Force Colonel in charge of the wing training. The Manager could not leave his work at CAFB to follow up in-plant. In summary, it was important that there be an in-plant manager who had the ability and authority to assure follow-through in support of off-site work and also to manage the total Customer Support Program.

Mr. Clemson was Assistant Supervisor of the Reports and Records Unit of the Aircraft Service Group. He spent most of his time in the home office receiving, evaluating, processing, and replying to field requests for information. These requests were received from the Air Force or from Convair Tech Reps in the field. A cumulative classification was maintained of field problems by type and area of ship. The Reports and Records Unit consisted of Mr. Clemson and three other employees.

The Design Groups of the Engineering Department received about 75 per cent of the field inquiries, Quality Control about 15 per cent, and the balance to other departments.

Mr. Clemson reviewed the replies to the requests to be certain that answers were as factual and straightforward as could be given. Replies could be prepared by any one of several hundred persons; so some control of replies was warranted.

Mr. Richards was General Supervisor of the Contract Spares Section. He was most emphatic that the spares functions should be better coordinated. He explained that his people were already assuming their new responsibilities for provisioning spares. Prior to the B-58 contract, his job was to submit drawings and technical data on all potential parts that could be spares to the Air Force at SAAMA (San Antonio Air Material Area), who would determine the items that would be spares.

On the B-58, Mr. Richards' people were selecting the spares and sending the list to SAAMA with the drawings and technical data. But at the same time, orders were released for purchase or manufacture. SAAMA had a specified number of days to object to Convair's selection. Mr. Richards said he had experienced no problems in working with SAAMA.

His complaints were directed at the scattered responsibility for spares. When the Air Force had the responsibility for selecting spares, the advantages of retaining the functional responsibilities in the basic departments were somewhat justified. On the B-58 Program he needed to be closer to the stock records in the GFP Section for analysis of usage on a current basis. He couldn't live with the old method of basing judgment on a Stock Balance and Consumption Report issued every 90 days by the GFP Section. This was Air Force procedure, but a procedure designed for a well-established, going program— not a developmental program like the B-58 would be up to ship 30 or so.

Furthermore, he had been delayed in making certain periodic reports to the Air Force because his information was supplied from one or more other sources, and because reconciliation and authentication took a good deal of his time. He said, " When something is everybody's business, it usually ends up by being nobody's business."

In addition to the provisioning activity, the Contract Spares Section consisted of the Spares Administrators who handled about every service and problem in connection with the spares portion of a contract.

There was a large clerical group which compiled spares " exhibits." These were the lists of spare items ordered under various contracts and funding arrangements. The lists were usually prepared from tablutating cards.

Mr. Camden, Assistant Manager of Material, was in charge of three sections of the Department: the Production Receiving and Stores Section, the Government Furnished Property (GFP) Section, and the Salvage Section.

Production was the largest section. It received, stored, and issued all materials procured by the Purchasing Section of the Material Department. Other than the clerical work associated with receiving, the Section was principally occupied in the physical storage and movement of production materials and parts.

The GFP Section had more extensive responsibilities in connection with parts furnished by the government. The GFP Section had need of a sizeable clerical staff to maintain stock record cards for parts, to issue a number of reports required by the Air Force, and to order parts not provisioned by the Contract Spares Section. There were two major categories of parts handled by the GFP Section: first, those furnished for production aircraft and, second, those for support of delivered aircraft. The inventories were physically segregated, and neither could be commingled with the Convair purchased inventories.

Mr. Camden had, until about a year ago, been in charge of only the GFP Section. He had had a number of years experience in this area of Air Force support. He knew the Air Force side of the operation and what was expected of the contractor. He explained that the GFP Section followed procedures set forth in Air Force manuals more closely than those of the Material Department. He saw no particular advantage for having the GFP Section in the Material Department. Rarely were items obtained from production sources through the Purchasing Section. SAAMA (or other AMAs) placed the purchase orders and contracts for all GFP items.

Mr. Camden had been placed in charge of the three sections to relieve the Manager of Material for more pressing problems in the purchasing area, which was receiving the major impact of the new Weapon-System Concept.

The Material Control Section, the third and very large portion of the Department, was under the very capable supervision of Mr. Jackson, Assistant Manager of Material. This Section was responsible for the records and paperwork associated with production material.

The Industrial Engineering Manager, Mr. Baker, had been in favor of consolidating the management of all warehousing activities in the Division to promote more uniform and better practices under a "top-notch" warehousing executive.

MISCELLANEOUS OBSERVATIONS

At the conclusion of the interviews, Mr. Alden attempted to evaluate what he had heard and to recollect some additional thoughts and experience that were related to the customer service problem.

WHAT IS CUSTOMER SERVICE?

Customer Service is a composite of a number of activities. Customer Service is evaluated by the customer; it is not a Convair measurement.

The principal basis for determining the success of a support program should be the degree of combat readiness attained for ships in the program. But there could be other factors which influence the customer.

The nearer we live with each level of customer personnel, the earlier we can detect unsatisfactory trends and take corrective action.

It is highly desirable that customer satisfaction be maintained at all times. It is a "current asset" in the business. Because customer satisfaction is determined by the customer's own evaluation—and often is intangible—perception by outsiders is difficult.

So this brings us down to the decision of what kind of people do we need in the Customer Service organization. Is technical competence, experience in customer operations and problems, knowledge of internal plant procedures of first importance? The type of organization and level of reporting can have a bearing on the effectiveness of customer service.

A BRIEF OUTLINE OF THE SPARES PROCEDURE:

Mr. Alden outlined the following steps representing the current spares process:

1. Provisioning consisted of selecting items to be supplied as spares, the quantity needed, and the delivery dates. Information was taken from drawings, technical data, flight programs, number of stocking bases or depots, and funds available. The Contract Spares Section provisioned B-58 spares and

submitted all data to SAAMA for review, and veto authority within approximately 30 days at no cost. Termination costs were applicable after 30 days.

2. Ordering proceeded at the time of selection. The Spares Parts Control (SPC) was prepared by Contract Spares. Among the several copies distributed, one was sent to the Purchasing Section of the Material Department for procurement of Purchased Parts or increase in the quantity of Raw Materials used in-plant. Another copy went to the Manufacturing Control Department, from where parts were ordered and scheduled, usually concurrent with lots of production parts and sub-assemblies.

3. Manufacturing Control also created a Tab card for each delivery quantity of each spare part number. About 30 days in advance of the date of delivery to the GFP Section, Manufacturing Control "pulled" the due deliveries and ran off an order list. In-plant manufactured items were filled from Manufacturing Control stock rooms and Purchased Parts were requisitioned from Material Stores.

4. All parts and assemblies were sent to the Manufacturing Control Accumulation Area adjacent to the Shipping Section of the Traffic Department in the main plant building.

5. The Accumulation Area checked items for obvious damage and correctness of part number and quantity, turned the orders over to the Shipping Section, and furnished data for a "Concurrency Report" issued by Manufacturing Control to show the status of deliveries or delinquencies.

6. The Shipping Section packaged and/or packed items adequately for the one-third mile trip to the GFP Section in Warehouse No. 4 in the northwest area of the Fort Worth reservation. The Transportation Section of the Traffic Department performed all in-plant movements.

Note: Spares items for other contracts were packaged according to AF instructions for preservation and occasionally export; adequately packed for movement by common carrier; and shipped to various AMAs. Subcontract production assemblies were shipped to the prime contractors. All shipments from the Division were handled through the Shipping Section.

7. When parts or material were moved from one AF "area of accountability" to another, the items were officially transferred on the government form for that purpose, DD250. In this case the B-58 parts were manufactured under a production contract of a cost-plus type. The accountability was transferred to a support operation which was funded separately and operated as a separate entity from production.

8. The GFP Section received the spares, maintained stock record cards, and accepted requisitions for issue to sub-store stock cribs. The GFP Warehouse No. 4 served in a similar capacity to a wholesale warehouse; AF terminology for this function was "AF Depot." The sub-store cribs were under the GFP Manager but physically located for convenience to flight operations. The number of such cribs would vary; one or more would be

located in Convair flight areas and at least one would be at CAFB when B-58's were delivered.

9. Every 90 days the GFP Section issued a "Stock Balance and Consumption Report," showing stock activity on all spares by contract. The GFP Section issued about 15 reports dealing with B-58 parts, generally on a monthly or quarterly basis. The Contract Spares Section issued about 12 reports in all. There was no outright duplication in reports, but verification of related data would have been much easier if all records were more accessible.

WAREHOUSING

Mr. Alden had not raised the question with Mr. Baker, but he had not seen any particular advantage in having one manager over all warehouses. The Material Handling and Methods Groups in Industrial Engineering were available for assistance. In the past three years, Mr. Alden had remarked to both Mr. Camden and the Foreman of Production Stores that he was favorably impressed with their warehouse operations and appearance.

LABOR FORECASTS

The forecasts of labor requirements for the GFP Section called for an increase from 225 in mid-1957 to 450 by 1959. The increase was proportionately greater in clerical personnel than stockmen. The emphasis would also shift from a current ratio of 20 per cent B-58 and 80 per cent all other contracts to 80 per cent B-58. The increase in personnel resulted not so much from an increase in volume of parts handled as from the management phase and additional responsibility on the B-58. The GFP Section served as a Government Depot on the B-58, acting as a sub-depot to SAAMA.

Labor forecasts for the Contract Spares Section showed an increase from 60 to 125 people for the same period, with 95 per cent of the work on B-58 contracts. This increase was due both to the increased responsibilities on the B-58 and the large volume at the beginning of a new prime contract.

AN ESTIMATE OF ORGANIZATION AND PERSONNEL REQUIREMENTS AT CAFB

Function	Responsibilities	Source of Personnel
Convair-CAFB Manager	All support activities at CAFB.	Present supervision or hire from outsdie (Est. No. of Employees: 4)
Maintenance and A & E Mechanics	Maintaining A/C and GSE- Field level. On-job instruction of AF crews.	Development Department Field and Service Mechanics (100)
Quality Control	Inspection and check-out of field-level operations. On-job instruction of AF-Quality Control personnel.	Modernization and Flight Line Inspectors (15)

AN ESTIMATE OF ORGANIZATION AND PERSONNEL REQUIREMENTS AT CAFB (con'd)

Function	Responsibilities	Source of Personnel
Tech Reps, Technical and General Assistance	Investigation of technical malfunctions. Preparation and follow-through on field reports. General assistance and support to AF in any capacity required.	Service Engineering, Engineering Design (15)
Tech Reps, Training	Formal training programs. Instruction and/or administration of classes. (Engineers, Mechanics, etc., may perform actual instruction.)	Service Engineering, Engineering Design, Development Mechanics (12)
Spares Reps.	Assist CAFB Supply personnel in determination of spares, and liaison with GFP Section.	Contract Spares (4)

AN ESTIMATE OF ON-SITE MANAGEMENT

It was estimated that the Manager of Customer Service and his in-plant staff would consist of about 50 people: Administrative 5, Maintenance and Engineering 15, Program Planning 9, Training 6, and Reports and Records 15.

CONTRACT ADMINISTRATION

Mr. Alden had talked to the Contract Administrators in Contract Spares. They felt that their work was separable from administration of the production contract and that they need not be a part of the Contracts Department. They pointed out that the Section had been physically separated for three years, being a five-minute walk between locations.

The Administrators of the production contract stated that there were occasions when closer coordination with the Contract Spares Section was desirable.

SERVICE ENGINEERING

Mr. Alden was concerned over the nucleus from which a new Customer Service organization would be established. The Supervisor of the Aircraft Services Group had expressed a desire to change positions and was being considered for the Engineering Department—Projects Section.

Looking at Mr. Baker's ideas of a Customer Service Department, there appeared to be considerable difference in the sizes of the organization elements that would be embodied in such an all-inclusive department. Would such a reorganization take place at one time? There was also the question as to what type of man should head the Department and how homogeneous these functions might be.

CUSTOMER SERVICE OBJECTIVES

In an interim meeting with Mr. Harrington, Mr. Alden submitted the following as the broad objectives of a customer support program:

• Develop an organization that will assure the customer superior follow-on service after delivery of Convair products.

• Maintain a high degree of combat readiness and a maximum service use record for Convair products.

• Keep the in-plant organization continually motivated to the customer's needs to effect a proper balance of customer service with other Division tasks.

• Assure good communications with the customer.

• Assure adequate supply of parts and services at minimum cost.

Mr. Harrington requested that the organization be resolved and any necessary changes be effected by 1 January 1958 or sooner. This was about four months away.

APPENDIX A

DIVISION STANDARD PRACTICE

Engineering Department—Service Section

PURPOSE
To define the channel of authority and the assigned functions of the Service Section of the Engineering Department.

CHANNEL OF AUTHORITY
This Section operates under the direction of the Chief of Service Engineering who reports to the Assistant Chief Engineer—Product Design.

SUMMARY
The Service Section fulfills Convair obligations with relation to developing design of, and furnishing service assistance for, mobile training units, ground handling equipment, special tools, service kits and service parts for delivered aircraft; provides operating personnel; prepares and issues applicable instruction paper and maintains necessary records for such service transactions.

RESPONSIBILITIES
Prepares and issues contractually required data, such as catalogs and handbooks, for the operation and maintenance of delivered aircraft and for the training of Air Force personnel.

Prepares and issues Installation Instructions and record of formal type Time Compliance Technical Orders for the incorporation of engineering changes on delivered aircraft.

Designs mobile training units, including maintenance instruction charts, for the training of Air Force personnel in the operation and maintenance of delivered aircraft and related aircraft equipment.

Designs special tools and ground handling equipment for the handling and maintenance of delivered aircraft and related aircraft equipment.

Maintains the channels through which all arrangements are made for Convair personnel to conduct business with, or provide any type of service to, the Strategic Air Command Air Force Bases.

Provides Field Engineers and Specialists to Air Force Bases to instruct and assist customer operating personnel in the proper operation and maintenance of delivered aircraft and related aircraft equipment.

Investigates all unsatisfactory operating or service reports and replies to the Air Materiel Command as required.

Maintains records of all unsatisfactory Government Furnished Aircraft Equipment and purchased items.

APPENDIX B

DIVISION STANDARD PRACTICE

Material Department—GFP Section

PURPOSE
To define the channel of authority and the assigned functions of the Government Furnished Property (GFP) Section of the Material Department.

CHANNEL OF AUTHORITY
The GFP Section operates under the direction of a General Supervisor, who reports to the Assistant Manager Material—GFP and Stores.

SUMMARY
This Section receives, stores, issues, keeps accountability records, and issues required reports on all GFP received by this Division, including the operation of the accumulation area and sub-stores for the B-58 Program.

RESPONSIBILITIES
Plans and schedules GFP requirements based on the GFP Master Schedule.

Receives and records incoming GFP shipments.

Checks material received against accompanying Packing Sheets and Freight Bills and distributes Receiving Reports for GFP items.

Stores GFP items in proper warehouse and storage areas.

Releases GFP items to Manufacturing Control stockrooms in regulated quantities based on schedule requirements.

> Note: Disbursement of GFP in specified areas, in accordance with production requirements and upon presentation of authorized paperwork, remains the responsibility of the GFP Section.

Maintains adequate inventory and accountability records.

Prepares government-required reports.

Obtains decisions concerning whether malfunctioning GFP items can be repaired by Convair or other companies, and maintains records showing location of items being repaired.

Takes physical inventory of GFP, as required.

Receives GFP removed from aircraft, makes proper GFP disposition, and receives and stores electronics and radio gear for reinstallation, as required.

Operates the Accumulation Area and Sub-stores for the B-58 Program.

APPENDIX C

DIVISION STANDARD PRACTICE

Contracts Department—Spares Section

PURPOSE

To define the channel of authority and the assigned functions of the Spares Section of the Contracts Department.

CHANNEL OF AUTHORITY

This Section operates under the direction of a General Supervisor, who reports to the Chief, Contracts Administration—Production and Modernization.

SUMMARY

Administers such functions of the Spares Program, Special Tools and Ground Handling Equipment Program, and Training Parts Program as are required to fulfill contractual obligations; negotiates and obtains required contractual deviations and coverages; prepares required fiscal reports and submits to concerned departments; submits recommendations to the customer of parts to be procured.

RESPONSIBILITIES

Analyzes prime and call contracts on spare parts, special tools, and training parts, and administers to ensure compliance of contractual obligations.

Coordinates with customer and affected departments to obtain required contractual deviations and coverages.

Prepares and submits to customer procurement changes on a progressive basis as engineering design changes are released.

Submits delivery schedule information on spare parts, special tools, and training parts equipment to the customer, and negotiates delivery schedules.

Advises concerned departments by issuance of Sales Orders of contractual obligations relative to Spares, Special Tools and Ground Handling Equipment, and Training Parts Programs.

Prepares fiscal fund reports for concerned departments and advises customer of the status of funds allocated.

Prepares and submits Spare Parts Breakdown, as required, on approved Engineering Change Proposals, including procurement recommendations.

Provides required spares representatives to customer field activities and company vendors' or subcontractors' plants to coordinate spares requirements and resolve spares problems.

Maintains official Air Force records of delivery of end items and provides current, comprehensive, and uniform information from negotiation stage through item completion to facilitate progressive contract closure.

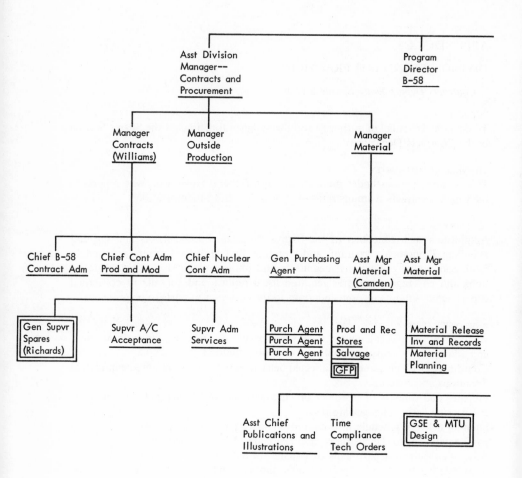

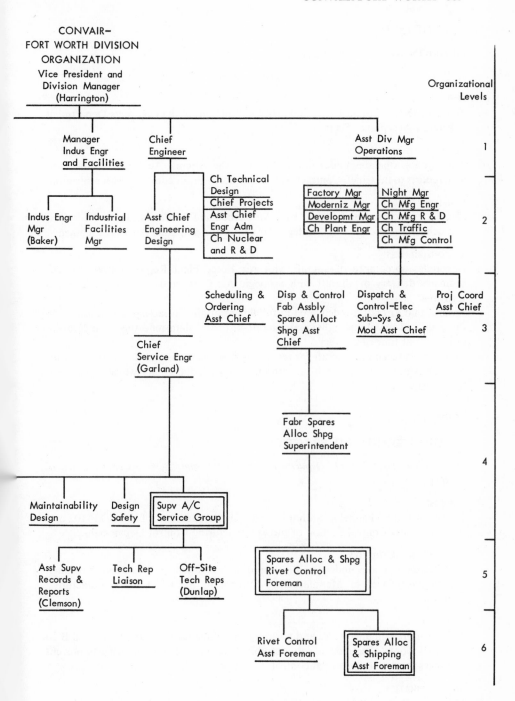

CONVAIR–
FORT WORTH DIVISION
ORGANIZATION
Vice President and
Division Manager
(Harrington)

Organizational
Levels

Manager
Indus Engr
and Facilities

Chief
Engineer

Asst Div Mgr
Operations

1

Indus Engr
Mgr
(Baker)

Industrial
Facilities
Mgr

Asst Chief
Engineering
Design

Ch Technical
Design
Chief Projects
Asst Chief
Engr Adm
Ch Nuclear
and R & D

Factory Mgr
Moderniz Mgr
Developmt Mgr
Ch Plant Engr

Night Mgr
Ch Mfg Engr
Ch Mfg R & D
Ch Traffic
Ch Mfg Control

2

Scheduling &
Ordering
Asst Chief

Disp & Control
Fab Assbly
Spares Alloct
Shpg Asst
Chief

Dispatch &
Control–Elec
Sub-Sys &
Mod Asst Chief

Proj Coord
Asst Chief

3

Chief
Service Engr
(Garland)

Fabr Spares
Alloc Shpg
Superintendent

4

Maintainability
Design

Design
Safety

Supv A/C
Service Group

Asst Supv
Records &
Reports
(Clemson)

Tech Rep
Liaison

Off–Site
Tech Reps
(Dunlap)

Spares Alloc & Shpg
Rivet Control
Foreman

5

Rivet Control
Asst Foreman

Spares Alloc
& Shipping
Asst Foreman

6

Figure 8.

APPENDIX D

DIVISION STANDARD PRACTICE

Contracts Department—Aircraft Acceptance Section

PURPOSE

To define the level of authority and assigned functions of the Contracts Department —Aircraft Acceptance Section.

CHANNEL OF AUTHORITY

This Section operates under the direction of the Aircraft Acceptance Supervisor who reports to the Chief, Contract Administration—Production and Modernization.

SUMMARY

Negotiates acceptance of aircraft with Air Force Plant Representative and coordinates delivery of aircraft with Strategic Air Command and other Air Force segments.

RESPONSIBILITIES

Negotiates acceptance of aircraft with Air Force Plant Representative and coordinates delivery of aircraft with Strategic Air Command and other Air Force segments.

Assures that aircraft are delivered in fulfillment of all contractual obligations.

Prepares and maintains individual aircraft historical data reflecting configuration of aircraft at time of delivery.

Coordinates receipt of aircraft for reconditioning programs, and through inventory of aircraft upon arrival establishes the property accountability which is assumed by Convair.

APPENDIX E

DIVISION STANDARD PRACTICE

Manufacturing Control Department—F/TF-102 and B-36 Assembly Control Section

PURPOSE

To establish this channel of authority and assigned functions of the F/TF-102 and B-36 Assembly Control Section of the Manufacturing Control Department.

CHANNEL OF AUTHORITY

This Section operates under the direction of a Superintendent who reports through an Assistant Chief of Manufacturing Control to the Chief of Manufacturing Control.

SUMMARY

This Section maintains stores and positioned stocking areas for F/TF-102 and B-36 Assembly Control Section and sub-assembly departments; expedites parts to prevent shortages; and maintains rivet control.

RESPONSIBILITIES

Maintains stockrooms and positioned stocking areas which furnish finished parts directly to assembly and sub-assembly departments.

Releases Operation Instruction Logs (Lists) and Operation Sheets to assembly and sub-assembly departments.

Maintains Assembly Zone Control Booths in assembly and sub-assembly departments.

Prepares and maintains control records, including call-outs for part receipts, irregular issuances, and schedule position.

Performs dispatching functions in assembly and sub-assembly departments.

Maintains rivet control.

Maintains Accumulation Area for check out of Spares and Service Kits.

Maintains an Accumulation Area for inter-division miscellaneous sales shipping items.

3. THE MERRIAM COMPANY*

—ROBERT W. CAMBRELENG

One afternoon in late June of 1962, Bill Pickens, industrial engineer of the Merriam Company,[1] was called into the office of his immediate superior, Walter Daly, the production manager.[2]

Daly began the conversation by saying, "Bill, I want to discuss a situation which has arisen in the production department. I don't think you are unaware of the fact that a lot of people feel Henry Hulbert isn't the right man for the assistant superintendent's position. The president and others have decided that I've got to fire Hulbert, or at least move him out of production. I had to call him in here this morning and tell him. He said he had no idea this was coming; he was stunned. Everyone wants to fire Hank, but I won't do it to him. I was talking with Tony Webster this morning, and we decided that you might be able to make use of Hank in your department."

Pickens was quite surprised by both the information and the proposal. His immediate reaction to the latter, based on his knowledge of Hulbert's very poor personality and his quality control record, was unsympathetic. Also, he was acutely aware that he was a much younger man than Hulbert, and that this might lead to difficulty between them. On the other hand, he reasoned silently, what he (Pickens) lacked in the way of production know-how could well be supplied by Hulbert who was vastly more experienced in these matters; between them, perhaps, they might do an outstanding job.

Hank Hulbert, who was a first cousin to Daly, was 47 years old, and a big hulk of a fellow with rough and gruff manner and little formal education. He had been with the company since its founding twenty years previously, and during this period had worked on every production operation; his last eleven years had been in supervisory capacity. Concerning the latter, when Daly

---

* Reprinted by permission of Professor Cambreleng.

[1] Names are fictitious.

[2] See Exhibit I for an abbreviated organization chart.

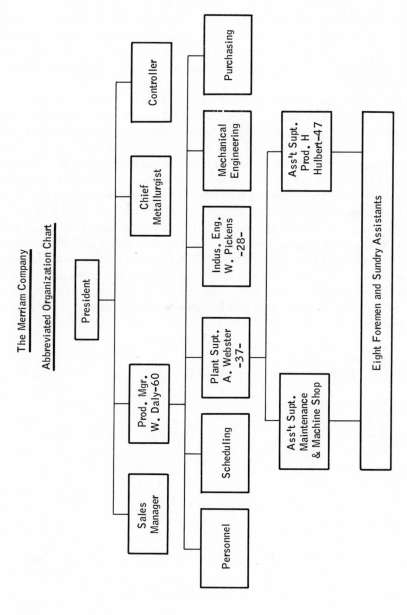

The Merriam Company

Abbreviated Organization Chart

President

Sales Manager

Prod. Mgr. W. Daly—60

Chief Metallurgist

Controller

Personnel

Scheduling

Plant Supt. A. Webster -37-

Indus. Eng. W. Pickens -28-

Mechanical Engineering

Purchasing

Ass't Supt. Maintenance & Machine Shop

Ass't Supt. Prod. H Hulbert—47

Eight Foremen and Sundry Assistants

Exhibit I

387

became foreman in 1951, Hulbert became his assistant; when Daly was appointed superintendent, Hank again was made assistant. However, when Daly was promoted to production manager in 1959, the president stepped in and refused to elevate Hulbert accordingly. Instead, the president selected Anthony Webster, then 34, with three years experience in mechanical engineering, to fill the plant superintendent's post vacated by Daly. Webster's promotion was based on his success in planning and supervising the construction of a branch factory in 1958; until that date, Tony had had no experience in supervision.

Daly continued his conversation about Hulbert with two arguments. Firstly, Pickens had recently been designated to carry out a program of in-process quality control involving several important projects; this program would require an increased staff, and he might be able to make good use of Hulbert here in view of the latter's tremendous technical experience acquired through twenty years of production work. Secondly, he stressed that company policy was never to discharge a man who had occupied so important a position as assistant superintendent without trying to make use of such talent as he possessed by transferring him to a less sensitive post; they could not turn out onto the street a man of that age and with that length of service.

Daly concluded his comments with, " Bill, I'm asking you to take Hulbert. You can say ' No ', but then he's fired. I've told him this. Also, he is aware that if he goes with you he'll take a pay cut. However, I think you can make use of him both to your own and his satisfaction. At least give him a six-month try."

EXTERNAL ORGANIZATIONAL ENVIRONMENT: SOCIAL, POLITICAL, ETHICAL, AND INTERNATIONAL ENVIRONMENTS

* *

1. THE ADHESIVE PRODUCTS LOCAL WELFARE FUND*

—ROBERT C. KIEKAMP

Mr. Anderson, supervisor of Employee Affairs for the Central Bedford Plant of the Adhesive Products Corporation attempted to disguise any indication of annoyance as he terminated a phone conversation. He buzzed his secretary and told her he would not take any more calls that morning. He had just received one of the many calls from employees who were complaining about the tactics used to solicit funds for the Local Welfare Fund. The 90% participation was something to be proud of all right, but he could not help wondering if the ill will generated by the solicitation tactics did not more than offset any improvement in community relations that may accrue. "I wonder," he said to himself, "if we don't carry this good citizen role a little too far. Should our corporate responsibility to the community include projects such as this, especially if morale of the employees and work effort are being sacrificed?" His thoughts then reflected back to the previous year when he had been deluged by the same type of written and verbal comments from employees expressing their dissatisfaction with the manner in which the drive had been conducted, especially the pressure tactics used by management during a resolicitation drive intended to get those employees to acquiesce who had not joined or had not contributed an adequate amount. The employees were approached again and again by their superiors until either the superior was satisfied that he had done all he could or the employee finally gave in. "Oh well, what's done is done," he said to himself and continued for the remainder of the morning to review the suggestions that had been submitted by employees the previous week. At noon he met with the local newspapers and representatives of various charities to receive an award on behalf of all employees for superior achievement during the fund drive. When Mr. Anderson returned to the plant the phone calls began again and continued for the remainder of the week. The

* Reprinted by permission of Professor Kiekamp.

389

pressure of phone calls, notes, and verbal comments was so great against the tactics used by management to obtain the enrollment and dollar participation goals in the Local Welfare Fund that by the end of the week he decided to review the entire situation in order to prepare what he considered proper recommendations to his management.

The Local Welfare Fund had been established back in 1952 by a popular vote of the employees of the Central Bedford Plant to stave off the numerous fund drives in the plant and to provide a convenient way of giving to worthwhile projects such as United Appeal, Heart Fund, March of Dimes, orphanages and over 100 other health, welfare, education, and charitable agencies. The money is allocated to the various causes by an elected Employee Board of Trustees. Each participating employee is given a window sticker to display at his home as evidence of his contribution to the Local Welfare Fund. The employee may, of course, contribute an additional amount at his home if he so desires.

The Adhesive Products Corporation is a large national manufacturing concern with operating, product oriented divisions decentralized throughout the United States and foreign countries. The management philosophy of the company is for strong decentralized management. Local Plant Management is thus urged to do whatever is deemed necessary to contribute the most to the community relations in which it operates. Almost every plant has a department manager who has spelled out, as part of his responsibilities, "Administering Employee Relations Programs in regard to, (1) maintaining and enhancing the company's good name and, (2) company objectives and policies with respect to public organizations."

The total Adhesive Products' employment at Bedford has averaged approximately 12,000. The Central Bedford Plant averaged just over 2,000. Until 1959, when the Central Bedford Plant percentage of employee participation hit 90%, after the first management "hard sell" drive, the Plant, consistently, had had the lowest percentage of employee participation in the Local Welfare Fund. A chart had been maintained by Mr. Anderson's Unit which indicated the following employee percentages of participation.

Year	%
1953	
1954	40
1955	45
1956	55
1957	60
1958	65
1959	90
1960	90
1961	80
1962	90

The Local Welfare Fund Campaign was kicked off by an article in the Plant Management Bulletin, dated October 12, 1963. The Management Bulletin is a plant-wide communications device distributed to all Managers and Supervisors at the plant. The article read as follows:

1963 LOCAL WELFARE FUND CAMPAIGN ANNOUNCED

The Central Bedford Plant Employees Local Welfare Fund Campaign was announced today by Mr. John Rigby, Manager, Industrial and Community Relations. Employee enrollment in the campaign will begin on October 17, 1963, and continue throughout next week.

The fund, as you know, serves two purposes: it helps Adhesive Products people here in Bedford to meet their community obligations in an economical and systematic manner; and it eliminates the need for numerous repeated solicitations in the plant.

Individual employee enrollment cards and other materials will be distributed to supervisors during the latter part of this week. Supervisors will then be asked, as they have been in past campaigns, to solicit new members for the LWF and to encourage greater contributions from old members during the period of October 17 through October 21.

Ninety per cent level of employee participation continues as the goal of the Bedford Plant. You may remember that this level of participation was achieved during the latter part of December 1959. However, due to normal attrition, reduction of forces, and a number of withdrawals, plant participation has slipped to an approximate 80% level. At this point, only some 250 new enrollments are needed to achieve our goal of 90%. Additionally, the Central Plant has set a dollar goal as well as a membership goal. The desired dollar level is $50,000 annually. Of course, it is up to each individual to determine how much to give—but more and more people are meeting the community wide objective of pledging one hour's pay every month. That's why it's known as "A Fair Share Pledge."

Strong management support of the campaign is required to successfully meet our 1963 goals.

On October 18th, the following article appeared in the Plant Management Bulletin. This device is a guide for current topics to be discussed in weekly departmental meetings and is distributed to all managers and supervisors.

A LITTLE WAY TO GO

A few weeks ago, during the Central Plant's prolonged effort to increase employee participation in their Local Welfare Fund, it became necessary to take some extreme action to awaken people to their responsibilities as employees and as citizens. Hopefully, no such action will be necessary this year because in the past few years some 80%–90% of the plant's employees have been made to recognize their obligations to their neighbors and their community.

While most employees have been taking giant steps forward in this matter, some have slipped back. This year we have only a little way to go to reach the 90%/$50,000 goal. However, slackers will be among us always and present you, the supervisor, with your current challenge. To this end we are reprinting the bulletin that was circulated last year.

SLEEPERS AND SLACKERS

In every kind of human activity, we observe, generally, two kinds of people—those who do what they ought to and those who do not. In politics we find people who vote and people who don't. There are those who take part in the activities of their church and those who do not. We find people who are interested in what their children do and those who couldn't care less. In short, most of us recognize our individual obligations; some of us, however, do not!

It is with this latter group that we are concerned here. And in this instance the activity we are concerned with is the Bedford Plant Local Welfare Fund. This group we can characterize broadly as sleepers or slackers. The sleeper just isn't aware of the human misery that exists in his community or how he can help alleviate it. We wonder sometimes how this one can make his way to and from work, since he obviously is so completely unaware of what goes on about him.

The slacker, though, knows what is needed and what he can do, but just doesn't care. He will take refuge in the excuse that his own needs are greater than his income, completely disregarding what it may be like for the family that has no income at all. Or he may say dogmatically that he doesn't believe in organized charity. What does he propose instead? Probably nothing. It's a convenient excuse for shirking his duty.

We've talked about people in general, now let's think about you, the supervisor, in particular. What have you done about waking up the sleeper, shaking him out of his lethargy? What have you done about breaking down the artificial defenses of the slacker? Perhaps some of you have been sleepers or slackers yourselves. Otherwise it would be impossible to account for the fact that some employee groups are at or near 100% membership in the Local Welfare Fund while others are 50% or less.

If you haven't done all you should to wake up or shake up the people who need it now is the time to do it! Go back to them again and again until you have demolished every excuse or defense that they have erected to salve their conscience.

OBJECTIONS YOU WILL HEAR

Q. I don't subscribe because too much of my contribution is used to pay administrative costs.

A. Not one penny of your contribution to LWF is used for such a purpose. All administrative cost is borne by the Company. Of the money which the LWF allocates to the United Appeal, only 3% is needed for the purpose of administration.

Q. I favor donating to specific charities rather than to a general fund.

A. Fine, designation forms are available at the Employee Affairs Office. You can designate one, two, or a dozen favorite charities.

Q. I like to see the good results of what I give.

A. The agencies of the United Appeal and those others supported in part by your LWF welcome the opportunity to show you what they are doing. Simply call anyone or all of them and they will arrange to inform you.

Q. I can't afford to give anything (or anymore) at this time.

A. Most employees recently received a pay increase of about 3% (September 12, 1963) and since that time the cost of living has been stable. You most certainly should be able to give something for the first time (a little more than you did last year).

Q. I give to my neighbor who solicits for United Appeal at my home.

A. Your neighbor will not solicit your home if you have the window sticker posted. You needn't be embarrassed even if he should knock because more and more people are giving systematically through payroll deduction at their place of employment. There's nothing wrong with giving at home as well as at work.

Q. Management just wants more membership so it can make a good show!

A. Yes, we are embarrassed about our rate of participation—aren't you?

Q. Why are we being treated like children? Why all the pressure?

A. Pressure is not being applied to those employees who have accepted their responsibility but only to those who, like children, have shirked theirs. The pressure doesn't embarrass us because our motive is good. We admit the pressure is unusual but it is not undue.

Q. I don't live in Lake County so why should I give at work?

A. Over the past few years, the Bedford Plant Local Welfare Fund has helped directly support 28 charity agencies in Bedford and surrounding communities and indirectly through the United Appeal and Community Chest, the Red Cross and 131 other health, education, and welfare agencies.

All during the week of the initial fund drive, October 17–21, the "News & Views," a one-sheet $8\frac{1}{2}'' \times 11''$, daily information sheet made available to all employees in the plant cafeteria, depicted a running measurement of participation by section. This consisted of a single bar horizontally graduated to 100%—each section was characterized, depending on per cent of participation, by such items as a rocket, jet plane, racer, car, and other symbols. The section in last place was indicated by a man pushing a wheel barrow. This gimmick was, of course, to create greater individual interest in and association with the drive.

This running measurement indicated on the 19th that the Industrial and Community Relations Department which publishes the "News and Views" was last—pushing the wheel barrow. This created employee comments regarding the fact that the department pushing the LWF drive was trailing and why should I break my back and etc. However, the I&CR Department was riding the first place rocket the next day, the 20th. They had divorced themselves as a department from one of their low subscribing units. This unit was depicted with the last place wheel barrow. This created more discussion as nobody knew when their unit was to be next to be singled out and pressure thus applied.

On October 25, 1963, an information bulletin distributed to all employees contained the following message in addition to a table showing percentage participation by each department and unit. The Information Bulletin is another plant-wide communications device utilized by the Industrial and Community Relations Department to disseminate information directly to the employee. Sufficient copies are prepared and delivered to work places so that each individual obtains one.

60 MORE EMPLOYEES—$5,500 MORE DOLLARS

The Bedford Plant's 1963 goals for employee participation and dollars pledged by employees to their Local Welfare Fund are within reach at the present time. The plant has been seeking 90% enrollment and contributions of $50,000 annually. At this time, only 60 more enrollments are needed to attain the first goal. Some $5,500 in pledges are needed, however, to reach the second goal.

The solution seems to be simple. Find 60 more employees who are willing to pledge $92.00 per year and we are there.

Not so simple really. Sixty or more employees may be enrolled shortly but looking at the problem realistically, it is not expected that each of these new members can or will pledge some $6.00 per month.

The alternatives, therefore, are few.

FIRST—change the goals! This will not be done!

SECOND—Go back to the employees who have not yet joined the vast majority of their fellow employees in supporting this community activity. This will be done!

THIRD—Go back to those employees who are contributing nominal sums, less than 40¢ per week or $2.00 per month. This will also be done!

The only exceptions in the re-solicitation will be those employees who, last week, enrolled in the fund for the first time and those who voluntarily increased their level of support. All other employees can expect to be approached by their supervisor very soon.

In support of the above re-solicitation for the LWF, a letter outlining the approach and requesting cooperation of department management was sent to each department manager by Mr. John Rigby, the Industrial and Community Relations Department Manager.

Mr. Anderson, Supervisor of Employee Affairs, responsible for following through on the LWF drive, prepared and submitted the following letter dated October 27, 1963, to all members of management with the appropriate IBM cards.

TO ALL MEMBERS OF MANAGEMENT:

Supplementing Mr. John Rigby's letter to all department managers dated October 25, 1963, the following information will serve as a guide to the subject above.

1. The key to the codes on the enclosed IBM list of all employees in your subsection is as follows:
A.   Column #4—number 1 represents hourly employees
              numbers 2-3-4-7 are weekly salaried
              numbers 5 & 6 are exempt salaried
              letter N indicates a new or changed deduction
              asterisk indicates no contribution
B.   Column #5—present amount of weekly contribution
C.   Column #6—present amount of monthly contribution
D.   Column #7—one shot deduction

2. Pledge cards registering IBM names of employees indicate that they did not voluntarily increase their contribution the first round and are still under one half hour's pay per month rate.

3. Unregistered cards are to be used by non-contributors and those who may have increased the first round but are still under the one half hour's pay per month rate.

4. The amounts on all cards should represent the new total contribution per pay period with emphasis on the fact that those paid weekly should indicate a weekly contribution.

5. Employees desiring to cancel contributions must submit a letter to Payroll to the effect, countersigned by their immediate supervisor.

6. Extra cards, window stickers, annual reports, designation forms and other material can be obtained from Employee Affairs.

7. All cards must be returned on a daily basis Friday, November 4, 1963.

The latest results of the drive were published on November 3 to all employees via an Information Bulletin. This bulletin carried a table showing not only the percentage of participation actually obtained to date by each department and unit, but also the percentage was calculated per department based on one half hour's pay per month per employee, summarized and compared with total actual amounts pledged. Some departments were over 100%. The majority were not. The table just described was accompanied by the following paragraphs:

LONG ON MEMBERSHIP—SHORT ON CASH

The Bedford Plant this morning achieved one of its 1963 goals in the Local Welfare Fund Campaign. Currently, 90.4% of the plant's employees are actively enrolled in and supporting the activities of their fund. Dollars pledged by employees thus far are still short of the quota needed to meet the committed and planned obligations of the fund.

Let's wrap up this campaign soon. If you are not a member—enroll now. If you can give more—pledge it now. Let's all support this very worthy activity as we are able.

Mr. Anderson, while replacing the file, believed that he now had sufficient insight and factual knowledge of the situation to allow him, once he had completed his analysis, to make appropriate recommendations to his management concerning the 1964 campaign and how it should be conducted.

2. HEWLETT-PACKARD COMPANY*

JOHN C. EWING

and

I. ROGER YOSHINO

In view of the establishment of the European Common Market, the management of the Hewlett-Packard Company, manufacturer of electronic instruments in Palo Alto, California, was considering the possibility of manufacturing some of the company's products in countries that were within this growing European market. This decision had been reached on the basis of their assessment of the potential growth of the European market and the several inducements offered by the Common Market to encourage U.S. firms to manufacture their products abroad.

In the spring of 1959, Mr. William R. Hewlett, Executive Vice-President of the company, had been asked by the executive committee to make preliminary recommendations concerning which form of overseas operations would be best suited to the needs of the Hewlett-Packard Company and in which of the six Common Market member nations its operations could be most effectively based.

Mr. Hewlett knew that the company had two alternative methods of manufacturing overseas—licensing or establishing their own subsidiary—and decided to investigate the advantages and disadvantages of each.

Licensing, he found out through reading and talking to his acquaintances experienced in foreign operations, had several advantages. By licensing manufacturing and marketing rights to overseas firms, Hewlett-Packard management would be dealing with going concerns that had market contacts, experienced management, and established organizations. The extent of Hewlett-Packard's participation would be the provision of technical know-how and some special equipment. Licensing would thus eliminate the tedious job of surveying the market, buying land, constructing plant facilities, selecting

* Reprinted from *Stanford Business Cases 1961–62*, Volume II, with the permission of the publishers, Stanford University Graduate School of Business. Copyright, 1962, by the Board of Trustees of the Leland Stanford Junior University.

personnel, and performing many other tasks which were required when a company established a manufacturing subsidiary overseas. Since licensing made it possible to combine U.S. technical know-how with the experience and skill of the local manufacturer, the adjustment of the product characteristics to local needs was made easier. Moreover, this form of operation was much more flexible because licensing agreements could be reviewed periodically and, if proved unsatisfactory, the company could terminate the agreements much more easily than it could discontinue a manufacturing organization. Thus, Hewlett-Packard's management believed that licensing was particularly attractive to a company like theirs which was relatively inexperienced in the field of foreign operations. Besides, they knew that a number of European manufacturers were quite anxious to enter into a licensing arrangement with a U.S. firm like Hewlett-Packard.

On the other hand, Mr. Hewlett had learned that licensing did have some serious limitations which had to be considered in making this decision. Lack of control over quality of products, distribution, and manufacturing policies often had in the past presented serious problems to U.S. licensors. There were also difficulties which could arise from misunderstandings due to differences in language, philosophy of business management, and commercial customs. The relationship between licensor and licensee was such that the attempts to iron out these problems were often difficult and demanded undue time and attention of already overworked executives of the licensor.

Mr. Hewlett also had noticed the following experience of one American licensor cited in an article appearing in the *Harvard Business Review:*[1]

"A large chemical company licensed a firm to manufacture and sell its products in a European country. The licensee pushed the parent company's name, brand and products and quickly built a substantial volume of business. But the United States company soon discovered that it was receiving only a negligible royalty for its participation in what had become a major market for its products, whereas the licensee was realizing tremendous profits. In order to retrieve control of the market which its own product and name had developed, the licensor was forced to buy a majority interest in the licensee's enlarged and prosperous company."

Most of these problems inherent to licensing would be avoided if a firm established its own manufacturing subsiduary. This form of operation had several attractive advantages. Primarily, the parent company retained tight control over the policies of its foreign subsidiary, particularly if the latter was wholly owned. It could set its own manufacturing as well as distribution policies and quality standard without being bound to the traditional ways of doing things which were frequently found in a foreign company, and most important of all, it could control its own destiny and reap maximum benefits from growth of the market. Establishing a manufacturing subsidiary also had

[1] Charles Henry Lee, "How to research the overseas market by licensing," *Harvard Business Review*, January–February, 1958.

its problems, however. It would be necessary to make long term financial, managerial and organizational commitments. Moreover, the parent company had to be prepared to make a large initial outlay for establishing the subsidiary and then sustaining its losses until the subsidiary became self-supporting. Risk factors also had to be considered inasmuch as there was always a possibility that the European Common Market, composed of the six independent nations, might collapse or its progress may be seriously retarded. In addition, the parent company had to assume entirely new managerial responsibilities connected with operating a foreign subsidiary. Although Hewlett-Packard had had substantial experience in export operations, its management believed that the nature and magnitude of the problems of management on an international scale were quite different.

Mr. Hewlett planned to take a fact-finding trip to Europe accompanied by his assistant and a lawyer in May, 1960. Prior to this trip, he hoped to reach a tentative decision on which of the two alternative methods of operation would be best suited to the company. He also was anxious to know what factors his group must consider in arriving at the recommendation of which of the six countries should be the center of Hewlett-Packard's European operations.

BACKGROUND OF THE COMPANY

The origin of the Hewlett-Packard Company dates back to the undergraduate college days of Bill Hewlett and Dave Packard. In their course of studies at Stanford University they became impressed with the opportunities in the field of electronic instrumentation. Following their graduation in 1934, the two spent several years gaining business experience and continuing their education. Mr. Hewlett, while engaged in graduate study, perfected a new type of audio oscillator. The first instruments were sold to acquaintances in the industry. Immediately, users compared enthusiastically this equipment with the cumbersome and expensive instruments offered by competitors. Mr. Hewlett presented the new oscillator at the 1938 Institute of Radio Engineers meeting in Portland. As a result of this presentation the chief sound engineer for Walt Disney Studios bought nine oscillators for the stereophonic sound presentation of "Fantasia."

Hewlett-Packard was officially organized as a partnership in 1939 with assets of $538. Production was started in Mr. Packard's garage. Initially, profit was ploughed back into the business, and the two partners concentrated on developing new instruments to broaden the base of their operation. Soon the need for more space became apparent and the business was moved to a concrete block building near its original site. In 1941 Hewlett-Packard obtained its first government contract from the Army for six signal generators. As the United States became increasingly involved in the war the company shifted its efforts to filling defense orders.

By 1943, one hundred people were working two shifts a day and sales reached $1,000,000. The volume of business reached a peak in 1944 when sales totaled $1.5 million and about a dozen different instruments were in regular production. The period immediately after the war was one of adjustment for the company's operations.

The firm incorporated in 1947 and sales again reached the 1944 level of $1.5 million. Operating as a corporation the company was able to meet the increasing needs for capital with a minimum of borrowing. During the same year the second major plant building was begun.

In the early 1950's the company introduced about 20 new products a year. With the advent of the Korean conflict the company again became involved in defense work. By 1952 about one half of the company's sales were of equipment that had been developed within the preceding three years. Although the company's increased level of business was not heavily dependent on direct sales to the government, the defense effort stepped-up the over-all demand.

Exhibit 1

Hewlett-Packard Company

Balance Sheet—October 31, 1958 and 1957

Assets	October 31	
	1958	1957
Current Assets:		
Cash	$644,880.43	$268,899.16
Notes and accounts receivable less provision for losses in collection:		
1958—$8,734.62, 1957—$9,897.70	4,734,143.20	3,475,258.44
Inventories:		
Finished goods and work in process, at approximate cost	3,833,566.42	4,001,993.87
Raw materials, at lower of cost or market	1,518,101.36	1,769,394.14
Deposits and prepaid expenses	95,438.41	76,659.83
Total Current Assets	$10,826,129.82	$9,592,205.44
Property, Plant and Equipment, at cost, less accumulated depreciation and amortization:		
1958—$2,083,533.00, 1957—$1,480,128.94	$4,883,724.92	$4,983,916.51
Other Assets:		
Securities, at cost (1957, $37,800.00 pledged to secure long-term note)	$47,800.00	$47,800.00
Deferred patent expense	33,622.02	33,622.02
Organization expense	3,960.05	3,960.05
Total Other Assets	$85,382.07	$85,382.07
Total	$15,795,236.81	$14,661,504.02

Exhibit 1 (cont.)

| | October 31 | |
Liabilities	1958	1957
Current Liabilities:		
Short-term notes payable	$ —	$1,100,000.00
Long-term debt maturing within one year	44,206.81	154,948.92
Accounts payable and accruals	2,428,221.24	1,885,211.90
Provision for federal taxes on income	1,757,872.91	1,768,042.78
Total Current Liabilities	$4,230,300.96	$4,908,203.60
Long-Term Debt:		
Mortgage payable, 4½% due 1963	$375,383.42	$419,591.11
Leasehold, 4½% due 1961	—	300,000.00
Other (1957, $24,154.20 secured)	—	56,654.20
Total Long-Term Debt	$375,383.42	$776,245.31
Reserve:		
Capital Stock bonus payable	—	$885,968.00
Capital Stock and Surplus:		
Common stock, par value $1.00 a share		
Authorized 5,000,000 shares; reserved		
for stock options 45,461 shares at		
October 31, 1958, 45,527 shares at		
October 31, 1957; issued and		
outstanding, 1958—3,055,373 shares		
1957—3,000,000 shares	$3,055,373.00	$3,000,000.00
Paid-in Surplus	830,595.00	—
Earned Surplus	7,303,584.43	5,091,087.11
Total Capital Stock and Surplus	$11,189,552.43	$8,091,087.11
Total	$15,795,236.81	$14,661,504.02

To provide needed working space, another major construction program which more than doubled the total area of the building, was undertaken in 1953. Employment increased from about 300 people in 1951 to about 700 in 1954. In 1957, the company completed construction on two large, ultra-modern buildings on the 40 acre site adjoining the Stanford University campus. Sales reached $27,000,000 and 1,500 people were employed in the organization.

Sales in 1958 went over $30 million, employment jumped to 1,700, and 12 new instruments were introduced. The product line then totaled 373 items. Complete financial statements for 1958 and a 10 year review of earnings are presented as Exhibits 1 through 4.

While the company in the past had not used acquisition of other companies to enhance its growth, it acquired in 1958 through an exchange of Hewlett-Packard stock 80% of the outstanding stock of the F. L. Moseley Company of Pasadena, California. The F. L. Moseley Company had in recent years enjoyed sales of about $1,500,000 from a line of X-Y recorders and related electronic instruments compatible with the Hewlett-Packard line.

PRODUCTS MANUFACTURED BY HEWLETT-PACKARD

Since its founding, the company's activities had been devoted to the design and manufacture of precision electronic measuring instruments. Although the firm manufactured close to 400 different types of instruments, the products fell into two broad categories. One category, which represented a fairly sophisticated engineering design, was basically an assembly type of operation from standard component parts. The other was equally complicated in design

Exhibit 2

Hewlett-Packard Company

Statement of Income—Years Ended October 31, 1958 and 1957

	October 31	
	1958	1957
Sales, net	$30,296,647.33	$27,948,789.65
Cost of goods sold	19,247,549.13	17,245,450.01
Gross profit on sales	$11,049,098.20	$10,703,339.64
Selling, administrative and general expense	6,562,678.56	5,738,327.93
Net profit from operations	$4,486,419.64	$4,965,011.71
Other Income	178,117.50	143,551.04
Total	$4,554,537.14	$5,108,522.75
Other deductions	83,610.65	110,074.57
Net income before provision for federal taxes on income	$4,580,962.49	$4,998,448.18
Provision for federal taxes on income	2,368,429.17	2,595,890.91
Net income before special charge	$2,212,497.32	$2,402,557.27
Special charge, net:		
Capital stock bonus to employees less federal taxes on income attributable thereto	—	425,264.64
Net income	$2,212,497.32	$1,977,292.63

Exhibit 3

Hewlett-Packard Company

Statement of Surplus—Year Ended October 31, 1958

	Paid-in	Earned
Balance, November 1, 1957	$ —	$5,091,087.11
Net income for the year		2,212,497.32
Excess of market value over par value of 55,373 shares of capital stock issued to officers and employees as a bonus	830,595.00	—
Balance, October 31, 1958	$830,595.00	$7,303,584.43

Exhibit 4

Year Review of Earnings
Years Ended October 31

	1958	1957	1956	1955	1954
Sales	$30,296,647	$27,948,790	$20,161,621	$15,338,179	$12,599,096
Other Income	178,117	143,511	109,403	74,349	59,914
Total	$30,474,764	$28,092,301	$20,271,024	$15,412,528	$12,659,010
Cost of Goods Sold	$19,247,764	$17,245,450	$11,990,207	$9,298,670	$8,516,446
Selling, Administrative and General Expense	6,646,289	5,848,403	4,541,827	3,203,014	2,577,405
Other Charges including Renegotiation Refund	—	—	—	36,787	73,375
Federal Taxes on Income	2,368,429	2,595,891	1,935,724	1,557,821	851,014
Total	$28,262,267	$25,689,744	$18,467,758	$14,096,292	$12,018,240
Net Income	$2,212,497	$2,402,557*	$1,803,266	$1,316,236	$640,770
Dividends Paid	—	$6,359	$250,000	$200,000	$150,000
Net Income per Share of Capital Stock**	$.724	$.786	$.590	$.431	$.210
Number of Employees	1749	1507	1169	765	700

	1953	1952	1951	1950	1949
Sales	$12,839,406	$10,952,980	$5,538,889	$2,301,744	$2,230,634
Other Income	43,361	41,441	24,802	11,841	9,682
Total	$12,887,767	$10,994,421	$5,563,691	$2,313,585	$2,240,316
Cost of Goods Sold	$7,996,778	$6,377,823	$4,075,280	$1,294,650	$1,238,849
Selling, Administrative and General Expense	2,290,537	2,278,643	363,548	658,553	570,153
Other Charges including Renegotiation Refund	20,908	—	—	—	—
Federal Taxes on Income	1,813,678	1,632,116	733,996	143,761	163,899
Total	$12,121,901	$10,288,582	$5,172,824	$2,096,964	$1,972,901
Net Income	$765,866	$705,839	$390,867	$216,621	$267,415
Dividends Paid	—	$60,000	$60,000	—	—
Net Income per Share of Capital Stock**	$.251	$.231	$.128	$.071	$.088
Number of Employees	622	573	491	195	145

* Before special charge, net of $425,264.64.
** Computed on the basis of 3,055,373 shares.

and required a great many special and precision parts, for which expensive tooling was required. The principal types of instruments include oscillators, voltmeters, signal generators, wave form analyzers, frequency measuring equipment, microwave and waveguide test instruments, and oscilloscopes.

EXPORT OPERATIONS

During the company's early stages its exports were handled by a local export house. This house, in turn, had representatives in various countries throughout the world. As the company grew, this method of distribution became unsatisfactory, and by agreement with the export house, the company took over the export operation by establishing an export department. Most of the overseas representatives were retained.

Hewlett-Packard's export market traditionally had run somewhere between 10% and 11% of their total sales. Due to the nature of the products, export sales were almost entirely to the more advanced countries. The company in 1959 had qualified sales representatives in 21 foreign countries. At that time, 60% of its foreign sales came from Europe, about 20% from Canada, and about 10% were divided between Australia and Japan. The remaining 10% was spread throughout the world.

APPENDIX

THE EUROPEAN ECONOMIC COMMUNITY (THE EUROPEAN COMMON MARKET)

I. GENERAL BACKGROUND

The European Common Market with headquarters in Brussels, went into operation on January 1, 1958. Its six members nation are Belgium, France, W. Germany, Italy, Luxemburg and the Netherlands. The Treaty of Rome, which created this group is both an economic and political instrument and provides a supernational organization to direct the activities of member nations. Of necessity, it sets forth principles and guidelines rather than detailed programs and mechanisms. According to the Treaty, the creation of the Common Market involves:[1]

1. gradual removal of all barriers to trade among the member countries, and the establishment of a common external tariff;
2. working out common policies in respect to agriculture, transportation, and the free movement of workers and capital;
3. drawing up rules to ensure free and equal competition within the community, to prevent distortions owing to national policies; and
4. taking steps to ensure the full use and development of the resources of the member states.

[1] First National City Bank of New York, *The European Common Market*, 1958, p. 7.

The four institutions supervising the common market have been modeled after those of the Coal and Steel Community.

A six-member Council of Ministers is endowed with final authority in coordinating national economic policies. During the early stages, all important decisions of the Council must be unanimous.

A nine-member Commission is to enforce the proper application of the Common Market rules and to make recommendations on key issues. But most of the Commission's major decisions are to be subject to the approval of the Council.

The Court of Justice, which the Common Market shares with the Coal and Steel Community is to adjudicate problems of treaty violation.

Exhibit A-1

Selected Economic Indicators of the EEC Nations and the United States

Country	Population mid-1958 (millions)	Labor Force mid-1957	G.N.P. mid-1958	Industrial Growth Rate 1948–'58 (%)	Average Hourly Wage 1957*
W. Germany	51.1	25.3	$72.4	13.0	$.74
Italy	48.6	20.4	$29.4	9.0	.59
France	44.6	18.9	$60.6	6.2	.89
Netherlands	11.2	4.2	$14.3	3.2	.60
Belgium	9.1	3.6	$11.2	n.a.	.81
Luxembourg	.3	.2	$.4	n.a.	n.a.
Common Market	164.9	72.6	$198.3	—	—
U.S.A.	174.1	70.7	$441.7	3.3	2.35

* Male employees in manufacturing including social charges.

Source: *European Common Market and Free Trade Area*, prepared by Rogers, Slade, and Hill, Consultant Marketing Management problems.

Exhibit A-2

Gross Domestic Fixed Capital Formation as Percent of Gross National Product

Country	Average Capital formation 1950–53	Average Capital formation 1954–57	Capital formation 1958
Belgium	15	16	16
France	16	18	18
W. Germany	19	23	22
Italy	19	21	21
Netherlands	20	23	23

Source: The First National City Bank of New York, *Europe Today*.

Exhibit A-3
Ownership of Consumer Durables

Number of Units per 1,000 Population, 1957

COUNTRY	BELGIUM	FRANCE	WEST GERMANY	ITALY	NETHER-LANDS	U.S.A.
Passenger cars	54	70	36	18	25	315
Motor cycles	23	41	48	43	16	3
Bicycles	325	190	315	145	450	143
Radio sets	249	233	277	131	264	890
Television	28	16	23	14	22	274
Refrigerators	53	49	39	20	10	265
Washing machines	151	56	45	6	104	235

Source: The First National City Bank of New York, *Europe Today*.

The Parliamentary Assembly, also shared with ECSC is to be a forum for debate and is to have advisory powers.

Over the transition period of twelve to fifteen years, all internal customs barriers and quota restrictions within the Community will be eliminated in the following three four-year stages.[2]

Stage 1 (1958–61)

Total internal tariff cuts on each product must be at least 25%; export duties and export quotas must be abolished within the Community; common external tariff to be applied in those cases where existing previous duty no more than 15% higher or lower than common tariff; in other cases the difference to be reduced by 30%. This stage may be prolonged if the Council does not unanimously decide to end it.

Stage 2 (1962–65)

Total internal tariff cuts on each product must be at least 50%; difference between remaining national tariffs and common external tariff to be cut by a further 30%. This stage may only be prolonged by unanimous vote of the Council.

Stage 3 (1966–69)

All internal tariff and quota restrictions on free movement of goods, men, services, and capital to be removed. Common external tariff to be applied. This stage may only be prolonged by unanimous vote of the Council: total transition period may not be prolonged by more than three years, and may even be shortened.

The pace at which the Treaty of Rome will be implemented will depend largely on the devotion to its ideals by the governments of the member nations. But the environment will be important, too. It is easier to do away with various

[2] European Community Information Service, *The Common Market at Work*, 1959, p. 18.

forms of trade restrictions when the economy is booming; however, any recessions may cause member nations to evoke escape clauses. Moreover the abolition of the trade barriers are likely to make the competition keener among the member nations. Although the Treaty provides for the alleviation of severe hardships that may be imposed on some industries, the transition period will present a great challenge to the member nations.

Exhibit A-4

Rate of Change in Productivity, Wage Rate, and Unit Cost
Among the Common Market Nations

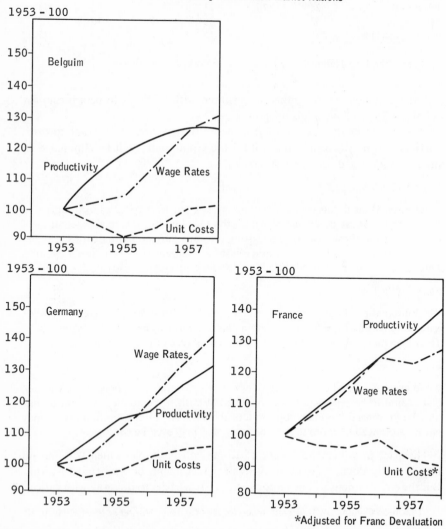

Exhibit A-4   (cont'd)

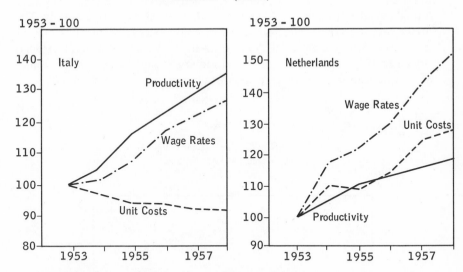

Source: Europe Today: The First National City Bank of New York.

To avoid giving an industry in any member country a relative competitive advantage over its counterparts in the other areas of the EEC because of the existence of inequitable taxes, the tax structures of the Six will have to be aligned. The existence of predominantly excise tax systems in some of the Six and of predominantly corporate tax systems in others will make this task more difficult.

Another great challenge will be meeting the balance of payment difficulties. Because the Treaty leaves the responsibility of coping with currency stability and the international balance of payments to the individual nation, the integration process will be temporarily suspended.

Several advantages are said to exist for an American firm considering entering into the Common Market either through licensing or establishing a manufacturing subsidiary:

1. Low cost of production.

Its primary component is the lower cost of European labor. At present, for example, the average hourly cost per male industrial worker in the common market countries equalled between 22 to 29% (depending on country) of similarly defined cost in the United States. In many cases the cost of primary materials and capital goods is also lower and thus further enhances the cost advantages given by wage differentials.

2. Avoidance of discriminatory tariff.

The establishment of the Common Market as a customs union with common external tariff will result in relatively greater discrimination against outsiders. In the case of the United States exporters to the Common Market countries, this discrimination will be especially pronounced since they tend to be directed more toward W. Germany than toward France and Italy. The former has relatively low tariffs and the common external tariff will represent an increase over present levels. Operating in the Common Market through either licensing or a manufacturing subsidiary is said to restore the ability of an American firm to compete successfully in the Common Market.

Exhibit A-5

World Exports of Common Market Countries
United States and Latin America

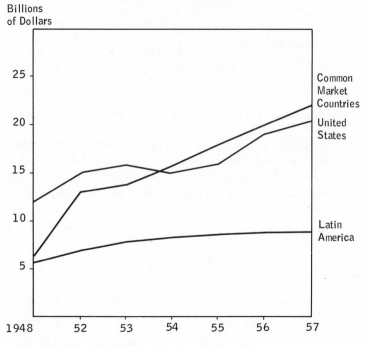

Source: Direction of International Trade – United Nations

3. Unified and expanding mass market.

The breaking down of tariff walls among the members of the Common Market and the setting up of common external tariff rates is creating for the firms within the Market the advantages of some protection from outside competition while at the same time opening to them a mass market exhibiting a tendency toward rapid growth. While both the area and the total population of the Common Market are somewhat smaller than the United States, they nevertheless make the use of mass market production and distribution techniques eminently feasible. Moreover, the market of the Community exhibits

the advantage of vigorous internal expansion. The rapid growth of the economies of member countries and the concurrent fast rise in the standard of
living are intensifying the demand for various products, especially in the field
of consumers' goods in general and consumers' durables in particular.

Exhibit A-6

Electric Component Exports to European Common Market Nations*

1954	Electron Tube	Electron Tube Parts	Inductors	Crystal Diodes Transisters	Capacitors	Resistors
Netherlands	$68,046	$29,481	$23,107	$16,076	$60,852	$17,173
Belgium	236,291	5,886	27,911	38,052	53,719	33,244
France	502,854	40,147	74,145	58,932	112,622	224,539
W. Germany	174,815	64,078	14,463	23,740	32,012	10,856
Italy	287,798	77,784	61,721	6,669	39,995	42,619
	$1,329,804	$217,376	$201,347	$143,469	$299,200	$328,431

$2,519,627

1957						
Netherlands	$74,610	$28,992	$15,429	$154,834	$76,388	$42,644
Belgium	184,045	1,077	128,049	194,806	142,258	51,699
France	446,523	250,248	163,569	723,866	156,391	244,658
W. Germany	321,908	78,307	20,402	153,694	70,361	80,398
Italy	818,928	202,427	547,594	413,104	79,154	152,843
	$1,846,014	$561,051	$875,043	$1,640,304	$531,552	$572,233

$6,026,167

1958						
Netherlands	$40,810	$205,582	$16,310	$672,372	$21,547	$105,122
Belgium	162,793	6,964	37,252	77,609	87,431	64,469
France	359,598	249,709	170,316	1,207,073	203,625	248,179
W. Germany	989,190	128,188	57,508	168,043	37,952	87,421
Italy	298,280	444,610	623,783	708,761	102,361	190,174
	$1,850,671	$1,035,053	$905,169	$2,833,858	$452,916	$695,365

$7,773,032

* Figures not available on Luxembourg.
Source: *Electronics*, May 8, 1959.

4. The Accessibility of Extra-Community Market.

Located in the heart of Europe, provided with a dense network of cheap
inland transportation means, and some of the largest seaports in the world,
the Common Market can offer any manufacturer easy access to outside markets in Europe, Asia, Africa and the United States.

5. Subsidies and Incentives granted by the Member countries of the Community.

Individual member countries have undertaken various measures designed

Exhibit A-7

Government expenditure and Defense expenditure of the Selected European Nations as % of National Income, 1957*

	Bel-gium	Den-mark	France	Ger-many	Italy	Nether-lands	Sweden	U.K.
National Income	100%	100%	100%	100%	100%	100%	100%	100%
Government Expenditure	26.6	19.4	30.4	17.4	24.7	25.8	24.5	32.4
Defense Expenditure	4.9	3.3	7.7	4.6	4.1	5.9	5.1	8.7

* % computed by the case writer. The original information was obtained from: *Statistical Yearbook 1958*, 10th Issue, Statistical Office of the U.N., New York, 1958.

Exhibit A-8

Patterns of U.S. Investment in the Common Market (Millions of dollars)

Types of Investment

Country	Manufacturing			Petroleum		
	1950	1958	% INCREASE	1950	1958	% INCREASE
Belgium–Luxembourg	35	89	154	17	47	176
France	114	270	137	75	179	139
W. Germany	123	315	156	38	164	332
Italy	19	91	379	37	110	197
Netherlands	23	48	109	43	126	193
Total	314	813	159	210	626	198

Country	All Others			Total Investment		
	1950	1958	% INCREASE	1950	1958	% INCREASE
Belgium–Luxembourg	13	27	108	65	163	159
France	28	78	179	217	527	143
W. Germany	43	95	121	204	574	164
Italy	7	63	800	63	204	319
Netherlands	18	51	168	84	225	168
Total	109	314	185	633	1,753	177

Source: First National City Bank of New York, *Europe Today*.

Exhibit A-9

**Return on U.S. Direct Investment in the European Common Market,
1956–1958**
(Earnings as percent of total investment)

| Country | Industry | | | |
	MANUFACTURING	OIL	OTHERS	TOTAL
Belgium–Luxembourg	12	9	20	12
France	10	11	11	11
W. Germany	17	4	19	13
Italy	15	5	11	10
Netherlands	7	6	26	8
Total EEC	13	7	16	11

Source: First National City Bank of New York, *Europe Today*.

to foster their economic development in general and that of their less developed or depressed areas in particular. Some of these measures apply generally to all new investors, domestic or foreign; others have been granted specifically to attract United States capital and apply only to American enterprises.

II. ELECTRONICS MARKET IN THE COMMON MARKET

1. Size of the potential market. Lack of detailed data makes it extremely difficult to estimate the size of electronics market in the Common Market. It has been reported by several sources that the total size of the market is between $16 to 18 billions[3] and a very rough estimate of the total market for types of products manufactured by the Hewlett-Packard is around $80 million, of which over $35 million comes from Germany. It must be recognized that these figures are very rough estimates and no accurate information is available.

The military market accounts for over 50% of the market in the United States; however, relatively small spending in the European countries make this market less significant than its counterpart in the United States. Nevertheless, defense labs, both military and civilian constitute an important segment of the potential market. NATO, France, Great Britain and Sweden, all do some weapon electronics research.

Electronic measuring instruments are used primarily in research and development laboratories of manufacturers of technical products. Civilian industries in communications, radio and T.V. products, as well as many basic industries such as steel, electric power, and others in the process of automating, all have need for measuring instruments. However, it is extremely difficult to quantify these potential demands.

[3] The total U.S. market for electronic products, including defense purchases, has been calculated at about $10 billions.

Exhibit A-10

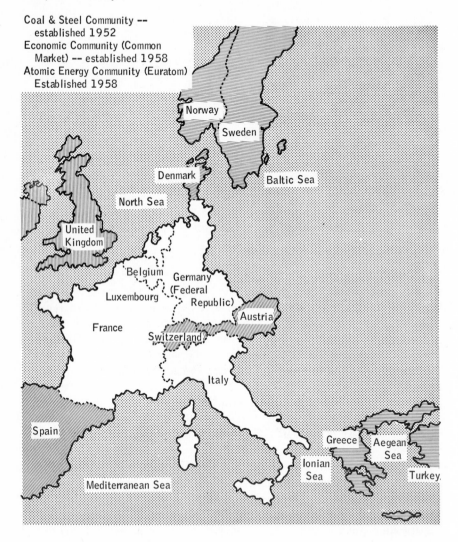

European Community

Coal & Steel Community --
  established 1952
Economic Community (Common
  Market) -- established 1958
Atomic Energy Community (Euratom)
  Established 1958

Norway

Sweden

Denmark

Baltic Sea

North Sea

United
Kingdom

Belgium

Germany
(Federal

Luxembourg

Republic)

Austria

France

Switzerland

Italy

Spain

Greece

Aegean
Sea

Ionian
Sea

Turkey

Mediterranean Sea

Members of the European Community—Also associated with the OEEC and GATT (white area) Belgium, France, Germany (Federal Republic), Italy, Luxembourg, and the Netherlands. Population—170 million area, 449,000 sq. miles.

Other Member Nations of OEEC (light shaded area) Austria, Denmark, Greece, Iceland, Norway, Portugal, Spain, Sweden, Switzerland, Turkey, United Kingdom.

2. Competition. The formation of the Common Market further strengthens the potential market as well as the competitive threat of European manufacturers to American producers in the electronics field. Full establishment of the Community will encourage European producers to specialize and produce on a scale which has previously been impractical because of limited internal markets, and as European manufacturing methods, marketing techniques, and product quality improve, American electronics firms will face competitive conditions in the Common Market more like those in the United States.

West Europe's electronics industry is still small by U.S. standards because of its late start. However, this need for a new start after the War has given attention to new ideas and techniques, so that the industry has kept up with the latest advances in the field despite its limited production volume. In fact, European electronics manufacturers are ahead of their American competitors in some respects.

Electronics firms in Britain, France and the Netherlands have done advanced work in almost all electronics areas, however, the most impressive advances in the past few years have been made by the German electronics industry. Although Germany and France will offer particularly tough competition in the years ahead, it is generally believed that the U.S. mass produced products of advanced types will always find a good European market.

Another source of competition is those U.S. firms operating in the Common Market. Most of the major competitors of the Hewlett-Packard Company have taken active interest in developing the European markets for their products.

STAGES OF BUSINESS
DEVELOPMENT AND GROWTH

* *

1. H & K DISTRIBUTING COMPANY:*
Organizing a New Business

CHARLES A. ANDERSON

and

P. R. JOHNSON

" Jack, sooner or later we are going to have to take the bull by the tail and look our problems right in the face." This was Bill Hazlet's way of telling his partner, Jack Kissock, that it was time to make some basic decisions relating to their new business, the H & K Distributing Company. Jack and Bill formed the H & K Company four months earlier, in June of 1960, to sell a product called the Hill Kat; a rugged motor scooter primarily designed for hunters and fishermen who desired mechanical conveyance into the back country.

The two principals believed that a review of the situation at this time was necessary because both had other businesses to look after, and it was becoming increasingly apparent that the H & K operation was going to require full-time management. Jack and Bill became interested in the cross-country motor scooter concept in 1959 when they became dealers in Butte, Montana, for the Tote Gote which was the first machine of this type on the market. The relationship with the Tote Gote distributor was unsatisfactory, however, with deliveries being slow and suggestions for improving the product receiving little or no attention. The amount of interest in the product evidenced by five sales in the first week that Jack and Bill sold the Tote Gote led them to the conclusion that here was a promising business opportunity. During the spring of 1960, the two decided that they would set up distribution for a similar but improved product if they could find someone to take on the manufacturing.

Mr. Blake West, proprietor of the Nu-Way Packmobile Company, heard of Jack and Bill's plans and contacted them in May, 1960. After initial discussions, West agreed to design and manufacture in Boise, Idaho, a machine to Jack and Bill's specifications. West was well versed in this type of product

* Reprinted from *Stanford Business Cases 1960*, Volume I, with the permission of the publishers, Stanford University Graduate School of Business. Copyright 1960 by the Board of Trustees of the Leland Stanford Junior University.

since at the time he was producing for the U.S. Forest Department a power-driven pack wagon called the Packmobile.

The agreement between Jack and Bill and Blake West was verbal. H & K Distributing Company was to be the exclusive distributor for the Hill Kat and the Packmobile. In effect, West owned the product while Jack and Bill owned the Hill Kat name and good will associated with the name. West retained full ownership of the Packmobile.

On June 10, 1960, Jack and Bill received their first eight Hill Kats; by August 24, they had received sixty-seven. By early September, sales had not materialized as expected and West had built up an inventory of fifty machines. He was at the time considering closing down the manufacturing operation and waiting for the distribution to catch up.

West had on several occasions reiterated his loyalty to Jack and Bill, stating that he was confident in their abilities, and as far as he was concerned his future in this business rested with their efforts to sell the product. Blake had borrowed $15,000 to get the operation started and believed his best chance to pay off this debt was through continuing his close relationship with Jack and Bill.

Bill Hazlet. Bill was born in South Dakota and moved to Butte in 1946. There he went into the linoleum business until 1951, when he moved to Boise, Idaho, to run two drive-in restaurants. In 1955, he tired of the restaurant business and returned to Butte and the linoleum business. Bill met Jack in 1957 and shortly thereafter the two agreed to share a building, Bill to sell floor and wall covering and Jack to sell Youngstown kitchens. There was no partnership agreement and, except for sharing the building, the two operated independently.

Bill was married and had five children. His linoleum business, for which he had a franchise with one of the large manufacturers, had not been overly successful, as shown by the following figures:

Linoleum Sales and Profits

	1957	1958	1959	1960 (est.)
Sales	30,000	35,000	16,000	14,000
Expenses*	27,500	31,500	18,500	17,500
Net Profit	2,500	3,500	(2,500)	(3,500)
(before taxes)				

* Includes a $400 a month salary for Bill.

A six-month strike at The Anaconda Company in Butte, which ended in January, 1960, caused the unusually poor showings in 1959 and 1960. Bill was reluctant, however, to predict any significant improvement in business conditions over the long run.

Jack Kissock. A native of Butte, Jack spent World War II in the Air Force and returned to Montana in 1946. When he was eighteen years old Jack acquired 1100 hours on a turret lathe in a night course at Butte High School. He had since become a journeyman carpenter and pursued this profession until 1951 when he moved from Butte to Lewistown, Montana, to become assistant manger of a lumber yard. He later took over the hardware end of the lumber yard but returned to Butte in 1957 to sell and install prefabricated kitchens. Jack was married and had three children. His wife worked as a registered nurse so he was not entirely dependent on his kitchen business. Jack held a franchise for the line he sold, and, like Bill, had not found the business overly profitable. Sales and profits (or losses) for 1957–1960 are shown:

Kitchen Sales and Profits

	1957	1958	1959	1960 (est.)
Sales	45,000	38,000	30,000	25,000
Expenses*	42,750	38,000	35,000	25,000
Net Profit	2,250	0	(5,000)	0

* Included a salary to Jack of $6,500 in 1957, $5,200 in 1958, and $3,600 in 1959. Jack estimated that he would draw between $3,000 and $4,000 out of the business in 1960.

Jack believed that his business could probably continue to break-even in spite of his activities with H & K Distributing Company. He could continue to make estimates on the weekends and hire a man as needed for installations. Bill faced a different situation in the linoleum business because the lower per job income for linoleum compared to kitchen sales required that he be in a position to make more customer contacts than could be handled on the weekends. Furthermore, a lower margin and a union requirement that Bill hire a full-time installation man added to the problems of managing the linoleum business.

ECONOMIC CONDITIONS IN BUTTE

A depressed economic condition in Butte was the major reason that Jack and Bill were seeking to either supplement their current income or find an entirely new endeavor. Butte was almost wholly dependent on the Anaconda Company which employed 3,500 of the local population. Gradual cutbacks in this company's mining operations at Butte had caused an area population drop from 60,000 in 1920 to 53,000 in 1958. Retail sales in Butte declined 2.6% between 1954 and 1958 while the overall state had increased 6.6% for the same period. Other major cities in Montana showed the following increases between 1954 and 1958:

Anaconda	15.1%
Helena	26.6%
Bozeman	24.3%
Great Falls	27.8%
Billings	12.6%

The sad state of business in Butte was further evidenced by a study in 1958 which showed vacant some 23% of the gross floor area within the city's central business district.

The Butte city council and city-county planning board had called in a firm of planning consultants to devise a master plan for the city's redevelopment, but Jack and Bill were not convinced that appreciable improvement was forthcoming.

THE PRODUCT

The Hill Kat, built similar to a motor scooter, was powered by a 3 h.p., 4 cycle gasoline engine. A belt drive provided the Hill Kat two speeds forward, a top speed of 10 mph, and sufficient power to climb a 45% slope. The machine which weighed about 115 lbs., could carry a 500 lb. load, including the rider. A special feature of the Hill Kat was an airplane balloon tire in the rear. This tire gave positive traction and took up much of the shock over rough spots. Jack and Bill tested the Hill Kat in one of the early Montana snows and found that this tire seemed to float over the surface. Under the same conditions a cleated tire tended to dig in and bury itself in the snow.

No patent application had been filed on the Hill Kat because the machine was apparently unpatentable. Blake West, the manufacturer, had previous experience in applying for patents on his Packmobile and stated that because the Hill Kat was an assembly of commonly manufactured parts, no protection could be had. The only identifiable components used in producing the Hill Kat were its Clinton engine and the oversized rear tire produced by the Goodrich Company. The Clinton Engine Company, with sales exceeding $35,000,000 in 1959, manufactured and sold under the Clinton name, a broad line of general purpose engines, outboard motors, and chain saws. Beyond ordering the needed engines there had been no contact with this company regarding the use of their product in the Hill Kat. The same was true with the Goodrich tire which was manufactured in special lots at the factory.

Bill and Jack believed that the Hill Kat had several distinct advantages over competitive machines. The airplane tire was one of these. The second was the transmission. The Hill Kat achieved its two speeds through a belt drive which eliminated the need for a clutch or gears. The shift had three positions—neutral, low, and high. The operator merely guided the shift lever to the desired speed and this action tightened the belt and started the Hill Kat forward. Jack and Bill reasoned that this system was superior to the centrigual clutch of some competitors because it allowed more pull at low speeds and also provided downhill braking through greater compression. They were also convinced that this type of drive was better than a geared transmission because it avoided the tremendous gear wear that would occur under the constant shifting required in hill climbing and cross-country travel.

MANUFACTURING

Blake West manufactured the Hill Kat in a 37 × 62 foot building located in Boise, Idaho, which was 480 miles from Butte. West estimated that the building was worth $15,000 and the tools and equipment, $5,000. He owned enough land that he could double the present plant should the need arise. Also, a 65 × 134 foot lot adjoining his property was available for purchase.

Manufacturing was primarily an assembly operation with the exception of the frame which had to be cut and welded from bar stock. Four men handled the manufacturing on a semi-assembly line basis. Components for from 10 to 20 Hill Kats were laid out and the workers moved from machine to machine assembling one part or component at a time. Two of the workers were welders, one a cutter-grinder, and the fourth, a general purpose man. The average wage rate for the workers was $2.48 an hour. Two of the men belonged to unions, but the shop itself was not unionized. West was seldom in the factory, spending most of his time with the Forest Service trying to convince them to place a large order for Hill Kats. So far he had been reasonably successful and only two modifications were required before the Hill Kat would meet the necessary specifications set out by the Forestry Department. One was the addition of a front wheel brake and the second was a requirement for some means of immediately disengaging the drive belt under emergency conditions. Without some such clutching arrangement it was necessary for the Hill Kat operator to grasp the shift handle and shift it into the neutral position. This only took seconds, but did require that one hand be taken from the handle bar, thus placing the rider at some disadvantage. West believed that a clutch control could be built into the handle bar grip similar to the existing accelerator mechanism.

Blake West estimated that working one shift with his present help and facilities he could ultimately turn out 25 Hill Kats a week. The top week to date had produced 20, but West did not believe the workers had yet reached the peak of their learning curve. He figured that direct labor and materials for the Hill Kat cost him $160.45. Of this total, $140 represented material costs.

Initially, West had run into trouble securing component parts for the Hill Kat. Most suppliers required that an order be placed two months prior to the expected delivery date. The parts for the first few runs were scrounged from local sources. After two months of production the supply problem had worked out and by the middle of August West was receiving a steady flow of needed parts. He estimated that on the 20th of August he had a $15,000 inventory. This represented finished and semi-finished Hill Kats, approximately 100 engines, and much smaller items as tires, belts, seats, and other components.

Except for $100 a month from other holdings and some rather unpredictable compensation from repairing trailers, West was entirely dependent on Hill Kat sales for his income. Production of the Packmobile, which was for the Forestry Service only, had reached a standstill. West estimated that the fixed costs of keeping his shop open were $200 a month. This figure included a small salary that West paid to his daughter for keeping the company's books, but not his own salary. So far West had not taken any money from the Hill Kat operation.

DISTRIBUTION

When Jack and Bill started out to set up distribution of the Hill Kat, they were uncertain of the approach to take. Several competitors were selling to distributors who went from town to town signing up dealers. Dealerships were supposed to be exclusive, but this policy had not been followed. This was one reason why Bill and Jack gave up their Tote Gote distributorship. After much thought the two decided to begin as sole distributor and see what success they would have in setting up dealers in Montana and neighboring states. If this method worked, Bill and Jack planned to shift their attention to setting up distributors in different parts of the country.

Bill and Jack agreed that one of them would go on the road at all times and the other would tend the kitchen and linoleum businesses. If, for instance, Jack was on the road and someone requested a kitchen estimate, Bill would take as much information as he could and set up an appointment for Jack on the weekend. The names and some of the details about the dealers that had been signed up by August 20 follow (a map of the area is attached as Exhibit 1.):

• *Bitter-Root Cannery, Hamilton, Montana.* Became the first dealer on July 1, 1960, by buying for resale three Hill Kats. No repeat orders had been received as yet. The Forest Service in the area would not allow the dealer to use local trails because of summer fire hazards. The dealer reported that he expected to make some sales in the fall.

• *Montana Lumber and Hardware, Louistown, Montana.* Purchased three Hill Kats on July 9, 1960. Business was combination hardware, sporting goods, and lumber. No repeat sales and no further contact as of August 20.

• *Dick Conklin, Lawyer, White Sulphur Spring, Montana.* Conklin, a jack-of-all-trades salesman, bought one Hill Kat on July 10, 1960, and had ordered two more since. Conklin contacted Jack and Bill regularly.

• *Petrolane Gas, Dillon, Montana.* Became a dealer by buying two Hill Kats on July 11, 1960. No repeat orders. Bill claims that "this one did not pan out." No further business was expected.

- *L. W. Smith Cabinet Shop, Anaconda, Montana.* Bought two Hill Kats on July 13, 1960. Smith had a nervous breakdown shortly after becoming a dealer. Bill intended to sign up someone else in Anaconda.

- *Singer Service Missoula Gas Station, Missoula, Montana.* Bought two Hill Kats on July 14, 1960. No repeat orders. Jack tried to contact dealer but found that "he wasn't there. He had taken his Hill Kat into the hills and hadn't returned yet—this looks like another loser."

- *Jim Burton, Billings, Montana.* Bought one Hill Kat on July 15, 1960. No repeat orders and no further communication.

- *Rug Motor Co., Whitefish, Montana.* Ford motor and farm implement dealer signed up as a Hill Kat dealer on July 27, 1960, and bought 6 Hill Kats at that time. "This one looks like a good prospect," said Jack. "We expect repeat orders soon. They are advertising on the radio. We have had no contact with them since they became dealers."

Exhibit 1

H & K Distributing Company
Dealer Locations

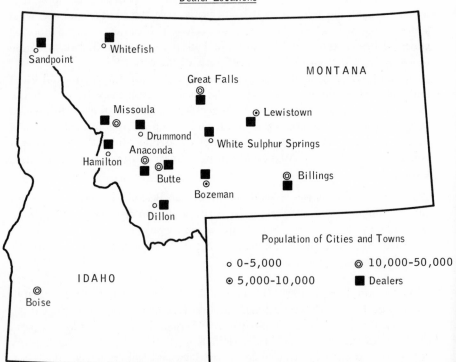

• *Harold King Auto Shop, Bozeman, Montana.* King bought two Hill Kats on August 4. No repeat orders yet, but Bill expected one within the week.

• *Drummond Swedes Bar and Sporting Goods, Drummond, Montana.* Bought two Hill Kats August 16, 1960. ". . . no chance for repeats yet," said Jack, " but I think this will be a good one."

• *Beaners Texaco Service, Sandpoint, Idaho.* Bought two on August 19, 1960. No chance for repeats yet.

• *Electric City Linoleum Co., Great Falls, Montana.* " Bought four on August 20, 1960—looks like a good one."

On August 26, 1960, Jack was in the process of setting up a motorcycle dealer in Helena, Montana, who was handling a competitive machine. " This guy claims," said Jack, " that our product is far superior to other machines. You should see him demonstrate the Hill Kat—he rides it up hills on the rear wheel without ever touching the front wheel on the ground."

Jack and Bill went cold into each city and talked to likely looking prospects. They drove a small German car behind which they pulled a chariot-like trailer which carried three Hill Kat demonstrators. Then ovelty of the rig was a natural for starting conversations and creating interest in the Hill Kat. When a group of people gathered around the car and trailer Jack and Bill would attempt to find out who in town might be potential dealers. They attempted to choose dealers who had facilities available for servicing the Hill Kats after they were sold. Jack liked to recall the way he signed up Drummond Swedes Bar and Sporting Goods as a dealer. While drinking a beer at the bar he got into an argument with an old timer over the virtues of the Hill Kat versus a horse. Soon everybody at the bar became interested and this went on for about half an hour. Finally, the bartender said to Jack, " Pal, you have me convinced—in fact, I'd like to become a dealer for you."

By the end of August neither Bill nor Jack had spent a full week on the road. Initially there were not enough machines to justify setting up a full-scale program for contacting potential dealers and the few days that they did spend on the road indicated that transportation costs were going to run too high. This discovery led to the purchase of the small German car and the construction of the trailer. Based on their experience to date, Jack and Bill estimated that it took one and one-half days to set up a dealer and each day on the road cost about $12.00 in out-of-pocket expense.

"What makes this whole thing look good to me," explained Bill, "is the potential snowballing of sales for us. If we could set up 100 dealers, say, and each sold one Hill Kat a month, we would come out with $4,500 gross margin."

Sales from June 15 to August 24 had been spotty. Figure 1 shows the purchases from the factory, Figure 2 shows the Hill Kat sold at retail through the Butte store, and Figure 3 the Hill Kat sold at wholesale to dealers.

Hill Kats Purchased from Factory[1]
($210.00)

June 10	8
June 28	9
July 9	10
July 17	12
July 21	2
July 26	20
August 24	6
	—
	67

[1] Until July 26, H & K bought *all* Hill Kats produced by factory. Factory was in late August geared to produce 10–20/week although this sales level (particularly repeat orders from dealers) had not yet been reached.

Hill Kats Sold at Retail Through Butte Store
($350.00)

June 18	2
June 24	1
July 1	1
July 15	1
July 22	1
August 1	1
August 3	1
August 4	1
August 24	1
	—
	10

Hill Kats Sold at Wholesale to Dealers
($255.00)

July 1	3
July 9	3
July 10	1
July 11	2
July 13	2
July 14	2
July 15	1
July 27	6
August 4	2
August 6	2
August 19	2
August 20	4
	—
	30

PRICING AND TERMS OF SALE

H & K Distributing Company purchased Hill Kats from the factory delivered in Butte for $210. Their suggested retail price was $350. This price was set after considering the price of competitive machines and comparable features. The H & K price to dealers was $255 delivered.

All sales to dealers were on a cash basis. Jack and Bill did not have the financing to offer credit nor did they particularly desire to in the initial stages of the operation. Blake granted Jack and Bill 10-day terms on purchases from the factory. The original plans required a dealer to buy a beginning nventory of three Hill Kats. In some cases, however, Jack and Bill relaxed the requirement to two machines when they felt the situation justified such action. On one occasion they set up a dealer with one Hill Kat, but required him to pay the retail price. They agreed to rebate the difference between the dealer and retail price when this individual sold three machines.

During the early part of August a party in Sandpoint, Idaho, contacted the H & K Company about becoming a jobber in the territory covering Eastern Washington and Western Idaho. Jack and Bill turned down the request for the time being because this was choice territory and they did not see how they could split the margin they were currently making and come out ahead. The request, however, did raise the questions of just how much of the distribution the two could handle alone and what the next step should be.

Other unsolicited inquiries about the Hill Kat such as the telegram shown below were beginning to come in.

STANFORD MONTANA AUG 23 1960

H & K DISTRIBUTING
1230 HARRISON AVE
BUTTE MONTANA
DEAR SIRS:
I RECENTLY SAW A HILL KAT IN ACTION AND BECAME VERY INTERESTED IN THE POSSIBILITIES OF THIS MACHINE. I OBTAINED YOUR NAME AS DISTRIBUTOR FOR THIS AREA AND WOULD YOU PLEASE SEND ME ANY INFORMATION THAT YOU HAVE AVAILABLE AND ADVISE THE PRICE. I HEAR THAT THERE ARE TWO OR THREE OTHER MACHINES OF THIS TYPE AVAILABLE, THE TOTE GOTE, A SCAMP OR SCAT OR SUCH. IF YOU ARE THE DISTRIBUTOR FOR THESE WOULD YOU PLEASE INCLUDE THE INFORMATION FOR THEM AND ALSO THE PRICES. THANK YOU.

VIVIAN L NUHFER
P O BOX 214
STANFORD MONTANA

COMPETITION

There were several competitive machines on the market—almost all being built and distributed in the states of Utah, Colorado, Wyoming, Idaho, and Washington. The Tote Gote, selling for $325 was the first machine on the market and had achieved the greatest market penetration. An article appearing in the August, 1960, issue of *Sports Afield*, featured the Tote Gote and stated that one distributor had during the past year sold over 400 machines in the state of Colarado alone.

The Blazer, manufactured and sold by a former distributor of the Tote Gote, appeared on the market also during the summer of 1960. This machine, which was priced to sell for $350, was patterned after the Tote Gote except that it had a geared transmission rather than a centrifugal clutch. Jack and Bill believed that the low gear in this machine was too slow (about one-half of Hill Kats) and that the high gear, which allowed a 25 mph top speed, was too fast.

On August 21, 1960, the Yard Marvel Manufacturing Company of Hillyard, Washington, announced a machine called the "Mountaineer". The Mountaineer, about which little was yet known, was priced at $245. A do-it-yourself machine called the Trail Cycle was on the market at a price of $290. Reports indicated that people who bought the do-it-yourself kit had experienced much trouble in keeping the machine operating.

Cushman Motors, a subsidiary of Outboard Marine Corporation, and one of the leading manufacturers of on-highway motor scooters, put out a deluxe mountain climber called the Trailster. The Trailster sold for $350. Jack and Bill did not believe this machine directly competed with the Hill Kat because of its price and weight. The Trailster weighed 252 pounds, compared to 115 for the Hill Kat. This became significant when one considered that the Hill Kat could be carried in the trunk of a car and handled by one person. Moreover, the danger of personal injury while riding over rough terrain increased with the extra weight of the machine.

ADVERTISING

Jack and Bill had made little provision for advertising the Hill Kat except in support of their local retail sales. They did have a number of handouts made which they gave to dealers. Locally they contracted the TV and radio spot advertisements. For $150 they bought 80, one-minute radio spots which featured various situations such as two beatniks talking about the Hill Kat. Also, they contracted for some TV spots which cost $250 and featured a short movie of the Hill Kat climbing a hill. Jack and Bill were disappointed with the service given by the TV station because they were not told when the spots would appear. Furthermore, the movie which was taken from the bottom of a hill did not give the desired illusion of climbing. Jack and Bill had hoped to simulate the Kaiser TV ad, where the jeep is shown surging up to the crest of a hill.

THE FUTURE

Events in the last several months had happened so fast that neither Jack nor Bill had taken the time to consider what was going to happen next. To more or less determine where they were at the end of August, Jack and Bill recapitulated what had taken place since the middle of June. Expenses during the period were:

Service (materials and outside labors)		
on Hill Kats sold at retail		$38.23
Advertising		
500 brochures	$60.60	
Fireman's dance ticket	2.00	
Accrued, to be used within next 60 days		
TV	250.00	
Radio	150.00	462.60
Dealer's license		20.00
Telephone		33.77
Invoices (printing)		14.07
Salary draw		
Jack	180.00	
Bill	150.00	330.00
		$898.67

Jack and Bill estimated that they had so far devoted 100 days to the H & K Company. The breakdown was 40 days of retail selling; 15 days of wholesale selling; 5 days of repairing Hill Kats and testing them; and 40 days of organizational activities (three trips to Boise to talk with West, building a trailer, assembling and adjusting machines).

A trial balance sheet as of August 30, 1960, produced the following:

Trial Balance Sheet

Assets			Liabilities	
Current			Accounts Payable	$2,900*
			Accrued Expenses	360
Cash		$218		
Inventory:			Long Term Debt (Car)	1,400
Hill Kats	4,910			
Demon's (3)	630			
Engines (1)	32			
Parts (Misc.)	25	5,597	Capital	3,640
Total Current		5,815		$8,300
Fixed Assets				
Plant	0			
Tools	20			
Trailer	275			
Car	2,070			
Development Expense	120			
Total Assets	$8,300			

* Owed to factory (10-day terms, but these had been relaxed).

Foremost in the minds of Jack and Bill, as they tried to assess their future, was to consider the type of organization to adopt and to decide what to do with their existing businesses. About this time Mr. Bill Wraith, a young Stanford MBA working for a large corporation in Butte, and one of the early Hill Kat buyers, indicated substantial interest in the operation. He was on friendly terms with Jack and Bill and often they asked him for advice on certain questions. Among other things, Bill Wraith suggested that the Hill Kat end of the business be incorporated. He offered to set up a board of directors to provide policy guidance and indicated that he would head up the board to lend whatever assistance he could in getting the business started. In return, he asked for a 25% share of the newly formed corporation's promotional stock. Bill suggested that "the board should be made up of individuals with legal, engineering, and managerial backgrounds; should meet monthly to review and appraise results and critical problems; and should make firm policy decisions as needed. As compensation, award each director 2% to 5% of the common stock, depending on the time they can spend and/or breadth of abilities they can contribute."

One of Bill Wraith's first suggestions was that Jack and Bill give serious consideration to setting up Hill Kat distribution on the East Coast. During his association with the Hill Kat operation Bill Wraith had interested a close friend and fellow Business School graduate in the product. Tom was moving to the East, where he was assuming responsibilities for running a small-size manufacturing operation. He offered to represent the H & K Company in New England, introducing the Hill Kat to the White and Green Mountain area. Tom Witter's business experience included sales, sales engineering, product management, sales management, and new product management (handling new inventions, patents, warranties).

DEVELOPING ADDITIONAL MARKETS

Among the ideas that were hoped would expand the market for the Hill Kat was introducing the product to the ranchers of the area. There were a number of large cattle ranches in Montana where such a machine could be used for irrigation and other purposes. In fact, Bill Wraith had spent a day "Hill Katting" with Larry Groomes, a rancher friend in Phillipsberg, Montana. Larry's reaction was enthusiastic to the point of indicating interest in becoming a dealer in the area. Phillipsberg was a ranching center and Larry thought he could be successful selling a Hill Kat "do-it-yourself" assembly kit. He indicated that most ranchers had welding and shop equipment and such a kit would appeal to them. Larry also suggested that in connection with using the Hill Kat for irrigating purposes he would like to experiment with a machine that used the airplane tire in the front as well as the rear.

Larry decided that rather than waiting for any product modifications he would take two of the regular machines and demonstrate them to neighboring ranchers. One week later he had taken orders for two Hill Kats and had two more almost sold. During the same week, Larry sketched out drawings for a rack to carry salt and distribute it to remote areas on his ranch and a rack for carrying iron fence posts, wire, and staples. He planned to build prototypes of these racks with his own welding equipment. In a phone conversation with Bill Wraith, Larry commented that his wife and son were constantly riding the Hill Kat. " Gosh, Bill," he said, " I think I'll need two of these for my own use, at least two. . . ."

Jack and Bill explored at some length the possibility of developing a group of Hill Kat accessories that would lend themselves to patent protection. The two reasoned that they could get the jump in a tensely competitive situation if the Hill Kat was the first to offer a trailer for hauling one or two machines behind a car, a side car, a power takeoff, a snow plow, and a track and ski rig for cross-country snow travel. Furthermore, there were related products that could be investigated once the marketing channels were established. Promotion of the Packmobile was considered along with a two-tracked " weasel " type machine (a " Swamp Kat ") that could be used for duck hunting, ice fishing, etc.

Jack and Bill received some bad news in early September when they attempted, at Bill Wraith's suggestion, to register their trade name and learned that the name Hill Kat conflicted with a previously registered name, " Hellcat." The Hellcat, manufactured in Colorado, was a self-propelled vehicle of the cart type that did not compete with the Hill Kat. The attorney that attempted the registration commented: ". . . in trademarks, phonetics are given much consideration and since Hill Kat and Hellcat sound so much alike I am reluctant to encourage your continued use of this trademark. Although the type of self-propelled vehicles are specifically different, the purchasing public is apt to jump to the erroneous conclusion that a motor scooter bearing the name Hill Kat is merely another product put on the market by the makers of the Hellcat."

2. BLOCKS INCORPORATED*[1]

—ROCCO CARZO, Jr.

For its first full year of operations (ending January 31, 1958) Blocks, Incorporated of Philadelphia, Pennsylvania, achieved a sales volume of $156,824, with assets valued at $185,439, and the second year (ending January 31, 1959) produced a sales volume of $353,909, with assets valued at $201,307. Sales for 1959, as forecast by the company management, are expected to exceed $400,000. James Marino, the president, and John Reilly, the secretary-treasurer, stated that their most critical problem was the shortage of funds. This problem has burdened the company since its birth. In fact, Marino and Reilly, the founders, recognized that they entered the business "undercapitalized."

The stated purpose of the founders was "... to manufacture and sell building materials." Their principal operations included the manufacture and sale of concrete and cinder building blocks. A minor but very profitable part of their business was that of middleman for other building materials and builder supplies. Both men had resigned from prominent positions held with one of their largest competitors (as of July, 1959). They formed their own company in order to realize the profits from their own labors and "know-how."

The nature of the business required the bulk of current assets to take the form of receivables and inventories. Furthermore, the high initial investment and obligations in plant and equipment produced a negative working capital position. (See Exhibits 1–2 for comparative statements.) According to the founders, this shortage has inhibited growth and restricted the company's entry into the more lucrative fields, such as builder's supplies and equipment.

The company executives estimated that they needed $100,000 to "get out of the woods." Accordingly, in July, 1959, they were actively negotiating

* Reprinted by permission of Professor Carzo.
[1] All names have been disguised.

with the Small Business Administration for that amount. Several attempts with banks for the $100,000, or fractions thereof, proved unsuccessful because of the negative working capital position and the fact that Blocks, Incorporated did not have enough property to secure notes. All but two of the notes payable shown on the latest financial statements are secured by equipment. The two unsecured notes represent money owed to raw material suppliers.

Mr. Louis Rud, a C.P.A. and a partner of the public accounting firm of Rud, Pal and Company, maintained the company's financial records, prepared financial analyses, and rendered general financial advice to the firm's executives. Mr. Rud, along with Marino and Reilly, prepared and submitted Exhibit 3 as part of the application for loan to the Small Business Administration.

ORGANIZATION AND PERSONNEL

Mr. Marino and Mr. Reilly started discussions on the possibilities of embarking on their own during the early part of 1956. Meetings with various bank officials were discouraging. Bank officers were not willing to authorize loans to a business that did not yet exist—especially where the prospective owners had so little capital resources. Machinery and equipment manufacturers and dealers were willing to accept notes and make leasing arrangements for 30 to 36 months primarily on their high estimation of the character, experience, and ability of Marino and Reilly.

To supplement their capital resources and technical knowledge, Marino and Reilly induced three other men to invest in the business. The company was incorporated January 4, 1957. James Marino and John Reilly each owned 30% of the authorized stock, while the other three stockholders owned the remaining 40%. James Marino, John Reilly and John Smith (one of the minor stockholders) made up the board of directors. The board met once a month. The board left the direction of the company almost exclusively in the hands of Marino and Reilly. A report of operations and conditions was made to stockholders once a year.

On December 17, 1956, contracts were signed with manufacturers for delivery of machinery, equipment, and storage bins. However, it was not until February 17, 1957, that management was able to negotiate a three-year lease with the Pennsylvania Railroad for 15 acres of property adjoining the "road's" main line with a "spur" leading directly to the plant site. The property was obtained at $65 a month. On February 18, 1957, 22,000 yards of dirt was moved so that construction could take place. With the basic building and machinery installed, the company started making blocks April 27, 1957.

Mr. Marino had received his B.S. degree in civil engineering from Penn State University in 1948. Subsequently he had worked for an engineering and construction firm and in 1950 was recalled into the Army to serve during

Exhibit 1

Blocks, Incorporated

Comparative Balance Sheet

Assets

	Jan. 31 1958	June 30 1958	Sept. 30 1958	Nov. 30 1958	Jan. 31 1959	April 30 1959
Current Assets:						
Cash	—	$ 1,424	$ 789	$ 1,214	$ 4,308	$ 972
Accounts Receivable	$23,602	50,546	54,095	50,539	21,324	41,558
Less: Reserve for Discounts	1,181	2,527	2,095	2,404	1,198	1,510
Reserve for Doubtful Accounts	1,575	1,576	1,575	1,576	640	1,346
Net Accounts Receivable	$20,846	$46,443	$50,425	$46,559	$19,486	$38,702
Inventories:						
Supplies	$2,315	$2,935	$2,950	$3,050	$ 3,050	$3,050
Building Materials	1,668	4,488	4,047	5,526	4,862	7,463
Aggregate	3,800	3,177	2,774	4,345	3,482	6,207
Finished Blocks	15,266	20,237	15,477	27,774	25,472	28,138
Total Inventories	$23,049	$30,837	$25,248	$40,665	$36,866	$44,858
Deposits with Public Utilities	650	650	650	755	755	755
Deposit on Block Machine—refundable within 1 year	600	600	600	600	600	600
Prepaid Expenses	8,296	4,420	4,693	4,661	3,890	4,648
Deferred Lease Rental on Block Machine Accessories			9,885	12,253	12,627	12,031
Loans to Employees	483	370	409	113	406	65
Loans to Officers	—	—	—	—	—	839
Total Current Assets	$53,924	$84,744	$92,699	$93,899	$78,938	$103,470
Plant and Equipment:						
Factory Building and Site Improvements	$41,057	$39,580	$40,614	$39,725	$38,836	$37,502
Factory Equipment	52,254	45,142	43,630	43,466	41,702	39,543
Materials Handling Equipment	10,793	7,774	9,926	8,960	8,593	8,043
Delivery Equipment	21,841	28,833	31,698	29,964	28,831	40,403
Office Equipment	310	285	269	260	250	501
Trailer	—	—	—	—	416	379
Net Depreciated Value of Plant and Equipment	$126,255	$121,614	$126,137	$122,375	$118,628	$126,371

	Jan. 31 1958	June 30 1958	Sept. 30 1958	Nov. 30 1958	Jan. 31 1959	April 30 1959
Other Assets:						
Deposit on Block Machine—Refundable after 1 year	$4,738	$4,538	$4,088	$3,450	$3,350	$3,200
Unamortized Portion of Incorporation Costs	522	467	435	413	391	359
Total Other Assets	5,260	5,005	4,523	3,863	3,741	3,559
TOTAL ASSETS	$185,439	$211,363	$223,359	$220,137	$201,307	$233,400

Liabilities and Stockholders' Equity

	Jan. 31 1958	June 30 1958	Sept. 30 1958	Nov. 30 1958	Jan. 31 1959	April 30 1959
Current Liabilities:						
Accounts Payable	$82,274	$109,582	$103,339	$70,872	$67,013	$82,380
Cash Overdraft	2,074	—	—	—	—	—
Notes Payable (Due Within One Year)	26,505	34,708	34,040	42,507	41,455	46,729
Payroll Taxes Payable	557	1,227	1,454	2,099	603	2,834
Penna. Sales Tax Payable	403	2,367	2,261	3,413	2,043	3,907
Accrued Payroll & Expenses	455	1,510	2,049	1,857	2,198	2,937
Loans Payable—Officers	1,921	—	—	—	—	—
Loans and Exchanges	1,813	1,708	8,307	1,729	1,301	500
Reserve for U.S. & Penna. Corporate Taxes	—	—	—	—	—	—
Penna. Capital Stock Tax	115	—	—	—	750	756
Total Current Liabilities	$116,117	$151,104	$151,450	$122,477	$115,369	$140,043
Long Term Liabilities:						
Notes Payable	36,089	32,038	24,120	41,098	34,804	34,867
Loans Payable to Officers	—	2,271	1,486	880	—	—
Total Long Term Liabilities	$36,089	$34,309	$25,606	$41,978	$34,804	$34,867
TOTAL LIABILITIES	$152,206	$185,413	$177,056	$164,455	$150,173	$174,910
Stockholders' Equity:						
Capital Stock	$41,200	$41,200	$41,200	$41,200	$41,200	$41,200
Capital Surplus	—	—	—	—	9,403	9,403
Retained Earnings:						
Balance, beginning of period (Feb. 1)	—	(17,879)	—	(7,966)	(7,966)	531
Net Income (or deficit) for period	(7,967)	2,629	5,103	22,448	8,497	7,356
Balance at end of period	(7,967)	(15,250)	5,103	14,482	531	7,887
TOTAL STOCKHOLDERS' EQUITY	$33,233	$25,950	$46,303	$55,682	$51,134	$58,490
TOTAL LIABILITIES AND STOCKHOLDERS' EQUITY	$185,439	$211,363	$223,359	$220,137	$201,307	$233,400

Exhibit 2
Blocks, Incorporated
Comparative Statement of Income and Expense

	2/4/57 to 1/31/58	2/1/58 to 6/30/58	2/1/58 to 9/30/58	2/1/58 to 11/30/58	2/1/58 to 1/31/59*	2/1/59 to 4/30/59
Income						
Sales	$162,977	$142,704	$258,122	$334,995	$368,600	$83,977
Less: Discounts	6,153	6,827	10,979	13,482	14,691	2,255
Net Sales	$156,824	$135,877	$247,143	$321,513	$353,909	81,722
Blocks			Cost of Goods Sold			
Material:						
Beginning Inventory—Aggregate	—	$3,800	$3,800	$3,800	$3,800	$3,482
Purchases of Aggregate	$78,235	43,948	80,093	106,695	119,768	29,086
Freight In	904	609	696	713	873	205
Total	$79,139	$48,357	$84,589	$111,208	$124,441	$32,773
Less: Ending Inventory—Aggregate	3,800	3,177	2,774	4,344	3,482	6,207
Cost of Materials Used	$75,339	$45,180	$81,815	$106,864	$120,959	$26,566
Labor	19,032	14,048	26,718	34,124	39,393	8,191
Factory Overhead	32,578	28,746	40,923	46,345	55,290	14,157
Total Cost of Production	$126,948	$87,974	$149,456	$187,333	$215,642	$48,914
Total Blocks Produced (#)	760,887	543,825	975,324	1,257,036	1,390,920	319,559
Cost per Block ($)	.1773	.1618	.1532	.1490	.155	.153
Beginning Inventory—Finished Blocks	—	15,266	15,266	15,266	15,266	23,472
Purchases of Blocks	—	437	564	564	487	1,039
Total Cost of Blocks Available for Sale	—	$103,677	$165,286	$203,163	$231,395	$73,425
Less: Ending Inventory—Finished Blocks	15,266	20,237	15,477	14,823	23,472	28,137
Total Cost of Blocks Sold	$111,682	$83,440	$149,809	$188,340	$207,923	$45,288

Building Materials:						
Beginning Inventory	$—	$1,668	$1,668	$1,668	$1,668	$6,862
Purchases	16,691	20,367	37,105	45,371	51,797	10,350
Material Available for Sale	$16,691	$22,035	$38,773	$47,039	$53,465	$17,212
Less: Inventory—Ending	1,668	4,488	4,047	5,526	6,862	7,463
Total Cost of Building Materials Sold	$15,023	$17,547	$34,726	$41,513	$46,603	$9,748
Total Cost of Goods Sold	$126,705	$100,987	$184,535	$229,853	$254,526	$55,036
Gross Income	$30,119	$34,890	$62,608	$91,662	$99,383	$26,686
Delivery Expenses	$22,949	$20,929	$33,559	$47,380	$55,573	$13,912
Selling Expenses	4,585	1,961	3,192	4,301	5,490	896
General and Administrative Expenses:	10,632	7,719	12,428	14,649	17,728	4,296
Total Expenses	$38,166	$30,609	$49,179	$66,330	$78,791	$19,104
Net Operating Income (Loss)	($8,047)	$4,281	$13,428	$25,332	$20,592	$7,581
Other Income	80	78	161	262	1,495	200
Other Expenses	—	$1,729	$2,479	$3,145	$3,822	$426
Net Income (Loss) Before Provision for Officers' Bonus and Corporate Taxes	($7,967)	$2,630	$11,110	$22,449	18,265	—
Less: Provision for Officers' Bonus	—	—	—	—	9,000	—
Net Income Before Provision for Corporate Taxes	—	—	—	—	9,265	—
Provision for U.S. and Pennsylvania Corporate Taxes	—	—	—	—	766	—
Net Income (Loss) Retained in Business	($7,967)	$2,630	$11,110	$22,449	$8,499	$7,355

*Note: 1. No Provision Has Been Made for Federal or State Income Taxes.

2. Depreciation in the Amount of $14,226.02 is Included in Above Statement.

Exhibit 3

Blocks, Incorporated

Projected Statement of Income and Expense

	1959	1960	1961	1962	1963
Income:					
Sales	$400,000.00	$500,000.00	$600,000.00	$700,000.00	$800,000.00
Cost of Goods Sold	270,000.00	330,000.00	380,000.00	455,000.00	520,000.00
Gross Income	$130,000.00	$170,000.00	$220,000.00	$245,000.00	$280,000.00
Expenses:					
Delivery Expenses	55,000.00	65,000.00	78,000.00	84,000.00	88,000.00
Selling Expenses	6,000.00	8,000.00	12,000.00	14,000.00	16,000.00
General and Administrative Expenses	20,000.00	25,000.00	30,000.00	35,000.00	40,000.00
Total Expenses	$81,000.00	$98,000.00	$120,000.00	$133,000.00	$144,000.00
Net Income Before Income Taxes	$49,000.00	$72,000.00	$100,000.00	$112,000.00	$136,000.00
Provision for Taxes	24,000.00	36,000.00	50,000.00	56,000.00	68,000.00
Net Income Retained	$25,000.00	$36,000.00	$50,000.00	$56,000.00	$68,000.00
Funds Available Through Depreciation Reserve	30,000.00	35,000.00	38,000.00	40,000.00	42,000.00
Less: Purchase of New Equipment	20,000.00	15,000.00	25,000.00	25,000.00	30,000.00
	$10,000.000	$20,000.00	$13,000.00	$15,000.00	$12,000.00
Income Available	$35,000.00	$56,000.00	$63,000.00	$71,000.00	$80,000.00

the Korean War. After his release in 1952 and until 1956, he had worked as general manager for Laino Bros., Inc., a manufacturer and seller of building blocks, materials, and supplies, and at the time of the case study, their largest competitor. In this capacity, Mr. Marino had managed practically all operations of the company. However, his primary concern was with production. A large portion of his time was spent in assuring that raw, in process and finished inventories were adequate to service production and sales. Also, he was concerned with production scheduling, which required the proper product-mix in quality, quantity and in time to meet customer demands. Marino supervised the development of work schedules, work assignments, employee recruitment, selection, training, placement and dismissal. Other matters such as pricing, bidding on large commercial jobs, and financial policy was generally reserved for the company owners. Laino Bros., Inc. was the firm where Marino had his first working relationship with Reilly. It was here that both men developed a great respect for each other's ability. James Marino, 38 years old, is married with two children.

John Reilly had to leave high school before graduation and help his widowed mother support their large family: His first big job was with the Reading Shipbuilding and Drydock Company as a crane operator. He held this position from 1937 to 1945. He and his wife successfully operated a grocery and meat retail store from 1946 to 1947. He had earned enough from this venture to purchase and operate a small trucking business. Subsequently, from 1953 to 1956, Reilly had worked as a building materials salesman for Laino Bros., Inc. Mr. Reilly said of this job: "This is where I found myself. I thoroughly enjoyed selling and was very successful. Builders and architects liked me personally—I could talk their language. That's what it takes in this business—selling yourself. Also, of great importance is customer service such as: prompt delivery, settling customer complaints quickly, carrying a builder on the books for several months when he is 'hard-up.' Price and quality are uniform throughout our competitive area." Marino said of Reilly: "He always had Laino Bros. 'sold out' and I firmly believe that it was through his efforts in selling and my efforts in production that Laino Bros. was able to expand so rapidly. This is why we went into business for ourselves—we wanted to enjoy the profits from our own efforts and abilities." John Reilly, 45 years old, is married with three children.

Joseph Pulaski, general foreman in charge of operations, after graduating from high school and holding various jobs, went to work for Laino Bros., Inc. from 1939 to 1941 when he was drafted into the Army. After the war in 1945, he returned to Laino Bros. as a truck driver. Shortly thereafter, he was promoted to yard foreman and worked directly under James Marino after the latter's employment. This relationship continued until 1957, whereby both men resigned from Laino Bros. to give birth to Blocks, Incorporated. Mr. Pulaski, 38 years old, is married with one child.

Characteristic of the building industry, sales for Blocks, Incorporated followed a seasonal pattern rising in the spring, peaking in the summer and fall months followed by significant declines during the winter months of December, January, February and March. Accordingly, a smaller work force is maintained during these slow months. Generally, however, with the one block making machine, approximately 24 employees were needed to operate two eight-hour shifts. Manning for the two shifts were as follows:

Day Shift		Night Shift
NO.	TITLE	NO.
1	General Foreman	
1	Block Machine Operator	1
1	Batch Mixer	1
2	Lift Truck Operators	1
1	Front-end Loader Operator	1
3	Cubers	3
	Watchman and Clean-up	1
7	Truck Drivers	

Marino said "... during the slow months we plan to layoff the six unskilled cubers and two truck drivers. We don't want to take the chance of losing our skilled workers so we keep them on and rotate them between driving equipment and cubing."

To say the very least, the first two and one-half years were hectic for Marino and Reilly. Besides undergoing the original stress and strain of negotiating for the plant site and equipment, the management had a $170,000 plant in operation with 10,000 square feet of floor space—including drying rooms for blocks—and all the latest block making and delivery equipment.

During these early years, their weak financial position forced Reilly and Marino to engage in every aspect of their business. "It seems we did everything" Reilly said, "we helped pour the footers for plant construction. Marino designed and drew the plans for the entire manufacturing plant and office. We had to train our entire work force." A large part of Mr. Marino's and Mr. Reilly's time was devoted to trying to raise additional funds to meet current obligations. Besides this, there were many details that needed constant attention. Both Marino and Reilly answered practically all phone calls. Most of these calls were customer orders. These orders were written on dispatch sheets. Both men dispatched trucks and filled out delivery slips. They typed, prepared envelopes, licked stamps, and mailed invoices. Besides performing such minor but necessary duties, they were constantly "checking jobs" to ensure customer satisfaction, meeting with salesmen, and soliciting new business. Probably their biggest and most embarrassing problem was "holding off the creditors." Much time was spent in negotiating and renegotiating their accounts payable. Both men had been working anywhere from 12 to 16 hours a day.

PLANT AND EQUIPMENT

For a list of plant and equipment and the schedule of depreciation, see Exhibit 4.

Exhibit 4

Schedule of Depreciation as at April 30, 1959
Straight Line Method Used

	Cost	Salvage	Basis	Rate (Months)	Deprec. 2/1–4/30
Trailer	$429.00	$129.00	$300.00	24	$37.50
Building and Leased Ground	29,573.90	3,573.90	26,000.00	300	260.00
Yard Improvements	3,144.23		3,144.23	60	157.21
Steam Room	14,786.94	3,786.94	11,000.00	36	916.67
Steel Racks	8,735.97	1,735.97	7,000.00	36	583.33
Boiler Equipment	1,793.61	293.61	1,500.00	72	83.33
Material Handling Equipment	12,308.05	1,308.05	11,000.00	60	550.00
Batcher and Accessories	24,888.66	2,888.66	22,000.00	84	785.70
Batcher and Accessories 2/1/59	330.05	30.05	300.00	84	10.71
Delivery Equipment	24,156.86	2,156.86	22,000.00	60	1,100.00
Delivery Equipment	13,390.00	1,390.00	12,000.00	60	600.00
Delivery Equipment 4/3	13,472.14	1,472.14	12,000.00	60	200.00
Steel Pallets	12,800.00	2,800.00	10,000.00	36	833.33
Mixer	6,143.46	643.46	5,500.00	84	196.43
Skip Hoist Hopper	3,796.72	596.72	3,200.00	84	114.29
Air Compressor	1,621.73	221.73	1,400.00	60	70.00
Office Equipment	339.58	39.58	300.00	60	15.00
Office Equipment 3/10	275.00	25.00	250.00	60	8.34
Welding Machine	195.92	20.92	175.00	60	7.78

PRODUCTION

According to Marino, the company was strongest in production and sales talent. Counting the time that Marino spent during summers part-time and full time at Laino Bros., plus the experiences of Reilly and Pulaski, the management of Blocks, Incorporated had about 25 years experience in the block business. Marino felt that the work force generally had the necessary skills to permit high productivity. Only three of the firm's employees belonged to a union. They were truck drivers and belonged to a local teamsters union.

Marino and Pulaski described the productive process as follows: One of the most important means of scheduling production of blocks in quantity, type and size, depends on the inventory of blocks in the yard. Both concrete and cinder blocks require a 28-day aging period in the yard to acquire the hardness and quality necessary for construction. The management of Blocks, Incorporated had decided that a minimum reserve of 50,000—3 5/8", 25,000—7 7/8", and 15,000—11 7/8", cinder and concrete blocks were needed at all times. When a particular block inventory reached these levels, production was scheduled to supplement these reserves to meet orders already on the books or promises of orders. Inventories were counted by visual estimation by either Marino or Pulaski.

Raw materials are purchased on open order. Suppliers were instructed to deliver five truck loads of slag (100 ton), four truck loads of cinders (80 yards), three truck loads of sand (36 ton) each day and one freight carload of cement (80 bbls.) every three days when the plant is operating two shifts. When the plant was working one shift, these shipments were reduced by one-half. Cement was delivered by freight car in bulk form to a siding adjacent to the manufacturing plant. From there, it is delivered to bucket elevator by an underground steel worm screw. The bucket elevator carries and dumps the cement to a gravity feed bin for storage and subsequent batching. Sand, slag, and cinders are delivered by truck to a second bucket elevator which carries the raw materials to the same gravity feed bin but a different partitioned section for storage and subsequent batching. When needed, the raw materials (technically called aggregates) were released into a combination weighing material aggregate batcher in proper amounts for mixing. When cinder blocks are being produced, one batch included: 400 lbs. of cement, 500 lbs. of sand, 1,800 lbs. of cinders and 1,400 lbs. of slag. When concrete blocks are being produced one batch included: 400 lbs. of cement, 1,400 lbs. of sand, and 2,900 lbs. of slag. In both cases, water is added until the batcher man determined by "feel" that the texture of the batch was "just right." In both cases, each batch was mixed for approximately five minutes. After mixing, the batch was dumped into an elevator bucket and elevated to a gravity feed storage bin on top of the block making machine. The automatic block making machine was of the latest design and produced a high quality block formed with vibration under pressure of 2,000 pounds. It took from eight to ten minutes to run each batch through the machine. Depending on the mold used, each batch was capable of producing: 115—7 7/8" blocks or 85—11 7/8" blocks or 196—3 5/8" blocks.

One man was required to offbear (or remove from the machine) the " green " (or wet) blocks with an air operated lift. The blocks were set on steel pallets. The air lift was capable of lifting two pallets at a time (see Exhibit 9). Each pallet carried three 7 7/8" blocks or two 11 7/8" blocks or six 3 5/8" blocks. The "green" blocks were then set on steel framed racks. There were 24 pallets to a rack and each rack was capable of holding: 72—7 7/8" blocks, 144—3 5/8" blocks, or 48—11 5/8" blocks. An operator-driven fork-lift truck then took the filled rack of " green " blocks to a steam room where live steam was used to dry and cure the blocks. It took approximately eight hours to dry and cure the blocks properly. There were five steam houses and when the plant was operating two shifts—eight steam houses could be filled a day. After drying and curing, the fork-lift truck operator delivers the racks to an area where the blocks are removed from the racks and stacked into what are called cubes by "cubers." The fork-lift truck operator is then able to lift the cubes by slipping the forward prongs of the fork-lift truck in the holes of the bottom layer of blocks. The cubes were then delivered to the yard for their 28-day storage period.

Loading of delivery trucks was a relatively simple operation. The fork-lift truck operator removed the cubes from their storage area and stacked them in a loading area. An operator would back the delivery truck to the stacked cubes. After inserting lifting bars the width of two cubes, the truck driver set the modern block loader and unloader in motion and lifted and placed the cubes on the flat bed delivery truck. Unloading was done similarly in reverse order.

MARKETING

The automatic block making machine was capable of producing approximately 80 different shapes and sizes of blocks. Basically, however, the bulk of sales had been of the following three core block sizes:

$$7 \ 5/8 \times 15 \ 5/8 \times 7 \ 5/8$$
$$11 \ 5/8 \times 15 \ 5/8 \times 7 \ 5/8$$
$$3 \ 5/8 \times 15 \ 5/8 \times 7 \ 5/8$$

Those products in which Blocks, Incorporated had operated as a distributor between manufacturer and builder included such items as lime, cement, sand, flue line, fire brick, dampers, concrete lintels, anchor bolts, wall ties, and window sash. According to Marino, "we sell everything a building contractor needs for his work—in all about 50 different products." All the products of Blocks, Incorporated were of standard quality. They were able to meet competition in all aspects of the business except in quantity. They were limited by the production of one machine and more so by the amount of delivery equipment. Although the block machine was capable of producing approximately 4,000,000 blocks per year (three eight-hour shifts per day—five days per week), the management was restricted to taking orders for less than 3,000,000 blocks. "We just don't have the working capital," Mr. Marino said. According to Marino "4,000,000 block sales with three-shift operation would require two more block unloading trucks ($16,000 apiece), another fork-lift truck, and $10,000 in cash to support slow turning receivables, i.e., have enough to meet current obligations. There is also the major capital requirement of maintaining a 28-day inventory of blocks." (See Exhibit 5 for monthly production and sales.)

Blocks, Incorporated has not been represented by any extensive sales promotion campaign. Their only advertisement, other than support of community drives, was in the yellow pages of the telephone directory. Most of the business was attributable to personal visits and the reputations of Messrs. Reilly and Marino. Both men had known most of the builders in the area—large and

Exhibit 5

	Production	Sales			
	BLOCKS	BLOCK	BLDG. MAT.	PA. SALES TAX	TOTAL ACCTS. RECEIVABLE
May 1957	72,972				
June	109,084				$5,129.05
July	74,568				24,436.91
Aug.	86,200				21,437.88
Sept.	87,577				18,201.40
Oct	82,356	$16,463.43	$3,033.83	$519.81	20,017.07
Nov.	80,316	18,175.43	3,944.04	570.79	22,690.26
Dec.	82,272	20,384.18	2,744.80	549.93	23,678.91
Jan. 1958	57,635	15,016.02	1,944.57	421.87	17,382.46
Feb.	no	12,029.00	889.84	338.28	13,257.12
March	production	15,825.66	2,086.29	432.29	18,344.24
April	184,299	24,049.06	3,868.18	619.81	28,537.05
May	221,190	35,414.36	7,189.31	1,209.41	43,813.08
June	109,236	33,613.30	6,879.01	1,112.01	41,604.85
July	124,292	32,835.10	6,408.38	1,132.86	40,363.19
Aug.	174,408	29,074.69	5,394.51	1,003.21	35,474.91
Sept.	132,699	35,123.10	6,664.63	1,235.86	43,023.59
Oct.	144,311	27,681.22	5,437.04	977.26	34,098.02
Nov.	136,503	36,525.70	7,270.43	1,301.51	45,097.64
Dec.	102,519	19,809.59	3,464.33	642.74	23,940.66
Jan. 1959	61,463	9,298.02	2,122.10	325.10	11,771.22
Feb.	134,216	14,784.35	1,963.68	445.26	17,193.29
March	129,370	24,395.91	4,245.62	807.20	29,448.73
April	118,436	31,538.48	7,122.70	1,236.82	39,960.79
May	195,672	33,226.77	7,945.24	1,371.98	42,543.99

small—on a personal basis. Mr. Reilly stated that he had obtained large orders by his frequent personal visits with architects. While the architects did not have the power to dictate what building supplier would get the contract for supplies, they could make recommendations which were usually followed by contractors. Reilly believed that personal salesmanship was the most important reason for his success in this endeavor. Big building projects or "commercial jobs" had generally represented about 50% of the company's sales. The remaining 50% was made up of sales that ranged from medium and small home building contractors to "do-it-yourself" consumers. Personal visits were the means employed to solicit orders from contractors. No effort was expended in seeking "do-it-yourself" business. Builders usually purchased on an open-order basis. After making a commitment or signing a contract, a builder would periodically phone his current needs in to the supplier. However, there were many small builders who requested shipment or purchased directly from the yard without any prior order or commitment.

The nature of the business and the uniformity of product quality required that prices be almost identical to that of competitors. There were enough competitors so that no one could dominate or successfully employ monopolistic practices. Builders were generally well informed because of the strong competition that existed among suppliers. The frequent calls of supplier salesmen, literature promulgated by manufacturers and the many national trade publications, provided builders with much information about prices, quality and any new developments that occurred in the industry. In this same manner suppliers were able to keep informed about competitor's prices, products, and general activities. Another characteristic that kept both builders and suppliers knowledgeable was the practice of public bidding required for government and institutional jobs and used by contractors in general.

For market information, the management relied on a number of sources. Much information about new construction was, of course, obtained from the frequent visits with builders and architects. From these visits, Reilly said, "I get many leads and meet many prospective customers." Another important source of information was the Dodge Report, published by the F. W. Dodge Corporation. The reports carry a wealth of information about building activity in an area of interest. The reports include such information as: name of proposed building project, number of units, value of project, the owner, the contractor, whether or not owner or contractor is taking bids, whether any sub-contracts awarded, address of owner and/or contractor, name and address of architect—if any. John Reilly said "I frequently just take a ride and look for excavations and/or building activity. I talk to anybody and everybody that might be a source of information."

The management of Blocks, Incorporated, estimated that their marketing area covers about a thirty-mile radius from their plant location. It includes Philadelphia, Delaware, Chester, and Montgomery counties in Pennsylvania. They do some business in the states of New Jersey and Delaware, but they tried to keep this to a minimum because of the expense involved in delivery.

Located within this marketing area, Marino estimated that there were 15 competitors with a total of 25 block making machines—each machine having an annual capacity of about 4,000,000 blocks. Blocks, Incorporated received its most intensive competition from five companies with a total of

10 block making machines. In this total marketing area, Marino estimated each operating machine was capable of a $500,000 production volume. Accordingly he felt that if each was realizing its full potential (and he believed they were), the market could conservatively be estimated at $150,000,000. Since Blocks, Incorporated only had one block making machine, he estimated that they were getting about 3% of the market.

Terms of sale employed by Blocks, Incorporated were 2/10, n/30. However, many of their accounts exceeded the 30-day limit and most took the discount, regardless of when the account was paid. The management felt obliged to accept these conditions and carry "bad" accounts because of the pressure of competition and their desire to establish good relations with builders.

FINANCE

Mr. Marino stated that he estimated Blocks, Incorporated's rate of sales growth at 30% improvement each year with 30% planned gross profit on total sales. However, he felt this rate of growth was dependent upon the funds available. Both he and Reilly firmly believed that they could sell all the company was able to produce. "Without the necessary delivery and production equipment, our company is restricted to relatively modest growth. With another $100,000, we could very easily realize 30% growth each year. With another $500,000, we could expand into such areas as the production and sale of ready-mix concrete, heavy duty concrete sewer pipe and the 'do-it-yourself' businesses."

Originally the company's financing had been solely through equity capital. Although Marino and Reilly had approached several potential investors about the possibility investment in the new venture, they were able to interest only three others. Mr. Reilly attributed this reluctance on the part of potential investors to several factors. Both he and Marino wanted to restrict ownership to people who they knew very well. Some of those approached were very close friends of the Laino brothers and they did not want to venture into a business that would compete directly with the Laino company. Others were just plainly afraid of the high initial investment required in plant and equipment. "There was just no getting around it, we had to start big," Reilly said.

The two founders and the three other stockholders invested $41,200 in the corporation. The directors authorized and issued 4,120 shares of common voting stock at $10 par value of which Marino and Reilly each owned 30%. After meeting with little success in raising sufficient funds through the sale of stock, the owners attempted debt financing but found that bankers were unwilling to take unsecured notes. The owners decided to go ahead on what they had. The construction of the factory building, the site improvement, and the deposit required for the block machine "ate up all our initial investment," said Marino. Besides this, the company incurred $152,000 in liabilities in order to operate in the first year. "That first year was terrible. We lost nearly $8,000. I didn't get much sleep that year," Reilly said. Subsequently as sales and profits grew, the founders had had several offers for the purchase of stock. However, Marino and Reilly refused. Marino said, "to hell with them! They wouldn't help when we really needed it. Now when we're about to see the light, they want to ride the gravy train. They just fortify our feeling that success is just around the corner."

The block making machine was obtained under a six-year leasing arrangement whereby Blocks, Incorporated was required to make an initial deposit of $5,000, refundable at the rate of $600 each year for five years. Besides the deposit, the company was required to pay one cent on each block produced up to one million blocks, and one-half of a cent on all blocks produced over the one million minimum—computed on a yearly basis. After the six years, the title of the block making machine and accessories would be transferred to Blocks, Incorporated, with the remaining $2,000 on deposit as consideration for the transaction. The accessories to the block making machine were leased by payments to the manufacturer at the rate of $1\frac{1}{2}$ mills per block produced. The block making machine was valued at $55,000 and the accessories at $22,000.

3. SOUTHERN FURNITURE PARTS COMPANY*

—FREDERICK A. BRETT

and

GEORGE E. PASSEY

The Southern Furniture Parts Company produces turned components for tables, chairs, beds, and other articles of furniture. The company was formed in 1947 by Frank Parker, a mechanical engineer, who after several years with a large company had decided he wanted a business of his own. Parker describes his present operation (sales passed the half-million dollar mark for the first time in 1962) as a medium size company in an industry characterized by many small companies.

Competition in the industry is keen and Parker reports that he early decided to emphasize quality at a fair price and to avoid competitive bidding which might result in the lowering of quality. At the outset, Parker employed only four men in addition to himself and had only two lathes in operation. The company prospered from the beginning and additional employees were added until the present work force of 26 men was assembled. Sixteen of these workers could be described as skilled and semi-skilled while the remainder are general laborers.

Supervision is exercised by Parker, his assistant Miss Palmer, and John Biddle, the factory foreman. Miss Palmer has been with the company for a period of thirteen years. Although her responsibilities appear to be of the usual administrative type, she has a thorough knowledge of the manufacturing process and when a new product is being produced can be found in the factory observing the operations. She appears to enjoy excellent rapport with all of the employees.

John Biddle, the factory foreman, has been with the company twelve years. He has worked in this industry for a period of fifteen years and is skilled in every phase of the operation. In the factory he instructs new workers in their responsibilities and when a new product is to be manufactured demonstrates the operations and procedures to be employed.

* Written for the Southern Case Writers' Association. Reprinted by permission of the Association and Professor Brett.

When an order for a new product comes to the factory, the first run appears to be less automated than when repeat orders are received. Miss Palmer indicated that the cost of automating for special jobs would exceed the labor cost for doing them less effectively if repetitive orders are not received. Plans for increasing the efficiency of production should repeat orders be received are germinated at the time the initial order is processed.

The operations performed by the workers in the factory are basically the same in principle, despite the particular product being turned out. Special drillings, and variations required for the particular end product, require versatility on the part of the work team. To this end, the workmen, especially the skilled workmen, are able to perform almost any of the operations in the factory. The majority of operations involve two-man teams and although the same team will at one time operate one piece of equipment and at another time shift to another piece, many of the men adjust very well to other pairings necessitated by labor turnover, illness and the like.

Since the formation of the company, Frank Parker has played a major role in the marketing of his products. Initially he had no assistance, however, in 1949 and 1952 commission salesmen were employed to find new business and service existing customers. In 1962, twelve customers purchased approximately 85% of the factory output. These customers are located in North Carolina, Ohio, Wisconsin, Tennessee, Mississippi, and Alabama. All but three of these customers market well-known nationally branded furniture. Parker reports no credit problems with no uncollectable accounts during the past seven years.

* * *

In June, 1963, backorders were on hand for approximately two months' work. The busiest season was still ahead and Parker found his reputation bringing several new accounts to him as well as an increased volume of orders from existing customers. He reports considering several possible courses of action: (1) continue to accept orders and put his factory on a two-shift basis; (2) refuse some of the less profitable orders and run the risk of losing one or two of his customers; or (3) enlarge the factory to meet the increased demand for his products. No consideration was given to a fourth alternative of raising the prices of his products as this had been tried in 1957 and several of his best customers had canceled their orders. Parker states that as competition is very keen in the industry, slightly higher prices can be charged only for high quality work and that any increase above the charge for quality will result in the canceling of orders.

The disadvantages of the alternative courses of action were voiced by Parker in discussing the situation:

A two-shift operation would require an additional qualified supervisor. Under present conditions, Parker spends from seven until eight each morning outlining the day's activities in the plant. Biddle takes over at eight and runs the plant until Parker returns after lunch. Most of Parker's mornings are taken up with other business matters including the commodity and security markets. If a two-shift operation were instituted, Biddle could handle the second shift but Parker would be tied to the plant from seven until three-thirty each day. Biddle is not enthusiastic about the prospects of supervising the second shift and no other present employee is deemed capable of assuming the duties of plant foreman without at least a year of intensive training. Additional workers would have to be trained and some personnel problems would undoubtedly arise from getting some of the skilled workers to work the night shift.

Refusing some of the less profitable orders and running the risk of losing one or two of his customers has two distinct disadvantages: (1) The present costing techniques make it almost impossible to determine just which orders are the most profitable because the arbitrary allocation of overhead as 100% of Direct Labor costs assumes a balance between processing times for all orders while in reality some orders require twice the labor time as others but may omit several of the processing steps. (2) What appear to be the profitable orders can not be separated by customers as each customer orders from six to fifteen different items from the company. Parker knows that many specialty items ordered are sold below cost but other orders from the same customer are very profitable.

Enlarging the plant would require additional capital investment. Ample funds are available from existing stockholders but Parker is not too sure that as good a return could be earned on the additional investment as is presently earned on the depreciated assets of the plant. If the plant is enlarged, the problem of maintaining a proper balance between the producing facilities used in the manufacturing process becomes of prime importance. Under existing conditions, bottlenecks often occur at the Planer, Moulder, and Dressing Machines (see Manufacturing Process below). Overtime on these machines has been used to eliminate this condition but Parker has found that this action results in bottlenecks at the Cut-off Saw, Rip Saw and Sanding machines. Of the above equipment, all but the Planer and Sanding machines are single unit installations. Thus, enlarging the plant means doubling the productive capacity of most of the processing stations as it is impossible to add small increments of production.

Another problem to be solved if additional equipment is installed is the rearranging of the plant lay-out. Very little floor space is available in the existing building and if more than two or three machines are added to the manufacturing process some of the operations will have to be moved to an adjacent building presently used for storage.

THE MANUFACTURING PROCESS

Operations involve receipt and preparation of the raw materials and the production process itself. Steps 1 through 3 are basically preparation stages while steps 4 through 14 deal principally with the production of the company's products.

1. *Stacking and Sorting of Lumber.* Upon arrival by freight car or truck the lumber is unloaded, sorted, and stacked in accord with its variety. Only Grade #1 common or better is purchased in Sap or Tupelo gum. Loads come in uniform thickness obviating the necessity for sizing. The company buys varying thicknesses from 4/4 to 6/4.[1] If a customer wants products produced from woods other than those which the company usually purchases, the material is specially purchased or on many occasions supplied by the customer. This operation is essentially a two man operation and is carried out by unskilled workers from the general labor pool.

2. *Kiln Drying.* With the lumber stacked on appropriate transfer trucks, it is introduced into a 40M foot capacity kiln. The lumber may remain in the kiln for periods varying from four to thirty days depending upon its condition, the final selected moisture content and the reaction of the particular batch to the drying process. The rate at which the lumber gives up its moisture is of great importance and moisture meters serve as guides for Parker and Biddle in arriving at the drying schedule.

3. *Lumber storage.* Upon removal from the Kiln, the lumber may be moved immediately to the factory for processing or it may be placed in storage. More frequently it is sent to storage in a warehouse maintained at approximately 10 degrees above atmospheric temperature in order to maintain the wood at the level of dryness desirable for the manufacturing process. The lumber remains on the transfer trucks for ease in moving and storing and will only be removed when it reaches the first stage of manufacture.

4. *Cut-off Saw (Station #1).* While the thickness of lumber will vary from 4/4 to 6/4 it is of random width and length. Work orders are issued to the operator of the cut-off saw and his assistant directing them to prepare a specified number of buggies[2] of lumber at specified length. The lengths processed in the factory vary from eighteen inches to six feet. In order to make maximal use of the incoming lumber several orders for different lengths are prepared simultaneously. Economy at this stage of operation is dependent in large part on the skill of the saw operator who can by judicious cutting cut the amount of scrap to a minimum. Short lengths (those less than eighteen inches) are removed by a member of the labor force and used to provide boiler fuel for heat in winter and for operation of the kiln and storage warehouse on a year round basis. Sawdust from this and succeeding operations is removed by an exhaust system and also utilized as fuel.

---

[1] Lumber is described as to thickness by reference to the basic unit of quarters of an inch, thus 4/4 is one inch lumber and 6/4 would be lumber one and one-half inches in thickness.

[2] By definition a buggy of lumber is a closely stacked rectangular solid measuring three feet high and three feet wide, varying in length from one to three unit lengths, depending upon instructions to the cut-off saw operator.

5. *Rip Saw (Station #2)*. Buggies of lumber in appropriate length are moved from Station #1 to the Rip Saw on hand trucks. The rip saw has an automatic feed and the operator and his assistant rip the boards to the widths specified in the work order. Widths usually vary from two to six and one-half inches. The operator of the saw and his assistant are constantly alert to reduce waste and when further ripping of a particular board will leave an essentially unusable piece of lumber it may be stacked for use on a subsequent order. Unusable scraps are sent to the fuel pile. Scraps which are too narrow to be of direct use are piled on special buggies and moved directly to the Gluing Process (Station #5) where laminates are produced and returned to the Rip Saw. Lumber ripped to the specified widths is then dispatched to the Planer (Station #3).

6. *Planer (Station #3)*. The Planer operation reduces the lumber to uniform thickness and planes it on one side. The machine is operated by two men; one places the pieces in the automatic feed, the second retrieves the pieces as they come from the machine and inspects them for defects such as knot holes. excessive warping and the like. Those which in the opinion of the inspector can be reduced in length or width and become usable on other orders will be returned to the Cut-off Saw or the Rip Saw. Those possessing defects which make them completely unusable are piled for removal to the fuel pile by the labor gang.

7. *Moulder (Station #4)*. Station #4, which is physically located a good distance from Station #3 involves again a two man operation. This machine dresses the lumber on both sides, further reducing thickness to the final desired thickness specified in the work order. A given initial thickness in lumber is always reduced to the same final thickness so that the number of settings required on this machine is minimal. Dressed lumber is piled on buggies as it comes from the Moulder and the buggies are then dispatched to the gluing presses, which are in the region of the Rip Saw.

8. *Gluing Presses (Station #5)*. Two rapid drying gluing presses are employed in this operation. Each press requires two men for operation. One of the men selects the material delivered from the Moulder for gluing and applies the glue. Pieces of wood with imperfections on the edges are suitable for outside positions on the cubes and are so placed by this worker. After the glue has been applied and the pieces stacked they are placed in the press by the second worker. The squares upon removal from the press are dispatched to the Dressing Machine (Station #6). A second operation, already noted under (5) involves the production of laminates from scraps brought from the Rip Saw. These scraps are laminated into boards about three feet in width and upon removal from the press are sent back to the Rip Saw from whence they will follow the sequence previously described.

9. *Dressing Machine (Station #6)*. The dressing machine dresses the squares on all four sides and produces squares of the proper dimension for the turning operation. This is again a two-man operation with the workman

who removes the finished pieces from the machine charged with a visual inspection to remove defective pieces before delivery to the Lathes for turning.

10. *Machining* (*Stations #7a through #7e*). Dressed squares are delivered to the machining station for processing on one or more of five lathes. The majority of forming operations in the plant, and all for the squares is accomplished on the lathes, even to the shaping of squared table legs on a special lathe with cam offset for its cutting tools. This operation is a one man process and is especially rapid. Although there are as many as 30 cutting tools in contact with a square on a single lathe, the squares are actually rotated as few as twenty to thirty times. Following the turning process the pieces are replaced on a buggy for delivery to the Sander (Station #8).

Two men who do not enter directly into the production process are required to set up the lathes for production and maintain the cutting tools in operating condition. The cutters are set up on fixed or rotating drive shafts which provide for the appropriate cuts. Initially, cutting assemblies are set up against profile templates made from blueprints. Most of the cutting assemblies are maintained intact for ready attachment to the lathes for repeat orders.

11. *Sander* (*Station #8*). Pieces delivered from the machining process are placed in the automatic sanding machine by a single operator who is also charged with inspecting the pieces. Defective pieces are sent, if judged repairable, to a bench where they are filled or otherwise repaired, and again returned to the sander. If judged beyond repair they are picked up by the labor gang for use as fuel. Pieces complete with this stage of work are sent immediately to the Packing and Shipping Department (Station #11). Items that must be fluted or drilled are sent to the appropriate station.

12. *Drilling Machine* (*Station #9*). About 10% of the products produced require drilling of holes for dowel pins or bolts before they are ready for shipping. Semi-automatic machinery capable of producing holes or slots and usually operated by a single worker are employed. Upon completion of this operation, items ready for shipping are sent to the Packing and Shipping Department (Station #11).

13. *Fluting Machine* (*Station #10*). About 25% of the furniture parts produced require fluting which is produced by mounting the piece on centers and utilizing a shaper with template. An index wheel is utilized to effect the proper degree of rotation between flutes. This is a one man operation. Following this process finished pieces are sent to the Packing and Shipping Department (Station #11).

14. *Packing and Shipping Department* (*Station #11*). Packing and shipping which includes a final inspection is a two-man operation. Two men who are brothers work as a team in this task. Most of the large items are shipped directly on buggies without further packaging. Smaller items are packed in cardboard boxes. A count is made of all finished items during the packing process. All orders have a five per cent over-or-under allowance. An initial

input of material at Station #1 is set at 320% of expected output[3] in order to meet the 5% overrun. Often this overrun is exceeded. The overruns in excess of 5% are stored against future orders for similar items and this inventory is used to adjust the initial input. If the items are not required again or if there are no repeat orders for the item, the pieces will be picked up by the labor gang for fuel. Because so much of the business in the plant involves repeat orders, storage space becomes acutely short on numerous occasions.

MANUFACTURING COSTS

Cost of materials makes up 60% of the cost of production. Direct Labor represents 20% of total cost and overhead is applied at 100% of the Direct Labor Cost. This overhead rate has not been adjusted since 1952. Frank Parker reports that although no attempt is made to cost each order, the total manufacturing expenses have been within ±2% of the Direct Labor Cost when an overall check is made at the end of each operating year.

The labor force, which as previously indicated numbers about 26 in total, is composed of about 16 workers who have been with the company more than five years. These 16 workers are the skilled and semi-skilled production workers. The remaining workers who belong to the general labor gang have employment records which range from 6 weeks to 7 years. Opportunity for advancement and increase in wages is rarely offered this group of laborers. The average age of the work force is about 30 years.

Both direct and indirect labor wage rates range from $1.15 to $1.67 per hour.[4] No incentive plan is in force. No attempt has been made to unionize the plant.

PRICING

Frank Parker or his assistant Miss Palmer assume responsibility for pricing on all orders. Prices are arrived at on a cost plus basis with a good deal of weight given to previous pricing of similar orders and experience under the previously quoted prices. A 6% profit figure is hoped for on each order. Some consideration is given to competitive pricing, but as previously noted the objective is to produce a superior product at a fair price even though the price happens to be a bit higher than the going market.

SCHEDULING AND ROUTING

Scheduling and routing instructions are given to the production workers at each station in terms of dimension specification, number of buggies required and the number of unit lengths per buggy. Machining instructions specify

---

[3] Finished furniture parts represent at best 40% of the input material. About 20% is converted to sawdust and 40 to 50% scrapped. Fuel recovery affords some economy with regard to lumber costs.

[4] Workers are considered part of the lumber industry which is one of the lowest paying industries in the United States.

the code number of the cutting assemblies if the order is a repeat order. In the event that the order is a new one, detailed instructions are given the set-up man who works rather closely with the lathe operator in the early stages of the machining process.

The scheduling and routing instructions are prepared by Parker in consultation with his foreman, John Biddle and Miss Palmer. Every attempt is made to process compatible orders together.

CORPORATE STRUCTURE

Parker started the company as a sole proprietorship in 1947, but in 1952 it was incorporated as a Delaware corporation. All stock in the company is retained by the Parker family. The board of directors is composed of Parker, his wife and his brother. Parker serves as president of the company as well as chief executive officer of the corporation.

FINANCIAL DATA

The company has no outstanding debt. Plant and equipment are depreciated on a ten year straight line basis. Over the past ten years the net profit has averaged 7% of gross sales. The range has been from 4% to 16% in 1957 and 1962 respectively.

Parker is well-satisfied with the profitability of the company and as the stockholders are satisfied with the dividends received on their investment, Parker is hesitant about changing his present operations. As Parker states it, "I wish business wasn't so good. I make all the money I need and am not anxious to take the risks of trying to make more!"

4. THE INSULATED WIRE AND CABLE CORPORATION*

—ERICH A. HELFERT AND

and

C. ROLAND CHRISTENSEN

"I don't see a growing future ahead in the telephone-wire business for a company like ours," remarked James Humphrey, president of The Insulated Wire and Cable Corporation, Philadephia. In 1956 more than 50% of Insulated's dollar volume came from independent telephone companies, to which it sold through distributors. Eight other lines accounted for the balance of sales. In the first five months of 1957, company income declined from the peak level attained during the previous year. During the same period, according to the National Electrical Manufacturers Association, industry sales were down 15%. (For financial data, see Exhibits 1 and 2. For comparative figures, see Industry Note.)

HISTORY

In 1938 a majority interest in Insulated stock had been purchased by Mr. Horace T. Humphrey, father of the current president. The elder Mr. Humphrey, who became chairman of the board, supervised several other businesses, among them a small firm making parts and supplies for telephone and power companies.

Although Insulated had prospered on the growing telephone market since its founding at the turn of the century, its financial and physical condition was poor after eight years of depression. Machinery had not been replaced, though the company had paid dividends of over $1 million a year during the 1920's.

In the first four years of Mr. Horace Humphrey's control, earnings were plowed back to improve the plant. With the declaration of war, however, all development of civilian products was dropped with what Mr. James

Humphrey described as "patriotic disregard for the future." The company won many awards and commendations for its part in the war effort.

After the war, research and development were re-emphasized. The company in 1944 had secured the services of a chemist and expert in extruded rubber-insulated wire. Elmer F. Lindgren; as works manager and head of the laboratory, he introduced a new continuous process and led the development of a series of telephone wires and cables insulated with synthetic rubber for increased durability.

The Korean conflict spurred volume during 1950, and in 1952 Mr. James Humphrey, who had become president in 1947, succeeded in borrowing $1,200,000 to initiate an expansion program. Within two years, plant space was almost doubled. The largest single investment, however, was about $450,000 for 11 continuous vulcanizing machines for rubber insulation. "We filled the plant with the latest machinery," commented Mr. Humphrey.

In the postwar period, several new product lines were added. Sales of telephone cable started in 1954. Electronic connectors and heavy-duty lighting cords were added in 1955, the latter being a patented portable cord, equipped with distribution plugs, connectors, and light bulb sockets, designed for use in ship repair work, oil well drilling, and in mines. This line was distributed through a wholly-owned subsidiary. Another subsidiary, acquired in 1956, put the company into the manufacture of printed electronic circuits. A third partly-owned subsidiary distributed Spira-Flex, a patented retractile cord set manufactured by Insulated and designed for use on telephones, taxicab microphones, and industrial machinery—e.g., where a dangling straight cord might annoy or endanger the user. This line was the company's second largest seller. (See Exhibit 3 for company sales by product lines, and Exhibit 4 for the ownership structure of subsidiaries.)

CURRENT PROBLEMS

In explaining his concern about the future telephone market. Mr. James Humphrey pointed to the dwindling number of companies in this field. He feared that the fast-growing General Telephone Corporation would absorb many of the independents. Since General Telephone had in 1956 acquired a 15% interest in General Cable Corporation (one of Insulated's competitors), Humphrey assumed this supplier would probably receive most of General Telephone's business. Most of the Bell System's requirements were supplied by its subsidiary, the Western Electric Company.

For many years in the past, Mr. Humphrey said, the independent telephone market had purchased up to 25% of its wire and cable needs from Insulated. He believed his product had an excellent reputation for quality and dependability in the communications field.

Another current problem, according to Mr. Humphrey, was Insulated's distribution policy. "Our concept of distribution is in a state of flux," he said. Until 1950 the company had relied on one national distributor, the Nation-

Exhibit 1

The Insulated Wire and Cable Corporation
Balance Sheets 1945 to 1956 (December 31)
(thousands of dollars)

Assets	1945	1946	1947	1948	1949	1950	1951	1952	1953	1954	1955	1956	5 Months Ended May 31, 1957
Cash	$199	$374	$752	$266	$153	$792	$1,085	$1,230	$799	$456	$281	$1,070	$1,430
Accounts and notes receivables	845	560	389	305	302	553	1,078	893	704	634	980	1,464	1,449
Inventories	634	1,026	835	794	1,022	1,241	1,766	2,086	1,707	2,269	2,808	3,056	2,181
Total Current Assets	$1,678	$1,960	$1,976	$1,365	$1,477	$2,586	$3,929	$4,209	$3,210	$3,359	$4,069	$5,590	$5,060
Noncurrent investments and receivables	$30	$25	$86	$99	$95	$95	$104	$106	$113	$119	$121	$130	$158
Plant and equipment	1,431	1,456	1,660	2,133	2,223	2,383	2,921	3,360	4,074	4,855	5,159	5,347	5,425
Less: reserve for depreciation	564	600	676	783	900	1,015	1,181	1,373	1,569	1,850	2,170	2,606	2,744
	$867	$856	$984	$1,350	$1,323	$1,368	$1,740	$1,987	$2,505	$3,005	$2,989	$2,741	$2,681
Deferred charges	30	34	53	44	41	55	55	63	76	84	75	109	73
Patents, at cost, less amortization	—	—	—	—	—	—	—	—	31	31	31	30	29
Total Assets	$2,605	$2,875	$3,099	$2,858	$2,936	$4,104	$5,828	$6,365	$5,935	$6,598	$7,285	$8,600	$8,001

Liabilities													
Bank loans (due within one year)	$301	$362	$338	$231	$100	$100	$100	$—	$—	$—	$—	$—	$—
Accounts payable	408	624	1,036	716	655	804	549	535	240	239	259	411	361
Employees' profit-sharing plan	—	430	—	—									
Federal taxes on income	982	997	336	178	676	1,251	1,285	562	115	89	245	219	348
Accrued liabilities	398	438	331	230	235	291	253	168	125	96	112	129	106
Total Current Liabilities	$2,089	$2,851	$2,041	$1,355	$1,666	$2,446	$2,187	$1,265	$480	$424	$616	$759	$815
Bank loans (due after one year)	$598	$681	$1,294	$1,444	$475	$275	$375	$—	$—	$—	$—	$—	$—
Reserves for inventory adjustment	—	—	—	—	1	1	—	5	—	—	—	—	—
Stockholders' investment:													
Common stock, par value $5	1,314	1,309	1,275	1,265	1,250	1,250	1,250	1,250	1,250	1,250	1,250	625	625
Capital surplus	97	94	25	14									
Earned surplus	3,911	3,665	2,650	2,520	2,544	2,393	2,016	1,584	1,206	1,184	1,233	1,491	1,165
Total stockholders' In.	$5,322	$5,068	$3,950	$3,799	$3,794	$3,643	$3,266	$2,834	$2,456	$2,434	$2,483	$2,116	$1,790
Total Liabilities	$8,001	$8,600	$7,285	$6,598	$5,935	$6,365	$5,828	$4,104	$2,936	$2,858	$3,099	$2,875	$2,605
Working capital	$2,971	$2,739	$2,028	$2,004	$1,544	$1,763	$1,742	$1,321	$997	$941	$1,360	$1,201	$863
Current ratio	2.42	1.96	1.99	2.48	1.93	1.72	1.80	2.04	3.08	3.22	3.21	2.58	2.06
Acid test	1.38	.89	.62	.80	.90	.87	.99	1.06	.95	1.35	1.85	1.23	1.28
Percent return on stockholders' investment	12.8*	24.9	7.2	5.0	10.1	15.5	19.8	18.1	2.2	0.5	22.4	18.0	6.2

* Annual basis.
Source: Company records.

Exhibit 2

The Insulated Wire and Cable Corporation
Income Statements 1945 to 1956
(thousands of dollars)

	5 Months Ended May 31, 1957	1956	1955	1954	1953	1952	1951	1950	1949	1948	1947	1946	1945
Net sales	$7,092	$19,444	$15,234	$10,084	$13,036	$13,141	$11,956	$8,659	$5,574	$5,705	$7,803	$6,155	$7,945
Materials	3,682	10,233	8,607	5,235	6,405	6,800	6,304	4,533	3,096	5,126	6,335	5,090	7,005
Labor	879	2,135	1,814	1,175	1,512	1,330	1,185	1,014	711				
Overhead	1,244	2,625	3,055	2,234	2,909	2,164	1,779	1,594	1,143				
Depreciation	180	361	325	304	250	215	169	120	116	103	91	78	216
Total cost of goods sold	$5,985	$15,354	$13,801	$8,948	$11,076	$10,509	$9,437	$7,261	$5,066	$5,229	$6,426	$5,168	$7,221
Gross Profit	$1,107	$4,090	$1,433	$1,136	$1,960	$2,632	$2,519	$1,398	$508	$476	$1,377	$987	$724
Selling, admin. and general expense	$258	$895	$834	$759	$746	$765	$593	$454	$438	$464	$485	$419	$407
Miscellaneous charges	187	159	71	61	50	37	23						
Contribution to profit sharing	44	450			121								
	$489	$1,504	$905	$820	$917	$802	$616	$454	$438	$464	$485	$419	$407
Operating income	$618	$2,586	$528	$316	$1,043	$1,830	$1,903	$944	$70	$12	$892	$568	$317
Dividend and other income	41	28	31	41	19	30	28	41	13	5	4	40	10
Net income before federal tax	$659	$2,614	$559	$357	$1,062	$1,860	$1,931	$985	$83	$17	$896	$608	$327
Federal income tax	363	1,354	275	166	679	1,295	1,285	471	28	5	341	227	216
Net income	$296	$1,260	$284	$191	$383	$565	$646	$514	$55	$12	$555	$381	$111
Cash dividends paid	$—	$128	$153	$190	$188	$188	$225	$138	$38	$75	$188	$63	$38
Stock dividends paid	—	88	—	—	—	—	—	—	—	—	625	—	—

	%	%	%	%	%	%	%	%	%	%	%	%	%
Net sales	100.0	100.0	100.0	100.0	100.0	100.0	100.0	100.0	100.0	100.0	100.0	100.0	100.0
Materials	51.8	52.6	56.5	51.9	49.2	51.8	52.7	52.4	55.5	89.9	81.2	82.7	88.2
Labor	12.5	11.0	11.9	11.7	11.6	10.1	9.9	11.7	12.8				
Overhead	17.3	13.5	20.1	22.2	22.3	16.5	14.9	18.4	20.5				
Depreciation	2.7	1.9	2.1	3.0	1.9	1.6	1.4	1.4	2.1	1.8	1.2	1.3	2.7
Total cost of goods sold	84.4	79.0	90.6	88.8	85.0	80.0	78.9	83.9	90.9	91.7	82.4	84.0	90.9
Gross profit	15.6	21.0	9.4	11.2	15.0	20.0	21.1	16.1	9.1	8.3	17.6	16.0	9.1
Selling, admin. and general expense	3.6	4.6	5.5	7.5	5.7	5.8	5.0	5.2	7.8	8.1	6.2	6.8	5.1
Miscellaneous charges	2.6	0.8	0.4	0.6	0.4	0.3	0.2						
Contribution to profit sharing	.7	2.3			0.9								
	6.9	7.7	5.9	8.1	7.0	6.1	5.2	5.2	7.8	8.1	6.2	6.8	5.1
Operating income	8.7	13.3	3.5	3.1	8.0	13.9	15.9	10.9	1.3	0.2	11.4	9.2	4.0
Dividend and other income	.6	0.1	0.2	0.4	0.1	0.2	0.2	0.5	0.2	0.1	0.1	0.7	0.1
Net income before federal tax	9.3	13.4	3.7	3.5	8.1	14.1	16.1	11.4	1.5	0.3	11.5	9.9	4.1
Federal income tax	5.1	6.9	1.8	1.6	5.2	9.8	10.7	5.5	0.5	0.1	4.4	3.7	2.7
Net income	4.2	6.5	1.9	1.9	2.9	4.3	5.4	5.9	1.0	0.2	7.1	6.2	1.4
Cash dividends paid	—	0.7	1.9	1.9	1.4	1.4	1.9	1.6	0.7	1.3	2.4	1.0	0.5
Stock dividends paid		0.5	1.0	—	—	—	—	—	—	—	8.0	—	—

Source: Company Records

Exhibit 3

The Insulated Wire and Cable Corporation

Sales and Gross Margin by Type of Product, Sales by Type of Distribution and Inventory Analysis
(thousands of dollars)

TYPE OF PRODUCT	3 Months Ended March 31, 1957	1956	1955	1954	1953	1952	1951	1950	1949
Telephone wire and cable	$2,480	$10,390	$8,304	$5,250*	$4,180	$4,100	$4,701	$4,346	$2,822
Flexible cords and wire	284	1,293	1,390	1,754	2,927	2,012	2,259	1,674	1,113
Power cable	45	—	—	—	—	—	—	—	—
Broadcasting cords and wire	94	474	360	276	405	749	343	354	134
Cord sets for telephones, appliances, etc.	357	1,160	1,635	1,639	2,518 }	1,892	2,036	2,040	1,247
Spira-Flex	979	4,461	1,625	496	621	4,388	2,617	245	258
Miscellaneous wire and cable	186	1,091	1,564	669	2,385				
Heavy duty cords	88	435	280	—					
Electronics connectors	38	140	76	—					
Total sales	$4,551	$19,444	$15,234	$10,084	$13,036	$13,141	$11,956	$8,659	$5,574

TYPE OF PRODUCT	%	%	%	%	%	%	%	%	%
Telephone wire and cable	54.5	53.5	54.5	52.1	32.1	31.2	39.3	50.2	50.6
Flexible cords and wire	6.2	6.7	9.1	17.4	22.4	15.3	18.9	19.3	20.0
Power cable	1.0	—	—	—	—	—	—	—	—
Broadcasting cords and wire	2.1	2.4	2.4	2.7	3.1	5.7	2.9	4.1	2.4
Cord sets for telephones, appliances, etc.	7.8	6.5	10.8	16.3	19.3 }	14.4	17.0	23.6	22.4
Spira-Flex	21.5	22.4	10.6	4.9	4.8	33.4	21.9	2.8	4.6
Miscellaneous wire and cable	4.2	5.6	10.3	6.6	18.3				
Heavy duty cords	1.9	2.2	1.8	—					
Electronics connectors	.8	0.7	0.5	—					
Total sales	100.0	100.0	100.0	100.0	100.0	100.0	100.0	100.0	100.0

*Sales of telephone cable started.

458

GROSS MARGIN BY TYPE OF PRODUCT (MAY 1957)

Product	Gross margin
Telephone wire and cable	15.9%
Flexible cords and wire	24.9
Broadcasting cords	22.4
Cord sets and Spira-Flex	7.7
Miscellaneous wire and cable	9.3
Heavy duty cords	1.1
Electronics connectors	−52.6

(No power cable made in May, the first order having been experimental)

Sales by Type of Distribution

	March 1957	March 1956
Nationwide Electric Company	29.7%	32.6%
Other distributors	26.0	27.9
Missionary salesmen (for distributors' accounts)	21.0	10.5
Direct sales		
Spira-Flex	21.5	22.3
Government	1.8	6.7
Total	100.0%	100.0

	$	%	$	%	$	%	$	%	$	%
	$934	52.9	$645	51.9	$453	44.3	$1,010	46.4	$767	44.9
	482	27.3	355	28.6	228	22.3	576	28.7	387	22.7
	350	19.8	241	19.5	341	33.4	500	24.9	553	32.4
Total	$1,766	100.0	$1,241	100.0	$1,022	100.0	$2,086	100.0	$1,707	100.0

INVENTORY ANALYSIS

	$	$	$	$
Raw materials	$549	$867	$1,396	$936
Work in process	406	636	805	621
Finished goods	1,226	1,553	607	712
Total	$2,181	$3,056	$2,808	$2,269

	%	%	%	%
Raw materials	25.2	28.4	49.8	41.2
Work in process	18.6	20.4	28.6	27.4
Finished goods	56.2	51.2	21.6	31.4
Total	100.0	100.0	100.0	100.0

Note: Sales by Electro-Print, Inc., not consolidated.
Source: Company records.

The Insulated Wire and Cable Corporation
Subsidiaries and Ownership

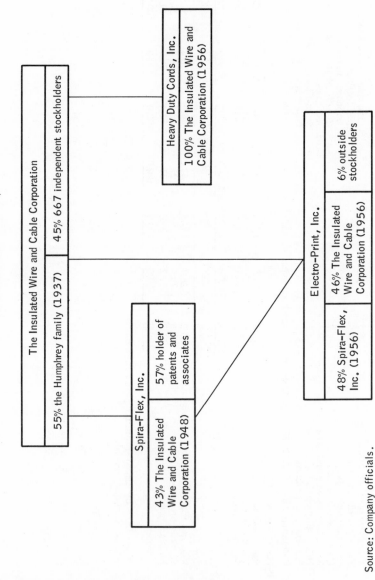

Source: Company officials.

Exhibit 4

460

wide Electric Company, to sell most of its products. "We had no sales control, and our sales department was occupied mainly with sales correspondence," Mr. Humphrey added. With sales and profits lagging, Insulated canceled Nationwide's exclusive contract, obtained three additional national distributors and about 60 independent local electrical distributors. The company also built up a "missionary" sales force of about 20 men. "We feel a lot safer with a field organization of our own, since we are in competition for the distributor's time and effort with 300 or more 'noncompetitive' manufacturers who supply his other products."

In discussing distributors, Mr. Humphrey said he believed their position in the industry might possibly be threatened by a trend toward direct selling. Depending on their product lines, some manufacturers had swung to this method almost entirely, whereas others tried to bolster the distributors' position by advertising their reliance on this channel. Mr. Humphrey stated, "Some of the distributors have been complacent instead of aggressive in selling wire products among their many other lines, and under an arrangement such as we had before 1950, it was awfully hard for them not to take advantage of the manufacturer—which is what happened." (For a breakdown of company dollar sales by channels, see Exhibit 3.)

Mr. Humphrey also commented on the company's current struggle for efficiency. In the past ten years, he indicated, the emphasis had been on research and development of better insulation materials, and the plant had been run "through the laboratory," in keeping with the main interests of the former works manager, Mr. Lindgren. "This did not help our costs any," said Mr. Humphrey, "and it was not until one year ago that poor earnings scared the gang into more efficiency and into paying more attention to costs."

Mr. Humphrey felt that the new works manager, Mr. Pearsall, who had come to Insulated in 1956 from the wire and cable division of a large company, was "picking up the ball in the production area and in related fields."

ORGANIZATION

In speaking of his management team and of their approach to company problems, Mr. Humphrey said, "We keep up mainly informal contacts. I myself tend to be away quite a bit. We have no regularly scheduled executive meetings; we start them periodically and then they are dropped again. I don't think that any problem here develops to such seriousness that the attention of everyone is required; rather, problems are solved by the individuals responsible. They meet informally when they feel it is necessary. General officers' meetings, when held, are thus mainly of an informative nature." (See Exhibits 5 and 6 for data on management personnel and the organization chart.)

Late in 1956 an organizational reshuffling occurred in the finance department when the previous treasurer had a nervous breakdown and left. His post was given to Mrs. Hazel Dickinson, Mr. Humphrey's cousin, while

Exhibit 5
The Insulated Wire and Cable Corporation
Background of Executives

Name	Title and Years with Company	Background
Horace T. HUMPHREY	Chairman of the Board (20 years)	Age 73; businessman, chairman of electrical equipment firm, father of president.
James V. HUMPHREY	President (18 years)	Age 48; Dartmouth '29, with father's electrical equipment firm (inspection, engineering, sales; v. p. in '37, pres. in '41). Director of Insulated since '39, president in '47.
Elmer F. LINDGREN	Vice President and Consultant (13 years)	Age 59; Chemist specialist in rubber technology and telephone wires. Formerly works manager and head of laboratory. Previously with large cable manufacturer.
Philip C. EDWARDS	Vice President—Sales (8 years)	Age 49; training as engineer and cost accountant, positions with three other cable manufacturers, last in sales. Joined Insulated as assistant sale manager.
Richard R. PEARSALL	Vice President and Works Manager (1 year)	Age 45; 26 years with large manufacturer's wire and cable division. Positions in shipping, planning, sales, purchasing, inspection. Plant manager there for 10 years.
Hazel S. DICKINSON	Treasurer (18 years)	Age 52; various positions in banks and loan offices, started in accounting department, appointed treasurer in 1956. Cousin of J. V. Humphrey.
Robert T. McPHERSON	Production Manager (21 years)	Age 46; various positions in plant. Production manager for 15 years.
Herman F. KAYSER	Controller and Assistant Treasurer (9 years)	Age 42; 7 years in general acct. office of railroad, 3 years with public accounting firm. Started as assistant controller.
John M. MARCHAND	Sales Manager (20 years)	Age 43; started in plant, various positions, later in sales department.
Edward B. JONES	Chief Engineer (18 years)	Age 39; started with Insulated after college in 1939 first in plant, then laboratory; chief chemist in 1941.
Ian F. BRIGHT	Purchasing Agent (17 years)	Age 40; started in plant, after 3 years started in purchasing, various positions.

Source: Interviews with individuals.

The Insulated Wire and Cable Corporation
Organization Chart

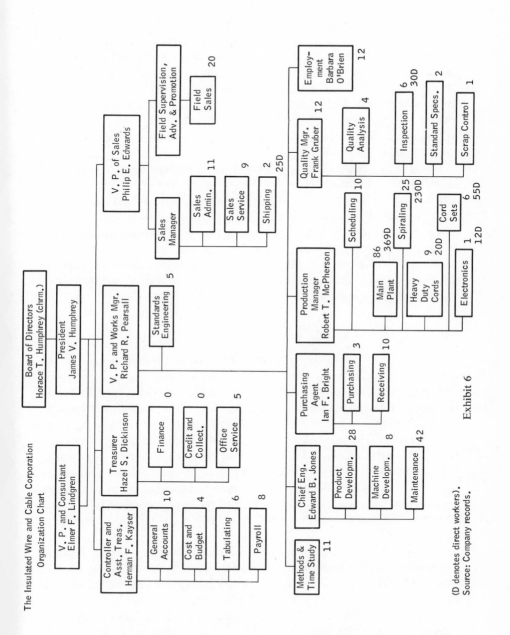

(D denotes direct workers).
Source: Company records.

Exhibit 6

accounting functions were turned over to Mr. Herman Kayser, who was appointed controller.

In December 1956 another major change occurred when Mr. Pearsall succeeded Mr. Lindgren as works manager. The latter was made a permanent consultant to the firm, and was to spend his full time observing technical developments in the industry, and participating in conventions and meetings. Mr. Humphrey pointed out that this assignment was best suited to Mr. Lindgren's interests and scientific background. "It is good to have someone watching all the time what goes on in the industry," he said, "because we were concentrating on our internal problems so much that we could not pay attention to outside trends."

Recent organizational changes were, Mr. Humphrey believed, conducive to improved cooperation. He pointed out that the new team in the financial area was now making cost data available to other departments in a more useful form—not just as historical information but on a day-to-day basis. "We are now working together rather than trying to win arguments all the time," he added. "There had been friction between personalities ever since the middle 1940's. Getting Mr. Pearsall was a great help because he does not just want things from people but actually works with them and helps them on their way."

NEW WORKS MANAGER

"When I came here in December 1956, I looked for the high spots of savings that could be made in this operation," said Mr. Pearsall. He had tried to cut inventories and costs of materials, to improve plant efficiency, and to impose restrictions on capital spending. Plans had also been made to overhaul the production department's organization and to improve controls and planning.

Inventories. "The first thing I did," said Mr. Pearsall, "was to check into the purchasing function, and I found no set policies with regard to procuring the company's major raw material, copper." He was able to reduce raw material inventories by $400,000 in two months by setting up more stringent controls and by keeping not more than 30 days' supplies on hand. What had happened was that the company had six months' supply of certain items and none of others.

"In times past anyone around here ordered anything he wanted, resulting in slip-ups like the purchase of one million metal contacts costing $30,000, which are still lying around today," Mr. Pearsall said. He had discovered excess inventories from a cash flow plotting, and found that "raw materials was the place to cut down." On his insistence, the accounting office had recently furnished him with a detailed breakdown of finished goods. The next step, he said, was to get a weekly breakdown of material ordered, on hand, and issued to the factory.

Materials Costs. In his drive for stricter controls on spending, Mr. Pearsall had reviewed the cost of some of the materials and supplies bought from other manufacturers to see whether they could be made at home or purchased elsewhere more cheaply. As a result, copper tinsel, which had cost $3.20 per thousand feet, was now obtained for $1.67; and wire terminals for cord sets, which had cost $6 per thousand, were expected to be renegotiated at $2.90. " I hope eventually to apply this kind of analysis to all of our supplies and look for more savings."

Operating Efficiency. Increasing the capacity of individual machines or operations and eliminating bottlenecks had been another major objective. Mr. Pearsall had found many places where output could be increased with existing equipment. For example, mixing of rubber insulating compounds was improved to the point where two shifts produced more than twice the output of the previous three-shift operation. Similarly, wire output in a bottle-neck department was increased from 25,000 to 44,000 units daily, even after a considerable reduction in work force. " There is still room for improvement," said Mr. Pearsall, who was beginning to analyze output and cost data for the previous year and compare them with present figures to tie down points of weakness.

Capital Spending. Mr. Pearsall had also demanded stricter controls on spending for capital equipment and had asked for detailed analyses of the merits of expenditures over $300. Furthermore, he required reports on the progress of capital projects. "From now on all unusual expenditures not directly connected with production orders must be approved by Mr. Humphrey and myself. I try to force people to be specific in their estimates, thus putting a damper on overoptimism."

In commenting on the $1,200,000 expansion program of 1952–1954, Mr. Pearsall indicated that he believed it was based on too much enthusiasm. He stated that processes in the industry had changed since the war. More plastic material was being employed, and the use of cold rubber had decreased. As a consequence, he indicated, of the 11 new continuous rubber insulating machines, one had never been used at all, and two more were only stand-bys. At the moment, only six machines were operating. Mr. Pearsall also mentioned the purchase of six new machines for automatic control of insulation thickness. It turned out that these machines, which had appeared on the market several years ago, were unsuitable because they used mechanical feelers which deformed the insulation when still soft. Recently Mr. Pearsall had ordered a new machine, employing electronics for process control, and he hoped to test it sufficiently before equipping all extruders with it.

Departmental Organization. Mr. Pearsall had also started to reappraise the organizational structure of the production department to check on duplication of effort. In the near future he planned to consolidate under one head the two departments making heavy-duty lighting systems and electronic connectors. From this move he hoped to get better use of supervisors, draftsmen, and toolmakers. Similarly, he planned to combine the departments making straight cord sets and Spira-Flex. Other contemplated changes included the consolidation of the standards engineering group (that drew up standards for a customer's order) and the methods and time study department.

Within the next year or two. Mr. Pearsall also hoped to move the new printed circuit operation into the company's main plant in order to "keep closer track of it." The lease on the present location, however, was not due to expire for two years. Currently the printed circuit operation was run by a chief design engineer. Mr. Pearsall stated that the company had a backlog of about $160,000 in orders for specialized circuits, but that he did not yet have personnel competent to turn out sufficient units of the quality required. "This is a matter of slow learning, and our biggest problem is technological. Our quality is not yet consistent."

Planning. "I am trying to get at least three months ahead in our planning on the production of major types of wire," Mr. Pearsall stated, "and in this connection I have asked for monthly budgets to be established by departments, estimating direct labor hours and other expenses, in order to arrive at a yardstick for performance. But these have been slow in coming. In my former position, I operated my plant on standards, and I hope to get them for this company eventually." Mr. Pearsall added that it was difficult to get the sales department to give estimates of sales by products, since it had in the past estimated only total dollar volume. "They are not yet coming up with detailed estimates which we must have for intelligent planning," he said.

He indicated that currently the tables had been turned in the relationship between sales and production. "They had been used to pushing production for more output during the sellers' market, whereas at the moment we estimate that we are operating at 60% of capacity and we have to push them to fill the plant with work."

Mr. Pearsall said the capacity of the plant was hard to measure in general terms, such as "miles of wire and cable," because of the varying product mix, which ranged from simple pastic-insulated wire to heavy cables 2 1/2 inches in diameter containing over 100 separate pairs of conducton. For rough planning purposes, however, it was estimated that the plant was capable of extruding about 30 million feet of plastic-covered single conductor per week and about 18 million feet of rubber-insulated conductor. This was the starting point for estimating the output of the braiding, cabling, and other special machines that would be employed in later steps.

In running his department, Mr. Pearsall held regular weekly departmental management meetings. "We have round-table discussions where we help each other on individual problems," he said. Mr. Pearsall felt the more regular meetings between the president and the vice president were desirable, but said Mr. Humphrey did not actively solicit them. "Not all people know of each other's activities, and I found in talking to my associates that they would welcome more frequent meetings. There is always the danger of forgetting to mention problems to all concerned on an individual basis. I have made it a practice to jot down things I consider important and at the best opportunity take them up with the people concerned."

Since joining the company, Mr. Pearsall recalled four management meetings, two of them dinner get-togethers. At one meeting sales policies had been discussed, such as pricing, discounts, profit margins, and the number of salesmen. One session had dealt with the electronic connectors, and decisions were made on what items to produce, what investments to make in the next year, and what government requests for engineering to accept. The most recent meeting reviewed the electronic connector line again, and the problems involved in new legal requirements for color-coding telephone cables.

Mr. Pearsall commented that Mr. Humphrey thought extensively about production problems and questions of design, patents, etc. "Basically, however, he is a financial man with a knack of raising money and promoting ventures," he added.

PROCESSES AND PLANT

As the first step in wire or cable production, wire was extruded from purchased copper bars by 12 machines, each capable of speeds up to 6,000 feet per minute. The drawn and heat-treated wire was next covered with tin, brass, or braided textile if destined for a rubber insulation, in order to protect it from corrosive rubber compounds. (For a production flow chart, see Exhibit 7.)

Wire. To make stiff wire, solid copper or copper reinforced with a steel core was used, the latter being purchased outside. For flexible applications, several fine wires were stranded together, while for extra softness, the company purchased "tinsel" conductors—e.g., extremely thin copper ribbons wrapped around textile threads, a number of which were then stranded together.

Next, these wires or strands were coated with either rubber or plastic insulating compounds. Before the war, natural rubber had been used for the most part, but Mr. Lindgren's introduction of new processes had made possible the use of synthetic rubber, which could be extruded cold as well as hot. The machines used for the purpose were over 100 feet long and produced insulated wire at speeds ranging from 25 feet to 650 feet per minute, depending on the thickness of the core and insulation.

The main plastic insulating compound was polyethylene; extrusion was made at high temperatures, and the finished wire was subsequently run through a long cooling bath. A wide variety of colors was available for coding multiconductor cables. Plastic wire insulation had been developed after the war, and it was estimated that at present about one-half of Insulated's footage was produced in plastic form.

Cable. To make cable, several insulated wires were twisted together into a single strand by cabling machines. Sometimes these strands also contained fiber threads or metal reinforcements, or they received a cotton

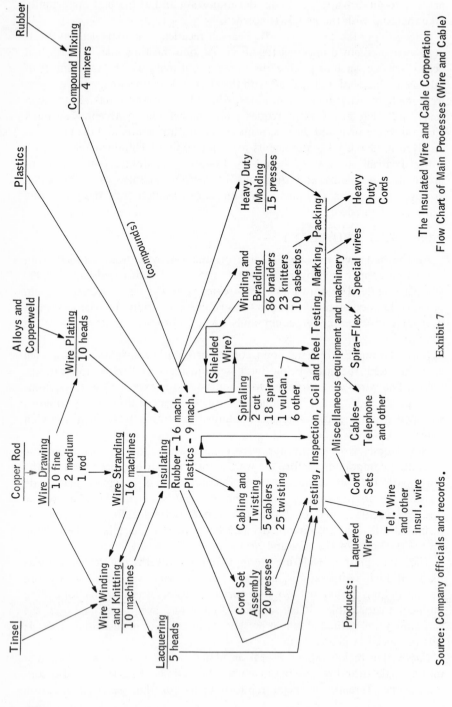

Source: Company officials and records.

Exhibit 7

The Insulated Wire and Cable Corporation
Flow Chart of Main Processes (Wire and Cable)

braiding, a lead or aluminum shielding, or a paper wrap. Depending on the type of cable desired, there were many other variations. Finally, a rubber or plastic coat was extruded onto the cable core by the same machinery used to insulate single wires.

Machinery. About 75% of the machinery in the plant was general-purpose equipment capable of producing standard telephone or other types of wire and cables. The remainder consisted of specialty machines used for making special telephone wires or spiraled cords. According to the plant management, the machines were of fairly modern design, and the processes employed were those generally found in the industry.

Quality Control. According to the production manager, Mr. Robert T. McPherson, quality depended on various factors, but mainly on uniform thickness of insulation and, to a lesser extent, on the insulating material used. Constant watchfulness was required of the operators to detect thickness variations early on account of the speed of the machines. Samples were taken from every reel and checked by the operator and his foremen as well as by inspectors who were independent in status from the production supervision.

Mr. Pearsall pointed out that each company developed its own formulae for insulating compounds and carried on research to secure improvements. He added, "The laboratory control of production at Insulated is greater than in most other places due to greater frequency of inspection both of the mixing of compounds and actual wire production." According to the sales vice president, the company, in contrast to many others, considered the Underwriters Laboratory standards as the minimum standard of quality and generally exceeded them.

Scrap trends, according to Mr. McPherson, gave evidence of increased efficiency and quality. He stated that the ratio of unusable wire and cable had dropped since 1955 from 11 1/2% of total weight of finished goods to 7% in 1957 and that rubber compound scrap had dropped from a total of 416,000 pounds in 1955 to 25,000 pounds for the first three months of 1957.

Labor. The plant was operated in three shifts under the supervision of 24 foremen. A force of close to 750 men worked on incentive wages that depended on the output of acceptable wire from the workers' machines. Unionized in 1946, Insulated enjoyed peaceful labor relations, except for minor grievances and a recent four-hour walk-out which Mr. Pearsall traced to his drive for efficiency. " For years they have gone along without insistence on efficiency, and now people feel they are working harder," he said, " but they will calm down when they find that I am fair in asking for a day's work." Wage negotiations and grievances were handled by Mr. McPherson along lines set by Mr. Pearsall.

SALES AND PROMOTION

Distribution. Mr. Philip C. Edwards, sales vice president, stated that the company was somewhat unique in the industry, inasmuch as it relied almost exclusively on distributors, except for sales to the government and other wire manufacturers. Other companies sold directly as well as through middlemen. "We try to sell on quality and not on price," he continued, "and we have a good reputation, but we must sell to our distributors just as hard as to final customers."

Commenting on the company's promotional sales force, Mr. Edwards explained that 6 of these 20 men were shared with Mr. Horace Humphrey's electrical equipment company. They were mainly used to promote Insulated's products with the salesmen of distributors and with final customers, and all their sales were made on the distributors' accounts. He felt that at least five additional men would be needed because present territories were too large for effective nation-wide coverage.

Mr. Edwards stated that the larger companies were increasing their sales forces, hiring mostly specialists in telephone or power wire. For example, one of the largest companies now had about 60 men in the field. He expected to add three men to Insulated's force within the next six months, after which he expected to hold off further expansion. Salesmen's yearly pay averaged about $7,500, depending on their experience.

The sales manager, Mr. Marchand, believed that selling wire depended greatly on personal contacts and relationships, and that much might be lost should the company change channels. He felt the best use for a promotional sales force was to bring Insulated and its products to the attention of distributors' salesmen.

Mr. Edwards explained that the company had about 60 independent local electrical distributors and 4 national distributors, including the Nationwide Electric Company. The latter's volume had remained unchanged since loss of its exclusive contract. Mr. Edwards felt that Insulated's strong adherence to selling through agents was a good point in the eyes of its outlets, since the company did not compete with them. Although it was an industry practice for a company to sell direct once an account reached considerable volume, Insulated turned over all accounts solicited by its missionary salesmen to its distributors.

A new development in distributor relations was the practice of consigning part of the stock, especially flexible cords which were sold over the counter to a great extent. "We got forced into consigning because one of our competitors started it," explained Mr. Edwards, "and it gave distributors greater stocks for immediate delivery. But not to let this practice get out of hand, we later changed our pricing policy from f.o.b. Philadelphia and started selling f.o.b. anywhere U.S.A. This forced the distributor to absorb freight charges if he shipped from consigned stock. After some complaints, we gave distributors 1% for freight absorption, but I think our move put a damper on excessive consignment." Finished goods inventories increased by about $375,000 as a result of the consignments. Mr. Edwards believed the increase above that amount constituted normal restocking after the extraordinarily high demand experienced in 1956.

Insulated, unlike some of its larger competitors, had no scattered warehouses. Such stocks as existed in the field were the inventories carried by distributors. The company did maintain sales offices at eight locations besides the home plant, including two in the Southeast and two in California, through which its missionary salesmen could be reached. The nine sales service men, however, were all at the home office. Their function was to answer letters, calls, and inquiries from distributors or customers, and to process orders.

Price. Pricing of Insulated's products was influenced by cost data as well as market conditions. Mr. Edwards indicated that the industry was peculiar in that prices for each standard product were set by an acknowledged leader, who was followed by all companies making the same item. He felt, however, that this practice was not the result of collusion; rather, the decisions of a sizable manufacturer influenced other companies "after the fact." Insulated was a price leader in the telephone wire field. Published list prices for standard products were merely suggestions to the distributors and were not enforced. Large volume orders were generally negotiated individually by the distributor or the missionary salesmen. "We are a high-cost producer," he injected, "being top-heavy on white-collar and engineering personnel. The result is that we have to be careful not to be underbid; at the same time we must cover our expenses. Sometimes we must be satisfied to get a contribution to overhead." (For company gross margins by type of products, see Exhibit 3.)

Mr. Edwards stated that the slump in wire demand early in 1957 had led to price cutting in the industry. There were instances of companies giving 20% off list for telephone cables, which was a great threat to Insulated's profit margins. In part, the price reductions were due to falling copper prices. He added, "Actually, I am trying to get away from tying our prices to that of copper, and the industry is thinking along these lines, too. If we can do that, we will have fewer fluctuations because customers will not attempt to hold off buying in times of falling copper prices, and vice versa."

Promotion. All advertising was done on a national basis and was placed mainly in two magazines, *Telephony* and *Telephone Engineering and Management*. The company employed colorful two-page spreads bearing a message of "quality and experience." Spiraled cords and flexible cord were also advertised off and on in magazines reaching purchasing agents, plant engineers, and railroad maintenance engineers. The advertising and promotion manager indicated that the company had become "advertising conscious" about nine years ago; he hoped to develop a more impressive campaign, employing specific examples of "end use" advertising as opposed to "catalogue" advertising that merely listed types of wire available. He also wanted an advertising budget of up to 2% of sales; present expenditures ran about $100,000 annually.

Promotions were directed mainly toward distributors' salesmen; they took the form of free road atlases, matches bearing Insulated's name, and—for display in distributors' shops and warehouses—wire display cases, signs, pamphlets, and clocks bearing Insulated's insignia. Approximately $10,000 per year was now spent on these activities, and the promotion manager hoped for an increase in this budget.

Forecasting. Mr. Edwards stated that forecasting the demand for company products was a difficult task, and the three-month estimates he attempted to give were revised monthly. Standard items were produced for stock, and special items were scheduled into production as needed.

PURCHASING

Each month the company used about 500,000 to 750,000 pounds of copper bars or wire, 30,000 pounds of natural rubber, 170,000 to 225,000 pounds of synthetic rubber (neoprene and other types), and between 60,000 and 100,000 pounds of various plastic molding compounds. In addition, many varieties of materials and supplies were bought, the most important being wire terminals, steel wire for reinforcement, copper alloys, and wooden cable reels.

Mr. Ian F. Bright, the purchasing agent, reported directly to Mr. Pearsall. He supervised three buyers and ten receiving clerks. According to Mr. Bright, the company was at no particular price disadvantage in buying raw materials, but during the unprecedented copper shortages of mid-1956, it had been necessary to pay premiums of up to 20% to cover the company's requirements. This experience had highlighted the need for developing a steady purchasing pattern with primary copper producers or custom smelters. Company emphasis was now directed toward this goal and away from reliance on middlemen.

Mr. Bright explained that most major raw materials were bought at the prices prevailing on the date of shipment. Copper wire bar was the major exception; it could be obtained at a price based on monthly average figures, published daily in the *Engineering and Mining Journal*. By using this average price, a company could buy on terms relatively unaffected by sudden short-term price fluctuations, and prices were the same for all buyers. Another exception was the relatively small amount of natural rubber, which was sometimes bought speculatively on a spot or forward position.

"We now try to buy on a monthly basis," said Mr. Bright, who explained that this was especially true of copper, for which he received monthly orders from the plant. He added that in the past year copper inventories had reached a three-month level. Some "scare" inventories, bought at unfavorable prices, were tying up company funds unnecessarily. For rubber, minimum levels had been established, and supply was replenished as need arose, generally on a monthly basis. Timing the purchases of plastic compounds, according to Mr. Bright, required some "juggling" to take advantage of carload lots, inasmuch as various types of plastic were not used in large enough amounts to warrant monthly ordering.

For the president, the works manager, treasurer, production manager, and scheduling department, Mr. Bright prepared monthly reports showing balances on hand, amounts on order, use of materials, and receipts. In addition, the accounting department kept a daily "black book" on purchasing activity. Clerks in the purchasing department maintained inventory records for major commodities and for minor supplies and materials that were kept under a minimum-maximum level system.

"In spite of the records, we must watch out or we will be caught short in certain items," said Mr. Bright. He recalled that in the fall of 1956 part of the telephone wire production had to be shut down for a week for lack of steel reinforcement wire. "Sometimes it is hard to keep in touch between purchasing and scheduling or with the storeroom. There are dozens of reasons for blunders, clerical and otherwise. For instance, we have a person out in the storeroom for only two out of the three shifts to control the issue of materials," he said.

ENGINEERING AND LABORATORY

The engineering and laboratory group had grown from a modest three-man team in 1939 to 36 persons. The maintenance force of 47 people was also under the chief engineer, Mr. Edward B. Jones. Four engineering groups were occupied with product development, specializing in plastics, rubber, cable design, and electrical properties of wires and cables. Another group carried on machine development, while several women technicians were occupied with product testing. The standards engineering group of five men, which wrote specifications for orders forwarded by the sales department, was to be placed under the chief engineer in the near future.

Originally, the engineering force had mainly concentrated on developing better rubber compounds and had also carried out "a smattering" of raw material inspection, according to Mr. Jones. Subsequently, however, the group was enlarged to include engineers capable of dealing with the electrical characteristics and properties required of communication wire and cables. In addition, as the variety of rubber and plastic compounds increased, so did control and test methods.

Mr. Jones explained that new product development rarely included pure research; rather, the engineers followed up ideas from the field sales force which was in contact with customers' needs. Occasionally members of the laboratory groups went out to visit customers and study their particular problems. The most recent contact with potential customers had been made by an engineer who had visited several power companies to study their power-cable requirements. Much direct contact was maintained between the standard engineers and the sales department, and the former relayed all research, development, and unusual problems to the laboratory.

New developments brought out by the company's engineers dated back to 1946, when a new type of insulation utilizing neoprene synthetic (rubber) for telephone wire was developed under Mr. Lindgren. Mr. Jones indicated that better and more durable insulation for telephone wires had been of concern to the telephone companies, which incurred high labor costs due to frequent replacement of the asphalt-covered, cloth-braided wires used at the time. The new neoprene insulation tripled the life of telephone wires and formed an important step forward in the application of synthetic rubber compounds to insulated conductors, In 1948 the company followed up this development with the introduction of flexible cords insulated with synthetic compounds, again resulting in an improvement of an existing product.

Even before the war, the company had experimented with plastic insulation, installing one of the first plastic extruders available. Extensive development of plastic wires was carried on after the war, both for civilian and military use. The spiraled cords acquired with the subsidiary had been improved, and the company was the first to get the Underwriters Laboratory approval for one of its new flexible cords. In 1953 the company began the manufacture of plastic-sheathed telephone cable with a design somewhat different from the ones then used in the industry. Eventually, the Rural Electrification Administration adopted these specifications as an industry standard. Later the company brought out distribution wires and self-supporting cables with the same specifications. One year ago, on the request of the sales department, a new method of color-coating cords, primarily for telephone hand sets, was developed.

Laboratory personnel and facilities were unusually numerous for a company of Insulated's size and allowed considerable attention to be given to methods engineering and product testing as well as to product engineering. Mr. Jones felt that his technical staff was superior in quality to that of most competitors, especially in view of the fact that the company had come out with a number of " firsts " in developing new items.

FINANCE AND ACCOUNTING

Mrs. Dickinson supervised credit and collection for Insulated and its subsidiaries. One of her current major concerns was integrating the office functions for the small printed circuits firm into the main office in such a way that Insulated's name would not be connected with that of its subsidiary for credit purposes. She also said that the Spira-Flex subsidiary, in contrast to Insulated, required "a lot of pushing" to collect from direct accounts, and that at times its three salesmen had to be restrained from selling to doubtful credit risks.

Accounting activities were in the hands of Mr. Kayser, who had been appointed assistant treasurer one month back. Facilities for record keeping included a small IBM punched card tabulating system which, according to Mr. Kayser, was put to increasing use. Currently it supplied all sales reports and analyses, production and scrap tabulations, finished goods inventory listings, payroll and deduction registers, burden distributions, accounts payable, and disbursements. Important exceptions were listings and breakdowns of raw material and work-in-process inventories, accounts receivable, which were handposted, and billings. It was hoped that these activities would be converted to machine tabulation within the next year and also that the machines would be used in cost work to a greater extent.

In this connection Mr. Kayser stated that one of the problems in the cost department was the reluctance of long-term employees to change the status quo. He said the man in charge of cost accounting had been with the company for 38 years and kept so many facts in his memory that it was often difficult to maintain adequate records. To meet this problem, Mr. Kayser had placed a younger man with cost accounting experience under the chief cost accountant, with the task of slowly reworking some of the methods employed.

In cooperation with the new works manager, several changes had been made in the department. Since the end of 1956, weekly breakdowns of finished goods had been furnished, showing delivery promises, total requirements, and stock on hand. In the same period, all products had been costed monthly. Actual materials and labor figures were collected, and output was determined. After allocating overhead on the basis of a "normal" 75% capacity rate, based on machine times, unit costs for each wire and cable type were determined and compared with estimates derived by the standards engineering group. Monthly reports were also compiled, showing sales volume and total cost for each product and also giving sales by product by distributor. Mr. Kayser hoped that eventually standard costs could be established for the major types of wire and cable, but he felt that a more exact basis for determining costs would first have to be established and some of the problematic practices of the past eliminated. For instance, payroll calculations were unduly complicated because changes in wage rates had been partly based on dollars and partly on percentage increases. The result was that rates for the same job sometimes differed among departments, and payroll calculation thus involved excessive detail. These irregularities would be difficult to straighten out because the union would resist any downward adjustments, whereas raising wages to the highest level paid would prove too costly.

Commenting on budgeting procedures, Mr. Kayser stated that "we have not been as alert as we could have been," and explained that, whereas annual budgets for the company as a whole were established, budgets for the individual departments were badly needed to help evaluate foreman performance and to establish closer cost responsibility. The accounting department was now in closer cooperation than ever with the factory and expected to be able to furnish any data the works manager might desire within the next year.

PROSPECTS OF PRESENT PRODUCT LINE

Telephone Wire and Cable. Mr. Humphrey stated, "At the moment Insulated is trying to keep the present market and even expand it, but in the long range it is slipping away from us. Our very competent works manager is getting our costs down, and our quality standing will help us for quite a while, but eventually we must put our ingenuity to work and broaden our lines. There is always the hope that some independent telephone companies will remain independent, but on the other hand there is no public resentment against bigness in the telephone business to stop the trend towards consolidation. Furthermore, the major suppliers of telephone equipment for the independents have directed their main interests toward military or industrial electronics, and one cannot expect much pressure on their part to preserve the independents as one of their markets."

Mr. Humphrey added that a glimmer of hope had arisen with the recent Supreme Court decision on the legality of du Pont's holdings of General Motors stock. He felt that possibly this decision, which opened up the field of vertical integration to the scrutiny of the government's "trust busters," might check the present merger rush in the telephone industry. "But it is too early to tell what is going to come of it."

Mr. Edwards commented on the shrinking telephone potential and said, "Every time one of the independent companies is bought up, we lose a customer, active or potential. Our market will dwindle unless we can get an arrangement to supply one of the two large companies. But this is unlikely. because of their own wire subsidiaries or interests." In addition, Mr, Edwards stated that the number of wire companies making certain types of telephone wire had increased. For example, since 1950 the number of companies making plastic-insulated telephone wires and cables had increased from five to thirteen, partly due to the fact that plastic extrusion required a much lower investment than rubber extrusion, he said.

Another problem in the telephone field was a requirement by the Rural Electrification Administration for color coding the various conductors in a telephone cable according to a set pattern. After January 1, 1958, cables with 60 or more conductors would have to be made by stranding together groups of conductors, but this could not be done on Insulated's present equipment. "I have been hollering my head off to get this machine in time, ever since the decision was announced several months ago," Mr. Edwards said, adding that delivery of the $55,000 cabler could not be expected for at least 18 months. Therefore, design of the machine would have to be entrusted to company engineers. If parts were subcontracted, the machine could be expected to operate within six months at the earliest. Mr. Edwards commented that he would like to stock up as soon as possible on the new color-coded cable to be ready for the change-over. "The sooner we get our stocks built up, the better. I hope we will straighten this out soon." The new machine would be usable for other purposes, including lighter types of power cables.

Flexible Cords and Wire. These products were turned out for a great variety of original and replacement applications. Distributors sold short lengths or whole reels of the cords to electrical equipment dealers and repair shops, or to manufacturers of electrical appliances.

Mr. Edwards stated that sales had decreased over the years because more manufacturers were producing these items. "Our major distributor now has eight sources of supply." Mr. Edwards hoped consignment would help sales of this line, which appeared better suited to over-the-counter selling than other company products. Moreover, sales had increased in test cases during 1956 when consignment was started. Mr. Edwards also hoped to widen the line through adding color-sheathed cords and possibly oil-proof cords. In addition, a line of large flexible cables, which regular distributors agreed to handle, had been developed and was expected to reach the market within a few months. However, Mr. Edwards was not sure about the market potential for these products.

Cord Sets. These products were flexible insulated cords containing one or more conductors; they were furnished with plugs, connectors, or hooks, ready for use on the handsets of telephones or on appliances of all sorts. Insulation materials varied greatly in this group. Except for supplying five old customers, Insulated had quit making cord sets for the original appliance market about two years ago, when it became apparent that large numbers of small manufacturers were undercutting quality and prices. Consequently, Insulated sold appliance cord sets for replacement purposes only. "We do not wish to downgrade our quality by producing two grades of wire," Mr. Edwards said. He believed that telephone cord sets had the same prospects as telephone wire in general. Occasionally the Bell System placed orders when its own facilities were operating at capacity, but the company could not count on this business.

Spira-Flex. "Our sales to this subsidiary took a big jump in 1956 when the Bell System ordered a large quantity of coiled telephone cords from them," commented Mr. Edwards. He added, however, that the line was "doomed" in the long run, not only because the basic patents had expired, but also because six companies had started producing their own line, including Western Electric Company. "I am afraid we may have dropped our prices a little too late," he injected. "They were somewhat inflated anyway due to our subsidiary's role as a middleman." He expected much tougher competition ahead.

Mr. Humphrey said the subsidiary was attempting to strengthen its direct sales force to exploit more fully the market for industrial applications. In addition, plans were made to combine distribution of the spiraled cords, the electronic connectors, and the printed circuits in one direct sales force. Direct sales were expected to result in lower prices to large users of these products.

Broadcast Wires. These products were flexible wires and cables, shielded with metal braiding, for use in sound systems and broadcast equipment. "Our competitors are selling below our prices because we are making too high and costly quality," said Mr. Edwards, who expected the line would be modified to correspond with market demands. With the increasing use of public address systems, music systems, and so forth, channels were shifting from specialized electronics distributors to general-line electrical distributors. "We did not have enough of a line to satisfy the specialist distributor," said Mr. Edwards. "We are basically a volume producer and must look for volume markets. We ought to be doing at least three times our present volume in this line, and we will have to concentrate on the right market." At the same time the number of competitors was growing, he said.

Heavy-Duty Lighting Cords. Mr. Edwards was hopeful about this recent addition to the line. Patents were held for commercial applications, which were mainly in shipyards at the moment. Mr. Edwards hoped eventually to extend uses to lighting coal mines. From the original patent acquired with the subsidiary, the company had developed in its heavy-duty cords the first explosion-proof plug and had secured approval by the U.S. Bureau of Mines. Mine owners had shown great interest, inasmuch as these systems would allow safe electrical lighting of coal mines for the first time. Expense was a consideration, however, since an average installation was expected to cost from $30,000 upwards. The company had also successfully demonstrated the heavy-duty lighting systems for use on oil derricks, where the corrosive influence of oil on insulation material had been a great problem. Mr. Edwards thought the company might be well advised to try to sell manufacturers of oil derricks on the use of heavy-duty cords, since success here would probably increase acceptance among derrick users. The systems were sold exclusively through one distributor. There was little competition in this field, except for government business, where patent protection did not apply.

Electronic Connectors. These products were generally small multiple-conductors, sockets, and plugs, mostly custom-made for military aircraft. They required precision assembly of small metal and plastic parts to be molded into shock- and temperature-resistant compounds of synthetic rubber or plastic materials. Mr. Humphrey hoped the company's developing experience in manufacturing these items might point the way toward a future market. "The industry has not come to the point of standardizing miniature cables and connectors as yet. We are trying to push the development of these products, since they have a military potential of $30 million annually." Mr. Humphrey said that several of the molding machines used for cord sets were adaptable for connectors, which had been originally developed by a designer hired by Insulated three years ago. The process of development had been difficult since the man's ideas "were not readily reduced to practice, and customer requirements were changing." Mr. Humphrey stated that the designer's optimism had resulted in a premature investment of about $300,000 in molds and a further investment in labor and supplies the size of which "I would rather not know." Mr. Humphrey hoped, however, that electronic office machines would eventually be built to make use of electronic connectors. He felt the company's efforts in this field would establish it firmly in the market, once the use of standard electronic connectors and wires became more generally accepted in civilian products.

Miscellaneous Wires and Cable. Mr. Edwards stated that this line consisted of specially designed, made-to-order items for both government and civilian uses. Individual contracts were obtained directly through bidding on a very competitive basis. The one most recently secured was part of a sizable order for military wire which had been distributed among three successful bidders out of a total of 20 companies. Bids had raised plus or minus 10% of the final average price. Insulated had to drop its price by about 4% to obtain part of the order, thus cutting the profit margin about in half.

Printed Circuits. Mr. Humphrey said that telephone switchboards were among the newer applications for printed circuits and that once the new subsidiary making this line could produce high-quality special products, there would be a market opening up. Radio and TV circuits were generally manufactured by captive shops, so Insulated would have to concentrate on special problems for both civilian automation and military electronics applications. Mr. Humphrey said that the engineering force of the subsidiary contained one specialist who had been a pioneer in the field. Major problems in running the operation, which employed an etching technique, were of a physical nature, and so far the subsidiary had turned out only $12,000 worth of circuits. However, a sizable backlog of several months' business was building up, he said.

PROSPECTS OF THE POWER CABLE FIELD

According to Mr. Edwards, power cable was the " only field in the business where there is any profit left and an attractive field because only a few quality manufacturers are in it." He said the company was currently interested only in "secondary" power cables, which carried voltages much lower than the 150,000 or more volts carried by overhead transmission cables. Secondary cables were used for distributing power within a power plant, for large lighting installations such as airports, railroads, and turnpikes, or for arc welding units.

Mr. Edwards stated that he and Mr. Pearsall, Mr. Humphrey, and Mr. Jones had informally discussed entering the power cable field. " I felt that getting into these cables, which are larger than the average cable used for communication purposes, would put us in a better position in terms of profit. Being a high-cost producer, it would be good for us to get into large-volume runs which would help to absorb overhead."

Mr. Edwards was not sure of the potential market for secondary power cables or of its percentage of the total power cable area. He indicated that one of Insulated's engineers had studied the requirements of several utilities and had found that power cables were made to specifications set by individual buyers. Each company had an informal list of suppliers for cables, and getting on these lists was an important forward step. Utilities generally bought direct, not through middlemen.

" It will be an uphill fight to get into this market," said Mr. Edwards, "and in addition we must change our sales policy in this area to direct selling only." He indicated that the present sales force could be used to call on power utilities. The six men shared with Mr. Humphrey's equipment company had sold wiring and switchboard accessories in this market, and Mr. Edwards hoped this relationship would facilitate entry into certain utility companies. He was not sure, however, of the extent of coverage obtained.

The characteristics of the market did not allow for large-scale promotion, Mr. Edwards continued. He said that confidence in Insulated's quality could best be won by talking about successful installations already made. "This is a slow process," he said. "We have to pick the companies off one at a time. We have a name in the telephone field, but not in power wire."

According to Mr. Lindgren, power utilities and railroads were characteristically reluctant to change suppliers where the reliability of purchased products affected the safety and comfort of their customers. He added that the company's experience had been strictly in communications, so a period of learning would be involved. He explained that the basic function of communications wire is to transmit weak electrical signals for long distances without interference from outside sources. Power wire is built for high voltage; it must withstand and dissipate heat, and must have low internal resistance. "We have always been specialty people selling insulation, not copper wire," he added, "and specialty manufacture even in this field will have to be our strength because the large volume of standard wire and cable, containing mostly metal, belongs to the copper or aluminum producer who can exert more control over metal prices."

Mr. Pearsall expected that power wire could be made in the plant, and he hoped that some of the presently idle rubber extruders could be adapted for use on this product by modifications costing about $15,000 per machine. He believed that rubber insulation would be used for quite some time to come, because plastic was attacked by electrical effects attendant on high voltage. The company would also need the large cabling machine for the color-coded telephone cables in order to accommodate the large-gauge wire used in power cables. However, Mr. Pearsall felt that concentration on the small and medium sizes comprising the secondary cable field would be necessary, inasmuch as very heavy cables required lead-curing, for which equipment would cost upwards of $175,000. "At any rate," he added, "we are entering an area where we shall have to gain different skills and experience." While the company could not draw aluminum wire on its present equipment without moderate modifications, Mr. Pearsall commented that this was no particular difficulty, because ready-drawn aluminum wire could be purchased outside.

The company's experience with power cable was limited to one order for airport lighting, which had been successfully filled, according to Mr. Edwards. A sizable order for another installation was lost because a large competitor underbid by an amount almost equal to the complete profit margin Insulated had tried to obtain.

Commenting on the meaning of the power cable field to the technical staff, Mr. Jones said he was not sure what the eventual scope of the company's activity might be. " We made studies of heavy portable power cables, such as those used in portable lighting installations for airports or arc welding," he said, " and our immediate objective is to go into cables not above 600 volts." He stated that presently available test equipment and engineering skills could cope with this first stage, but going into higher voltages and larger sizes would require new facilities. He recalled no discussion of using aluminum conductors which were sweeping the field of overhead transmission cables, and commented that Insulated's current interest in power cables was probably due in part to the excess capacity available on rubber insulating equipment.

Mr. Humphrey hoped for an eventual entry into the power cable field. He added, however, that "actually we have not done as much long-range planning as we should have, and so far we have not set a schedule for the introduction of new items in that field."

5. ADELL CHEMICAL COMPANY*

—NORMAN J. KAYE

After five years of phenomenal growth the Adell Chemical Company was preparing to take another step toward expansion of its production facilities in 1959. Expansion was a relatively recent development with the company. A new plant of 40,000 square feet was built in 1957 at Holyoke, Massachusetts, followed by an addition of 20,000 square feet shortly thereafter at the same location.

However, Adell Chemical Company did not always have this enviable problem of expansion. Mr. Jacob L. Barowsky, the founder and president of Adell Chemical Company, developed an all-purpose, heavy duty, liquid detergent in 1933. Throughout the years he had sold his product to the industrial consumer market. Mr. Barowsky had also periodically promoted his detergent to the household consumer market during this time. Unfortunately his latter efforts proved unsuccessful until 1954.

In 1954, Mr. Barowsky launched an unorthodox promotion and distribution campaign. His advertising program was focused on a one-year saturation spot television contract. Initially this contract consisted of 30 one-minute commercials per week at hard-to-sell off-hour times. Because of limited financial backing he necessarily restricted this effort to one Holyoke TV station. After saturating the consumer with the merits of the product, salesmen approached food wholesalers and large chains in the area to exploit the created demand. Mr. Barowsky further encouraged demand at the retail level by establishing a self-regulated fair trade price policy and by offering a cooperative advertising allowance of 15c per case to the retailer. (See Exhibit 1 which is the price list to wholesalers.) The immediate success of the campaign and the product, Lestoil, prompted Mr. Barowsky to increase his TV spot saturation from one station to all stations covering a given market. The company

* Reprinted by permission of Professor Kaye.

Exhibit 1

Adell Chemical Company

PRICE LIST

Lestoil, the All-Purpose Liquid Detergent

Size	Pack	Cost per Case (to Wholesaler)	Suggested Price to Grocer	Fair Traded Retail Price
Pint	24	$6.53	$7.10 case	$.37 each
Quart	12	5.74	6.24	.65
½ Gallon	6	5.52	6.00	1.25
Gallon	4	6.62	7.20	2.25
5 Gallon Can	1	8.10	8.80	11.00

WAREHOUSES IN ALL PRINCIPAL CITIES
F.O.B. delivered Terms: 2% 10 days, net 30.
Shipped by truck from Holyoke, Massachusetts or from our nearest warehouse.
Truckload—36,000 lbs or more—Shipped to one location from factory—additional 2% discount allowed.
ADVERTISING ALLOWANCE: 15¢ per case (on contract).
MINIMUM SHIPMENT: 25 case quantities.
LESTOIL, INC., Holyoke, Mass.
 a subsidiary of Adell Chemical Company

found that generally its sales volume corresponded to density of population in any given area. Mr. Barowsky felt, however, that to jump to large population centers would have created too many fringe area distribution problems simultaneously. As each new fringe area developed, the company moved out from market to market. This decision logically developed into a geographically contiguous expansion. In the next five years, the company continued its successful marketing ideas.

Sales skyrocketed from an estimated $500,000 in 1954 to $31,000,000 in 1958 (see Exhibit 2). Geographically the sales area covered over 50% of potential Lestoil users. It extended across the northeast section of the United

Exhibit 2

Adell Chemical Company

Although exact sales figures of Lestoil are not disclosed, the following estimates are fairly reliable.

Year	Sales ($000)
1953	$450 (industrial)
1954	500
1955	1,000
1956	2,500
1957	12,500
1958	31,000

States as far west as Wisconsin and southward through Kentucky and Virginia. It included the provinces of Ontario and Quebec and the Maritimes in Canada. Only once did the expansion deviate from its market-to-market plan. In January of 1958, Lestoil penetrated Puerto Rico, Bermuda, and southern Florida (see Exhibit 3). Initially, the Holyoke plant supplied all Lestoil customers directly. Later the company adopted a system of using public warehouses

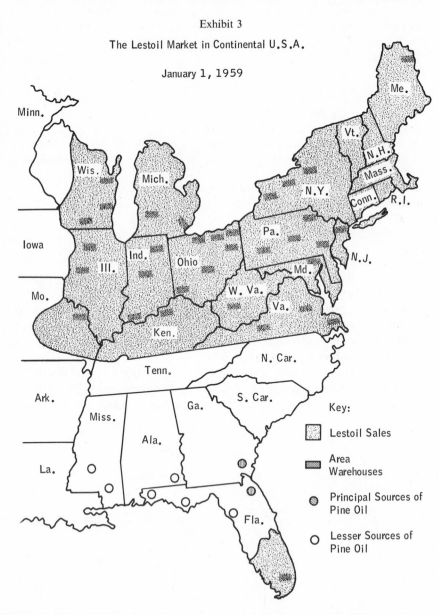

Exhibit 3

The Lestoil Market in Continental U.S.A.

January 1, 1959

Key:

▦ Lestoil Sales

▦ Area Warehouses

◉ Principal Sources of Pine Oil

○ Lesser Sources of Pine Oil

for storing and handling in more remote areas. This system provided the same instant delivery of Lestoil to its customers throughout the area it served. (See Exhibit 3 for warehouse locations.)

By late 1958, the production of Lestoil had expanded from its "two-man basement operation" to a million dollar highly automated plant. The plant operated four semiautomated lines on one shift, concentrating primarily on pint and quart bottles for household consumers. The layout included a four-bay shipping platform and a large concrete receiving platform. Employees very often worked overtime to meet the current demand. The receiving platform frequently was called upon to handle as many as eight shipping trucks on an emergency basis with less efficiency than the bays built for that purpose. About 35 salesmen handled the field contacts, over 100 clerical and office personnel maintained the organization, and less than 70 production workers carried on the mixing and bottling processes of Lestoil. Plant labor cost comprised about 2% of total costs.

The plant was not unionized. The lack of unionization may very well have been because of Mr. Barowsky's concern for his workers. He proudly admitted to the fact that, "Every employee knows he can come and talk with me and they do it too." Liberal wage rates and excellent employee benefit plans demonstrated the sincerity of his feelings.

Over the period of rapid expansion, Mr. Barowsky directed all phases of the company's activity. The entire success story of Lestoil was his in every detail. However, to aid in his decision making, Mr. Barowsky gradually developed a staff of executives in accounting, advertising, public relations, traffic, and other management areas. When the occasion called for it he also employed consultants in appropriate fields.

Above all, Mr. Barowsky built his operation around his family. Adell was a closed corporation, completely owned by the members of the family. All of them acted as directors of the company. In addition, various members of the family took an active part in its operation. Mr. Isaac L. Eskenasy, a son-in-law and executive vice-president, guided such functions as research, production, and sales. Mr. Aaron L. Kingsberg, another son-in-law and comptroller, had charge of all legal aspects of the business and headed Jackson Associates created by Adell as an advertising agency to handle the Lestoil account. Mr. Barowsky's wife contributed her efforts to advertising, promotion, and, to a great extent, public relations. Mrs. Edith Eskenasy, a daughter, had the primary function of handling the confidential accounting of the firm. Mrs. Dorothy Barowsky, widow of Mr. Barowsky's son, Seymour, carried her responsibility with Jackson Associates. The entire family felt that their close association was an important satisfaction derived from the company's operation. Mr. Barowsky, with undisguised pleasure, said, "The whole family works together very closely. Sometimes some of us have to be away for a few days, but we all live here in Holyoke and most of the time we work right here."

During 1958, Mr. Barowsky and his young organization faced several new developments as direct outgrowths of Adell's expansion. First, his product and promotion caught the eye of his competitors. Colgate, Lever Brothers, and Procter and Gamble entered the market with similar products.[1] The big three used Lestoil's advertising technique on a national scale, introducing products called "Genie," "Handy Andy," and "Mr. Clean" respectively. Genie had especially concentrated its promotion on the West Coast.

Exhibit 4

Adell Chemical Company

Advertising Expenditures by Selected Competitors on All-Purpose Liquid Detergents in 1958

Company	Product	Spot TV Liquid Detergent	Total TV All Products
Adell Chemical Co.	Lestoil	$12,339,090	$12,339,090
Colgate	Genie	319,840	33,855,990
Lever Brothers	Handy Andy	740,730	38,537,230
Procter & Gamble	Mr. Clean	421,300	84,471,710
Texize Chemicals, Inc.	Texize	3,619,020	n.a.

Sources: *Sponsor, Food Field Reporter.*

Exhibit 5

Adell Chemical Company

Lestoil Advertising Budget Breakdown for 1957 and 1958

Media	1957 ($000)	1958 ($000)	% Increase
Measured:			
Newspapers	$100	$350	250%
Business publications	29	64	211
Spot Television	7,665	12,339	61
Outdoor	1	50	450
Total	$7,794	$12,803	64%
Unmeasured:			
Point of sale	20	30	50
TV-Talent production	45	70	56
Direct mail	6	10	67
Merchandise material	20	30	50
Cooperative advertising	446	535	20
Total	$537	$675	26%
Total expenditure	$8,331	$13,478	62%

[1] Because of practical reasons Lestoil's formula was not patented.

Other smaller competitors were also invading the field, typical of which was Texize Chemicals, Inc. Following in the footsteps of Lestoil's product and promotion, "Texize" established a strong market in the South and Southeast (see Exhibit 4).

Second, the popularity of spot television increased the demand to the point where rates on this type of television contract were boosted upward. Lestoil management estimated that from 1956 to 1958 alone, rates on spot television contracts had risen 25%. Mr. Eskenasy estimated that advertising expenditures ran as high as one-third of sales and Adell's advertising budget was primarily TV (see Exhibit 5). Mr. Kingsberg also noted that as Adell expansion moved into more sparsely populated areas the cost of advertising per sale necessarily had to rise. Both men admitted that there possibly were areas in which Lestoil operated at a loss but dismissed this lightly since the company's policy was such that it had to operate at a loss in new areas until a certain point of saturation was reached.

Third, rising transportation costs became evident. The preponderance of raw material came into the plant by rail. All finished product left the plant by truck. The shipping costs of raw material were fairly set. In fact, because of the geographic location of Lestoil's most critical ingredient, pine oil (see Exhibit 3 for sources of pine oil), there was little difference in shipping costs for the company's raw material to any part of the continental United States. However, the company employed and took advantage of various competitive modes of transporting its finished product; that is, truck, piggyback and fishy-back. The aggressiveness with which the company approached the problem, however, could not offset the fact that its finished product's delivery distances increased with each new contiguous market. Typical of the way in which transportation costs increased is the following illustrative example of the cost of shipping a cwt. of Lestoil from Holyoke to its expanding market.

	To Boston	To Cleveland	To Chicago
Truck transport	$0.33	$.96	$1.23
Warehouse and local cartage	0.00	.47	.47
Total	$0.33	$1.43	$1.70

To further accentuate this situation the traffic department prepared a schedule of transportation costs around a hypothetical Lestoil plant in Chicago showing substantial savings to the company (see Exhibit 6).

Lastly, the transportation costs entered into inventory investment. Several factors brought this about. Mr. Barowsky, aware of the consequence of a production stoppage at his one-plant operation, decided to maintain a six-to-eight-weeks' supply of finished product. The existing plant space was pressed with a crowded office and the necessity of storing raw materials, especially pine oil, Lestoil's distinctive ingredient. As a result, the bulk of finished product inventory had to be carried in the public warehouses used by the company.

Exhibit 6

Adell Chemical Company

Truck Load Rates in Effect in 1958 via Truck and Piggy-back

Holyoke to Minneapolis, Minnesota		Chicago to Minneapolis, Minnesota	
	$1.59 cwt.*		$.60 cwt.
Whse. and ctge.	.47	Whse. and ctge.	.47
	$2.06 cwt.		$1.07 cwt.
Holyoke to St. Louis, Missouri		Chicago to St. Louis, Missouri	
	$1.42 cwt.		$.38 cwt.
Whse. and ctge.	.47	Whse. and ctge.	.47
	$1.89 cwt.		$0.85 cwt.
Holyoke to Chicago, Illinois		Chicago to Chicago	
	$1.23 cwt.		$0.25
Whse. and ctge.	.47		
	$1.70 cwt.		

* Cost per cwt × .4 equals cost per case.

The company was financially able to open a new plant in another location without difficulty. Yet Mr. Barowsky firmly insisted that his young organization was not ready for developing a production center at this time. He felt that his product was well established and that he should continue to pursue his proven technique of expansion. He stressed the easy control of everything in a one-plant operation and added, "I'm not really interested in building an empire!"

6. LYALL SHOE CORPORATION (A)*

—GORDON DONALDSON

and

JAMES D. FLECK

Lyall Shoe Corporation was incorporated in 1928 as Lyall Chain Stores, Inc. and initially was comprised of a group of retail stores formerly operated by Jeremiah Douty and Company. In 1929 and 1930 it acquired Smythe Brothers Shoe Company, Inc., a shoe manufacturer and Simplex Shoe Company, a retailer. From its inception the Smythe family held control. The stock has been listed on the American Stock Exchange since 1936 and the Smythes continued to hold effective control with over 40% of the outstanding common stock. (Selected Financial Data, Exhibit 1.)

In its early stages the primary corporate emphasis was on the manufacturing side of the business. The company was primarily a manufacturer of men's shoes and the stores were a means of distributing this production. During the 1930's little executive talent or energy was devoted to the development of the retail merchandising portion of the business.

During the Second World War, the company moved almost entirely into government business, and relationships with peacetime customers were allowed to deteriorate. There was a lack of planning for the postwar period coupled with a belief that prewar conditions would return. The president's letter in the 1943 financial statement stated, "The reconversion to normal peacetime business in the shoe industry will not be a serious factor and it is expected that the world-wide demand for shoes will be substantial."

In 1947, 32-year old Mr. Walter Gordon, a vocal advocate of radical changes, was appointed vice president. For his years Gordon had considerable experience in the shoe business. During high school and college he had worked part time selling shoes in a Margot Bros. retail shoe store. In 1936, after graduating from Northwestern with a B.S. in Commerce, Gordon went to work full time in the head office of the Margot Bros. retail shoe chain as an

* Copyright 1963 by the President and Fellows of Harvard College. Reprinted by permission.

assistant buyer. Two years later he came to Lyall Shoe at the request of a Lyall executive who had previously been with Margot Bros. For the next three years Gordon worked in the retail division of Lyall. While there he recommended many changes including more emphasis on women's shoes and retailing in general and less emphasis on manufacturing. Gordon's superiors did not respond favorably to his suggestions. In 1941 Gordon resigned and submitted to Mr. John Smythe, the Chairman of the Board, a written statement presenting his analysis of Lyall Shoe and his suggested program for the future.

Exhibit 1
Lyall Shoe Corporation
Selected Operating and Dividend Figures for the Twelve Months Preceding the End of Each Fiscal Period

Year	Sales (000)	Net Profit (000)	Depreciation (000)	Cash Dividends* (000)
1958	$8,400	$52	$105	$31
1957	6,900	27	85	31
1956	6,300	78	77	32
1955	5,700	7	73	14
1954	5,200	(102)	67	59
1953	5,600	36	63	59
1952	5,700	(26)	65	89
1951	6,200	130	56	118
1950	7,000	82	67	73
1949	8,500	(278)	93	0
1948	11,400	(124)	108	0
1947	11,900	75	104	0
1946	11,500	346	104	0
1945	11,000	157	102	0

* Stock dividends were declared in 1956 (5%), 1957 (5%).

This must have made an impression upon Mr. Smythe, because in 1944 he prevailed upon Gordon to leave his position as merchandising manager of Basel's Inc., a shoe chain based in Nashville, and go with Lyall's manufacturing subsidiary, Smythe Bros., to expedite war orders. In 1945 Gordon was put in charge of the retailing of women's shoes for Lyall. He continued to impress Smythe, and, when Lyall's Board refused an opportunity to purchase a small shoe manufacturing and retailing firm, Smyth bought it himself at Gordon's urging. The results were so favorable and the situation at Lyall was becoming so critical that in late 1947 Smythe received sufficient support to remove the president and two top executives and to install Gordon as the operating head with the title of vice president.

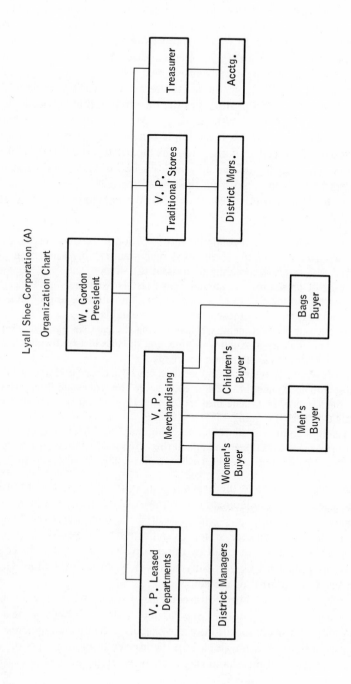

Lyall Shoe Corporation (A)

Organization Chart

Exhibit 2

491

Gordon believed that a strong retail distribution network was the key to future success. He felt that management approached policy from the viewpoint that they could sell everything they could make, whereas his approach was that they could make or buy everything they could sell. In addition he saw changes in the market to which Lyall was not reacting. There was a fast growing market for women's style merchandise. The higher priced men's shoes were now being bought in exclusive men's shops and Lyall was unable to compete in price with larger manufacturers such as Melville Shoe Corp. (over 700 Thom McAn retail stores) in the medium- and low-priced fields.

In June 1948, Mr. John Smythe died, and Mr. Gordon no longer had the support necessary to have his ideas implemented. However, sizeable losses in 1948 and 1949 helped in convincing the Board to accept Mr. Gordon's recommendation that manufacturing facilities be liquidated and that men's shoes be gradually eliminated from their retail stores.

The president's letter in the 1949 statement commented on their liquidation policy as follows:

The manufacturing division continued in this period to account for the over-all unprofitable showing while the retail stores made money, increasing their profits as compared with the corresponding six months of 1948.

At the time of presenting the annual report last November, your Officers and Directors committed themselves to a program of elimination of unprofitable operating units, and expansion of those found to be profitable.

Carrying out this committment, we have during the past six months completed the closing of our factory in Auburn, Maine, and the loss incurred which has been taken in this report, was greater than anticipated.

The cut sole plant in Saybrook, Connecticut, has been closed and nearly all of the merchandise and equipment has been used or sold. The real estate there, which we own, is in the hands of real estate brokers for sale. However, it is now partly rented and is practically self sustaining.

As the result of continued unprofitable operations your Directors voted to sell or otherwise dispose of additional manufacturing division facilities. We have been offering these for sale, but have received no definite offers to date.

By early 1950, the last of the firm's manufacturing plants had been liquidated. However, strong differences between Mr. Gordon and the manufacturing oriented members of the Board prevented the company from following any clearly defined course of action over the next five years. In 1956 Mr. Gordon acquired control of Lyall by purchasing with associates the controlling block of stock held by Mr. Smythe's widow. Since that time, Gordon has been firmly in control of the company.

Gordon has assumed control of a company with 58 stores spread mainly through the northeast section of the United States. Within the next year Gordon modified the composition of the executive group by replacing those men who would not or could not adapt themselves to his concepts of selling shoes with experienced merchandising executives from outside.

Exhibit 3
Lyall Shoe Corporation
Number of Outlets

At Fiscal Year End	Leased	Owned	Franchised	Total
November 30, 1956	1	64	0	65
November 20, 1957	20	64	0	84
May 31, 1958	31	62	3	97
May 31, 1959 (proposed)	37	54	12	103

Exhibit 4
Lyall Shoe Corporation (A)
Distribution of Footwear: Sales of Manufacturers' Branded and Unbranded Footwear by Types of Retail Channels

	Sales in Millions of Dollars	
	1958	1948
Shoe Stores	*$2,138*	*$1,467*
Single units—brands chiefly	884	621
2–10—brands chiefly	356	264
11 or more—unbranded chiefly	890	582
General Mdse. and Apparel	*$1,508*	*$1,395*
Single units—brands chiefly	525	676
2–10—brands chiefly	255	252
11 or more—unbranded chiefly	728	467
Leased Departments	*$308*	*$170*
Brands chiefly	176	130
Unbranded chiefly	132	40
Catalog and Direct Sales	*$84*	*$58*
Brands	25	19
Unbranded	59	39
Total Sales	*$4,030*	*$3,090*
Brands	2,221	1,962
Unbranded	1,809	1,128

Source: National Shoe Manufacturers Association.

One of the most far reaching of Mr. Gordon's early moves was the decision to lease shoe departments in discount department stores. This was by no means an innovation since leased departments had been in existence for many years and general merchandise discount houses were well established (see Exhibit 5). However, there was much vocal reaction by wholesalers and retailers to manufacturers who sold to discount outlets. Since Lyall did not manufacture, they were not concerned with the reactions of retail customers and

Exhibit 5

Lyall Shoe Corporation
Balance Sheet
(thousands of dollars)

	Dec. 1 1945	Nov. 30 1946	Nov. 29 1947	Nov. 30 1948	Nov. 26 1949	Dec. 2 1950	Dec. 1 1951	Nov. 29 1952	Nov. 29 1953	Nov. 27 1954	Nov. 26 1955	Dec. 1 1956	June 1 1957	May 31 1958
CURRENT ASSETS														
C & Mktb. Securities	$130	$131	$176	$381	$285	$685	$625	$787	$674	$493	$357	$526	$447	$509
AR	391	331	486	460	265	49	24	23	23	25	21	55	27	68
I-Mfg. Div.	1,202	1,799	2,044	1,288	323	28	—	—	—	—	—	—	—	—
Ret. Div.	908	1,161	1,383	1,310	1,381	1,600	1,827	1,331	1,337	1,404	1,473	1,838	1,649	2,539
Other	—	—	—	—	—	—	—	—	36	27	28	39	27	38
Total Current	$2,631	$3,422	$4,089	$3,439	$2,254	$2,362	$2,476	$2,141	$2,070	$1,949	$1,879	$2,458	$2,150	$3,154
CSV Life Ins.	$40	$45	$31	$33	$36	$39	$41	$47	$51	$54	$59	$64	$67	$71
Other	86	122	102	94	138	110	71	72	27	25	27	29	49	60
FIXED ASSETS														
Machining and Equipment	$239	$235	$220	$185	$55	$10	$—	$—	$—	$—	$—	$—	$—	$—
Stores & Equipment	715	804	832	884	926	1,049	1,114	1,220	1,235	1,326	1,388	1,466	1,532	1,572
Other	35	75	79	92	20									
Less Depreciation	(625)	(673)	(710)	(721)	(644)	(642)	(676)	(666)	(678)	(711)	(734)	(787)	(794)	(855)
Total Assets	$3,121	$4,030	$4,643	$4,006	$2,785	$2,928	$3,149	$2,814	$2,705	$2,643	$2,619	$3,230	$3,004	$4,002
CURRENT LIABILITIES														
Notes Pay-Bank	$—	$222	$805	$638	$—	$—	$—	$—	$—	$—	$—	$222	$—	$500
Accounts Pay	134	296	556	342	94	275	344	285	195	300	273	583	585	1,070
Taxes Pay	193	328	178	103	77	58	151	59	67	54	56	66	71	123
Due Employees	70	70	66	31	30	20	23	13	8	8	9	11	11	—
Other	40	84	83	56	30	27	71	12	13	18	23	44	28	41
Total Current	$394	$1,000	$1,688	$1,170	$231	$380	$589	$369	$283	$380	$361	$926	$695	$1,734
Other Liabilities	2	5	6	8	8	8	7	5	6	8	10	11	3	7
Capital Stock	1,168	1,296	1,296	1,296	1,296	1,290	1,290	1,290	1,290	1,290	1,290	1,373	1,373	1,441
Surplus	1,355	1,729	1,653	1,532	1,250	1,250	1,263	1,150	1,126	965	958	920	933	820*
Total Liabilities and Net Worth	$3,123	$4,030	$4,643	$4,006	$2,785	$2,928	$3,149	$2,814	$2,705	$2,643	$2,619	$3,230	$3,004	$4,002

* Revaluation to market price and loss on sale of securities totaling $62,000 charged to surplus.

since the leased departments were not located in the same areas as their own traditional stores they would not be competing with them.

One of the criteria for picking the location of a discount house at that time was that it not be too close to an existing discount store. This usually meant that initial sales were substantial and there was not the long build-up period usually associated with retail stores selling at nondiscount prices. Therefore, Gordon thought profits could be generated much more quickly than through the establishment of new retail stores. He also reasoned that the lower margin resulting from discount prices would be more than offset by a higher volume of sales and a faster turnover of merchandise resulting in a higher return on investment. In addition, there was a postwar shift in buying patterns to suburban stores and shopping centers where discount houses were normally located. Gordon did not think that traditional Lyall stores could compete in these markets with discount houses. Therefore, if Lyall wanted to share in this new market, they would have to do it through the discount stores. In the spring of 1956, Lyall leased the shoe department in a pilot venture of a successful ready-to-wear chain. The experiment was profitable and by November of 1958 the number of leased discount store departments had jumped to 30.

At the same time, Gordon placed the 58 traditional stores under close scrutiny. He decided to sell or liquidate those that did not have a profit potential. These included stores with less than $50,000 per annum sales, poor locations, onerous leases, and less than 40% before tax profit on inventory investment. By November of 1958 negotiations were being completed to sell 11 of the stores and as leases expired or opportunities to sell arose, Gordon intended to continue pruning the traditional outlets.

Organizationally the leased departments were put under Vice President Bert Wise, and the traditional stores remained under Vice President David Bentley, who was also responsible for all merchandising. Even though Gordon thought that the growth possibilities were mainly in the expansion of discount self-service departments, he also felt that the traditional store still catered to an important segment of the women's shoe market that demanded and was willing to pay a premium for personal service and fitting, pleasant surroundings, and downtown locations. However, no new stores had been acquired by November 1958.

The traditional stores were typically located in downtown shopping areas, at street level, with glass fronts for shoe display purposes. The store was staffed by a manager, sometimes an assistant manager, and one or two clerks, depending upon the season. Since shortly after the war, these stores had sold only women's shoes and accessories such as gloves, belts, etc. Lounge chairs were provided for the customers and the shoes were brought to her by a sales clerk.

The average store had sales of $100,000 per year, required an inventory of $25,000, and an investment in fixtures and leasehold improvements of $25,000 at cost, on the average. Although the gross margin (40%-45%) was higher than that for leased stores, the operating costs were proportionately higher still, resulting in a slightly lower net profit per sales dollar.

Lyall did very little initial styling of its own. It had what it called "creative copying ability in women's shoes." This they described as the ability to offer to the consumer a "popularly priced shoe" in a reasonable image of its "higher priced sister."

Lyall did not advertise merchandise in their traditional stores. They felt that they did not have a dense enough coverage in any one area to make advertising pay off locally. They also felt that point of sale displays and salesmanship were much more influential in the purchase of popularly priced shoes. (Most of the Lyall's shoes fell into the $3.00–$7.00 range.) Since they felt that the window display was their advertisement, they handled the setting up of store windows through a subsidiary professional display house. In this way they set up seasonal style themes and carried them out throughout their stores. While some of the store managers complained about the lack of media advertising, Lyall was not alone in this policy. Shoe Corporation of America (657 stores) advertised branded products sold through its own outlets and other retailers, but did not do local advertising for women's shoes. Morse Shoe, Inc. (70 stores), and Morton—two women's shoe specialists comparable to Lyall—also did no media advertising.

On the other hand, Edison Bros. Stores (322 stores) had advertising expenditures of approximately 1 % of sales. Several regional chains with large concentrations of stores in one area, such as National Shoe (125 stores in New York City) did advertise significantly. Gordon felt, however, that Lyall's stores were spread out too much to be able to support effective advertising.

He believed too that centralized control of as many functions as possible was essential to the profitability of a chain retail store. The following is a list prepared by head office of the various functions which it performed for each store:

1. Purchase all merchandise, trade fixtures, supplies and all other items that may be required by you in your business; the price to you of all of the foregoing shall be the cost to us of the items purchased.

2. Design styles for the merchandise purchased.

3. Receive and store the merchandise purchased.

4. Prepare the merchandise purchased for shipment to, and for sale in, your store. This will include, among other things, inspection, pricing, numbering, boxing, labeling, ticketing, packing, and distribution (of such merchandise).

5. Plan and advise with respect to store and window display.

6. Formulate and supervise merchandising policies and sales promotions.

7. Plan, supervise, and design all advertising material.

8. Furnish the services of an insurance, a real estate, and a construction and maintenance department.

9. Have supervisors visit your store at regular intervals and make recommendations with respect to operations.

10. Maintain inventory records and a set of books of account and perform all necessary clerical and bookkeeping services in connection therewith.

11. Assist and advise you with respect to personnel and labor relations problems.

Centralized purchasing provided the expertness of a highly qualified buyer with many high level contacts in the supplying firms. In addition, the buyer and his staff were able to minimize the style risk inherent in women's shoes. Lyall bought from many suppliers, including a large number of smaller suppliers who were able to expand their production quickly if an item proved successful. This enabled Lyall to follow successfully a cautious buying policy with quick reaction to early sales acceptance. They were then able to reorder in time for the fashion season and thus capitalize on the " racehorses " of the industry.

A high proportion of the shoes were shipped into Lyall's warehouse, where they were prepared for sale and repacked in smaller lots for shipment to the individual stores.

The vice president of retail stores had four district sales managers reporting to him. Each of the district sales managers had two or three area sales managers who were also store managers of a large store in the area. Through this network, constant contacts were made with the stores. These contacts enabled management to check on the operations of the stores and also gave the store managers an opportunity to feed back useful information on customer reactions.

Perpetual inventory records were kept in New York showing inventories at each of the stores. Weekly reports were sent to New York by the stores indicating sales for the week. On the basis of this information, the head office staff decided what each store would receive the following week and periodically, through the cumulative effect of these records, revised old orders or placed new ones with suppliers. While the individual store managers had no authority to purchase, set up displays, etc., the more successful ones were listened to and their recommendations were taken into account in setting limits.

In the leased departments buying and display were also under the control of head office, but an advertising allowance of 2% of sales to the discount chain involved was usually incorporated into the lease. While this advertising would often promote shoes, its main purpose was to bring traffic to the stores. Lyall would supply mats and copy for their allotted space, but was subject to the dictates of the discount house when differences of opinion occurred.

The leased discount departments did not carry the Lyall name on the outlets. The typical leased departments was a self-service section of a large discount house. Wide aisles were arranged to accommodate many more shoppers at one time than would be possible in the conventional store. The shoes were arranged in racks and display counters for easy access by the customer. A minimum of clerks were available for fitting and completing the sale when necessary. The emphasis was on displaying in an attractive and appealing manner as many shoes as possible.

The average leased department had sales of $200,000 per year and required 3,000 square feet of space. The lower gross (22%–28%) was more than offset by lower operating expenses and a higher net profit margin, averaging between 3% and 4% on sales after taxes, had been typical. The rental charge was usually 6% of sales plus the additional advertising charge of 2%. Other expenses brought occupancy costs up to 8.75% of sales. The average investment in inventory and fixtures (minor) was $38,000. Most leases were for five years with escape clauses for low volume and renewal clauses subject to renegotiation of rent. While traditional stores carried only women's shoes, the leased departments carried a complete line of men's and children's shoes as well.

By November of 1958, sales were at an annual expected level of $10 million with leased departments accounting for one-half of the volume evenly divided between women's shoes on the one hand and children's and men's on the other.

APPENDIX: EXHIBIT 6

1958 BASIC ANALYSIS OF THE LEATHER AND SHOE INDUSTRIES[1]

Shoes

DEMAND

Growth of population is expected to continue as the principal factor affecting demand for shoes and footwear. Because these articles are necessities, shoe producers are likely to be affected to a lesser degree by swings in the business cycle; the percentage of income expended by consumers for shoes rises during recessions, and lags during advances.

The following points are important in appraising the longer-term prospects for the industry:

1. Based on income trends, plus projected increase in population, it is possible that unit consumption of shoes in the U.S. may increase by as much as 40% in the next decade.

2. The shoe industry is considered to be moving into stronger hands, since the number of shoe manufacturing companies decreased by some 15% in the past five years. This pattern, reflecting need for stronger finances and more efficient manufacture and distribution, doubtless will contribute to more emphasis on research, both in products and processes.

3. Production per man in U.S. shoe factories is 50% higher than in the best comparable foreign plants. Rapid style changes and wide ranges of sizes and widths also insulate the domestic shoe industry from foreign competition.

4. Technological progress in the shoe industry has been important. Nylon heels on women's shoes, for example, outlast leather by four to one.

[1] Reprinted by permission from *1958 Basic Analysis of the Leather and Shoe Industries*, Standard & Poor's Corporation, New York, N.Y.

5. Shoe prices now, against those a decade ago, make a more favorable comparison than prices in most consumer goods industries.

Per capita consumption of shoes in the U.S. is higher than that in any other country. In 1957, U.S. consumption was 3.45 pairs per capita, against 2.77 in the United Kingdom, 2.72 in Canada, and 2.55 in Australia, the other three largest shoe consumers on a per capita basis. Annual consumption in the U.S.S.R. is estimated at 0.85 pairs per capita, Brazil 1.00, and Japan 0.38.

PER CAPITA CONSUMPTION

In the past, spectacular advances in consumption of shoes were notably absent. Per capita consumption of shoes in 1927, for example, some three decades ago, was about 2.80 pairs per year in the U.S. After rising to 2.92 pairs in 1929, and falling to 2.53 in 1931, consumption advanced irregularly to a peak of 3.62 pairs in 1946, including military. From a post-war low of 3.11 in 1949, per capita consumption rose to some 3.49 in 1957 (see Table 1). Practically all of the gains in per capita consumption of shoes were in the women's, misses' and childrens' categories. Per capita consumption of men's shoes over the past several decades decreased slightly on balance.

Women normally buy four or five pairs of shoes per annum. The volume of men's shoe sales is too modest to support the average shoe retailer, and for this reason, most of the shoe retailers have expanded their distribution of women's and misses' shoes. At first sign of a downturn in business, the head of the family starts to economize. Sales of women's shoes decrease only when the economizing becomes critical. Children's shoe sales at the same time increase consistently, and nothing short of a severe crisis in the family budget retards sales of this division.

LEADING PRODUCERS

Since comparatively little capital is required to start a shoe factory, the bulk of production is accounted for by a large number of small, highly-competitive units. According to the Bureau of Census, there were 900 shoe producers in the U.S. in 1954. The largest 500 producers made approximately 94% of the shoes, while the smallest 400 accounted for only 6%. In 1957, the eight largest companies combined did approximately 30% of the total business and the 15 largest about one-third. Imports and exports normally account for only about 1% to 2% of domestic shoe requirements and production, and are expected to continue relatively unimportant.

Domestic manufacturers that accounted for roughly one-half of 1% or more of total shoe production in 1957 were as follows: International Shoe Co. (8.5%); Endicott Johnson Corp. (6.1%); General Shoe Corp. (4.8%); Brown Shoe Co. (4.9%); Shoe Corp. of America (1.9%); J. F. McElwain Co., owned by Melville Shoe Corp. (1.4%); U.S. Shoe Corp. (1.1%); Craddock-Terry Shoe Co. (1.0%); Consolidated National Shoe Corp. (1.0%); Green Shoe Manufacturing Co. (0.7%); Sudbury Footwear, Inc. (0.6%); Wolff Shoe Manufacturing Co. (0.5%); Muskin Shoe Co. (0.5%); Kesslen Shoe Co. (0.-%); H.O. Toor Shoe Corp. (0.5%); Ettelbrick Shoe Co. (0.5%); Lown Shoes, Inc. (0.5%).

The largest manufacturer outside the United States from a unit volume standpoint is believed to be the group of shoe enterprises controlled by the Bata interests. Extremely low-cost producers, the Bata factories are situated strategically near markets, including the population centers of countries such as India and Egypt.

Shoe-producing facilities added after World War II raised U.S. capacity to over 600 million pairs in 1946. Subsequently, there were some plant shutdowns as deferred requirements for shoes became satisfied and a larger proportion of disposable income was diverted to the purchase of hard goods. Nevertheless, rated capacity in

Table 1

Estimated Consumption of Shoes by Major Types
(Pairs per Capita)

	Women's	Men's	Misses' and Children's	Boys' and Youth's	Infants and Babies'	All Other	Total
1957	4.47	1.74	5.09	1.61	1.98	0.46	3.49
1956	4.45	1.81	5.19	1.48	1.99	0.46	3.51
1955	4.42	1.75	5.33	1.53	2.05	0.45	3.50
1954	4.21	1.68	5.37	1.46	2.14	0.41	3.36
1953	4.11	1.80	5.27	1.35	2.17	0.40	3.34
1952	4.17	1.78	5.11	1.35	2.12	0.38	3.31
1951	3.93	2.02	4.82	1.20	2.06·	0.37	3.25
1950	3.92	1,83	4.87	1.29	2.26	0.40	3.25
1949	3.68	1.80	4.50	1.30	2.43	0.36	3.11
1948	3.70	1.89	4.77	1.40	2.37	0.35	3.15
1947	3.70	1.92	4.55	1.57	2.28	0.33	3.43
1946	4.36	1.98	4.86	1.68	2.58	0.49	3.62
1945	4.00	1.26	4.98	1.59	2.67	0.47	3.22*
1944	3.64	1.37	4.55	1.85	2.50	0.50	3.12*
1943	4.13	1.80	3.98	1.77	2.20	0.50	3.38*
1942	3.79	2.04	4.09	1.67	2.37	0.59	3.45*
1941	3.61	2.15	4.18	1.56	2.21	0.47	3.29*
1940	3.57	2.09	3.79	1.40	2.18	0.42	3.15
1939	3.61	2.05	3.74	1.46	2.14	0.40	3.13
1938	3.60	2.08	3.53	1.48	2.06	0.41	3.13
1937	3.69	2.18	3.35	1.45	2.06	0.48	3.25
1936	3.51	2.16	3.19	1.44	1.96	0.48	3.14
1935	3.26	2.07	3.09	1.47	1.85	0.44	2.96
1934	3.11	1.96	2.07	1.55	1.67	0.43	2.83
1933	2.99	1.80	2.78	1.57	1.53	0.41	2.68
1932	2.85	1.70	2.80	1.56	1.51	0.38	2.56
1929	3.20	2.11	3.14	1.86	2.05	0.36	2.92

* Excludes shoes for military purposes.

Source: Boot and Shoe Recorder.

1958 was indicated above the 600 million figure. During periods of high consumer income—such as 1955 and 1956—shoe production should run at or fairly close to rated capacity. However, the industry is capable of manufacturing considerably more shoes from present facilities than "capacity" figures indicate.

From 1946 to 1957, the total number of shoe manufacturers held fairly stable, despite the trend towards acquisition of smaller concerns by larger companies. Most leading producers have acquired "captive" retail outlets for at least a portion of their output, primarily through purchase of shoe-store chains, direct financing of retailers, or acquisition of smaller competitors. This trend promises a more integrated and stronger shoe industry.

LEADING RETAILERS

According to the Census Bureau, there were 23,847 stores in operation in the U.S. in 1954, and about one-quarter of the outlets were owned by organizations operating eleven or more stores. Divergent trends have been in evidence during postwar years.

Table 2

Production of Shoes by Major Types

(In Millions of Pairs)

	Women's	Men's	Misses' and Children's	Boys' and Youths'	Infants and Babies'	All Other	Total
1958	—	—	—	—	—	—	E573.0*
1957	274.2	104.3	76.7	24.2	37.7	80.5	597.6
1956	273.4	106.9	74.4	21.8	37.2	78.1	591.8
1955	270.9	103.7	74.5	22.1	38.0	76.2	585.4
1954	245.1	94.7	68.8	19.7	36.9	65.2	530.4
1953	237.9	100.7	71.4	18.1	37.9	66.0	532.0
1952	247.2	103.9	67.0	18.7	36.7	59.7	533.2
1951	214.1	107.1	56.9	14.6	34.1	55.1	481.9
1950	236.1	103.4	61.9	16.7	38.6	65.8	522.5
1949	207.2	97.8	55.0	16.9	36.5	60.9	474.3
1948	205.3	105.4	58.9	17.3	38.4	54.3	479.6
1947	210.6	107.5	55.8	19.8	36.4	49.7	479.8
1946	234.9	104.2	53.9	20.6	37.8	74.3	525.8†
1945	196.0	68.7	54.4	15.9	35.0	74.3	443.9†
1944	185.3	68.8	45.7	17.3	29.1	70.2	417.4†
1943	195.7	84.7	33.8	19.8	25.4	59.0	418.5†
1942	181.7	102.1	41.3	17.1	25.7	75.2	443.0†
1941	184.9	120.5	47.9	19.2	28.8	82.4	483.1†
1940	167.5	102.7	40.8	15.3	21.8	56.2	404.2
1939	179.6	104.0	44.0	16.9	24.1	55.6	424.1
1938	164.0	97.0	40.2	17.1	21.3	51.1	390.7
1937	171.4	103.4	39.8	17.5	22.8	57.1	412.0
1936	168.0	104.1	36.8	16.6	21.6	68.1	415.2
1935	151.8	99.9	37.3	17.8	21.2	55.8	383.8
1934	138.0	91.7	34.5	17.3	19.5	56.1	357.1
1933	136.5	89.2	33.2	20.0	18.6	53.0	350.4
1932	121.1	75.3	33.6	18.1	15.7	49.5	313.3
1929	134.2	95.0	39.9	22.9	23.8	45.5	361.4

† Excludes shoes for military purposes, which were as follows: 1946 3.2; 1945 47.2; 1944 50.5 1943 46.9; 1942 40.9; 1941 15.3.

* E—Estimated.

Source: U.S. Department of Commerce and Boot and Shoe Recorder.

During most of the period, the family type of shoe store has declined in importance, although they account for over half of the total. The specialized store, particularly for women, has grown in popularity. However, the sharp rise in the volume of retail business done in suburban areas has encouraged the large shoe chains to concentrate on stores catering to all members of the family.

Table 3
Shipments of Leather and Leather Products
(In Thousands of Dollars)

	1947	1955	1956
Leather tanning and finishing	1,004,970	666,935	661,931
Finished cattle hide and kip side leathers	646,105	405,210	417,410
Finished calf and whole kip leathers	107,747	74,529	67,537
Finished sheep and lamb leathers	91,674	65,762	64,369
Other finished leathers	146,920	90,245	81,478
Rough, russet and crust, leathers	12,524	N.A.	N.A.
Industrial leather products	52,267	79,986	88,737
Industrial leather belting	21,993	12,553	12,875
Leather backing	20,011	56,080	63,128
Other, including textile leather	10,263	N.A.	N.A.
Footwear, cut stock and findings	294,135	268,375	278,030
Boot and shoe cut stock	198,539	164,188	164,788
Other boot and shoe findings	95,596	104,187	113,242
Footwear, except rubber	1,712,761	1,876,454	2,000,706
Men's, youth's, and boys dress shoes	522,910	528,814	558,708
Men's work shoes, including moccasins	97,523	128,591	149,474
Women's, misses', and children's shoes	924,304	937,839	990,485
Infants' and babies' shoes	57,176	72,002	74,463
Athletic shoes, except rubber soled, canvas top	19,926	N.A.	N.A.
Playshoes	77,973	174,827	181,102
All other, except rubber and house slippers	12,952	N.A.	N.A.
House slippers	75,390	105,343	118,341
Dress gloves and mittens, all leather	44,992	N.A.	N.A.
Work gloves and mittens, all leather	16,370	20,186	N.A.
Suitcases, briefcases, bags, and trunks	127,863	190,002	198,397
Women's handbags and purses	161,080	191,796	200,497
Leather billfolds, wallets, and key cases	37,060	68,387	69,002
Saddlery, harness, and whips	18,817	N.A.	N.A.

N.A.—Not available.

Source: Annual Survey of Manufacturers, U.S. Dept. of Commerce.

Among the companies operating the largest number of shoe outlets are the following, with approximate number of stores: Melville Shoe Corp. (1,018 outlets including 788 Thom McAn stores and 219 Miles Shoe stores); Brown Shoe Corp. (685 outlets, with 406 through E. R. Kinney, which it controls, 190 through Wohl Shoe Co. and 89 Regal Shoe); Shoe Corp. of America (676 outlets excluding A. S. Beck, in large part through Shiff Shoe Co. and Gallenkamp Stores Co.); General Shoe Corp. (over 600); Endicott Johnson Corp. (about 540); Edison Bros. Stores, Inc. (330, including 144 under the name Baker's); A. S. Beck Shoe Corp., controlled by Shoe Corp. of America (231); Butler's Inc. (148); Nunn-Bush Shoe Co. (120); National Shoes, Inc. (136); Cannon Shoe Co. (110); H. C. Godman Co. (100); Florsheim Shoe Co., owned by International Shoe Co. (about 100); and John Irving Shoe Corp. (106).

Table 4
Shoe Production of Five Leading Companies
(In Thousands of Pairs)

	Brown Shoe	Endicott-Johnson	General Shoe	Int'l Shoe	Melville* Shoe
1957	29,105	34,223	30,000**	50,952	—
1956	26,908	36,342	27,500**	53,434	—
1955	25,018	35,757	26,000**	52,314	9,100†
1954	22,471	31,714	25,380	50,775	8,500†
1953	24,060	35,367	19,512	55,557	9,000†
1952	21,475	—	—	53,341	—
1951	19,591	—	16,274	48,333	8,535
1950	22,116	—	16,643	51,565	9,548
1949	19,600	—	15,070	47,904	10,311
1948	20,590	—	15,397	54,602	10,658
1947	19,526	—	16,149	54,044	11,017
1946	17,400	—	15,985	47,365	11,599
1945	18,609	—	13,415	52,651	8,841
1944	17,720	—	12,520	53,921	8,397
1943	18,050	—	12,028	50,133	8,797
1942	17,352	—	10,608	54,984	11,857
1941	15,803	—	9,629	56,609	12,221
1940	11,798	—	7,392	45,427	10,933

* Retail sales

† Estimated production.

Source: Company reports.

MERCHANDISING POLICIES

Distribution and merchandising policies in the shoe industry generally are sound. Around half of total output is distributed to retail outlets by manufacturers, about 25% is accounted for by producers' wholesale branches, and some 25% is handled by independent distributors. Under this arrangement, the industry has been able to gear production relatively close to retail demand. The retailer's markup varies considerably in individual instances, but generally is around 40% of retail price.

Based on a U.S. Bureau of Census study sponsored by the National Shoe Manufacturers Association and the New England Shoe & Leather Association, the average retail price of all U.S. footwear sold in 1957 was $6.10 a pair, unchanged from 1956.

About half the shoes in 1957 sold for $4.80 or less. In 1956 about half sold at $4.97 or less. Half the men's shoes in 1957 sold at $9.45 or less; in 1956, $9.50. The comparable "midway" prices in the case of women's were $4.71 in 1957, and $4.78 in 1956.

In most years, there has been a noticeable absence of pressure on retail prices in periods of slack demand. However, the buyer's market that developed in 1953–1954 resulted in greater emphasis on marketing policies. Many leading companies increased advertising and promotional expenses and now concentrate on production of medium and lower-priced footwear.

Table 5
Shoe Production by States
(Per Cent of Total)

	Mass.	Me.	N.H.	N.Y.	Penn.	Ohio	Ill	Mo.	Tenn.	Wis.	Other	Total U.S.
1957	16.6	8.2	6.8	14.7	13.1	3.5	4.8	10.5	4.1	2.7	15.0	100.0
1956	17.4	8.3	7.1	14.5	12.4	3.6	4.9	10.4	4.0	2.7	14.7	100.0
1955	18.0	8.2	7.2	14.8	12.3	3.4	5.0	10.0	4.3	2.8	14.0	100.0
1954	18.7	8.1	7.1	15.8	11.0	3.0	5.2	10.6	4.1	3.0	13.4	100.0
1953	17.9	8.0	7.7	15.6	10.7	3.4	5.7	11.5	—	3.2	16.3	100.0
1952	17.1	7.4	7.9	16.3	10.3	3.8	6.0	12.0	—	3.3	15.9	100.0
1951	16.9	7.0	7.7	17.8	10.4	4.0	5.5	11.6	—	3.3	15.8	100.0
1950	17.5	6.6	7.9	17.5	10.2	3.7	5.9	11.4	—	3.4	16.9	100.0
1949	17.5	5.8	8.2	17.9	9.9	3.8	6.1	11.9	—	3.7	15.3	100.0
1948	17.4	5.3	7.7	18.7	8.6	3.8	6.7	13.3	—	3.8	14.7	100.0
1947	17.0	6.0	8.0	18.0	8.0	4.0	7.0	14.0	—	4.0	14.0	100.0
1946	20.7	6.1	8.2	19.0	8.2	3.3	6.6	11.4	—	3.5	13.0	100.0
1945	19.6	5.6	8.3	20.8	7.8	3.3	6.9	11.6	—	3.6	12.3	100.0
1940	18.9	6.5	9.2	17.7	8.9	3.7	7.1	11.3	—	3.9	12.8	100.0
1935	19.6	6.6	7.8	21.7	5.7	4.3	7.0	11.3	—	4.4	11.6	100.0
1931	24.0	4.7	7.5	23.1	4.4	3.1	7.2	12.3	—	4.1	9.6	100.0
1929	23.4	4.3	6.9	21.7	4.8	3.3	7.5	13.3	—	4.8	10.0	100.0
1925	22.3	5.2	5.5	22.5	5.2	4.6	22.2		—	5.2	7.3	100.0
1919	35.3	5.8	6.9	19.0	7.1	5.4	3.2	8.0	—	3.4	5.9	100.0
1909	41.4	3.3	9.0	10.0	6.2	6.6	2.9	9.1	—	2.6	8.9	100.0

Source: U.S. Department of Commerce.

Because of the highly seasonal character of the business, practically the entire installed capacity of the shoe trade is needed to meet the normally heavy demand during the spring and fall peaks. The fact that costs are normally flexible (as discussed later) discourages excessive production during the slow between-season periods. As a result, there are few prolonged periods of production greatly in excess of actual consumption requirements.

STYLE ELEMENT

Style is important in merchandising women's shoes. The greater emphasis on style rather than on quality developed during the early thirties, when competition for business brought drastic changes in the price structure, increasing the volume in low-priced brackets and reducing sales of high-priced lines.

This shift in emphasis increased per capita consumption of women's shoes from less than three pairs in the 1920's to approximately 4.47 in 1957. Strong emphasis

Table 6
Percentage of Shoes Produced with Leather Soles

Year	%	Year	%	Year	%	Year	%
1957	34.4	1949	56.5	1941	75.5	1933	73.6
1956	36.3	1948	65.0	1940	73.3	1932	94.9
1955	37.0	1947	73.3	1939	73.4	1931	80.0
1954	38.0	1946	74.2	1938	77.0	1930	85.2
1953	40.0	1945	56.7	1937	78.8	1929	88.2
1952	42.0	1944	54.9	1936	80.4	1928	89.3
1951	44.0	1943	69.3	1935	79.0		
1950	51.0	1942	78.2	1934	74.4		

Source: U.S. Department of Commerce.

Table 7
Athletic Shoes Production by Types
(Pairs)

	1955*	1956*	1957*
Baseball—Regular	721,555	750,000	760,000
Baseball—Little League	155,713	170,000	180,000
Football	436,503	475,000	480,000
Track	138,343	140,000	150,000
Soccer	2,274	2,500	2,800
Bowling	423,080	450,000	470,000
Boxing	19,835	20,000	20,000
Basketball—leather uppers	5,001	5,500	6,200
Skating—Ice	1,043,029	1,120,000	1,170,000
Skating—Roller	448,153	495,000	520,000
Golf	29,448	33,000	35,000
Ski boats	3,910	4,200	4,400
Crew shoes	14,876	15,000	15,300
Umpire shoes	235	250	280
Total	3,441,955	3,680,450	3,813,980

* Partly estimated.

Source: The Athletic Institute.

will continue to be placed on styling of women's footwear. However, an offsetting factor in the uptrend in women's shoe demand has been a steady to downward trend in consumption of men's shoes. Because of this adverse trend, the trade is become more conscious of style in men's shoes, particularly in regard to sports' footwear.

Styles in women's shoes, like those in other women's apparel, normally change often, thus increasing costs and inventory risks. Some of the large manufacturers concentrate the bulk of operations in men's shoes, since earnings in this division usually are the more stable.

Style changes add to the manufacturer's hazards, but also have a favorable side. Modern shoes, particularly women's shoes, are largely a product of fashion. Shoes vary not only with the season, but also with the different social functions in the course of the day. Even the styles of men's shoes differ seasonally. In a smaller degree, fashion has done to the shoe industry what it has done to the dress industry.

SHOE PRICES

Demand, although relatively stable, reflects broad changes in consumer purchasing power, and prices tend to fluctuate with the consumer's ability to buy. Raw materials and labor are the chief costs in the manufacture of shoes, with leather and wages usually accounting for roughly 50% and 35%, respectively, of wholesale prices. Therefore, leather and hide prices and wages play important parts in determining shoe prices. Shoe prices are sensitive to changes in leather prices, but fluctuate less widely.

Table 8

Number of Stores of Leading Shoe Chains

	Shoe Corp. of America	Edison Bros. Stores	E.R. Kinney Co.*	Melville Shoe Corp.		Shoe Corp. of America	Edison Bros. Stores	E.R. Kinney Co.*	Melville Shoe Corp.
1957	656	322	385	1,018	1948	326	202	308	547
1956	625	297	360	947	1947	306	188	310	519
1955	591	267	352	886	1946	315	180	306	519
1954	528	251	344	834	1945	301	170	317	536
1953	511	245	327	794	1944	284	169	330	549
1952	485	237	324	739	1943	284	166	338	556
1951	467	228	318	577	1942	288	168	339	579
1950	440	220	311	560	1941	294	162	346	659
1949	332	213	305	560	1940	285	142	343	666

* Controlled by Brown Shoe Co.

Source: Company reports.

OPERATING COSTS

Piece-work wage scales and leased machinery, uncommon in other mechanized industries, give shoe makers a relatively flexible cost structure. Nearly all of the machinery used to produce shoes is owned by a few concerns—United Shoe Machinery is the largest—and is leased to shoe manufacturers on a rental basis. Under a United States Supreme Court Ruling, United was required, beginning in late 1954, to offer all types of its machinery for sale as well as for rental. However, most shoe producers have continued to lease machinery, as rentals are paid in proportion to actual output, thus eliminating the necessity of periodic charges for idle plant equipment and holding depreciation and obsolescence expenses to a minimum.

The wage structure also is favorable from an operating point of view. Unlike the fixed patterns in most industries, the wages of a relatively large percentage of the workers are on a piece-work basis. Thus, in periods of declining demand, when production necessarily must be reduced, wage costs also decline. In 1946 and 1947, a few shoe companies, including International negotiated wage contracts which included automatic increases and decreases in wage rates in accordance with fluctuations in the cost-of-living index. This practice is not widespread nor do many companies grant a guaranteed work week.

Table 9
Employment and Hourly Earnings (Wages)
Leather and Shoe Industries

	Production Workers (thousands)			Hourly Earnings (cents)		
	Leather*	Footwear†	All Mfg.	Leather*	Footwear†	All Mfg.
1957	38.4	219.1	12,911.0	195.0	149.0	207.0
1956	38.4	221.5	13,195.0	187.0	144.0	198.0
1955	40.1	223.6	13,061.0	181.0	134.0	188.0
1954	39.3	219.0	12,589.0	176.0	133.0	181.0
1953	42.4	225.8	13,833.0	171.0	132.0	177.0
1952	41.9	222.7	13,144.0	162.0	127.0	167.0
1951	43.3	218.4	13,155.0	155.0	123.0	159.0
1950	46.5	229.4	12,317.0	144.1	113.8	146.5
1949	45.2	226.2	11,596.2	139.1	109.6	140.1
1948	49.5	234.8	12,717.0	134.5	108.5	135.0
1947	51.5	235.5	12,794.0	124.4	102.2	123.7
1946	—	—	12,105.0	108.8	93.0	108.4
1945	—	—	12,859.0	98.2	82.3	102.3
1944	—	—	14,607.0	93.9	76.8	101.9
1943	—	—	15,014.0	87.9	71.7	96.1
1942	—	—	12,854.0	81.3	65.6	85.3
1941	—	—	10,877.0	70.8	57.8	72.9
1940	—	—	8,811.0	64.7	52.6	66.1
1939	—	—	8,192.0	63.4	50.3	63.3

* Establishments primarily engaged in tanning, currying and finishing sole and belting leathers and upper and lining leathers.

† Except rubber.

Source: U.S. Department of Labor.

Accounting practices of most leading shoe companies are conservative and provide protection against any serious decline in earnings because of inventory losses. Some companies, notably General and Brown, value inventories at lower of cost or market, while others, such as International and Melville, use the Lifo (last in, first out) method of inventory valuation. Endicott Johnson's practice of taking a definite amount of stock as normal and carrying it at a low fixed price limits the unsettling effect of the usually wide changes in hide prices.

Two recent developments have had a moderate effect on shoe manufacturing costs. In 1955, United Shoe announced that, under its new machine leasing agreements, repair and service charges would no longer be included in the basic rental charge but would be computed separately, and that the basic monthly rental charges were being increased. In addition, the increase in the minimum wage to $1 an hour on March 1, 1956, appears to have affected the shoe industry to a greater extent than the average industrial concern. However, in the aggregate, these added direct costs probably do not amount to more than several cents for the average pair of shoes.

Table 10
Shoe Prices—Average Factory Value
(Dollars Per Pair)

1958*	$3.53	1950	$3.44	1942	$2.33	1935	$1.66
1957	3.58	1949	3.46	1941	1.94	1349	1.71
1956	3.60	1948	3.72	1940	1.80	1933	1.57
1955	3.43	1947	3.72	1939	1.68	1932	1.68
1954	3.54	1946	3.01	1938	1.71	1931	2.05
1953	3.61	1945	2.42	1937	1.80	1930	2.39
1952	3.56	1944	2.40	1936	1.71	1929	2.58
1951	3.96	1943	2:41				

* Through September.

Sources: U.S. Department of Commerce (1946 to date) and Tanners' Council of America (1929–1945).

Piece-work wage rates, coupled with machinery rentals based on production and conservative accounting practices, help to maintain profit margins in good times and bad, and offset to some extent the adverse effects of wide swings in raw material prices.

EARNINGS

Primarily because of comparatively steady volume, sound merchandising policies, and flexible costs, earnings of leading shoe producers have been relatively stable. A large number of mergers since World War II have tended to distort the earnings picture for a number of the companies covered in this Survey. In general, however, profit margins have remained narrower than during World War II.

According to figures for 1954 reported by the Internal Revenue Service, 897 footwear manufacturing establishments (other than rubber) realized a 4.36% profit on gross income of $1,904,141,000 for the year. For the preceding year, the profit realized was 3.92% on sales of $2,009,982,000 reported by 1,042 reporting factories. The percentage of profit to gross was about 70% above that realized by an average of 970 reporting factories for the period 1935-1939.

According to the Internal Revenue Service, based on 982 income tax returns for 1955, 707 shoe manufacturers in that year earned a total of $105 million, and at the same time, 275 had losses, indicated at an aggregate of $5 million. Total receipts for all 982 units were $2,085,838,000.

7. LYALL SHOE CORPORATION (B)*

—GORDON DONALDSON

and

JAMES D. FLECK

During 1958 Walter Gordon, president of the Lyall Shoe Corporation (see Lyall (A)) was approached by a business broker to see if Lyall was interested in purchasing a men's shoe manufacturing firm. Lyall's volume in men's shoes had grown from 8% to 12% of total sales in the last three years and Gordon wondered if the time to re-enter the manufacturing field had arrived.

At one time Lyall had manufactured medium and higher priced men's shoes, but had liquidated their manufacturing division in the late 1940's after sizeable losses and a shift in emphasis from men's to women's shoes in their retail stores.

Lyall had never manufactured women's shoes, and Gordon was definitely not interested in taking on the tremendous style risks involved. However, medium and low-priced men's shoes were another thing. While there were style changes, they were not as extreme and the price concessions required to move older styles were not as severe. In addition, there had been important changes in Lyall's methods of distribution in the last two years.

After Gordon had acquired control of Lyall in 1956, the company had moved strongly into the leasing of shoe departments in discount stores. These departments offered a complete range of medium and low-priced shoes. As a result of this, Lyall bought close to a million dollars worth of men's shoes in the last twelve months with prospects of a substantial increase as new leased departments were opened. Upon finding out that the company for sale made low-priced men's shoes and boots, Gordon decided to investigate the opportunity.

The V. R. Shakee Company was an old family company started in 1908. The son and son-in-law of the founder each held 50% of the common stock. They were both over fifty and there were no members of the family interested in carrying on the business. The company had one plant composed of six large four-story frame buildings located on a rail siding one-half mile from downtown Portland, Maine. It had been leased from an investment group composed of prominent local businessmen. The original building had been erected for Shakee and additions made as needed.

The company employed approximately 500 persons, of which 60% were female. Direct production work required 400 people of whom 200 were skilled; 145 were semiskilled; and 55 were unskilled. Most of the work force were over forty with many years of seniority. The workers were not unionized. The average rate of pay based on piecework incentive was $1.50 an hour. Cutters, the operation requiring the highest degree of skill, earned up to $100 per week.

Portland had long been a shoe manufacturing center and there were also several tanneries within a fifty-mile radius. It was a labor surplus area. Experienced workers were available on short notice. Many workers lived on small acreages outside of town, enabling them to support themselves during work shortages and layoffs.

Shakee made shoes to customers' specifications upon order only and did not stock finished shoes for subsequent sale. The customers could pick from 100 different designs for which Shakee had lasts, dies, and patterns. The company owned most of its equipment which it had purchased since the 1954 Supreme Court ruling on leased shoe machinery. Of its civilian shoe sales, approximately 50% went to jobbers, 25% to chain stores, and 25% to mail-order houses. The sales force consisted of a sales manager and three salesman handling about 130 accounts in total.

After meeting with the owners of Shakee, Gordon had established that Mr. Shakee wished to retire; that Mr. Hart (the son-in-law of the founder) would remain up to five years to assist new management, if desired; that they were willing to sell the stock at the book value indicated by the adjusted May 31, 1958, Balance Sheet (see exhibit).

The Balance Sheet had been adjusted to include the value of certain assets. Shakee had written off all capital acquisitions at the time of purchase. An appraisal company had put depreciation-adjusted replacement values on these assets of approximately twice the amounts shown in the Balance Sheet (Exhibit 1). The final amounts were arrived at by the owners and Gordon thought that these were reasonable values for the assets in question.

From an analysis of the operating statements for the past five years (see Exhibit 2), Gordon gathered data to help him in estimating a return on investment and a payback for the business.

In talks with his banker, Gordon obtained a promise that, if the purchase was consummated, the bank would grant a five-year loan of $1,500,000 at 5% payable $100,000 every six months and then a $500,000 final payment. Gordon had previously attempted to get additional financing to open up leased departments at a faster rate, but had difficulty due to the lack of a profitable history. He felt sure that through a judicious use of assets he would be able to generate a positive cash flow from the acquisition of Shakee which would aid in the financing of new leased departments.

Exhibit 1

V. R. Shakee Company

Adjusted Balance Sheet,
May 31, 1958

Current Assets		
Cash	$408,633	
Accts. Rec.	727,405	
Inventories	571,947	
Mktbl. Securities (market price)	123,375	
Prepaid Insurance	22,649	
Total Current Assets		$1,854,009
Other Assets		
CSV Life Insurance	$134,499	
Right of Reduction Fund	13,320	
Advances to Employees	901	$148,720
Fixed Assets		
Land	$2,775	
Warehouse	10,183	
Machinery and Fixtures	305,250	
Improvements—Leased Premises	7,547	
Lasts, Dies and Patterns	11,100	$336,855
		$2,339,584
Current Liabilities		
Accts. Pay and Accrued Items	$205,072	
Reserve for Taxes	43,693	
Dividends Payable	11,717	
Accrued Vacation Pay	24,420	
Accrued Pension Plan	17,760	
Total Current Liabilities		$302,662
Captail		
Preferred (4,000 shares $100 Redeemable)	$400,000	
Common (3865 npv)	286,500	
Surplus	1,350,422	
Total Capital		$2,036,922
		$2,339,584

Gordon was not concerned about providing new management for Shakee. Gordon's younger brother was a director and vice president of Wrightson International, a company which performed the buying function for a large retail shoe chain in Chicago. Wrightson controlled the manufacturing of several shoe plants and, although Bud Gordon had not had manufacturing experience, he was familiar with manufacturing problems. Walter Gordon had always been impressed by his younger brother, but had never had a big

Exhibit 2

V. R. Shakee Corporation

Short Form Profit and Loss Statement for the Periods Indicated

	6 months Ended 5/31/58	Years Ended				
		11/30/57	11/30/56	11/30/55	11/30/54	11/30/53
Sales (Net of Returns, Allowances and Discounts)	$2,068	$4,746	$5,082	$4,393	$3,883	$4,134
Cost of Goods Sold	1,911	4,332	4,619	3,997	3,625	3,781
Gross Profit from Sales	157	414	463	396	258	353
Other Operating Expenses	62	111	96	113	107	100
Operating Profit	95	303	367	283	151	253
Net Other Charges	6	34	22	36	(23)	5
Net Profit before Extra Compensation and Federal Taxes on Income	89	269	345	247	174	248
Extra Compensation						
Owners	24	93	113	89	33	56
Others	11	53	74	62	21	23
TOTAL	35	146	187	151	54	79
Net Profit Before Federal Taxes on Income	54	123	158	96	120	160
Federal Taxes on Income	19	65	82	69	39	70
Net Profit	$ 35	58	76	27	81	99

NOTE: It has been the Company's practice to write off fixed assets in the year of acquisition and the foregoing statements include such chargeoffs. Had depreciation been provided, in conformity with the Company's Federal Tax Return deductions, chargeoffs would have been reduced as follows:

Fiscal year ended November 30, 1957 $18
Fiscal year ended November 30, 1956   14
Fiscal year ended November 30, 1955   29
Fiscal year ended November 30, 1954   (6)
Fiscal year ended November 30, 1953   3

enough job to lure Bud from Wrightson. Gordon felt sure that Shakee would interest Bud and that with Hart's assistance he would do an excellent job.

On the other hand, Gordon had been so definite about Lyall going out of the shoe manufacturing business that he wanted to consider carefully the implications of purchasing Shakee before proceeding further.

8. EASTERN STATES FARMERS' EXCHANGE, INC.*

—JOHN C. PARK

At the 1960 (January) Annual Meeting of the National Council of Farmers' Cooperatives held in Atlanta, some executive officers of Eastern States Farmers' Exchange, Inc. (hereinafter called "ES"), were having a social conversation with the counterparts of Cooperative Grange League Federation Exchange, Inc. (hereinafter called "GLF"). Among the subjects they covered was a possible consolidation of the two farmers' cooperatives. This led to a meeting of the presidents and general managers of ES and GLF at Ithaca, New York, on June 17, 1960. This meeting recommended a study to determine whether savings for members could be made by forming a jointly owned cooperative, and the recommendation was approved by the boards of directors of the two cooperatives.

Subsequently, numerous meetings were held and many studies were attempted, but it was not until August 1, 1963 when a serious effort was instigated, with a renewed vigor, toward a possible merger. On this day, a so-called "two-phase program" was drafted. The first phase was to draw up a framework of a new organization in line with the objective of developing an "ideal" farmers' cooperative for the future, and the second phase was to see whether the present two organizations could possibly be consolidated into such an ideal cooperative.

With this program in mind, a joint committee of directors of both organizations (four from each) was appointed to settle on the make-up of the new board and the method of election, and to deal with broad membership problems. At the same time, one officer from each of the two cooperatives, Mr. A and Mr. B, were selected to develop ideas on the physical make-up of the new organization and most importantly to report the findings as to the feasibility and the possible advantages and disadvantages of the contemplated

---

* Reprinted by permission of Professor Park.

merger to the general managers,[1] employing the best consulting firms available.

The background and the current situation of the two organizations are described in the following pages. If you were consulted, how would you advise Messrs. A and B as to the contemplated merger?

HISTORY

Eastern States Farmers' Exchange, Inc. (ES), a cooperative purchasing and marketing association, was incorporated in Massachusetts on January 23, 1918. In its first two years of service, ES supplied farmers in Massachusetts, Connecticut, Rhode Island, New Hampshire, and Vermont. Its service was largely that of a broker handling feed ingredients. In the following years the service territory was expanded to Delaware (1922), Maine (1924), and Pennsylvania (1926). Service to Maryland developed soon thereafter, and recently part of Ohio was added.

Fertilizer and seed services followed feed in the early 1920's. Farm supply was added in 1934. Agricultural chemicals were introduced as part of farm supply, then took on a full status in 1949. ES started production of its own fertilizer in the Army Base in Boston in 1932, and agricultural chemical blending facilities were developed in West Concord, Massachusetts, in 1944.

Through most years of ES history, it had been the policy of the organization to concentrate on purchasing services. Marketing services were begun in 1959, however, and recently included local grain, eggs, and potatoes.

Cooperative Grange League Federation Exchange (GLF), a farmers' purchasing and marketing cooperative, was founded in 1920 by the New York State Grange, Dairymen's League Cooperative Association, N.Y., and the New York Farm Bureau Federation. Two years later, GLF services were extended to New Jersey and the northern counties of Pennsylvania. The territory had remained the same since then, but supply services had greatly expanded to include nearly every commodity used on the farm except field machinery; and marketing services for farm products had been added.

In the beginning, GLF bought supplies for its members, and very few facilities were owned by the cooperative. Through the years, however, plants and warehouses had been built or bought wherever owning the facilities would provide better control of quality, lower costs, or service not otherwise available to farmers.

Although the geographical service territory did not expand, business diversification continued, and by 1955 GLF was no longer a farmers' cooperative, per se, but was greatly enlarged to be more like a general cooperative, including lines such as oil refinery, pipeline and tanker investment, insurance,

---

[1] In the given cooperative organizations, the office of general manager was the highest paid executive office, equivalent to the office of presidency in an ordinary (noncooperative) corporation. The office of presidency in the given cooperatives was equal to the chairmanship of board of directors.

finance, etc. Farmers were, however, still the primary customers of the cooperative.

BUSINESS AND SERVICE SYSTEM

Both ES and GLF provided purchasing and marketing services to farmers. A summary of distribution by commodity items for the two organizations is described in Exhibit 1. As to the current service territory, ES dealt with the

Exhibit 1
Eastern States Farmers' Exchange, Inc.
Summary of Distribution by Commodity Items, ES and GLF, 1963

ES	Item	GLF
$61,070,469	Feed and Grain	$91,900,000
13,047,095	Fertilizer and Lime	22,600,000
3,472,520	Agricultural Chemicals	
4,781,706	Seed	9,200,000
8,191,596	Farm Supplies	22,000,000
10,866,337	Marketing	17,800,000
—	Petroleum	21,600,000
—	Home and Garden Supplies	4,100,000
—	Miscellaneous Items	5,400,000
(2,407,273)	Less Discounts Allowed	—
—	Less Inter-divisional Transactions (est.)	(23,644,047)
$99,022,450	Total	$170,955,953

farmers in the six New England states, Delaware, central and southern Pennsylvania, and parts of Maryland and Ohio; on the other hand, GLF provided service to the farmers in New York, New Jersey, and the northern tier counties of Pennsylvania. See the map in Exhibit 2. If the merger were to be materialized, the new cooperative would be the largest one of its kind not only in the country, but probably in the whole world.

For the calendar year ending December 31, 1963, ES' business volume in purchasing and marketing operations was $99,022,450, and GLF's volume was $206,217,851[2] for the fiscal year ended June 30, 1963 (and the GLF

Exhibit 2

Eastern States Farmers' Exchange, Inc.

Service Territories, ES and GLF, 1963

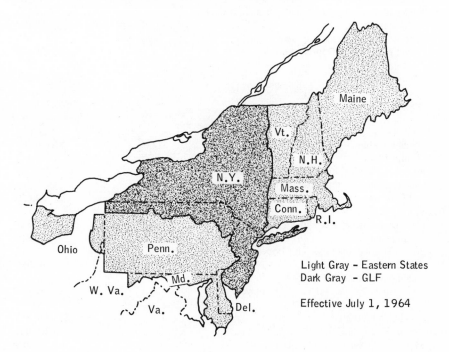

Light Gray – Eastern States
Dark Gray – GLF

Effective July 1, 1964

affiliated cooperatives as a whole had about $159 million worth of business in addition during the said period). Certainly, the combined business volume after merger would have a tremendous magnitude, but the managements estimated that for the initial years of joint operation the volume would not greatly exceed $300 million which was about the same amount of the current business of ES and GLF put together. The relative strength of financial condition of the two was shown in Exhibits 3, 4, 5, and 6.

[2] Including net sales of products marketed for patrons: $35,261,898.

Exhibit 3
Eastern States Farmers' Exchange, Inc.

Balance Sheet, September 30, 1963

ASSETS

Cash		$889,797
Accounts and Notes Receivable		4,975,128
Inventories		15,441,734
Prepaid Expenses and Supplies		1,032,024
Total Current Assets		$22,338,683

OTHER ASSETS

Noncurrent Receivables		219,604
Springfield Bank for Cooperative Stock		595,155
Advice of Retains and Capital Stock from Other Cooperatives		67,171
Land, Buildings and Equipment	$40,621,418	
Less Reserve for Depreciation	17,129,972	23,491,446
Deferred Charges		9,034
Total Assets		$46,721,093

LIABILITIES

Loans Payable	$3,100,000
Facility Loan	518,182
Accounts Payable and Accrued Expenses	2,479,489
Facility Note and Purchase Contracts Payable— Within one year	2,650
Total Current Liabilities	$6,100,321
Facility Loan	5,181,818
Equity Holders of Acquired Cooperatives— Due after one year	81,396
Facility Note and Purchase— Contracts Payable—Due after one year	72,950
Total Liabilities	$11,436,485
PATRONS' Equity, 12/31/62	33,286,088
1963—NINE MONTHS' ACCUMULATED SAVINGS	1,998,520
	$46,721,093

The service system, or the cooperative business organization, was markedly different between the two. ES was an integrated, centrally controlled establishment, financed by both businessmen and farmers. Originally, it functioned solely as a purchasing cooperative. At present, the purchasing division had responsibility for purchasing and processing feed, agricultural chemicals, fertilizer, seed, and for purchasing and warehousing farm supplies as well.

Exhibit 4

Eastern States Farmers' Exchange, Inc.

Cooperative Grange League Federation Exchange, Inc.
and Consolidated Subsidiaries
(Excluding GLF Affiliated Cooperatives)

Balance Sheet, September 30, 1963

ASSETS

Currents Assets		
Cash		$ 1,692,468
Accounts and Notes Receivable		24,117,525
Inventories		30,247,933
Prepaid Expenses		581,413
Total Current Assets		$56,639,339
Investments		
Due from Local GLF Affiliates	$1,333,445	
Other Investments—Net	7,817,998	
Total Investments		$ 9,151,443
Fixed Assets		
Land, Buildings and Equipment—Cost	$35,080,410	
Less—Allowance for Depreciation	15,375,742	
Total Fixed Assets—Net		$19,704,668
Other Assets		
Organization Expense		33,942
TOTAL ASSETS		$85,529,392

LIABILITIES AND NET WORTH

Current Liabilities		
Notes Payable, Principally to Banks		$ 8,395,000
Current Installments of Long-Term Debt		808,000
Accounts Payable and Accrued Expense		14,810,919
Federal Income Taxes		1,155,388
Patronage Refunds Payable		633,006
Total Current Liabilities		$25,802,313
Long-Term Debt		
Notes Payable		2,931,113
4% Debentures due 1/1/1966		1,441,800
Minority Interest in Consolidated Subsidiaries		547,124
Net Worth		
Capital Stock	$26,498,960	
Revolving Fund Certificates	4,261,710	
Retained Margins	23,458,977	
Undistributed Margins—3 months	587,395	
Total Net Worth		54,807,042
TOTAL LIABILITIES AND NET WORTH		$85,529,392

Exhibit 5

Eastern States Farmers' Exchange, Inc.

Five-Year Statement of Operations Ending with December 31, 1963

	1959	1960	1961	1962	1963
Sales	$89,955,130	$91,610,057	$94,076,895	$97,642,923	$99,022,450
Gross Margins	6,104,290	8,340,154	8,340,911	8,601,154	15,202,024
Selling and Administration	4,675,060	5,714,885	5,449,155	6,003,719	12,778,874
Other Income	51,858	171,041	99,268	357,569 ⎱	−505,992
Other Deductions	8,403	99,229	53,960	114,515 ⎰	
Net Margins before Distribution	1,472,685	2,787,081	2,937,064	2,840,489	1,917,158

Exhibit 6

Eastern States Farmers' Exchange, Inc.
Cooperative Grange League Federation Exchange, Inc. and
Consolidated Subsidiaries
(Excluding GLF Affiliated Cooperatives)

Comparative Statements of Operations
Year Ending June 30th

	1959	1960	1961	1962	1963
Sales	$179,009,648	$172,584,494	$175,755,394	$196,290,870	$206,217,851
Gross Margins	11,631,880	11,955,372	12,741,045	14,208,923	15,993,586
Selling, Administrative and General Expenses	6,717,322	7,389,146	8,147,357	9,419,676	10,362,105
Other Income	1,568,717	1,637,524	1,303,887	1,543,467	1,587,685
Other Deductions	1,994,882	902,628	533,327	710,117	1,466,334
Net Income Before Distribution	4,488,393	5,301,122	5,364,248	5,622,597	5,752,832

The marketing division operated potato, grain, and egg marketing services, and the area service director had responsibility for eight retail service areas. In these service areas there were 112 service centers, including nine branches and 313 local representatives.

The 112 service centers, which contributed about 65% to the total volume were facilities for providing feed, fertilizer, and other farm supplies on a retail basis to farm patrons as well as other services, such as fertilizer spreading, grinding, and mixing, and feed deliveries. In general, the 313 local representatives, which added the remaining 35% to the total volume, acted in much the same manner as a manufacturer's agent, taking orders from farmers and seeing that these orders were filled. They were not employees of ES, but were franchised agents. Eighteen of these local representatives had service-center facilities of their own.

On the other hand, GLF was the parent cooperative of a complex system of subcooperatives. It functioned as an operating cooperative, directly

Exhibit 7
Eastern States Farmers' Exchange, Inc.
Subsidiaries, ES and GLF, 1963

ES	Adams Country Fruit Packing and Distributing Company, Inc. (ES owned 100% of common voting stock.)
GLF	Allied Seed Cooperative, Inc. (GLF owned 100% of common voting stock.) Comank Corporation (Noncooperative corporation, GLF owned 100% of common voting stock.) Cooperative GLF Credit Corporation (GLF owned 100% of common voting stock.) Cooperative GLF Holding Corporation (GLF owned 100% of common voting stock.) Curtice-Burns, Inc. (Noncooperative corporation, GLF owned 58% of common voting stock.) GLF Insurance Company (GLF owned 100% of common voting stock.) GLF Petroleum Corporation (Noncooperative corporation, GLF owned 100% of common voting stock.) 211 Cooperative GLF Service Corporations (GLF held in trust 100% of common voting stock.) 64 Cooperative GLF Petroleum Corporations (GLF held in trust 100% of common voting stock.) 2 Cooperative GLF Marketing Corporations (GLF held in trust 100% of common voting stock.)

In addition GLF had considerable sums invested in a number of affiliates. The following were some of the investments:

Texas City Refining, Inc. (GLF investment: $2,550,000, the present book value: $4,107,000).

United Cooperatives (GLF investment: $406,000 and $1,137,000 had been received as cash refunds),

Fertilizer Manufacturing Cooperative (GLF investment: $294,000),

Select Seeds (GLF investment: $96,000),

Empire Livestock Marketing, Inc. (GLF investment: $102,000),

P and C Food Markets, Inc. (GLF investment: $638,000, the market value: $1,502,000),

Mohawk Airlines (GLF investment: $915,000, the market value: $1,305,000), and

Seneca Grape Juice Corporation (GLF investment: $115,000).

engaged in product manufacturing, processing, and distribution, and whole-sale purchasing, and marketing of commodities. It was also the trustee-holder of all the outstanding common stock of some 277-member GLF cooperative associations operating in local communities within its service territory. The local member cooperatives of the system in 1963 consisted of 211 service store cooperatives, 64 petroleum distributing cooperatives, and two marketing cooperatives, which served as distribution outlets for about 65% of GLF's total product and service volume. The common stock of each member cooperative was held by GLF under a trustee-ownership arrangement which provided for operating management of the local cooperatives. The GLF management maintained general supervision and control of the operations of the retail cooperatives under an annual management agreement.[3]

Exhibit 8
Eastern States Farmers' Exchange, Inc.
Plant Facilities, ES and GLF, 1963

ES			GLF	
LOCATION AND YEAR OF ESTABLISHMENT (OR PURCHASE)	NET BOOK VALUE (IN $1,000)	PLANT FACILITIES	LOCATION AND YEAR OF ESTABLISHMENT (OR PURCHASE)	NET BOOK VALUE (IN $1,000)
1. Buffalo, N.Y., 1925	$4,029		1. Albany, N.Y., 1932	$1,300
2. Huron, Ohio, 1952	6,603	Feed	2. Binghamton, N.Y., 1950	140
3. N. Franklin, Conn., 1964	745	Mills	3. Bordentown, N.J., 1946	2,200
4. Manchester, N.H., 1964	555		4. Buffalo, N.Y., 1930	4,800
E. Butler, Pa.,		Seed	1. Bordentown, N.J., 1946	$50
1. —vegetable seed, 1961	$117	Process-	2. Buffalo, N.Y., 1921	260
2. —field seed, 1963	267	ing	3. Plymouth, Ind., 1950	80
		Plants	4. Warners, N.Y., 1955	360
1. Cambridge, Mass., 1937	$545	Fertilizer	1. Albany, N.Y., 1935	$465
2. Detroit, Maine, 1958	698	Plants	2. Batavia, N.Y., 1929	268
3. Kittanning, Pa., 1951	435		3. Big Flats, N.Y., 1940	343
4. Wilmington, Del., 1940	278		4. Bridgehampton, N.Y., 1952	130
5. York, Pa., 1945	484		5. Bridgeton, N.J., 1937	109
			6. Canastota, N.Y., 1937	186
			7. Englishtown, N.J., 1947	104
			8. Lyons, N.Y., 1942	195
			9. Middletown, N.Y., 1947	9
			10. S. Kearny, N.J., 1936	279
			11. Union City, Pa., 1953	260
			12. Yardville, N.J., 1939	145

[3] All told, GLF had 284 subsidiary entities, and owned 100% of common voting stock of all of them, except one, Curtice-Burns, Inc., of which GLF owned 58% of common voting stock. On the other hand, ES had only one subsidiary. See Exhibit 7.

Exhibit 8—(cont'd)

1. Spring Garden, Pa., 1955	$387	Farm	1. Albany, N.Y., 1936	$55
2. W. Concord, Mass., 1944	376	Supply	2. Caledonia, N.Y., 1940	91
		Plants	3. Canton, N.Y., 1940	46
			4. Cortland, N.Y., 1961	79
			5. Oneida, N.Y., 1939	49
			6. Owego, N.Y., 1939	33
			7. Port Jervis, N.Y., 1940	111
			8. Warren, Pa., 1941	28
(None)		Bulk Fuel	1. Albany, N.Y., 1956	$352
		Terminals	2. Brewerton, N.Y., 1949	98
			3. Dupont, Pa., 1954	156
			4. Marcy, N.Y., 1961	199
			5. Newburgh, N.Y., 1946	97
			6. Ogdensburg, N.Y., 1950	94
			7. Rochester, N.Y., 1950	150
			8. Tonawanda, N.Y., 1949	184
			9. Vestal, N.Y., 1954	177
1. Brockton, Mass., 1959	$4	Egg	1. Buffalo, N.Y., 1932	$52
2. Derry, N.H., 1959	100	Grading	2. New Paltz, N.Y., 1962	167
3. Doyleston, Pa., 1964	30	and	3. Waverly, N.Y., 1961	239
4. E. Butler, Pa., 1961	74	Packing	4. Weedsport, N.Y., 1955	91
5. Groton, Vt., 1961	9	Plants		
6. Hamden, Conn., 1959	56			
7. Providence, R. I., 1959	111			
8. Springfield, Mass., 1959	130			
1. Ellington, Conn., 1938	$340	Research	(None)	
2. Feeding Hills, Mass., 1940	43	Farms		

The remaining 35% of GLF sales and service volume went through independent retail dealers and independent cooperatives authorized to distribute GLF products and furnish GLF services. Most of these were designated as "GLF agent-buyers." In 1963 there were more than 300 independent dealers serving GLF patrons in areas where GLF-managed local cooperatives were not in operation. The plant facilities of ES and GLF are compared in Exhibit 8.

MANAGEMENT

The managerial organizations of ES and that of GLF did not exactly coincide with one another. For the organizational charts, see Exhibits 9 and 10. But the heterogeneity in this was quite moderate, compared to the differences that existed in their managerial philosophy or attitude. ES had been historically very conservative, particularly in earlier years. Through the years it

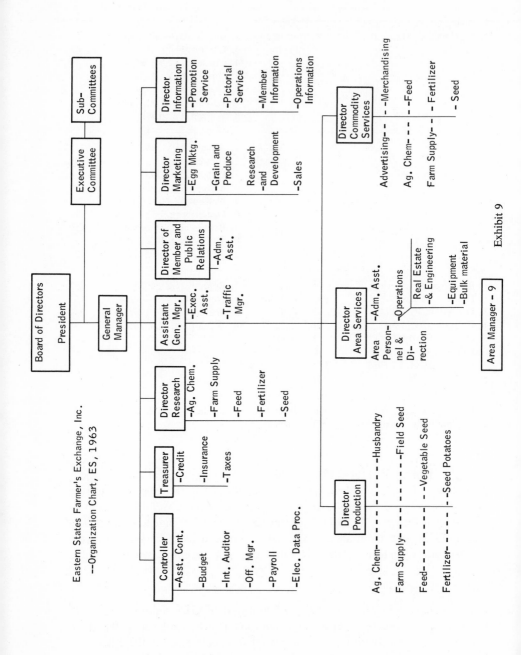

Eastern States Farmer's Exchange, Inc.
--Organization Chart, ES, 1963

Exhibit 9

524

Eastern States Farmers' Exchange, Inc.
Organization Chart, GLF, 1963

Exhibit 10

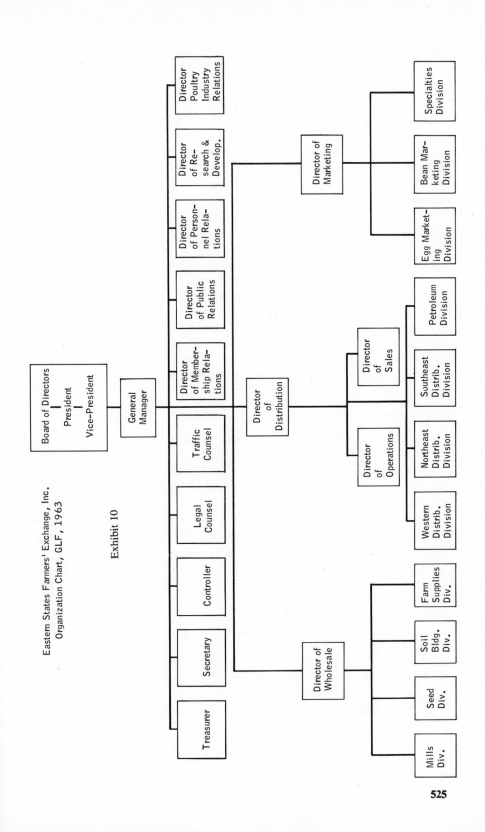

held pretty much to the mainstays of the farm supply business, and until 1959 ES had no credit business, for example. Some called ES a "pure" (if not old-fashioned) farmers' cooperative. GLF management, on the other hand, had been quite aggressive. While concentrating on its existing lines, it had a history of bold action moving into new lines, such as petroleum, insurance, and suburban services, and a wide range of marketing activities.

Yet, there is a somewhat parallel historical development of the two organizations. Both systems operate extensive production and warehousing facilities for livestock feed, seed, fertilizer, farm chemicals, and farm hardware. Their members it must be recalled were chiefly dairy, poultry, and crop farmers. Recently, members of both cooperative managements were reexamining their traditional question: how to provide better services to northeastern agriculture, so that their customers could hold their own in changing times and meet the competition of other regions; and both were seriously contemplating a merger between the two to achieve this end. Both saw the great opportunities offered by consolidation, but both realized at the same time the many problems that could arise in effecting a merger between two cooperatives with differing outlooks and attitudes. Each realized that the advantages and disadvantages offered by merger were interwoven in a complex web.

MERCHANDISING POLICY

ES had historically operated as a true cooperative, extending the principles of self-help and "value-in-use" in its operations. As late as 1954, an officer of the cooperative stated publicly that ES "is truly a cooperative purchasing service and not a merchandising business even though goods are exchanged for money." It traditionally had relied upon its directors and its members, as well as operating personnel, to promote services and products offered. Its annual meetings were run in a much more conservative manner than those of GLF, and its publications reflected this basic conservatism.

On the other hand, GLF had placed an increasing emphasis on merchandising, selling goods to farmers, initially to build up business in off seasons, but later to generally promote sales throughout the year. They had a planned program of special promotions, as well as fairly aggressive sales action at all times. In fact, besides a director of sales and sales managers in each of the departments and divisions of distribution services, there were sales personnel in wholesale services to "sell" manufactured materials to the retail outlets. GLF had at times been criticized by farmer members for being too aggressive a merchandiser. Some members felt that it was difficult for them to distinguish GLF merchandising policies from those of private companies.

EXPANSION PROBLEM

ES had relatively more room to expand in the farm supply fields within its own territory. It also had a foothold in Ohio that could be exploited. Expanding one's share of the market, however, would not be an easy proposition. Even though ES was gearing up to be a more effective competitor, an expansion to a new area (e.g., Ohio) would be costly. Offering a broad range of farm-supply products and services would be one area of expansion. Petroleum, for example, could be added, as well as a wider line of specific farm-supply items. But, here again, in adding more products and services, ES would face both market development costs and costs of starting a new venture or acquiring a going concern in the field.

ES also could expand its farm product marketing services, which probably would be the largest immediate opportunity for expansion. But, this was a low-margin field, and one that could be fairly restricted by the limits of the service area. It also could go more heavily into areas of indirect benefit to farmers, expanding its suburban services, for example. However, it had more room to expand within the traditional farm cooperative lines of activity than did GLF before it was forced to turn to indirect services as the only feasible alternatives for growth.

Expansion problems also confronted GLF. This organization also would have difficulty in expanding its total share of the farm supply market in its own territory. Trends in the markets for the various farm-supply products and services were mixed, but on the average would increase only slightly in the immediately following years, as the number of farms decreased. This meant that the growth rate in the total farm-supply sector of the GLF complex would tend to level off, and might actually decline in some areas. Because of its diversity, GLF had nearly exhausted the possibilities for extending into other areas in which they might be of direct service to the production side of agriculture.

GLF could do more in the marketing area than it had done, but the service territory could be quite restrictive in many marketing activities, and margins were very very slim in most of the farm-product marketing areas. Some better opportunities were available that would be of indirect benefit to farmer members. Expanding insurance activities, doing more reinsurance, as well as putting together more successful ventures in the suburban service areas were examples. Most of these activities were relatively high-margin operations that would bring in proportionately greater returns than the farm-supply activities. However, for many of the operations that could be performed in this area, the service territory would have little relevance.

MERGER ADVANTAGES AND DISADVANTAGES TO ES

The advantages and disadvantages to each of the two cooperatives were difficult to view clearly. They were largely hypothetical in nature, and were without statistical indications. If ES were to be consolidated with GLF, advantages to ES would accrue mainly from possibilities for reducing plant costs in some area—feed and seed in particular—and from sharing the merchandising skill of the GLF organization in areas such as fertilizer, seed, farm supplies, and small animal foods. These advantages, however, were rather speculative, though they appeared to be reasonably favorable. In addition, the benefits ES would receive by joining existing GLF services such as petroleum and insurance services which were new to ES, would present a real opportunity and challenge. And, with GLF, there would be improved purchasing and marketing strength, as well as a greater financial strength to operate.

Exhibit 11

Eastern States Farmers' Exchange, Inc.

Cost Comparison, Selected Items, ES and GLF, 1962-1963

	ES	GLF
(A) Estimated Per Ton Costs of Producing Fertilizers		
Plant Costs	$5.46	$8.70
Administrative Costs	0.85	2.54
Sub-Total	$6.31	$11.24
Depreciation	1.13	1.35
Total	$7.44	$12.59
(B) Estimated Average Costs Per Ton for Producing Feed		
Plant Costs	$ *	$5.16
Administrative Costs	*	1.17
Sub-Total	$7.20	$6.33
Depreciation	1.20	0.41
Total	$8.40	$6.74
(C) Estimated Costs Per Dollar of Sales of Seeds		
Cost of Sales	$0.81	$0.78
Plant and Administrative Costs	0.18	0.12
Total	$0.99	$0.90

* These costs were combined in the financial statement.

On the other hand, ES would not be benefited by GLF's higher average plant costs of producing fertilizer. See Exhibit 11. That is, the merger would make possible a considerable reduction in GLF's plant costs and lower the combined average plant cost, but this would still be substantially higher than the current ES average.

MERGER ADVANTAGES AND DISADVANTAGES TO GLF

Should the contemplated merger become a reality, GLF's cost of production might also be lowered, but unlike the case with ES, the cost reduction might be spread across the board, that is, in all sectors of activity: feed, fertilizer, seed, farm-supplies, petroleum, insurance, finance, and all the rest. Exhibit 11 indicates some of the more important cost comparisons. The greatest advantages for GLF, however, would be securing a larger market territory in which they could further demonstrate their successful marketing experience in many areas, such as (direct service areas) fertilizer, seed, farm-supplies, pet and small animal food; (indirect service areas) insurance, finance, and suburban services.

One main drawback GLF might experience would be the element of conservatism in policy-making injected by the ES forces. As a consequence, new combined policy might be less effective and less workable to their taste. In addition, a serious disadvantage might be possible disruption of relations with GLF's partners in several joint ventures, such as Texas City Refinery, the Fertilizer Manufacturing Cooperative, and Curtice-Burns, Inc. (a fruit and vegetable processor). And, an increase in size and a move to other territories also could affect some of GLF's traditional relationships with other cooperatives and farm organizations in some localities.

ADDITIONAL MERGER ADVANTAGES AND DISADVANTAGES APPLICABLE TO BOTH ES AND GLF

It appeared that there were some further advantages and disadvantages applicable to both cooperatives. On the favorable side of the ledger, greater usages of some facilities could be made. For example, plants located as listed could operate nearer their capacities: Huron (Ohio, ES, feed), West Concord (Mass., ES, farm supplies), Waverly (N.Y., GLF, small animal foods), Wilmington (Delaware, ES, fertilizer); Cortland (N.Y., GLF, farm supplies), Bordentown (N.J., GLF, feed), and Buffalo (N.Y., GLF, feed). (See Exhibit 8.)

Another advantage would be a substantial savings, through potential reduction in duplicated overhead functions (producing as well as distributing), management, and administrative functions and personnel.[4] Research and development activities which modern farming required at an ever-increasing rate, could also be pooled together for greater achievements. The greatest benefits, however, would come from an improved effectiveness in all areas— an improved base for moving into new activities. With increased competition to be expected in many areas, the combined resources would be better equipped to compete than either cooperative would be separately.

A larger market for possible greater business volumes would be an attractive and tempting factor. However, the rate of growth would not be uniform

---

[4] True, two duplicative offices, for example, could be combined into one. But, the new, single office might require larger salary and staff expenses for the added responsibility. Therefore, the possible cost reduction along these lines might not be as great as one could expect.

in all areas, and the rate of margin might not remain favorable in all lines. In some, farm-supply products and services, for example, the rate of growth might stagnate and even decline, and the rate of margin might be depressingly slim, as the size enlarged. Furthermore, the cooperatives would have adjustments to make, perhaps at a greater expense, in serving the larger market.

On the other side of the ledger, probable elimination of some of the plant and service facilities which proved to be duplicative, or relatively inefficient, or necessitated due to a re-arrangement, would create rather severe capital losses; and the relocation of home offices (that is, establishment of whole new central office facilities at a site different from the present home office locations) would be costly.

Furthermore, if the new organization failed to capitalize on the advantages of potential and expected efficiencies in combined operation, or became too cumbersome through unskillful management, or developed management conflicts in a power struggle, or failed to take advantage of other opportunities that were expected to accrue through the merger, the potential advantages would be lost. Also a lack of decision as to how to choose business ventures to be entered by the new cooperative could be a source of difficulty after the merger.

And, only for a short-run or temporary consideration, there would be high initial costs in "selling" the merger to members and in effecting several phases of the consolidation. For example, putting the two heterogeneous accounting and controlling systems onto a common base and making it ready for more merchandising would be expensive. Furthermore, some extraordinary expenses might be increased beyond initial expectations, in getting the new organization established as a going concern.

NEW HEADQUARTERS AND EMPLOYEE RELOCATION

The home office of ES was currently located at West Springfield, Massachusetts and GLF at Ithaca, New York. The board of directors of the two cooperatives said that if the merger was to be the answer, a study should be made to determine the best location for the centralized headquarters. Consequently, several factors were evaluated in detail in the selection of a prospective site. Among the factors considered were proximity to operations and patrons, transportation facilities—both surface and air—community facilities and operating costs.

Out of several cities studied, Syracuse, N.Y. was considered to be the most suitable one. If the merger actually took place and the new offices located in Syracuse, it would incur a considerable amount of expense to disconnect, displace, load, move, and reinstall the involved equipment. In selling those items which would not be needed in Syracuse, or in their old units, financial losses might be incurred. Should the new company decide to build a completely new set of buildings, it would be doubly costly. The current home office buildings and facilities were quite handsome and sufficient for ES and GLF separately. And the communities of West Springfield and Ithaca, with their active Chambers of Commerce, were literally begging the cooperatives not to desert them. ES and GLF were the most important employers in their cities employing about 500 each.

If the home office were relocated in Syracuse (or any other new location) it would be the cause of considerable discomfort to many employees now working at West Springfield and Ithaca. As a consequence, both ES and GLF might lose a number of competent and experienced employees permanently. This, of course, could not be calculated in terms of dollars as to its magnitude Even assuming all would be willing to move to Syracuse, it could still develop a considerable amount of ill-feeling among employees, when it came to who would survive and hold the one position between the two counterparts in almost every classification of office. Compare the organization charts in Exhibits 9 and 10, as a small sample.

The top managements were hopefully expecting to realize about $4 million savings by eliminating duplicative staff members, but obviously this could be accomplished only at the expense of victims and casualties, however systematically and sympathetically administered to make the best use of their manpower. True, some new positions might possibly be created, yet the total number of employees after the merger would be substantially smaller than the total number at present.

MEMBERSHIP

One fundamental difference between ES and GLF was their definition of membership. ES was a nonstock cooperative based on patronage membership, which was a more traditional and common form of membership in the world of cooperatives. A member is defined as a farmer who had purchased or marketed products through ES in the previous calendar year. The ES member built up an equity by his purchases, but this was not negotiable. One member had one vote, regardless of the magnitude of the equity accumulated to his account. There were approximately 82,000 members in 1962. The classification of members is shown in Exhibit 12.

ES retained about one third of its earnings, or " savings " as the cooperative preferred to call them, for capital uses, and distributed the rest as a cash refund to member patrons at the annual rate of approximately 2.39% of the member's purchase volumes. Each member was kept informed on this amount of equity or " retains " that he built up in the cooperative, but they were, as indicated above, non-negotiable and would only be distributed in the case of complete dissolution of the cooperative. No certificates of indebtedness or equity were ever issued.

On the other hand, GLF was a stock cooperative based on stock membership, and had promoted the sale of common and preferred stock of various types of members to assure a stronger member participation in the organization.

Exhibit 12

Eastern States Farmers' Exchange, Inc.

Annual Purchases of Members, ES and GLF, 1961–1962

Range	Number	Per Cent	Cumulative Per Cent	Dollar	Per Cent	Cumulative Per Cent	Average Purchases
				– ES –			
Under 1,000	67,010	81.8		$ 11,482,879	14.9		$ 171
1,000— 5,000	11,459	14.0	95.8	26,480,243	34.3	49.2	2,311
5,000—10,000	2,331	2.9	98.7	15,945,863	20.7	20.7	6,841
Over 10,000	1,138	1.3	100.0	23,260,857	30.1	30.1	20,440
	81,938	100.0		77,169,742	100.0		$ 940 (Av.)
				– GLF –			
Under 1,000	47,244	63.3		$ 12,204,014	9.0		$ 258
1,000— 5,000	20,529	27.5	90.8	50,152,436	36.9	45.9	2,443
5,000—10,000	4,833	6.5	97.3	33,141,321	24.4	70.3	6,857
Over 10,000	2,014	2.7	100.0	40,279,189	29.7	100.0	20,000
	74,620	100.0		$135,776,960	100.0		$ 1,818 (Av.)

The thinking here was that financial involvement would make for a stronger and more loyal member than non-financial involvement. A farmer qualified for a membership first by purchasing non-transferrable common stock. Each member had one vote, and only one vote, whether he possessed a single share or 400 shares, which was the top limit per farm family. There were 74,620 members in 1962.[5] See Exhibit 12 for the composition of members.

Retained savings of GLF were not earmarked to individual member accounts, as was the case with ES, but they were reserved in unallocated form. After adequate reserves had been retained, the remaining savings were distributed in cash as dividends on common stock (up to 6%) and preferred stock (5%), and in the form of so-called "revolving fund certificates" (at the rate of 0.5% per annum in recent years) which represented patronage refunds—noninterest-bearing, nontransferrable—and were redeemable in full or in part at such times as the board of directors might determine. Thus, GLF members had stock equity which drew dividends plus revolving fund certificates which were more or less "near-money."

These divergent definitions of membership between the two cooperatives brought about problems in the merger consideration. Assuming the new organization would be a Delaware corporation, the managements were carefully comparing some of the more outstanding differences between stock cooperative corporations and membership cooperative corporations. Under a stock cooperative corporation, the following disadvantages were enumerated: (1) Delaware required approximately 50% of the stockholders to change the articles of incorporation. (2) Selection of directors from each could not be made mandatory as the full member body voted on a single ballot. (3) The image of an agricultural cooperative would be somewhat diminished. (4) Conditions of membership might be more difficult to state and operate. (5) The corporate fees cost more. And (6) in view of the fact the ES was not a stock corporation, it was feared that if the current ES members were required to purchase stock shares, say at $25 or $50 per share, as the new membership would demand under this plan, a substantial number of members might not purchase stock, thus they would cease to be members, decreasing the total number of members accordingly. Particularly some of the member farmers who did less than $1,000 per year business with the cooperative might refuse to purchase stock—and this would generate some concern—for these members made up more than 80% of the total members.[6] (See Exhibit 12.)

[5] There were about 117,000 common stockholders on record in 1962, all of whom were members by definition, but only 74,620 were currently users of the cooperative.

[6] Strictly speaking, the proposals and discussions of possible merger were largely originated and oriented by the managements, not by the members. Although it was constantly publicized to the members that the managements and the boards only work for "what is good for the members at large," some members might not necessarily understand, nor agree with the managements, as to the needs and problems of merger.

And, some members of GLF, as well as of ES, might question their accumulated retained savings over the years, withheld by the cooperatives ($35,284,608; ES, $24,046,372: GLF,

Under this membership cooperative corporation, on the other hand, the following disadvantages were considered. (1) Investment from outside the cooperative would be more difficult as the cooperative terminology would not be the same as a stock corporation. For example, a term such as " common (or preferred) stock " could not be used to outside investors. (2) Public groups unrelated to agriculture would not understand, or readily accept, the membership cooperative corporation, as they were familiar with the stock corporation. (3) It might be more difficult to qualify membership cooperative corporation in some states, and (4) it would also not be possible to mortgage property, in some states, without court approval.

Unlike most ordinary (non-cooperative) corporations, but like most cooperatives, ES' and GLF's boards of directors were composed entirely of their own members. ES had 53 directors and GLF 14. In terms of composition, election procedures, policy making power, the frequency of meetings, etc., the two boards (as well as their subordinating local boards) were, once again, quite different. The most serious problem in forming one board out of the two, however, would be solving the human elements involved as to who would stay and who would depart. Apparently, everyone on the boards was able, willing, and anxious to remain on the new board (other than normal retirement for old age), though none of them were paid to serve, except for a modest compensation *per diem* for attending meetings. (No paid-officer in the managerial staff was on either of the boards.)

GLF, being the larger of the two would undoubtedly nominate more to the big board than ES could, if the merger was to be accomplished. This meant that the great majority of the current board members of ES would be dismissed, and the experienced and ambitious members would feel uncomfortable as they were " tested " in the process of elimination. So, if the consolidation were effected, a human drama, similar to that among the employees of the two organizations, and difficult to handle, might develop.

---

as of September 30, 1963—see Exhibits 3 and 4, pp. 6 and 7), interpreting that the termination of ES and GLF as separate entities would constitute a dissolution, thus the accumulated retained savings, the undistributed patrons' equity, should be refunded at the time of merger.

Legal counsel, however, took the position that the proposed merger would not require a dissolution of any part, but simply be a grand combination of the two cooperatives, and the members' retained savings would be carried intact onto the new books of the new organization; thus refunding would be unwarranted and unnecessary.

Nevertheless, those members who did pay income taxes on their credited retained savings in the past might still argue, and as they found no possible way of " getting back " any part of them, some might withdraw membership, perhaps with ill-feeling. Should this ever happen, the total number of members would experience another wave of shrinkage. The managements, however, were absolutely confident to state that this kind of questioning or request for refunding would be unlikely to arise on the part of their members.

LAW

The legal staff of ES began studying the legal implications for the contemplated merger, and soon found many problems. To cite a few, it was ascertained that, without passage of a special bill, the New York state law did not permit a cooperative incorporated in the state (GLF) to merge with a membership corporation (ES). And it was determined that under the Delaware law, a strict interpretation would require a two-thirds vote of all members before the merger could be effected. In the event that a two-thirds vote was required, the staff were to develop a procedure for reducing the membership and authorize proxy voting. Later, however, they were informed by an outside law firm that a vote of three-fourths of the members present at the coming annual members' meeting would be sufficient.

The accounting procedure for dealing with a merger between the cooperatives posed many problems, some of which were closely related to legal entanglements. The most significant accounting problem was to determine whether the combining of the two organizations would qualify for one legal procedure called "pooling of interests." This procedure was essential in order to permit the carrying forward of the very significant amounts of retained margins of ES and GLF on the balance sheet of the surviving merged cooperative. The ordinary "pooling" situation basically involved the exchange of stock for stock, and would not contemplate the issuance of a disproportionate amount of cash or cash equivalents such as debentures or the substantial "bail out" of prior stockholders. In this connection, the most important criteria established to qualify for "pooling" were the continuity of ownership and the continuity of management.

The common stockholders of GLF, on a dollar-for-dollar basis, would have the opportunity of exchanging their present aggregate stockholdings in GLF (par value, $5 per share) for new common stock, say, $25 per share, and the balance in "membership debentures" in the newly created corporation. To the extent that the present common stockholders of GLF would become common stockholders of the new corporation, there would be a "continuity of ownership." However, to the extent that the present GLF stockholders would not make such exchange for whatever reason (because the aggregate par value of their present GLF stockholdings were not an aggregate $25 and they might not wish to pay up in cash the difference between such stockholdings and $25, or because they might be opposed to the merger for whatever reason), there would be a "continuity of ownership."

The farmer patrons of ES would be individually entitled to purchase some shares, say, one share of common stock, par value $25 (or whatever denomination) per share, and "membership debentures" in the new organization. However, to the extent that these people would not exercise this right of purchase of common stock for whatever reason, there would be no "continuity of ownership." There would be no question, however, that both ES and GLF contemplated that there would be "continuity of management." The question was on the matter of "continuity of ownership" but unfortunately the situation was unorthodox and without precedent.

9. PEERLESS POULTRY PROCESSING, INC.*

—VERN H. VINCENT

Walter Harmon obviously was disappointed as the others left his office after a two-hour meeting on July 29, 1963. He had presented the arguments for the $250,000 expansion of the processing plant to the best of his ability. But the decision was made to study the proposal further, especially with respect to securing the necessary funds from outside sources.

Harmon knew that Art Yeager, manager of the processing plant, would be waiting impatiently at his office telephone thirty miles away. He called Yeager at once and found himself doing all of the talking except for a flat statement of resignation: "Well, I guess we can just keep limping along."

By "limping along" Yeager referred to the fact that the business was not showing a satisfactory profit, that volume had declined at the processing plant during the first half of 1963 to the extent of producing a net loss for the year ended June 30, 1963, even though a reasonable profit appeared to have been earned during the first half of the fiscal year. Both the volume and the profit "spread" on broiler processing had declined during fiscal year 1963; this virtually forced an effort to process a greater number of turkeys in order to avoid ruinous idle capacity and the failure to cover even the amount of overhead costs—those which declined little with reductions in the level of operations. New, greatly enlarged facilities for quick freezing were needed in order to process turkeys in volume. The freezing facilities available did not permit proper freezing of even a small quantity of turkeys.

Harmon had been for about two years the general manager of agricultural operations for a group operating in three counties in northern Arkansas. In this capacity he served six corporations. Each of these corporations had a manager directly responsible for operations, who reported to Harmon. Besides the processing plant, two other corporations were involved in poultry

* Prepared for the Southern Case Writers' Association. Reprinted by permission of the Association and Professor Vincent.

activities: Rollins Poultry Company, which operated the poultry farms and Rollins Feed Mill. The latter firm produced and delivered feed only for the Rollins farms—poultry and others.

Peerless Poultry Processing, Inc. began operations March 1, 1957, about the time agricultural activities for the group began to expand rapidly, especially in poultry. The corporations engaged in agriculture were not subsidiary corporations of Peerless Manufacturing Corporation, but they were affiliated, being owned and controlled by the same group, composed largely of executives of Peerless Manufacturing. (Two of these executives had met with Harmon during the evening of July 29, previously mentioned.)

John Rollins was the founder and controlling stockholder of Peerless Manufacturing Corporation. In the early days of World War II he moved to Arkansas from a neighboring state to establish a small factory. During the next twenty years he was successful in building a profitable, expanding business and a capable group of executives and employees.

Early in the 1950's agriculture in northern Arkansas began to attract the interest of Rollins. He was challenged by the adverse conditions as to terrain; but he thought the presence of relatively cheap mountainous land and of many marginal farmers would support expansion in agriculture, especially with poultry and beef cattle. Rollins, on his own account, purchased over the years many thousands of acres of farm land, trying to secure either large farms or several small ones adjacent to form a large acreage. He and his executives established new corporations to conduct operations, but major decisions were made by those responsible to Rollins for policy in Peerless Manufacturing Corporation.

The scale of operations in poultry farming increased greatly. In the largest complete year to date, in terms of volume, the year ended June 30, 1962, the Rollins farms turned over to the processing plant more than 110,000 turkeys and about 3½ million broilers. That particular year turned out to be something of a disaster for the farms, however, because of sharply reduced prices. In July, 1963, about 650,000 broilers were being grown on the farms, and the annual turkey volume had moved up to about 300,000 birds. The farms were capable of carrying far more broilers than this number, but price prospects not being favorable in the spring of 1963 for broilers, the decision was made to double the number of large turkeys to be produced—from 100,000 to 200,000. Thus the facilities for raising young birds were utilized fully— broilers having given way as necessary to accommodate turkey poults.

In July, 1963, there were 125 employees at the processing plant, which had a capacity of 5,000 young chickens (broilers) per hour. The plant was designed primarily to handle broilers in large volume. Turkeys could be dressed there as well as broilers, but facilities for quick freezing turkeys were inadequate. Only 15,000 pounds could be frozen properly in 24 hours—considerably less than a truck load of turkeys. If volume were to be maintained at even a tolerable level in the processing plant during the last half of 1963, the turkeys from the Rollins farms would have to be dressed and frozen there. Except for a short period before the Thanksgiving Day and Christmas holidays, only a small number of turkeys could be marketed from the plant as ice-packed birds. Those turkeys which were to be held for any length of time had to be frozen.

This shift in "product mix" toward turkeys and away from broilers had produced the problem faced by Harmon and Yeager. Harmon himself had initiated this change. Not only had turkeys been more profitable than broilers to the farm, but the processor's "spread" for overhead and profit was running about two cents a pound on turkeys as compared to less than one-fourth cent on the broilers. The shift was expected to effect a fuller utilization of the capacity of both the farms and the plant. Without a commitment as to the new freezing facilities, Harmon had been willing to make the change for the sake of the farm alone, but he had hoped the processing plant could benefit also, from a better utilization of capacity during four or five months of each year.

The Rollins operation extended over a distance of about 45 miles. Peerless Manufacturing Corporation was located at Maryville, Arkansas. The headquarters for the farming enterprises—as well as several farms—was at Boydstun, about 15 miles to the southwest. Southwest of Boydstun about 24 miles were the feed mill and additional farming units at Spring Creek. The processing plant and several poultry farms were located at Auburn, which was 30 miles west of Boydstun and 30 miles northwest of Spring Creek.

Harmon felt that operations were spread too widely for maximum efficiency; friends reminded him jokingly that "you can't get out on the road anywhere without seeing a Rollins feed truck." If the processing plant were being located in 1963, it would be placed at or near Boydstun. The location at Auburn came when there was a good supply of broilers being produced in the area by farmers. After the 1960–61 year production declined greatly, and buyers had to range widely to secure broilers. The feed mill was located at Spring Creek primarily because of the availability there of adaptable unused buildings and a railroad.

Walter Harmon was fully conscious of changing economic conditions in the poultry industry. He had been involved with the poultry industry, first in Georgia then in Mississippi, during most of his adult life. He had worked as a feed and poultry dealer, as a processor, and as a poultry breeder and hatcheryman before joining Rollins in May, 1961. He had gained wide experience in dealing with farmers and farm workers and had dealt successfully with many chain store executives in connection with sales. He had seen the "squeeze" on the poultry producer tighten steadily and relentlessly during the 1950's—especially on small producers.

IMPORTANT CHANGES IN THE POULTRY INDUSTRY, 1948–63

Poultry meat production increased greatly in the United States during the fifteen years ending in 1963. Between 1948 and 1962 broiler production increased almost sixfold from 1,200 million pounds to 6,850 million pounds. Turkey production increased almost threefold from 650 million pounds to 1,880 million pounds, at the peak in 1961. Broilers recorded gains in every year, and turkey production expanded in all years except four: 1948, 1953, 1955, and 1962.

The uptrend in poultry production resulted from a complex of factors which affected both supply and demand. On the one hand, producers were willing to offer increasing supplies of poultry even though consumer prices were declining—because the cost of producing and marketing poultry was declining also. The cost reduction was brought about largely by spectacular advances in nutrition, genetics, disease control, and management. Other developments, however, were important, including changes in the organization, structure, and financing of the broiler, turkey, and retail food industries, as well as some downward movement in the price of poultry feed.

At the same time, the average consumer was willing to use more and more poultry as prices fell. Also, the consumer demand for poultry after 1950 grew because of increased availablity, convenience, and quality. The growth in population of the United States and in its per capita incomes and the improvement in exports, especially to Europe, also supported the rapid increase in production. (In contrast, the consumption of red meats was rather stable, on a per-capita basis, during a comparable period—pork and lamb and mutton declining moderately and beef and veal declining slightly after 1956, following a moderate increase during 1948–55.)

Most large grocery stores came to sell poultry every day in the week instead of merely for weekends or holidays. Poultry was offered in an increasingly wide variety of easy-to-use forms. These included ready-to-cook birds (both whole and cut-up), poultry parts, canned poultry, poultry pies, and poultry incorporated into other convenience foods. Quality was improved through genetics and better feeding and management and through Federal inspection of processing. As recently as the mid-1950's most of the fowl delivered in New York City was sold after the removal of only blood and feathers.

Changes in the production of market eggs during the 1948–63 period were not comparable to changes in meat production. Though trends toward lower cost and more efficient production were evident here also, along with drastically lower prices, the overall volume was barely maintained. Largely because of changing attitudes toward the importance of eggs in the diet, the per-capita consumption of eggs in the United States declined over this period.

PRICE DECLINES

The spread between producer costs and revenues narrowed markedly during the same fifteen-year period. Producer's gross income from all poultry products in the United States (including products consumed on farms) declined from $3,573 million in 1948 to $3,333 million in 1962. The peak was reached in 1951 at $3,982 million. (Meat products constituted about 40 per cent of this total in 1948; about 42 per cent in 1951; and 47 per cent in 1962.) At the same time, of course, the physical volume of the products and the cost of earning this gross income both increased enormously. Early in 1963 one speaker put the matter this way: In the last ten years broiler prices have been cut ten cents per pound, but the farm price has declined seventeen cents.

The adjustments which poultry meat producers made during the 1948–62 period to their changing economic environment are summarized below:

	Commerical Broilers Slaughtered			Turkeys Slaughtered		
	POUNDS (LIVE) (MILLIONS)	AVE. PRICE (CENTS)	VALUE (MILLION DOLLARS)	POUNDS (LIVE) (MILLIONS)	AVE. PRICE (CENTS)	VALUE (MILLION DOLLARS)
1948	1,127	36.0	405	561	46.8	263
1949	1,570	28.2	443	760	35.2	267
1950	1,945	27.4	533	820	32.9	270
1951	2,415	28.5	689	938	37.5	351
1952	2,624	28.8	756	1,060	33.6	356
1953	2,904	27.1	786	1,011	33.7	340
1954	3,236	23.1	747	1,161	28.8	334
1955	3,350	25.2	844	1,090	30.2	329
1956	4,270	19.6	838	1,259	27.2	342
1957	4,683	18.9	886	1,360	23.4	319
1958	5,431	18.5	1,002	1,348	23.9	322
1959	5,763	16.1	925	1,440	23.9	345
1960	6,017	16.9	1,014	1,471	25.4	373
1961	6,836	13.9	947	1,883	18.9	356
1962	6,913	15.2	1,049	1,628	21.6	352

Clearly farmers were producing more for less. The national price averages tend to hide some of the pressures placed on farmers to produce for less. For example, in 1961 when the average price received for broilers was 13.9 cents, the lowest monthly average price on a national basis was 11.8 cents in October; during that month farmers in the North Georgia area received only 10.4 cents, an amount less than the cost of feed, according to experts. (The cost of each baby chick amounted to about 3 cents per pound in the broiler.)

Regional differences are quite significant in broiler and turkey production. The transportation cost on processed birds reduces the farm price which can be paid. Regional cost differences—primarily feed transportation, heating, and labor—influence the cash-cost position of producers and thereby the point at which an individual producer may decide (or be forced) to decrease his volume or cease production entirely, at least temporarily.

REGIONAL SHIFTS

One of the adjustments made by poultry producers was that of regional shifting. During the period 1955–62 very significant declines in production, and in rank among producing states, occurred in Connecticut, Massachusetts, New Jersey, New York, and Ohio; and most of the broiler expansion in output was found in Georgia, Arkansas, Alabama, North Carolina, and Mississippi, the composite gain being 160 per cent in this area. In 1961 these five states produced 55 per cent of the country's broilers.

Turkey production became more specialized regionally, also. In 1950 the ten leading states produced 64 per cent of the country's output; in 1962 the ten leading states produced about 75 per cent. In 1962 California and Minnesota raised almost one-third of the country's turkeys. From 1950 to 1962 the largest production gains were made by the four leading turkey producing states of California, Minnesota, Iowa, and Wisconsin. Production of turkeys declined in twenty states, led by Oregon, Pennsylvania, Washington, New York and Maryland.

Feed and the cost of its transportation are relatively more important in turkeys than in broilers. Capital investment (long-term) and labor cost are relatively more important in broilers. In addition excesses of heat and humidity in an area have a more significant effect on turkeys than on broilers.

LARGE-SCALE PRODUCTION

A second adjustment made by poultry meat producers to adverse conditions was an increased scale of operations. The labor used per 100 pounds of broilers declined in the United States from an average of 3.10 hours in 1950–51 to 0.98 hours in 1960–61. This improvement in productivity was accomplished by a move toward larger production units, which permitted the use of labor-saving buildings and equipment—largely automatic equipment for feeding, watering (including medication), and temperature-control.

In broiler production, the definition of an efficient unit expanded during the 1948–62 period from about 10,000 birds to about 50,000 birds, though the overall average remained much lower. The fixed-capital investment in capacity at this level approximates $1.00 per bird. The size of the most efficient processing equipment unit increased approximately the same as the production unit, and equipment continuously became more mechanized.

Over 90 per cent of the United States production of turkeys in 1959 came from farms which raised over 3,200 turkeys, and farms raising 10,000 or more turkeys accounted for more than 70 per cent of the total. Only about half as many farms raised turkeys in 1959 as in 1954; the average number of birds per farm increased from 370 to 953. (These facts were developed for the year 1959 in the last U.S. census for agriculture.)

Turkeys are raised (after being started in a brooder house) primarily on the range during late spring, summer and early fall. Then very little shelter is necessary, and usually none is supplied even in sections where considerable rain may fall during the range period. After the period of brooding, virtually all of the long-term requirement is for land. Fences, automatic water fountains and large-capacity, waterproof feeders ordinarily are provided. Hence the investment in fixed assets is small except for land, which usually can be used for some other purpose if not for ranging turkeys. However, most growers must have short-term credit because of the need to put $3 to $4 into each bird, prior to maturity, in terms of cash-costs. This small emphasis on long-term capital commitment (for individuals already farming) makes easier the development of large-scale operations in turkeys, provided the farmer's reputation as a good operator and a good financial risk permits him to secure the short-term credit necessary.

It is well recognized in the poultry industry, for either chickens or turkeys, that the significance of the disease problem, as well as the inherent risk, increases more than proportionately to an increase in flock size. Only exceptional care and emphasis on disease control can offset this additional hazard in large flocks.

INTEGRATION

Another response of poultry meat producers to adversity was integration. This development was related to the increased scale of operations. Most farmers in the poultry-expanding sections of the United States who could be attracted by an opportunity to raise poultry commercially had little more to offer than land and labor. Frequently the initiative was taken by feed-mill representatives, who agreed to furnish baby chicks, feed, and medicines on credit to encourage the plunge into broiler raising; also, some help was often provided with respect to securing credit for initial building construction. When the birds were sold, the feed mill sponsor accepted the proceeds to the extent necessary to cover the debt, frequently picking up the birds in trucks and delivering them to his own processing plant or one having a working agreement with him. The existence of a supply of so-called marginal farmers in the South undoubtedly contributed to the rapid increase of broiler production there during the post-war period.

This process of integration in broiler feeds, raising, and processing became more rapid and more all-pervading as the "squeeze" on producers became tighter. Farmers had many losses, even cases where cash-costs were not covered by revenues. This result could be expected where a serious disease outbreak occurred, but it often happened even in the absence of this adverse development. Milling companies frequently had to contract to provide such producers with a minimum guarantee to keep them operating. In the early days this minimum might be five cents a bird to cover labor and fixed costs such as depreciation, insurance, taxes, and interest on investment. Over the years, as the size of flocks increased—with the consequent reduction in labor time per bird—this minimum guarantee declined.

After suffering serious losses from minimum guarantees given to farmers who later "earned" them through poor performance, misfortune, or poor broiler prices, many milling companies refused to give such guarantees in contracts. Some of these firms simply ceased to do business in the area. Many of the large milling companies developed incentive programs for their integrated farmers, the formula being built around the ratio of feed conversion in the flock. Keeping the ratio of feed to pounds of broiler marketed at a small figure became the farmer's objective, since he was rewarded in the contract formula for having a low conversion ratio. Many experts argue that this sort of incentive—rather than a salary—is necessary to secure the dedication needed in the care of chickens.

Processing companies gradually had to enter more aggressively into the integration picture of broilers. As the "squeeze" became tighter, especially in 1961, many feed mills—usually the smaller and more poorly financed ones—had to drop out of broiler production and either quit business or accept with resignation the reduction in volume of their own activities. This development left processing plants with idle capacity in many sections of the United States. Many of these companies attempted to keep up the volume of their activities by encouraging farmers to grow broilers under contract with them. In recent years, a processing firm and a feed company have often entered into a kind of partnership agreement with a broiler grower by which each was allowed his "costs" and shared in the profits or losses on a predetermined percentage basis. The extension of credit to the farmer for baby chicks and feed is a characteristic of this kind of contract, usually by the processor and miller jointly. Typically the farmer assumes more risk than under the older minimum-guarantee arrangement, but he is in a position to earn more if successful.

Commercial broiler production was said to be virtually 100 per cent integrated in 1963. Many speakers and writers have blamed integration for the price troubles of the broiler industry. They allege that integration has produced an automatic pressure toward more production and more capacity for production: Feed mill firms and processors having their capacities established, and a resulting large amount of overhead or fixed costs, must try to do whatever is necessary to maintain a profitable operating level—so long as they have a reasonable expectation of receiving something more than their variable costs in return. It is argued that this process of integration causes a loss of flexibility in the broiler industry, production adjustments responding very slowly to price declines.

One writer late in 1961 correctly predicted that broiler output would not decline in 1962 after the disaster of 1961: "Despite the weakened financial position of the firms backing broiler production, the same forces which encouraged output in 1961 will be evident in 1962. . . . Physical facilities to support sustained or even increased production are available." He added that only about 84 per cent of commercial broiler housing had been utilized even in 1961—capacity which had not yet been diverted to other use to a significant extent. He described the broiler business as being an integrated structure, which tended to make leaving the business and returning quite difficult: The producer-processor sees his competitors as being under like financial pressure and he expects some of them eventually to give up; and with the prospect of that eventual improvement, he continues to operate at near capacity.

It is clear that this writer assumed that the producer-processor was faced with a given market price and that his own output was too small to influence the price in the market. Actually many farmers, part of the integration picture, left their buildings idle during much of 1962 and 1963. News stories in 1963 described modern poultry buildings being torn down in New Jersey to lower the assessment of the farm for property taxes and, also, many other buildings being considered for lease by large, national feed milling companies for operation on their own account with hired labor because not enough growers on a contracted basis could be secured. News reports from Georgia indicated that some idle broiler buildings were being converted for integrated operation as commercial egg farms—also that some integrated operations were expanding into commercial egg production because of the reduced level of opportunity for profitable expansion in broiler production.

Turkey production did not by 1963 lend itself to the type of integrated, large-scale production used for broilers, especially in the Southeast. (It is more seasonal in nature, though freezing turkeys obscures this fact from consumers.)

After an investigation of the broiler industry in 1962, a Subcommittee Report of the U.S. House of Representatives recommended that integration and contract growing be reduced in the industry by legislation. This report also blamed the retailing practice of using broilers as loss leaders for difficulties in the industry.

On the other hand, experts in the field frequently stated that further concentration of control in the broiler industry (and in turkeys also, though more slowly) was both necessary and inevitable. The argument held that 75 per cent of the broilers were turned out by 90 companies in 1962, that the corresponding number was 200 as late as 1959, and that the number must become small enough that a production unit (for selling) can have a bargaining power equal to that of major retail organizations. In some areas groups of farmers have established cooperatives to increase the concentration of selling power.

One expert, writing for January, 1963, publication, predicted that large producing groups—with processors at the selling end—would control output more and more. (With this development, supply could be adjusted to price more efficiently.) Also, he saw the gradual increase in the percentage of poultry meat frozen as providing a less perishable product and an increased independence of chain-store buyers. He predicted, also, that further-processing (beyond ordinary dressing and freezing) activities would have to be concentrated in the hands of large processors for efficiency in production and promotion and selling, tending to produce more concentration.

EXPORTS

United States poultry exports reached a new high in 1962. This increase was concentrated in the first half of the year, in anticipation of new trade regulations by countries in the Common Market, effective July 1. Total exports of fresh and frozen poultry increased from 25 million pounds in 1955 to 263 million pounds in 1962. Exports of broilers and fryers (largely to the Common Market) increased from almost 24 million pounds in 1958 to almost 173 million pounds in 1962. During this period exports of turkey (largely to the Common Market) expanded from 5.2 million pounds to 36.9 million pounds.

Exports represented 7 per cent of domestic broiler production in June, 1962, but only 3 per cent in October of that year. The new Common Market trade regulations had a more severe effect on United States broiler exports than on turkey exports—largely because turkey production within the Common Market and in Denmark were negligible. Drastic declines in broiler exports to Europe seemed inevitable, though the federal government continued to make the poultry tariff a major issue in trade negotiations in 1963.

West Germany, the principal foreign poultry market of the United States in 1962, illustrated the impact of the new trade regulations. Total import levies against U.S. broilers increased from less than five cents a pound early in 1962 to about 12½ cents early in 1963. Importers' total cost for broilers rose from 37 cents per pound to 44 cents and for turkeys from 41 cents to 52 cents.

GOVERNMENT INTERVENTION

By 1959 much agitation had developed in the poultry industry for intervention on the part of the federal government in an attempt to overcome the difficulties of operators. The plea was usually made for the independent farmers being forced out of production by declining prices. Several Congressional Committees and Subcommittees held hearings on the problems of the poultry industry. Finally, the Agricultural Act of 1961 provided for the proposal to farmers of a national marketing order for turkeys—to be effective if approved by two-thirds of the farmers eligible to vote, for the 1963 production year. The voting in June, 1962, led to a rejection of the proposal. About 42 per cent of the producers voting favored the order; their votes represented 50 per cent of the total pounds of live-weight turkey production being voted by producers. The rejected program provided for a limitation on production increases in turkeys.

The 1961 Act also provided for support by the U.S. Department of Agriculture of poultry prices by the purchase, when considered advisable by the Secretary of Agriculture, for the school lunch program of dried eggs, frozen turkey, and frozen cut-up broilers. In 1962, under this program, the government purchased 43 million pounds of turkey as compared with 60 million in 1961. Purchases in 1962 were 5 per cent of the September-December production, and 1961 purchases were 6 per cent of the output in those months. In the two years the government spent about the same for broilers as for turkeys: 60 million pounds for 1962 and 45 million pounds for 1961—for a total of about $31½ million.

THE PROBLEM: DETAILS

The meeting of July 29 at Boydstun was the fourth formal meeting of executives of Peerless Manufacturing Corporation with Walter Harmon concerning the volume problems of the processing plant and the expansion proposal. Art Yeager, the manager of the processing plant, had attended two of the meetings, but he had not arranged to leave his work in time to attend this one. This was to have been the "decision" meeting. Robert Andrews, Vice-President for Administration, and William Robertson, Executive Vice-President, attended the meeting for Peerless Manufacturing Corporation.

THE PROPOSAL

Each of the conferees had a copy of the original proposal—which had been written in May by Harmon:

HISTORY

Peerless Processing began operations on March 1, 1957. Initial 15 months operations were unprofitable due to problems associated with procurement of sufficient live production and establishment of profitable sales outlets.

During fiscal 1959 and succeeding years operations improved and reasonable profits have been realized until fiscal year ending 6/30/63. In 1963 net profits to January 1 were $40,000. Since that time due to lower operating margins, broiler processing has been unprofitable in most areas of the country. This has reflected in severe losses up to April 1, 1963. Since that time margins have improved and changes in marketing techniques have enabled us to break even weekly and we anticipate future small profits in processing chickens.

The Arkansas-Missouri area immediately adjacent to the plant has been declining in chicken population for the past several years. Present plans are to increase this production of broiler chickens and turkeys through additional growing by Rollins Poultry Company and contracting with poultry farmers by Rollins Feed Mill, both affilitated companies. This increase will help to avoid the losses incurred in the first quarter of 1963 by making more volume available to the processing plant.

Turkey processing since its inception in 1959 has been consistently very profitable, even though facilities to properly freeze the produce have been inadequate. This has made it impossible to do a good enough job of freezing turkeys so that they could be certified Grade "A" by USDA and limiting the number of possible sales outlets, resulting in a loss in profits of from 01¢ to 03¢ per pound at various times.

PROPOSAL

Construct as addition to the plant of a *liquid freezing* and *blast freezing* facility capable of freezing 100,000 pounds of turkeys per day, storage facilities at −10 degrees for 400,000 pounds of turkeys, additional processing and dock area to complement this. This will enable us to expand our turkey processing operation to 8,000,000 pounds per year and will also provide additional badly needed space to diversify our broiler chicken processing operation into phases which are more profitable, such as fresh and frozen cut-up birds, squabs, and capons.

Live production of turkeys is available in an area within a satisfactory distance of the plant including approximately 4,000,000 pounds available from affiliated Rollins Poultry Company.

Cost of this facility will be:

Equipment	$50,000
Building and Assoc. Facil.	200,000
	$250,000

We propose two financing arrangements: #1—$400,000 loan to be secured by a mortgage on building and equipment valued at $600,000 net. This will enable us to release a $150,000 note presently secured by securities pledged by Peerless Manufacturing Corporation of Maryville, Arkansas (an affiliated company). #2— $250,000 loan to be secured by a mortgage on building and equipment valued at $600,000 net.

Estimated Cash Flow on Investment

	Profit	Depreciation	Total
1963/64	$130,000	$15,000	$145,000
1964/65	140,000	15,000	155,000
1965/66	190,000	15,000	205,000
Total	$460,000	$45,000	$505,000

OPERATING DATA

During the meeting Harmon presented additional figures designed to show how much more profitable the processing plant would be if the $250,000 were expended as proposed.

Through June 30, 1963, the plant had processed poultry as follows—in thousands of pounds, dressed weight:

Year Ended	Turkeys	Broilers	Broilers— Own Farms' Percentage
June 30, 1958	1,124	8,654	40
June 30, 1959	406	14,409	38
June 30, 1960	1,168	14,212	45
June 30, 1961	1,632	14,815	48
June 30, 1962	2,213	14,637	65
June 30, 1963	2,071	13,862	55

The percentage figures given for output from Rollins farms applied to broilers only, since all of the turkeys processed came from these farms. Birds were sold to the processing plant by Rollings farms at the going market rate and picked by trucks from the processing plant. Harmon stated that, on the average, turkeys had a dressed weight of 80 per cent of live weight, while broilers "dressed out" 74 per cent.

Harmon explained also that during the last year about 1,300,000 pounds of turkey had been dressed and frozen at the plant, while just under 775,000 had been sold fresh—that is, ice-packed—and that the latter figure represented all the firm could hope to dress and sell in fresh condition. He stated also that the greater part of the frozen turkeys packaged had been inefficiently frozen so as to sell at a discount. With the quick-freezing room overloaded in order to freeze a minimum processing unit (a truckload) the skin of the frozen bird took on a dark or reddish color; too slow freezing at the surface caused fluid in the flesh of the bird to be drawn, early in the freezing process, close enough to the skin to cause discoloration.

Harmon's statement in the proposal that "reasonable profits have been realized until fiscal year ending 6/30/63" referred to statements presented in condensed form as follows:

Thousands of Dollars

Statements Dated	FIXED ASSETS (NET)	REVENUES	VARIABLE EXPENSES	FIXED EXPENSES	NET INCOME *LOSS
June 30, 1958	$429	$3,168	$3,130	$119	$81*
June 30, 1959	492	4,100	3,838	184	78
June 30, 1960	429	4,595	4,349	192	54
June 30, 1961	378	4,625	4,382	183	60
June 30, 1962	350	4,205	4,031	157	17
June 30, 1963					5

*Estimated

The increase of fixed assets in 1959 arose from the fact that additional units of labor-saving cleaning and finishing equipment were added during that year. The amounts stated for net income were after-tax figures; also, interest actually paid, amounting to about $10,000 per year, was deducted. On all balance sheets the amount of working capital shown was negligible; current assets averaging about $200,000 were approximately offset by outstanding current liabilities. The principal cause of the decline in fixed expenses in 1962 was that much of the automotive equipment became fully depreciated. Depreciation of all fixed assets amounted to about $35,000 (included in "fixed expenses") in fiscal year 1958.

While Harmon realized that the classifications of expenses as between fixed and variable were necessarily only approximations—the fixed group being partially variable and the variable expenses as a group being fixed to some extent—he thought the built-in errors in both directions would roughly offset each other for the type of decisions necessary in his plant with respect to volume of activity. (He remarked, "I know one thing—that fixed overhead is really big enough to hurt us.") For example, maintenance workers, inspectors, and clean-up personnel were treated as variable, although reduced activity would clearly not reduce these costs proportionately.

The key to Harmon's calculations was that for every extra turkey the plant had processed, on the average, 2 cents per pound had been contributed to overhead, profit, and income taxes.

	Pounds
Estimated fiscal 1964 broiler turkey production, 100,000 birds averaging 7.5 pounds each, dressed	750,000
Estimated 1963 large turkey production, 200,000 birds averaging 17 pounds each, dressed	3,400,000
Estimated total for fiscal 1964	4,150,000
Estimated pounds to be sold fresh	800,000
Estimated pounds to be frozen	3,350,000
Less: Amount frozen in fiscal 1963	1,300,000
1964, increase from new equipment	2,050,000
At 2c spread per pound	$41,000

Harmon stated that this $41,000, coming from the use of less than 50 per cent of freezing capacity (estimated at 8,000,000 pounds annually), might well keep the processing plant from going into the red in fiscal 1964. "We can sell our turkeys on foot," he said, "but I hate to hand that spread to some other processor while our plant has the idle dressing capacity." He added that the plant could dress 20,000 pounds of turkeys an hour, which "leaves plenty of time even during the busy turkey season for dressing all the broilers we'll ever want to process during that period." Turkey flocks were usually planned so that there was a concentration of maturity during the middle 10 weeks of the busy turkey season (about the last $4\frac{1}{2}$ months of the year). The ideal time to slaughter a mature turkey extended over only about one week.

Harmon did not consider securing sales outlets for his poultry to be a big problem except for the freezing capacity. Birds sold were identified as Peerless products. Harmon used sales brokers very little. He dealt with smaller chain stores but did not control enough volume to negotiate with large chain retailers; inefficient freezing restricted his turkey market considerably. His estimates showed that the improved quality of freezing with the new facilities might easily eliminate "upwards of $10,000 now being lost through discounts on discolored frozen turkeys."

Peerless Processing stored frozen turkeys at public storage facilities in Springfield, Missouri. Even with the new capacity proposed, this practice would continue. However, Harmon thought storage facilities provided in the plan for 400,000 pounds would largely eliminate the need to use public storage for turkeys dressed during about half of the year. In addition, being able to keep a supply of frozen turkeys at the plant during the busy season would reduce costs by eliminating transfers. Harmon estimated that it cost .6 cents a pound just to transport and move birds in and out of public storage and that the planned storage capacity would have a turnover rate of three times a year, for a saving of $7,200 (1,200,000 pounds at .006).

Harmon had estimates even more specific as to fixed overhead cost: In a well-run plant this cost should be about .98 cents per pound of poultry dressed; and, also, "I think our dressing plant can qualify in this category." He had figures showing that savings on fixed overhead of $36,000 a year would amortize the $250,000 investment proposed at 8 per cent in ten years and that this saving could be accomplished by an increase in poultry dressed annually of 3,800,000 pounds. He put this increase in perspective by explaining that " we have increased turkeys by 1,700,000 pounds just this year." He would have to increase by 2,100,000 more.

This further increase would require raising a total of about 400,000 large turkeys. Robertson raised questions at this point, primarily, in every discussion: Though the processing plant had not been doing badly until the last two years, the poultry farming operation (aside from the feed mill) had been performing poorly as to profits rather consistently. His stock question was: "Can we afford to risk doubling the poultry farm operation"? Harmon's standard answer had been: "We have had trouble with turkeys only one year —the loss of 1962-fiscal year from falling prices. If turkey prices stay up to last year's level, our 1963 increase will make fiscal-1964 a good year. Of course, we did have disease problems with broilers a couple of years and a lot of trouble with prices—that's what hurt the farm so much."

Harmon's well considered personal conviction was that the main thing his poultry farming enterprise had to do was to be careful not to expand too much in what eventually turned out to be a "bad year." Sometimes such a misfortune might ruin an operator, he admitted; but in the main all the good producer had to do was stay as efficient as other good operators to stay in the game: "By and large, turkey production adjusts pretty well to price changes: and there will always be a lot of turkeys raised—on which the efficient can make a profit, on the average."

Harmon considered the turkey operation of Rollins farms an efficient one. The standard direct costs he used in evaluating the performance on each flock (5,000 to 10,000 turkeys) were:

COST ITEM	Cents per pound, live weight	
	HENS	TOMS
Poult	.04	.026
Feed	.12	.115
Labor	.0155	.0090
Fuel	.0030	.0025
Power	.0005	.0005
Medicine, etc.	.0075	.0060
Litter and grit	.0015	.0010
Supervision	.0025	.0020
Housing and equipment	.0020	.0015
Less: Manure (at estimated value)	.0015	.0015
Total direct costs	.1910	.1620

On the average, male birds reached their ideal finished weight at 27 pounds; females, at 15 pounds. All of the cost items except supervision and housing and equipment were charged directly to each flock in the bookkeeping process. The two items of exception were allocated among flocks on the basis of pounds of feed consumed. Total direct costs had rather consistently been held close to these standards in Harmon's experience, seldom having been more than one-half cent greater in a particular flock.

Additional overhead items were allocated to the cost of raising turkeys and raising broilers but not to each flock. These amounted to 2.5 cents a pound in turkeys in 1962, and Harmon's estimates showed that they would come to 1.5 cents a pound in the 1963 flock, being reduced by the increased volume in turkeys. This category included indirect labor, travel, insurance, taxes, vehicles, depreciation on buildings, machinery and land improvements, laboratory expense, "growing" administrative costs, miscellaneous expenses, and unused building rent. The last item was present, because overhead on certain buildings was charged to poultry at standard; the adjustment to actual was made to the accounts at the end of each year.

Harmon knew that further expansion in turkeys raised could not be accomplished without much more capital commitment to the farms. Already about $350,000 had been committed (short-term capital) in the decision to raise 100,000 more turkeys in 1963. Both brooding facilities and suitable range land were rather fully utilized. Broiler operations could be reduced further to solve the brooding problem, but this would not permit a large further increase in turkeys. More land could be purchased, but he knew no such plans were being considered.

Harmon believed, however, that in the long-run turkeys could be raised fully as cheaply in pole-type houses, under confinement, as was possible on the range—and probably there would be better control over diseases. His figures showed that a seven-year amortization of the buildings could be accomplished at 8 per cent on the alternative value of the range land for grazing beef cattle. Considering the difficulty of getting capital for farming, however, Harmon was willing to dismiss the pole-shelter alternative.

Harmon considered the only really practical alternative to "limping along" to be that of getting the expansion of the plant immediately and then setting out to build the necessary capacity into the farming operation by the increase of broiler chickens and turkeys through "contracting with poultry farmers by an affiliated company," as stated in his proposal. There were plenty of broiler houses in the vicinity of Auburn standing idle during either all or part of each year. There was plenty of range land for turkeys, also, as well as brooder houses in which to start the poults. In July, 1963, 50,000 turkeys and 50,000 broilers were being raised on this "contract" basis. There was no Rollins-owned land in the vicinity of Auburn. In working with farmers around Auburn, Harmon and his turkey and broiler managers had found in the spring of 1963 that farmers were loath to re-enter the poultry business under the type of contract formerly used by feed mills in the vicinity. As the broiler manager had told Harmon: "They have been hurt by such contracts before; they just won't take the risk on broiler costs and prices." So the Rollins Feed Mill cooperators of 1963 were working on what was essentially a piece-work basis—a certain amount per bird per week being received by them for their labor, land, buildings, and equipment. The rate for turkeys was $1\frac{1}{2}$ cents per week per growing turkey. The Rollins Feed Mill trucks delivered feed to the turkey range hoppers just as they did to turkeys on land owned.

In the conference Robertson was critical of calling this a "contract arrangement." Harmon admitted that Rollins Feed Mill carried all of the risk. He believed that this method of payment had some advantages over a conversion-ratio type of formula, because farmers seemed distrustful of an arrangement which they often could not understand in detail and because, as he said, "They used to work out ways to beat the formula, such as swapping feed— giving feed to a neighbor when it was not going to matter anyway and receiving it back when there was something to be gained." Harmon believed their cooperating farmers had sufficient incentive: They had to keep their turkeys living to receive their $1\frac{1}{2}$ cents a week, and "they know very well that we will drop them if they don't do a good job." He believed that to date good farmers had been attracted to their proposition. But he observed that labor on the Rollins farms averaged costing 20 to 25 per cent less per bird than was being paid to contract farmers. Harmon was convinced that production, especially in turkeys, could be expanded in the Auburn area under the 1963 plan of the Rollins Feed Mill—possibly tripled in 1964 provided the plant expansion materialized. He was counting on still further expansion in the contract program in succeeding years.

Harmon was enthusiastic about the improvement in the dressing operation to be gained from the plant expansion. Peerless since April 1 had marketed an increasing number of chickens as cut-up broilers, ready to cook, although the plant was already too crowded for routine dressing operations. He had found that the additional spread for processing broilers cut-up was quite significant and that fewer birds, failing to meet standards, had to be discounted in price. Such unimportant factors as body shape did not matter in cut-up birds.

After the conference and after his call to Art Yeager, Harmon reflected on events of the meeting. He was pleased that he was permitted by executives of Peerless Manufacturing to carry on the farming operation as he saw fit: "They told me when I took this job that they would turn me loose; and they did. I just go to them when I'm in trouble. And I am now."

Yes, he believed the Peerless executives regarded his ability and judgment highly; but it seemed awfully hard to get money out of them. On the other hand, they had found $350,000 to finance the current expansion in turkey growing. Both Robertson and Andrews had argued that "each corporation should stand on its own two feet." But Harmon had countered with his opinion that the processing corporation had been undercapitalized in the beginning with capital stock of only $175,000. He was sure that funds for the expansion could be secured within the corporate organization or by using its credit.

Harmon still could not see the logic of the statement of Andrews that "we like to seen ten cents out of each sales dollar staying in the business as profit —or at least the possibility."

Robertson had quoted some expert who had written to the effect that integration, which was complete in broilers, would move rapidly into turkey production. "We know," Robertson had said, "that processors and feed milling companies have always wanted volume and can make money out of it—take the year of 1961 for instance. Traditionally they have got a reasonable spread regardless of low prices. But maybe things are changing. Processors took a beating the next year on broilers because of severe competition for the small volume in many parts of the country." He had closed with a question: "Do we want to become even more firmly locked in than we are now in farming?" Harmon had replied with two questions: "Do you want us to try to sell the processing plant and let someone else make that two cents? Who would buy a broiler processing plant at Auburn now—even a very modern one like ours?"

Harmon saw his job as being an interesting and challenging one, though sometimes discouraging. His work seemed never to be finished. At the end of the meeting on July 29, he had completed a twelve-hour day. After calling Yeager he still had to call two of his farm managers. He frequently did not take time for lunch. On this Monday he had spent four hours with three men from a major feed manufacturing firm, who were seeking a source of good feeder pigs in volume. Though he had a purchasing specialist for the agricultural enterprises and a farm-product sales specialist, he seemed always to be involved in sales decisions. Next week he would have to make a trip to points in New Jersey and to New York City in connection with August and September turkey sales—a program being complicated by the failure to start the processing plant expansion.

10. KELLYS' DATA PROCESSING CENTER*

—JACK T. DOBSON

Kellys' Data Processing Center was established April 1, 1957, in Tallahassee, Florida. It is a wholly owned subsidiary of Kellys' Printers, Inc. of Orlando, Florida. Kellys' Printers, Inc. have branch offices in Apopka and Tallahassee. Controlling interest in Kellys' Printers, Inc. is held by two brothers, John and Carl Kelly. That company was originally organized by their father, who had retired and handed down the operations of the company to his two sons. John Kelly's office was in Orlando.

The Tallahassee branch of Kellys' Printers, Inc. was primarily a sales office with a small printing plant. Carl Kelly was in charge of this branch. Most of its sales were to customers utilizing data processing equipment. Therefore, the salesmen were quite well informed of data processing procedures and systems.

The sales manager of the Tallahassee branch of Kellys' Printers, Inc., was a Mr. James T. Grant. Mr. Grant is a graduate of Rutgers University and is 48 years of age. He was formerly a sales manager with UARCO, Inc. UARCO, Inc. is a well-known and rather large producer of business forms used primarily for data processing. Through many years association with UARCO, Mr. Grant had acquired a great deal of knowledge in his field. He has a reputation of being one of the better systems and forms men in the United States.

Kellys' Printers, Inc. is an agent for the products of UARCO, Inc. within the Northern Florida and Southern Georgia areas. Through this connection they became acquainted with Mr. Grant. Kellys' Printers offered Mr. Grant the job as sales manager in Tallahassee. The offer was accepted.

After several years in Tallahassee Mr. Grant expanded the sales of Kellys' Printers, Inc. tremendously. Through his training, five subordinate salesmen

* Reprinted by permission of Professor Dobson.

became well versed in forms design and data processing systems. Mr. Grant's duties brought him into contact with many of the top men in data processing, among which was a consultant, Mr. Glen H. Hancock. He and Mr. Hancock became well acquainted and enjoyed good business relations for a number of years. Mr. Grant and Mr. Hancock had a great deal of respect for one another because of their ability within their respective vocations.

Mr. Hancock is a graduate of Florida State University with a major in accounting. He is 31 years of age. He had approximately ten years experience in the data processing field in both governmental and private industry activities. He was quite influential in modernizing and standardizing accounting procedures and data processing systems within Florida State government. He also served in the capacity as a consultant for many governmental and private concerns.

Mr. Hancock and Mr. Grant began to consider the possibility of organizing a data processing center in the Tallahassee area. After a considerable analysis, Mr. Grant felt that such a venture should be closely coordinated with Kellys' Printers, Inc. His reasoning was that due to tightening of State purchasing laws in the area of printing and forms purchases, such an arrangement would be more profitable to Kellys' Printers, Inc. The disadvantage brought about by revisions in the State purchasing law could be overcome by selling a package deal to customers which would include both their data processing and form needs. The customer would be billed by the data processing center which in turn would pay for the printing through a billing from Kellys' Printers, Inc. Such an arrangement would provide a tremendous boost in sales to Kellys' Printers, Inc. because a great deal of their business is from state government. Grant and Hancock believed that Kellys' Printers would be interested in financing the proposed data processing venture.

Mr. Grant approached the Kelly brothers about the idea of the data processing center. His argument was convincing. The brothers agreed to organize Kellys' Data Processing Center. They were told that the initial operating costs would be high and operations for the first three years would be at a loss. Mr. Grant anticipated that at the end of three years the company would be at a break even point, and thereafter would develop into a very profitable operation. It was expected that the new company would provide Kellys' Printers, Inc. with a considerable increase in sales.

ORGANIZATION (Exhibit 1)

Upon organizing Kellys' Data Processing Center, the Kelly brothers gave Mr. Grant the job as general manager in addition to his sales management duties with Kellys' Printers, Inc. They also employed the part-time services of Mr. Hancock as a consultant. Mr. Hancock's duties were to price all jobs sold by Kellys' Data Processing Center, to analyze and correct all proposals to prospective customers by the sales force and such other consulting duties that may arise. Another agreement was made effective when the Data Processing Center started producing a profit. At that time Mr. Hancock was to become general manager on a full time basis. He would also be given part interest in the company.

Mr. Doyle Ernest, age 25, was employed as the supervisor of the data processing labor force. He also performed the technical and functional phases

Exhibit 1

Kellys' Data Processing Center
Organizational Chart, 1957

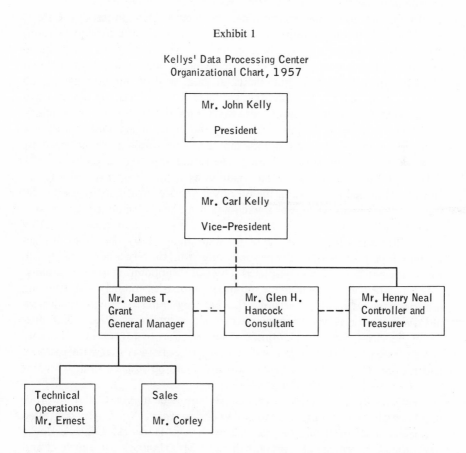

of the business until such time as business was sufficiently large to employ additional people. Mr. Ernest had several years in the data processing field. He was well known by Mr. Hancock and Mr. Grant, who agreed that he could do a good job for the company.

The salesman, Mr. Tom Corley, age 30, is a graduate of the University of Georgia, and had been associated with a data processing service in Atlanta, Georgia. At the time of his employment as salesman with the new company, he was a sales trainee in the data processing service bureau operated by the International Business Machine Corp., in Atlanta.

Two keypuncher operators were employed to perform the clerical task for Mr. Ernest. These were a Mrs. Jane Bower and Mrs. Peggy Jones. Both had a great deal of experience in keypunching and clerical duties and were approximately 28 years of age.

The bookkeeping was to be performed on a part-time basis by the bookkeeper of Kellys' Printers, Inc. Kellys' Data Processing Center was located in a building adjacent to Kellys' Printers, Inc.

Just before the formal establishment of Kellys' Data Processing Center, Mr. Hancock and Mr. Grant visited several State agencies to inquire about their data processing needs. These agencies were informed of the plans to organize a data processing service center which would be able to handle all of their data processing requirements. A great deal of interest was created about the new venture. Several State agencies expressed a desire to enter into contracts at the earliest possible date. Mr. Grant and Mr. Hancock estimated that these contracts, if consummated would bring a revenue to the new company of several thousand dollars monthly. This would place the company on a profit paying basis immediately. The future appeared very bright.

When Kellys' Data Processing Center was formally opened, Mr. Grant and Mr. Hancock followed up the proposed offers of contracts by the several state agencies in an attempt to make them firm. Several small contracts were signed and the services were performed immediately on a continuing monthly basis. However, due to cut-backs in state budgets by the State Budget Commission, as a result of an economic recession, the larger contracts, which were anticipated, were not completed. This was disappointing to the company.

Sales efforts were then made in other industries, namely the trucking industry, the medical profession, the banking industry, textile concerns, utilities and various other concerns which might have a need for a data processing service. After several months of sincere effort by Mr. Grant, a number of new customers were added. Mr. Grant's forecast was that with patience and proper sales technique, new customers could be added to put the company on a sound profit making basis.

Mr. Grant turned most of the sales activity over to Mr. Corley in order that he might devote more time to Kellys' Printers, Inc. Mr. Corley consulted frequently and for prolonged periods with Mr. Hancock. Corley's duties were to design systems and present them to Mr. Hancock for approval and pricing. Mr. Corley, however, was unable to develop sound proposals. As a result, Mr. Hancock had to spend a great deal of time designing systems for Mr. Corley. After several months Mr. Hancock recommended to Mr. Grant that Mr. Corley be relieved of his duties and that a new salesman be employed who had the experience and ability necessary to sell data processing systems. Mr. Grant was reluctant to release Mr. Corley. Instead, he added on to the sales force on a part-time basis, five form salesmen with Kellys' Printers, Inc. This arrangement appeared satisfactory due to the background of the forms salesmen and the many contacts they had in performing their daily task.

This new sales program created additional interest, particularly in the Southern Georgia area. On many occasions Mr. Grant and Mr. Hancock would accompany the salesmen to follow up any lead for data processing service. At first, these efforts proved rather fruitless. However, it was anticipated that after a rather long and extensive sales effort several large contracts would be executed for the data processing service.

Kellys' Printers, Inc. had planned to utilize the services offered by the Data Processing Center to modernize its own record keeping in its three plants in Florida. They desired to purchase the service of the Data Processing Center for all their accounting and statistical needs. They realized the advantages of good sales analysis and other management reports and wished to take advantage of them in their printing business. Rather extensive sales analysis reports were developed by the Center. These proved very beneficial to Kellys' Printers, Inc.

Mr. Hancock made a trip to all the plants operated by Kellys' Printers, Inc. for the purpose of designing and submitting a complete procedural manual for each plant that would take care of all the companies, systems and accounting needs. Upon completion of the task, a meeting was held in Orlando, Florida, at the home office of Kellys' Printers, Inc. At the meeting were John and Carl Kelly, Mr. Grant, Mr. Hancock and the Controller, Mr. Henry Neal. The procedural manuals were reviewed and found satisfactory. They were approved and the service was to be purchased from Kellys' Data Processing Center. This business arrangement would help put the Data Processing Center on a profitable basis.

Mr. Neal, the Controller of Kellys' Printers, Inc., was quite opposed to the data processing venture. He was a man of approximately 60 years of age and had been considering retirement for several years. However, this retirement had been postponed a number of times. He gave no support to the plan to utilize the services of Kellys' Data Processing Center. In fact, he objected to the original establishment of that company.

An effort was made by the Data Processing Center to start converting the account procedures of Kellys' Printers, Inc. Some success was attained in the Tallahassee branch by Kellys' Data Processing Center because of its location and the interest of that branch in the Data Processing Center. However, due to lack of internal support for the data processing program in the other plants, the complete conversion was delayed several months. Mr. Hancock informed the Kelly brothers that it was essential that support be given to the proposed system and suggested that they require their subordinates to give it proper implementation. In the months that followed, the Kelly brothers failed to give the system the attention necessary. They felt that it was the controller's duty to follow through and insure its success.

In 1959, two years after the organization of Kellys' Data Processing Center, the Florida State Legislature passed additional amendments to the State Purchasing Law. These amendments added a considerable number of restrictions to the purchases of printing and business forms by the State and County governments. As a result the sales of Kellys' Printers, Inc. reduced drastically. They began to shift their sales effort to private industry with little success. After a few months it became necessary to release three salesmen. Mr. Grant had become quite disturbed with the management of Kellys' Printers, Inc. and began considering re-locating with some other company.

Kellys' Data Processing Center was very near the break even point, after two years of operation. However, the conversion of Kellys' Printers, Inc. procedures by Kellys' Data Processing Center had still not been completed. The Kelly brothers appeared to have less interest in requiring their employees to accept the new procedures. In fact they were considering discontinuing Kellys' Data Processing Center.

At the end of 1959, Kellys' Printers, Inc. closed down its printing plant in Tallahassee. The equipment was moved to Orlando and utilized in the plant there. Mr. Grant resigned as sales manager and accepted a sales manager position with his former employer, UARCO, Inc., with his office in Miami, Florida.

Talgquin Electric Co-op, Inc., of Quincy, Florida, who had been a prospective customer of Kellys' Data Processing Center decided to enter into a contract for the data processing service. This contract would place the center soundly in a profitable operation. It further could open the door for other small utility companies throughout the North Florida and Southern Georgia areas to use the facilities of Kellys' Data Processing. Utilities were considered one of the better and more profitable customers for data processing businesses.

The Kelly brothers were undecided about the future of Kellys' Data Processing Center. Kellys' Printers, Inc. now had only Mr. Hancock and Mr. Corley in its Tallahassee office. Carl Kelly had moved to Orlando to join his brother in the operation of the plant and home office there. The loss of Mr. Grant thrust the burden of the data processing center upon the Kelly Brothers. They were considering several possibilities for the Data Processing Center. They were trying to decide whether to continue the operation in Tallahassee or to move it to Orlando. The move to Orlando would result in the loss of several local customers. Another consideration was to temporarily discontinue the business and re-open it later in Orlando. A third consideration was to permanently discontinue Kellys' Data Processing Center. A meeting was called on January 15, 1960, in Orlando at which time a decision was to be reached.

AUDIT APPRAISALS
AND CONTROLS

* *

1. BLAIR, INC.*

—C. L. MITCHELL

"This proposal should tidy up the various controls that have developed over the years, so long as we take our time to insure that the plan is prepared carefully and we don't rush into it. I assume we won't start until 1965 for the 1966 budget year."

"I only hope that it is a more realistic plan than the salary budget."

"Another sign of growing pains!"

"If Mr. Strong thinks it may be needed I'll wager my future that it will be both fruitful and possible."

"How can I predict sales of a custom-built product?"

The above was a sample of remarks from the 12 members of the executive and managerial staff of Blair, Inc., following a meeting on July 14, 1964, at which Mr. Strong, the President, had proposed that the executive and managerial staff consider the adoption of an overall budget "as a means of coordinating the various existing controls of the company, so that we can continue to enjoy increasing sales, profits and bonuses."

Blair, Inc. was the earliest American manufacturer of high-quality ovens and furnaces for laboratories and industry. The development of the first American scientific ovens and furnaces can be traced to a request by a scientist at the University of Chicago for an oven for chemical laboratory application. This request had been made to Mr. H. E. Blair who was operating a sheet metal business near Chicago. The inventive genius combined with the craftsman pride of Mr. Blair resulted in the development of an effective oven for the laboratory purposes. Over the years, the quality reputation of the products of the company spread, and requests for high-quality ovens were received from laboratories throughout the country.

During and after World War I, the major source of laboratory equipment from Germany was eliminated. As a consequence the demand for

* Reprinted by permission of Professor Mitchell.

all types of domestically produced laboratory equipment, including the company's ovens and furnaces, increased dramatically. Shortly after World War I, Mr. Blair wished to retire and convinced Dr. C. L. Bright to accept the shares of the company in repayment of the advances he had made to Mr. Blair to finance the expansion of the company. Doctor Bright did not disturb the operating management established by Mr. Blair and restricted his activity to the financial affairs of the company, and continued to follow this policy until his death in 1955.

In the early 1920's the company began production of a line of commercial ovens and furnaces for industry and began distributing their products through laboratory supply dealers. Concurrently Doctor Bright appointed a young instructor in mechanical engineering from Northwestern University, Mr. A. Strong, to take over the operation of the company. Mr. Strong was soon faced with a problem of resurgence of German competition and to counteract this activity began to expand the product line with related high-quality products and to advertise. This sustained merchandising program combined with an active research and development plan resulted in a gradual expansion of the company's sales and profits over the next two decades.

During World War II, the company consolidated its market position and began development of infra red heaters which were marketed commercially in 1946. New product development continued and by 1964 the company had a product line of ovens, furnaces, infra red heaters and allied products representing 40%, 32% and 28% respectively of total dollar sales. An analysis of the company's price lists follows:

Price Range	Number of Items
$ 100–$ 200	168
$ 200–$ 400	112
$ 400–$ 800	90
$ 800–$1,600	114
$1,600–$3,200	128
$3,200–$6,400	6

In addition custom designed installations were constructed for up to $30,000. According to Mr. Golis, the executive vice president, the company held a dominant position in the domestic market for high-quality ovens and furnaces in 1964 and was one of the major suppliers of infra red heaters. The balance of their products were developed to serve the specialized needs of their customers and in the majority of cases were purchased in a finished state. Approximately one-half of their sales were made to 100 laboratory supply dealers of which 15 transacted 80% of the business. The balance of the sales were made directly to hospitals, laboratories and commercial customers through sales offices maintained in New York, Washington, Atlanta, Chicago, Los Angeles, and Dallas. The growth of sales by product group is presented in Exhibit 1.

Exhibit 1

Blair Incorporated

Growth of Sales by Product Group

(1950 = 100)

Year	Ovens & Furnaces	Infra Red Heaters	Other	Total
1950	100	100	100	100
1954	130	225	190	153
1956	147	300	270	188
1958	188	400	380	235
1960	192	530	500	281
1961	194	570	560	307
1962	212	710	670	355
1963	240	880	800	421

The responsibility for advertising and sales promotion of the company's products was shared by Mr. Markin and Mr. Golis. Mr. Markin was responsible for working with the advertising agency in designing and placing advertisements in trade magazines and for preparing news releases on new-product development. Many of the news releases found their way into the "new product" section of the trade magazines. Mr. Markin also arranged for company participation in exhibits at professional conventions. At the beginning of each year, the proposed advertising and convention display expenditures for the next 12 months were estimated by Mr. Markin in consultation with Mr. Strong.

Mr. Golis was responsible for all marketing activities, except advertising, in consultation with Mr. Strong. Over the past decade the company had opened sales offices in six major cities and planned to expand this coverage. However, to be consistent with the company's policy of quality he had deferred opening a new office until a salesman had been trained in the central sales office for at least a year. In 1964 one sales trainee was on the central staff and might be ready to go into the field within six months.

Until 1963 all salesmen were paid a commission on sales with a guaranteed minimum and reimbursed for traveling expenses, since they operated from their homes the only other field office expenses were sundry supplies and telephone charges.

Since the salesmen did not acquire a high level of technical competence, members of the technical staff were regularly called to assist them when a customer had a complex installation.

Effective January 1, 1964, all salesmen were paid a base salary ($9,000–$14,000) plus expenses and in addition received a commission on sales in excess of quota. The quota for each sales territory was based on a conservative judgment of the sales potential, so that a normal salesman would be expected to earn a fairly substantial commission in addition to his salary.

At the beginning of each year Mr. Golis prepared a sales forecast for each of the two major product lines and for miscellaneous products. Since he was unable to establish a market potential for the company's products, he relied on the previous year's sales and his own feeling about the future. With the wide range of products and fluctuating demands, he did not feel that his forecast was very reliable.

In 1961, Acme Laboratory Supply, a major laboratory supply dealer in the United States, began a program of vertical integration and purchased the shares of a small laboratory oven and furnace producer in New York State. Six months later Acme dropped the Blair line and marketed its own brand through a marketing staff of 150 salesmen, many of whom were sales engineers. During 1961 and 1962, Acme salesmen did not actively promote their line of ovens and furnaces, since production was limited. During 1963 and 1964, the expansion of the production facilities of its subsidiary had been accomplished and Acme had recently begun to allow a discount of 30% to customers on standard makes of ovens and furnaces.

High quality and tailor-made products were the hallmark of Blair ovens and furnaces resulting in small quantity production to customer order, and a high ratio of white to blue-collar workers. Of the 300 employees of the company in 1964, 40% were engaged in production and the balance in sales, research and development, quality control, customer service and engineering. An organization chart of the company is presented in Exhibit 2. The specialized skills of the company's personnel have been developed by informal "in service" training programs. The manager of production estimated that it takes four years' service with the company for an employee to attain an adequate level of performance in the factory. To retain these skills the company maintains a steady level of employment and has not laid off any workers because of lack of production in the last 36 years. When sales outstrip normal production capacity of 40 hours per week (five eight-hour days), the company operates a six-day week or subcontracts some of the work. No temporary help is employed in the factory. According to union agreement all time in excess of 40 hours per week is paid a premium of 50% of regular wages. Throughout 1963, and the first quarter of 1964, the plant operated six days a week. The combination of security of employment, interesting work, ample fringe benefits, specialized skills and above average wages have resulted in a very stable labor force. Evidence of this stability is found in a very low labor turnover, absence of strikes—none in 18 years—and the large number of long-service employees—40% with more than 15 years' service.

The two production plants of the company are located in a Chicago industrial suburb about a mile apart. The infra red heaters are produced in plant #2 and the balance of production (and the majority of the employees) is located in the main plant adjoining the engineering, sales and executive offices. Plant #2 is in the path of a throughway which is expected to be constructed by 1966. The main plant is a two-story structure with a basement

Blair Incorporated
Executive and Managerial Staff

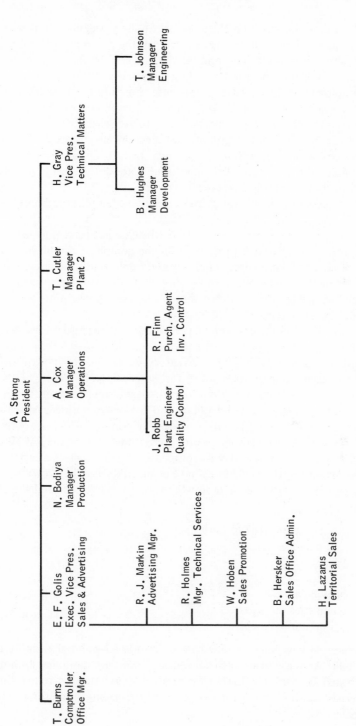

Exhibit 2

and contains the machine shop, electrical shop, welding shop, sheet metal shop, the polishing and plating department, the painting and coating department, shipping and receiving and the shop office. Mr. Bodiya, the production manager, is responsible for scheduling the work and supervising and training the employees. He is assisted in this latter function by six working foremen, members of the plant union, who have no disciplinary or directive authority over the men in their departments. The jobs are scheduled for each employee under the direction of Mr. Bodiya and the working foremen give help to the employees when required and encourage them to do an honest day's work. Both Mr. Bodiya and Mr. Cox have doubts about the ability of the working foremen to accomplish this latter function.

Mr. Cox is responsible for plant and methods engineering, purchasing and inventory control, quality control, industrial engineering and the stockrooms. Since joining the company late in 1963 Mr. Cox has been engaged in formalizing the quality control procedures of the company, establishing standard bills of material, labor time standards and implementing a reservation ordering system for inventories. In solving this latter problem he has worked closely with Mr. Burns, the comptroller, who is planning to establish a standard cost system.

For many years the company has maintained a perpetual inventory system of all raw materials, purchased parts and manufactured subassemblies. This record was used as a basis for inventory valuation, for control over theft, for cost accounting purposes and for purchasing. For each of the 20,000 items in the inventory, Mr. Finn, the purchasing agent, establishes minimum, maximum quantities, reorder points and reorder quantities. At least once a year these inventory guides are reviewed by him and if necessary revised. In 1963 the perpetual inventory records were transferred to the I.B.M. machine and every other working day the purchasing agent receives a report of items in the inventory whose balances have changed during the previous two days. This report shows for each item where a change has occurred the following data:

1. Issues for the year to date
2. Old balance
3. Issues
4. Receipts
5. New balance
6. Quantities on order
7. Minimum balance

When the new balance falls below the reorder point the report indicates this fact. At the end of each month an inventory summary is prepared as illustrated in Exhibit 3. Except for products purchased for resale, the cost of materials has accounted for one-third of the selling price for a number of years.

Exhibit 3
Blair Incorporated

MAY

Categories	Budget	USAGE FOR MONTH	USAGE YEAR TO DATE	INVENTORY MAY 31, 1964
1. Automatic Controls	18 000 00	9 253 34	49 713 49	17 525 05
2. Bibbs, Valves, Gauges, etc.	10 000 00	4 160 27	22 128 26	9 315 76
3. Burners	1 000 00	249 98	1 247 94	1 075 31
4. Elect. Fitting & Accessories	6 000 00	1 348 59	10 145 93	6 737 93
5. Brass, Iron & Sweat Fittings	7 000 00	3 033 87	17 679 53	8 039 46
6. Gaskets, Nameplates, Paints, Miscellaneous	6 000 00	1 282 81	8 750 80	7 436 88
7. Heating Elements	12 000 00	5 151 99	28 113 60	14 136 19
8. Brass, Rod, Pipe & Tubings: Copper Tubing	13 000 00	3 449 99	19 984 65	13 182 74
9. Carbon Steel Pipe, rings, bars, plates	5 000 00	1 026 37	5 548 62	3 712 24
10. Screw Machine Products	9 000 00	2 223 27	13 111 06	9 078 13
11. Copper Sheets, Brass Sheet	15 000 00	5 097 11	29 686 46	16 289 29
12. Stainless Sheet, Monel Sheet	10 000 00	2 672 20	14 231 72	10 703 47
13. Solders	4 000 00	4 403 49	12 674 57	9 132 17
14. Meters & Accessories	16 000 00	3 502 58	18 577 75	15 842 63
15. Infra Red Small Components	25 000 00	11 315 16	50 057 67	30 231 55
16. Heater Stock	1 500 00	110 16	1 425 72	1 919 84
17. Heater Cartridges	4 000 00	19 999 95	105 481 07	5 007 47
18. Misc. Packaged finished goods	8 000 00	2 152 12	13 465 96	13 012 06
19. Castings, Unfinished	1 000 00	512 45	2 271 31	923 77
20. Castings, Finished	25 000 00	15 137 86	87 942 80	28 529 47
21. Sub-Assemblies (less Heating Elements)	40 000 00	34 091 29	212 542 76	46 099 60
22. Spinning & Stampings	10 000 00	2 088 90	14 194 01	11 394 90
23. Infra Red Heaters (Finished goods)	1 000 00	7 893 57	32 008 07	4 764 56
24. Floor Stock	5 000 00	11 522 62	52 064 64	2 650 16
25. Filter Elements	6 000 00	998 80	7 354 34	2 518 53
26. Shipping Materials	5 000 00	1 247 36	6 695 56	6 077 50
27. Full Open Door Ovens	15 000 00	3 978 35	35 194 28	17 671 85
28. Plastic Fittings & Pipe	11 000 00	8 594 39	41 199 64	15 962 31
29. Cartridge Components	15 000 00	4 262 35	19 663 72	12 974 12
30. Jackets & Components	15 000 00	4 437 86	20 291 86	15 684 34
31. Resistance Wire	40 000 00	21 981 48	96 131 70	46 141 35
32. Fasteners	4 000 00	1 300 59	5 576 67	2 982 99
99. Miscellaneous	10 000 00	1 682 92	14 743 78	7 374 68
TOTAL MATERIAL INVENTORY	373 500 00	200 164 04	1069 899 94	414 128 30

When Mr. Cox's department has completed the preparation of standard bills of material it is planned that the inventory will be divided into reserved and nonreserved categories. As soon as a sales order is received, a standard bill of material will be prepared, the information entered in the I.B.M. machine and the items listed segregated by category in the purchasing agent's report. In this way the purchasing procedure may begin when the sales order is received, not when the issues are made to production. There is normally a two-week lag between the receipt of the sales order and the issue of the production order while the engineering details are being prepared. By implementing this system, it is expected that fewer inventory shortages will occur and at the same time the margin of safety can be reduced. According to the purchasing agent most of the material can be delivered by the company's suppliers on two weeks' notice.

When Mr. Burns, the comptroller, joined Blair, Inc., in 1951, the bookkeeper maintained only an elementary set of double entry financial accounting records which were used by the auditors to prepare quarterly financial statements in which the inventories were estimated. Mr. Burns was appointed specifically to provide Mr. Strong with accurate financial statements at the end of each month. Over the next five years Mr. Burns worked with the manufacturing and purchasing departments to develop a job cost accounting system. Under this system material was requisitioned by the worker for each job as required, and each worker made a notation of the time worked on each job. The material requisition slips were passed on to the perpetual inventory records for pricing and recording and then passed to the accounting department where they were sorted and accumulated for each job. The payroll department reconciled the men's job time slips with their clock cards, recorded the wage rates and passed them to the accounting department where they were sorted by job number. When the accounting office was advised that the job had been shipped or at the end of the accounting period, the material requisitions and the labor time tickets were totalled for each job, an overhead rate was applied and the total cost compared to the sales price. At the end of each month a list of the cost and sales prices of jobs completed during the month was prepared and forwarded to Mr. Strong who inquired further about any unusual items. It was found that many of the inquiries made by Mr. Strong were attributable to mechanical errors in the system. To overcome these mechanical errors and to facilitate control over production inefficiencies, the company is in the process of implementing a standard cost system.

The executives of the company, with the exception of Mr. Cox who joined the company late in 1963 from the management services division of Ernst and Ernst, have a long record of service with the company. Details of the age and length of service of the executive and managerial staff and number of employees under their authority are presented in Exhibit 4. In the majority of cases these men have held their present positions since joining the company. To reward this group for their contribution to the company's progress, Mr. Strong introduced a bonus plan in 1963. Under this plan 8% of net income before income taxes is allocated to the members of this group at the end of each year.

In January 1964, Mr. Strong perceived that the growth of the company was resulting in a breakdown of communication and control so necessary in an organization producing a quality custom built product. To provide formal channels of communication within the company, a sounding board and

Exhibit 4

Blair Incorporated

Age and Length of Service and Numbers of Employees under Authority of Executive and Managerial Staff as of December 31, 1963

Name	Age	Length of Service (years)	Employees
A Strong	53	31	300
N. Bodiya	52	36	97
T. Burns	52	12	25
A. Cox	49	1	24
T. Cutler	48	18	31
R. Finn	49	22	3
E. Golis	55	28	54
H. Gray	42	15	57
R. Holmes	41	9	6
D. Hughes	45	5	9
T. Johnson	52	23	24
R. Markin	47	22	1
J. Robb	54	22	5

training ground for executives, and as a means of evaluating executive potential and performance, Mr. Strong established 13 committees. In establishing the committees, Mr. Strong made it clear to the committee chairman that, within the limitations of duration and frequency of meetings established by him, the committee chairman was responsible for the agenda of the meetings and its membership. In no case was the function of decision making to be delegated to the committee—the members were to perform only an advisory

Exhibit 5

Blair Incorporated

MEMORANDUM
To: Staff

SUBJECT: OPERATING COMMITTEES

For quite some years we have had conference groups, in some areas of our operation, meeting periodically to discuss problems in these specific areas, reviewing progress made in the immediately preceding period and setting up a program for the next succeeding period. These committee conferences have been very successful and we are now expanding this program to other areas of our operation.

Below is a listing of Committees with members and meeting dates. Changes may be made from time to time as the need requires.

1. *Sales Promotion* (1 hour)
E. F. Golis, Chairman
Strong, Markin, Gray, Holmes, Cutler, Hersker, Hoben, Lazarus
Quarterly, 2nd Tuesday, 9:30 a.m.; March, June, September, December

2. *Advertising and Publicity* (3 hours)
R. J. Markin, Chairman
Arthur, Golis, Hoben, Strong
Monthly, 3rd Tuesday, 9:30 a.m.

3. *Research, Development, Engineering and Technical Service* (3 hours)
H. Gray, Chairman
Golis, Cutler, Holmes, Johnson, Markin, Strong, Hughes
2nd Thursday, Monthly, 9:30 a.m.

4. *Industrial Design* (3 hours)
H. Gray, Chairman
Jones, Golis, Cutler, Markin, Hughes, Holmes, Johnson, Strong
Monthly, 3rd Thursday, 10:00 a.m.

5. *Export* (1 hour)
B. Martin, Chairman
Golis, Strong, Markin
Quarterly, 4th Tuesday, 9:30 a.m.; January, April, July October

6. *Industrial Engineering and Labor Relations* (1 hour)
A. Cox, Chairman
Cutler, Bodiya, Strong, Burns
Monthly, 4th day of each month, 9:30 a.m.

7. *Manufacturing and Operation* (2 hours)
A. Strong, Chairman
Bodiya, Cutler, Cox, Robb, Gray, Finn
Monthly, 5th day of each month, 9:30 a.m.

8. *Materials, Inventory Control and Expediting* (1/2 hour)
R. Finn, Chairman
Bodiya, Cox, Cutler, Towl, Burns
Weekly, every Monday, 2:00 p.m.

9. *Costs Reporting* (1/2 hour)
T. Burns, Chairman
Cox, Bodiya, Finn, Johnson, Hughes, Cutler, Gray, Strong, Golis
Quarterly, 2nd Tuesday, 9:30 a.m.; February, May, August, November

10. *Foreman's Conference* (1 1/2 hours)
N. Bodiya, Chairman
Cutler, Cox, Robb, Park, Peterson, Raymond, Trodden, Van Eck
Monthly, 2nd Wednesday each month, 2:00–4:00 p.m.

11. *Product Change and New Product Manufacturing Committee* (1/2 hr)
R. Holmes, Chairman
Cutler, Johnson
Monthly, 4th Tuesday, 9:30 a.m.

12. *Order Process Committee* (1/2 hour)
B. Hersker, Chairman
Burns, Johnson, Towl, Cox, Salmon, Cutler
Monthly, 4th Wednesday, 9:30 a.m.

13. *Lab. Program* (1/2 hour)
H. Gray, Chairman
Kennedy, Dearden, Hughes
Monthly, 2nd Friday, 9:30 a.m.

function. The initial membership of the committees and the duration and frequency of the meetings is included in Exhibit 5. Each committee was required to keep formal minutes, one copy of which was given to Mr. Strong. Mr. Strong is an ex-officio member of each committee and if any questions arise when he reads the minutes of the committee, Mr. Strong calls the chairman for further elaboration.

During 1963 the plant worked a six-day week and Mr. Strong had received numerous requests for additional salaried personnel. The personnel increases plus overtime payments had resulted in a 10% increase in salaries. To minimize this significant element of overhead (salary, wages and fringe benefits account for approximately one-third of sales revenue) and at the same time to begin to delegate responsibility, he introduced a salary budget, effective January 1, 1964, for which each member of the executive and managerial staff was partially responsible. The amount of the budget for each responsibility center was based upon the number of salaried staff at the beginning of the year at the current salary rates. At the end of the first quarter of 1964 the salaries paid exceeded the budgets in many cases because of overtime payments. A number of the executive and managerial staff commented on the arbitrary way whereby the budget had been established.

Due to the reactions of some of the executive and managerial staff to the salary budget, Mr. Strong did not want to force an extension of the budget idea. On the other hand, he had a feeling that an overall budget might be useful at this stage in the company's growth. To get the reactions of his executive and managerial staff to this idea, he introduced the idea as the last item on the agenda of a staff meeting of August 1964, advising the staff that "he was considering starting an operating plan and wanted their reactions." An active but rather disjointed discussion followed his remarks and it soon became apparent that the staff did not understand fully the proposal which Mr. Strong had made and were unwilling to commit themselves to an opinion on it. After 10 minutes discussion, Mr. Strong adjourned the meeting advising the staff that he would place the subject on the agenda of the next meeting in September.

2. DAVIS PAINT COMPANY LTD.[*][1]

—JOHN R. KENNEDY

and

DONALD H. THAIN

On October 19, 1961, Mr Glenn Wood was appointed acting president of the Davis Paint Company. Mr Wood has been assigned to this job on a temporary basis for "no more than six months" by the board of directors of the Davis Paint Company's U.S. parent company, the Rogers Paint Corporation. His appointment followed the unexpected death on October 6, 1961, of Mr. Ross Baker, who had been president of the Davis Company since 1943. Mr. Wood, aged 65, was previously the vice-president of manufacturing of the Rogers Paint Corporation.

In explaining the reasons for Mr. Wood's assignment, the president of the Rogers Corporation made the following remarks to his board of directors: "The sudden and unexpected loss of Ross Baker has confronted us with several serious problems in our Canadian operation. As some of you will recall, our decision in 1943 to make him president of Davis was a compromise. Most of us thought he lacked some of the qualities and abilities necessary to solve the problems in the Davis operation. To the people in his organization he was always more a friend than a boss and leader. As a result, he was never able to get his people to do some of the things they should have been doing. On the other hand, everyone in the organization up there saw him as the logical choice for president. There is no doubt in my mind that he was the only man there who could keep his associates of that time working together. To have brought in an outsider would have caused a minor rebellion. . . .

"At any rate, due to his personality and the feelings of some of his top people, we never got to the bottom of some of the key problems in Davis the way we might have. In spite of what we might perhaps call our lack of atten-

[1] Disguised name.

tion to his operation, Baker was able to improve the profit picture every year until 1953, after which profits started to fall. As you know, I made three or four trips up to Toronto to find out what was going on. As I have already reported to you, every time I looked into his problems, I got the story that the falling profits and return on investment were due to the unhealthy condition of the Canadian paint industry. As we got the picture, it was a story of cut-throat price competition, new and small companies capturing regional markets on a price basis, too much capacity in the industry, slackening consumer demand, consumer confusion about new paints, discount outlets and private branders working havoc in our distribution picture, the impossibility of getting and keeping good people, the uncertainties of the Canadian economy, and so on. Of course, from Baker's point of view, what this all amounted to was a situation about which he could do little if anything! Things were tough, but it wasn't the fault of his people—or so he said. I honestly don't think we ever got to know what was really going on up there. In fact I don't think Baker knew what was going on at the working level in his operation. Now, I may sound somewhat negative but I don't mean to be. In many ways he did a good job. Moreover, everything he said may be true. But, I think we must take a closer look at the whole situation. With this in mind, I recommend that we hold off appointing a new president on a permanent basis and send Glenn Wood to Toronto as acting president to appraise the operation. I think you'll all agree that Glenn has the personality and abilities to make a penetrating examination of the Davis Company. We should give him about three or four months to look things over and come back to us with recommendations for both the short and the long term. While he's up there he can also run the operation on an interim basis. He'll have a chance to watch the key people in operation. This way he'll be better able to size up what's going on."

This recommendation was accepted unanimously by the board and, on October 23, Mr. Wood arrived on the scene in the Davis Paint Company head office to carry out his assignment.

Mr. Wood had wide business experience. After graduating from college with a degree in engineering, he had gone to work as a foreman in the automotive company for which he had worked during his summers while at college. Within three years he had risen to the position of plant superintendent. At age 29, he had taken a job in production with a medium-sized food company. Because of his pleasing personality, ability, and hard work, he had risen through the production side of the business to the position of executive vice-president. In the late 1930's he left the food company to join a management consulting firm which he left "temporarily" to straighten out some serious management problems for the Rogers Corporation. After a minor stroke in 1947, he decided to stay with Rogers permanently as vice-president in charge of manufacturing and research.

He was scheduled to retire in October 1961 but had agreed to putting off his retirement in order to take on the assignment in Davis Paint Company. Since joining the Rogers Corporation, he had made several trips to the Davis Company to discuss specialized manufacturing and research problems with Davis personnel. He was well liked apparently by all in the Davis organization who had met him.

"I've been here about three weeks now," explained Mr. Wood in his Toronto office on November 10, 1961. "I'm approaching the point where I should begin to organize my notes and impressions of this operation in preparation for presenting my conclusions and recommendations to our board. Since coming here, I've spent most of my time talking to the key people about the company and its operations and problems. Although I'm getting a different story from each one of them, a general picture is beginning to shape up.

"This organization is getting old. From our top management group [see Exhibit 1] we lose Bolton next year, Chalmers the following year, and Taylor six years from now. Due to the way the operation has been run—low salaries, little if any management development, negligible management supervision—there really isn't any middle management. How we'll replace Chalmers and Bolton I'm not sure. We'll probably have to go outside for someone to replace Chalmers. I know that Hodges thinks he's all set to replace Bolton but Hudson is a better man. I can sense from the way Hudson talks that he will probably leave if he doesn't get Bolton's job. Although Hudson looks good when compared with others in the sales organization, he has many weaknesses—the lack of policies, control, and results in sales are bad. Taylor has the ability to do a good job but he's developed a negative attitude to anything new and is now lagging badly in his knowledge of and interest in new developments. I think his negative attitude to anything that's new is a decided liability. Chalmers is basically a bookkeeper, which is a tragedy because he's bright and active and could have made a first rate financial planning man if he had been given the chance. At this point he is a product of his environment. If the top man in an organization and his key people don't understand and won't use modern management fundamentals, no one else in the organization will have a chance. Thomas, the plant manager, is perhaps the most able of the group. He and Hudson would be prime candidates to run this operation if either had any broadening experience. However, as things stand now they know only their own jobs, and have never had the opportunity to get involved in the rest of the business.

"Incidentally, you have to remember that in my position it's tough to keep your perspective in evaluating people. I may be overrating both these men simply because they look good when compared to the rest in this organization.

"Looking at the overall picture here, we face a tough job in getting control of this operation. No one seems to be managing anything. As these people see it, the market dictates sales and production, competition decides prices, the lab decides quality, and the pile of paper work and confusion of daily operations rules out time for planning and thinking. We've got to face up to some serious realities—a sick industry, lack of management, declining sales and

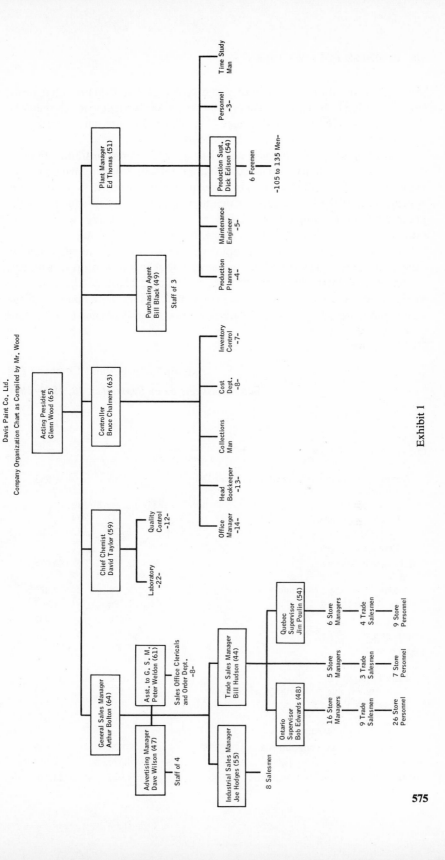

Davis Paint Co. Ltd.
Company Organization Chart as Compiled by Mr. Wood

Acting President
Glenn Wood (65)

General Sales Manager
Arthur Bolton (64)

Chief Chemist
David Taylor (59)

Controller
Bruce Chalmers (63)

Purchasing Agent
Bill Black (49)
Staff of 3

Plant Manager
Ed Thomas (51)

Advertising Manager
Dave Wilson (47)
Staff of 4

Asst. to G. S. M.
Peter Weldon (61)
Sales Office Clericals
and Order Dept.
-8-

Laboratory
-22-

Quality
Control
-12-

Office
Manager
-14-

Head
Bookkeeper
-13-

Collections
Man

Cost
Dept.
-8-

Inventory
Control
-7-

Production
Planner
-4-

Maintenance
Engineer
-5-

Production Supt.
Dick Edison (54)
6 Foremen
-105 to 135 Men-

Personnel
-3-

Time Study
Man

Industrial Sales Manager
Joe Hodges (55)
8 Salesmen

Trade Sales Manager
Bill Hudson (44)

Ontario
Supervisor
Bob Edwards (48)

Quebec
Supervisor
Jim Poulin (54)

16 Store
Managers

9 Trade
Salesmen

26 Store
Personnel

5 Store
Managers

3 Trade
Salesmen

7 Store
Personnel

6 Store
Managers

4 Trade
Salesmen

9 Store
Personnel

Exhibit 1

575

profits, lack of control on inventory and receivables, and many other problems. It's going to be tough to get this operation on the right track. It will take time, good people, effort and money. Even then, I'm not sure whether the payoff will be worth all the trouble and cost.

"In my opinion, top management has no greater responsibility than to divert assets and activity from areas that are producing a low return on investment to areas that will yield a higher return on investment. If we come to the conclusion that the future of the Canadian paint industry in general, or the prospects for this company in particular, are not encouraging, we'll have to examine the possibility of diversification, merger, or selling out.

"As I understand it from our people here, many of the top managers in the Canadian paint industry are very unhappy about low return on investment, falling profits, increasing competitions, a declining share of the consumer expenditures, and many other basic problems. If things are as bad as all the complaining would seem to indicate, somebody should begin to take con-

Exhibit 2 Davis Paint Company Ltd.
Balance Sheets as at September 30, 1953–1961

	1953		1954		195
ASSETS					
Current Assets					
Cash		$ 37		$ 38	$
Accounts Receivable less Reserve for Bad Debts		968		963	1,0
Inventories					
Raw materials	$ 381		$ 389		$ 380
Goods in Process	82		74		36
Finished Goods	1,061	1,524	1,143	1,606	1,158	1,5
Prepaid Expenses		17		17	
Total Current Assets		$2,546		$2,624	$2,6
Fixed Assets					
Land, Buildings, Machinery & Equipment		2,768		2,889	3,0
Less: Depreciation		1,289		1,397	1,5
		1,479		1,492	1,5
TOTAL ASSETS		$4,025		$4,116 $4,35	$4,1
LIABILITIES:					
Current Liabilities					
Bank Loan		$ 271		$ 270	$ 2
Accounts Payable & Accrued Liabilities		507		493	5
Income Tax Reserve		141		135	1
Total Current Liabilities		$ 919		$ 898	$ 8
NET WORTH					
Capital Stock: 60,000 common shares		600		600	6
Surplus		2,506		2,618	2,7
TOTAL LIABILITIES AND NET WORTH		$4,025		$4,116	$4,1

structive action. To me, constructive action means getting out of the paint business either partially and gradually, or totally and suddenly. If we come to the conclusion that it is almost impossible to make an adequate return on investment, we should sell out. If the situation isn't that black, diversification into other lines might give us the profit potential we need. However, I don't want to recommend drastic changes until I am convinced they are necessary. I rather have the impression that the quality of management is so low in the Canadian paint business that great profits could be made by a company that would fire deadwood, get top quality people, and sharpen up its approach to the problems of making money. Maybe they have all been doing things the wrong way for so long that they can't break out of the rut!''

EARLY HISTORY OF THE DAVIS PAINT COMPANY LTD.

The Davis Paint Co. was founded in Toronto in 1902 by Mr. Richard Davis. Initially, the firm was small and Davis took an active part in manufacturing

	1956		1957		1958		1959		1960		1961
	$ 56		$ 57		$ 60		$ 61		$ 64		$ 63
	1,107		1,211		1,243		1,299		1,376		1,427
$ 394		$ 403		$ 411		$ 409		$ 415		$ 419	
67		78		106		79		97		103	
1,255	1,716	1,265	1,746	1,347	1,864	1,450	1,938	1,465	1,977	1,454	1,976
	14		12		13		12		12		8
	$2,893		$3,026		$3,180		$3,310		$3,429		$3,474
	3,130		3,239		3,347		3,461		3,563		3,646
	1,607		1,718		1,824		1,939		2,059		2,172
	1,523		1,521		1,523		1,522		1,504		1,474
	$4,416		$4,547		$4,703		$4,832		$4,933		$4,948
	$ 373		$ 393		$ 458		$ 451		$ 496		$ 481
	535		562		583		579		591		594
	124		110		111		132		108		94
	$ 996		$1,065		$1,152		$1,162		$1,195		$1,169
	600		600		600		600		600		600
	2,820		2,882		2,951		3,070		3,138		3,179
	$4,416		$4,547		$4,703		$4,832		$4,933		$4,948

and selling. However, under Davis' direction, the firm grew and, when Davis died in 1922, annual sales were approximately $600,000. On Richard Davis' death, ownership and management control passed to his only son, Arnold, who at that time was 29 years old. Although he was assisted by a chemist, accountant, production foreman, and sales manager, all of whom worked with his father, Arnold quickly assumed the position of leadership in the organization. He personally controlled all aspects of the company's operations, but concentrated his efforts particularly on developing retail distribution, an area which his father had neglected. Sales and profits grew rapidly in the 1920's, with a high of $1,200,000 in sales and $100,000 in profits being reached in 1929. Sales dropped sharply during the depression and, although the firm remained in strong financial condition, losses were sustained in 1931, 1932, and 1933. Much of the reason for the 1931–1933 losses was attributed by later management to Arnold Davis'· policy of "keeping on many old timers who had been hired by his father, even though sales did not justify such charity."

Arnold Davis was killed in a hunting accident in October 1935. Ownership of the firm passed to his wife and children, Because of the young age of the children, control of the firm was, in effect, left in the hands of Mrs. Davis. Mrs. Davis appointed the sales manager, Mr. Whit Newman, president. However, without Mr. Arnold Davis' leadership, Mr. Newman and his associates were not able to operate effectively and the firm, which earned a net profit of $30,000 in 1935, barely broke even in 1936, and incurred a loss of $20,000 in 1937. As a result of advice from several outside sources, Mrs. Davis sold the firm in 1938 to the Rogers Paint Corporation, a large U.S. paint manufacturer. Rogers' principal move after acquiring Davis was to retire Mr. Newman and to replace him with Mr. Charles Wahl, a plant manager from their own organization. In the following years, there developed a fairly close liaison between the two firms at the technical level, and a minimum of three of Davis' seven man board of directors were always officers or directors of the Rogers Corporation. However, since Rogers' top management heavily emphasized a policy of decentralization in regard to all their subsidiaries, the management of Davis was expected to operate almost completely on their own, except for an annual review of profit and loss statements and balance sheets. When Mr. Whal retired in 1943, he was succeeded by Mr. Ross Baker, previously sales manager of the Canadian organization. There was no further interchange of personnel between the two companies until Mr. Wood arrived on the scene in October 1961.

The firm's Toronto plant was, by industry standards, relatively modern. Production facilities were located in a large building in 1947 adjacent to the old plant, which was a motley collection of additions to a small original structure dating from 1891. When the new plant was built, the laboratory, general offices, and warehousing facilities were relocated in some of the newer section of the old plant, and some parts of the old plant were demolished to

Exhibit 3

Davis Paint Company Ltd.

Statement of Profit and Loss for the Years Ending September 30, 1953–1961

	1953 ($000's)	%	1954 ($000's)	%	1955 ($000's)	%
Sales	$6,457	100.00	$6,389	100.00	$6,553	100.00
Cost of Goods Sold	4,175	64.66	4,148	64.93	4,236	64.64
Raw Material Cost	$2,784	43.11	$2,741	42.90	$2,802	42.76
Packages	382	5.91	380	5.95	386	5.89
Direct Labor	482	7.47	480	7.51	490	7.48
Quality Control	86	1.34	87	1.36	92	1.41
Depreciation	96	1.49	97	1.52	97	1.48
Other Manufacturing Expenses	345	5.34	363	5.68	369	5.63
Gross Margin	2,282	35.34	2,241	35.07	2,217	35.36
Selling Expense	847	13.11	880	13.77	961	14.65
Selling*	367	5.68	355	5.55	342	5.22
Sales Administration	110	1.70	112	1.75	113	1.72
Office Expenses	104	1.61	104	1.63	106	1.62
Advertising & Sales Promotion	185	2.87	192	3.01	193	2.94
Sales Outlets*	63	0.97	94	1.47	169	2.57
Other	18	0.28	23	0.36	38	0.58
Warehousing	104	1.61	118	1.84	119	1.82
Shipping	112	1.73	114	1.79	127	1.94
Research	132	2.04	137	2.14	144	2.19
Administrative	362	5.62	371	5.80	374	5.72
Other Expenses						
Bank Interest and Charges	32	0.50	30	0.47	32	0.49
Bad Debts	48	0.74	40	0.62	45	0.69
Other	68	1.05	69	1.09	73	1.11
Other Income	(5)	(0.08)	(6)	(0.09)	(5)	(0.08)
Net Profit Before Taxes	$582	9.02	$488	7.64	$447	6.83
Taxes	289	4.48	241	3.77	220	3.37
Net Profit	$293	4.54	$247	3.87	$227	3.46

579

Exhibit 3—(continued)

	1956 ($000's)	%	1957 ($000's)	%	1958 ($000's)	%
Sales	$6,923	100.00	$6,955	100.00	$7,176	100.00
Cost of Goods Sold	4,416	63.79	4,426	63.64	4,534	63.18
Raw Material Cost	$2,892	41.78	$2,893	41.60	$2,970	41.39
Packages	411	5.94	414	5.96	429	5.98
Direct Labor	532	7.68	531	7.63	543	7.56
Quality Control	93	1.34	95	1.36	95	1.32
Depreciation	87	1.26	100	1.44	94	1.31
Other Manufacturing Expenses	401	5.79	393	5.65	403	5.62
Gross Margin	2,507	36.21	2,529	36.36	2,642	36.82
Selling Expense	1,063	15.36	1,133	16.28	1,178	16.42
Selling*	338	4.88	327	4.70	329	4.58
Sales Administration	119	1.72	126	1.81	132	1.84
Office Expenses	117	1.69	118	1.70	119	1.67
Advertising & Sales Promotion	249	3.60	293	4.21	304	4.24
Sales Outlets*	202	2.92	228	3.28	253	3.53
Other	38	0.55	41	0.59	41	0.57
Warehousing	129	1.86	145	2.09	156	2.17
Shipping	144	2.08	154	2.22	169	2.35
Research	139	2.01	143	2.06	153	2.13
Administrative	391	5.63	398	5.72	401	5.58
Other Expenses						
Bank Interest and Charges	34	0.49	37	0.53	39	0.54
Bad Debts	50	0.73	60	0.86	74	1.03
Other	80	1.16	78	1.13	78	1.10
Other Income	(6)	(0.08)	(5)	(0.07)	(6)	(0.08)
Net Profit Before Taxes	$ 483	6.97	$ 386	5.54	$ 400	5.57
Taxes	238	3.44	189	2.72	196	2.73
Net Profit	$ 245	3.53	$ 197	2.82	$ 204	2.84

Exhibit 3—(continued)

	1959 ($000's)	%	1960 ($000's)	%	1961 (000's)	%
Sales	$7,347	100.00	$7,428	100.00	$7,304	100.00
Cost of Goods Sold	4,522	61.55	4,640	62.47	4,538	62.13
Raw Material Cost	$2,934	39.94	$2,995	40.32	$2,935	40.18
Packages	444	6.04	453	6.10	443	6.07
Direct Labor	539	7.34	559	7.53	542	7.42
Quality Control	97	1.32	102	1.37	98	1.34
Depreciation	106	1.44	105	1.42	104	1.43
Other Manufacturing Expenses	402	5.47	426	5.73	416	5.69
Gross Margin	2,825	38.45	2,788	37.53	2,766	37.87
Selling Expense*	1,226	16.69	1,265	17.03	1,298	17.77
Selling*	324	4.41	328	4.42	331	4.53
Sales Administration	135	1.84	136	1.83	139	1.90
Office Expenses	121	1.65	125	1.68	128	1.76
Advertising & Sales Promotion	317	4.31	324	4.36	330	4.52
Sales Outlets*	285	3.88	309	4.16	321	4.39
Other	44	0.60	43	0.58	49	0.67
Warehousing	170	2.32	177	2.38	172	2.36
Shipping	181	2.46	188	2.54	191	2.62
Research	142	1.94	147	1.98	148	2.03
Administrative	428	5.82	434	5.84	441	6.03
Other Expenses						
Bank Interest and Charges	46	0.63	52	0.70	58	0.79
Bad Debts	57	0.78	56	0.75	64	0.87
Other	80	1.08	76	1.02	63	0.87
Other Income	(7)	(0.09)	(6)	(0.08)	(6)	(0.08)
Net Profit Before Taxes	$ 502	6.82	$ 399	5.37	$ 337	4.61
Taxes	248	3.37	196	2.64	161	2.20
Net Profit	$ 254	3.45	$ 203	2.73	$ 176	2.41

Exhibit 4

Davis Paint Company Ltd.

Selected Data on Davis Operations 1953–1961

	1953	1954	1955	1956	1957	1958	1959	1960	1961
After Tax Income as % of Net Worth	9.43%	7.67%	6.86%	7.16%	5.66%	5.74%	6.92%	5.43%	4.66%
Current Ratio	2.77	2.92	3.13	2.90	2.84	2.76	2.85	2.87	2.97
No. of Day's Sales in Average Receivables	53.25	55.13	54.92	55.78	60.82	62.41	63.14	65.70	70.01
No. of Day's Sales at Cost in Average Inventory	131.49	137.71	137.00	135.96	142.75	145.31	153.44	153.94	159.01
Capital Expenditures ($000's)	$124	$121	$125	$116	$109	$108	$114	$102	$83
Depreciation ($000's)	$107	$108	$109	$101	$111	$106	$115	$120	$113
Dividends ($000's)	$135	$135	$135	$135	$135	$135	$135	$135	$135
No. of Company Owned Retail Outlets	5	7	13	16	19	21	24	26	27

provide outside yard storage. In 1952, an addition to the newest section of the plant was constructed and the laboratory facilities were shifted to this area.

Davis' sales increased rapidly after 1945, rising 70% between 1945 and 1953. This sales growth rate slowed considerably in the 1953–1961 period, the profit margin suffered a general decline (see Exhibits 2 and 3), and the company's share of the total paint market declined from 6% to 5%.

1961 sales were $7,304,000, a drop of 2% over the previous year. Profits decreased 13% and return on invested capital dropped from 5.43% in 1960 to 4.66% (see Exhibit 4), the lowest since 1940.

Davis competed in both the industrial and trade sales paint field. Company executives estimated that the company's sales by type of customer were roughly as follows:

Exhibit 5

Davis Paint Company Ltd.

Estimated Sales Analysis by Type of Customer and/or Product Group

Type of Customer and/or Product Group	% of Total Sales
Industrial Sales	
Industrial (product finishes)	23
Trade Sales	
Dealer Organization	44
Retail Sales to Consumers Through Company Outlets	8
Direct sales of Maintenance Products	11
Direct Sales to Painting Contractors	6
Private Label Business	8
	100%

They also estimated that trade sales were "probably more profitable than industrial sales."

Davis sold industrial finishes to over 2,500 accounts of which 1,500 were considered active in that they actually had purchased paint during the previous year. Approximately 35% of the firm's 1961 industrial sales were accounted for by sales to two automotive, four appliance, and two agricultural implement manufacturers.

From 1950 to 1955, Davis' sales of industrial finishes had grown at approximately the same rate as that of the firm's trade sales products. However, in 1958, due primarily to increased competition, the firm had lost over $250,000 worth of product finish business and it was not until 1961 that industrial sales topped the 1957 dollar level.

Davis brand trade sales products were sold to the public through nearly 1,200 independent outlets and 27 company-owned outlets in Ontario, Quebec, and the prairie provinces. The total number of dealers had been increasing by about 25 a year in recent years, but the company controller stated that this figure was not too significant, because each year some existing dealers switched sales emphasis away from Davis products to competitive lines, although still continuing to carry Davis products. He also said that approximately 30% of the dealers accounted for 80% of Davis' business through dealers. The company outlets, located in major market cities, acted as local warehouses for all dealers in their "territory". However, Davis brand merchandise was shipped direct from the plant to a few large volume independent dealers in Toronto and to the one large retail organization that carried Davis brand products. Dealers in British Columbia and the Maritimes were sold through hardware distributors, located in Vancouver and Halifax respectively.

The private brand business came from one large department store chain, one mail order house, two automotive supply chains, and six builders' supply chains.

The maintenance figure of 11% (see Exhibit 5) was made up of direct sales of maintenance finishes to industry, government, institutions, and commercial establishments.

The painting contractor figure of 8% consisted of direct factory sales to approximately 25 painting contractors in the Toronto market.

Company outlets and independent dealers also sold Davis products to the maintenance and professional painter market. The company made no attempt even to estimate what proportion of their dealer or company outlet sales were made to these groups.

The Davis trade sales product line was an extensive one. The line included about 100 different basic types of products and, within each of these product classifications, there were as many as six ranges of quality and up to 30 different pre-mixed colours. In total the company carried approximately 900 different products in inventory. This figure did not include different package sizes, which ranged from one to four per product.

Included in the trade sales product line were two colour systems. One system was used for Davis brand products and utilized 12 pre-mixed colours and 10 colourants. This system, first marketed by the company in 1958, required a dealer to use a tinting machine. Davis offered their dealers the choice of a large machine which sold at cost ($500) or rented ($22.50 a month), and a small machine which was sold at cost ($110) only. The large machines automatically measured out preset amount of colourants and would mix some 1200 shades of paint. The manually operated smaller machine used a limited number of colourants and could mix some 700 shades of paint. In 1961, all company-owned outlets and 47 independent dealers had the large tinting machine, while approximately 125 dealers had purchased the smaller machine. The company had also developed a tube tinting system for its private label brands. In this system small tubes of colours were added to one of two base colours and some 400 standardized shades of paint could be mixed. Both the company and their dealers viewed these colour systems as an addition to, rather than a replacement for, the company's existing range of pre-mixed colours.

In the product finishes field, the company carried a few "standard" items, but most products were custom formulated to individual customer specifications. Davis stocked a few of these custom formulated items to give better customer service. In addition, the firm frequently produced extra gallonage on industrial orders, when it was anticipated that there would be further orders for small quantities. By stocking these overruns, the company could avoid the high costs incurred by the production of small batch sizes. Overruns which were not sold as anticipated were normally sold as "specials" through the dealer organization.

When Mr. Wood first arrived at Davis, he tried to find an organization chart so that he could quickly familiarize himself with the overall organization. After being informed by Mr. Chalmers that no organization chart was available, Mr. Wood compiled his own (see Exhibit 1). He also had Mr. Chalmers prepare a list of all management reports used in the firm (see Exhibit 6). Mr. Wood then spent considerable time talking with each of the six key men in the company. After meeting with these men and investigating their records in company files, Wood jotted down notes about their background and his perception of them as individuals and managers.

SALES MANAGER: ART BOLTON—1961 SALARY, $21,000

Art Bolton, aged 64, joined the Davis Company as an industrial salesman in 1934 because the Davis Company offered the only job he could find at that time. He had risen to the position of sales manager on the basis of his record as an oustanding salesman. During his years as Sales Manager, he had frequently proven his ability as the best salesman in the company and still enjoyed getting out to "make tough sales calls". He spent about 60% of his time in the field where he was well liked, especially by many of the company's older industrial account contacts, distributors, and dealers. He was a free spender who liked to "eat and drink well" when he was with customers. He was short tempered, honest, and outspoken. Although he usually took the customer's point of view when dealing with the head office departments, he "buried the hatchet quickly" after most disagreements with other head office personnel.

In discussing his approach to the sales force, Bolton made the following comments: "Our salesman turnover is very low for the paint business. One of our trade salesman has been with us over 40 years. Our sales objectives differ from those of our big competitors. I have always sold by building a personal relationship and that's what I expect my men to do. I'm convinced that it's the key to success in any part of the paint business. I'm not sold on all this merchandising material for dealers. Basically, they have to sell paint for themselves. When our salesmen make calls, they provide technical information, listen to problems, and try to help as much as possible. If the dealer

Exhibit 6

Davis Paint Company Ltd.

Reports Received by Top Management Personnel

Name	Frequency	Report Information
Mr. Baker	Monthly	Profit and loss statement.
Mr. Bolton	Monthly	Industrial sales for month; Trade sales for month by outlet, by distributor, and other; and Total Sales for month; Cumulative total sales for current year and previous year's cumulative sales to same date.
Mr. Hodges	Monthly	Industrial sales for month by salesmen and total; Monthly sales for each of the firm's eight largest industrial accounts; Cumulative total sales for current year and previous year's cumulative sales to same date.
	Yearly	Total compensation, by salesman.
Mr. Hudson	Monthly	Sales by company outlet, by territory, and total trade sales. Cumulative trade sales for current year and previous year's cumulative sales to same date. Salesmen's and store managers' travelling expenses, by individual.
	Yearly	Total compensation by salesman, by store manager.
Mr. Thomas	Monthly	Sales forecast for following month. Total production in dollars; Direct labour costs for each of five "cost centres". Overhead expenses in eight classifications. Average costs per batch produced (on a per gallon basis).
Mr. Chalmers	Monthly	All reports received by other members of management. Percentage analysis of age of accounts receivable, by company outlet, and total.

wants help, we'll give it to him. But we don't try to tell him how to run his operation. Most dealers have been in business long enough that there is no sense in us trying to push them around. Give them the products they can sell at a reasonable price, and hope for the best. Don't ever let anyone tell you that any other approach is better."

"We are not interested in salesmen's reports," continued Mr. Bolton, "What we want is results. Since you don't get results filling in reports, we don't have them."

Bolton was due to retire in less than a year and it was common knowledge in the company that he had never declared himself in favour of either Hodges or Hudson as his successor. He had told Thomas confidentially that he was afraid either Hodges or Hudson would leave if the other were singled out as the next sales manager. Since he thought there were no well-trained, adequate replacements for either Hodges or Hudson, he aimed to prevent the succession problem from coming to a head until its solution would not be his responsibility.

CONTROLLER: BRUCE CHALMERS—1961 SALARY, $15,600

Bruce Chalmers, aged 63, had come to work for the Davis Company as a mail boy in 1912 when he was 14 years of age. Those who knew him best thought of him as being conscientious in his work and intensely loyal to management. He had progressed through the accounting department from the level of junior clerk through the jobs of chief clerk in charge of accounts receivable, accounts payable, and payroll. Except for two years during the depression, when he worked as a labourer in the plant, he had always been in the accounting department. He had taken special extension courses in book-keeping and cost accounting. Over the years, he had suggested many ways of improving the control set up in the company but these suggestions nearly always fell on unreceptive ears. Because of his deep loyalty to top manage-ment, the rejection of his ideas did not seem to bother him visibly. He some-times repeated stories about the reactions of Messrs. Arnold Davis, Charlie Wahl, and Ross Baker, who had told him in effect, "You can't afford a lot of fancy accounting systems in a paint company. Even if you could, what good would they do?" Chalmers possessed a great deal of native shrewdness and sound common sense.

He had often clashed, sometimes seriously, with Art Bolton. On the surface, these clashes were usually sparked by the sales organization cutting prices to the point where sometimes only the cost of the material was covered with little, if any, contribution to overhead. Occasionally, the conflict between the two became so intense that others in the organization suspected that the two saw each other as rivals for the presidency of the company. At any rate, Chalmers sometimes left no one in doubt that Bolton and his "free-spending, price-cutting salesmen would sell the company the river for a thousand gallon paint order." It was evident that Chalmers' attitude to Bolton was echoed in his dealings with Hodges and Hudson who were both viewed by Chalmers as having many "of the same short-comings as their boss." Chalmers' relation-ships with other key personnel were cordial, perhaps to some extent because they had few occasions to be drawn into conflict with him.

CHIEF CHEMIST: DAVID TAYLOR—1961 SALARY, $12,800

Taylor, aged 59, had taken a job with Davis in the laboratory in 1925 immediately after taking a master's degree in chemistry at a large university. His work from the late 1920's to the early 1940's had earned him the reputa-tion as one of the "brilliant young paint chemists in North America." He had stayed with the Davis Company in spite of many attractive offers from other companies.

Taylor was extremely proud of Davis' reputation in the trade for top quality products. He firmly believed that the success of Davis depended on its ability to keep quality standards high, and its ability to fit top quality pro-ducts to specific application problems. When water-thinned paints came on the market, his group already had been doing development work on them for some time. As a result of his group's experience, Taylor had opposed the idea that Davis should put them on the market at all, because he did not feel that a water-thinned paint was a superior product. Although Taylor had been prevailed upon by Baker to speed up development work, the firm was several years late in getting a water-thinned product on the market because of Taylor's adamant stand that no product should be put out that did not meet the firm's high quality standards. A somewhat similar situation had taken place with the introduction of the company's first new colour system. The firm was behind most of its competitors in getting a colour system on the market because Taylor had insisted that "all the bugs be worked out" before introduction. In recent years, some of Taylor's associates had begun to suspect that Taylor's increasingly rigid viewpoint on quality in the trade sales area was a coverup for his lack of interest in any developing trade sales product innovations that were needed because of changing consumer buying habits. Taylor had been bitterly opposed to the firm's 1950 policy of selling lower quality paints to those customers who requested them and which provided large volume business.

"If firms like Davis set the industry standards of quality," he said in 1961, "We cannot compromise our standards by selling inferior quality products at the same time. By doing so, we jeopardize our good name and confuse the customer. We simply can't afford to do that—the Arctics[1] of the industry are doing enough damage."

PLANT MANAGER: ED THOMAS—1961 SALARY, $15,600

Thomas, aged 51, had joined the company in 1952. He had previous wide production experience in other companies. Because of his earlier contacts with Thomas, Thomas had, in many respects, become Wood's closest advisor in the investigation of the company.

Thomas was regarded by his colleagues as being progressive and able, though he had been exposed to general management problems in other companies for which he had worked, the organizational structure and method of operation at Davis had confined him solely to the production area.

Mr. Thomas stated that his ability to do an effective production planning job was severely hindered by available sales information. "When I first came to this firm," he said, "I worked hard to have some sort of budgeting system set up for manufacturing. At that time, no budgeting was done for the plant. I finally convinced Mr. Baker that budgeting should be done. He got quite keen on it and for the 1954 year everybody—and I mean everybody—made up monthly budgets for the whole year. Unfortunately, everybody's budget was based on the sales department's forecast that sales would go up by 5% over 1953. When sales actually dropped, everybody threw their budgets in the wastepaper basket and that was that! Now, on the 20th of each month, I get a lump sum sales figure forecast for the following month. It is not a very good

[1] Arctic Paint was an Ontario paint manufacturer with estimated sales of about $2,000,000 a year. Arctic's trade sales products were heavily promoted by one of Canada's largest department store chains, in giant two-for-one sales (e.g. one gallon for $8.40, two gallons for $9.40).

figure to work with, but it's better than nothing. I would like, at least, to get a forecast of sales by product for three months in advance, but we don't have the system to develop the necessary information and Baker didn't think that the potential savings merited the cost of putting the system in, although Bruce Chalmers would be happy to install it. The big block, though, is Bolton. He thinks that detailed forecasts are a waste of time."

Thomas felt that the sales force, in general, did not have enough technical background to do an adequate job. " By this I don't mean that they should necessarily sell the technical properties of the product. But they should know what products can do what jobs. And, particularly in the industrial area, our salesmen seem to lack any ability to judge which of our standard products would be acceptable to the customer. They always want to sell a custom product and this creates problems for both the lab and ourselves. In addition, as I see it, the most important skill in selling product finishes is the ability to do a good job in communicating the customer's needs to the lab in such a form that they can do a proper job. By and large, our industrial sales force doesn't have this ability. Consequently the lab has to do extra work and Taylor keeps saying he needs more staff, while Hodges complains that the lab is doing a lousy job."

Thomas thought Davis should have diversified "long ago" into some business that "either utilizes the knowledge of our lab or provides sales to counteract our sales peaks." He considered that pigments, plastic molding, and ceramic coatings were all good diversification possibilities.

INDUSTRIAL SALES MANAGER: JOE HODGES—1961 SALARY $13,800

Joe Hodges was a technically oriented engineer who had joined the Davis Company as an industrial salesman in 1949. He had previously worked for a competitor and a raw materials supplier. He was hired by Davis primarily because of his wide contacts in the trade.

Much of Hodges' time in the office was spent in making pricing decisions and in personally seeing that orders got out "as promised." About 50% of Hodges' time was spent trying to develop new large industrial accounts and he was a firm believer that the best way to break into this area was to "develop a product and give it to the customer in sufficient quantities that he can test it extensively."

Hodges also believed that the supplier that could give fast delivery of product finishes gained an advantage over competitors. Consequently he liked to carry overruns to give this service.

Hodges thought that lab personnel were unrealistic in their approach to the formulation of product finishes. " No matter what price we want the product built to, Taylor's boys always come up with a formulation that is priced too high. Then it has to be scaled down or we're left with very little to play around with in pricing. Moreover, we can't seem to get it through their heads that a lot of manufacturers want a paint that makes their product more saleable, but don't give a damn how long it lasts once it is sold to the end user. Their approach seems to be pitched always to the customer that wants a long-lasting high quality paint."

TRADE SALES MANAGER: BILL HUDSON—1961 SALARY, $12,000

Hudson, aged 44, joined the Davis Company in 1945. He had previously sold chain store accounts for a large marketing oriented soap manufacturer. He was encouraged to join Davis in 1945 by a friend in the armed services who had been a foreman in the Davis factory. Hudson was progressive, hard-working, and ambitious. Several of the men in the trade sales force had been hired and trained by him and he was confident that "his new men" formed an adequate nucleus. It was rumoured that he had unwisely admitted to his foreman friend that he "would fire half the salesmen working for this company tomorrow if he had the chance" and that "Bolton doesn't know what the hell is going on in this business but he only has a short time to go, so why bother him with the facts of life."

Although Hudson had proven himself to be able in carring out orders, especially from Ross Baker whom he had respected a great deal, his ability as a marketing strategist was questionable. According to Hodges "the mixed-up smorgasbord of a distribution setup that we have is largely the product of Hudson's thinking. If he would do what makes sense instead of what he thinks the top brass wants, we'd be better off." However, many attributed such statements by Hodges to his growing fear that Hudson was better equipped to succeed Bolton than he was.

Hudson spent much of his time in the field. "Probably too much," he said, "but many of my decisions must be based on my feel for the situation, and I find that you lose that feel if you don't stay close to the field. I had trouble trying to get this across to Ross Baker. Being a technical man, he couldn't understand why everything couldn't be put on a slide rule."

ROSS BAKER

From his conversations with members of Davis management and his own limited prior knowledge of the late president, Mr. Wood also developed a picture of Ross Baker.

Ross Baker had joined Davis in 1927 after graduating with a master's degree in chemistry from an eastern Canadian university. He had started work in the lab but had been switched into quality control work in the plant within a year. Part of this job involved dealing with product finish customers on quality control problems. Baker had shown such an aptitude and liking for this job that, within a short time, he was working full time as the firm's "trouble-shooter salesman" on difficult product finish accounts. In the interval between the death of Arnold Davis and the sale of the firm to the Rogers Paint Corporation, Ross Baker had acted as Davis' sales manager, although he was not given the title. After Rogers purchased Davis, Baker was officially appointed sales manager and when Mr. Wahl retired in 1943, Baker had moved up to the position of president.

Baker had been well-liked and respected by all members of Davis' management. His one close personal friend in the company had been the chief chemist, David Taylor. The friendship dated back to 1927 when Baker and Taylor had worked together in the lab.

Although Baker had spent most of his years with Davis in non-technical areas of the firm, he had always maintained an active interest in the technical aspects of paint and paint applications. Both Bolton and Chalmers told Wood about the times that they had been out with Baker and Baker pointed out some wall or sign where the paint had failed. Baker would then speculate as to the composition of the paint and the technical reasons for its failure.

All members of Davis' management spoke of Baker's interest in having the firm produce only quality paint products. For many of his years as president, Baker had maintained and built up the Davis reputation in this regard. However, as a result of the pressure on sales that developed in the mid-1950's, Baker, according to his associates, had modified this policy "with great reluctance" because, "If the only way we can increase sales is to add lower quality lines, then we have no alternative."

Mr. Wood next began piecing together the key factors in the firm's operation.

INDUSTRIAL SALES

There were eight salesmen in the industrial sales organization, all of whom were located in Ontario and Quebec. One man worked almost exclusively with appliance manufacturers, the others were assigned to territories and were responsible for developing product finish and large volume maintenance finish business.

The sale of product finishes involved contact with the purchasing agent and/or personnel in the customer's plant to determine types of finishes used, general levels of quality, and conditions of applications. After sizing up the situation, the salesman would try to visualize a product that would do the same job at less cost, a different system that would enable the manufacturer to do the painting job with lower labour cost, or a combination of both. The salesman then transmitted the product requirements to the lab so that they could develop a suitable product by modifying an existing formulation or by developing a new formulation. After the lab developed a product, it was costed and, after consultation with the salesman, Mr. Hodges would set the price which would be quoted to the customer. On potentially large orders and on all bid business, the final pricing decision was made by Mr. Bolton and had frequently been made in collaboration with Mr. Baker.

In those instances where the lab developed a product finish for a manufacturer that differed to a large extent from the product he was already using.

Davis usually supplied the firm with a quantity of the new product so that the manufacturer could test it.

Salesmen were expected to make regular calls on customers using Davis products, both to make sure that the products were performing satisfactorily, and to attempt to sell other Davis products to the customer for other paint requirements.

The salesmen's job in selling specialty maintenance finishes was similar to that of product finishes. However, a good part of the maintenance finish business involved the sale of standard Davis products. The salesman's job in this instance was to determine the customer's plant requirements, sell the customer the right product, or, if the paint was bought on a bid basis, ensure that Davis got an opportunity to bid.

Wood found it difficult to determine whether or not the industrial salesmen were doing a satisfactory job since they did not submit call reports, nor was any regular or formal appraisal made of them. Mr. Wood "guesstimated" that the industrial salesmen made two or three calls a day.

Five of the eight industrial salesmen had at least some university education; all had worked or trained in either the lab or quality control for periods of from three months to four years each before becoming salesmen. Four of the men had originally joined the firm in the technical area. Industrial salesmen were paid a basic salary ranging from $350 to $500 a month plus a 0.5% commission on their first $150,000 of annual sales and 1.0% on anything above this figure. The company provided the salesmen with cars and paid all travelling and business expenses.

The firm had a record of a fairly high turnover of industrial salesmen but Hodges estimated that it was no higher than for other paint firms. Most men leaving the firm either went to a materials supplier, joined another paint firm, or went to staff technical positions. Hiring of new men was done by Hodges, subject to the approval of Bolton.

TRADE SALES ORGANIZATION

Prior to 1951, the firm had used distributors and dealers exclusively for the distribution of Davis brand products. In 1951, the firm embarked on a policy of supplementing this system with company stores. In 1961, there were 27 company outlets with sales ranging from $60,000 to $300,000.

Company outlets fulfilled a dual purpose. Each outlet acted as a warehouse for company dealers in a surrounding "territory." They also served as retail outlets for Davis products. In addition to Davis paint products, all outlets carried stocks of brushes, rollers, and miscellaneous painter supplies, which were purchased from outside firms for resale. Small dealers did purchase some of these supplies through Davis, but most dealers could purchase direct from the manufacturer at lower prices.

Each outlet was staffed by a manager and one or more clerks. In addition, about half the outlets had salesmen working a specified part of the outlet's territory. These salesmen were directly responsible to the manager of the store to which they were connected.

Although store managers were responsible for the total operations of their outlet, their primary job was that of a trade salesman. In his territory or his part of the outlet's territory, he was expected to develop new dealers, to service existing dealers, and to develop maintenance and professional painter business for both the dealers and the company outlet. Mr. Hudson stated that "Probably three-quarters of a store manager's time should be spent outside his store making calls on, and for, dealers, and developing maintenance business for his own store. The other quarter should be used in ensuring that the operations of his outlet are running smoothly."

Company outlet managers were paid a base salary of $250 a month plus— 1.5% of all sales through their outlet up to $150,000 and 2% on all sales above this figure. In addition, under a new system instituted in 1960, they received a bonus of 5% of the gross profit of their operations.

The compensation of individual store managers in 1961 ranged from $3,900 to $9,000, with an average of about $7,000.

Trade salesmen attached to company outlets received a base salary of $200 to $250 a month plus 2% on all sales up to $100,000 plus 3% on all sales above this figure. Salesmen's compensation ranged from $3,800 to $8,600. All trade salesmen and store managers were provided with cars travelling expenses. Store clerks who also acted as warehousemen and records clerks, received salaries ranging from $200 to $375 a month. Twelve of the store managers had formerly been trade paint salesmen with Davis, five had formerly worked in other areas of the firm, and ten had been hired from outside the firm. About a dozen store employees had been previously employed elsewhere in the company. Two other store employees were former trade salesmen that Bill Hudson had taken off the road because of their poor sales records. Both had over 20 years of service. Hudson said that: "I didn't feel we could fire them. We kept them for so long that now we're obligated to them. They're both conscientious, but damn it they just can't sell."

The final decision on the hiring of all trade salesmen and store managers was made by Hudson. Store personnel were hired by store managers subject to supervisory approval. Head office also hired some store personnel, but these people were never placed in stores without the approval of the store manager. Recommendations for salary increases for store personnel were made by store managers to Hudson who, in almost all instances, approved them.

The territories of trade salesmen working out of company outlets in Ontario and Quebec were set by the supervisors. The supervisors were responsible for initiating all recommendations for salary increases or territory salesmen and movement of territory personnel between territories for up to store manager.

All new store personnel were trained by the store managers. New trade salesmen with no prior experience in the paint business usually spent some time in the order department before going on the road. However, most training of these men was left to the store managers.

Davis salesmen appointed to the position of store manager were normally brought to head office for a day or two for separate briefing sessions with Hudson and Chalmers. Depending on their background, store managers hired from outside the firm, and Davis employees promoted to store manager from outside the sales group, spent periods ranging from two days to two weeks with the head office sales and accounting personnel on an informal training program.

The 22 company outlets in Ontario and Quebec serviced about 900 of the company's 1,200 independent dealers. Total operations in each province were under the direction of a supervisor. Mr. Hudson considered these supervisors as "adequate in dealing with salesmen and dealers, but both have trouble in adapting their thinking to meet the problems encountered in the retail side of our operation."

Both distributors were old friends of Art Bolton so he handled all of the firm's relations with them. Although the five western outlets reported directly to Hudson, he rarely travelled to the West, preferring to let Mr. Bolton see these outlets in his trips to the west coast.

Mr. Hudson handled all of the management contacts with the firm's private label accounts, although one of the sales office staff handled many of the details. This same man also handled details connected with direct sales to painting contractors, although the actual selling was done by either Mr. Hudson or the Ontario supervisor, Mr. Edwards.

In discussing Davis' system of distribution, Hudson said, "As I understand it from Art, we originally got into company outlets because Baker heard how well Rogers was doing with them in the U.S. Although Art disagrees, I think the move was probably a good one, although it does pose some problems. I don't think we can go on opening company outlets and still keep opening independents, or holding our existing ones. Despite Baker's contention that it would be easy to sell dealers on the fact that we can give faster delivery service from local outlets, most of them have a built-in resistance to any supplier competing directly with them. This can be overcome, but you really have to watch what your outlets do. At Baker's insistence, we pushed a promotional sale last fall in Toronto featuring our top line exterior house paint at 20% off. Many dealers didn't go along with the idea because they didn't feel that such a promotion made any more money for them, although it might sell more paint for us. These dealers were sore as hell when our own stores went ahead with the promotion.

"Baker was keen to get our Davis lines into these new discount chains that are opening up in Toronto. I didn't push it, but I don't think we should do it. This isn't because I don't think discount outlets aren't going to sell paint. They are. But we're selling a top quality line, and people buying that type of paint are willing to pay extra for service that discount stores don't give. I'm quite willing to go in on a low quality private brand basis, but, by and large, the new discount outlets want, and need, the big brand names."

Mr. Hudson and Mr. Hodges held different opinions as to the level of selling and calibre of salesman needed for their own and the other's organization. Mr. Hodges felt that selling industrial paint products was a technical job, and that the prime requisite for a salesman selling industrial paint products was a sound technical background. He considered "pushing paint to dealers" a much lower type of selling and thought that very little sales ability was required for the job.

Mr. Hudson thought this viewpoint as "just so much hogwash." "Selling a dealer on changing his line," he maintained, "is the highest form of salesmanship there is. The salesman has to talk the dealer into taking a loss in selling out his existing line and replacing it with a line, that, in most instances, differs very little from the old one, And the dealer then has to switch his customers away from the old line, which is like admitting he was wrong all those years when he told them that it was the best paint available. No sir, the salesman that can get his paint line into a store is the real salesman."

Mr. Hudson thought industrial paint salesmen were "prima donnas." "Most of them," he said, "don't even consider themselves to be salesmen. They like to refer to themselves as technical representatives or some such name. Most of them don't like travelling, don't make enough calls, and, if they can't offer the customer a better price or hold out the carrot of a special product, they're dead!"

Mr. Hudson admitted that the calibre of his sales force and store personnel was not what he would have liked it to be. He attributed this to a lack of training and the poor selection policies and outdated methods used by his predecessors. "I had a hell of a time convincing Baker that sales training didn't consist of filling the salesman full of technical information, and just as much of a problem in convincing Bolton of the need for any training at all! At the moment, I'm trying to upgrade our personnel but it's a difficult job because we don't pay enough money to be able to attract good men. Our only consolation here is that most of our competitors don't either. In addition, I have a problem in that this firm has a policy of not firing incompetent people. I agree that if we've made a mistake on a man for 15 years, we have an obligation to him. But I don't feel that the company outlets should be the resting place for everybody else's problem, and this has been so up to the present— I've got enough problem people of my own to take care of."

Hudson also admitted that he engaged in some selling practices of which he did not personally approve, and of which Mr. Baker had been unaware. "Ross Baker always had the heat on for more sales. At the same time, he was a big man in the C.P.V.L.A. and always stressed the idea that we should get sales through "clean competition." In my books the two aren't compatible. Baker wanted sales and new dealers, so I got them. But to get them, I had to do things of which he didn't approve. Insofar as possible, I tried to arrange it so that he would never find out. In the last few years, I bet we've opened a dozen dealers by putting in the opening order with no payment for twelve months and another year to pay. I don't like selling that way, but Baker wanted sales, so I did my best to get them."

ADVERTISING

Approximately half the firm's advertising dollars were spent on newspaper advertisements, primarily in those areas where the company outlets were located. Two campaigns were run yearly, the larger of the two campaigns featured Davis exterior finishes and ran in the spring and early summer. A smaller campaign ran in the early fall and featured Davis interior finishes. All advertisements were black and white and the themes for the 1961 campaign were "quality," "ease of application," and "paint in any weather." Some promotional advertising was also done for company outlets. The remaining 50% of the firm's advertising dollars were used for price lists, colour cards, dealer signs, and in-store promotional material.

Davis' advertising manager, Mr. Wilson, considered that the firm's media advertising fulfilled two objectives:

1. It kept Davis within the group of brands that had "quality acceptability"; i.e., less selling was required at the retail level because the retail clerk did not have to overcome consumer reluctance to purchase an unknown brand.

2. It provided the sales force with an excellent sales point in their efforts to get the Davis line into new outlets.

Mr. Wilson did not feel that salesmen used the in-store promotional material as efficiently as they might. "Most paint dealers are poor merchandisers," he said. "Our salesmen are supposed to sell dealers on the idea that it pays to merchandise, and encourage them to use display materials by offering to do the display work. However, a lot of our in-store material is just dumped on the dealer by the salesman and never gets used."

Mr. Wilson was also responsible for label designs. He stated that he would like to do a major job of redesigning the firm's labels, which he felt were poorly coordinated and lacked visual appeal. "They look old fashioned," said Mr. Wilson. "We have a different design for practically every product and most of them are cluttered and drab. Bill Hudson agrees that they should be changed but Mr. Baker liked the present labels, which he felt minimized the chance that the consumer or the retail clerk would pull the wrong product off the shelf. He also felt that the present labels gave the customer the impression of a quality product, and that the use of decorator colours and clean designs on the labels would mar the image of quality."

PRICING AND CREDIT

The company put out a retail and dealer price list for the dealer organization. The minimum volume discount off dealer list was 10% and this ranged up to a cumulative 20%, 10%, and 5% discount for dealers with purchases over $25,000 a year.

Distributors purchased at dealer list less 20%, 10%, and 7.5%. Company outlets were authorized to give "competitive discounts" up to dealer list to painting contractors and purchasers of maintenance products in their territory. Any manager wishing to give larger discounts was required to get approval from his supervisor. Supervisory or head office approval was also required for all special prices, volume discounts, or credit terms that a store manager might wish to give to existing or new dealers in his territory. Head office credit approval was required for all new dealer, professional painter, or direct maintenance accounts.

The company's suggested retail sales prices were usually within $0.25 a gallon of most large competitors' prices for similar products and quality. Individual prices of trade sales products were not reviewed on a regular basis, with reference to costs. The company generally followed the price leadership of the "big two" and when either of these firms announced a general price increase, Mr. Hudson and Mr. Bolton met to decide whether or not the firm would make a general price increase at that time.

When new trade sales formulations were developed or major changes in existing trade sales formulations were proposed, the firm's cost man developed an estimated manufactured cost figure based on a probable annual sales volume. This cost figure was used by Messrs. Hudson, and Bolton as one factor to consider in their decision. However, competitors' prices for similar products were normally given much greater weight in the final pricing decision because of both Hudson's and Bolton's belief that "we can't afford to get out of line on prices."

When a custom formulation was developed, it was sent to the firm's cost department. A cost man worked out the material costs based on current material prices. From the salesman's estimate of the probable order size, and his own knowledge of what machines and time would be required to make the product, the cost man computed a direct manufacturing cost. To this he added a factor for overhead which was computed by multiplying his estimated direct labour hours by the quarterly overhead figure expressed as a rate per direct hour. Packing costs were also added in. Finally, he added 15% for "profit," divided the total figure by the total gallons used in the computations, and arrived at a rate per gallon. This figure, along with the estimated order size, was used by Messrs. Hodges, Bolton, and Baker as the basis for their final decision as to what price the firm would submit.

Once a price was established for a custom formulation, it was not normally reviewed on subsequent orders unless a customer requested a "better price."

Quite frequently, when the inventory records were checked, it was found that the firm was currently selling below full manufactured cost. In some cases the price would subsequently be raised, but in many others, the price was either kept at the old level or reduced slightly "to keep the business."

PURCHASING

The purchasing department was made up of Mr. Bill Black, the purchasing agent, and three assistants. Mr. Black and his staff worked closely with the production planner to ensure that sufficient quantities of the several hundred types of raw material used by the firm were on hand to meet production requirements. The purchasing department also worked closely with lab personnel so that, where possible, substitutions could be made in formulations which would result in lower raw material costs. Some raw materials purchased by the firm were traced on the commodities markets, but the firm, as a matter of policy, did no speculative purchasing. According to Mr. Black, two factors dictated this policy:

1. Speculation in commodities tied up working capital.
2. Mr. Baker's personal conviction that, since the firm had to purchase these materials in any case, the possible savings from speculation were not worth either the risk or time involved.

Mr. Wood concluded that Mr. Black and his staff were doing a highly competent job. Although Mr. Black had responsibility for spending approximately $3,000,000 a year, Mr. Wood did not feel that the purchasing agent's job was a top management one. "It's not difficult to do a good job as a purchasing agent," was the way Mr. Wood put it. "It's simply a matter of getting to know sources of supply, delivery dates and prices, and then making sure that we get the right material here on time."

TECHNICAL SERVICES

Mr. Taylor was responsible for the establishment and maintenance of quality control standards in the plant, production quality standards, new product development, and basic material research. He also acted as technical advisor to the purchasing department and, since his department was responsible for investigating complaints of product failures in the field, he spent some of his time following up complaints in the Toronto area.

The firm did relatively little materials research because of their connection with Rogers, which did extensive research in this area.

The quality control group worked in the plant to ensure that all products met the predetermined standards of quality and performance. They were not always popular with plant or sales personnel because of their insistence on thoroughness, which occasionally interfered with tight delivery schedules.

One lab group worked closely with the industrial salesforce in the development of custom formulations. Mr. Taylor reported that it was difficult to keep lab costs down for work done in this area because:

1. The extra work involved in reformulation as a result of salesmen not telling the lab precisely enough just what product was needed.

2. Salesmen frequently brought requests for formulation development to the lab for products whose order size, once received, was so small that the development cost exceeded the income from the order. "I can't really blame the salesmen," said Mr. Taylor. "After all, their income is tied to sales. But I do think they could use more discretion."

A system had been instituted whereby a cost estimate was made for all requests by salesmen for formulation development work. These were sent to Mr. Hodges who, after discussing the sales situation and probable order size with the salesman, would accept or reject the requests. Although the system did eliminate some expense, the problem still existed for two reasons.

1. Salesmen tended to be overoptimistic on the potential volume of the order.

2. Many requests for product formulations for small volume orders were approved because they came from customers who bought other larger volume products. This policy was justified on the grounds that "You've got to do it to keep the large business because if you don't, somebody else will."

Mr. Taylor did not disagree with this policy but was "extremely put out when we spend a couple of thousand dollars developing a new system for a firm and then once we have it working, they go out and see if they can get somebody else to give them a better price on the product."

New product development work in the trade sales area was devoted to the improvement of existing products and to the development of new products. To guide them in their work, the people in this group depended on feedback from the sales-force, information from suppliers, the firm's own basic research group, and the Rogers' technical staff. Extensive testing of new trade products was carried out before they were put on the market. This was true even for products already tested by Rogers because, in Mr. Taylor's words, "A product developed for the U.S. market does not necessarily stand up in Canada because of our vastly different climate."

Mr. Taylor was extremely upset by the firm's advertising of a new water-thinned synthetic resin exterior house paint put on the market in 1961. The advertising for this product had used a "paint in any weather" theme and in Mr. Taylor's opinion, had implied that it was a one-coat paint product. "This simply isn't true," said Mr. Taylor. "The product can be applied in a wider variety of weather conditions than existing oil base exterior paints, but a coat of oil base primer *must* be used first. Further, this primer has to be applied to a dry surface. Our labels clearly indicate these facts, but a lot of people are going to be left with a bad taste in their mouth. Already the complaints are coming in."

PRODUCTION

When the Davis plant was built in 1947, the layout was designed to fit the firm's product mix of that time. Since then, the addition of new equipment to meet changing production requirements and to effect materials and labour savings had resulted in a layout which created materials handling problems. Thomas had submitted, for several years running, a capital expenditures budget in which he estimated that the firm, by spending $90,000 on plan modernization, could effect annual cost savings of $60,000. Mr. Baker, however, had decided against the expenditures because "of the firm's need to conserve its funds for working capital requirements."

The plant operated one shift a day, five days a week during the winter months. During the peak season in late spring and early summer, partial two shift operation was used, with the day shift working five one-half days a week. Thomas estimated that, with the firm's existing product mix and seasonal production cycle, plant capacity was at about $8,500,000 in sales. An additional investment of $150,000 would increase this figure 20% and level year round production a further 50% to 60%.

In discussing his job, Mr. Thomas stated that "You don't really need to be technically oriented. It helps, of course, but the ability to handle people and plan production is far more important. Since I'm blocked to a large degree on the planning side, my interest is focused primarily on the people problems."

Paint was put into production by the following method. Inventory reorder points had been established for all trade sales products and those industrial products that the firm considered "standards." Production batch sizes had also been developed. Boty the inventory reorder points and batch sizes were initially determined when the product was first put on the market and upward adjustments made if out-of-stock positions developed with any frequency. Decisions on changes in batch sizes or reorder points were made by Mr. Thomas after consultation with Mr. Hudson or Mr. Hodges. When customer orders for a product brought the inventory below the reorder point, the inventory clerk sent the production planner's office a slip showing the product number and indicated batch size. The planner then scheduled the product into production and had batch tickets made up.

All re-orders for industrial products were checked by the sales office to see if overruns were in stock. Orders which could not be filled from stock were sent to Mr. Hodges and he determined the batch size.

The average production cycle for a paint product in the Davis plant was from three to ten days. According to Mr. Thomas, the worker skills required for most production jobs were minimal, and new workers could be trained in a very short time. The job of tinting, however, required a man with a good working knowledge of paint technology, and the ability to perceive small variations in shades and colours.

Production was carried out under the direction of a plant superintendent and six foremen. Mr. Thomas stated that his production superintendent did a good job but that he was not "promotable material because he does not have the ability to plan ahead." The six foremen were in charge of resin manufacture; grinding, standardizing, and filling (two); colorants, product finishes; and labelling and shipping. Thomas reported that it was extremely difficult to develop supervisory help from production workers. "The type of worker we attract just doesn't seem to have what it takes to be a foreman," he said, "Twice in the last three years I've been a short a foreman for fairly lengthy periods of time, because we had no one of promotable calibre. Both times I finally filled the job with an outside man."

The permanent work force of slightly over a hundred men was expanded by about a third in the peak summer months. The permanent work force was fairly stable but trained tinters, who were in short supply in the industry, were often lost to smaller firms.

The plant was unionized but union relations were good. Mr. Wood thought that this was both a result of Mr. Thomas' approach to management and the fact that the firm paid workers at a rate somewhat above the industry average. From his experience in paint production, Wood estimated that the worker efficiency in the Davis plant was above average for the industry.

Thomas had a good working relationship with Taylor but was not always on the best of terms with the sales managers, particularly Joe Hodges. These disagreements usually stemmed from the fact that, when delivery problems arose, the sales managers frequently went direct to the foremen and tried to get them to push the product through production, instead of working through the production superintendent, Mr. Edison, or the expediter.

Mr. Thomas thought that significant inventory and production savings could be effected if the firm were more realistic on its product policy. "This is especially true in the trade sales area," he said. "For instance, we sell two water-thinned interior paints of comparable quality and application properties. One has a latex base (vehicle) and the other a polyvinyl chloride base. Despite the fact that most people in the firm consider the PVC product to be superior, we offer both because Hudson says that we'll lose sales if customers ask for a "rubber" base paint, and we don't have one.

"To my mind, we also produce too many variations of what is essentially the same product. Just because you sell a product under a different label or give a guy a special price doesn't mean that it is profitable to change the product. If we offered just two, or at the most, three ranges of quality for a given product and just used different labels where necessary, I'm sure that we would save money overall, even if we made less money on some products than we do now.

"What we really need in this firm is a man working full time on this whole problem of simplification of the product line and inventory control. As it stands now, the personnel in this firm are spread too thin to do any work on it. I suggested the idea a couple of times to Ross Baker but he felt that the problem didn't merit hiring a man full time."

THE CONTROLLER'S DEPARTMENT

Mr. Chalmers was responsible for all operations connected with finance, cost, and inventory records, as well as credit, collections, and the firm's relationship with the bank. Although Mr. Chalmers would like to have devoted more of his time to financial planning and the development of better records and systems for reporting and control, he realized that there was "no point in developing systems that people won't buy or use. In any case, most of my time is spent working on day-to-day problems and in trying to keep things up to date."

In 1960, Mr. Chalmers had managed to get Mr. Baker interested in the idea of installing data processing equipment. However, after preliminary investigation, the idea had been abandoned. Mr. Chalmers said that the decision was based on the reasoning that "the equipment would cost more than our present system, and it was doubtful that we could use it effectively because of our multi-product operation. We also heard that several other paint companies had put in equipment and had later thrown it out because it wouldn't do the job."

ACCOUNTS RECEIVABLE AND COLLECTIONS

Customer billing for sales through the firm's Quebec outlets was done by a small clerical group located in one of Davis' Montreal outlets. Each of the five company outlets in western Canada did its own billing. All other sales were billed from the firm's Toronto offices.

In recent years, the receivables outstanding over ninety days had grown as a percentage of total receivables (see Exhibit 7). Mr. Chalmers attributed this to the fact that "a lot of independents are now being squeezed for working capital and are leaning more and more on us. This problem isn't exclusive to our company by any means."

The trend by both industrial customers and dealers to carrying lower inventories had meant that the average invoice size had dropped 20% in eight years to $55 in 1961.

At Mr. Baker's urging, Mr. Chalmers had been trying to hold down the number of clerical staff in recent years. Mr. Chalmers reported that his had made it difficult to keep up to date on billing during the peak summer season and, as a result, both accounts payable and the firm's bank loan were higher during this period than they might normally be (see Exhibit 8).

Exhibit 7

Davis Paint Company Ltd.

Percentage Analysis of Age of Outstanding Accounts Receivable as at September 30th for Selected Years

	1953	1955	1957	1959	1961
Current Items (not yet billed)	30.4%	37.2%	36.5%	37.0%	44.3%
1–29 days	34.5	24.5	23.8	21.9	15.0
30–59 days	14.5	10.6	10.3	13.2	10.4
60–89 days	7.0	8.2	8.4	8.8	6.7
Over 90 days	13.6	19.5	21.0	19.1	23.6
TOTAL	100.0%	100.0%	100.0%	100.0%	100.0%

The firm had a full time credit man and a full time collections man. The credit man, who reported directly to Mr. Chalmers, was responsible for giving credit approval on all new accounts and setting credit limits. Credit decisions on larger accounts were often made by Mr. Chalmers after consultations with one or more of the sales managers.

The collection man, Mr. Norton, had overall responsibiity for all collections. He was assisted by one of the clerks in the Montreal accounting group, who handled all collections of accounts billed by that office. Most of Mr. Norton's time was spent in collection work connected with accounts billed through

Exhibit 8

Davis Company Ltd.

Selected Accounts by Month for the 13-Month Period Ending September 30, 1961

Month	Sales (000's)	Accounts Receivable (000's)	Inventory (000's)	Bank Loan (000's)	Accounts Payable (000's)
September	$612	$1,376	$1,977	$496	$591
October	565	1,212	1,849	300	628
November	439	1,164	2,025	223	612
December	349	1,043	2,271	257	723
January	448	1,155	2,340	538	714
February	532	1,246	2,421	758	684
March	603	1,473	2,353	1,112	745
April	756	1,680	2,298	1,218	658
May	836	1,798	2,355	1,330	885
June	751	1,749	2,331	1,227	881
July	666	1,757	2,256	1,247	763
August	750	1,519	1,954	671	603
September	607	1,427	1,981	481	594

head office. Although sales personnel were not responsible for collections, Mr. Norton frequently relied on the managers of the company's western outlets in western Canada to do collection work for him.

Mr. Chalmers thought that the firm's bad debt experience was "probably higher than the industry average." He thought that this stemmed from the fact that the firm, as a matter of policy, took a fair number of marginal credit risks. As a group, painting contractors were the worst credit risks, accounting for up to 40% of the firm's yearly bad debt loss.

Although industrial accounts generally paid their bills more promptly than did dealers, the firm's bad debts records showed that more dollars were annually written off for industrial accounts than were written off for dealer accounts.

PRODUCTION COST SYSTEM AND INVENTORY CONTROL

Actual costs were collected for each batch that was produced. The product was then charged into inventory at a figure which represented actual direct costs, plus a manufacturing overhead cost which was calculated by multiplying the direct labour hours spent producing the batch by an overhead rate. The overhead rate was determined quarterly by dividing total factory overhead expenses by total direct labour hours. The company used an average cost system for inventory records. For purposes of determining the profitability of company outlets, shipments to them were charged out at the average cost per gallon figures which appeared in the records at the time the shipments were made.

The variance between actual and allocated factory overhead costs was computed monthly. A portion of this variance was charged to company outlets, the amount being determined by multiplying the variance figure by the ratio of dollar shipments to company outlets divided by total production costs. The variance allocated to each outlet was computed by multiplying the figure obtained in the previous step by the ratio of shipments to each company outlet divided by shipments to all company outlets. The remaining difference between the total variance and the variance charged to company outlets was charged to a head office variance account.

Physical inventory was taken once a year. Plant inventories were costed out at the year-end average cost figures contained in the inventory records. Differences between actual quantities and book quantities were written off at the average cost. Physical counts of inventory in company outlets were also made and figures forwarded to head office where they were costed out in the same manner as the plant inventory. No calculation of inventory losses in company outlets due to theft or other reasons was possible, because the company outlets did not maintain perpetual inventory records. "This is Bolton's influence," said Chalmers. "Anytime anyone mentions paper work, he's up in arms. His attitude has rubbed off on store managers to some extent and occasionally we have trouble with a store manager because he 'forgets' that his daily report listing total cash sales, charge sales by customer, and total sales must be sent in at the end of each day.

"We also have an obsolete inventory problem. No real effort is put in during the year to get rid of small quantities of broken lines and overruns. And shipping doesn't always send out the oldest stock first. We catch some of these things when we do our year-end stock-taking and each year write down inventory to the tune of $20,000 to $30,000. This figure could be reduced if the problem was given continual attention.

"You know," continued Mr. Chalmers, "I'm becoming more and more convinced that overcapacity isn't the real problem in the paint business. We're really a variable cost business, and margins are more critical than volume. In spite of what the sales staff will say, I feel that selective price increases could be made. Further, the sales managers never consider the idea that both margins and profits could be increased by dropping both low margin business and the people it takes to produce and sell it. I'm sure that Arnold Davis would never have looked at the business this way, but perhaps there is no other alternative if we want to stay in paint business."

3. WORTHY COMPANY (A)*

—HAROLD D. JANES

The Worthy Watch Company of Kentucky was founded in 1889, and by 1920 had established itself as a "quality house" manufacturer of jeweled watches and watchcases.

In 1953, the Worthy Watch Company, hereinafter frequently referred to as Worthy, began a product diversification program which included the establishment of a committee to study and recommend acquisition of additional plant facilities. In 1955, Worthy purchased the Stretchband Company located in Rhode Island—a producer of gold-filled and stainless steel watchbands. At the time of this purchase the average employment in the Worthy plant was 2000. Stretchband employed approximately 350.

Two months after the Stretchband purchase—now operated as a wholly owned subsidiary—the President (of Worthy) called a regular Saturday morning staff meeting of his vice presidential personnel.[1] The personnel concerned in this case are delineated in the organizational chart on page 607.

---

* Prepared for the Southern Case Writers' Association. Reprinted by permission of the Association and Professor Janes.
[1] Additional information about the President's staff can be found in Appendix A.

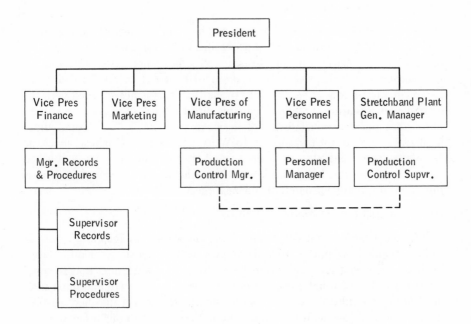

The President called the meeting to order and stated: "Gentlemen, there are two important items on the agenda this morning. *First,* the General Manager of our Stretchband plant, Mr. Joe Hudnal, is concerned about the scheduling requirements imposed upon his organization. He states that we do not give him enough 'lead time' on the more complicated gold-filled watchbands. He, also, believes that his organization gets the tough jobs and that we subcontract the easy work to our competitors. He contends that this makes it difficult, if not impossible, to show profit improvement. Mr. Hudnal commented about the mix-up on the watchband shipment last week. He said the reason they didn't include the stainless steel bands resulted from an apparent misinterpretation of instructions during a phone conversation between their Production Control Supervisor and our Production Control Manager.

"*Second,* our Manager of Records and Procedures, Mr. Charles Platte, has reported that he is unable to improve the efficiency of his department because the personnel department keeps filling employment orders with unqualified, substandard help. Charlie stated, 'We have to fire them faster than Personnel can hire them for us. The referrals are just not good, and it adds up to the fact we do not have enough help to do our job, and frankly what help we do have isn't very good.'"

"Gentlemen, I welcome your comments on these problems."

The officials present commented as follows:

THE VICE PRESIDENT OF PERSONNEL

" You all know the personnel department hires on the basis of the job order. We have job descriptions and job specifications for each job. Personnel administers the basic aptitude tests to all office applicants. Mr. Platte's accusations do not surprise me even though I have not been informed of his complaints until now. It would seem to me that if he is not satisfied with the employment situation, I should hear this direct from him. I am sure you all know that our personnel tests are designed to help us 'weed out' those applicants who do not measure up to Worthy standards. Our tests meet the requirements for reliability and validity, and are based on our own established norms. In any event, I will check with Personnel and be prepared to discuss this situation in greater detail at our next meeting."

THE VICE PRESIDENT OF MANUFACTURING

"Yes, we have subcontracted some jobs, but we should keep a few outside sources available. Suppose Stretchband gets tied-up in a strike or other labor trouble? We have tried to give our outside sources a work mix, that is, some easy jobs and some tough jobs, but perhaps we have given Hudnal more than his share of the difficult work. This may be due to the fact that he turns out the complicated jobs with less follow-up and rework than our other sources.

"As far as lead time is concerned, if we could give Joe extra time we certainly would. The way our system works we couldn't give him an extra week. For that matter we have been more lenient with Stretchband than with our other suppliers. No one else seems to be complaining about our lead time requirements. You all know it takes six and one-half months to produce a watch, and about two months to complete a new band order. We (at the main plant) experience a variety of complicated problems and still manage to come up with profit improvements. For example, last month the tool and die department was asked to make drills as fine as 28/10,000ths of an inch in diameter that are accurate to 3/100,000ths of an inch, and this was accomplished. However, I will discuss Hudnal's problem with our Production Control Manager and see if we can improve this set-up."[2]

THE VICE PRESIDENT OF FINANCE

"Gentlemen, I want you to know that Charles has not indicated these problem areas to me. I have given him a wide latitude to run his department, and to make changes as he deems necessary.

---

[2] The production control function is decentralized. Scheduling and control are coordinated by each staff department. The production control section in each plant is responsible for: (1) Machine loading, (2) Assignment of due dates. (3) Keeping an account of the flow of material and work in process. (4) Working with the main plant production control in determining economic lot sizes. Stretchband makes a limited number of band designs and varies production mix as directed by the main plant production control.

" He has only been with us for seven months, and is trying to do his best and make a good showing. He is well aware that our increased sales volume requires an increase in his staff, but apparently he is experiencing some difficulty in this area.

" Before we hired Charles we were in considerable trouble with our records and procedures set-up, and it is my understanding that he was to be given a free hand to straighten it out."

THE VICE PRESIDENT OF MARKETING

"There seems to be a lack of coordination between manufacturing, production control, personnel, and Charlie's department.

"I want you to know that marketing has already committed the company to an increased sales volume in watches, quicker delivery dates, and a wider variety in the new jeweled watch line, including matching bands.

"What really worries me is the increased cost of labor (85% of the watch is direct labor), and the highly elastic demand for our product."

AFTER THE MEETING WAS ADJOURNED

Walking back to their respective offices, the V.P. of Manufacturing commented to the V.P. of Personnel, "Where in the hell does marketing get the impression that they can dictate commitments to me! As I see it, it is up to them to sell what we make and not vice versa."

The V.P. of Personnel, commented, "I agree with you, I better head towards the personnel department. Charlie is probably bucking for that top finance job, and thinks he can impress Jim (the President) by his direct approach."

LATER THAT SAME WEEK

The Vice President of Personnel had several talks with the Personnel Manager, and assembled the following information:

1. Several exit interviews of the women terminated by Records and Procedures are reproduced in Appendix B.

2. All of the women hired for Records and Procedures, over the past three months, had at least two years of high school, and 70% were high school graduates. All women employed in records and procedures scored in the upper fifty percentile group on their aptitude and clerical tests.[3]

3. The Personnel Manager had talked with, and had the opportunity to observe, both the Supervisor of Records and the Supervisor of Procedures.

It was the opinion of the Personnel Manager that the Supervisor of Records, a 28-year-old college graduate in liberal arts, supervised "too closely." That

---

[3] Factored aptitude test series included: judgment, perception, numbers, office terms, and spelling.

is, he was always checking up on his employees. He was extremely general in his employment job orders and specifications, and when questioned about this his comment to the Personnel Manager was, "Personnel ought to know all about the jobs in the plant. Just get me qualified girls—you know what I mean." This Supervisor had previously been employed in the company's

Exhibit 1
Labor Turnover

Month	Records Department			Procedures Department		
	HIRES	TERMINATIONS	TOTAL	HIRES	TERMINATIONS	TOTAL
January	0	0	16	0	0	7
February	0	0	16	1	1	7
March	0	1	15	0	0	7
April	2	1	16	0	1	6
May	0	0	16	1	0	7
June	3	1	18	2	1	8
July	4	2	20	1	1	8
August	4	3	21	2	0	10
September	6	5	22	2	2	10
October	6	7	21	3	2	11
November	4	6	19	2	4	9
December	7	9	17	2	4	7
TOTAL HIRES— Term's	36	35		16	16	
TOTAL EMPLOYMENT			17			7

SUMMARY OF RECORDS DEPARTMENT TERMINATIONS
Discharges	23
Resigned	6
Moved out of State	2
Maternity Leave..........................	1
Miscellaneous...........................	3
	35

SUMMARY OF PROCEDURES DEPARTMENT TERMINATIONS
Discharges	4
Resigned	9
Moved out of State	1
Maternity Leave	0
Miscellaneous.............................	2
	16

management training program and he had completed about two-thirds of his training when (at the request of the Vice President of Finance) he was shifted to his present assignment.[4]

The Supervisor of Procedures was recruited by his boss (Charlie Platte) from Charlie's former company. He is 36 years of age, has been with the company for five months, and has two years of college training in business administration. The new employees in his department claim that he gives them very little, if any, direction. Once they are hired they are on their own. Only in recent weeks have the new girls been assigned to work with senior members of the department. This constitutes in the eyes of the Supervisor, on-the-job training. This form of training has not, however, reduced the labor turnover in his section. Three new girls in his section complained that the senior employees seem to "look down" on new hires, and it is very difficult to break into their inner circle.

4. The Personnel Manager summarized the labor turnover figures from official records (see Exhibit 1).

APPENDIX A

INFORMATION ABOUT THE PRESIDENT

He has twenty six years of company service, and has served as the President for the past eighteen years. He graduated (Bachelors degree in Liberal Arts) from a well known Ivy League college, and was immediately hired as an understudy and protégé of the former Worthy President. Prior to his present assignment he served Worthy as a Foreman, Supervisor of Inspection, and Superintendent of Manufacturing. He is considered, by his staff, as a competent man. He is cordial but sometimes has a reserved manner that is interpreted by middle management as "stand-offish." It is generally conceded that he rarely shows partiality or prejudice. He is forty-seven years of age.

INFORMATION ABOUT THE VICE PRESIDENT OF FINANCE

He has thirty-five years of company service, and has served as V.P. of Finance for the past nineteen years. He is a self-educated man, and an avid reader. Prior to his present assignment he served Worthy as a Chief Accountant & Controller. He frequently tells his associates that he looks forward to retirement next year. He is sixty-four years of age. He is cordial, but somewhat "formal," that is, he is restrained in his dealings with his associates and subordinates. He has an exceptional grasp and competency in the area of economic and fiscal matters. A few associates consider him to be somewhat of a "nit-picker," but all would say he works in harmony with the president's staff and the employees.

---

[4] Worthy maintains an anti-nepotism policy in employment practices.

INFORMATION ABOUT THE VICE PRESIDENT OF MANUFACTURING

He has twenty-one years of company service, and has served as V.P. of Manufacturing for the past six years. He is self-educated—graduated from high school and has continued to supplement his education by reading technical periodicals, and a planned program of study. Prior to his present assignment, he served Worthy as a General Foreman (10 years), and following this as Superintendent of Manufacturing (5 years). He is forty-five years of age. Associates view him as having a dominating type of personality, but with a pleasing manner. He often jokes about his weight and his waistline (5′ 8″— weight 210 pounds).

INFORMATION ABOUT THE VICE PRESIDENT OF MARKETING

He has four years service with the company, and has served these four years as the Vice President of Marketing. He earned a bachelors degree from a large midwestern university, and has completed much of the coursework toward the Master's degree. His past service has been at the top management level of a large scale electronics firm (Director of Marketing). He is forty-four years of age. Associates consider him a very persuasive person, but some have stated that he sometimes "rubs" people the wrong way due to his outspoken and controversial opinions. He is considered to be extremely knowledgeable in his field.

INFORMATION ABOUT THE VICE PRESIDENT OF PERSONNEL

He has eight years of service with the company, and has served all of this time as the V.P. of Personnel. He was formerly a V.P. in charge of Industrial Relations for a large Steel company. He is forty-five years of age. He completed two years of college, and has continued to pursue a program of self-education. Associates consider him curt, "driving", egotistical, and persuasive. He is a brilliant master bargainer with the six national unions represented at Worthy. His analytical ability is respected by top management and the unions. At times he is "rough" spoken and sardonic.

INFORMATION ABOUT THE STRETCHBAND PLANT GENERAL MANAGER

At the time of Stretchband's purchase by Worthy, he was the Executive Vice President of Stretchband. He was persuaded to remain as the General Manager. The President of Stretchband was retired at the request of the Worthy President. The General Manager's job is the top line position at Stretchband. He is a college graduate, holding the bachelors degree in mechanical engineering from a large northeastern university. He is fifty-one years of age. The Worthy staff considers him as enthusiastic about his job, even tempered, and loyal to the organization. He is sometimes rather brusque, but most always manages to make a favorable impression. He is quick to grasp new ideas, and is very adaptable.

APPENDIX B: VERBATUM EXIT INTERVIEWS

FEMALE EMPLOYEE "A"—RECORDS DEPARTMENT

Personnel Manager: I just received a call from the Records Supervisor. He said he was sending you to Personnel, and that you will no longer be needed in his section. Is this correct?

Employee: Yes, sir. I have only worked in his section for one week. I just can't understand his attitude. After the first day the only words he ever spoke to me were, "You don't seem to be catching on to the job very well." He assigned me to do order filing, and, without exaggeration, he didn't spend more than twenty minutes telling me what I was to do.

Personnel Manager: Were you satisfied with your job?

Employee: No, I don't believe so. I never really knew what I was to do. I never received any training of any kind. Things aren't so bad for me though—my husband works. I'll find another job. This isn't the only factory in town.

FEMALE EMPLOYEE " B "—RECORDS DEPARTMENT

Employee: My supervisor told me to report down here to you.

Personnel Manager: Did he say why you were to report here?

Employee: He said I was being laid off.

Personnel Manager: How long have you worked for the company?

Employee: Two weeks.

Personnel Manager: When an employee is laid off this means that she has seniority, and that there is some reasonable chance of her being recalled to work. You must have misunderstood your supervisor. Are you sure he didn't tell you that you were being terminated?

Employee: No, he said laid off.

Personnel Manager: Let me call him, and get this straightened out.

Records Supervisor: No, I didn't say she was laid off. I told her she was discharged because her work was not up to standard.

Personnel Manager: Your supervisor tells me that you were informed by him that you were discharged.

Employee: That's not the way I understood him. It doesn't make any difference anyway. Things are in such a mess in his section it's a wonder he hasn't been discharged.

Personnel Manager: What do you mean—such a mess?

Employee: Well, the supervisor would tell me to do one thing and the older employees would tell me not to do it that way because it would take too long. It seemed to me that work directions were always being changed.

Personnel Manager: Isn't that part of the Records section's job to see that the most efficient ways are devised for record keeping? And, wouldn't this in itself require some changes?

Employee: He (Records Supervisor) never explained it to me that way, but I can see where this could be so. Why don't you have a talk with him and get him straightened out?

FEMALE EMPLOYEE " C "—RECORDS DEPARTMENT

Employee:	I certainly don't think it's fair to be hired and terminated in the same month. I've worked in other places and Worthy is the worst.
Personnel Manager:	What do you mean the worst?
Employee:	Why, just last week the Vice President of Marketing, I think that's who he was, came down and borrowed an invoice I was working on, and that's the last I saw of it. When I told my supervisor what had happened he told me, " Why did you let him take the invoice," and I said no one ever gave me the authority to tell a V.P. what he could take.

Later that same week my boss told me that Friday would be my last day—they wouldn't need me any more. If you ask me he (Records Supervisor) didn't have the nerve to tell the Marketing V.P. what to do, and he is blaming me for his own shortcomings.

I guess I'm glad to be leaving. I never did like the way he looked at me. |

FEMALE EMPLOYEE " D "—RECORDS DEPARTMENT

Personnel Manager:	My secretary told me that you will be leaving us today.
Employee:	Yes, my boss told me last week that they were going to reduce his department, and that he was sorry, but since I was one of the last hired. I would have to be one of the first to go.
Personnel Manager:	Were you satisfied with your job?
Employee:	Yes, Sir.
Personnel Manager:	No complaints?
Employee:	No—I just wish they didn't have to cut back employment.

FEMALE EMPLOYEE " E "—RECORDS DEPARTMENT

Employee:	Can you imagine that young " brat " you all call a boss telling me I shouldn't spend so much time in the rest room!
Personnel Manager:	Are you being terminated today?
Employee:	I guess you could call it that. I'm being " let go."
Personnel Manager:	You say you are being " let go." Do you know why?
Employee:	I suppose it's that argument I had with him about the rest room. Last week he saw me waiting around by the calculator, and I told him I was waiting to do my invoice price extensions. He told me that there were other things to do besides standing around.
Personnel Manager:	Well, were there?
Employee:	Like what? No one gives help up there. I managed to stay here two months by asking the senior girls how to look busy. They all seemed to look busy, but when I offered to help them out one girl told me if the boss caught her without work she might get the ax.
Personnel Manager:	Did you observe any other problems?
Employee:	In my opinion, the supervisor plays favorites.
Personnel Manager:	For example?

Employee: For one thing the older girls have the new desks, and better equipment. The older girls (in terms of seniority) have better assignments—I mean they have plenty to keep them busy. They all stay within their own group. They eat lunch together —bowl in their own group—and even come to work in their own car pool.

That's all I have to say.

FEMALE EMPLOYEE "A"—PROCEDURES DEPARTMENT

Personnel Manager: I understand you are resigning?

Employee: That's correct. At first I liked my new job. I had a wonderful friend to work with, and she helped me a great deal. Two weeks ago she was transferred to another assignment. Lately they seem to change things so much I get all mixed-up. It's just not enjoyable to work this way.

Personnel Manager: Did your supervisor try and explain these changes?

Employee: He is certainly willing, but that man has so much to do—why, he only takes one-half hour for his lunch. You all work him too hard.

FEMALE EMPLOYEE " B "—PROCEDURES DEPARTMENT

Personnel Manager: Your boss called me and said you are resigning, is this correct?

Employee: Yes, Sir.

Personnel Manager: Would you care to tell me why? Perhaps there is a misunderstanding I can help clear up. You have almost six months' service.

Employee: I don't think you could do anything, but I told my supervisor the reason.

Personnel Manager: What was the reason?

Employee: I don't like to work under pressure. It isn't that my boss pushes me, but the work keeps stacking up, and we keep working overtime. My doctor told me that it's making a nervous wreck out of me. My husband told me that when I keep complaining about my work (to him)—then I better quit.

FEMALE EMPLOYEE " C "—PROCEDURES DEPARTMENT

Employee: I just finished talking with your secretary.

Personnel Manager: Aren't you two neighbors?

Employee: Yes we are. She is the one that told me about this job four weeks ago.

Personnel Manager: Your record indicates you are being discharged?

Employee: I know it sounds bad, but I just don't seem to fit into the job.

Personnel Manager: What were you doing?

Employee: I did most of the proofreading of the new procedures—made up procedures manuals for all the departmental Foremen, and saw to it that they all received copies. This past week I was assigned to work with a girl who does the art lay-out work on production control forms.

Personnel Manager: And?

Employee: Well, the proofreading job was about completed, and I told my boss I didn't think I could do very well on the lay-out type of work. He checked with me every day for the past week, and we agreed that I had better resign. He said there wasn't any other work he could assign me to. You know I can't type very well.

Personnel Manager: He marked the termination slip as discharged.

Employee: What difference does it make?

Personnel Manager: When you resign you initiate the action. When you are discharged, it is your boss who takes the action.

Employee: I think it sounds better to say terminated, don't you?

Personnel Manager: That depends upon what caused the termination. I'll call your supervisor, and get the correct interpretation on the record.

Employee: Thank you. I'll appreciate it.

4. WORTHY COMPANY (B)*

—HAROLD D. JANES

The Superintendent of Production, Mr. Al Buhrow, phoned the Personnel Manager, "Paul, we are going to have to take some action on this solicitation raffle. I understand that you are aware that this is going on. Let's have lunch together today and compare notes."

The Personnel Manager, Mr. Paul Jordan, was aware of the overall problem, and had talked with the General Foreman concerned (Mr. Bob Brown) that same morning. The participants involved are represented on page 618.

---

* Prepared for the Southern Case Writers' Association. Reprinted by permission of the Association and Professor Janes.

Worthy Company (B)

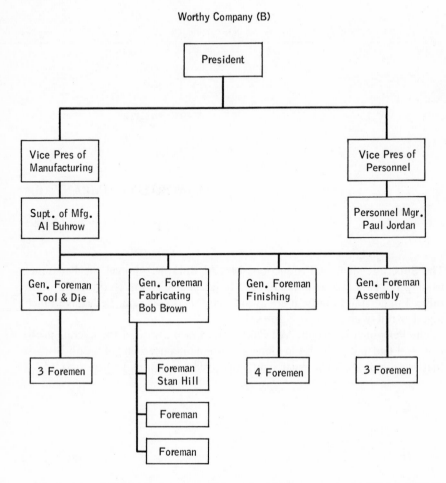

Both Al and Paul were aware of the rule which was a part of the company rule book. This rule stated: No selling or advertising of any merchandise shall take place on company property.[1] This was followed by another statement (in the same rule book): all business dealings within a department, or between departments must be approved by departmental supervision.

AT LUNCH

"You know Paul, that I feel as sympathetic as any man. It's a terrible thing that happened to Stan Hill's wife. Their family doctor said it's multiple sclerosis, and I understand Stan's wife is almost completely paralyzed. She can only speak with great difficulty. Our company doctor told me that little is known

---

[1] Sale of cokes and candy in vending machines are excluded. All employees have a copy of the rule book.

about this disease, but a national foundation has been working on the medical problems begging solution."

Paul stated, "I was aware of this Al, Bob Brown came to my office this morning and told me that last week the Fabricating department employees took up a donation for Stan's wife, and got about $150. Bob indicated this would certainly help, but it would not be near enough. Now Stan's fellow foremen have been closing their eyes to a "Help Stan" raffle sale, that soon threatens to spread across the entire plant. Stan told me last week that they may take his wife to Mayo Clinic, and the expenses are about to put him to the wall."

Paul continued, " My understanding is that three of Stan's senior employees purchased a Leica camera, two portable radios and several smoked hams, and they are selling chances at twenty-five cents each—all proceeds going into a fund. They even have an employee committee to see that all funds are accounted for, and that no one makes a dime on this."

Al stated, "That's the same story I got from Brown. He said he (Brown) realized it was against company rules, but the employees had such a genuine respect and willingness to help Stan, that he didn't want to be the one to stick his neck out and say, 'Stop this practice.'"

Paul continued, "I think we should solve this. I'm not anxious to push this type of a problem up to the V.P. level."

Al agreed that he and Paul should work out a solution to this situation.

PART V

BUSINESS MANAGEMENT
SIMULATION GAME

* *

1. POLICY DECISION MAKING AND BUSINESS MANAGEMENT GAMES*

—CHARLES R. KLASSON

Today well over 100 computerized and noncomputerized business management games, also known as "business simulations," are in use in a growing number of universities and businesses across the country.[1] Since their introduction as an educational tool in 1956 by the American Management Association, considerable progress has been made in the advancement of this methodological approach to developing the decision-making capabilities of individuals preparing themselves to assume managerial responsibilities and the practicing executive.[2] Beyond the educational benefits of simulation, its value as a research tool has been recognized and exploited by a growing number of advocates of simulation systems techniques. Already an increasing

---

* Contributed by Professor Charles R. Klasson, Graduate School of Business, The University of Texas, Austin, Texas.

[1] For the most comprehensive surveys, evaluations, and bibliographies now available on business games, see: *Proceedings of the National Symposium on Management Games* (Lawrence, Kansas: University of Kansas Center for Research in Business, May, 1959), *Simulation and Gaming: A Symposium* (New York: American Management Association, Management Report No. 55, 1961); *Proceedings of the Conference on Business Games as Teaching Devices* (New Orleans: Tulane University, School of Business Administration, April 26–28, 1961); K. J. Cohen and E. Rhenmen, "The Role of Management Games in Education and Research," *Management Science* Vol. 7, No. 2 (January 1961), pp. 131–166; Paul S. Greenlaw *et al.*, *Business Simulation* (Englewood Cliffs, N.J. Prentice-Hall, Inc., 1962); J. M. Kibbee *et al.*, *Management Games* (New York: Reinhold Publishing Corporation, 1961); J. L. McKenney, "An Evaluation of a Business Game in an MBA Curriculum," *The Journal of Business*, Vol 35, No. 8 (July 1962), pp. 278–86; M. Shubik, "Bibliography on Simulation, Gaming, Artificial Intelligence and Allied Topics," *Journal of the American Statistical Association*, Vol. 55, No. 292 (December 1960), pp. 736–51. For a survey on the use of games in American Collegiate Schools of Business see: C. R. Klasson, "Business Gaming: A Progress Report," *Academy of Management Journal*, Vol. 7, No. 3 (September 1964), pp. 175–188.

[2] F. C. Riccardi *et al.*, *Top Management Decision Simulation: The AMA Approach* (New York: American Management Association, 1957).

number of business firms use simulation to (1) examine and study complex management planning and control systems at all organizational levels in order to improve their present effectiveness in future design, (2) enable managers and workers alike to study organizational and technical systems in order to improve their abilities to operate them, and (3) gain executive acceptance of proposed operational programs by permitting them to review potential results through simulating testing of a plan.

Without question, one of the greatest contributions made possible by business management games has been that of offering a means of understanding the field of "corporate policy decision making" or the job of top management. Policy decisions determine the over-all success or failure of a business, since they normally deal with and affect all aspects of business operations. For this reason earlier methods of exposing trainees to the job of top executives largely were limited to describing what top executives did and what they should do. No way existed to examine in depth the interrelatedness of a complex set of decision variables entering into making a final choice as to over-all corporate objectives, plans, policies, and competitive strategies. Neither did the trainee fully comprehend the true nature of the class of non-structured problems confronting the chief executive officers nor the pressures of uncertainty which materially reduces the level of confidence connected with a particular course of action selected.

While no panacea, business management games did offer at least a "methodological means" for studying in a *more* analytical manner the task environment and problems confronting the "policy maker." Even though the business student or practitioner may never assume the responsibilities of top management in either large or small enterprises, an understanding of the complex economic, technical, and human processes which characterize the operation of any business are both fundamental and essential to one's effective performance within a company. So this chapter has two broad aims:

1. to describe first the meaning of business management games, and
2. second, to discuss how they can be used to demonstrate in a dynamic manner the area of corporate policy decision making.

BUSINESS MANAGEMENT GAMES

Those interested in designing games had three fundamental problems to solve: (1) to permit trainees to make decisions of the kind made by top executives, (2) to duplicate the conditions and forces or executive task environment in which decisions would have to be made, and (3) to supply the trainees with information relative to the outcome of their decisions and the status of the new executive task environment.

ELEMENTS OF SIMULATOR

Then regardless of the specific educational objectives sought or type of simulators used, all business games have three basic elements, which vary in complexity, that can be identified readily—decision-making tasks and procedures, an executive task environment, and a performance information system. Considered together these elements form a "simulator model" of a complete business operating in a given industry (total enterprise simulator) or some functional area as finance, marketing, or production (functional simulator). To illustrate, physical simulators like link trainers and wind tunnels are designed to simulate realistic physical environments in which both pilot and aircraft could be expected to perform.

AN ILLUSTRATION

The pilot trainee makes decisions about flying his link trainer in response to environmental conditions while attempting to maintain a given course and altitude. Information regarding the effectiveness of these decisions through time are displayed on an instrument panel which reflects the magnitude of deviation of the trainer's simulated flight from planned flight. Hopefully, learning occurs regarding the aerodynamics of the link trainer and the skills necessary to fly it successfully so that an effective transfer of knowledge can be made to the real aircraft in an accelerated manner.

In contrast to physical simulations, as illustrated by the link trainer example, symbolic systems simulations, the kind useful to managerial training, usually consist of a series of mathematical representations (logical and algebraic) which replicate certain business variables and their presumed interrelationships. Operation of this model through a series of discrete time periods is accomplished by the model acting on the input data (decisions of players) and computing and displaying operating results. Figure 1 shows the basic model elements of a business management simulation.

Decision making tasks and procedures. A business management game involves a group of trainees who are required to manage a hypothetical company or some part of it with the objective of training in mind. Thus game participants play the role of managers, and thus decision managers. Decisions made by participants based on an analysis of constantly changing situational factors, and within the administrative structure of their respective organizations, provide the input information to the simulated model of the executives' task environment. Normally, a number of companies participate in a particular industry, which results in an interactive competitive exercise. That is, within every industry depending upon market structure, a group of companies actively compete for market share and a dominant industry. position. Therefore, before final decisions are made, serious attention must be given to how competitors may react to a company's past decisions and anticipated future actions. For example, "How will a competitor react to another price reduction on our part?" In brief, the decisions of participants in one company affect the decisions and outcomes of decisions made by participants in other companies.

In most business management games, a large variety of decision variables must be acted upon during each period of play by the trainees. Typical

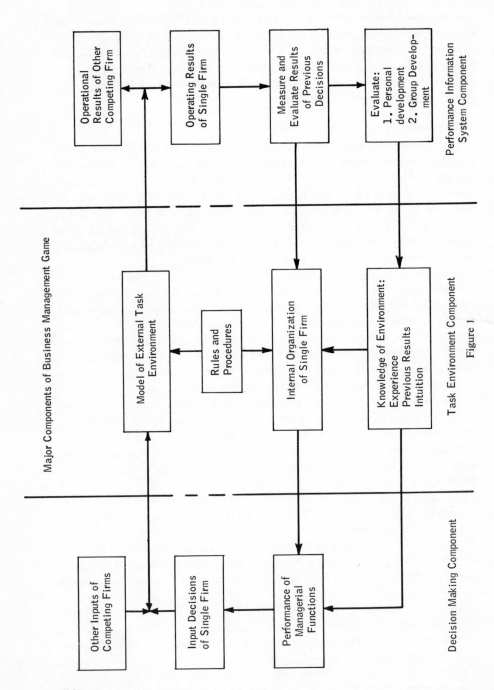

Major Components of Business Management Game

Operational Results of Other Competing Firm

Operating Results of Single Firm

Measure and Evaluate Results of Previous Decisions

Evaluate:
1. Personal development
2. Group Develop-ment

Performance Information System Component

Model of External Task Environment

Rules and Procedures

Internal Organization of Single Firm

Knowledge of Environment:
Experience
Previous Results
Intuition

Task Environment Component

Figure 1

Other Inputs of Competing Firms

Input Decisions of Single Firm

Performance of Managerial Functions

Decision Making Component

decision variables include product prices, level of advertising, promotional programs, sales force employment, capital equipment purchases, production scheduling, manpower utilization, bank loans, planned plant expansion, market development, and salesmen incentives, to mention a few.

As seen in Figure 1, there are a number of procedural decision rules which regulate how participants can act out their managerial roles. They exist simply because a simulation is an abstraction of real life. While restrictive in nature, such rules, if accepted objectively, do not measurably detract from potential learning experiences or opportunities for experimentation in the performance of managerial functions.

Executive task environment. The executive task environment is a basic element of any game and consists of two components: (1) external competitive environment and (2) internal organizational environment. Together these represent the executive task environment in which an executive must manage. Attempts to replicate this environment will vary in complexity according to educational goals sought. As more detail is built into the model, a greater degree of realism can be achieved up to a certain point.

As in every industry, chief executives are constantly trying to learn as much as possible about the character of their external environment. Knowledge of the state of this ever changing environment is essential to corporate planning so a viable adjustment can be made between the actions taken by the firm and the environmental threats and opportunities existing in the foreseeable future.

Even though an executive may be fully appraised of the status of external affairs, he may not be able to act decisively due to a hostile internal administrative environment. While the administrative organization of participants into a functioning company is largely a matter of their own doing, the net result is the presence of (1) human hostilities, conflicts, and failures to perform on schedules, (2) seemingly restrictive administrative entanglements and procedures, (3) seemingly inadequate communication systems, (4) seemingly a lack of willingness to cooperate on the parts of others, and other organizational conditions which in total replicates the internal environment in which an executive must learn to live and cope successfully.

Performance information system. Response of the external environment to actions of the players is calculated by the predetermined relationships in the model and are indicated by output information normally in the form of balance sheets, operating profit and loss statements, market reports, and various status reports. Such feedback information serves to evaluate the decision processes of the players and to reflect the worthiness of courses of action taken in terms of results achieved. From Figure 1 it is apparent that one of the major values of business simulation is the fact that participants have an opportunity to learn of the results of decisions made in terms of outcome achieved. From this they can evaluate their own personal development as well as the development of the group which functioned together to achieve results. This experience can then be used to improve the performance of participants, each in his respective decision-making area.

REAL AND SIMULATED EXPERIMENTATION

Beyond providing a trainee with an opportunity to enter the decision-making process, perhaps the most important characteristic of any business management game is that it permits experimentation and testing of basic managerial principles, proposed corporate plans, policies, and procedures prior to actual implementation. In the business world the alternative to "simulate an experimentation" is "real experimentation." In a parallel sense, trainees for many years prior to the introduction of simulation techniques were forced to accept at face value many so-called sound principles of business management without adequate proof or explanation of their validity.

Real experimentation at best is a process of "trial and error," in which all the resources of past experience, knowledge, and judgment are brought to bear on a problem. Having thoroughly studied all the information connected with a particular problem, a manager and/or his staff at some point selects one solution or another. Then the selected solution is simply applied, on the assumption that it is the best alternative available. It if fails to resolve the problem, the implementation solution may be modified or completely disregarded for another, better one.

The fact is that no solution can be considered "optimal" or "best" until tried under actual business circumstances. To find a so-called best solution many firms are forced to test their plans through experimentation with real operational plans, managers, and other resources. Ultimately, all plans must be evaluated this way. And in some instances of certain business situations experimentation is the only alternative, even though it may result in a very inefficient operation and the creation of additional unforeseen problems. Clearly, this approach often leaves the business executive apprehensive about the outcome of certain programs, because of the unavoidable uncertainty connected with them.

One of the most significant values of business games is that it permits trainees to study business problems to an extent not possible in any other way. Repeated testing of the model, with new values being assigned to model variables, allows managers to identify and study various outcomes resulting from a particular plan. This at least lets a trainee study an operating model under varying conditions that contain many different variables and inter-relationships.

In short, business management games provide a laboratory environment within which business education can be carried out. A realistic objective of laboratory training is to develop more competent managers with known degrees of development in specified areas. Laboratory training offers a unique and highly effective training methodology because it provides:

1. a more realistic training environment,

2. an incentive for a high degree of personal commitment and achievement,

3. a means for generating unstructured, yet pertinent problematic training situations and exercises as a means for trainees to examine critically their own behavior and responses to problematic situations through various feedback situations, and

4. a basis for generalizing from various learning and experiences.[3]

TOTAL ENTERPRISE SIMULATION

Total enterprise or general management's games focus upon the decisions and problems of the chief or top executive of a business firm, as already mentioned. They are designed to give participants experience in making business decisions at a top executive level, a level at which decisions in one functional area will interact with those made in other areas in the firm. One of the difficulties involved in the solution of corporate-wide problems is the compartmentalized thinking that traditional organization structures and standardized procedures tend to impose upon managers of the involved departments. Normally each manager is motivated by departmental objectives which often conflict with objectives in other departments. Solutions to such top management problems generally are only reached through compromise. Everyone gives and takes, with the end result being something less than the best economic solution from the over-all company viewpoint. Due to the existence of this well-known problem, general management games provide an opportunity for trainees to gain and appreciate an understanding of this interactional problem.

KINDS OF LEARNING POSSIBLE

Generally, what can a trainee learn from participating in a management game? This question is not easily answered. As with most training techniques and methods, the trainer often accepts "face validity"—the method seems to work well and the trainees like the device. Little has been done by way of scientifically determining exactly what can be taught and how well it is taught via simulation. But the results speak for themselves. Most trainees speak favorably about their experience, which generally includes all or part of the following benefits:

1. An ability to work effectively and willingly with other people including superiors, peers, and subordinates

2. An ability to collect, organize, and use necessary information in the process of making decisions

3. An ability to forecast and develop operational plans, the consequences of which can be estimated

[3] See Chris Argyris, "A Brief Description of Laboratory Education," *Training Directors Journal*, Vol. 17, No. 10 (October 1963), pp. 4–9.

4. An ability to develop in an initial form executive judgment which normally takes years of actual experience to acquire

5. An ability to appreciate the meaning of calculated risk and to make decisions under various conditions of uncertainty

6. An ability to understand complex functional interrelationships within a company

7. An ability to consider and formulate corporate long-range plans, policies, and product-market strategy as well as operational ones

8. An ability to analyze problems systematically and to use appropriate analytical tools and techniques for their solutions.

Next, let us examine some of the specific uses to which a total enterprise simulation can be put in learning more about the economics of the firm and the policy decision making role of the manager.

PLACING THEORY INTO PRACTICE

The subject of Business Policy deals with two major problem areas confronting top management of a company: (1) formulation of corporate strategies, and (2) implementation of selected strategies. The significance of each of these problem areas can be demonstrated vividly to participants of business management games in a variety of different ways. The particular approach used will depend on the kind of simulation used, the time available, and the specific educational objectives to be achieved. The following kinds of experiences mentioned are intended to illustrate the kinds of knowledge which can be gained about the subject area of Policy and the problems encountered with placing theory into practice.

FORMULATING CORPORATE STRATEGIES

A major set of business decisions often called "strategic decisions" involves the choice of organizational goals, determination of appropriate policies, and development of operational plans for achieving goals within policy directives. Broadly, these decisions describe a company's strategy for competing in a given task environment. It represents management's considered judgment as to how limited resources can be used best in exploiting market opportunities and/or minimizing a variety of competitive threats at an acceptable level of risk. It represents a set of resource allocation decisions to products and markets in hopes of realizing a given rate of return on invested capital. It represents a series of trade-offs between short-run profitability and long-run growth or perhaps between market position and product line expansion. It represents a conservative, adaptive, or innovational philosophy of business operations. And finally it represents some level of executive confidence in estimating future states of affair with sufficient accuracy so that operational plans may yield hoped-for results.

While all the above notions sound nice and worthy to the interested student of Policy, their true meaning and significance are experienced when the gaming participant is requested by the Chairman of the Board of Directors of a simulated company to formulates a corporate strategy in fact. Developing a finalized corporate plan expressible in the form of a pro forma profit and loss statement and balance sheet can be a very frustrating although enlightening experience. Gaming participants become aware sooner or later of a number of problems they must live with when engaged in strategic planning. Strategic planning is inherently complex, with no simple set of procedural rules to follow. Other than describing what needs to be done, few books even attempt to explain the process by which corporate-wide plans are arrived at. Moreover, it is a continuous process involving (1) the setting of environmental boundaries, (2) searching for information about present state of a defined environment, (3) forecasting future states of the environment, and (4) using gathered information to prepare a master corporate plan.

Setting environmental boundaries. Identifying the boundaries of a firm's *task environment* bears importantly upon: (1) gathering useful and timely planning information, (2) minimizing the cost of collecting, storing, and handling this information, and (3) recognizing the economic opportunity cost of various alternative oportunities. Today this remains an unsolved problem for many firms. Faced with such questions as, "What should be done?" "What do we want to be?" "What can we be?" trainees in a simulation setting at some point learn the true meaning and value of setting economic objectives. To say objectives are important is rather academic and meaningless in and of itself. Meaning is attached when a participant is forced to identify specific industries along with statements about desired and achievable levels of performance within selected markets. With the large number of factors bearing on such decisions coupled with the presence of uncertainties, the difficulty of this undertaking is quickly recognized, especially when a multi-product firm is involved.

Searching for information. When and how does a company start searching for information to satisfy strategic planning requirements? A variety of needs and events trigger search procedures, for example, decreased sales, poor profits, customer complaints, and growing inventories. But participants become aware of the need to develop systematic management information systems capable of (1) supplying timely information about their current and projected task environment and (2) responding to the demands of users for information about internal conditions and operations. Gaming participants quickly learn that there is a decided difference between collecting statistical data, a factual accounting of some transaction, and the collating of this data into knowledgeable and useful information for planning and control purposes. A manager must develop his own information system which both generates and supplies information for definite decision problems. For the system to be effective it must also receive *and* supply information to the company-wide information system; it must be "on-line."

Forecasting future environments. Imperfect knowledge of future conditions makes managerial decision-making difficult. Participants learn the sole purpose of forecasting is to reduce the amount of uncertainty connected with making strategic decisions. As the degree of uncertainty increases due to management's inability to foresee and prepare for future conditions, decisions become more imperfect at all managerial levels, resulting in decreasing economic returns to invested resources. Often a highly unstable environment, for example, defies the most conscientious projections of managers with a firm suffering serious consequences. To learn that a manager seeks to minimize his forecasting error rather than to maximize the accuracy of his forecast is also an enlightening experience.

Using information and forecasts. Once having ordered information, having stated appropriate assumptions about future states of affairs, the creative task of preparing a corporate master plan is at hand. Defining the most desirable relationship between a firm and its task environment in such a way as (1) to facilitate the formulation of current operational planning and (2) to enable the continuation of developmental planning into the future turns out also to be a difficult responsibility at best for the conscientious gaming participants. Assuming the generation of good planning information, a manager still must enter into the creative task of using it to his advantage and to the disadvantage of his rivals.

Some behavioral observations. In the process of formulating a viable corporate strategy, behavioral implications of managing soon become visible to the gaming participant. While the economic data may indicate overwhelmingly one course of action, the personal value structure of the gaming president may lead to yet another course of action. Or the acting president may fail to fulfill his leadership role; as a result, the driving force so necessary to purposeful group action is absent. Or all gaming officers may assert such aggressive functional behavior that one stalemate after another occurs, with a consequence of delayed action and a faltering market position. Or failure of one executive to accept willingly a high level of risk can result in many lost opportunities. When the Chairman of the Board summarily rejects the proposed corporate master plan, what impact does this have upon the willingness of an executive group to modify or re-plan operations? These and many other types of organizational processes can be observed and dealt with by the gaming participants. Surprisingly enough, these experienced patterns of behavior are not unlike those found in the business world, including the continual pressures of inadequate time, unplanned for results, an unending stream of problems, and constant conflicts of opinions and perceptions.

But somehow, some kind of master corporate plan that includes (1) a statement about the simulated firm's economic objectives, (2) a statement of standards, and (3) a statement about the product-market strategy necessary to accomplish economic objectives is formulated, as illustrated in Figure 2.

Top Management Developmental and Operational Planning Framework

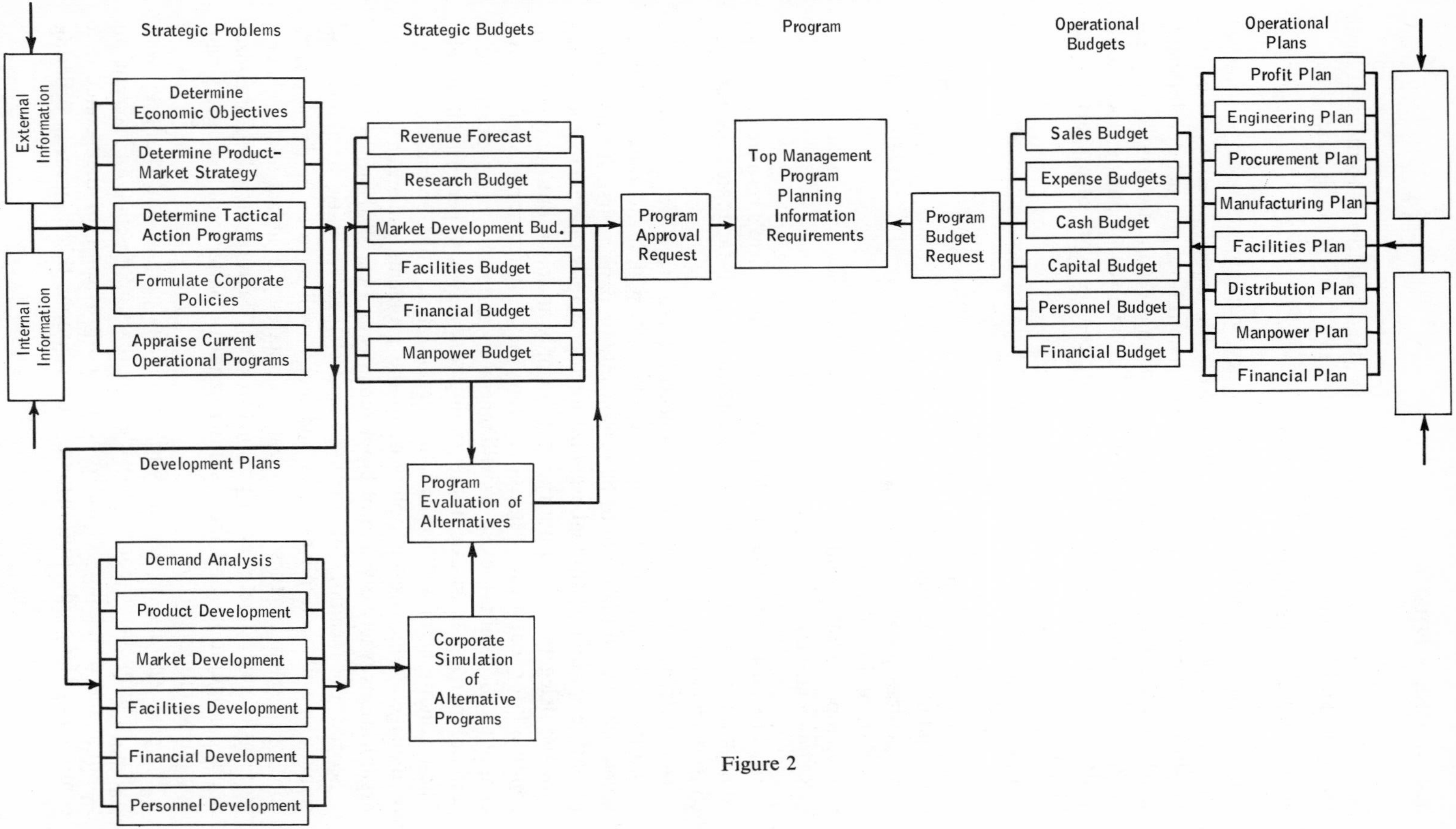

Figure 2

The simulation permits ultimately (1) a testing of strategies to discover their strengths and weaknesses, and (2) a revising of them through time.

IMPLEMENTING CORPORATE STRATEGIES

Once certain strategic decisions are made, participants need to translate them into a specific *tactical action program* for implementation. In brief, a product-market strategy (whether market penetration, product development, market development, or product and/or market diversification) must be translated into a product-market program. This involves preparing operational budgets and time-phase schedules of activities. The work of preparing a detailed:

1. profit plan
2. engineering plan
3. procurement plan
4. manufacturing plan
5. facilities plan
6. distribution plan
7. manpower plan, and
8. financial plan

brings into clear focus the problems of mobilizing a firm's resources through some kind of an administrative organization which facilitates the resource conversion process.

Designing operations. Problems concerning the structure of information, authority, and responsibility flows must be dealt with if the above set of detailed operational plans are to be responsibly prepared. First, it will become patently clear that traditional organizational principles relating to good structure and delegation of authority represent only an initial but not a sufficient condition for cooperative group action. As a functioning organization, communications must exist, a willingness to cooperate must exist, and a common purpose must exist if the gaming company is to perform effectively. These conditions of a dynamic living organization must be created by acts of managers which reflect solutions to the problems generated by formal organizations where division of labor remains as a classical principle.

Second, the meanings of organizational change, stability, flexibility, and stagnation will come alive. Ways and means will have to be developed to cope with each of these organizational states. Organizational behavior patterns of subordinates are a product of many factors, including organizational configurations and the resulting behavior patterns of executives who operate within them.

Planning operations. Developing operational plans and budgets with which to implement corporate-wide programs represents an exercise in detailing and dovetailing operative tasks and providing for their concurrent control. For the production manager, for example, this may mean ordering materials and parts, scheduling and dispatching shop orders, scheduling men and machinery to these orders, and developing a system for monitoring actual work-in-process. In brief, the gaming participants come to learn that operational planning information involves identifiable, measurable, and controllable transactions concerning personnel, facilities, supplies, equipment, work-in-process, products, and/or customers. Each of these above elements becomes a specific part of an operational plan and is usually stated in terms of quantity, quality, cost, and coordinated time standards.

Controlling operations. Failure to recognize the kinds of control information necessary to constrain and regulate actual operations inevitably leads to a high cost inefficient business. Participants have the opportunity to experience first hand the conditions which develop in the presence of either an effective or ineffective control system. Moreover, business management games can be used to demonstrate that a communications control system regulates systems performance by (1) supplying information which functions to cause and guide actions to achieve a predetermined goal and (2) gathering information feedback about the manner in which these events transpire. Quickly the gaming observer can become sensitive to how information affects behavior of each part of a business system and serves to connect or disconnect discrete parts of the system.

EVALUATING DECISIONS AND RESULTS

Decisions yield results. Following a decision period, which normally represents one quarter or three months of real time operations, gaming participants eagerly await news of their successes or failures in accomplishing stated objectives. Whatever the nature of the results, they need to evaluate and explain existing performance gaps as well as successes in order that realistic plans can be prepared for succeeding quarters of operations. Unless time is spent on this kind of activity, chances are small that subsequent decisions will be correct in view of the changing nature of market forces and internal supply capabilities. A number of useful insights can be gained from such re-appraisals, besides explanations to the Board Chairman as to why sales, costs, and profit expectations were not realized. Some of these are now examined.

Assessing company's strategy. Did it work? If not, why not? When answers to these questions about a company's strategy are arrived at, some conclusions normally can be drawn:

1. Assessing opportunities and competition. Often market opportunities are not properly identified due to poor market information and/or the inability to predict accurately a highly instable task environment. In addition, failure to assess properly the strengths of competing firms diminishes the chance of success of a company's strategy.

2. Assessing corporate capabilities. To exploit any market opportunity, a company needs to know exactly what industry performance requirements

need to be met in order to be successful. Strategies which fail to compare a company's financial, technical, and managerial resources with those required to compete in a given industry are poorly formulated and have a high probability of failure.

3. Assessing merits of over-all planning. Even good plans may fail to materialize. By recognizing this fact, trainees come to appreciate the limitations of advance planning due to the impossibility of accurate forecasting. There is no way to determine exactly what a competitor will do under varying market conditions. However, the true value of any strategy can be revealed to gaming participants—as providing management with a number of possible future business environments, none of which would seriously jeopardize the survival of the firm if anticipated correctly. Strategies serve to minimize the inevitable adjustments which will be required to a changing task environment. Strategies provide acceptable and defensible limits within which such changes can be profitably executed.

Optimization internal strategies. In any organization, resources are ideally allocated among principal functional areas to insure some optimal realization of over-all company goals. Gaming results vividly point out the inherent difficulties associated with this aim. Marketing policies and strategies, if granted top priorities, can drastically reduce the effectiveness of research and development and production policies and procedures. And all of the latter strategies can be nullified by an organization's conservative financial policy or one imposed by financial institutions. Often in the real business world it is impossible to develop an optimal capital structure because of external money and market constraints. Participants in the simulation are exposed to numerous deterrents to a truly integrated form of business operation, including the desire for functional rather than organizational success.

Estimating errors. Yesterday's decisions generate tomorrow's operating problems for many organizations. The kinds and magnitude of these problems depend upon the size of the estimating errors originally made. To illustrate consider this example. High sales estimates may call for a large increase in the production of a product. This in turn can generate increased working capital requirements to finance direct labor and direct material costs. If actual sales for the planning period are, say, 30 per cent below estimates, some distinct problems are generated. First, sales revenue drops, creating an unanticipated cash flow problem—especially if a company is in a tight cash position and dependent upon current sources of operating funds. Second, excessive inventories, both raw material and finished goods, may force curtailment of productive programs which may generate lay-off costs, higher per unit fixed costs for current production, and thus higher production break-even points. Third, pressure to move finished good inventories may result in price concessions that in turn further aggravate the cash flow problem. While hypothetical, this set of operational problems is rather typical of difficulties that come into being because of incorrect decisions about future states of affairs. Participants come to appreciate the need to explore the consequences of alternative levels of operations and to take steps to minimize the number and size of estimating errors in *key* or *critical areas* of operations. Too, they understand why many real business firms never seem to have time to consider tomorrow's business and to engage in developmental planning. The reason is simple. Executives spend most of their time on operational problems as their company's strategic gap continues to grow and the company continues to become less profitable and competitive.

Formulating policies. How are decision rules formulated that permit sufficient opportunism at acceptable levels of risk and still provide for continuity and consistency in executive thought and action? Formulation of corporate policies is a necessary and vital reponsibility of management. The absence of product line, price, market, and financial policies, to mention a few, all contribute to the estimate errors mentioned above. Beyond the time pressures and changing character of business, there is another reason why policy remains a major problem area of administrators. How are useful policies formulated? Participants in a simulating exercise can examine the factors which enter into formulating effective decision rules. Beyond recognition that effective policies are vital and difficult to formulate, let alone enforce, the knowledge is acquired that experience, which implies time, in an industry is a necessary prerequisite to policy formulation.

SOME CONCLUDING REMARKS

And so goes company life from one quarter to the next. Gaming participants rise to new sets of problems in new and ever changing environments. New plans are developed only to be changed by the forces of the market place and the ability of company management to act on and react to them.

As a manager assuming a given role in a quasi-realistic training setting, each gaming participant can learn about his own analytical capacities and administrative behavior if he is willing to look introspectively at himself. Admitting the limitations of any simulation regardless of how simple or complex it may be, both trainer and trainee can gain as much or as little from the experience as they care to put into it. While the setting surely is different as well as the rewards and penalties for level of performance achieved, the problems are essentially the same as in the business world. The kinds of experiences mentioned above merely represent a limited sample of the potential that exists for developing an understanding of the management function of the firm. Rise to the occasion, and the rewards, I am sure, will be worthy of the effort. But, as in the business world, a truly high price is paid for continuing success.

2. BUSINESS GAMES— PLAY ONE!*

—G. R. ANDLINGER

The grooming of executives for positions of increased responsibility has always presented a dilemma to business. To qualify for any top-level job, a man must have "sound business judgment," "breadth of vision," "ability to integrate parts of the business," and related skills. Yet how is he able to acquire these qualities before he is in a top-level job? Of course, books, training courses, rotation programs, and work on committees can give a man some exposure to the problems of making the transition from the operational to the judgmental level. But the fact remains that only through experience can he develop real skill in making decisions at the top level.

Business gaming is the first promising attempt to provide this experience by simulating the real-life operations of a business and forcing the participants to cope with the same kind of problems that face the top management of a company. By stripping away nonessentials, a game makes it possible to simulate several years of a company's life in one to two days.

A business game can be defined as a set of rules that corresponds to the economics of a business as realistically as possible within the limitations of a game structure. This type of gaming, which can aptly be called "operational gaming," has no relation to "game theory," which is a theoretical approach to the solutions of conflict situations. Operational gaming is essentially simulation and thus provides a framework for making trial-and-error decisions rather than for evolving an optimum strategy.

Recently both the American Management Association and McKinsey & Company, Inc., have developed operational games. The focus of this discussion will be on McKinsey's experimental "Business Management Game." The first version of this game was developed by the author, prior to joining

* Reprinted by permission from the *Harvard Business Review*, March–April 1958, pp. 115–125.

McKinsey, and by Jay R. Greene, now with the General Electric Company's Computer Department.

Both the AMA game and McKinsey's game include the same key elements of a business—marketing, production, research and development, and so forth. The AMA game, however, deals essentially with a consumer goods environment, while the Business Management Game deals with capital goods companies. In addition, the Business Management Game introduces the realistic element of time lags between decision making and results, and lends itself to playing under informal "do-it-yourself" conditions.

In this article I shall:

1. Outline and explain the basic concepts of the Business Management Game.
2. Show how it can be played in a company with only a small amount of easy-to-reproduce equipment—*not* an electronic computer. (Thus businessmen can conveniently evaluate its usefulness.)
3. Indicate how gaming can be used as a supplement to management development programs in the vital area of decision-making experience.

BASIC OBJECTIVES

Games are as old as man. Usually their basic objective is entertainment. The Business Management Game, however, aims not at entertainment but at learning. Other differences between it and a game like Monopoly, for example are:

• The degree to which it approaches reality.
• The degree to which the players' experience, judgment, and skill—as opposed to luck—influence the outcome.

If any business game is to serve a purpose beyond that of a fascinating toy, there must be some transfer of learning from the game situation to reality. While there probably is some such transfer from playing a generalized business game that mirrors "any company" and not a particular firm, an executive could derive infinitely greater benefit from a game that permits him to practice guiding the destiny of his own company or one in his own industry—which, unfortunately, is unavailable at this early stage in the development of business gaming. The success of specific war games, which the military has been using for years to simulate combat situations for the training of officers, however, holds great promise for similar applications in business in due course.

The Business Management Game is a case in point. We started it in 1956 with the idea of applying war-gaming techniques to business. In the course of the year we tested, modified, and retested the game many times to develop a fine balance between realism and playability. The more closely a game resembles reality, the more cumbersome it becomes—until it is no longer playable. Hence, there is a need to compromise. Also, we designed the game to be relatively stable. No extreme strategy can result in sudden success; yet players can gain outstanding success if they are good enough—or bankruptcy if they are not careful.

The game is partly deterministic and partly probabilistic. Some results are determined directly by the action of the players; others are, to varying degrees, subject to chance or probability. The weight of the elements in the game is such that the longer the game, the smaller the influence of luck.

SETTING UP THE GAME

This game incorporates the key elements of a one-product capital goods company which is competing with one or two other companies for the same market. These elements, which I shall define in detail later, are:

- The Market
- Marketing
- Advertising
- Research and Development
- Production
- Finance
- Competition

PLAYERS & UMPIRES

The game may be played with either two or three teams, or "companies"; and for this description I shall assume a three-company game. Players are generally divided into teams of three to four men each, although it is possible to play the game with just one man on a team. The teams, each running a company, are placed in separate rooms. Company organization may be left to the players—that is, a team may adopt a committee management approach; or it may assign a specific responsibility to each player, naming a president, a controller, a sales manager, and a production manager.

If the game is played by three teams, an umpire group of three or four who know the game is required. They have full information about the game, each company's actions, and the state of the market. Thus, they calculate the operating results of each team's set of decisions. All their decisions are dictated by the rules of the game, except that they decide the trend of the market at the beginning of the game (see "The Market" in the section on rules of play).

TOOLS & MATERIALS

The three basic tools of the game are: random number tables, the game board (see Exhibit I; this can easily be copied or reproduced in black and white), and the decision form (see Exhibit II).

Exhibit 1   Game Board and Symbols

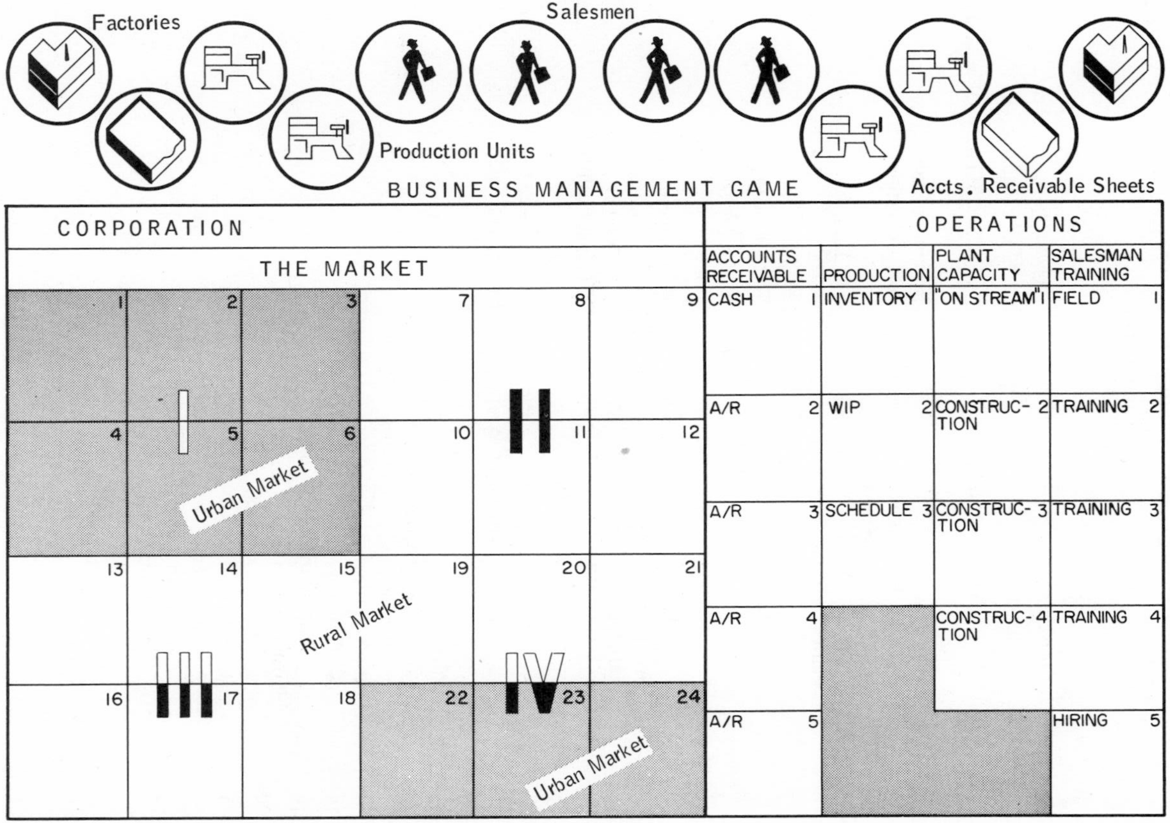

Salesmen

Production Units

Factories

Accts. Receivable Sheets

BUSINESS MANAGEMENT GAME

CORPORATION

THE MARKET

1	2	3	
4	5	6	
13	14	15	
16	17	18	

Urban Market

Rural Market

Urban Market

7	8	9
10	11	12
19	20	21
22	23	24

Urban Market

OPERATIONS

ACCOUNTS RECEIVABLE	PRODUCTION	PLANT CAPACITY	SALESMAN TRAINING
9 CASH	1 INVENTORY	1 ON STREAM	1 FIELD	1
A/R	2 WIP	2 CONSTRUC- TION	2 TRAINING	2
A/R	3 SCHEDULE	3 CONSTRUC- TION	3 TRAINING	3
A/R	4	CONSTRUC-4 TION	4 TRAINING	4
A/R	5		HIRING	5

641

Exhibit II
Decision Form

_____ *Corporation*   *Quarter*_____ *Year*_____

SALES	TOTAL ASSETS	DISPOSITION OF CASH

SALES

1 _____
2 _____
3 _____
4 _____
5 _____
6 _____
7 _____
8 _____
9 _____
10 _____
11 _____
12 _____
13 _____
14 _____
15 _____
16 _____
17 _____
18 _____
19 _____
20 _____
21 _____
22 _____
23 _____
24 _____
_____

TOTAL ASSETS

Cash   _____
Accounts Receivable   _____
Inventory—Finished Goods _____
          —WIP   _____
Plant   _____

Total Assets   _____

WORK IN PROCESS

Fixed Cost   _____
Variable Cost   (____)* _____
Total WIP

DISPOSITION OF CASH

Beginning Cash   _____
A/R Collections   _____

Total Income   _____

Total Expenses   _____
WIP Cost   _____

Plant Investment   _____

Total Outgo   _____
Endging Cash Balance   _____

PROFIT AND LOSS STATEMENT
Units

	Units		
Sales			
Beginning Inventory	____	____	_____
Production	____	____	
Total Inventory	____		_____
Less Units Sold	____		_____
Ending Inventory	____		
Gross Margin			_____
Hiring Expenses	_____		
Salaries	_____		
Advertising	_____		
Research and Development	_____		
Factoring Expense	_____		
Staff Work	_____		
Total Expenses	_____		
Net Profit			_____

The random number tables, which can generally be found in statistical textbooks, are used by the umpire group only. Each of the umpires should have one. Serving much the same purpose as the throwing of dice, they provide the answers to all questions in which probability is a factor. For instructions on how to use these tables, see the section on "Umpire Routine" at the end of this article.

Each team has a game board, preferably about 20 by 30 inches, which represents the physical operations of its company. The left-hand half of the game board represents the market, with the tinted areas representing urban markets, the white areas rural markets. Each square is a customer. The right-hand half represents operations; the spaces in the vertical columns indicate that decisions made during one time period do not become effective until some time in the future. At the beginning of each period all operations move *up* one space. For example:

When a salesman is hired, he is put on the lowest space in the "Salesman Training" column. After four time periods allowing for hiring and training time, he has arrived at the top space and may be put into the field (left-hand half of the board).

In addition to the game board, various symbols are needed to represent resources. For this purpose, physical models or drawings on slips of paper will suffice. The maximum number needed for a three-company game is approximately:

Salesmen	60
Factories	20
Production units	300
Accounts receivable sheets	250

The decision form shown in Exhibit II is the financial reflection of a company's operations. The extreme left-hand column is provided so that the umpires can inform a company of the customers from whom it has received sales during the past time period. The other sections correspond fairly closely to standard financial forms. For every time period, each team will need two decision forms and one sheet of carbon paper, so that the umpires can keep a copy.

Actually, the use of the decision form is optional. The game could be played with poker chips or paper money, with some loss in educational value but with a reduction in the time needed for play and less chance of error.

TIME PERIODS

Each time period represents one-quarter of a year. For inexperienced players, the period should be about 20 minutes. As players gain familiarity with the rules and mechanics of the game, however, the quarters should be shortened to no more than 15 minutes.

The players make decisions at the beginning of each time period and enter them on the decision form or give them orally to the umpires. The umpires then collect the decision forms, calculate the impact of each company's decisions on those of the others, enter the results of these calculations on the decision forms, and return the forms to the teams. After reviewing these results, the teams decide on new courses of action, and the cycle starts again.

Each time the teams receive their operating results, they are given the next "quarter" deadline. If a company misses the deadline set by the umpires, its sales volume is automatically reduced to zero for that quarter.

PREGAME PREPARATION

Before the game is started, players should be given a general description of the rules and the mechanics of game play. This article could serve this purpose if the instructions to the umpire were deleted.

In addition, it is helpful to provide the history of a company in the game, as reflected in its financial statements, for a period of perhaps two years. The experience of one company in a previous game could serve this purpose. This gives the players an opportunity to analyze the past, gain a better understanding of the game, and plan a definite course of action before starting play. If this is done, all teams start with the same company history; otherwise, all companies simply start with $400,000 of capital.

WINNING & LOSING

It should be emphasized that the purpose of playing this game is not to win it but to learn from the experience. (Over a period of time, of course, winning can be considered one measure of learning.) To avoid an overly competitive atmosphere, it is helpful to have each team spell out its general objectives and its management philosophy at the beginning of play and then elicit each team's own evaluation of the soundness of its policy framework at a postgame critique session.

A company's progress is judged by changes in its total assets, profits, sales volume, and share of market. The necessary information is taken from the operating results of each company and plotted by the umpires on large boards at the end of each time period. The results of the successive time period are then totaled to determine the company's position at the end of the game.

Critique sessions held at the end of a game can often be the most fruitful and stimulating aspect of the experience. Generally, critique sessions should be divided into four parts:

1. Umpire review of game results and general observations.
2. Self-critique by each company team.
3. Outline of the strategy each company would adopt if there were a "next time," to point up specific game lessons learned.
4. General discussion of the training value of the game in terms of each participant's decision making in reality, pointing up general lessons learned.

RULES OF PLAY

In this section I shall give a brief general description of each game element and the specific values, rules, and probabilities that define each element in quantitative terms. Instructions for the umpires are included at each point; but remember that they should not be given to the players.

THE MARKET

The market is made up of 24 customers. Each customer's potential is different; in any one time period, a few customers are not buying any units, while others may buy four or five units (at $10,000 per unit) *if* a salesman is able to make a sale.

The market is dynamic, so the customer potentials change. If the market is growing, they change upward; should the market be hit by a recession, however, they may drop drastically. The long-term trend of the market is announced to the players; short-term fluctuations are not. If a company is interested in finding out what the total market potential is in any time period, a $2,000 expenditure for market research will buy this information from the umpires.

The 24 customers divide geographically into four regions on the game board, each region containing six accounts. This geographical division allows a company to do local advertising (see the section on "Advertising the Product") and conduct market research in only one region at a time. Such market research which tells a company the potential of each customer in the region and permits the pinpointing of the direct selling effort (see the section on "Marketing the Product"), may be obtained by paying the umpires $30,000 for "staff work."

In addition to the separation into geographical regions, the market breaks down into one rural and two urban markets. The significance of this distinction is that in an urban market, where a salesman can make more calls per day, he has two chances of making a sale during each time period, while in the rural market he has only one chance.

If at the end of a year a company desires to find out what portion of the total market it has been able to capture, it may buy share-of-market information from the umpires for $2,000,

MARKETING THE PRODUCT

Units are sold by salesmen, who call on the 24 accounts in the market. In an urban market a salesman may make two calls per quarter; and in a rural market, only one.

In the presence of an umpire, the sales manager of a company points to the accounts he wants to call on. The umpire will tell him, after examining the random number table, whether a sale is made or not. How many units are sold to a customer will depend on competitive action. The completed decision form, returned to the company by the umpire at the end of the particular period, contains the actual sales results by accounts.

Wherever a salesman has two calls, he must make the second call on any of three to eight accounts adjacent to the first square called on; that is, he may not jump across territories. If no sale is made on the first call, he may, of course, call on the same account again during the same quarter. Furthermore, there is no limit to the number of salesmen who may call on one account in one time period. Between quarters, salesmen may be moved to any accounts that the company wishes them to cover during the next quarter.

Each time a salesman makes a call, he has a certain fixed probability of making a sale. This chance of making a sale may be increased in one of three ways or a combination thereof:

• A company may intensify its direct selling effort by having more than one salesman cover one account as described above. In such a case, if the first salesman makes a sale, the second one may move to any adjoining account for his calls.

• A company may support a salesman's effort by advertising (see "Advertising the Product").

• A company may attempt to improve its product by spending more money for a research and development effort (see "Research and Development").

Every salesman costs $10,000 to hire and then $1,000 per quarter in salary. (Since the product he will be selling is a high-price, complicated unit, it takes one year to train a salesman before he may be sent out into the field.) There is a possibility that a salesman will resign, in which case the umpire informs the company of this loss.

ADVERTISING THE PRODUCT

Product advertising in any quarter increases the salesmen's chances of making a sale. It covers only the region or regions (I, II,III, and IV on the game board) that the company designates, and it is effective in the current quarter only. Advertising costs $3,000 per page per region, and a company may buy up to five pages of advertising in any region in any quarter.

RESEARCH & DEVELOPMENT

If a company can develop a superior product, it gains a competitive advantage. Usually research and development have to be fairly continuous to achieve a product improvement, but a "crash program" may yield results in a relatively short time. The minimum research effort per quarter costs $10,000, but a company may invest more than that in multiples of $10,000.

The umpire notifies the company immediately when its research and development program has produced results, and all units scheduled for production in that quarter are considered to be equipped with the improvement. To find out the extent to which customers will prefer an improved product, $5,000 of market research (obtained from the umpires) is needed.

Of course, these ground rules can be altered to fit a company's situation more closely—just as the ground rules for other aspects of the Business Management Game can. A company manufacturing equipment for railroads may well want to use different units of research expenditure than would a company making dies for plastic products. The length of time necessary to get results from research also varies greatly from company to company, as does the cost of research to measure customer reactions to new products. These and other rules can—and in many cases should—be tailored to the realities of the industry.

The umpires will tell a company as soon as a competing team introduces an improved product in the market. The players can then counter with a stepped-up marketing effort or a crash research and development program.

If a company is interested in finding out the total industry research and development expenditures for the past year, such information is available from the umpires for $1,000.

INCREASING PRODUCTION

The initial plant which each company must build costs $150,000, and it has a maximum throughput of 5 units each quarter. From then on a company may add other production lines for $30,000 each. But each such $30,000 increment will increase the maximum throughput by 5.

A company must pay for increased capacity as soon as it decides to start construction. Construction time is nine months (three time periods), and only after completion (that is, when the top space under " Plant Capacity " is reached) may the first unit be put into " work in process " for the new production line. The companies are not allowed to sell or otherwise dispose of excess capacity.

The total lead time in producing units in a company's plant is six months. First, production is scheduled, and this involves no financial outlay. Then in the next quarter units are put into " work in process " and must be paid for. In the subsequent quarter these units come off the production line, are added to inventory, and may be sold.

Total production cost contains a fixed and a variable element. The fixed cost is incurred each quarter, regardless of how many units are produced. At a maximum capacity of five units per quarter, the fixed cost is $6,000, and the variable cost per unit is $3,000. As capacity is increased by additional production lines, fixed costs rise and the variable cost per unit decreases. If a company, prior to adding a line, wants to know the exact costs it will incur at the next higher level of capacity, it can get that information from the umpires for $2,000, but otherwise the umpires will inform the company what production costs are when the new line goes into production.

Units are added to inventory at actual cost. When a unit is sold, however, it is deducted from inventory at the average cost (total inventory investment divided by number of units in inventory).

FINANCIAL MANAGEMENT

The management of a company's available capital is of critical importance. Each company starts with $400,000 of capital and can grow only through reinvested earnings. Profitability will be in direct relation to the skill with which the various parts of the business are kept in harmony with each other to achieve sound growth.

The price per unit of product is fixed at $10,000. When a sale is made, accounts receivable are increased by the total amount of the sale, and on the game board an accounts receivable symbol is placed on the fifth space in the "accounts receivable" column. Every quarter this symbol is moved up one space until after four quarters it reaches the top space and becomes cash. Competitive pressure in the industry forces the extension of credit; hence the one-year collection lag.

If a company is short of cash, accounts receivable may be factored to get cash immediately. The cost of doing this is 20% of the amount factored.

RULES FOR COMPETITION

Each company competes for the same accounts with the same product. If only one company sells a customer, it gets all of his business; but if two or more make a sale, the customer splits his business as follows:

1. If the customer potential splits evenly *into multiples of* $10,000, it is divided equally; e.g., $20,000 to be split between two companies or $30,000 to be split among three companies. Otherwise follow steps (2) and (3).

2. In an uneven split the odd $10,000 (or $20,000 in a three-way split) goes to the company (or companies) with the greater advantage in advertising and/or improved product. For example:

Case	Number of companies selling a customer	Potential	Split
A	2	$10,000	To the one company with the greater advantage.
B	2	30,000	$10,000 to each; the odd $10,000 as in Case A.
C	3	10,000	As in Case A.
D	3	20,000	$10,000 each to the two companies with the greater advantage.

3. In the event there is no differentiation in advantage to decide an uneven split as in (2), the odd amount over what can be divided equally is declared "no sale" in that quarter.

It is of course the duty of the umpires to make these divisions when necessary, always remembering that the split is even where possible and otherwise is determined by relative advantage in advertising and/or improved product, as set forth above.

To make the income and expense items of all categories easily available to the players and the umpires, use the summary in Exhibit III.

UMPIRE ROUTINE

The foregoing description of game rules gives an indication of the scope of, and the steps in, the umpiring process.[1] The role of the umpires is vital in this

---

[1] *Note:* Umpire's instructions omitted from text in this reprint.

Exhibit III
Summary of Income and Expense Items

Selling price per unit	$10,000
Salesmen:	
(a) Hiring expense per salesman	$10,000
(b) Salary per quarter, whether in the field or in training	$1,000
Advertising:	
One page of advertising (covering one region) per quarter (with a maximum of five pages per quarter per region)	$3,000
Plant:	
(a) Initial plant (maximum throughput of five units per quarter)	$150,000
(b) Each additional production line (maximum throughput of five units per quarter)	$30,000
Research and development:	
Minimum per quarter (with no upper limit)	$10,000
Production (at five units of throughput):	
(a) Fixed cost per quarter	$6,000
(b) Variable cost per unit per quarter	$3,000
Staff work (information):	
(a) Total market potential	$2,000
(b) Share of market	$2,000
(c) Total industry R & D expense	$1,000
(d) Production costs in advance	$2,000
(e) Market research for one region	$30,000
(f) Market research to test new product	$5,000
Penalties:	
(a) Factoring of accounts receivable	20%
(b) Missing of a deadline set by umpires	no sales

game, so they must understand all these rules clearly. Exhibit IV gives in detail the routine that umpires should follow in each time period.

When the umpires finish the cycle of steps in Exhibit IV, they begin over again. Q skillful umpire group can handle the steps in approximately five to seven minutes, which, assuming fifteen-minute deadlines, means that each company has about ten minutes to review its operating results, decide on a new course of action, and record it on the decision form.

Each of the three umpires determines sales results, completes financial forms and records, and so forth for one company, but they should be rotated among the companies periodically. A fourth or " head" umpire may determine the credit on split sales, plot sales results, and set the deadlines; if only three umpires are available, however, they perform these functions as a group.

CONCLUSION

After having played the Business Management Game, the participants might want to change certain rules or adopt others to adapt this game more closely to the characteristics of the real environment. I have previously indicated the kinds of changes that might be made for research; similar ones might be made for the effectiveness of advertising, salesmen's salaries, sales prices, production costs, and other elements of the game. Executives may gain added insight from this process of analyzing the key factors and variables in a company's operation and translating them into game rules.

Exhibit IV

Steps in the Umpiring Process

Step	Procedure
1.	Change market potential.
2.	Examine random number table for loss of salesmen.
3.	At deadline, go out to your assigned company.
4.	Collect filled-in decision form.
5.	Examine random number table to determine whether or not there is a sale for each call of the company's salesmen, and record each sale with a mark in the appropriate account space on the decision form.
6.	Return to umpires' room.
7.	Determine split-sale credits.
8.	Complete decision form (sales, ending inventory, gross margin, profit, accounts receivable, and total assets).
9.	Write information on market research or other requested staff work on slips of paper.
10.	Add new R & D expenditure to previous company total for this item.
11.	Examine random number table for product improvement, if any.
12.	Set next deadline
13.	Keep carbon copy of decision form.
14.	Go out to assigned company and: (a) Return completed decision form (b) Give out any information the company has paid for (c) Inform company of next deadline.
15.	Return to umpires' room.
16.	Chart the following operating results for the past quarter for the company: (a) Total assets (b) Profit (c) Sales volume (d) Share of market.

The Business Management Game itself can be played with a number of variants. A simpler version, for example, with only very minor changes, can be played on a cash basis instead of with an accounting record like the decision form. The amount of information that is given the players may also be varied. The main thing to keep in mind is that, since the game does not call for automatic computation, the game elements, parameters, and interactions should be kept relatively simple.

There probably is no better way for an executive to learn about gaming and to judge the usefulness of business games than to participate in one. Men who have done this in the past have felt that, apart from being a fascinating and a thought-provoking experience, business gaming can potentially make a unique contribution to management skill in the following important ways:

1. A top-management business game forces the adoption of an over-all point of view and, to a functional specialist, drives home the need for coordination and balance in a business.

2. The need to exercise judgment and make decisions without "complete" information is a powerful stimulus to mental discipline, decisiveness, and a healthy willingness to take risks.

3. The complexity and time pressure of the game provide a lesson in the importance of effective organization and the delineation of areas of responsibility.

4. Finally, by putting a premium on the development of objectives and long-range plans for a company's future and on the thoughtful integration of planning with financial capability, the game gives meaning to these aims—in the case of many participants, for the first time.

In this connection it is revealing to examine the play of a typical game. Thus, ten completed decision forms reflecting the operating history of a company for the first two and one-half years of operation show that the players have to accumulate a certain amount of actual experience before they begin to operate with a real plan. This history also shows that, as in any new venture, the beginning is erratic and entails some period of loss. It is not until the next phase of the game—between three to seven years of operation—that rapid growth, mature game planning, and the tough competitive battles begin.

But a generalized business game such as the Business Management Game must be considered only a beginning. A good deal of further experimentation is desirable. In time we should be able to develop specific games—games that simulate the functioning of one specific company and its major competitors. The training value of such games and the amount of insight and skill which can be derived from them may be a genuine "breakthrough" in executive development.

INDEX